Understanding The Scriptures

A Complete Course On Bible Study

The Didache Series

The Didache

[DID-uh-kay]

The *Didache* is the first known Christian catechesis. Written in the first century, the *Didache* is the earliest known Christian writing outside of Scripture. The name of the work, *"Didache,"* is indeed appropriate for such a catechesis because it comes from the Greek word for "teaching," and indicates that this writing contains the teaching of the Apostles.

The *Didache* is a catechetical summary of Christian sacraments, practices, and morality. Though written in the first century, its teaching is timeless. The *Didache* was probably written by the disciples of the Twelve Apostles, and it presents the Apostolic Faith as taught by those closest to Jesus Christ. This series of books takes the name of this early catechesis because it shares in the Church's mission of passing on that same Faith, in its rich entirety, to new generations.

Below is an excerpt from the *Didache* in which we see a clear example of its lasting message, a message that speaks to Christians of today as much as it did to the first generations of the Church. The world is different, but the struggle for holiness is the same. In the *Didache*, we are instructed to embrace virtue, to avoid sin, and to live the Beatitudes of our Lord.

My child, flee from everything that is evil and everything that is like it. Do not be wrathful, for wrath leads to murder, nor jealous nor contentious nor quarrelsome, for from all these murder ensues.

My child, do not be lustful, for lust leads to fornication, nor a filthy-talker nor a lewd-looker, for from all these adulteries ensue.

My child, do not be an interpreter of omens, since it leads to idolatry, nor an enchanter nor an astrologer nor a magical purifier, nor wish to see them, for from all these idolatry arises.

My child, do not be a liar, for lying leads to theft, nor avaricious nor conceited, for from all these thefts are produced.

My child, do not be a complainer, since it leads to blasphemy, nor self-willed nor evil-minded, for from all these blasphemies are produced.

Be meek, for the meek will inherit the earth.

Be long-suffering and merciful and guileless and peaceable and good, and revere always the words you have heard.[1]

The *Didache* is the teaching of the Apostles and, as such, it is the teaching of the Church. Accordingly, this book series makes extensive use of the most recent comprehensive catechesis provided to us, *The Catechism of the Catholic Church*. The *Didache* series also relies heavily on Sacred Scripture, the lives of the saints, the Fathers of the Church, and the teaching of Vatican II as witnessed by the pontificate of John Paul II.

---

1. Swett, Ben H. "The Didache (The Teaching)." © January 30, 1998. http://bswett.com/1998-01Didache.html

Understanding
The Scriptures

A Complete Course On Bible Study

Author: Scott Hahn, Ph.D.
General Editor: Rev. James Socias

MIDWEST THEOLOGICAL FORUM
Woodridge, Illinois

Published in the United States of America by

Midwest Theological Forum
1420 Davey Road
Woodridge, IL 60517

Copyright, ©2005 Rev. James Socias
ISBN 1-890177-47-4 UTS
Revised First Edition

Nihil obstat
Reverend John G. Lodge, S.S.L., S.T.D.
Censor Deputatus
July 13, 2004

Imprimatur
✠ Most Reverend Edwin M. Conway, D.D.
Vicar General
Archdiocese of Chicago
July 19, 2004

The Nihil obstat and Imprimatur are official declarations that a book is free of doctrinal and moral error. No implication is contained therein that those who have granted the Nihil obstat and Imprimatur agree with the contents, opinions, or statements expressed. Nor do they assume any legal responsibility associated with the publication.

Author: Scott Hahn, Ph.D.
General and Managing Editor: Rev. James Socias
Editorial Board: Rev. James Socias, Scott Hahn, Ph.D., Emmet Flood, Kimberly Kirk Hahn, Mike Aquilina
Design and Production: Marlene Burrell, Jane Heineman of April Graphics, Highland Park, Illinois

Acknowledgements

Excerpts from the English translation of the *Catechism of the Catholic Church* for the United States of America copyright ©1994, United States Catholic Conference, Inc.–Libreria Editrice Vaticana. Used by permission.

Excerpts from the English translation of the *Catechism of the Catholic Church: Modifications from the Editio Typica* copyright ©1997, United States Catholic Conference, Inc.–Libreria Editrice Vaticana. Used by permission.

Scripture quotations contained herein are adapted from the Catholic Edition of the Revised Standard Version of the Bible, copyright ©1946, 1952, 1971, and the New Revised Standard Version of the Bible, copyright ©1989, by the Division of Christian Education of the National Council of the Churches of Christ in the United States of America, and are used by permission. All rights reserved.

Citations of official Church documents from Neuner, Josef, SJ, and Dupuis, Jacques, SJ, eds., The Christian Faith: Doctrinal Documents of the Catholic Church, 5th ed. (New York: Alba House, 1992). Used with permission.

Excerpts from Vatican Council II: The Conciliar and Post Conciliar Documents, New Revised Edition edited by Austin Flannery, O.P., copyright ©1992, Costello Publishing Company, Inc., Northport, NY are used by permission of the publisher, all rights reserved. No part of these excerpts may be reproduced, stored in a retrieval system, or transmitted in any form or by any means—electronic, mechanical, photocopying, recording or otherwise, without express permission of Costello Publishing Company.

All maps on pages 89, 90, 98, 112, 115, 121, 138, 171, 172, 174, 175, 181, 192, 209, 211, 224, 231, 234, 249, 253, 265, 279, 280, 293, 295, 297, 329, 333, 351, 357, 413, 433, 448, 465, 466, 467, 468, 507, 519, copyright ©1997 Lion Hudson plc/Tim Dowley and Peter Wyart, trading as Three's Company. Used by permission. All rights reserved.

Disclaimer: The editor of this book has attempted to give proper credit to all sources used in the text and illustrations. Any miscredit or lack of credit is unintended and will be corrected in the next edition.

Library of Congress Cataloging-in-Publication Data
Hahn, Scott.
    Understanding the Scriptures: a complete course on Bible study/author, Scott Hahn;
general editor, James Socias.—1st ed. p. cm.—(The Didache Series)
    Includes index.
    ISBN 1-890177-47-4 (alk. paper)
    1. Bible—Hermeneutics.   2. Bible—Textbooks.   3. Catholic Church—Doctrines.
    I. Socias, James. II. Title. III. Series.
BS476.H235 2005
220.6'1—dc22   2005002832

The Ad Hoc Committee to oversee the Use of the Catechism, United States Conference of Catholic Bishops, has found this catechetical text, copyright 2005, to be in conformity with the *Catechism of the Catholic Church.*

Printed in Canada

Contents

Contents

Contents

Contents

Contents

ABBREVIATIONS USED FOR THE BOOKS OF THE BIBLE

Old Testament

Genesis	Gn	Tobit	Tb	Hosea	Hos
Exodus	Ex	Judith	Jdt	Joel	Jl
Leviticus	Lv	Esther	Est	Amos	Am
Numbers	Nm	Job	Jb	Obadiah	Ob
Deuteronomy	Dt	Psalms	Ps(s)	Jonah	Jon
Joshua	Jos	Proverbs	Prv	Micah	Mi
Judges	Jgs	Ecclesiastes	Eccl	Nahum	Na
Ruth	Ru	Song of Songs	Sg	Habakkuk	Hb
1 Samuel	1 Sm	Wisdom	Wis	Zephaniah	Zep
2 Samuel	2 Sm	Sirach	Sir	Haggai	Hg
1 Kings	1 Kgs	Isaiah	Is	Zechariah	Zec
2 Kings	2 Kgs	Jeremiah	Jer	Malachi	Mal
1 Chronicles	1 Chr	Lamentations	Lam	1 Maccabees	1 Mc
2 Chronicles	2 Chr	Baruch	Bar	2 Maccabees	2 Mc
Ezra	Ezr	Ezekiel	Ez		
Nehemiah	Neh	Daniel	Dn		

New Testament

Matthew	Mt	Ephesians	Eph	Hebrews	Heb
Mark	Mk	Philippians	Phil	James	Jas
Luke	Lk	Colossians	Col	1 Peter	1 Pt
John	Jn	1 Thessalonians	1 Thes	2 Peter	2 Pt
Acts of the Apostles	Acts	2 Thessalonians	2 Thes	1 John	1 Jn
Romans	Rom	1 Timothy	1 Tm	2 John	2 Jn
1 Corinthians	1 Cor	2 Timothy	2 Tm	3 John	3 Jn
2 Corinthians	2 Cor	Titus	Ti	Jude	Jude
Galatians	Gal	Philemon	Phlm	Revelation	Rv

ABBREVIATIONS USED FOR DOCUMENTS OF THE MAGISTERIUM

AAS	*Acta Apostolica Sedis*	FC	*Familiaris consortio*
CA	*Centesimus annus*	GS	*Gaudium et spes*
CCC	*The Catechism of the Catholic Church*	LG	*Lumen gentium*
CCEO	*Corpus Canonum Ecclesiarum Orientalium*	LH	*Liturgy of the Hours*
CDF	Congregation for the Doctrine of the Faith	PG	J. P. Migne, ed., *Patrologia Graeca* (Paris, 1857-1866)
DS	Denzinger-Schönmetzer, *Enchiridion Symbolorum, definitionum et declarationum de rebus fidei et morum* (1965)	PL	J. P. Migne, ed., *Patrologia Latina* (Paris, 1841-1855)
DV	*Dei Verbum*	STh	*Summa Theologiae*

Foreword

The Bible is a huge and compelling book, full of smaller and no less moving books. Written thousands of years ago in languages few of us today can read, it converts hearts but can also challenge and puzzle our understanding. In the Bible—like no other book—generations of our ancestors have found the meaning of life. In the Bible—as in no other book—we find the meaning of our own lives.

The Scriptures can be difficult. They don't spell out their meaning in an easy, question-and-answer format. So when we read the Bible, we need a guide.

Scott Hahn has seen this need and put together a wonderfully valuable guide in *Understanding The Scriptures: A Complete Course On Bible Study.*

Over the last 20 centuries, no book has been researched, pondered, and prayed over as intensely as the Bible. Dr. Hahn has done all these things himself; but, more importantly, he has studied the work of the many generations of Christians and Jews who have gone before him. Then he gathered the best of all that study to help you in your own reading.

By the end of this book you will be very well acquainted with the word "covenant," and you'll know how important it is in your life. Covenant is the handle that helps us grab hold of all the vital history contained in the Bible. Indeed, God's covenant with humanity defines the "story line" that holds all of Scripture together, from beginning to end. Indeed, God's covenant encompasses the meaning and the means of our salvation, and that's why the Bible's "story line" is often called "salvation history." The story of Sacred Scripture turns on the life of one person: Jesus Christ. He is the Messiah promised, expected, and prayed for in the Old Testament. In the New Testament, He is the Savior come to fulfill all those hopes. Jesus unites the two testaments and makes them one book, one Bible.

Yet Jesus himself never wrote a book. Instead he established a Church to bring salvation to every generation, through His sacraments and His teaching. That's very good news for us. Maybe the most important thing to learn from Dr. Hahn's guide is how important the Church is in our understanding of the Bible. Read the last chapter of St. Luke's Gospel, and you'll see that Jesus Himself most clearly and powerfully "opened up" the Scriptures only in the context of the "breaking of the bread"—what we today know as the Mass, the Eucharist, or the Liturgy. That's where we disciples continue to "know Him" and grow in our understanding of the Holy Bible.

A very significant group of Bible scholars, the Pontifical Biblical Commission, recently wrote: "it is above all through the liturgy that Christians come into contact with scripture....In principle, the liturgy, and especially the sacramental liturgy, the high point of which is the eucharistic celebration, brings about the most perfect actualization of the biblical texts....Christ is then 'present in his word, because it is he himself who speaks when sacred scripture is read in the Church' (*Sacrosanctum concilium* 7). Written text thus becomes living word."

Because we're Catholic, we need to become biblically literate. We need to know the Bible well because we hunger for abundant life—because we want to know Jesus, which is the same thing. Scott Hahn does a superb job of feeding his readers with the Word of God in this immensely useful guide.

✠ **Charles J. Chaput,** O.F.M. Cap.
Archbishop of Denver

This book is dedicated
to my Godchildren:

Andrew Klika
Christopher Carter
Thomas Martin
Michael Sherman
Jaki Cavins
and Joseph Mitch

— Scott Hahn

In the beginning God created the heavens and the earth.
The earth was without form and void,
and darkness was upon the face of the deep...

Genesis 1: 1-2

And God said, "Let there be light"; and there was light.
And God saw that the light was good;
and God separated the light from the darkness.

Genesis 1: 3-4

God called the dry land Earth,
and the waters that were gathered together he called Seas.
And God saw that it was good.

Genesis 1: 10

"*Let us make man in our image, after our likeness...*"

Genesis 1: 26

Chapter 1

What is the Bible?

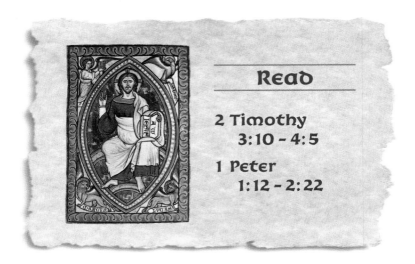

Read

2 Timothy
3:10 - 4:5

1 Peter
1:12 - 2:22

The revelation of God in Jesus Christ is transmitted through Scripture and Tradition as one common source. The Tradition includes the Scriptures which are a privileged expression of the Tradition. "Sacred Scripture is the speech of God as it is put down in writing under the breath of the Holy Spirit. And Tradition transmits in its entirety the Word of God which has been entrusted to the apostles by Christ the Lord and the Holy Spirit" (DV 9). The Word of God in written or oral form is interpreted authentically by the magisterium of the Church. Scripture—the Bible—has to be read and explained in the Church.

The Bible is the *inspired* and *inerrant* Word of God. In seventy-three books, it gives us the history of God's plan for our salvation, beginning with the creation of the world and ending with the beginnings of the Christian Church. Together with the teaching of the Church, the Bible tells us what we need to know in order to be saved.

Although the Bible is made up of many books, together those books tell one story. God created us perfect in the beginning, but our first parents, through their free will, sinned and brought death upon themselves and their descendants. The rest of the Bible tells how God gave human beings the means to salvation. We learn how God chose the people of Israel to lead all people back to himself, and how God the Father completed that work in his only-begotten Son, Jesus Christ, and his sacrifice on the Cross. Finally, we learn the truth about the end of history: good triumphs, evil fails, and the People of God live forever in paradise. That is the story of our faith.

Sacred Scripture is not the *only* authority for our faith, as Scripture itself tells us. The Church was founded by Jesus Christ to keep the *living Tradition* of the faith alive. As Catholics, we believe that the Church is not simply a religious institution that preserves tradition. At Pentecost, after the death and resurrection of Christ, God poured out the Holy Spirit upon the Apostles, and because of that gift, the Holy Spirit continues to dwell in and guide the Church. The teaching of the Church opens up all the riches of the Bible to us. Because we have the living truth of the Church, we can read Scripture with more confidence, more understanding, and more freedom.

What Catholics Believe About The Bible

- **The inspired Word of God comes to us through Sacred Scripture.**
- **The living Word of God also comes to us equally through the living Tradition of the Church.**
- **The infallible Word of God as transmitted by Scripture and Tradition has been entrusted solely to the living Magisterium of the Church which exercises its authority in the name of Jesus Christ.**

Sacred Scripture is inspired and inerrant. "Inspired"—from a word meaning "breathed in"—means that God himself guided the authors who wrote the books of the Bible. The writers' intellects were enlightened directly by the action of the Holy Spirit to write what God wanted and nothing more. This process took place over several thousand years. The Spirit moved them to write without in any way impairing their freedom to write what was in their intellects. Though God is the principal author of scripture, the human authors are also true authors because they acted as free, subordinate, intelligent instruments of the Holy Spirit.

"Inerrant" means that it does not err: properly understood, Scripture always teaches truth, never error. "Since, therefore, all that the inspired authors, or sacred writers, affirm should be regarded as affirmed by the Holy Spirit, we must acknowledge that the books of Scripture firmly, faithfully, and without error, teach that truth which God, for the sake of our salvation, wished to see confided to the Sacred Scriptures" (Vatican II, *Dei Verbum* 11).

Reading Sacred Scripture is, in a way, like receiving the Eucharist. In both cases, the Word of God comes directly to us. The *Catechism of the Catholic Church* (103) tells us that "the Church has always venerated the Scriptures as she venerates the Lord's Body. She never ceases to present to the faithful the bread of life, taken from the one table of God's Word and Christ's Body."

For the Catholic believer the Word of God alone is supreme. But the Scriptures are not the only source for God's Word, as the Scriptures themselves will tell you.

In 2 Thessalonians 2:15, St. Paul reminds the Thessalonian believers that they must hold fast to the traditions that the apostles have passed down either in writing or by word of mouth. "So then, brethren, stand firm and hold to the traditions which you were taught by us, either by word of mouth or by letter." Sacred Scripture and Sacred Tradition form one source from which the Word of God comes to us, as the New Testament itself tells us.

The true interpretation of both Sacred Scripture and Sacred Tradition is expressed in the infallible teaching of the Church, the Magisterium. "Infallible" means that, because of the divine help of Christ himself, the Church cannot teach error in matters of faith.

The Great Qumran Isaiah Scroll, ca. 100 B.C., is the oldest complete manuscript of any book of the Bible. Remarkably similar to the standard Hebrew text, it provides overwhelming proof of the accuracy of the Book of Isaiah we read today.

In order to preserve the Church in the purity of the faith handed on by the apostles, Christ who is the Truth willed to confer on her a share in his own infallibility. By a "supernatural sense of faith" the People of God, under the guidance of the Church's living Magisterium, "unfailingly adheres to this faith" (LG 12; cf. DV 10). (CCC 889)

The mission of the Magisterium is linked to the definitive nature of the covenant established by God with his people in Christ. It is this Magisterium's task to preserve God's people from deviations and defections and to guarantee them the objective possibility of professing the true faith without error. Thus, the pastoral duty of the Magisterium is aimed at seeing to it that the People of God abides in the truth that liberates. To fulfill this service, Christ endowed the Church's shepherds with the charism of infallibility in matters of faith and morals. The exercise of this charism takes several forms: (CCC 890)

"The Roman Pontiff, head of the college of bishops, enjoys this infallibility in virtue of his office, when, as supreme pastor and teacher of all the faithful—who confirms his brethren in the faith—he proclaims by a definitive act a doctrine pertaining to faith or morals....The infallibility promised to the Church is also present in the body of bishops when, together with Peter's successor, they exercise the supreme Magisterium," above all in an Ecumenical Council (LG 25; cf. Vatican Council I: DS 3074). When the Church through its supreme Magisterium proposes a doctrine "for belief as being divinely revealed" (DV 10 § 2), and as the teaching of Christ, the definitions "must be adhered to with the obedience of faith" (LG 25 § 2). This infallibility extends as far as the deposit of divine Revelation itself (cf. LG 25). (CCC 891)

Divine assistance is also given to the successors of the apostles, teaching in communion with the successor of Peter, and, in a particular way, to the bishop of Rome, pastor of the whole Church, when, without arriving at an infallible definition and without pronouncing in a "definitive manner," they propose in the exercise of the ordinary Magisterium a teaching that leads to better understanding of Revelation in matters of faith and morals. To this ordinary teaching the faithful "are to adhere to it with religious assent" (LG 25) which, though distinct from the assent of faith, is nonetheless an extension of it. (CCC 892)

What does it mean to say the Bible is divinely inspired?

The Holy Spirit enlightened the intellects of many different specific authors over thousands of years so they could conceive all that which God wanted them to write and nothing more. Divine inspiration infallibly moved the will of each sacred author—without impairing his freedom in any way—to write what was in his intellect. Divine inspiration assisted the human author to use the correct language and expressions to describe what was being infallibly written.

This means God is the principal author of Scripture; the human authors are also true authors. These sacred authors were free, intelligent, subordinate instruments of the Holy Spirit. Because of this, each book of the Bible is inspired and can at the same time be called the work of God and of the human author. There is nothing in Scripture not inspired by God. "All scripture is inspired by God and profitable for teaching, for reproof, for correction, and for training in righteousness" (2 Tm 3:16).

The Holy Spirit, principal author of the Bible, can guide human authors in the choice of expressions in such a way that the latter will express a truth the fullest depths of which the authors themselves do not perceive. This deeper truth will be more fully revealed in the course of time and discerned in the Church under the guidance of the Holy Spirit.

Periods Of Bible History

The Old Testament Period – 4000 B.C. to 400 B.C.

The Inter-Testamental Period – 400 B.C. to 4 B.C.

The New Testament Period – The A.D. Period

4000 B.C. to 2120 B.C.	The Primeval Period
2120 B.C. to 1900 B.C.	The Patriarchal Period
1900 B.C. to 1400 B.C.	The Egyptian Period
1400 B.C. to 1050 B.C.	The Tribal Period
1050 B.C. to 900 B.C.	The Davidic Period
900 B.C. to 600 B.C.	The Assyrian Period
600 B.C. to 540 B.C.	The Babylonian Period
540 B.C. to 330 B.C.	The Persian Period
330 B.C. to 170 B.C.	The Greek Period
170 B.C. to 70 B.C.	The Maccabean Period
70 B.C. to 100 A.D.	The Roman Period

The Gezer Calendar, a limestone tablet listing the agricultural year, is one of the oldest Hebrew inscriptions dating to the time of Solomon, late 11th to early 10th century B.C. The city of Gezer was given to Solomon by the Pharaoh of Egypt as part of the dowry for Solomon's marriage to an Egyptian princess. David had left Gezer unconquered out of respect for Egypt's claim to the city.

Because we have both Scripture and Tradition, interpreted for us by the Magisterium, the *Catechism* tells us (108), "The Christian faith is not a 'religion of the book.'" Instead, Christianity is a religion of the Word of God, and the Word of God—Jesus Christ—is still living today and will live forever.

But Scripture is the way we come to know who Jesus is. As St. Jerome declared, "Ignorance of Scripture is ignorance of Christ." If you want to feel at home in the Kingdom of God, then the Bible is your map. If you want to understand whom you receive in Holy Communion, then you need to understand how God was preparing his people for centuries before he finally gave us the Bread of Life in the Eucharistic Liturgy.

> All Sacred Scripture is but one book, and this one book is Christ, "because all divine Scripture speaks of Christ, and all divine Scripture is fulfilled in Christ" (Hugh of St. Victor, *De arca Noe* 2, 8: PL 176, 642: cf. ibid. 2, 9: PL 176, 642-643). (CCC 134)

"For the Word of God is living and active," says Hebrews 4:12, "sharper than any two-edged sword, piercing to the division of soul and spirit, of joints and marrow, discerning the thoughts and intentions of the heart." To live in a way that truly pleases Jesus Christ, we need to study—and meditate on—the Bible. That is the only way to get to know what Jesus Christ is like.

How The Bible Was Written

- **The Bible was written by inspired human writers in their own styles.**
- **The human writers of the Bible wrote only what God wanted them to write.**
- **The whole Bible, properly interpreted by the Church, is true and completely without error.**

The Bible is a collection of many works written by different authors at different times and in different languages. Those different authors had different ways of thinking and writing. Some of them wrote beautiful poetry, as in the Psalms. Others, like St. Luke, wrote detailed history based on accurate research. Some, like Ezekiel, had symbolic visions that they wrote down. Some simply recorded facts, like the catalog of the tribes of Israel recorded in Numbers. Some books are written in a very simple style; others, like Ecclesiastes, are philosophical and intellectual. Just as with writers of other books, the personalities of the authors come through in what they wrote.

The works which make up the Bible are different from other writings. Even though they were written by human authors, the ultimate author of the whole Bible is God. The human authors wrote in their own styles, but they wrote what God wanted them to write. So, unlike any human book, the Bible is completely free from error. Of course, we need to remember that the Bible is teaching us the way to salvation. The sacred authors presented their message in ways the people of their own time could understand, so sometimes their ideas of physics or astronomy seem outdated to us. But the real truth that God wanted us to learn is presented without error. Everything in it is true.

> The inspired books teach the truth. "Since therefore all that the inspired authors or sacred writers affirm should be regarded as affirmed by the Holy Spirit, we must acknowledge that the books of Scripture firmly, faithfully, and without error teach that truth which God, for the sake of our salvation, wished to see confided to the Sacred Scriptures." (CCC 107)

King David, the youngest of the eight sons of Jesse, is credited with the authorship of the Psalms. His story is told in 1 Samuel 16 through 1 Kings 2:12. King David reigned ca. 1000-960 B.C.

That doesn't mean everything in Scripture is easy to understand. But the Church, guided by the Holy Spirit, helps us understand how to find the truth in the books of the Bible in light of the living Tradition.

How did that inspiration work? Inspiration is one of the great mysteries of our faith—a mystery very much like the mystery of the Incarnation of God in Jesus Christ. Like Christ himself, the inspired books of the Bible are fully human and fully divine. The two natures are inseparably united but still distinct. Jesus Christ, the Word of God incarnate, took on the weakness of human flesh, becoming a true man. In the same way, the Bible, the Word of God inspired, takes on the weakness of human language, becoming a book that humans can understand.

The Bible Is Sacred Literature

- **The sacred authors used literary techniques to express their meaning.**
- **We cannot understand the whole meaning of Scripture without understanding those literary techniques.**

The Bible is sacred literature because God is its author. Because Sacred Scripture is written in human language, it is possible for humans to understand it. Understanding it correctly, however, sometimes requires some preparation.

The first thing to remember about Scripture is that it is *literature*. That means it uses literary forms and techniques to convey its meaning. Unless we understand how those forms and techniques work, we cannot understand the meaning the inspired authors wanted to convey to us.

For a good example of how the sacred authors convey meaning with literary techniques, turn to the very beginning of Genesis. When creation begins, the earth is "without form and void"; then the first thing God creates is light.

Now turn to Jeremiah 4:23, and see how Jeremiah describes the destruction brought on by God's judgment against Judah:

> I looked on the earth, and lo, it was
> waste and void;
> And to the heavens, and they had no light.

Reading only the verse in Jeremiah gives us some of the meaning. Reading it with the beginning of Genesis in mind, however, brings out much more of the meaning. Jeremiah uses the same words as in Genesis. The destruction is so terrible, Jeremiah is saying, that it completely undoes the work of creation!

There are many different kinds of literature (stories, poems, dialogue, figurative language, and others) in the Bible, and the sacred writers used many different literary techniques. Because they lived at different times and had different personalities, they used those techniques differently. Those differences make reading Scripture endlessly fascinating.

Prophet Jeremiah lamenting the destruction of Jerusalem.

We also need to remember that the Bible is *ancient* literature. Even the most recent books of the New Testament were written almost two thousand years ago. The authors of Scripture did not write the same way modern authors write. To understand what they meant to say, we have to understand the way they saw the world.

> In Sacred Scripture, God speaks to man in a human way. To interpret Scripture correctly, the reader must be attentive to what the human authors truly wanted to affirm and to what God wanted to reveal to us by their words (cf. DV 12 § 1). (CCC 109)

> In order to discover *the sacred authors' intention*, the reader must take into account the conditions of their time and culture, the literary genres in use at that time, and the modes of feeling, speaking, and narrating then current. "For the fact is that truth is differently presented and expressed in the various types of historical writing, and in other forms of literary expression" (DV 12 § 2). (CCC 110)

The Bible Is Religious

- **The sacred authors see everything in the light of religion.**
- **Because God sees the whole truth, Bible history is the only truly objective history.**
- **All Bible history is really salvation history.**

We also need to remember that the Bible has a different purpose from other human literature. The Bible is religious. Although the sacred writers told great stories and wrote great poetry, all that literary technique was in the service of the religious purpose of the Bible.

In discerning the meaning of inspired Scripture it is traditional to distinguish two senses, the literal and the spiritual (CCC 115-119). The literal sense is that which the authors intended to express; historical and linguistic analysis, by shedding light upon the processes which gave rise to the biblical texts help to determine this sense which is also intended by God as principal author of the Scriptures and to determine the direction of thought expressed by the text. The spiritual sense is the meaning expressed by the biblical texts when read under the influence of the Holy Spirit in light of the mystery of Christ. There should be no contradiction between the two senses of Scripture; they belong together because scholarship together with faith is needed to enable us to grasp the religious meaning of Scripture.

People today usually think of religion in terms of personal experience. But that isn't how the authors of the Bible—or other ancient peoples—saw it. The word "religion" comes from a Latin word meaning "binding." To the ancients, religion was what held everything together. Their view of history, culture, politics, and everything else was a religious view.

Because of that view, the Bible writers don't write history the way we write history. We see history as a list of important events—wars, treaties, inventions, and so on. The main characters in our history are kings, presidents, and generals.

Although we pretend to write "objective" history—history that tells just the facts—all our history is biased. Even by deciding which facts are important, we make biased decisions. There's no getting around that personal bias in ordinary history, because every history has to be written from some point of view.

But there is one point of view that's completely unbiased. God sees everything exactly the way it is. The Bible writers tell history from God's point of view.

To the Bible writers, the important thing about history is what it tells us about God's relationship with his people. Many of the most important characters in Bible history seem to be just ordinary people—not emperors, not kings, not even governors or mayors. Jesus himself, the Son of God, looked like an ordinary carpenter's son to the people around him. But those ordinary people carried God's message, and that made them more important than all the mighty emperors who fill our history books. Because God sees history objectively, the Bible often ignores the emperors and concentrates on the people who were really important.

In fact, all the history in the Bible is really "salvation history"— the history of how God's plan to save us unfolded through the ages.

Does the Bible contain any errors? Is everything in the Bible true?

Since He is perfect, God can neither deceive nor be deceived. Scripture is affirmed as true by God. Because both the human author and the Holy Spirit are true authors of Scripture, the inspiration of the Holy Spirit guarantees Scripture is free from error.

Scripture is true and contains no errors because God Himself is the true author of all its parts by divine inspiration given to the human writers. The word "inspiration" is chosen to indicate the Holy Spirit "breathed" into the writers what he wished them to write.

Archaeological Periods And Biblical Events

Paleolithic (Old Stone Age)	Before 10,000 B.C.	Genesis 1-11
Mesolithic (Middle Stone Age)	10,000-8000 B.C.	Genesis 1-11

Neolithic (New Stone Age)
    Pre-Pottery Neolithic
    Pottery Neolithic
	8000-4500 B.C.
	    8000-6000 B.C.
	    6000-4500 B.C.
		Genesis 1-11

Chalcolithic (Bronze/Stone Age)	4500-3150 B.C.	Genesis 1-11

Bronze (or Canaanite)
  Early Bronze
    I
    II
    III
    IV
  Middle Bronze
    I
    IIA
    IIB
  Late Bronze
    I
    IIA
    IIB
	3150-1200 B.C.
	  3150-2200 B.C.
	    3150-2850 B.C.
	    2850-2650 B.C.
	    2650-2350 B.C.
	    2350-2200 B.C.
	  2200-1550 B.C.
	    2200-1950 B.C.
	    1950-1750 B.C.
	    1750-1550 B.C.
	  1550-1200 B.C.
	    1550-1400 B.C.
	    1400-1300 B.C.
	    1300-1200 B.C.
		Genesis 1-11
		
		Abraham
		Jacob enters Egypt
		
		The Exodus
		  and Conquest

Iron (or Israelite)
  Early Iron
    IA
    IB
  Middle Iron
    IIA
    IIB
    IIC
	1200-586 B.C.
	  1200-1000 B.C.
	    1200-1150 B.C.
	    1150-1000 B.C.
	  1000-800 B.C.
	    1000-900 B.C.
	    900-800 B.C.
	    800-586 B.C.
		
		David becomes King
		
		Israel and Judah Fall
		(722 and 586 B.C.)

Babylonian (Persian) (or Late Iron)	586-332 B.C.	Babylonian Captivity (586-539 B.C.)

Hellenistic (Greek)
  I
  II (or Hasmonean/Maccabean)
	332-37 B.C.
	  332-152 B.C.
	  152-37 B.C.	

Roman
  I (or Herodian)
  II (or Middle Roman)
  III (or Late Roman)
	37 B.C.-324 A.D.
	  37 B.C.-70 A.D.
	  70-180 A.D.
	  180-324 A.D.
		
		Jesus Christ

Byzantine (Early Church Age of Roman Empire)	324-640 A.D.	

What "Salvation History" Is

- **God has always had a plan to save us.**
- **Salvation history is the story of how that plan works in history.**
- **We can look at all salvation history as a series of seven covenants between God and his people.**

From before the beginning of time, God had a plan to save us all from our sin. The Bible, taken as a whole, tells us the history of that plan of salvation. That's what we mean when we say "salvation history": the story of how God's plan to save us was worked out over thousands of years. But salvation history is different from other kinds of history; it deals not only with the past but also with the *future*. Because God's Word has been revealed to us, we know how the plan of salvation will keep working until the end of time.

One good way of looking at salvation history is to see it as a series of *covenants* between God and us. In the Old Testament, a covenant was an agreement between God and mankind made through individual persons. A *covenant* is similar to a contract, but it is much more than merely a contract. A covenant establishes bonds of sacred kinship: it

The third covenant is with Abraham and his whole tribe. Abraham is the Ancestor of Israel and a model of one who has faith.

unites the participants in a family relation. A contract is a temporary business agreement, meant to last as long as current circumstances make it necessary. God's covenant unites persons in a union that is meant to last. A corporation is a contract; a marriage is a covenant.

Salvation history is the story of how we, sinful humans that we are, have been brought into God's covenant family. We can see seven covenants between God and us in salvation history. (The number seven is a symbol of covenant completeness in Scripture, so it is especially appropriate here.) Each covenant is made through a covenant mediator, and although each covenant reflects a promise God makes to all humanity, each covenant takes the form of a wider social relationship.

1. The first covenant we read about in the Bible is the covenant with Adam. In Hebrew, the name "Adam" is also used to refer to the whole human race. So this first covenant is really the one from which all the other covenants spring.

2. The second covenant is with Noah and his household after the flood.

3. The third covenant is with Abraham and his whole tribe.

4. The fourth covenant is with the whole nation of Israel through Moses.

5. The fifth covenant is with all the nations through David and Solomon.

6. The sixth covenant is the New Covenant with all humanity through Jesus Christ.

7. Finally, at the end of time, there will be a seventh covenant for all eternity.

When you learn to see salvation history this way, it will be easy to make sense of the Bible as a whole. That's what this book is about. You'll learn to see how every part of the Bible fits as part of God's plan for our salvation.

Covenant History

The first covenant we read about in the Bible is the covenant with Adam. In Hebrew, the name "Adam" is also used to refer to the whole human race. So this first covenant is really the one from which all the other covenants spring.

With Each Additional Covenant, The Relationship Between God and Humanity Is Manifested Through A Wider Form Of Human Relationship.						✝
Covenant Mediator	Adam	Noah	Abraham	Moses	David	Jesus
Covenant Role	Husband	Father	Tribal Chief	Judge	King	Royal High Priest
Covenant Form	Marriage	Household	Tribe	Nation	National Kingdom	Catholic Church
Covenant Sign	Sabbath	Rainbow	Circumcision	Passover	Throne	Eucharist

The Church Will Be Our Guide

- **The Bible can be hard for us to understand.**
- **The Church was created by God to teach us what we need to know.**

The Bible is a large and sometimes difficult book. All of it was written over several thousand years, by writers who lived in times very different from ours. Without help, we might misunderstand what some of the Bible writers are trying to tell us.

But we are not left without help. The Church, founded by Jesus Christ himself, and guided by the Holy Spirit interprets the Bible without falling into error. Just as Christ promised, the Catholic Church is always here to teach us how to understand the Bible in light of the living Tradition.

Without that help, we would be lost. If we had no divinely guided teacher to help us, we would be left with human interpretations of the Bible. And those human interpretations disagree. If we want to follow the Word of God and understand Sacred Scripture, then we must learn what our Mother the Church teaches.

In 382 A.D. the Pope commissioned scholar and churchman Jerome (St. Jerome) to make a new translation of the Bible into Latin from the Greek and Hebrew. This translation is known as the Vulgate, from the Latin *vulgata editio*, roughly translated "edition for common circulation."

What is the Canon of the Bible?

The books of the Bible are inerrant under the guidance of divine inspiration. Therefore, only God can reveal which books He has inspired. The list of inspired books is called the canon from the Greek for "measuring rod." In order for a book to be included in the canon, it must be divinely inspired. The Church has answered the question of the inspiration of a book by turning to Sacred Tradition. The Magisterium interprets Tradition with the assistance of the Holy Spirit.

The Church, from Her beginning, has held the books of the Bible to be inspired. "By means of the same Tradition the full canon of the sacred books is known to the Church, and the Holy Scriptures themselves are more thoroughly understood and constantly actualized in the Church" (Vatican II, *Dei Verbum* 8).

Important documentary evidence from the early Church comes from the Councils of Carthage in the fourth century and from the ordinary Magisterium afterwards, including the Council of Florence in 1441. The Council of Trent in 1546 solemnly defined the canon of Scripture.

How The Canon Came To Be

- **The "canon" of Scripture is the list of books proper for reading in the Liturgy.**
- **The whole Church, meeting in a general council (Trent), decided on the canon.**
- **It was by the apostolic Tradition that the Church discerned which writings are to be included in the Canon (CCC 120).**

The Bible is divided into two sections: the Old Testament and the New Testament. The Old Testament is made up of books that were written before the time of Christ; the New Testament books were written after the time of Christ. Both parts are equally important. As we'll soon learn, the New Testament does not cancel the Old Testament. On the contrary, the New Testament writers themselves constantly refer to the Old Testament as "the Scriptures."

But how the Bible was written is only half the story. Many other books were written during that time besides the ones that ended up in the Bible. How did the Church decide which books belonged in the Bible and which books didn't? For that matter, what did it mean to say that a book was part of the Scriptures?

The answer to that last question has to do with the celebration of the liturgy. The liturgy is the service of the Church, and the center of the liturgy is the celebration of the Eucharist.

When the early Christians met, they celebrated the liturgy in two parts: the Liturgy of the Word and the Eucharist. Anyone could attend the Liturgy of the Word, but only baptized Christians could stay for the Eucharist. (We still keep the same division today, although we no longer ban non-Christians from the church when we celebrate the Eucharist.)

In the Liturgy of the Word, the early Christians heard readings from the Scriptures, just as we do today. The Old Testament scriptures were the same ones Jewish congregations heard in their synagogues—in fact, many early Christians continued to go to the synagogues until the synagogue authorities banned them. But they also heard letters from the Apostles and stories from the life of Christ. Which of these new books were suitable for reading in the liturgy? That was the question the early Church had to answer.

The "canon" is the answer to that question. Under the guidance of the Holy Spirit, the Church came up with a list, or "canon," of approved books. The inclusion of a book in the canon meant it was divinely inspired. ("Canon" is a Greek word meaning "measuring rod" or "rule.") Other books were rejected because they were not divinely inspired.

In the Old Testament, the Church accepts some books as canonical that Jewish tradition does not regard as Scripture. These books are called "deuterocanonical," from a Greek word meaning "second canon":

Tobit	**Sirach (Ecclesiasticus)**	**2 Maccabees**
Judith	**Baruch**	**Parts of Daniel**
Wisdom	**1 Maccabees**	**Parts of Esther**

Protestant churches usually follow later Jewish tradition, so most Protestant Bibles omit those books. But according to the Catholic Church, these deuterocanonical books have the same authority as the rest of the books of the Bible; they are part of Scripture. These books offer, quite explicitly, certain doctrines which are recognized as Catholic teaching and practice. For example, the book of 2 Maccabees shows conclusively the concept of creation and that Jewish believers prayed for the souls of the dead many years before the coming of Jesus Christ. The book of Tobit demonstrates the existence and action of guardian angels.

There was a division among the Jewish scholars between the Septuagint or Alexandrian canon, a collection of forty-six books translated into Greek by seventy Jewish scholars, and the Palestinian canon which did not contain the deuterocanonical books. Protestant churches usually follow the Palestinian tradition, thus most Protestant Bibles omit those deuterocanonical books. The Catholic Church has determined the deuterocanonical books have the same authority as the rest of the books of the Bible.

The Canon Of Scripture

This is the complete list of all the books in the Bible, as determined by the Catholic Church.

The Old Testament

Genesis	1 Chronicles	Wisdom	Jonah
Exodus	2 Chronicles	Sirach	Micah
Leviticus	Ezra	Isaiah	Nahum
Numbers	Nehemiah	Jeremiah	Habakkuk
Deuteronomy	Tobit	Lamentations	Zephaniah
Joshua	Judith	Baruch	Haggai
Judges	Esther	Ezekiel	Zechariah
Ruth	Job	Daniel	Malachi
1 Samuel	Psalms	Hosea	1 Maccabees
2 Samuel	Proverbs	Joel	2 Maccabees
1 Kings	Ecclesiastes	Amos	
2 Kings	Song of Solomon	Obadiah	

Many Bibles put the two books of Maccabees after Esther. With that arrangement, all the historical books of the Old Testament are grouped together. On the other hand, the books of Maccabees make a good historical introduction to the New Testament, so there are good reasons for both arrangements.

The New Testament

Matthew	Ephesians	Hebrews
Mark	Philippians	James
Luke	Colossians	1 Peter
John	1 Thessalonians	2 Peter
Acts of the Apostles	2 Thessalonians	1 John
Romans	1 Timothy	2 John
1 Corinthians	2 Timothy	3 John
2 Corinthians	Titus	Jude
Galatians	Philemon	Revelation

SUPPLEMENTARY READING

John Paul II, *Fides et Ratio*

10. Contemplating Jesus as revealer, the Fathers of the Second Vatican Council stressed the salvific character of God's Revelation in history, describing it in these terms: "In this Revelation, the invisible God (cf. Col 1:15; 1 Tm 1:17), out of the abundance of his love speaks to men and women as friends (cf. Ex 33:11; Jn 15:14-15) and lives among them (cf. Bar 3:38), so that he may invite and take them into communion with himself. This plan of Revelation is realized by deeds and words having an inner unity: the deeds wrought by God in the history of salvation manifest and confirm the teaching and realities signified by the words, while the words proclaim the deeds and clarify the mystery contained in them. By this Revelation, then, the deepest truth about God and human salvation is made clear to us in Christ, who is the mediator and at the same time the fullness of all Revelation."

11. God's Revelation is therefore immersed in time and history. Jesus Christ took flesh in the "fullness of time" (Gal 4:4); and two thousand years later, I feel bound to restate forcefully that "in Christianity time has a fundamental importance." It is within time that the whole work of creation and salvation comes to light; and it emerges clearly above all that, with the Incarnation of the Son of God, our life is even now a foretaste of the fulfillment of time which is to come (cf. Heb 1:2).

The truth about himself and his life which God has entrusted to humanity is immersed therefore in time and history; and it was declared once and for all in the mystery of Jesus of Nazareth. The Constitution *Dei Verbum* puts it eloquently: "After speaking in many places and varied ways through the prophets, God 'last of all in these days has spoken to us by his Son' (Heb 1:1-2). For he sent his Son, the eternal Word who enlightens all people, so that he might dwell among them and tell them the innermost realities about God (cf. Jn 1:1-18). Jesus Christ, the Word made flesh, sent as 'a human being to human beings,' 'speaks the words of God' (Jn 3:34), and completes the work of salvation which his Father gave him to do (cf. Jn 5:36; 17:4). To see Jesus is to see his Father (Jn 14:9). For this reason, Jesus perfected Revelation by fulfilling it through his whole work of making himself present and manifesting himself: through his words and deeds, his signs and wonders, but especially though his death and glorious Resurrection from the dead and finally his sending of the Spirit of truth."

This page is from a parchment codex, ca. 1505. A codex (Latin for "book") is a handwritten book from late Antiquity or the Middle Ages. The codex was an improvement over the scroll. Because it was single pages stitched together with leather, it could be opened flat at any page, allowing easier reading, and both sides could be written on. Parchment and vellum were made from fine calf skin, sheep skin or goat skin. Parchment is named after the city Pergamon where it was first invented. In the Middle Ages, calf and sheep skin were the preferred materials for making parchment in England and France, goat skin was more common in Italy.

VOCABULARY

BIBLE
Scripture. The collection of all the canonical books. The Bible is divided into two parts: the Old Testament, made up of books written before the coming of Jesus Christ, and the New Testament, made up of books written after the coming of Jesus Christ.

CANON
The list of inspired books. Greek for "measuring rod."

CATHOLIC
Universal. Catholic can describe the Church or one of her members.

CHURCH
The faithful. This can refer to the Roman Catholic Church or an individual diocese.

COVENANT
An agreement that establishes a sacred family bond between persons. A covenant is more than a contract; a contract establishes a temporary relationship beneficial to both parties, whereas a covenant is intended to bind both persons in kinship forever.

INERRANT
Making no mistakes or errors. Scripture is inerrant; that is, it always teaches truth, never falsehood.

INFALLIBLE
Incapable of failing. The Bible and the teaching of the Church are infallible because of a special protection by God.

INSPIRED
Guided by God. From a word meaning "breathed in." The human writers of Scripture wrote in their own language, but through God's inspiration they wrote what God intended them to write and nothing more.

MAGISTERIUM
The teaching authority of the Church which, guided by the Holy Spirit, interprets Scripture and Tradition.

PROTESTANT
A Christian not in communion with the Church. A Protestant owes allegiance to one of the reform movements, most of which began in the 1500s.

SALVATION HISTORY
The story of God's plan to save humanity from the consequences of sin. This plan begins with Creation, is unfolding now, and will continue until the end of time.

SCRIPTURE.
See Bible.

TRADITION
The living transmission of the message of the Gospel in the Church.

Before the printing press was invented in 1455, the Bible was copied by hand on stone, clay, leather, papyrus and vellum. Special scribes developed intricate methods of counting words and letters to insure that no errors could be made.

STUDY QUESTIONS

1. Name the two original sources for Catholic teaching.

2. What is the Bible?

3. What is Tradition?

4. What does "inerrant" mean?

5. What does "inspired" mean?

6. What is the divinely chosen interpreter of Scripture?

7. What does "infallibility" mean?

8. What is the purpose of the Magisterium?

9. Who exercises the supreme Magisterium?

10. What does the phrase "in a particular way" mean in reference to the teaching authority of the pope?

11. Who is the author of the Bible?

12. Explain the meaning of number 107 of the *Catechism of the Catholic Church*.

13. How did the authors of the Bible differ from many people today in their view of religion?

14. Why do we say the Bible is "objective history"?

15. What is "salvation history"?

16. How does salvation history differ from all other history?

17. What is a "covenant"?

18. How many covenants has God made with his people?

19. What does the word "canon" mean?

20. List the three sources used to determine canonicity.

21. List the five rules for determining correct scriptural interpretation.

22. What are "deuterocanonical" books?

23. In what covenant period are we living?

PRACTICAL EXERCISES

1. Numbers 75 to 78 of the *Catechism of the Catholic Church* explain how divine revelation has been passed on to us from the very beginnings of the Church in two distinct but not separate ways; Sacred Scripture and Tradition are the one common source making present the revelation in the Church. How does the *Catechism* distinguish between these two sources of Revelation? How does the "continuous line of succession" from the Apostles to our present day bishops assure us that we are receiving the same truths which were received by the Church two thousand years ago?

2. There are many passages in the Bible which may be interpreted differently by different people. One such passage is Luke 12:51-53. Try to come up with two possible interpretations for the meaning of Jesus' words: "Do you think I came to give peace on earth? No, I tell you, but rather division; for henceforth in one house there will be five divided, three against two and two against three; they will be divided, father against son and son against father, mother against daughter and daughter against her mother...." How can we be sure of what Jesus was trying to tell us? What special quality does the Magisterium of the Church have which allows it to aid us?

FROM THE CATECHISM

80 "Sacred Tradition and Sacred Scripture, then, are bound closely together, and communicate one with the other. For both of them, flowing out from the same divine well-spring, come together in some fashion to form one thing, and move towards the same goal" (DV 9). Each of them makes present and fruitful in the Church the mystery of Christ, who promised to remain with his own "always, to the close of the age" (Mt 28: 20).

82 As a result the Church, to whom the transmission and interpretation of Revelation is entrusted, "does not derive her certainty about all revealed truths from the holy Scriptures alone. Both Scripture and Tradition must be accepted and honoured with equal sentiments of devotion and reverence" (DV 9).

85 "The task of giving an authentic interpretation of the Word of God, whether in its written form or in the form of Tradition, has been entrusted to the living teaching office of the Church alone. Its authority in this matter is exercised in the name of Jesus Christ" (DV 10 § 2). This means that the task of interpretation has been entrusted to the bishops in communion with the successor of Peter, the Bishop of Rome.

104 In Sacred Scripture, the Church constantly finds her nourishment and her strength, for she welcomes it not as a human word, "but as what it really is, the word of God" (1 Thes 2: 13; cf. DV 24). "In the sacred books, the Father who is in heaven comes lovingly to meet his children, and talks with them" (DV 21).

132 "Therefore, the 'study of the sacred page' should be the very soul of sacred theology. The ministry of the Word, too — pastoral preaching, catechetics, and all forms of Christian instruction, among which the liturgical homily should hold pride of place — is healthily nourished and thrives in holiness through the Word of Scripture" (DV 24).

135 "The Sacred Scriptures contain the Word of God and, because they are inspired, they are truly the Word of God" (DV 24).

2653 The Church "forcefully and specially exhorts all the Christian faithful...to learn 'the surpassing knowledge of Jesus Christ' (Phil 3: 8) by frequent reading of the divine Scriptures....Let them remember, however, that prayer should accompany the reading of Sacred Scripture, so that a dialogue takes place between God and man. For 'we speak to him when we pray; we listen to him when we read the divine oracles' (DV 25; cf. Phil 3: 8; St. Ambrose, *De officiis ministrorum* 1, 20, 88: PL 16, 50)."

A page from the *Biblia Pauperum*, ca. 1470. The *Biblia Pauperum* or Poor Man's Bible is thought to have been used by poorer members of the clergy to prepare sermons. Each page of the *Biblia Pauperum* illustrates a subject from the life and Passion of Christ, two parallels from the Old Testament, and witnesses from among Biblical personages. In the woodcut illustrated here, we see the Temptation of Christ in the center panel, Jacob and Esau on the left, and the Temptation of Adam and Eve on the right.

The Old Testament

You need to understand the Old Testament before you can understand the New Testament.

Chapter 2

The Old Testament

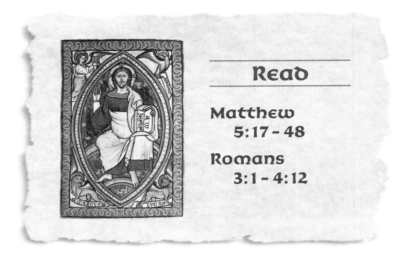

Read

Matthew 5:17 - 48

Romans 3:1 - 4:12

Why does a Christian need to know about the Old Testament? The very first verse of the New Testament answers that question:

The book of the genealogy of Jesus Christ, the son of David, the son of Abraham.
(Mt 1:1)

A long list of the human ancestors of Jesus comes next, starting with Abraham. That "genealogy" (a Greek word that means the study of ancestry) is a summary of Old Testament history. The first thing to know about Jesus Christ, Matthew tells us, is how he is related to the Old Testament.

Even Matthew's words echo the Old Testament. In Genesis 5:1, our translation says, "This is the book of the generations of Adam." In the Greek translation of the Old Testament—the translation the early Christians used—"generations" is the same word as "genealogy" in our translation of Matthew 1:1. Matthew is showing us that Jesus Christ is the new Adam, and that the story that began with Adam ends with Christ.

You need to understand the Old Testament before you can understand the New Testament, just as you need to understand algebra before you can understand trigonometry.

The Old Testament is a complete library of everything that was best in the literature of Israel. Since the people of Israel were the Chosen People of God, the best of their literature is more than human literature. It is divinely inspired.

Together, the books of the Old Testament tell the story of the long journey toward salvation—a journey that leads straight to the New Testament, where the promises of the Old Testament are *fulfilled.*

The New Testament *fulfills* the Old Testament: that is, it completes and accomplishes all the promises of the Old Testament Scriptures. It doesn't cancel the Old Testament. The Old Testament is still just as much Sacred Scripture as it was before the coming of Christ. "Think not that I have come to abolish the law and the prophets," Jesus said in his Sermon on the Mount. ("The law and the prophets" is the way Jewish tradition referred to the Scriptures of the Old Testament.) "I have come not to abolish them but to fulfill them. For truly, I say to you, till heaven and earth pass away, not an iota, not a dot, will pass from the law until all is accomplished."[1]

> The Old Testament is an indispensable part of Sacred Scripture. Its books are divinely inspired and retain a permanent value (cf. DV 14), for the Old Covenant has never been revoked. (CCC 121)

> Indeed, "the economy of the Old Testament was deliberately so oriented that it should prepare for and declare in prophecy the coming of Christ, redeemer of all men" (DV 15). "Even though they contain matters imperfect and provisional" (DV 15), the books of the Old Testament bear witness to the whole divine pedagogy of God's saving love: these writings "are a storehouse of sublime teaching on God and of sound wisdom on human life, as well as a wonderful treasury of prayers; in them, too, the mystery of our salvation is present in a hidden way" (DV 15). (CCC 122)

"The Tree of Jesse"
Artists of the Middle Ages were inspired by Isaiah 11: 1-3 for the family tree of Jesus Christ. The tree grows from a sleeping Jesse. Among the tree branches sprout the kings of Judah and the Old Testament prophets. The tree is crowned with The Blessed Virgin Mary and Infant Jesus.

The first notable example of this popular theme is attributed to Abbot Suger (1081-1151). In 1144, he commissioned a stained-glass window for the Abbey of St. Denis near Paris. This window was destroyed over time, but a version (25 ft x 9 ft) was installed in Chartres Cathedral in 1150 and survives intact to this day.

"There shall come forth a shoot from the stump of Jesse, and a branch shall grow out of his roots. And the Spirit of the Lord shall rest upon him, the spirit of wisdom and understanding, the spirit of counsel and might, the spirit of knowledge and the fear of the Lord. And his delight shall be in the fear of the Lord." (Is 11: 1-3)

The Books Of The Old Testament

The forty-six books of the Old Testament are arranged by type. There are four main types:

1. **Law**
2. **History**
3. **Wisdom**
4. **Prophecy**

Of course, not every book has only one type of writing in it. Much of the most important history is in the books of the Law, for example, and some of the books of wisdom also contain important words of prophecy. But the books are arranged according to their most important functions.

The Law

God gave Moses the Ten Commandments on Mount Sinai in the Book of Exodus.

The first five books of the Bible were considered the most important in the Jewish tradition. Traditionally, they are known as the Books of the Law, or the Torah. Moses is traditionally said to have been the author, so they are also called the five Books of Moses. Finally, because there are five of them, they are sometimes called the Pentateuch, from the Greek word for "five volumes."

Genesis (Greek for "beginning") tells the story of the creation of the world and the beginning of the nation of Israel. It explains the origins of the people and customs that most concerned the Israelites. Many of the most famous stories in the Bible are in Genesis—Adam and Eve, Noah's flood, Abraham and Isaac, Joseph's coat of many colors. The book ends with Joseph and his brothers—founders of the Twelve Tribes of Israel—living in Egypt, where their families grow and prosper.

Exodus (Greek for "going out") tells the story of the Israelites' escape from Egypt (where they had become slaves) and their wandering in the desert on the way to Canaan, the Promised Land. It also includes the most important laws of the Old Testament: the Ten Commandments, which God gave to Moses on Mount Sinai. And it tells how the people of Israel fail to live up to their unique relationship with God, so that a new, lesser law has to be given for them.

Leviticus (so named because it has to do with the Levitical priests of Israel) is a book of laws, most of which have to do with religious observances. Every detail of their worship life is made explicit, because the Israelites have proved that they cannot be trusted to worship God properly.

Numbers is so named because it gives a census of all the tribes of Israel. But it also tells the story of their forty years in the desert, and their constant rebellion against the authority of God and of his prophet Moses.

Deuteronomy is Greek for "second law." It repeats some of the laws in the earlier books: for example, the Ten Commandments are repeated from Exodus. It also gives new laws specifically about how the Israelites will live in the Promised Land. In fact, the heart of Deuteronomy is a new constitution for the state of Israel. Finally, it gives a prophetic road map of Israel's history—a prophecy that will be fulfilled in the historical books that follow.

J, E, D, and P

In the 1800's, scholars studying the Pentateuch tried to figure out what original sources had gone into the final books. They gave each source a name, usually known by its initial. The most popular scheme identified four sources: J, E, D, and P.

J, the "Jehovist" or "Yahwist" source, was identified in passages that frequently use the Divine Name, Yahweh (given as "Jehovah" in earlier translations). It was thought to represent the perspective of Jews in Judah in about the tenth or ninth century B.C.

E, the "Elohist" source, was seen in passages that most commonly referred to God as "Elohim," the Hebrew word for "God" or "gods." It was thought to represent the perspective of believers in the northern kingdom of Israel in the ninth or eighth century B.C.

D, the "Deuteronomistic" source, was identified as the original author of Deuteronomy, who was believed to have written in the seventh century B.C., about the time of Josiah's reforms (see Chapter thirteen of this book).

P, the "Priestly" source, was thought to be a later editor who revised all five books to reflect the concerns of the Jerusalem priesthood after the return from the Babylonian Exile.

Of course, it was no news that the books of the Pentateuch were compiled from earlier sources. The sacred authors themselves sometimes cite their sources, many of which are older books that are no longer available.

In spite of the hard work of Scripture scholars, any attempt to identify the sources of Scripture is only scholarly conjecture and speculation. Some saw the sources as oral traditions preserved by different groups in different times of Israel's history. Now, many scholars believe that a much more complex mixture of sources went into those books. No one will ever know for certain what the sources were, and each new generation of scholars will build up a slightly different theory. The Pontifical Biblical Commission, however, responded to a question of Cardinal Suhard in 1948 regarding the authorship of the Pentateuch. The Commission taught we can be confident that whatever the time frame of the sources, Moses was the substantial influence as author and legislator in the Pentateuch.

As Christians, we have the certainty of faith that Scripture is divinely authored and teaches no error in faith, morals or history which communicates the crucial and determinative events of salvation. The books *as we have them now* are Sacred Scripture, not the original sources that might have gone into them. When we have trouble understanding Scripture, or when one passage seems to contradict another, humility should teach us to seek patiently for better understanding, to not give up and declare that Scripture is in error.

The books of the Pentateuch were named by the Jews of Palestine according to the opening Hebrew words:

1. **Bereshith:** "In the Beginning…"
2. **We'elleh Shemoth:** "And these are the names…"
3. **Wayyiqra':** "And he called…"
4. **Wayyedabber:** "And he spoke…"
5. **Elleh Haddebarim:** "These are the words…"

History

The next group of books tells the history of the people of Israel, from the conquest of Canaan through the end of the kingdoms of Israel and Judah and on to the restoration of Jerusalem. (In many Bibles, the two books of Maccabees are included in this group, which brings the history up to the time just before the Roman Empire.) Some of the books, like Judges, cover long periods of history; others, like Ruth, tell the story of one person who led a holy life.

Joshua tells how the Israelites — led by Joshua, the successor of Moses — began their conquest of Canaan.

Judges continues the story of the conquest of Canaan after the death of Joshua. It tells how, time and again, the people of Israel were unfaithful to God, and how as punishment God let them fall into the hands of their enemies. But each time, when they repented, God sent a "judge" to be their leader and save them.

Ruth, set in the time of the Judges, tells the story of a foreign woman who converts to the worship of the True God. At last she marries Boaz, a wealthy Israelite. Her great-grandson David would be king of Israel, which means that Ruth is also one of the human ancestors of Jesus Christ.

1 Samuel tells the tragic story of the first King of Israel, Saul. Anointed king by the prophet Samuel, he starts out well, but loses God's favor by his disobedience. He involves all Israel in a long civil war with his successor, David.

2 Samuel continues the story of David after the death of Saul. God's everlasting covenant with David makes Jerusalem the religious center of the world. David builds the nation of Israel into a strong power, but he also suffers the consequences of his sins.

And David went up from there, and dwelt in the strongholds of En-gedi.
(1 Sm 23: 29)

1 Kings continues with the reign of David's son Solomon, who makes Israel a mighty empire and is famous for his wisdom. Much of the book is taken up with the most important event of Solomon's reign: the building of the Temple of the Lord in Jerusalem. But Solomon and his successors fall into idolatry, and God sends great prophets to rebuke them. The most famous of those prophets is Elijah.

2 Kings tells how Israel's two kingdoms, Judah and Israel, grew more deeply divided by falling away from God and turning to foreign idols. Finally God permitted both kingdoms to be conquered and destroyed.

And Elisha sent a messenger to him (Naaman), saying, "Go and wash in the Jordan seven times, and your flesh shall be restored, and you shall be clean." (2 Kgs 5: 10)

1 Chronicles tells much of the same history contained in 1 and 2 Samuel, but from another point of view. It emphasizes the religious aspect of David's reign, notably his preparations for the building of the Temple.

2 Chronicles continues where 1 Chronicles left off, retelling some of the same events that were recorded in 1 and 2 Kings. Most of the emphasis is on the kingdom of Judah.

Ezra tells how some of the Jews are allowed to come back to Jerusalem after a long exile in Babylon, and how they rebuild the Temple and try to restore the pure worship of the True God.

Nehemiah continues the story begun in Ezra, telling how the returned exiles restore the city of Jerusalem and promise to live by the Law of Moses. Much of the book is taken from the personal memoirs of the governor Nehemiah.

Tobit is the story of a pious man who, even in exile, scrupulously follows the Law. His son is also faithful to the Lord, and the story ends with the son rich and happily married.

Judith tells how a heroic woman saves Israel by a clever strategy. The book is careful to point out that her success comes because she trusted in God.

Esther tells about a heroic Israelite woman who becomes Queen of Persia. She saves the Jewish exiles from the plots of evil enemies.

Wisdom

There are several different kinds of books in this section. Most of them are written in verse. Some, like many of the Psalms, are poems in praise of God. Others, like Proverbs, tell us how to face our everyday problems.

Job is a long poem that asks a hard question: Why does God let bad things happen even to people who have done nothing wrong? Most of the book is a long debate between Job's friends, who believe that God always rewards the good and punishes the bad, and Job himself, who insists that life does not always work that way.

Psalms is a collection of religious poems or songs, many of them attributed to King David. The greatest religious poetry ever written is in this book, and we still hear words from the Psalms every time we celebrate the liturgy.

Proverbs is a collection of wise sayings, many of them attributed to King Solomon. Each saying gives us some important truth in a short and memorable form.

Ecclesiastes is a long meditation on the "vanity"—that is, the complete pointlessness—of worldly things. Nothing in this world is ultimately worthwhile, the author says, and the only thing a good person can do is trust in God.

"For I know that my Redeemer lives, and at last he will stand upon the earth; and after my skin has been thus destroyed, then from my flesh I shall see God..." (Jb 19: 25-26)

Song of Solomon is the world's most famous love poem, in which a bride and groom alternately speak of their love for one another. Since the earliest times, the Church has seen the poem as an allegory of Christ's love for his Church.

Wisdom, whose full title is the Wisdom of Solomon, is a poem in praise of wisdom, with a long section on how patient God has been with human folly..

Sirach is a book about how to live a good life. The author tells us how to live in the real world without compromising our faith in God.

What is Wisdom Literature?

The Wisdom books—sometimes called didactic or poetic—consist of Job, Psalms, Proverbs, Qoheleth (Ecclesiastes), Song of Songs, Wisdom, and Sirach (Ecclesiasticus). These books in general neither recount stories advancing the history of the People of God nor make prophecies about the future.

The Wisdom Literature tells stories—some poetic in nature—about the greatness of God, the justice and mercy of God, the futility of hoping in things of this world, and the like. Proverbs and Sirach are purely didactic (teaching), giving wise sayings and principles intended to guide us in our lives.

The most widely known of these books is Psalms. The Book of Psalms, traditionally attributed to David, was familiar to all Jews as the Prayer Book of the Temple. Jesus prayed psalms with The Twelve on many occasions. "The Responsorial Psalm . . . is an integral part of the Liturgy of the Word" (Introduction to *Lectionary for Mass* 19). The Book of Psalms is also a common source of Entrance, Offertory, and Communion Antiphons within every Mass.

Prophecy

Prophets are sent by God to bring his words to his people. Often the prophets warned Israel of disasters to come if the people did not return to the True God. But when the disasters did come, God sent his prophets with messages of comfort, promising that he would save his people. Many of the prophets predicted the coming of the Messiah, God's anointed one, who would lead his people out of bondage. Christians know that their predictions came true in Jesus Christ.

"For to us a child is born, to us a son is given; and the government will be upon his shoulder, and his name will be called 'Wonderful Counselor, Mighty God, Everlasting Father, Prince of Peace.'" (Is 9: 6)

Isaiah has some of the clearest prophecies of the coming of Christ in the whole Old Testament. The first part of the book warns of the disaster that will befall Judah if the people do not turn back to God. The rest of the book, possibly edited and compiled during the Exile, promises redemption to the people even though they have sinned.

Jeremiah is called by God to foretell the destruction of Judah and call on the people to repent. They hate him for what he said. We know a lot about Jeremiah because this book, unlike most of the prophets, gives us many details of his life.

Lamentations is a book of poems (attributed to Jeremiah) bemoaning the destruction of Jerusalem. Some scholars think these poems were used in Jewish liturgies celebrated on the site of the destroyed Temple.

Baruch, supposed to have been written at Babylon by a disciple of Jeremiah, prophesies a New Covenant with the people of Israel—this time an everlasting covenant. It also contains a lot of wise advice similar to what we find in the Wisdom books.

Ezekiel wrote at about the same time as Jeremiah. His book is full of strange visions, in which the message from God is given in symbolic pictures. But, even though he foretells destruction, his message is ultimately one of hope: no matter how impossible it seems, God can bring dead Israel back to life.

Daniel tells the story of a Jewish prophet who gained a high place in the court of Babylon during the Exile. The book also records his prophecies. Some of his prophecies, like Ezekiel's, come in the form of strange visions.

Isaiah's scroll reads: *"Ecce virgo concepiet et pariet filium et vocabitur nomen eius Emmanuel."*
"Behold, a young woman shall conceive and bear a son, and shall call his name Emmanuel." (Is 7: 14)

What is Prophetic Literature?

The Prophetic books consist of Isaiah, Jeremiah, Lamentations, Baruch, Ezekiel, Daniel, Hosea, Joel, Amos, Obadiah, Jonah, Micah, Nahum, Habakkuk, Zephaniah, Haggai, Zechariah, and Malachi.

A prophet is one who is called by God or speaks on God's behalf, announcing His message. Thus Prophetic Literature is a collection of those prophets' writings and their judgments which warn of divine retribution, calling Israel to repentance while offering hope to those who repent.

The prophets from Hosea to Malachi are traditionally known as the "Minor Prophets." That doesn't mean their messages are less important. They are called "minor" (Latin for "smaller") only because their books are shorter.

Hosea tells us not only the prophet Hosea's words, but also the story of his marriage. His wife was unfaithful, but he took her back nevertheless. His marriage is a metaphor for God's relationship with Israel: Israel is unfaithful, but God takes her back.

Joel warns of the divine judgment that will come to Judah. But he also speaks the famous words that have comforted God's people ever since: "Return to the LORD, your God, for he is gracious and merciful, slow to anger, and abounding in steadfast love." And he foretells a time when the Spirit of God will be poured out on all people.

Amos brings a stern message of repentance to Israel at the height of the Northern Kingdom's prosperity. Naturally, that doesn't make Amos very popular—Israel seems to be doing just fine. But his predictions of doom will soon come true. Nevertheless, he also predicts a time when the ruined kingdom of David will be restored.

Obadiah, the shortest book in the Old Testament, foretells the downfall of Edom, traditional enemy of Judah. Edom takes advantage of the destruction of Jerusalem, but God brings justice at last.

Jonah tells a story about a very reluctant prophet who tried to run away when God sent him to the wicked city of Nineveh. You can't run away from God, of course, as Jonah finds out. The story gives us a good idea of how hard it must have been to be God's chosen prophet.

Micah pronounces judgment against the wicked who take bribes and exploit the poor. But he also foretells that a savior will come to rule Israel—and that savior will come from the little town of Bethlehem.

Nahum foretells the end of Nineveh, the center of the bloody Assyrian Empire. Nineveh the conqueror will be conquered, because the Lord himself is against her.

Habakkuk again pronounces judgment against the wicked, but also preaches comfort to the righteous, who will live by faith.

Zephaniah moves beyond Israel and Judah to pronounce God's judgment against the whole earth. But he also brings a message of joy: the judgments against God's people will be taken away, and "he will renew you in his love."

"When my soul fainted within me,
I remembered the Lord;
and my prayer came to thee, into thy holy temple."
(Jon 2: 7)

The last three prophets come from the time after some of the Jews had returned from exile in Babylon.

Haggai leads the effort to rebuild the Temple in Jerusalem. He chastises the people for living in luxury while the Lord's house is in ruins.

Zechariah, who lives at the same time as Haggai, also works to have the temple rebuilt. In his visions he sees the coming of a new king to Zion, "humble and riding on an ass, on a colt the foal of an ass."

Malachi warns the returned exiles that God is not satisfied with just the forms of worship. Those who prosper by evil do not please God with token offerings from their ill-gotten goods. But he predicts the coming of the Lord's messenger, who will be "like a refiner's fire," purifying his people.

The two books of the Maccabees fill in the gap between the Prophets and the New Testament. They tell the story of a revolt led by the family of the Maccabees against the Greek rulers of Palestine, who tried to force the Jews to worship pagan gods. Many Bibles place these books at the end of the historical books, between Esther and Job.

1 Maccabees tells the story of the Maccabean revolt as a historian would tell it, starting with the background (Alexander the Great's conquest of the East) and telling the events in order.

2 Maccabees tells part of the same story from a religious point of view. Everywhere, the author sees the hand of God in the successes of Judas Maccabeus and his brothers.

Finding the Date

We count our years from the birth of Christ…from the birth of the King of kings. We say, for example, that something happened in 2000 B.C. (B.C. stands for "before Christ") if it happened two thousand years before the birth of Christ. If something happened two thousand years *after* the birth of Christ, we say it happened in 2000 A.D. (A.D. stands for *anno domini,* Latin for "in the year of Our Lord"). Christians began using this system of dates several hundred years after the time of Christ, and most historians today believe that there was some error in calculating the exact date of Jesus' birth.

The ancient Israelites—like most ancient peoples—did not number their years from a fixed calendar date. Instead, they counted the years from the beginning of the reign of the current king, or from some important event in the recent past. To find out how their dates fit in the dating system we use, historians have to add together the reigns of kings and make certain assumptions about the length of generations. For that reason, many dates given for events in Scripture are only conjectures. Sometimes, when the Bible mentions an event whose date we know for certain, we can use that event to date things that happened before and after it.

Above left: Copper prutot coin, 40 B.C., reads "Of King Herod" year 3 of reign. Historical artifacts assist us in dating events in the Bible.
Above right: Battle scene from the Alexander Sarcophagus, ca. 300 B.C., discovered in Sidon, Turkey.

Quick Outline of Old Testament History

The books of the Old Testament were written over the course of many centuries. Together, they give us the history and literature of Israel from the beginning of time to about a century before the coming of Jesus Christ.

By reading the books of the Old Testament, we can get a very good idea of which events happened in what order. Sometimes we see the same events from two points of view, as in the books of Kings and Chronicles or the books of the Maccabees. In those cases, it's even easier to tell exactly what happened.

Finding dates for those events is another matter. Obviously, the authors of the Old Testament didn't use our current dating system. We count years forward and backward from the birth of Christ, but God hadn't told the Old Testament writers exactly when the Messiah would come. So we have to rely on internal evidence—what is in the Bible—and outside sources to come up with dates we can understand for the events in the Bible.

Most of the events from the books of Samuel forward can be dated fairly precisely. The further back in history we go, the harder it is to find outside sources to compare to the events in the Bible. Nevertheless, the Bible itself gives us detailed genealogies and chronologies that we can use to work backward from the dates we do know. This chronology attempts to synchronize all of the chronological data supplied (and implied) from many Old Testament passages. Such a task is not easily done, since there are so many ambiguities and alternate datings in extra-biblical and ancient Near Eastern sources.

1. THE BEGINNING to 1635 B.C. (B.C. means "Before Christ")

Genesis

It's impossible to date the early events in the book of Genesis. Once we get to Abraham, though, we can at least make some good guesses:

ca. 2120 B.C. God calls Abram (later Abraham) to go to the land of Canaan. The time of the Patriarchs begins.

ca. 1906 B.C. Jacob and his sons go to Egypt.

ca. 1836 B.C. Joseph dies in Egypt.

2. THE EXODUS AND THE JOURNEY TO THE PROMISED LAND (1571 B.C. to 1406 B.C.)

Exodus

Leviticus

Numbers

Deuteronomy

Job

ca. 1571 B.C. Moses is born.

ca. 1484 B.C. Traditional date of the events in the book of Job.

ca. 1446 B.C. God appears to Moses; Israelites escape from Egypt.

ca. 1406 B.C. Moses dies within sight of the Promised Land.

"…and she named him Moses, for she said, 'Because I drew him out of the water.'" (Ex 2:10)

"And Joshua turned back at that time, and took Hazor, and smote its king with the sword; for Hazor formerly was the head of all those kingdoms."
(Jos 11:10)

3. THE CONQUEST OF CANAAN AND THE TIME OF THE JUDGES (1406 B.C. to about 1120 B.C.)

Joshua

Judges

Ruth

ca. 1406 B.C.   Israel begins the conquest of Canaan under Joshua.

ca. 1366 B.C.   Joshua dies.

ca. 1350-1050 B.C.   Traditional date of the events in the book of Ruth.

ca. 1120 B.C.   Samson is born.

4. THE UNITED KINGDOM (1050 B.C. to 930 B.C.)

1 Samuel

2 Samuel

1 Kings (through chapter 11)

1 Chronicles

2 Chronicles (through chapter 9)

Psalms

Proverbs

Ecclesiastes

Wisdom

ca. 1155 B.C.   Samuel is born.

ca. 1050 B.C.   Saul becomes first king of Israel.

ca. 1010 B.C.   David becomes king.

ca. 970 B.C.   Solomon becomes king.

ca. 930 B.C.   Solomon dies.

Inspired by 1 Samuel 18:10, Rembrandt's *Saul and David* shows the old king half-mad with grief because the LORD has withdrawn his favor from him and bestowed it on David. As David soothes the weeping king with his harp, the king's hand rests on his javelin. "...for he thought, 'I will pin David to the wall.'"

5. THE DIVIDED KINGDOM (930 B.C. to 588 B.C.)

1 Kings
(from Chapter 12 on)

2 Kings

2 Chronicles
(from Chapter 10 on)

Tobit

Isaiah

Jeremiah

Hosea

Joel

Amos

Obadiah

Jonah

Micah

Nahum

Habakkuk

Zephaniah

"And he (Elijah) arose, and ate and drank, and went in the strength of that food forty days and forty nights to Horeb the mount of God." (1 Kgs 19: 8)

ca. 930 B.C.	Rehoboam becomes king.
ca. 926 B.C.	Ten northern tribes revolt against Rehoboam; kingdom divided into Israel and Judah.
ca. 912 B.C.	Elijah begins to prophesy.
ca. 896 B.C.	Elijah taken up into heaven.
ca. 721 B.C.	Assyrians conquer Israel and take ten tribes into captivity.
ca. 705 B.C.	Traditional date of the events in the book of Tobit.

6. THE BABYLONIAN CAPTIVITY (586 B.C. to 536 B.C.)

Judith

Lamentations

Ezekiel

Daniel

ca. 586 B.C.	Babylonians destroy Jerusalem and carry Judah into captivity.
ca. 539 B.C.	Cyrus conquers Babylon.

7. THE RETURN FROM EXILE (537 B.C. to 442 B.C.)

Ezra

Nehemiah

Esther

Haggai

Zechariah

Malachi

Sirach (Ecclesiasticus)

The Cyrus Cylinder
On this clay cylinder, the Persian King Cyrus tells the story of how he took the ancient capital city of Babylon in 539 B.C. He writes with great pride how he brought peace and tolerance to the region and allowed the Jews who had been living there as exiles to return home to Jerusalem. (see Ezr 1: 2-4)

ca. 537 B.C. Decree of Cyrus allows Jews to return to Jerusalem.

ca. 515 B.C. Second Temple built

8. THE REVOLT UNDER THE MACCABEES (336 B.C. to 133 B.C.)

1 Maccabees

2 Maccabees

ca. 336 B.C. Alexander the Great begins conquests.

ca. 175 B.C. Antiochus Epiphanes becomes king.

ca. 167 B.C. Persecution of the Jews; revolt begins

ca. 164 B.C. Temple rededicated

ca. 134 B.C. John Hyrcanus becomes high priest

"Eleazar…saw that one of the beasts was equipped with royal armor…and he supposed that the king was upon it….He got under the elephant, stabbed it from beneath…but it fell to the ground upon him and there he died."
(1 Mc 6: 43–46)

King Antiochus IV, *Epiphanes* was determined to completely destroy all worship of the "One True God" by the Jews. It was his belief that public acts of extreme cruelty would discourage the Jews from following their God. (1 Mc 60-61)

His mistake was to underestimate the devotion and faith of the Israelites. Thus (led by one Jewish family) began the bloody struggle known today as The Maccabean Revolt…The Hasmonean Period…The Period of Independence (168-135 B.C.).

What Typology Is And How It Works

The Church, as early as apostolic times (cf. 1 Cor 10:6, 11; Heb 10:1; 1 Pt 3:21), and then constantly in her Tradition, has illuminated the unity of the divine plan in the two Testaments through typology, which discerns in God's works of the Old Covenant prefigurations of what he accomplished in the fullness of time in the person of his incarnate Son. (CCC 128)

The Old Testament contains more than simply the history of Israel. Everywhere in the Old Testament, we see things that make us think of the New Testament.

Everything in the Old Testament was written before the coming of Christ. But God himself is the true author of the books of the Old Testament, and God sees all of history at once. God is also the author of history itself. In fact, God writes history the way we write books. God sees—and creates—all history as a unity. Although we, who live in time, see history as a series of different periods with different characters, we see it that way because of our time-limited minds. God, who never changes, works the same way throughout history, and from the beginning of time his plan of salvation never varied.

So when we Christians look at the Old Testament, we see many things that point forward toward the New Testament, or toward other events in the Old Testament. Some of those things are simply predictions. For example, we can see that Old Testament prophets predicted the coming of Jesus Christ, and the sufferings he would have to endure for our salvation.

But—because God is the author of history—events in history also point forward to other events. For example, we say that Abraham's sacrifice of Isaac points forward to God's sacrifice of his own Son on the cross.

That does not mean that the story in the Old Testament has no meaning by itself. On the contrary, we must first understand the story the way the original readers understood it. But we can use that story as an analogy to help us understand Christ. And because God is the author of history, the analogy is more than an accident. It shows us that God works the same way throughout history, gradually unfolding his master plan to save his people.

When something in history points forward to something else in the future, we call the earlier thing a *type* of the later thing. So, for example, we say that Isaac was a "type" of Christ.

The study of the "types" in the Old Testament is called "typology." Typology is one of our most important tools for understanding the Old Testament. With so many books written at so many different times, the Old Testament can seem huge and bewildering. But when we see how God works the same way over and over, leading up to the climax of his plan in the death and resurrection of Jesus Christ, then the Old Testament makes even greater sense as a whole.

The Old Testament's sacrifice of Isaac by Abraham points forward to the New Testament's sacrifice by God of his son.

Typology is not an obscure technical idea. It is simply a normal way of teaching by analogy—explaining the new in terms of the old. God introduces us to new ideas in ways we can already understand.

SUPPLEMENTARY READING

Hippolytus, *Commentary on the Psalms*

1. The book of Psalms contains new doctrine after the law which was given by Moses; and thus it is the second book of doctrine after the Scripture of Moses. After the death, then of Moses and Joshua, and after the judges, David arose, one deemed worthy to be called the father of the Savior, and he was the first to give the Hebrews a new style of psalmody, by which he did away with the ordinances established by Moses with respect to sacrifice, and introduced a new mode of the worship of God by hymns and acclamations; and many other things also beyond the law of Moses he taught through his whole ministry. And this is the sacredness of the book, and its utility. And the account to be given of its inscription is this: for as most of the brethren who believe in Christ think that this book is David's, and inscribe it "Psalms of David," we must state what has reached us with respect to it. The Hebrews give the book the title *Sephra Thelim* [Book of Praises] and in the Acts of the Apostles it is called the "Book of Psalms" (the words are these, "as it is written in the Book of Psalms" [Acts 1:20]), but the name of the author in the inscription of the book is not found there. And the reason of that is, that the words written there are not the words of one man, but those of several together.

Irenaeus, *Against Heresies*, 4:32

2. For all the apostles taught that there were indeed two testaments among the two peoples; but that it was one and the same God who appointed both for the advantage of those men (for whose sakes the testaments were given) who were to believe in God, I have proved in the third book from the very teaching of the apostles; and that the first testament was not given without reason, or to no purpose, or in an accidental sort of manner; but that it subdued those to whom it was given to the service of God, for their benefit (for God needs no service from men), and exhibited a type of heavenly things, inasmuch as man was not yet able to see the things of God through means of immediate vision; and foreshadowed the images of those things which now actually exist in the Church, in order that our faith might be firmly established; and contained a prophecy of things to come, in order that man might learn that God has foreknowledge of all things.

"And when he sits on the throne of his kingdom, he shall write for himself in a book a copy of this law…" (Dt 17:18)

VOCABULARY

FULFILL
To complete or accomplish totally.

GENEALOGY
The study of ancestry. A list of someone's ancestors.

LAW
A rule of conduct enforced in a society. Also the traditional name (in Hebrew, "Torah") of the first five books of the Old Testament, also known as the Pentateuch or the Books of Moses. These five books are called the Law because they contain many rules and regulations, including the Ten Commandments.

OLD TESTAMENT
The forty-six books of Scripture written by Israelites before the coming of Jesus Christ.

PENTATEUCH
The first five books of the Old Testament. From the Greek word for "five."

PROPHET
One who speaks the message of God to the people. Some prophets foretold future events, while others preached against the unholiness of their own time.

TYPE
An event or person in Scripture that points forward to a later event or person. The type has similar virtues or other qualities as its fulfillment.

TYPOLOGY
The study of types in Scripture.

WISDOM LITERATURE
A style of Hebrew literature that meditates on important truths. Wisdom literature utilizes poems, teachings, and other means of communicating these truths.

STUDY QUESTIONS

1. Who came to fulfill the Old Testament?

2. Which two historical figures does Matthew mention as ancestors of Jesus Christ at the beginning of his Gospel?

3. Where is the Old Testament perfected?

4. What does the New Testament accomplish?

5. What does Jesus' genealogy indicate?

6. What are the four main types of books in the Old Testament?

7. Which books are known as the books of the Law?

8. What are other names for the books of the Law?

9. What does the word "Pentateuch" mean?

10. What do the Historical books describe?

11. What are the Wisdom books?

12. Which book includes many religious poems attributed to David?

13. Which three books of the Old Testament are named for women?

14. Why are the books from Hosea to Malachi called "Minor Prophets"?

15. What can we discover from reading the Old Testament?

16. What are biblical types?

17. How did Old Testament writers date events?

18. What are the names of the four sources which contributed to the compilation of the Pentateuch?

19. What is a "heresy"?

20. What were the points made by Hippolytus?

21. What points were made by Irenaeus?

PRACTICAL EXERCISES

1. It is very important for Christians to realize the significance of the Old Testament and all that it has to teach us. An example of someone who didn't is Marcion, who was born in 110 A.D. Marcion believed that the Old Testament was so scandalous and crude that it should be cut out of Christianity completely, and that the New Law of Christianity rendered the Old Testament void anyway. Was Marcion's way of thinking correct? How did his thinking differ from that of the Church? How does the *Catechism of the Catholic Church* respond to this way of thought in points 121-123?

2. If God is the ultimate author of Scripture, why is there sometimes more than one book that tells us about the same events? For instance, 1 and 2 Chronicles are books in the Old Testament that repeat much of the same history that is told in 1 and 2 Samuel and 1 and 2 Kings. Why do you think it is important that we hear some of the events in Scripture from more than one point of view?

FROM THE CATECHISM

292 The Old Testament suggests and the New Covenant reveals the creative action of the Son and the Spirit, (cf. Ps 33:6; 104:30; Gn 1:2-3) inseparably one with that of the Father. This creative co-operation is clearly affirmed in the Church's rule of faith: "There exists but one God…he is the Father, God, the Creator, the author, the giver of order. He made all things by himself, that is, by his Word and by his Wisdom," "by the Son and the Spirit" who, so to speak, are "his hands" (St. Irenaeus, *Adv. haeres* 2, 30, 9; 4, 20,1: PG 7/1, 822, 1032). Creation is the common work of the Holy Trinity.

304 And so we see the Holy Spirit, the principal author of Sacred Scripture, often attributing actions to God without mentioning any secondary causes. This is not a "primitive mode of speech," but a profound way of recalling God's primacy and absolute Lordship over history and the world, (cf. Is 10:5-15; 45:5-7; Dt 32:39; Sir 11:14) and so of educating his people to trust in him. The prayer of the Psalms is the great school of this trust (cf. Ps 22; 32; 35; 103; 138; *et al*).

1094 It is on this harmony of the two Testaments that the Paschal catechesis of the Lord is built, (cf. DV 14-16; Lk 24:13-49) and then, that of the Apostles and the Fathers of the Church. This catechesis unveils what lay hidden under the letter of the Old Testament: the mystery of Christ. It is called "typological" because it reveals the newness of Christ on the basis of the "figures" (types) which announce him in the deeds, words, and symbols of the first covenant. By this rereading in the Spirit of Truth, starting from Christ, the figures are unveiled (cf. 2 Cor 3:14-16). Thus the flood and Noah's ark prefigured salvation by Baptism, (cf. 1 Pt 3:21) as did the cloud and the crossing of the Red Sea. Water from the rock was the figure of the spiritual gifts of Christ, and manna in the desert prefigured the Eucharist, "the true bread from heaven" (Jn 6:32; cf. 1 Cor 10:1-6).

FROM THE CATECHISM continued

1962 The Old Law is the first stage of revealed Law. Its moral prescriptions are summed up in the Ten Commandments. The precepts of the Decalogue lay the foundations for the vocation of man fashioned in the image of God; they prohibit what is contrary to the love of God and neighbor and prescribe what is essential to it. The Decalogue is a light offered to the conscience of every man to make God's call and ways known to him and to protect him against evil:

> God wrote on the tables of the Law what men did not read in their hearts (St. Augustine, *En. in Ps.* 57, 1: PL 36, 673).

2465 The Old Testament attests that *God is the source of all truth.* His Word is truth. His Law is truth. His "faithfulness endures to all generations" (Ps 119: 90; cf. Prv 8: 7; 2 Sm 7: 28; Ps 119: 142; Lk 1: 50) (Mt 5: 33). Since God is "true," the members of his people are called to live in the truth (Rom 3: 4; cf. Ps 119: 30).

2585 From the time of David to the coming of the Messiah, texts appearing in these sacred books show a deepening in prayer for oneself and in prayer for others (Ezr 9: 6-15; Neh 1: 4-11; Jon 2: 3-10; Tb 3: 11-16; Jdt 9: 2-14). Thus the Psalms were gradually collected into the five books of the Psalter (or "Praises"), the masterwork of prayer in the Old Testament.

2586 The Psalms both nourished and expressed the prayer of the People of God gathered during the great feasts at Jerusalem and each Sabbath in the synagogues. Their prayer is inseparably personal and communal; it concerns both those who are praying and all men. The Psalms arose from the communities of the Holy Land and the Diaspora, but embrace all creation. Their prayer recalls the saving events of the past, yet extends into the future, even to the end of history; it commemorates the promises God has already kept, and awaits the Messiah who will fulfill them definitively. Prayed by Christ and fulfilled in him, the Psalms remain essential to the prayer of the Church (cf. *General Instruction of the Liturgy of the Hours* 100109).

This miniature depicting King David is from the *French Bible of Hainburg*, one of the finest illuminated manuscripts ever created. The *French Bible* was published in Northern France between 1300 and 1320 A.D.

Endnote

1. Mt 5: 17-18.

Chapter 3
The Creation of The World

*All of creation is a great temple
for the worship of God the creator.*

Chapter 3

The Creation of The World

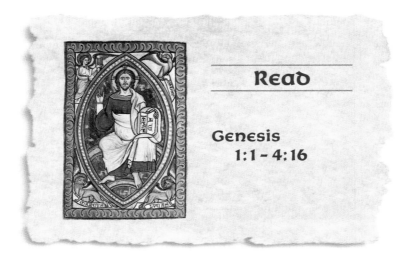

Read

Genesis
1:1 – 4:16

"In the beginning," Genesis tells us, "God created the heavens and the earth."

Everything that exists was created by God. The first chapter of the first book in the Bible is a poetic narrative that tells us what we need to know to understand why God created. When we outline it, we can see how carefully constructed it is:

In the beginning God created the heavens and the earth. The earth was without form and void, and darkness was upon the face of the deep; and the Spirit of God was moving over the face of the waters.

Days 1-3: Creating Form

First Day: TIME

And God said, "Let there be light"; and there was light. And God saw that the light was good; and God separated the light from the darkness. God called the light Day, and the darkness he called Night. And there was evening and there was morning, one day.

Second Day: SPACE

And God said, "Let there be a firmament in the midst of the waters, and let it separate the waters from the waters." And God made the firmament and separated the waters which were under the firmament from the waters which were above the firmament. And it was so. And God called the firmament Heaven. And there was evening and there was morning, a second day.

Third Day: LIFE

And God said, "Let the waters under the heavens be gathered together into one place, and let the dry land appear." And it was so. God called the dry land Earth, and the waters that were gathered together he called Seas. And God saw that it was good. And God said, "Let the earth put forth vegetation, plants yielding seed, and fruit trees bearing fruit in which is their seed, each according to its kind, upon the earth." And it was so. The earth brought forth vegetation, plants yielding seed according to their own kinds, and trees bearing fruit in which is their seed, each according to its kind. And God saw that it was good. And there was evening and there was morning, a third day.

Days 4-6: Filling The Void

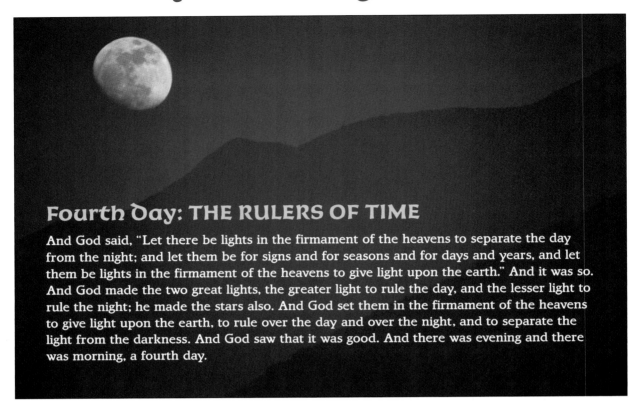

Fourth Day: THE RULERS OF TIME

And God said, "Let there be lights in the firmament of the heavens to separate the day from the night; and let them be for signs and for seasons and for days and years, and let them be lights in the firmament of the heavens to give light upon the earth." And it was so. And God made the two great lights, the greater light to rule the day, and the lesser light to rule the night; he made the stars also. And God set them in the firmament of the heavens to give light upon the earth, to rule over the day and over the night, and to separate the light from the darkness. And God saw that it was good. And there was evening and there was morning, a fourth day.

Fifth Day: THE RULERS OF SPACE

And God said, "Let the waters bring forth swarms of living creatures, and let birds fly above the earth across the firmament of the heavens." So God created the great sea monsters and every living creature that moves, with which the waters swarm, according to their kinds, and every winged bird according to its kind. And God saw that it was good. And God blessed them, saying, "Be fruitful and multiply and fill the waters in the seas, and let birds multiply on the earth." And there was evening and there was morning, a fifth day.

Sixth Day: THE RULERS OF LIFE

And God said, "Let the earth bring forth living creatures according to their kinds: cattle and creeping things and beasts of the earth according to their kinds." And it was so. And God made the beasts of the earth according to their kinds and the cattle according to their kinds, and everything that creeps upon the ground according to its kind. And God saw that it was good. Then God said, "Let us make man in our image, after our likeness; and let them have dominion over the fish of the sea, and over the birds of the air, and over the cattle, and over all the earth, and over every creeping thing that creeps upon the earth." So God created man in his own image, in the image of God he created him; male and female he created them. And God blessed them, and God said to them, "Be fruitful and multiply, and fill the earth and subdue it; and have dominion over the fish of the sea and over the birds of the air and over every living thing that moves upon the earth." And God said, "Behold, I have given you every plant yielding seed which is upon the face of all the earth, and every tree with seed in its fruit; you shall have them for food. And to every beast of the earth, and to every bird of the air, and to everything that creeps on the earth, everything that has the breath of life, I have given every green plant for food." And it was so. And God saw everything that he had made, and behold, it was very good. And there was evening and there was morning, a sixth day.

Man is made to live in communion with God in whom he finds happiness: "When I am completely united to you, there will be no more sorrow or trials; entirely full of you, my life will be complete" (St. Augustine, *Confessions* 10, 28, 39: PL 32, 795). (CCC 45)

Day 7: God Rested

Seventh Day:
THE SABBATH COVENANT WITH CREATION

Thus the heavens and the earth were finished, and all the host of them. And on the seventh day God finished his work which he had done, and he rested on the seventh day from all his work which he had done. So God blessed the seventh day and hallowed it, because on it God rested from all his work which he had done in creation.

Creation: A Covenant With The Universe

So what is the real purpose of the creation story?

We can see some of the most important ideas in just a few phrases. "In the beginning, God created the heavens and the earth."

We see how God creates, by the power of his Word. He simply speaks the world into being. That same Word of God became flesh and dwelt among us. In the New Testament, we discover that the Word is not some impersonal utterance; it is the Son of God, our Savior.

"The earth was without form and void." There was no structure on earth, and no one to live there. One way of looking at the creation account is to see it as two sets of three days. In the first three days, God creates the place, the structure of the earth. In the second three days, God creates the inhabitants to fill it. In other words, God first creates forms and then fills them with inhabitants.

- **On the first day, God creates day and night.**
- **On the second day, God creates the sky and the sea.**
- **On the third day, God creates the land and the vegetation.**

These first three days see the creation of the environments in which God's creatures will live.

Day and Night (Time)	Sky and Sea (Space)	Land and Vegetation (Life)

In those first three days, God has created a world fit to live in. He has provided the threefold form of earthly life. Day and night give us time; sky and sea give us space; land and vegetation give us a place to live.

The next three days correspond to the first three.

- **On the fourth day, God creates the sun to rule the day, and the moon and stars to shine at night.**
- **On the fifth day, God creates the birds and the fish to fill up the sky and the sea.**
- **On the sixth day, God creates the beasts of the field, and finally human beings, to live on the land with its vegetation.**

These next three days, in other words, see the creation of the *rulers* of the environments created in the first three days.

Sun and Moon *rule over*	Birds and Fish *rule over*	Humans and Animals *rule over*
Day and Night	Sky and Sea	Land and Vegetation

So on the first three days, God establishes a form. On the second three days, God creates the inhabitants for each of the realms he created in the first three days.

Finally, on the seventh day, God rests.

The Hebrew word that means "to swear a covenant" is based on the Hebrew word for seven. Someone who said "I swear a covenant" in Hebrew was literally saying "I seven myself."

So in creating the world in seven days, God is swearing a *covenant* with the universe. He is not just the master, and we are not just slaves. He is more than creator, and we are more than his creatures. If God had stopped on the sixth day, we would be only creatures: we would be slaves and private property of God. But God went on. "So God blessed the seventh day and hallowed it, because on it God rested from all his work which he had done in creation." God invited us into that rest, because that rest represents the covenant relationship that he establishes with his creation.

The Sabbath rest crowns creation as a roof crowns a temple:

SABBATH COVENANT WITH CREATION		
Sun and Moon *rule over*	Birds and Fish *rule over*	Humans and Animals *rule over*
Day and Night	Sky and Sea	Land and Vegetation

All of creation is a great temple for the worship of God the creator.

> Thus the revelation of creation is inseparable from the revelation and forging of the covenant of the one God with his People. Creation is revealed as the first step towards this covenant, the first and universal witness to God's all-powerful love (cf. Gn 15: 5; Jer 33: 19-26). And so, the truth of creation is also expressed with growing vigor in the message of the prophets, the prayer of the psalms and the liturgy, and in the wisdom sayings of the Chosen People (cf. Is 44: 24; Ps 104; Prv 8: 22-31). (CCC 288)

Understanding Time As Part Of Creation

"In the beginning, God created the heavens and the earth." What was God doing before he created? It's a hard question. St. Augustine had a simple answer:

"Nothing. He didn't have the time."

What St. Augustine meant was that time and space are things that exist for creatures, but not for the Creator. God fills all of time.

We speak of God as "omnipresent," which means that he is everywhere. And that, in turn, means that God cannot move. Why not? Because in order to move, God would have to go from someplace where he is to some other place where he is not. But there is no place where he is not. God is not stuck in one place; rather, God fills space to overflowing. Space cannot contain the infinite glory of God. We can move, because most of the universe is made up of places where we are not. But God cannot move.

The same thing is true for time. Time is an experience of limited creatures like us. We move forward in time, as we see it, because most of time is made up of moments that for us either have already passed or have not come yet. But God fills all of time. Just as God cannot move anywhere in the universe because he is everywhere to begin with, so for God, the past, the present, and the future are one simultaneous moment, one eternal present.

Creation Is Good

Some people—even some who call themselves Christians—believe that matter is evil and only spirit is good. The soul, they say, is good, but the body is only a necessary evil we need to get through this world.

The first chapter of Genesis contradicts that idea. Every time God creates something, the creation story tells us that "God saw that it was good." And in the end, "God saw everything that he had made, and behold, it was very good."

Matter as well as spirit, body as well as soul—both are positive goods that are created by God for good. They are ultimately the instruments God uses to redeem us.

If we sin with our bodies, God turns around and uses Christ's body to redeem us and to restore us to a relationship with himself. In fact, the goodness of matter is one of the foundations of the seven sacraments, all of which make use of material things for spiritual ends.

Is It True?

Is it literally true that God made the world in six days?

Many Christians think that six days means six "days" as we know days today. Other people say the creation story is just a myth, a made-up fable that isn't true at all.

The Catholic Church has always taught that everything in the Bible is true; so the creation story must be true. Some Christians believe that "six days" means six literal days. Most Catholic interpreters, however, do not take that view.

Hebrew history was not written the same way we write history today. Modern historians write down a series of events—battles, plagues, elections—just as they happened, from start to finish. Scripture, on the other hand, gives us *religious* history. The sacred writers use different literary forms, with many symbols and figures. The important thing for them was not merely to give us an accurate knowledge of historical events, but to tell us the truth about our relationship with God. In the creation story, they were not trying to tell us *how* creation was done. They had no interest in the exact physical forces and mechanics that went into creation. Instead, Genesis 1 is primarily meant to show us *why* God created.

The same is true of the rest of the story of human beginnings.

The account of the fall in *Genesis* 3 uses figurative language, but affirms a primeval event, a deed that took place *at the beginning of the history of man*. Revelation gives us the certainty of faith that the whole of human history is marked by the original fault freely committed by our first parents (cf. Council of Trent: DS 1513; Pius XII: DS 3897; Paul VI: AAS 58 (1966)). (CCC 390)

"*If there was time, You made it, for time could not pass before You made time...*
If there was not any time, there was not any 'then.'"

(*St. Augustine, Confessions, XI, 12–13*)

The Creation Of Human Beings In The Image Of God

As the very last act of creation, God creates human beings.

> Then God said, "Let us make man in our image, after our likeness; and let them have dominion over the fish of the sea, and the birds of the air, and over the cattle, and over all the earth, and over every creeping thing that creeps upon the earth." So God created man in his own image, in the image of God he created him; male and female he created them.

What does it mean to say that we were created in God's image and after his likeness?

1. **God is our Father.** The next time Genesis uses the terms "image" and "likeness" together, it's speaking of Adam becoming the father of Seth: "When Adam had lived a hundred and thirty years, he became the father of a son in his own likeness, after his image, and named him Seth" (Genesis 5:3). We were created with the ability to have a loving relationship with God, our father. We were given "the inner harmony of the human person, the harmony between man and woman" (CCC 376) from the moment our existence began.

2. **We are like God.** We have intelligence, free will, and the capacity to love. Furthermore, God made our nature unlike any other. As human beings, we find ourselves somewhere between the angels and the beasts, with physical bodies and rational souls. Our love in our families is an image of the love and life of the Trinity—Father, Son, and Holy Spirit.

3. **Human life possesses great sacredness.** Too often, we make the mistake of valuing people according to what they can do for society. The Nazis made that mistake, and it is at the heart of the tragedy of abortion and euthanasia in our own time. Old or young, healthy or sick, every person is sacred because every person is created in God's image. Even someone who has committed a horrible crime is still created in the image of God. No human is beyond redemption.

4. **Our work has special value.** Our dignity does not come from what we do. Our work has dignity because we bear the image of God. *Work itself is not a curse,* even though it is cursed with toil because of Adam's sin, as we'll see shortly. God himself labored to bring creation into existence. We are called to work in imitation of God our Father.

> Being in the image of God the human individual possesses the dignity of a person, who is not just something, but someone. He is capable of self-knowledge, of self-possession and of freely giving himself and entering into communion with other persons. And he is called by grace to a covenant with his Creator, to offer him a response of faith and love that no other creature can give in his stead. (CCC 357)

Adam and Eve were created in original justice. They were full of sanctifying grace and had dominion over their passions and over the earth. They had perfection of mind and will coupled with freedom from death and sickness. They were immortal.

The Marriage Covenant

Not only did God create us in his image, but he also created us *male and female.*

> And God blessed them, and God said to them, "Be fruitful and multiply, and fill the earth and subdue it; and have dominion over the fish of the sea and over the birds of the air and over every living thing that moves upon the earth."

"Be fruitful and multiply" means more than just to reproduce. God created man and woman as equal but complementary persons, meant to join in a family relationship sealed by the marital covenant. Marriage is not man-made. Marriage is divinely instituted the very moment man was created *male and female.*

In Matthew 19, when the Pharisees probed and questioned Jesus about divorce, he went right back to Genesis. There he set straight and made clear the doctrine of marital indissolubility: "What God has joined together, let no man put asunder." God is the one who creates marriage. Mere humans cannot break it up. Marriage was created to be permanent, lifelong, and indissoluble. More than that, it was created to be *fruitful.*

We are, in a sense, co-creators with God in the act of marriage. Marital love in the covenant of marriage is life-giving, not just accidentally or incidentally, but intrinsically. That is the divine intention, for the two to become one—and then three and four and five....

God is a family, an infinite family of three persons. God created the human family in his own image and likeness. How can finite beings be an image of an infinite family? By becoming three, four, five, a million, ten million, twenty million, thirty million, and so on. We are called to be fruitful and multiply in the image of God, not just biologically but psychologically and socially in love and virtue.

Man and woman have been *created*, which is to say, *willed* by God: on the one hand, in perfect equality as human persons; on the other, in their respective beings as man and woman. "Being man" or "being woman" is a reality which is good and willed by God: man and woman possess an inalienable dignity which comes to them immediately from God their Creator (cf. Gn 2: 7, 22). Man and woman are both with one and the same dignity "in the image of God." In their "being-man" and "being-woman," they reflect the Creator's wisdom and goodness. (CCC 369)

God Our Father

Among all the Scriptural texts about creation, the first three chapters of Genesis occupy a unique place. From a literary standpoint these texts may have had diverse sources. The inspired authors have placed them at the beginning of Scripture to express in their solemn language the truths of creation—its origin and its end in God, its order and goodness, the vocation of man, and finally the drama of sin and the hope of salvation. Read in the light of Christ, within the unity of Sacred Scripture and in the living Tradition of the Church, these texts remain the principal source for catechesis on the mysteries of the "beginning": creation, fall, and promise of salvation. (CCC 289)

We have seen in the first chapter of Genesis that all the universe was created as a temple. But if it is a temple, where is the holy place? Where is the priest? The second chapter of Genesis answers those questions.

The first chapter of Genesis in Hebrew speaks of God as Elohim, God the creator. Now the story begins to call God Yahweh, God the Covenant Lord. In many Bible translations, including the one used in this book, the sacred name Yahweh is translated as "Lord," in small capitals.

In the day that the Lord God made the earth and the heavens, when no plant of the field was yet in the earth and no herb of the field had yet sprung up—for the Lord God had not yet caused it to rain upon the earth, and there was no man to till the ground; but a

> mist went up from the earth and watered the whole face of the ground—then the LORD
> God formed man of dust from the ground, and breathed into his nostrils the breath of life;
> and man became a living being. And the LORD God planted a garden in Eden, in the east;
> and there he put the man whom he had formed. And out of the ground the LORD God
> made to grow every tree that is pleasant to the sight and good for food, the tree of life
> also in the midst of the garden, and the tree of the knowledge of good and evil. **(Gn 2:4-9)**

Genesis 1 describes how *Elohim* called the universe into existence; now Genesis 2 tells us how *Yahweh* acted closely and personally, forming Adam out of the ground and placing him in the Garden of Eden. The difference in names reflects a difference in how the author looks at what God is doing. "Elohim" suggests the infinite power of the Creator, while "Yahweh" suggests God's covenant love—the love of the Father for us, his children.

> The LORD God took the man and put him in the garden of Eden to till it and keep it. And
> the LORD God commanded the man, saying, "You may freely eat of every tree of the
> garden; but of the tree of the knowledge of good and evil you shall not eat, for in the day
> that you eat of it you shall die."

Here God gives Adam his instructions. He is to till the garden (even in paradise there was work!) and to "keep" it—the word literally means to "guard" it, as though Adam might have to defend it from intruders. In fact, Adam will be a priest—the Hebrew words for "till" and "keep" are the same words the priests of God would later use to describe their duties. In the Garden of Eden, God has created a holy place where he meets his priest, Adam, face to face.

But his role as priest was about to be put to the test.

Adam could eat the fruit of any tree in the garden, including the tree of life. There was only one exception: the tree of the knowledge of good and evil.

> Then the LORD God said, "It is not good that the man should be
> alone; I will make him a helper fit for him."

Now the story goes on to tell how God brings every creature to Adam, and Adam names each one of them. By bringing him the animals one by one, God shows Adam that he is *different* from the animals. "But for the man there was not found a helper fit for him."

> So the LORD God caused a deep sleep to fall upon the man;
> and while he slept took one of his ribs and closed up its place
> with flesh; and the rib which the LORD God had taken from
> the man he made into a woman and brought her to the man.
> Then the man said,

> "This at last is bone of my bones and flesh of my flesh; she
> shall be called Woman, because she was taken out of Man."

> Therefore a man leaves his father and his mother and cleaves to his wife, and they
> become one flesh. And the man and his wife were both naked, and were not ashamed.

> Man and woman were made "for each other"—not that God left them half-made and
> incomplete: he created them to be a communion of persons, in which each can be "help-
> mate" to the other, for they are equal as persons ("bone of my bones...") and comple-
> mentary as masculine and feminine. In marriage God unites them in such a way that, by
> forming "one flesh" (Gn 2:24), they can transmit human life: "Be fruitful and multiply, and
> fill the earth" (Gn 1:28). By transmitting human life to their descendants, man and woman
> as spouses and parents cooperate in a unique way in the Creator's work (cf. GS 50 § 1).
> **(CCC 372)**

The Fall

Genesis 3 starts with an ominous new character:

> Now the serpent was more subtle than any other wild creature that the LORD God had made. He said to the woman, "Did God say, 'You shall not eat of any tree of the garden?'" And the woman said to the serpent, "We may eat of the fruit of the trees of the garden; but God said, 'You shall not eat of the fruit of the tree which is in the midst of the garden, neither shall you touch it, lest you die.'" But the serpent said to the woman, "You will not die. For God knows that when you eat of it your eyes will be opened, and you will be like God, knowing good and evil." So when the woman saw that the tree was good for food, and that it was a delight to the eyes, and that the tree was to be desired to make one wise, she took of its fruit and ate; and she also gave some to her husband, and he ate.

So Adam and Eve both disobeyed God. Why?

The Hebrew word used to describe the "serpent," *nahash,* implies something much more deadly than a garden-variety snake. It is used throughout the Old Testament in reference to powerful evil creatures.

- **Numbers 21 uses the term to describe "fiery serpents" that attack the Israelites in the desert.**
- **In Isaiah 27:1 the term in depicting the great mythical dragon, the Leviathan.**
- **Job 26:13 uses *nahash* in reference to the great sea monsters.**

Wherever it appears, the word usually refers to something that bites, often with venom. The serpent here is more than just subtle: it is deadly, a liar, and a murderer.

> Scripture witnesses to the disastrous influence of the one Jesus calls "a murderer from the beginning," who would even try to divert Jesus from the mission received from his Father (Jn 8:44; cf. Mt 4:1-11). "The reason the Son of God appeared was to destroy the works of the devil" (1 Jn 3:8). In its consequences the gravest of these works was the mendacious seduction that led man to disobey God. (CCC 394)

Spiritual Death

God said "the day you eat of the tree [of knowledge] you shall die." The serpent said, "You will not die." Who was right?

On the surface it appears that the serpent was right. After all, Adam and Eve did not fall dead after they ate the fruit—they ran and hid. In every lie, there is an element of truth. The truth in Satan's lie was this: you will not die a physical death once you eat the fruit.

Adam and Eve lost something greater than natural life when they sinned; they lost supernatural life, original holiness, and original justice. Losing this life is true death—a death much worse than any they would have experienced had they simply lost their bodily lives. Confronted with the choice of preserving their earthly lives on the one hand or surrendering the supernatural life in their souls on the other, Adam and Eve chose to love themselves more than God.

> Following St. Paul, the Church has always taught that the overwhelming misery which oppresses men and their inclination towards evil and death cannot be understood apart from their connection with Adam's sin and the fact that he has transmitted to us a sin with which we are all born afflicted, a sin which is the "death of the soul" (cf. Council of Trent: DS 1512). Because of this certainty of faith, the Church baptizes for the remission of sins even tiny infants who have not committed personal sin (cf. Council of Trent: DS 1514). (CCC 403)

Here it is helpful to recall Jesus' words, "And do not fear those who kill the body but cannot kill the soul; rather fear him who can destroy both soul and body in hell" (Mt 10:28).

> This dramatic situation of "the whole world [which] is in the power of the evil one" (1 Jn 5:19; cf. 1 Pt 5:8) makes man's life a battle:
>
> > The whole of man's history has been the story of dour combat with the powers of evil, stretching, so our Lord tells us, from the very dawn of history until the last day. Finding himself in the midst of the battlefield man has to struggle to do what is right, and it is at great cost to himself, and aided by God's grace, that he succeeds in achieving his own inner integrity.[1] (CCC 409)

Everything the serpent had said was right—but in a twisted way. Adam and Eve didn't die *physically* when they ate the fruit—but they died spiritually. In the "dour combat," they had lost the battle. And their eyes were opened—but to the shame of their own nakedness and sin. They knew that they had sinned against God. And like every disobedient child, they ran and hid from their Father.

"Where Are You?"

When Adam and Eve hear God coming they hide themselves. God asks a series of puzzling questions.

"Where are you?" (Gn 3:8).

"Who told you that you were naked?" (Gn 3:11).

"Have you eaten of the tree of which I commanded you not to eat?" (Gn 3:11).

"What is this that you have done?" (Gn 3:13).

Why would God, all-powerful and all-knowing, ask such questions? Doesn't he know the answers? Of course he does. God is giving Adam and Eve every chance to come to him and confess their sin. Instead they hide and make excuses for disobeying God.

Adam begins by blaming his wife. But he also blames God himself. "The woman whom *you* gave to be with me, she gave me fruit of the tree and I ate" (Gn 3:12). Eve turns around and blames the serpent for tricking her into eating the fruit: "The serpent beguiled me, and I ate" (Gn 3:13).

The First Gospel

God then curses the serpent, adding a promise to send one who will conquer the serpent. "I will put enmity between you and the woman, and between your seed and her seed; he shall bruise your head, and you shall bruise his heel" (Gn 3:15). The serpent will wound the Redeemer, but not seriously, biting His *heel*. The Redeemer will issue the final blow to the serpent, bruising his head.

Early Christian writers called this the "First Gospel" (*Protoevangelium*). Furthermore, they saw the term the "seed of the woman" as God's promise of a future Redeemer:

> The Christian tradition sees in this passage an announcement of the "New Adam" who, because he "became obedient unto death, even death on a cross," makes amends super-abundantly for the disobedience of Adam (cf. 1 Cor 15:21-22, 45; Phil 2:8; Rom 5:19-20). Furthermore, many Fathers and Doctors of the Church have seen the woman announced in the *Protoevangelium* as Mary, the mother of Christ, the "new Eve." Mary benefited first of all and uniquely from Christ's victory over sin: she was preserved from all stain of original sin and by a special grace of God committed no sin of any kind during her whole earthly life (cf. Pius IX, *Ineffabilis Deus*: DS 2803; Council of Trent: DS 1573). (CCC 411)

The Curse

By their sin, Adam and Eve brought suffering into the world. Sin is the reason for suffering. All the good things God planned for us will now be tainted by suffering. Because of their sin, God warns Adam and Eve that:

- When we carry out God's wish for us to "be fruitful," childbirth will be painful.

- Our family life will still be an image of God's love, but relationships will be marred by sin.

- Work—which was designed to be a joy—will be toil; it will not always be fruitful, but may bring forth thorns and thistles. Labor will be carried out with difficulty, in sweat.

- Even life itself will end in suffering. Physical death is inevitable.

How did the sin of Adam become the sin of all his descendants? The whole human race is in Adam "as one body of one man" (St. Thomas Aquinas, *De Malo* 4, 1). By this "unity of the human race" all men are implicated in Adam's sin, as all are implicated in Christ's justice. Still, the transmission of original sin is a mystery that we cannot fully understand. But we do know by Revelation that Adam had received original holiness and justice not for himself alone, but for all human nature. By yielding to the tempter, Adam and Eve committed a *personal sin*, but this sin affected the *human nature* that they would then transmit *in a fallen state* (cf. Council of Trent: DS 1511-1512). It is a sin which will be transmitted by propagation to all mankind, that is, by the transmission of a human nature deprived of original holiness and justice. And that is why original sin is called "sin" only in an analogical sense: it is a sin "contracted" and not "committed"—a state and not an act. (CCC 404)

This is the curse Adam and Eve brought on themselves—and on all of us—by their sin. That curse was not, however, an act of revenge. God's wrath is not the *opposite* of God's love: rather, his wrath is a *manifestation* of his love.

When we disobey the Father's law, we refuse his love. But we cannot escape it; we simply seal ourselves off from it so that we cannot enjoy it. We only feel burned by it until we open ourselves to it again. That opening up is *repentance*, and God's wrath is meant to lead us to repentance.

Repentance thus involves a change of thinking and living. We do not see suffering as evil in itself any longer. By seeing it as part of God's plan to teach us love, we can embrace suffering as a needed remedy for sin.

Instead of being God's revenge on Adam and Eve, the curse was the *cure* for their illness.

Evil

Once evil had entered the world, it took firm root. Adam and Eve, thrown out of paradise, had two sons, Cain and Abel. And the very next thing we read is the story of how Cain killed Abel. Evil had entered the world to stay.

Why did Cain kill Abel? Cain was angry because Abel's sacrifice had been acceptable to God, but his own had not. Why not? It was because of Cain's own attitude. Sacrifice was no good if it didn't go along with a right mind.

> The LORD said to Cain, "Why are you angry, and why has your countenance fallen? If you do well, will you not be accepted? And if you do not do well, sin is crouching at the door: its desire is for you, but you must master it." (Gn 4:6-7)

Cain's sacrifice was unacceptable because he had not mastered sin. His sin was envy—one of the traditional seven deadly sins, and one of the most dangerous. Envy is the sin of resenting the blessings of others: "It's not fair," says the envious person. Cain saw himself as persecuted: God wasn't being fair to him. Even after God confronted him with his sin, he moaned that "my punishment is more than I can bear." Yet God would not abandon Cain to total destruction. He would be punished by being made a wanderer, but God would protect Cain also.

> The doctrine of original sin, closely connected with that of redemption by Christ, provides lucid discernment of man's situation and activity in the world. By our first parents' sin, the devil has acquired a certain domination over man, even though man remains free. Original sin entails "captivity under the power of him who thenceforth had the power of death, that is, the devil" (Council of Trent (1546): DS 1511; cf. Heb 2:14). Ignorance of the fact that man has a wounded nature inclined to evil gives rise to serious errors in the areas of education, politics, social action (cf. John Paul II, CA 25), and morals. (CCC 407)

Creation And Evolution

The first thing the Bible tells us is that God created the heavens and the earth, so Christians believe that God created the whole universe. In addition to this, here are important truths of faith found in Genesis which the Church requires us to accept. Some of these are:

- That matter was created out of nothing by God at the beginning of time.

- That the creation of human beings—however humans arose in history—was an act of special creation by God. God breathed a human soul into Adam.

- That woman is formed from the body of man, from his very self.

- That all humanity is descended from Adam and Eve. *common source*

- That Adam and Eve were created without sin. *mitocondrial Eve*

- That Adam and Eve were commanded to be obedient to God.

- That Adam and Eve sinned against this command.

- That, as a result of that sin, our ancestors fell from their state of sinless innocence.

- That, even at the time of the Fall, God made clear the promise of a future Redeemer.

The creation account in the Bible tells us God is the origin of the material which makes up the universe.

Evolutionists attempt to explain, scientifically, how man and animals came to be by an examination of the material universe, and the Church does not oppose research and discussions on the part of men of experience in science and sacred theology in regards to evolution insofar as it relates to the origin of the human body coming from pre-existent material.

However, when a statement of evolution appears to conflict with the Bible, the Church will indicate the truth Catholics must believe.

When the theory of evolution opened the door to the possibility of polygenism—the belief there were many sets of first parents on the earth—this was a contradiction of a truth contained in the Bible.

To counter this and other false beliefs, Pope Pius XII wrote the encyclical *Humani generis* in 1950 to counter false opinions concerning Catholic Doctrine. In the encyclical he states, "the faithful cannot embrace that opinion which maintains either after Adam there existed on the earth true men who did not take their origin through natural generation from him as from the first parent of all or that Adam represents a certain number of first parents."

To accept polygenism would have led directly to the denial of original sin.

An initial in Genesis from the *Neapolitan Luxury Bible,* 1360, Naples; a lavishly illustrated Latin text of the Vulgate.

The question about the origins of the world and of man has been the object of many scientific studies which have splendidly enriched our knowledge of the age and dimensions of the cosmos, the development of life-forms and the appearance of man. These discoveries invite us to even greater admiration for the greatness of the Creator, prompting us to give him thanks for all his works and for the understanding and wisdom he gives to scholars and researchers. With Solomon they can say: "It is he who gave me unerring knowledge of what exists, to know the structure of the world and the activity of the elements . . . for wisdom, the fashioner of all things, taught me" (Wis 7:17-22). (CCC 283)

The great interest accorded to these studies is strongly stimulated by a question of another order, which goes beyond the proper domain of the natural sciences. It is not only a question of knowing when and how the universe arose physically, or when man appeared, but rather of discovering the meaning of such an origin: is the universe governed by chance, blind fate, anonymous necessity, or by a transcendent, intelligent, and good Being called "God"? And if the world does come from God's wisdom and goodness, why is there evil? Where does it come from? Who is responsible for it? Is there any liberation from it? (CCC 284)

SUPPLEMENTARY READING

John Paul II, *Mulieris Dignitatem*, III: 7

By reflecting on the whole account found in Genesis 2:18-25, and by interpreting it in light of the truth about the image and likeness of God (cf. Gn 1:26-27), we can *understand* even *more fully what constitutes the personal character* of the human being, thanks to which both man and woman are like God. For every individual is made in the image of God, insofar as he or she is a rational and free creature capable of knowing God and loving him. Moreover, we read that man cannot exist "alone" (cf. Gn 2:18); he can exist only as a "unity of the two," and therefore *in relation to another human person.* It is a question here of a mutual relationship: man to woman and woman to man. Being a person in the image and likeness of God thus also involves existing in a relationship, in relation to the other "I." This is a prelude to the definitive self-revelation of the Triune God: a living unity in the communion of the Father, Son and Holy Spirit.

At the beginning of the Bible this is not yet stated directly. The whole Old Testament is mainly concerned with revealing the truth about the oneness and unity of God. Within this fundamental truth about God the New Testament will reveal the inscrutable mystery of God's inner life. *God,* who allows himself to be known by human beings through Christ, is the *unity of the Trinity:* unity in communion. In this way new light is also thrown on man's image and likeness to God, spoken of in the Book of Genesis. The fact that man "created as man and woman" is the image of God means not only that each of them individually is like God, as a rational and free being. It also means that man and woman, created as a "unity of

the two" in their common humanity, are called to live in a communion of love, and in this way to mirror in the world the communion of love that is in God, through which the Three Persons love each other in the intimate mystery of the one divine life. The Father, Son and Holy Spirit, one God through the unity of the divinity, exist as persons through the inscrutable divine relationship. Only in this way can we understand the truth that God in himself is love (cf. 1 Jn 4:16).

The image and likeness of God in man, created as man and woman (in the analogy that can be presumed between Creator and creature), thus also expresses the "unity of the two" in a common humanity. This "unity of the two," which is a sign of interpersonal communion, *shows that the creation of man is* also marked by a certain likeness to the divine communion (*"communio"*).

The prologue page to Genesis from a Parisian "Pocket Bible," mid-13th century; a handy type of Bible which was so popular that hundreds were produced and distributed by booksellers instead of monastic scriptoria, thus playing a central role in promulgating this version of the Bible which included the Prayer of Manasseh.

VOCABULARY

ADAM

The first man and our first father. He committed the first sin. The name "Adam" was also used in Hebrew to refer to humanity in general.

CREATION

The act by which God brought the universe and all its inhabitants into being out of nothing. The universe that God created. Creation is good, yet has been corrupted by sin. The scientific theory that species were created as they are.

DOCTORS OF THE CHURCH

Christian men and women whose teachings are especially valuable.

EDEN

The name of the garden in which God placed Adam and Eve.

ELOHIM

The Hebrew word for God as Creator.

EVE

The first woman and our first mother. She committed the first sin. Eve was created from the rib of Adam, and thus woman—unlike the animals—is man's equal and complement.

EVOLUTION

The scientific theory that species came to be as they are by a gradual process of change and development. God created all matter, and the creation of human beings is a special act of creation.

FATHERS OF THE CHURCH

The great theologians of the early Church after the apostles. The Patristic age, named for these Fathers ("*patri*" in Latin), lasted until about the seventh century.

IMAGE

A likeness or picture. Each person is made in the image of God; that is, like God insofar as having intelligence, free will, and the capacity to love.

PROTOEVANGELIUM (*Protoevangelion*)

The announcement of a future Redeemer to Adam and Eve after their Fall. Greek for "first Gospel."

SABBATH

The day of rest in imitation of God resting on the seventh day of creation. The Sabbath is sacred, a sign of God's covenant with creation.

SERPENT

The form taken by Satan in the Garden of Eden. The Hebrew word refers to a fearsome, murderous creature.

VOID

Empty. Without form. The state of the world before God gave it form and created beings to fill it.

YAHWEH

God's personal Name, often translated as "Lord" in English. Scripture often uses it to emphasize God's personal, covenantal relationship with people.

God separates the day from the night. Detail from the *Utrecht Luxury Bible*, 1430, Netherlands. Illuminated manuscripts from Utrecht were so coveted that artists from other countries demanded an import ban on them.

STUDY QUESTIONS

1. According to Genesis, what was the condition of earth before creation began?

2. On what day did God create human beings?

3. What did God do the day after creating human beings?

4. What name does the Hebrew text use for God in the story of the Garden of Eden?

5. How did God create a form during the first three days of creation?

6. How does God's creation during the second three days relate to his creation from the first three days?

7. What was the importance of God's rest on the seventh day?

8. From what is the revelation of creation inseparable?

9. What does "omnipresent" mean?

10. List four consequences of the fact that humans were created in God's image and likeness.

11. What are the effects of being in God's image for us?

12. To what does grace call us?

13. When was marriage instituted?

14. What relationship did God establish between man and woman?

15. How was marriage created?

16. What does CCC 289 list as the truths of creation?

17. Explain the purpose of marriage as noted in CCC 372.

18. Who are considered the "New Adam" and the "new Eve" according to CCC 411?

19. What sets the transmission of life by Adam and Eve distinct from that of the animals?

20. Read Genesis 4:1-5. Why was Cain's sacrifice not as acceptable as Abel's was?

21. What death did Adam and Eve suffer through their sin?

22. Why did God ask Adam and Eve, "Why have you done this?"

23. List the effects of Adam's sin.

24. How did the sin of Adam become the sin of all his descendants?

25. How is God's wrath a manifestation of his love for us?

26. What was the sin of Cain?

27. Can we accept the argument there were many sets of first parents?

Adam and Eve with the Serpent, Spanish school, 12th century.

PRACTICAL EXERCISES

1. God is our Father who created us in his own image and likeness. Explain how he takes care of us in our setbacks, in our sufferings, in our frustrations, and in our failings. How is this care fatherly?

2. In the story of the fall, the serpent tempts Adam and Eve with the chance to be like God. Adam and Eve sin by choosing power for themselves instead of God's love. How is this first sin like all others? What are some temptations that the devil uses to draw young people today away from God? Can these temptations be related to the one faced by Adam and Eve?

3. God created us in his own image (Gn 1: 27). In your life, how do you present yourself to others as an image of God? What does this mean to you? What are some ways you could show others what it means to be an image of God?

4. "Man with all his noble qualities, with sympathy which feels for the most debased, with benevolence which extends not only to other men but to the humblest living creature, with his god-like intellect which has penetrated into the movements and constitution of the solar system — with all these exalted powers — Man still bears in his bodily frame the indelible stamp of his lowly origin." This quote from Charles Darwin's *The Descent of Man* offers one of the more striking points of the theory of evolution, where it is concluded that humans have evolved from lesser animals like the apes. Does this theory fit in with the creation story we find in Genesis? Can someone be a Catholic and believe in evolution? Why would we say that it is fine to believe in evolution of the body but not in evolution of the soul?

An illustration from the *Bibles moralisée*, a French commentary on the Old and New Testament, early 13th century.

Artists often depicted God as a cosmic architect, measuring out the universe with a compass.

FROM THE CATECHISM

294 The glory of God consists in the realization of this manifestation and communication of his goodness, for which the world was created. God made us "to be his sons through Jesus Christ, according to the purpose of his will, *to the praise of his glorious grace*" (Eph 1: 5-6), for "the glory of God is man fully alive; moreover man's life is the vision of God: if God's revelation through creation has already obtained life for all the beings that dwell on earth, how much more will the Word's manifestation of the Father obtain life for those who see God" (St. Irenaeus, *Adv. haeres* 4, 20, 7: PG 7/1, 1037). The ultimate purpose of creation is that God "who is the creator of all things may at last become 'all in all,' thus simultaneously assuring his own glory and our beatitude" (*Ad gentes* 2; cf. 1 Cor 15: 28).

355 "God created man in his own image, in the image of God he created him, male and female he created them" (Gn 1: 27). Man occupies a unique place in creation: (I) he is "in the image of God;" (II) in his own nature he unites the spiritual and material worlds; (III) he is created "male and female"; (IV) God established him in his friendship.

705 Disfigured by sin and death, man remains "in the image of God," in the image of the Son, but is deprived "of the glory of God," (Rom 3: 23) of his "likeness." The promise made to Abraham inaugurates the economy of salvation, at the culmination of which the Son himself will assume that "image" (cf. Jn 1: 14; Phil 2: 7) and restore it in the Father's "likeness" by giving it again its Glory, the Spirit who is "the Giver of Life."

1147 God speaks to man through the visible creation. The material cosmos is so presented to man's intelligence that he can read there traces of its Creator (cf. Wis 13: 1; Rom 1: 19 f.; Acts 14: 17). Light and darkness, wind and fire, water and earth, the tree and its fruit speak of God and symbolize both his greatness and his nearness.

1602 Sacred Scripture begins with the creation of man and woman in the image and likeness of God and concludes with a vision of "the wedding-feast of the Lamb" (Rv 19: 7, 9; cf. Gn 1: 26-27). Scripture speaks throughout of marriage and its "mystery," its institution and the meaning God has given it, its origin and its end, its various realizations throughout the history of salvation, the difficulties arising from sin and its renewal "in the Lord" in the New Covenant of Christ and the Church (1 Cor 7: 39; cf. Eph 5: 31-32).

2402 In the beginning God entrusted the earth and its resources to the common stewardship of mankind to take care of them, master them by labor, and enjoy their fruits (Ex 20: 15; Dt 5: 19; Mt 19: 18). The goods of creation are destined for the whole human race. However, the earth is divided up among men to assure the security of their lives, endangered by poverty and threatened by violence. The appropriation of property is legitimate for guaranteeing the freedom and dignity of persons and for helping each of them to meet his basic needs and the needs of those in his charge. It should allow for a natural solidarity to develop between men.

2566 *Man is in search of God.* In the act of creation, God calls every being from nothingness into existence. "Crowned with glory and honor," man is, after the angels, capable of acknowledging "how majestic is the name of the Lord in all the earth" (Ps 8: 5; 8: 1). Even after losing through his sin his likeness to God, man remains an image of his Creator, and retains the desire for the one who calls him into existence. All religions bear witness to men's essential search for God (cf. Acts 17: 27).

Endnote

1. GS 37 § 2.

The Early World

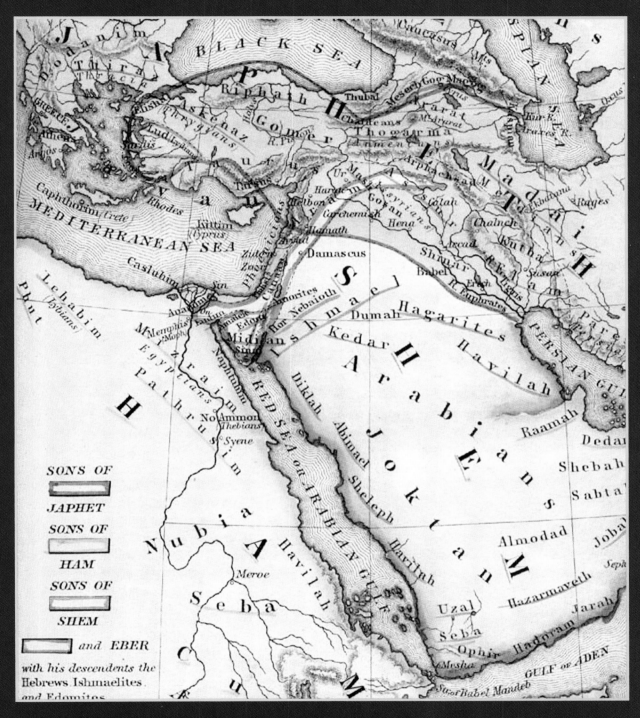

Noah and his sons are all descendants of Adam.
They carry original sin with them.

Chapter 4

The Early World

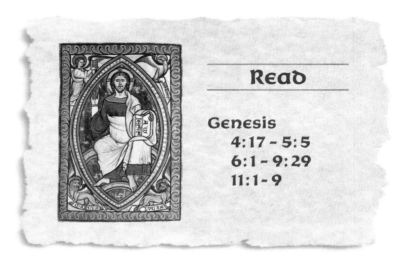

Read

Genesis
4:17 - 5:5
6:1 - 9:29
11:1 - 9

The Evil Line Of Cain

- **The descendants of Cain seek only personal glory in a world of sin and violence.**
- **Seven generations from Adam, the line of Cain reaches its evil peak in Lamech.**

After Cain is punished by God, he is banished from the land and he goes to the land of "Nod," which means "wandering." There he has a son named Enoch. After that, he builds a city and names it after Enoch.

In fact, Scripture credits Cain's line with inventing most of the things that make civilization possible. Another descendant of Cain, Tubal-cain, was the inventor of metalworking. And Tubal-cain's half-brother Jubal "was the father of all those who play the lyre and pipe."[1]

But the descendant of Cain who gets the most space in this list is Lamech. He came seven generations down. Seven is not only a covenant number: seven often is a symbol of perfection in the Bible.

Lamech had two wives—the first record of bigamy or polygamy in the Bible. And in Genesis 4:23-24, we hear a little song Lamech made up for them.

> Lamech said to his wives,
> "Adah and Zillah, hear my voice,
> You wives of Lamech,
> hearken to what I say:
> I have slain a man for wounding me,
> a young man for striking me.
> If Cain is avenged sevenfold,
> truly Lamech seventy-seven-fold."

The first murder: Cain killed Abel out of envy—one of the traditional seven deadly sins, and one of the most dangerous.

Lamech has defied God's will. The marriage covenant is the primary covenant, a holy institution created by God. But Lamech treats women as if they were objects to be possessed. And he treats men as objects, too, killing them whenever he feels like it.

Instead of treating other people as images of God, Lamech and his followers live in a world of wars and bloody revenge. Seven generations down from Adam through Cain, the line of evil has reached its ugly completeness.

Lamech's code of revenge is exactly the opposite of God's intention. In the Septuagint, the Greek translation of the Old Testament that the New Testament writers used, "seventy-seven fold" is translated "seventy times seven." Jesus would turn the song of Lamech on its head when he answered Peter's famous question:

> Then Peter came up and said to him, "Lord, how often shall my brother sin against me, and I forgive him? As many as seven times?" Jesus said to him, "I do not say to you seven times, but seventy times seven." (Mt 18: 21-22)

Christians multiply forgiveness as disproportionately as Lamech multiplied his revenge.

And the Lord said, "What have you done? The voice of your brother's blood is crying to me from the ground. And now you are cursed from the ground, which has opened its mouth to receive your brother's blood from your hand." (Gn 4: 10-11)

The Righteous Line Of Seth

- **The descendants of Seth work for God's glory instead of their own.**
- **The People of God are his children, just as Seth was Adam's child.**

Meanwhile, Adam and Eve had another son named Seth. Now we hear about his line—the faithful followers of God.

When Seth had a son, he named him Enosh. "At that time men began to call upon the name of the LORD" (Gn 4:26).

That phrase "to call upon the name of the LORD" means to worship God. Notice the difference between Cain's line and Seth's line. Cain named a city after his son to make a name for himself. But when Seth has a son, his work is not for himself but rather for God. The men of Cain's line care only about their own glory. But Seth's descendants, God's people, put the glory of God first.

This is where the City of God begins and God's covenant family finally begins to progress. We start almost with a new beginning in Chapter 5: "When God created man, he made him in the likeness of God." Then Adam fathered a son, Seth, again "in his own likeness, after his image."² In other words, Seth was Adam's son in the same way that Adam was God's son. God isn't just our Creator. God is our Father as well.

Here we see two completely contrary cultures. The family of Cain reached its evil completeness in the murderous tyrant Lamech, whereas the family of Seth was built on worshiping God, "calling upon the name of the LORD."

Seth was Adam's son in the same way that Adam was God's son. God isn't just our Creator. God is our Father as well.

The Sons Of God And The Daughters Of Men

- **The line of Seth is tempted by the sinful practices of the Cainites.**
- **Breaking the marriage covenant, they spread evil throughout the world.**

Those two groups—the Cainites and the Sethites—had to live on the same earth. As long as there is evil, pride, and injustice, there will be no harmony.

The descendants of Cain saw the whole world in terms of wars and personal glory. On the other hand, the descendants of Seth, although they worshiped God, still had the seeds of sin in them that we all inherit from Adam and Eve.

So we read at the beginning of Genesis 6, "When men began to multiply on the face of the ground, and daughters were born to them, the sons of God saw that the daughters of men were fair and they took to wives such of them as they chose."

Who are the "sons of God?"

God created Adam in his own image and likeness, and Adam fathered a son named Seth in his own image and likeness. The "sons of God," then, must be the family of Seth, that family of God that built itself up, calling upon the name of the Lord. In other words, they are the original Church, God's family.

The "daughters of men," on the other hand, are the descendants of Cain. We know that in the seventh generation of the wicked Cainites, Lamech became a polygamist, taking however many women he wanted. Now the descendants of Seth were tempted by that same sin. They "took to wife such of them as they chose," implying that polygamy has entered into the line of Seth, the covenant family of God.

Sin is becoming institutionalized. We'll find, as we get further into the Old Testament, that breaking the marriage covenant always brings God's judgment every time. In fact, the very next verse (Gn 6:3) tells us that God decided then to shorten our lives.

> "Then the LORD said, 'My spirit shall not abide in man forever,
> for he is flesh, but his days shall be a hundred and twenty years.'"

But that didn't stop the spread of evil. The book goes on to tell us, "The Nephilim [or "giants"] were on the earth in those days, and also afterward, when the sons of God came in to the daughters of men, and they bore children of them. These were the mighty men that were of old, the men of renown."[3]

In Hebrew, "the men of renown" is literally "the men of *shem*," the men of the "name"—which is what the word "shem" means. They were wicked tyrants who were making a name for themselves. As the lines of Seth and Cain intermarried, the whole world came to be dominated by the descendants of Lamech—unjust, violent men, building a culture of pure evil.

We see the result in Genesis 6:5-6.

> "The LORD saw that the wickedness of man was great in the earth, and that every
> imagination of the thoughts of his heart was only evil continually. And the LORD was sorry
> that he had made man on the earth, and it grieved him to his heart."

The Flood

- **The wicked violence of the human race provokes God to send a great flood.**
- **One righteous man is saved, along with his family and representatives of every beast and bird.**

With the lines of Cain and Seth mixed up, almost the whole world had gone over to the side of evil. Genesis tells us that "the earth was filled with violence."[4] There was one righteous group left: Noah, his wife, his three sons, and their families. "Noah was a righteous man, blameless in his generation" (Gn 6:9).

So God decided to make a new beginning, starting the human race over again with Noah as the founder. "I will blot out man whom I have created from the face of the ground, man and beast and creeping things and birds of the air, for I am sorry that I have made them."

Noah, therefore, was instructed to build an "ark"—a giant boat capable of carrying his family and enough animals to repopulate the earth. God would send a great flood, but Noah would be safe, and God promised, "I will establish my covenant with you" (Gn 6:18).

We see the number seven throughout the story of the Flood. Noah took seven pairs of each clean animal, seven pairs of each bird, and one pair each of all the rest,[5] and they followed him into the ark. Then God shut the door behind them. After seven days, the flood came.

The rain poured down from the sky, and water came up from the deep. For forty days and forty nights it rained. Forty is another important symbolic number in Scripture. Periods of trial and repentance often come in forties in the Bible; later we'll see how Israel wandered forty years in the desert, and how Jesus fasted forty days. Even now, the season of Lent, our yearly time of repentance and fasting, takes up forty days in the Church calendar.

For 150 days,[6] there was nothing but water. Then at last the waters started to recede, and in the seventh month the ark came to rest on Ararat, a mountain in what is today eastern Turkey.[7]

But what condition was the rest of the world in? Noah sent out a raven to see whether there might be dry land yet. The raven "went to and fro until the waters were dried up from the earth." Then he sent out a dove, and the dove returned to him. After seven days, he sent out the dove again, and this time the dove came back with an olive leaf. Now Noah knew the waters had begun to go down. The next time he sent out the dove, seven days later, it did not come back.[8]

Finally Noah released his passengers, and the animals spread out to repopulate the earth. Then he built an altar to offer sacrifice to the Lord. Like Adam, Noah would be the priest for his whole family—which, after the Flood, was all that was left of humanity.

Above: Noah builds the ark to God's specifications: 300 cubits long, 50 cubits wide, and 30 cubits high. Traditional pictures of the ark show something shaped like a boat. However, the Hebrew word for "ark" is "tebah," meaning "box" or "chest" and may suggest the actual shape of the ark. A box shape would seem more practical for stability and volume and consistent with the narrative, considering the nature of the deluge.

Did The Flood Really Happen?

For a long time, Bible scholars tried to prove that there had been a flood over the whole earth, while scientists simply ignored the Bible story. But more recently, scientists and Bible scholars have been coming closer to agreement. Many geologists and archaeologists now think that the story of the Flood refers to a real geological event. Meanwhile, anthropologists point out that similar stories of a disastrous flood—and one family who survived it—are found in cultures all over the Middle East and Europe.

Archaeologists point out that Mesopotamia, the part of the Middle East where civilization first developed, sometimes went through terrible floods. A layer of flood deposit at Ur, one of the most ancient cities in Mesopotamia, showed that the city had been wiped out in some great disaster. Later in the book of Genesis, we read that Abraham, the ancestor of all the people of Israel, came from Ur. He and his family might easily have carried the true story of the Flood at Ur with them when they moved west.

One of the most interesting theories puts the Flood farther back than that. In a book called *Noah's Flood,* two marine archaeologists point out that the Black Sea was an isolated lake until a few thousand years ago. Some of the first steps toward civilization were taken around that lake. When the Mediterranean Sea broke through (perhaps during a great storm), the water came in so suddenly and violently that all the towns and villages were under water in a few days. We know from other evidence that Oral Tradition can preserve a story accurately for thousands of years. The book suggests that this Black Sea flood was the source of the story of Noah and of all the other flood stories. Since the book was published, surveys have found whole towns on the floor of the Black Sea.

Neither of those theories necessarily contradicts the literal sense of the Bible. The Hebrew word translated as "world" in the Flood story could also mean "country," so the sacred writers might have meant that the land as far as anyone could see was submerged.

Of course, the question of where the story came from is not really important to understanding the Bible. The important thing is to understand what the story says about our relationship with God.

Mount Ararat, the tallest peak in modern Turkey, is a snow-capped dormant volcanic cone, located in far northeast Turkey, 10 miles west of Iran and 20 miles south of Armenia. The mountain rises 16,945 feet above the surrounding plains. The Book of Genesis identifies this mountain as the resting place of Noah's Ark after the great flood.

"Ararat" is a version of the name "Urartu" from the Hebrew Torah written by Moses which only included the consonants "rrt."

The Covenant With Noah

- **Noah and his family after the Flood are the beginnings of a new creation.**
- **Christians see the Flood as a "type" of baptism.**

It was a new creation. The human race was founded again, with a righteous man as its founder. But had the Flood eliminated sin? No! He might have been righteous, but Noah was not perfect. Like every human, he inherited the sinful nature of Adam and Eve.

God knew, of course, that we would sin again. "I will never again curse the ground because of man," God said after Noah's sacrifice—not because the line of Noah was without sin, but for exactly the opposite reason: "for the imagination of man's heart is evil from his youth."

Then God blessed Noah and his family, saying to them, "Be fruitful and multiply, and fill the earth."⁹ Those are the same words God spoke to Adam and Eve at the dawn of creation. As he did with Adam and Eve, God gave Noah and his family dominion over the living things of the world.

In fact, the story of Noah and the story of Adam are so similar that we can see a literary genius at work. The inspired author uses literary parallelism to leave us no doubt that the Flood begins a new creation.

God's covenant with Noah and all creation, the rainbow, touches the plain at the foot of Mount Ararat.

After Noah's sacrifice, God established his promised covenant with Noah and his family. God gave them the earth and all its goods, to have dominion over them. But there were conditions. A covenant goes two ways: a blessing for abiding by its conditions, and a curse for breaking it. "For your lifeblood I will surely require a reckoning; of every beast I will require it and of man; of every man's brother I will require the life of man. Whoever sheds the blood of man, by man shall his blood be shed; for God made man in his own image."

God promised Noah that he would never again destroy the world by a flood. As a sign, he placed the rainbow in the sky. When the rainbow appears after a storm, God told Noah, "I will look on it and remember my covenant which is between me and you and every living creature of all flesh that is upon the earth." The rainbow is a universal sign. By making the rainbow the sign of the covenant, God shows that this covenant ultimately applies to all creation—as did the covenant with Adam.

> God made an everlasting covenant with Noah and with all living beings (cf. Gn 9:16). It will remain in force as long as the world lasts. (CCC 71)

Christians see the Flood as a "type"—a symbolic precursor in history—of Christian baptism. The story in Genesis tells us in a symbolic way what happens when a Christian is baptized. Our old world of sin is washed away, and we are created anew, reborn in the waters of baptism. Like Noah, we still carry the potential of sin with us after baptism, but we have received God's blessing and his promise that he will not destroy us.

Another Story Of The Flood

When archaeologists found ancient Babylonian tablets that told a familiar-sounding flood story, the whole world seemed to be in an uproar. Here, as part of the Epic of Gilgamesh, was a flood story many centuries older than the oldest Bible manuscripts. Yet the story it told was clearly similar to the story of Noah. Right away, some people jumped to the conclusion that the story of Noah must be "derived" from this older flood story.

Of course, a few moments' thinking is enough to show that their conclusion won't hold water. The story of Noah in its present form was written down later, that's true. But it could well be the record of an oral tradition that goes back thousands of years. The flood story in Gilgamesh might just as easily be derived from oral traditions of the Noah story.

What the story does prove, however, is that some story of a worldwide flood was known all over the Middle East. In fact, anthropologists have found Flood stories, and flood heroes like Noah, all over the world. It seems that every culture preserves the memory of some great catastrophe long ago.

In the Gilgamesh story, the gods have decided to destroy humankind with a great flood. But one of the gods rebels and decides to save one man and his family. He tells Utanapishtim, the man who takes the place of Noah in the story, to build a boat, and to gather all the beasts of the field into the boat.

Then comes the horrible storm, and everything is wiped out except Utanapishtim and his boat. The destruction is so horrible that even the gods are quivering like dogs.

After seven days, the storm subsides, and the boat comes to rest on a mountain. To see if there's any dry land about, Utanapishtim releases a dove, but the dove comes back. Then he sends out a swallow, but the swallow comes back as well. Finally he sends out a raven, and the raven doesn't come back. Knowing that the waters have gone down, Utanapishtim releases all the animals and offers a sacrifice to the gods.

Clearly this is a version of the same story as the one about Noah—especially the details about sending out birds to see if the flood has gone down. But although the story has some of the same details, it doesn't have the same point at all. In the Gilgamesh story, the gods are capricious tyrants battling against each other, and they bring on the flood for no good reason. (In one version of the story, the gods decide to destroy humanity because people make too much noise, and the gods can't get any sleep at night.) Utanapishtim is saved mostly because one of the gods wants to undermine the other gods. In the Noah story, it is the wickedness of human beings that brings justice from the one true God, and Noah is saved because of his righteousness.

Above inset: A relief traditionally identified with the ancient King Gilgamesh of Uruk; from the palace of Sargon II, ca. 720 B.C.

Clay tablet with the flood story from the Epic of Gilgamesh, one of eleven tablets which were in the collection of the Assyrian king, Ashurbanipal, 7th century B.C.

The Curse On Canaan

- **Sin is not washed away by the Flood.**
- **Ham's sin brings a curse on his son Canaan, ancestor of the Canaanites.**

Once the flood waters receded, Noah and his family had to start from the beginning. They had to find food for themselves and their animals. Noah became a farmer, and one of his crops was grape vines. At harvest time, he made wine from the juice of the grapes. In Genesis 9: 20-27, we read the result of Noah's drunken celebration:

"Noah was the first tiller of the soil. He planted a vineyard; and he drank of the wine, and became drunk, and lay uncovered in his tent. And Ham, the father of Canaan, saw the nakedness of his father and told his two brothers outside.[10]

"Then Shem and Japheth took a garment, laid it upon both their shoulders, and walked backward and covered the nakedness of their father; their faces were turned away, and they did not see their father's nakedness. When Noah awoke from his wine and knew what his youngest son had done to him, he said:

'Cursed be Canaan;
    a slave of slaves shall he be to his brothers.'
He also said, 'Blessed by the LORD my God be Shem;
    and let Canaan be his slave.'"[11]

In spite of the universal Flood, sin was not destroyed in the world. Noah and his sons are all descendants of Adam; they carry original sin with them. Ham's disrespect undermined his father's

authority at a time when his was the *only* authority. His sin earned a curse on his descendants—in particular on Canaan, regarded as the father of the Canaanites, hated enemies of Israel.

Noah therefore gave his blessing to Shem—one of two cases in Genesis where the first-born son didn't succumb to pride and end up being passed over in favor of his younger brother. (The other case would be Abraham.)

The role of the first-born is always very important in a patriarchal society. When the family is the main unit of society and the father is the leader of the family, what happens when the father dies? Human mortality would create a crisis of leadership in every generation. The first-born is the natural mediator between the father and the rest of the children—the one who teaches the others what the father's rules are. When the father dies, he is in a natural position to be the leader of the family.

But God chooses his servants according to his wisdom, not according to our rules. One of the recurring themes in Genesis is the preference for a younger son as heir instead of the first-born. It starts right at the beginning, when Seth becomes Adam's heir instead of Cain. That is why Shem and Abraham stand out: they are the only two first-born sons in Genesis who follow the "usual" pattern.

Shem's family would be the foundation of the People of God. Remember that the word "shem" means "name" in Hebrew.

Above: *The Drunkenness of Noah* by Giovanni Bellini, ca. 1515

TABLE OF NATIONS according to Genesis 10

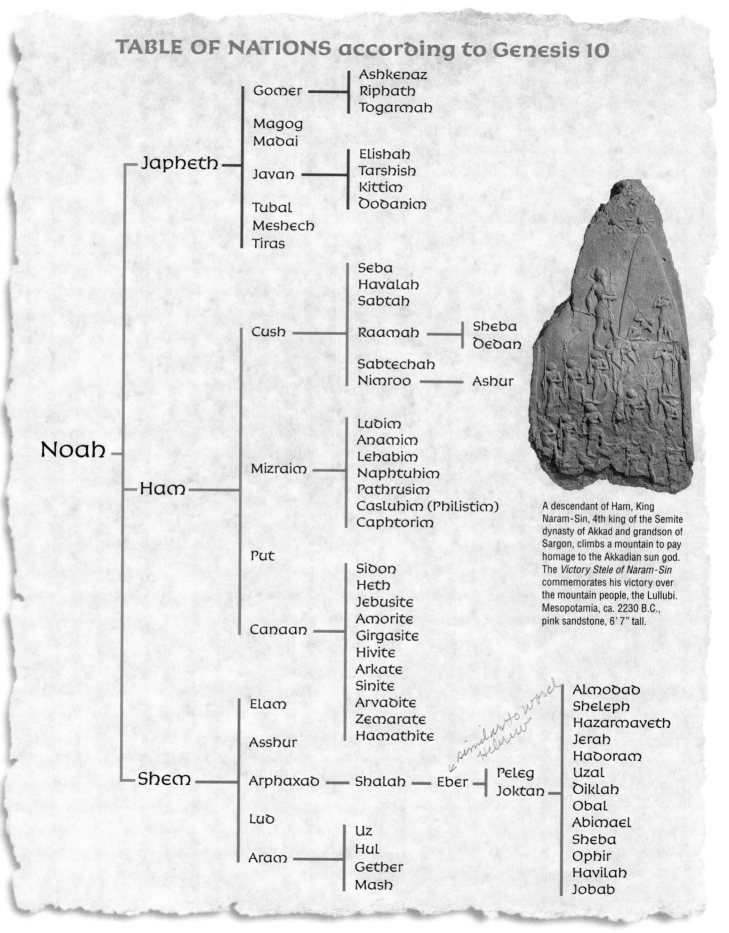

Noah

Japheth
- Gomer
  - Ashkenaz
  - Riphath
  - Togarmah
- Magog
- Madai
- Javan
  - Elishah
  - Tarshish
  - Kittim
  - Dodanim
- Tubal
- Meshech
- Tiras

Ham
- Cush
  - Seba
  - Havalah
  - Sabtah
  - Raamah
    - Sheba
    - Dedan
  - Sabtechah
  - Nimrod
    - Ashur
- Mizraim
  - Ludim
  - Anamim
  - Lehabim
  - Naphtuhim
  - Pathrusim
  - Casluhim (Philistim)
  - Caphtorim
- Put
- Canaan
  - Sidon
  - Heth
  - Jebusite
  - Amorite
  - Girgasite
  - Hivite
  - Arkate
  - Sinite
  - Arvadite
  - Zemarate
  - Hamathite

Shem
- Elam
- Asshur
- Arphaxad — Shalah — Eber
  - Peleg
  - Joktan
    - Almodad
    - Sheleph
    - Hazarmaveth
    - Jerah
    - Hadoram
    - Uzal
    - Diklah
    - Obal
    - Abimael
    - Sheba
    - Ophir
    - Havilah
    - Jobab
- Lud
- Aram
  - Uz
  - Hul
  - Gether
  - Mash

similar to word Hebrew

A descendant of Ham, King Naram-Sin, 4th king of the Semite dynasty of Akkad and grandson of Sargon, climbs a mountain to pay homage to the Akkadian sun god. The *Victory Stele of Naram-Sin* commemorates his victory over the mountain people, the Lullubi. Mesopotamia, ca. 2230 B.C., pink sandstone, 6' 7" tall.

The Arrogance Of The Children Of Ham

- **All the Israelites' enemies are said to be descendants of Ham.**
- **By building the Tower of Babel, the Hamites were again trying to usurp the authority of Shem.**

The section that follows (Chapter 10 of Genesis) is what Bible scholars call the "Table of Nations," because it tells which nations came from each of Noah's sons. The most interesting list is the descendants of Ham. Egypt, Canaan, Philistia, Assyria, and Babylon all come from Ham's line. In other words, all the nations that were the enemies of the Israelites are descendants of the wicked Ham. The people of Israel would see this list as a rogues' gallery of evil oppressors.

On the other hand, the descendants of Shem would be the ancestors of the People of God. His great-grandson, Eber, gave his name to the Hebrews.

After the genealogies comes another of the most famous stories in Genesis — the story of the Tower of Babel. The descendants of Ham who settled in the Plain of Shinar (ancient Mesopotamia, which is modern Iraq) decided to make a name for themselves. "Come, let us build ourselves a city, and a tower with its top in the heavens, and let us make a name for ourselves, lest we be scattered abroad upon the face of the whole earth."[12]

Again, that word "name" in Hebrew is "shem." The Hamites are saying they intend to make a "shem" for themselves. In other words, they're rebelling against the covenant authority of Shem, the first-born son of Noah. The tower-builders think they can reach heaven by themselves, without following God's way.

Of course, God intervened to put a stop to their scheme. God had sworn a covenant oath never to destroy the world by a flood again. Instead, he confused their language.

Before this time, the Bible tells us, all people had spoken the same language. But suddenly they couldn't understand each other. They had to give up the project. The city they had started to build, however, remained. It would be known as Babel or Babylon, and it would become the symbol of everything that was evil and decadent.

> This state of division into many nations is at once cosmic, social, and religious. It is intended to limit the pride of fallen humanity (cf. Acts 17:26-27), united only in its perverse ambition to forge its own unity as at Babel (cf. Wis 10:5; Gn 11:4-6). But, because of sin, both polytheism and the idolatry of the nation and of its rulers constantly threaten this provisional economy with the perversion of paganism (cf. Rom 1:18-25). (CCC 57)

Meanwhile, the people of Shem went on worshiping God properly. Finally, after a few more generations, we come to one of the central figures of the Old Testament. His name was Abram, and through him God was about to perform the impossible.

Above: *The Tower of Babel* by Pieter Bruegel

The Real Tower Of Babel

The most impressive thing in any Mesopotamian city would have been its ziggurat, a huge pyramid-like structure with a temple on top.

Archaeologists tell us that these temple-mounds were more than high buildings. They were representations of the mountains where the gods were believed to live. The ziggurat was an artificial mountain of the gods. By building the ziggurats, the Mesopotamians thought they were literally reaching heaven.

In fact, the ziggurats were so important to their religion that, in Mesopotamian mythology, the cities and their ziggurats existed before human beings were created.

Many scholars believe that the story of the Tower of Babel refers to the huge ziggurat that was built in Babylon. Like the Hamites in the story of Babel, the people who built the ziggurats thought they could build a tower to heaven.

The ziggurat of Ur in southern Iraq dates to 2100 B.C.

An artist's concept of a Babylonian market scene at the Gate of Ishtar and the imposing presence of a ziggurat.

nohę ꝛeqner appellaur ꞇ ꞇ ꞇ ꞇ ꞇ dr yaꞇꞇjo nohę ſnomni aꞇru
arpaar ſprur lumꞇꞇ ꞇ quum nꞇn rolur lurar ſnumaur ꞇra .
ꞇ ſmponꞇra ꞇ prophꞇꞇubra arunꞇar ſncuaucliꞇmo uguꞇ
hꞇꞇ uꞇa faꞇꞇꞇꞇ nor ꞇqurꞇꞇꞇ ꞇ poruꞇꞇꞇ ſpre ꞇolur quum
uboporꞇꞇ ur ꞇꞇꞇꞇꞇꞇ munum domo ꞇuu ꞇulbuꞇur ꞇra quꞇu
nꞇꞇꞇum uꞇꞇꞇ u.. ꞇꞇ ꞇfuꞇꞇuꞇꞇꞇa ꞇ rolur dꞇn ꞇꞇbꞇ bꞇrꞇ ꞇubꞇrdo ꞇꞇꞇꞇuꞇ

"He waited another seven days, and again he sent forth the dove out of the ark; and the dove came
back to him in the evening, and lo, in her mouth a freshly plucked olive leaf;
so Noah knew that the waters had subsided from the earth."
(Gn 8: 10-11)

SUPPLEMENTARY READING

Second Vatican Council: *Dei Verbum*

CHAPTER IV: THE OLD TESTAMENT

14. In carefully planning and preparing the salvation of the whole human race the God of infinite love, by a special dispensation, chose for himself a people to whom He would entrust his promises. First he entered into a covenant with Abraham (see Gn 15:18) and, through Moses, with the people of Israel (see Ex 24:8). To this people which he had acquired for himself, he so manifested himself through words and deeds as the one true and living God that Israel came to know by experience the ways of God with men. Then too, when God himself spoke to them through the mouth of the prophets, Israel daily gained a deeper and clearer understanding of his ways and made them more widely known among the nations (see Ps 21:29; 95:1-3; Is 2:1-5; Jer 3:17). The plan of salvation foretold by the sacred authors, recounted and explained by them, is found as the true word of God in the books of the Old Testament: these books, therefore, written under divine inspiration, remain permanently valuable. "For all that was written for our instruction, so that by steadfastness and the encouragement of the Scriptures we might have hope" (Rom 15:4).

15. The principal purpose to which the plan of the old covenant was directed was to prepare for the coming of Christ, the Redeemer of all and of the messianic kingdom, to announce this coming by prophecy (see Lk 24:44; Jn 5:39; 1 Pt 1:10), and to indicate its meaning through various types (see 1 Cor 10:12). Now the books of the Old Testament, in accordance with the state of mankind before the time of salvation established by Christ, reveal to all men the knowledge of God and of man and the ways in which God, just and merciful, deals with men. These books, though they also contain some things which are incomplete and temporary, nevertheless show us true divine pedagogy. These same books, then, give expression to a lively sense of God, contain a store of sublime teachings about God, sound wisdom about human life, and a wonderful treasury of prayers, and in them the mystery of our salvation is present in a hidden way. Christians should receive them with reverence.

16. God, the inspirer and author of both Testaments, wisely arranged that the New Testament be hidden in the Old and the Old be made manifest in the New. For, though Christ established the new covenant in his blood (see Lk 22:20; 1 Cor 11:25), still the books of the Old Testament with all their parts, caught up into the proclamation of the Gospel, acquire and show forth their full meaning in the New Testament (see Mt 5:17; Lk 24:27; Rom 16:25-26; 2 Cor 14:16) and in turn shed light on it and explain it.

"Then Noah built an altar to the Lord,... and offered burnt offerings on the altar." (Gn 8:20)

VOCABULARY

ABEL

Adam and Eve's second son. Murdered by his brother Cain.

ARK

The large ship built by Noah to save his family and two of every animal from the Flood.

The box (Ark of the Covenant) in which the Ten Commandments were kept.

BABEL, TOWER OF

A tall building proposed by the Hamites in order to "make a name for themselves." God responded to their challenge by confusing their languages, so the project could never be completed.

BIGAMY

Being married to more than one person at the same time. A perversion of the marriage covenant.

CAIN

Adam and Eve's first son. The first murderer. His descendants carried a line of evil in contrast to the descendants of Seth, the People of God.

FLOOD

The destruction of the world by water, from which only Noah, his family, and the animals escaped. The Flood is a type of baptism, through which sin is destroyed.

HAM

Noah's rebellious son. The ancestor of Israel's enemies.

LAMECH

A descendant of Cain. The first bigamist. His revenge demonstrates how far evil had developed in the world.

NOAH

The righteous man who, with his family and the animals, survived the Flood.

PARALLELISM

A literary technique in which similarities between events or terms is used to point out similarities of ideas.

POLYGAMY

The practice of having multiple wives. A perversion of the marriage covenant. Polygamy always leads to evil consequences in Scripture.

SETH

Adam and Eve's third son and eventual heir. His line carried on the true worship of God in contrast to the evil line of Cain.

SHEM

Noah's first-born son and heir. Ancestor of the Israelites and related tribes. Hebrew for "name."

SHINAR, PLAIN OF

Mesopotamia, or modern Iraq; the land settled by the descendants of Ham.

And God said, "This is the sin of the covenant which I make between me and you and every living creature that is with you,.... I set my bow in the cloud,..."
(Gn 9: 12–13)

STUDY QUESTIONS

1. Where does Cain go after his banishment?

2. Who is Lamech?

3. Who is the first bigamist mentioned in Scripture?

4. How did the descendants of Cain differ from those of Seth?

5. What was the downfall of the descendants of Seth?

6. In Genesis 6, who were the "sons of God"?

7. In Genesis 6, who were the "daughters of men"?

8. Why did God shorten the lives of men?

9. During this period, whose family remained righteous?

10. What was the sign of the rainbow?

11. How long did the rain last during the Flood?

12. What was the first thing that Noah did when he got off the ark?

13. How is the flood considered a precursor of Baptism?

14. What is Ham's sin?

15. Who are Ham's descendants?

16. Who are the descendants of Shem?

17. Why are Ham's descendants punished when they try to build the Tower of Babel?

18. How does God punish the tower builders?

19. What does Babylon symbolize?

PRACTICAL EXERCISES

1. Chapter three ended with Cain murdering Abel because of envy. As punishment, Cain was banished from the land and his descendants were caught up in sin and violence. Explain why Cain and his descendants were punished so harshly for the murder he committed. Do people today still value life the way that God wants them to? How does this topic tie into abortion or euthanasia?

2. Many inventions that make civilization possible have been attributed to Cain's line and held in disdain because of the evil that has come from them. How do you feel about the use of technology for civilization? What are some of the risks and benefits of technology?

Finally, what are some good and some bad effects that have come from inventions such as television, the internet, or video games?

3. The Flood was a punishment for the chosen people because they had turned away from God. God decided, however, to also use the Flood as a means to save mankind. In order to do this, he made a covenant with Noah as he had done with Adam. Look back to chapter two and read about God's covenant with Adam. How was that covenant similar to the covenant God made with Noah? List as many similarities as you can. What are the differences?

FROM THE CATECHISM

56 After the unity of the human race was shattered by sin God at once sought to save humanity part by part. The covenant with Noah after the Flood gives expression to the principle of the divine economy toward the "nations," in other words, towards men grouped "in their lands, each with [its] own language, by their families, in their nations" (Gn 10:5; cf. 9:9-10, 16; 10:20-31).

701 *The dove.* At the end of the Flood, whose symbolism refers to Baptism, a dove released by Noah returns with a fresh olive-tree branch in its beak as a sign that the earth was again habitable (cf. Gn 8:8-12). When Christ comes up from the water of his baptism, the Holy Spirit, in the form of a dove, comes down upon him and remains with him (cf. Mt 3:16 and parallels). The Spirit comes down and remains in the purified hearts of the baptized. In certain churches, the Eucharist is reserved in a metal receptacle in the form of a dove (*columbarium*) suspended above the altar. Christian iconography traditionally uses a dove to suggest the Spirit.

845 To reunite all his children, scattered and led astray by sin, the Father willed to call the whole of humanity together into his Son's Church. The Church is the place where humanity must rediscover its unity and salvation. The Church is "the world reconciled." She is that bark which "in the full sail of the Lord's cross, by the breath of the Holy Spirit, navigates safely in this world." According to another image dear to the Church Fathers, she is prefigured by Noah's ark, which alone saves from the Flood (St. Augustine, *Serm.* 96, 7, 9: PL 38, 588; St. Ambrose, *De virg.* 18, 118: PL 16, 297B; cf. already 1 Pt 3:20-21).

1664 Unity, indissolubility, and openness to fertility are essential to marriage. Polygamy is incompatible with the unity of marriage; divorce separates what God has joined together; the refusal of fertility turns married life away from its "supreme gift," the child (GS 50 § 1).

2259 In the account of Abel's murder by his brother Cain (cf. Gn 4:8-12), Scripture reveals the presence of anger and envy in man, consequences of original sin, from the beginning of human history. Man has become the enemy of his fellow man. God declares the wickedness of this fratricide: "What have you done? The voice of your brother's blood is crying to me from the ground. And now you are cursed from the ground, which has opened its mouth to receive your brother's blood from your hand" (Gn 4:10-11).

"...*Cain brought to the Lord an offering of the fruit of the ground, and Abel brought of the firstlings of his flock....*" (*Gn 4:3-4*)

Endnotes	
1. Gn 4:21.	7. Gn 8:3-4.
2. Gn 5:3.	8. Gn 8:6-12.
3. Gn 6:1-4.	9. Gn 9:1.
4. Gn 6:11.	10. Gn 9:20-22.
5. Gn 7:2-3.	11. Gn 9:23-27.
6. Gn 7:24.	12. Gn 11:4.

Chapter 5
Abraham, Our Father

*God used the descendants of Abraham
to bring salvation to the world.*

Chapter 5

Abraham, Our Father

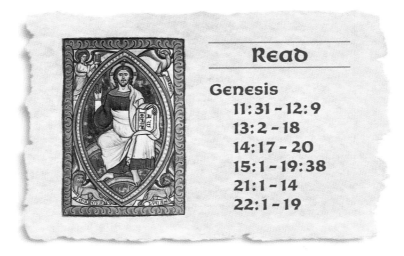

Read

Genesis
  11:31 – 12:9
  13:2 – 18
  14:17 – 20
  15:1 – 19:38
  21:1 – 14
  22:1 – 19

The builders of the Tower of Babel tried to make a great *name*—in Hebrew, *shem*—for themselves without God's help. But God had already chosen a descendant of Shem to become the new father of his people. Immediately after the story of the Tower of Babel, the book of Genesis gives us a detailed list of the descendants of Shem (Gn 11:10-27), ending up at Abram. "Abram" was his name then, but he is more familiar as "Abraham," the father of a multitude of nations.

The Life Of A Nomad

- **Abram came from Ur, an important center of civilization in Mesopotamia.**
- **When he was a young man, Abram went with his father to Haran.**
- **In Haran, seventy-five-year-old Abram heard God calling him to go to Canaan.**

By the time Abram was born, his family was living in Ur, an ancient city in Mesopotamia. Ur was a great port city, with a towering ziggurat, thousands of houses and shops, and merchants from all over the world speaking every language.

Some of those merchants came by ship from places as far away as India. But Terah and his family—including his eldest son Abram—were probably caravan traders from the west. They were used to the idea of making long journeys over land, grazing their cattle along the way.

Terah had three sons: Abram, Nahor, and Haran. They all grew up and married. Haran died young, leaving behind a son named Lot. Terah seems to have raised his grandson Lot as his own son, and Lot and his uncle Abram developed a close relationship.

Then Terah decided to take his family away from Ur. Scripture tells us only that "they went forth together from Ur of the Chaldeans to go into the land of Canaan." (Archaeology supplies one possible reason: if the traditional dating of Abram's life is correct, Terah and his family might have left just when a new conqueror who hated western nomads like Terah and Abram took over in Ur.)

But when they came to the town of Haran, Terah settled there, abandoning his trip to Canaan. Haran was very much like Ur—a bustling market city where traders from all over the world came to sell their wares. It was a city where Terah could resume his familiar way of life.

So Terah and his family settled in Haran, and they prospered there. Terah died in Haran, and Abram grew old.

It was when he was already an old man that Abram's story really began. When Abram was seventy-five years old, he heard a call from God.

> Now the LORD said to Abram, "Go from your country and your kindred and your father's house to the land that I will show you. And I will make of you a great nation, and I will bless you, and make your name great, so that you will be a blessing. I will bless those who bless you, and him who curses you I will curse; and in you all the families of the earth shall be blessed." (Gn 12:1-3).

> When God calls him, Abraham goes forth "as the LORD had told him" (Gn 12:4); Abraham's heart is entirely submissive to the Word and so he obeys. Such attentiveness of the heart, whose decisions are made according to God's will, is essential to prayer, while the words used count only in relation to it. Abraham's prayer is expressed first by deeds: a man of silence, he constructs an altar to the Lord at each stage of his journey. Only later does Abraham's first prayer in words appear: a veiled complaint reminding God of his promises which seem unfulfilled (cf. Gn 15:2f.). Thus one aspect of the drama of prayer appears from the beginning: the test of faith in the fidelity of God. (CCC 2570)

The Promises To Abram

God is pure mystery

- **God promises Abram land, kingship, and worldwide blessing.**
- **Each of these promises will be fulfilled in another covenant later in history.**
- **God will reinforce each promise with a covenant oath.**

There are three promises here at the beginning of Genesis 12.

Moses **1. LAND AND A NATION.** "Go to the land that I will show you," God says. As Abram will find out, the land God will show him is Canaan. Jewish legend had it that the land of Canaan was originally meant to belong to Shem, but Ham and Canaan had usurped Shem's birthright. God will make a great nation of Abram, and the first thing a nation needs is land.

David **2. KINGSHIP AND A NAME.** "I will bless you, and make your name great." Making his *name* (in Hebrew, *Shem*) great meant founding a dynasty, giving Abram political authority and power. God has thrown down the proud tyrants of Babel, and now he intends to build a kingdom on humble, faithful Abram.

Jesus **3. BLESSING FOR ALL NATIONS.** "In you all the families of the earth shall be blessed."[1] God isn't just promising to give Abram some local prestige among the tribes of Canaan. Impossible as it must sound to Abram, God will use Abram to bring salvation to the whole world. The whole human family, torn apart by sin, will be brought back together again through the line of Abraham.

As we'll see in the chapters to come, these three promises are actually fulfilled in three more covenants later in history.

1. The promise of **LAND AND A NATION** will be fulfilled in the covenant with **Moses.**
2. The promise of **KINGSHIP AND A NAME** will be fulfilled in the covenant with **David.**
3. The promise of **BLESSING FOR ALL NATIONS** will be fulfilled through **Jesus Christ.**

The very first verse of the New Testament, Matthew 1:1, reminds us that the whole plan of salvation goes back to Abraham: "The book of the genealogy of Jesus Christ, the son of David, the son of Abraham."

> In order to gather together scattered humanity God calls Abram from his country, his kindred and his father's house (Gn 12:1), and makes him Abraham, that is, "the father of a multitude of nations." "In you all the nations of the earth shall be blessed" (Gn 17:5; 12:3 (LXX); cf. Gal 3:8). (CCC 59)

God would reinforce each of these promises individually with covenant oaths at three different points in Abraham's life.

"When they had come to the land of Canaan, Abram passed through the land to the place at Shechem,…Then the Lord appeared to Abram, and said, 'To your descendants I will give this land.'" (Gn 12:5-7)

Abraham's Migration In The Near East, ca. 2120 B.C.

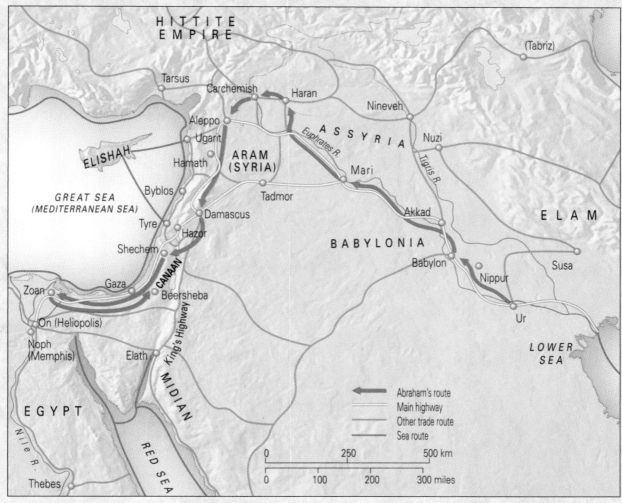

HITTITE EMPIRE

(Tabriz)

Tarsus

Carchemish   Haran

Nineveh

Aleppo

A S S Y R I A

Ugarit

Nuzi

ELISHAH

ARAM (SYRIA)

Euphrates R.

Hamath

Mari

Tigris R.

GREAT SEA (MEDITERRANEAN SEA)

Byblos

Tadmor

Akkad

E L A M

Tyre

Damascus

Hazor

B A B Y L O N I A

Shechem

Babylon

Susa

Gaza

Beersheba

Nippur

Zoan

On (Heliopolis)

Ur

LOWER SEA

Noph (Memphis)

Elath

King's Highway

Nile R.

E G Y P T

M I D I A N

RED SEA

Thebes

CANAAN

→ Abraham's route
Main highway
Other trade route
Sea route

0   250   500 km
0   100   200   300 miles

From Abram To Abraham

The book of Genesis explains Abram's name change as a change in meaning—"Exalted Father" (Abram) to "Father of a Multitude" (Abraham). Some linguists suggest that the name change had another significance as well. Abram, they say, was an East Semitic form of the name, a form that Abram would have used in Ur. Abraham was the West Semitic form of the same name. By taking the western form of the name, Abraham showed the world that he belonged permanently in Canaan, the land in the west that God had given him.

Abraham Journeying Into The Land of Canaan by Gustave Doré

The Journeys Of Abraham In Canaan, ca. 2100 B.C.

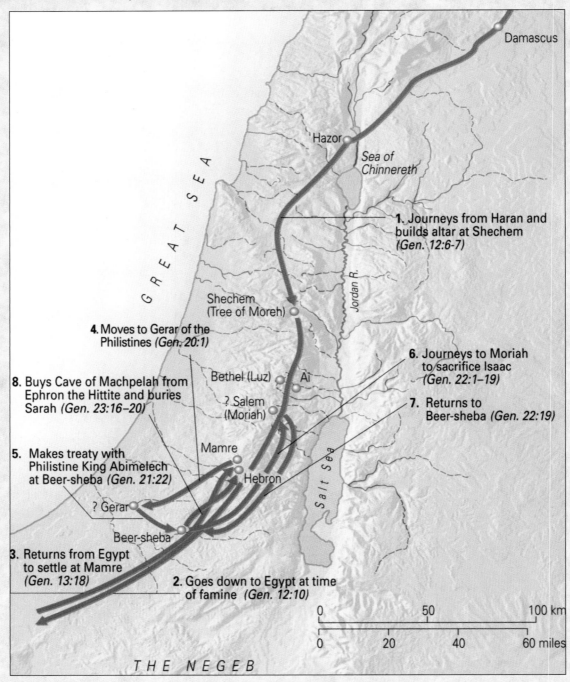

Damascus

Hazor

Sea of Chinnereth

GREAT SEA

Jordan R.

1. Journeys from Haran and builds altar at Shechem *(Gen. 12:6-7)*

Shechem (Tree of Moreh)

4. Moves to Gerar of the Philistines *(Gen. 20:1)*

Bethel (Luz)   Ai

6. Journeys to Moriah to sacrifice Isaac *(Gen. 22:1–19)*

8. Buys Cave of Machpelah from Ephron the Hittite and buries Sarah *(Gen. 23:16–20)*

? Salem (Moriah)

7. Returns to Beer-sheba *(Gen. 22:19)*

Mamre

5. Makes treaty with Philistine King Abimelech at Beer-sheba *(Gen. 21:22)*

Hebron

Salt Sea

? Gerar

Beer-sheba

3. Returns from Egypt to settle at Mamre *(Gen. 13:18)*

2. Goes down to Egypt at time of famine *(Gen. 12:10)*

0		50		100 km

0	20	40	60 miles

THE NEGEB

1. God's Oath: Land And A Nation

- **Abram believes God's unlikely promise of an heir.**
- **By a common ritual of the time, God swears a covenant oath to give Canaan to Abram's descendants.**

God's promise to Abram was hard to believe: Abram had no children, he was an old man already, and his wife, Sarai, had never been able to conceive. How could he have a dynasty with no descendants?

In Abram's time, having a multitude of descendants was considered the greatest possible blessing. Abram must have wondered why he seemed to be cursed. His journeys to Egypt and other places made him very wealthy,[2] but it was all meaningless if he had no son to carry on his name.

Once again, God came to Abram with a promise of great things. But this time Abram dared to ask how the promise could possibly be fulfilled.

> After these things the word of the LORD came to Abram in a vision, "Fear not, Abram, I am your shield; your reward shall be very great." But Abram said, "O LORD God, what wilt thou give me, for I continue childless, and the heir of my house is Eliezer of Damascus?" And Abram said, "Behold, thou hast given me no offspring, and a slave born in my house will be my heir." (Gn 15:1-3)

Abram's questions were perfectly reasonable. But God was about to do something extraordinary, something beyond human reason.

> And behold, the word of the LORD came to him, "This man shall not be your heir; your own son shall be your heir." And he brought him outside and said, "Look toward heaven, and number the stars, if you are able to number them." Then he said to him, "so shall your descendants be." And he believed the LORD, and he reckoned it to him as righteousness. (Gn 15:4-6)

Even though it might have seemed very unlikely, Abram still believed God's promise. But he wanted more assurance about the land. "How am I to know that I shall possess it?" Abram asked.

Now comes a scene that seems very strange to modern readers. To understand it, we need to know how oaths were sworn in the ancient Near East.

In the time of Abram, and for many centuries afterwards, a serious oath was usually sealed with a sacrifice. We know from ancient inscriptions that the animals in a way represented the people who were swearing the oath. "If I break this oath," the people were saying, "may it be my blood spilled on the ground instead of this animal's." An especially solemn way to swear an oath was to cut the sacrifice in two and then walk between the two halves of the sacrifice.

So in answer to Abram's question, God told him, "Bring me a heifer three years old, a she-goat three years old, a ram three years old, a turtledove, and a pigeon."[3] Abram brought all the sacrificial animals, and he cut each of the three large animals in half. All day long he guarded the sacrifices. When the sun began to go down, Abram fell into a deep sleep, and God appeared to him again, repeating the promise that Abram's descendants would possess Canaan—though only after being delivered from bondage in a foreign land. (The foreign land would be Egypt, as the book of Exodus will tell us.)

> When the sun had gone down and it was dark, behold, a smoking fire pot and a flaming torch passed between these pieces. On that day the LORD made a covenant with Abram, saying, "To your descendants I give this land, from the river of Egypt to the great river, the river Euphrates, the land of the Kenites, the Kenizzites, the Kadmonites, the Hittites, the Perizzites, the Rephaim, the Amorites, the Canaanites, the Girgashites and the Jebusites."

The firepot and torch represented the presence of God himself. By passing between the halves of the sacrifices, God was swearing a covenant oath with Abram, solemnly promising that the land would be his.

Lippi's *Circumcision* of Christ depicts the fulfillment of God's covenant with Abraham in Genesis 17: 9-14.

Zakr - remember (zakear) to

2. God's Oath: Kingship And A Name

- **Sarai and Abram try to speed up God's plan by having Abram take another wife.**
- **God swears a covenant oath that kings will come from Abram's line.**
- **Abram's name is changed to Abraham.**
- **Circumcision is an outward sign of the covenant between God and Abraham.**

But it was hard to believe that Sarai would ever have children. She was far too old. After they had lived ten years in Canaan, Sarai started to think that God might not have meant that Abram's heir should come through her.

One of the customs of the time (remember that the corrupt institution of polygamy had spread all over the world) was that a woman could give her servant to her husband, then claim the child as hers. Sarai had an Egyptian maid named Hagar. "Behold now," she said to Abram, "the Lord has prevented me from bearing children; go in to my maid; it may be that I shall obtain children by her."[4]

Abram did as Sarai suggested, and Hagar did conceive a son. He was named Ishmael, and for Abram's sake God made a great nation of him, too: he became the father of the Arabs. But God's plan would be accomplished through Abram and his real wife, Sarai. Ishmael was not the heir Abram had been promised. Yet by this time Abraham was eighty-six years old, and Sarai only about ten years younger. Ishmael must have seemed like his only chance.

Ishmael's descendants on Ch. 25, 12-17

Thirteen years later—when Abram was ninety-nine years old—God appeared to him again.

> When Abram was ninety-nine years old the LORD appeared to him, and said to him, "I am God Almighty; walk before me, and be blameless. And I will make my covenant between me and you, and will multiply you exceedingly." Then Abram fell flat on his face; and God said to him, "Behold, my covenant is with you, and you shall be the father of a multitude of nations. No longer shall you be called Abram, but your name shall be Abraham; for I have made you the father of a multitude of nations. I will make you exceedingly fruitful; and I will make nations of you, and kings shall come forth from you. And I will establish my covenant between me and you and your descendants after you throughout their generations for an everlasting covenant, to be God to you and to your descendants after you. And I will give to you, and to your descendants after you, the land of your sojournings, all the land of Canaan, for an everlasting possession; and I will be their God." (Gn 17:1-8)

Here God confirms the second part of the promise to Abram: kingship and a name. Kings will spring from his line, and he will be known as "Father of a Multitude"—Abraham instead of Abram. But there was more to this covenant than God's promise. Once again, there would be an external sign of the covenant.

> And God said to Abraham, "As for you, you shall keep my covenant, you and your descendants after you throughout their generations. This is my covenant, which you shall keep, between me and you and your descendants after you: Every male among you shall be circumcised. You shall be circumcised in the flesh of your foreskins, and it shall be a sign of the covenant between me and you. He that is eight days old among you shall be circumcised; every male throughout your generations, whether born in your house, or bought with your money from any foreigner who is not of your offspring, both he that is born in your house and he that is bought with your money, shall be circumcised. So shall my covenant be in your flesh an everlasting covenant. Any uncircumcised male who is not circumcised in the flesh of his foreskin shall be cut off from his people; he has broken my covenant." (Gn 17:9-14)

Circumcision, a permanent marking of the flesh, would be the sign of the covenant between God and his people. The descendants of Abraham will bear the mark of the covenant forever.

Finally, God had a very surprising promise for Sarai.

> And God said to Abraham, "As for Sarai your wife, you shall not call her name Sarai, but Sarah [that is, "Princess" or "Queen"] shall be her name. I will bless her, and moreover I will give you a son by her; I will bless her, and she shall be a mother of nations; kings of people shall come from her." (Gn 17:15-16)

This was too much even for faithful Abraham to believe.

> Then Abraham fell on his face and laughed, and said to himself, "Shall a child be born to a man who is a hundred years old? Shall Sarah, who is ninety years old, bear a child?" And Abraham said to God, "O that Ishmael might live in thy sight!" God said, "No, but Sarah your wife shall bear you a son, and you shall call his name Isaac." (Gn 17:17-19)

The name Isaac means "he laughs" in Hebrew. Abraham laughed when he heard that he would have a child at his age. Later on, Sarah would laugh as well when she heard it.

But Abraham took his covenant with the Lord seriously. The very same day, Abraham had himself and all the males in his family circumcised—including Ishmael, who was thirteen years old. Circumcision at thirteen was the Egyptian custom; the Israelites who originally heard this story would see right away that Ishmael, the son of a slave-concubine, was not an Israelite, but an outsider—in other words, the promise God made to Abraham would not be fulfilled through Ishmael.

Some time afterward, the promise was repeated in a strange way. Abraham saw three strangers approaching his camp by the oaks of Mamre. Like any good hospitable Easterner, he ran out to meet them and begged them to stop for a while.[5]

They looked like ordinary travelers. But one of them was God himself, and the other two were his angels. "I will surely return to you in the spring," the Lord said, "and Sarah your wife shall have a son." Sarah, listening by the door of the tent, laughed to herself. She was far too old to have children. But the Lord, who heard her laughter, assured her that she really would have a son by spring.[6]

> Against all human hope, God promises descendants to Abraham, as the fruit of faith and of the power of the Holy Spirit (cf. Gn 18:1-15; Lk 1:26-38, 54-55; Jn 1:12-13; Rom 4:16-21). In Abraham's progeny all the nations of the earth will be blessed. This progeny will be Christ himself (cf. Gn 12:3; Gal 3:16), in whom the outpouring of the Holy Spirit will "gather into one the children of God who are scattered abroad" (cf. Jn 11:52). God commits himself by his own solemn oath to giving his beloved Son and "the promised Holy Spirit…[who is] the guarantee of our inheritance until we acquire possession of it" (Eph 1:13-14; cf. Gn 22:17-19; Lk 1:73; Jn 3:16; Rom 8:32; Gal 3:14). (CCC 706)

Above: *Abraham and the Three Visitors.* The three visitors are considered by some to represent the Trinity.

Sodom And Gomorrah

- **Abraham bargains with God for the fate of Sodom.**
- **Sodom is so wicked that only Lot and his daughters are saved from the destruction.**
- **The children of Lot by his own daughters are the founders of two of Israel's worst enemies.**

Abraham was God's choice to found the People of God, so Abraham needed to know how the Lord dealt with unrighteousness. The cities of Sodom and Gomorrah had built up such a sinful reputation that God had decided something had to be done. God would make an inspection tour to see whether the rumors were true. (Of course, God knew the truth about Sodom and Gomorrah, but he was relating to Abraham in a human way that Abraham could understand.)

But Abraham's nephew Lot was living in Sodom. That gave Abraham a strong interest in the place. And so—in a moving scene that Abraham's descendants must have loved to tell around the campfire—Abraham pleaded with God as would a child with his father. "Suppose there are fifty righteous within the city," he began, and God assured him that the place wouldn't be destroyed if there were fifty righteous.

Then Abraham thought for a moment. "Suppose five of the fifty righteous are lacking? Wilt thou destroy the whole city for lack of five?" God assured him that the place wouldn't be destroyed if there were forty-five righteous.

"Suppose forty are found there," Abraham continued, and so on. He finally talked God down to ten. If there were ten righteous people there, God wouldn't destroy the city.[7]

Abraham might have thought he had saved Sodom. After all, Lot and his family were there, and there were at least six of them, counting future sons-in-law. But what the two angels found when they reached Sodom was every bit as bad as the rumors said it would be.

Lot himself had kept some of the family's virtue. He showed the same hospitality to the strangers that Abraham had shown them, taking them in and offering them a night's rest under his roof. But the people of Sodom surrounded the house and demanded that Lot turn over his guests. They made their intentions perfectly clear: to rape the strangers.[8]

> Homosexuality refers to relations between men or between women who experience an exclusive or predominant sexual attraction toward persons of the same sex. It has taken a great variety of forms through the centuries and in different cultures. Its psychological genesis remains largely unexplained. Basing itself on Sacred Scripture, which presents homosexual acts as acts of grave depravity (cf. Gn 19:1-29; Rom 1:24-27; 1 Cor 6:10; 1 Tm 1:10), tradition has always declared that "homosexual acts are intrinsically disordered" (CDF, *Persona humana* 8). They are contrary to the natural law. They close the sexual act to the gift of life. They do not proceed from a genuine affective and sexual complementarity. Under no circumstances can they be approved. (CCC 2357)
>
> The number of men and women who have deep-seated homosexual tendencies is not negligible. This inclination, which is objectively disordered, constitutes for most of them a trial. They must be accepted with respect, compassion, and sensitivity. Every sign of unjust discrimination in their regard should be avoided. These persons are called to fulfill God's will in their lives and, if they are Christians, to unite to the sacrifice of the Lord's Cross the difficulties they may encounter from their condition. (CCC 2358)
>
> Homosexual persons are called to chastity. By the virtues of self-mastery that teach them inner freedom, at times by the support of disinterested friendship, by prayer and

sacramental grace, they can and should gradually and resolutely approach Christian perfection. (CCC 2359)

Lot hardly knew what to do. In that time, people thought there was almost no worse sin than a sin against hospitality. A homosexual rape is a grave enough sin, but Lot had invited the strangers in; that meant they were under his protection. He would be responsible if something bad happened to them. He tried to reason with the mob. He even offered his own daughters if the mob would leave the strangers alone. That was not the right thing to do, but Lot was desperate, and the mob was threatening serious violence. In fact, it took a miraculous intervention by the angels to evade the mob: they struck everyone blind and pulled Lot back into the house, shutting the door behind him.

No more investigation was needed after that demonstration. The angels warned Lot that they would destroy the city, and he would have to get his family out quickly. Lot gave the news to his sons-in-law, but they did not take him seriously. And when the time came to flee, even Lot lingered longer than he ought to have. The angels had to drag him out of the city, along with his wife and daughters. "Flee for you life," they told him; "do not look back or stop anywhere in the valley; flee to the hills, lest you be consumed."[9] God showed his mercy by allowing the innocent to escape.

"Then the Lord rained on Sodom and Gomorrah brimstone and fire from the Lord out of heaven;... But Lot's wife behind him looked back and she became a pillar of salt." (Gn 19: 24, 26)

The angels meant their instructions to be taken seriously. Lot and his daughters just barely escaped the destruction. Lot's wife stopped for a moment to look back, and turned into a pillar of salt.[10]

Everything Lot had was destroyed, and everything that he had considered civilization was gone. The blooming plain with its prosperous cities was a sunken, barren wasteland with a poisonous lake in the middle—the lake we call the Dead Sea. He cowered with his daughters in a mountain cave, afraid to go back to the lowlands after the horrendous catastrophe.

To Lot's two daughters, lost in a cave far from anyone else, it seemed like their father was the last man on earth. "Our father is old," they said, "and there is not a man on earth to come in to us after the manner of all the earth."[11]

So they came up with a wicked scheme. They got their father drunk and tricked him into fathering their children. The results of these two incestuous unions were sons who would be the fathers of two more nations, the Moabites and the Ammonites—hated enemies who would try to destroy Israel at every opportunity.

> *Incest* designates intimate relations between relatives or in-laws within a degree that prohibits marriage between them (cf. Lv 18:7-20). St. Paul stigmatizes this especially grave offense: "It is actually reported that there is immorality among you...for a man is living with his father's wife....In the name of the Lord Jesus...you are to deliver this man to Satan for the destruction of the flesh..." (1 Cor 5:1, 4-5). Incest corrupts family relationships and marks a regression toward animality. (CCC 2388)

The Sea of Sodom

With a salinity of 26-35%, the Dead Sea is truly dead. Ten times as salty as the world's oceans, its shoreline is the lowest point of dry land on earth at 1300 feet below sea level. 7 million tons of water evaporate daily.

The Story Of Lot

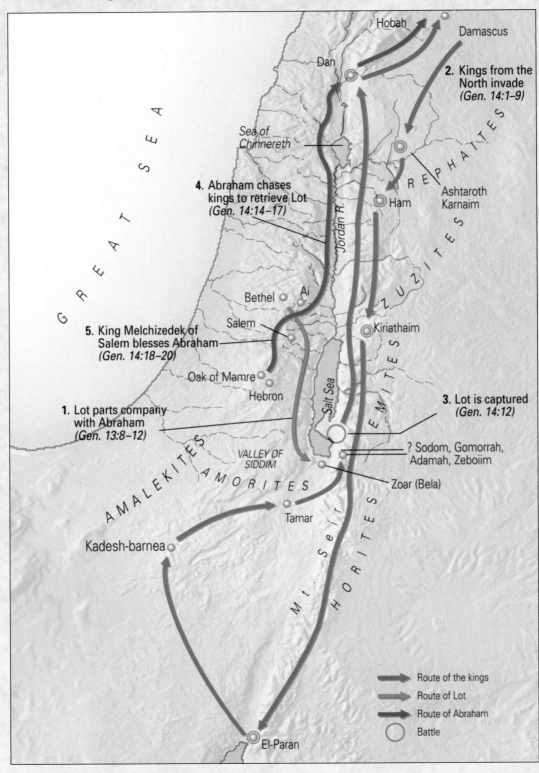

Hobah

Damascus

Dan

2. Kings from the North invade *(Gen. 14:1–9)*

G R E A T S E A

Sea of Chinnereth

R E P H A I T E S

4. Abraham chases kings to retrieve Lot *(Gen. 14:14–17)*

Ham

Ashtaroth Karnaim

Jordan R.

Z U Z I T E S

Bethel   Ai

Salem

5. King Melchizedek of Salem blesses Abraham *(Gen. 14:18–20)*

Kiriathaim

E M I T E S

Oak of Mamre

Salt Sea

Hebron

1. Lot parts company with Abraham *(Gen. 13:8–12)*

3. Lot is captured *(Gen. 14:12)*

? Sodom, Gomorrah, Adamah, Zeboiim

A M A L E K I T E S

A M O R I T E S

VALLEY OF SIDDIM

Zoar (Bela)

Tamar

Mt. Seir

Kadesh-barnea

H O R I T E S

El-Paran

→ Route of the kings
→ Route of Lot
→ Route of Abraham
◯ Battle

3. The Binding Of Isaac And God's Third Oath

- **Abraham gains a son in Isaac but loses Ishmael to Sarah's jealousy.**
- **When God tells him to sacrifice his only remaining son, Abraham obeys.**
- **The sacrifice of Isaac is a type of the sacrifice of Christ.**

When spring came, Sarah gave birth to a son and named him Isaac, just as the Lord had promised. It certainly was a joyous occasion—but it ended up splitting Abraham's family apart.

Sarah saw Ishmael mocking her son Isaac. "So she said to Abraham, 'Cast out this slave woman with her son; for the son of this slave woman shall not be heir with my son Isaac.'"[12] Perhaps she had forgotten that Abraham's double marriage was her idea in the first place. Throughout Genesis, whenever someone breaks the marriage covenant by taking more than one wife, the result is always jealousy and pain.

"And the thing was very displeasing to Abraham on account of his son," the book tells us. Abraham loved his son Ishmael. But God told him that Ishmael would also become a great nation. However, it was Isaac that would carry on the divine covenant.[13]

Ishmael and his mother were thrown out into the wilderness, where Ishmael grew up and married an Egyptian woman, and we hear nothing more of him for a while. Now Abraham had only one son left. As he watched the boy grow into a young man, all his hopes depended on Isaac.

> After these things God tested Abraham, and said to him, "Abraham!" And he said, "Here am I." He said, "Take your son, your only son Isaac, whom you love, and go to the land of Moriah, and offer him there as a burnt offering on one of the mountains of which I shall tell you." (Gn 22:1-2)

Here is where we see the real depth of Abraham's faith. He would certainly rather have offered himself as a sacrifice than his only remaining son. And we know that he was willing to bargain with God over the destruction of Sodom. But here he simply responds.

> So Abraham rose early in the morning, saddled his ass, and took two of his young men with him, and his son Isaac; and he cut the wood for the burnt offering, and arose and went to the place of which God had told him. On the third day Abraham lifted up his eyes and saw the place afar off. The Abraham said to his young men, "Stay here with the ass; I and the young man will go yonder and worship, and come again to you." And Abraham took the wood of the burnt offering and laid it on Isaac his son; and he took in his hand the fire and the knife. So they went both of them together. And Isaac said to his father Abraham, "My father!" And he said, "Here am I, my son." He said, "Behold, the fire and the wood; but where is the lamb for a burnt offering?" Abraham said, "God will provide himself the lamb for a burnt offering, my son." So they went both of them together. (Gn 22:3-8)

Above right: Abraham Casts Out Hagar and Ishmael.

Notice that Isaac carries the wood for his own sacrifice. He is not a little boy; but rather a strong man. And Abraham has left his servants behind: he is alone with Isaac, an ancient man about to sacrifice his strong young son. If Isaac wanted to fight back, he certainly could.

> When they came to the place of which God had told him, Abraham built an altar there, and laid the wood in order, and bound Isaac his son, and laid him upon the altar, upon the wood. Then Abraham put forth his hand, and took the knife to slay his son. (Gn 22: 9-10)

By the time his father was tying him up, Isaac knew what was happening. Remember that Abraham was already an old man. How was he able to tie up a strong young man and lay him on the altar? There can be only one explanation: Isaac himself cooperated. The sacrifice was not only Abraham's; Isaac himself was a willing participant. The Jewish writing known as 4 Maccabees shows us that ancient Jewish readers saw the story that way: "Remember whence you came, and the father by whose hand Isaac would have submitted to being slain for the sake of religion."[14]

As for Abraham, he could only have faith. If God chose, he could raise Isaac from the dead (see Heb 11: 19). Meanwhile, Abraham could only resign himself to the will of God.

But the story has a happy ending.

> But the angel of the LORD called to him from heaven, and said, "Abraham, Abraham!" And he said, "Here am I." He said, "Do not lay your hand on the lad or do anything to him; for now I know that you fear God, seeing you have not withheld your son, your only son, from me." And Abraham lifted up his eyes and looked, and behold, behind him was a ram, caught in a thicket by his horns; and Abraham went and took the ram, and offered it up as a burnt offering instead of his son. So Abraham called the name of that place The LORD will provide; as it is said to this day, "On the mount of the LORD it shall be provided." (Gn 22: 11-14)

The people who surrounded the ancient Israelites practiced human sacrifice all the time. In particular, they sacrificed their own children to their horrible idols. But the people of Israel would remember this story and know that their God never demanded human sacrifice, that the Lord's own angel had stayed Abraham's hand when he was about to kill his son.

For Christians, the story has far more significance. The Church Fathers saw the sacrifice of Isaac as a type of the sacrifice of Christ.

Isaac	Christ
A father offers his beloved son.	The Father offers his beloved Son.
The son submits to the father's will.	The Son submits to the Father's will.
Isaac carries the wood for his own sacrifice.	Jesus carries his own wooden cross.
God himself provides the sacrifice.	God himself provides the perfect sacrifice.

The mountains of Moriah were the hills around Jerusalem. On one of the peaks, the Temple would later be built, where the whole nation of Israel would offer its sacrifices to God. On another one, Golgotha, Jesus would offer himself as the last sacrifice.

Because of Abraham's faith, God swears an oath to deliver the last and most incredible part of his promise: that all the nations of the world will be blessed through Abraham.

> And the angel of the LORD called to Abraham a second time from heaven, and said, "By myself I have sworn, says the LORD, because you have done this, and have not withheld your son, your only son, I will indeed bless you, and I will multiply you as the stars of heaven and as the sand which is on the seashore. And your descendants shall possess the gate of their enemies, and by your descendants shall all the nations of the earth bless themselves, because you have obeyed my voice." (Gn 22:15-17)

At last, it seemed, the promised blessings had arrived. Abraham lived to a good old age, and by the end of his life he had seen his son married and well established. It must have seemed as though the hard times were over, and his descendants would have only to enjoy the blessings God had promised.

But the hard times were not over. Abraham's descendants would sin and fail over and over again. Still, God had not forgotten his covenant. In spite of their sins and failings, God was using the descendants of Abraham to bring salvation to the world.

The Dome of the Rock mosque in Jerusalem is built upon the Temple Mount which is thought to be the site where Abraham took Isaac to be sacrificed. Salem is believed to be Jerusalem and Mount Moriah the hill on which the Temple stood.

The Cave of Machpelah in Hebron was purchased by Abraham as a burial place for his wife Sarah. He paid 400 shekels of silver to Ephron the Hittite. (Gn 23) Later, Abraham, Isaac, Rebekah, Jacob and Leah were buried here. Jewish people are allowed to visit only 10 days a year.

SUPPLEMENTARY READING

Augustine, *City of God*, XV: 25:

The anger of God is not a disturbing emotion of his mind, but a judgment by which punishment is inflicted upon sin. His thought and reconsideration also are the unchangeable reason which changes things; for he does not, like man, repent of anything he has done, because in all matters his decision is as inflexible as his prescience is certain. But if Scripture were not to use such expressions as the above, it would not familiarly insinuate itself into the minds of all classes of men, whom it seeks access to for their good, that it may alarm the proud, arouse the careless, exercise the inquisitive, and satisfy the intelligent; and this it could not do, did it not first stoop, and in a manner descend, to them where they lie. But its denouncing death on all the animals of earth and air is a declaration of the vastness of the disaster that was approaching: not that it threatens destruction to the irrational animals as if they too had incurred it by sin.

Commentary, Genesis 12: 1-6

God's call to Abraham (the name he would give him instead of Abram: cf. 17: 5) marks the start of a new stage in his dealings with mankind, because his covenant with Abraham will prove a blessing to all nations. It means that Abraham has to break earthly ties, ties with family and place, and put his trust entirely in God's promise — an unknown country, many descendants (even though his wife is barren: cf. 11: 30) and God's constant protection. This divine calling also involves a break with the idolatrous cult followed by Abraham's family in the city of Haran (apparently a moon cult) so as to worship the true God.

Abraham responds to God's call; believing and trusting totally in the divine word, he leaves his country and heads for Canaan. Abraham's attitude is in sharp contrast with the human pride described earlier in connection with the tower of Babel (cf. 11: 19), and even more so with the disobedience of Adam and Eve which was the cause of mankind's break with God.

The divine plan of salvation begins to operate by requiring man to make an act of obedience: in Abraham's case, he is asked to set out on a journey. The plan will reach its goal with the perfect obedience shown by Jesus "made obedient unto death, even death on a cross" (Phil 2: 8), whereby all mankind will obtain the mercy of God (cf. Rom 5: 19). Everyone who listens and obeys the voice of the Lord, all believers, can therefore be regarded as children of Abraham. "Thus Abraham 'believed God, and it was reckoned to him as righteousness.'" So you see that it is men of faith who are the sons of Abraham.

God Testing Abraham – This parchment folio is from the Velislav Bible, ca. 1341, one of the most comprehensive medieval illustrated Bibles. The Bible is narrated by 800 paintings with Latin captions. The original manuscript is in the National Library of the Czech Republic.

VOCABULARY

ABRAHAM
A descendant of Shem; founder of the Hebrew nation.

ABRAM
The original name of Abraham.

ANGEL
A messenger from God. Angels are pure spirit. In Scripture, their appearances are usually terrifying.

CIRCUMCISION
The visible sign of God's covenant with Abraham. Circumcision set the People of God apart from other nations.

ISAAC
Son of Abraham and Sarah; born when they were very old. Although Isaac was not Abraham's first son, he was the only child born of Sarah, Abraham's wife, making Isaac the heir of God's promises.

ISHMAEL
Abraham's son by Hagar, Sarah's servant. The founder of the Arab tribes.

GOMORRAH
See Sodom.

LOT
Abraham's nephew. He settled in the prosperous plains, leaving Abraham in the wilderness of the hill country.

MORIAH
The mountains around Jerusalem, where Abraham went to offer his son Isaac as a sacrifice.

SARAH
The wife of Abraham and mother of Isaac.

SARAI
The original name of Sarah.

SODOM
Along with Gomorrah, one of the cities of the plain destroyed by God because of wickedness. Lot had settled there, but was warned by angels to flee.

UR
A city in the Plain of Shinar, the original home of Abraham.

"Abraham planted a tamarisk tree in Beersheba and called there on the name of the LORD, the Everlasting God." (Gn 21: 33)

STUDY QUESTIONS

1. In what city did Abram grow up?

2. Who were Abram's brothers?

3. How old was Abram when he first heard God's call?

4. What lesson can we learn from Abraham's submissiveness to God?

5. What were the three promises God made to Abram?

6. Through which three of Abraham's descendants are these promises fulfilled?

7. What does Matthew 1:1 remind us?

8. Why did a firepot and a torch pass between Abram's sacrifices after he had questioned God about his promises?

9. What was the sign of God's covenant with Abram?

10. What were God's promises to Abraham?

11. What was to be the sign of the covenant between God and his people?

12. How old was Sarah when she was told she would have a son?

13. What was the sin of Sodom and Gomorrah?

14. How should those who have homosexual tendencies be treated?

15. Who was Lot and why did he have to leave his city?

16. How are God's actions at Sodom and Gomorrah signs of his judgment and mercy?

17. Why were Ishmael and his mother thrown out into the wilderness?

18. In what ways was the proposed sacrifice of Isaac a "type" of the Lord's sacrifice on the cross?

19. What city was built on the mountains of Moriah?

"Do not lay your hand on the lad or do anything to him;
for now I know that you fear God,..." (Gn 22: 12)

PRACTICAL EXERCISES

1. A recurring theme in the story of Abraham is his humble obedience to God. Two great examples of this obedience are Abraham's answer to God's call and his willingness to offer his only son as a sacrifice when God asked. What are some ways in which we can show humble obedience to God? How could this obedience help us in our prayer? How could it help us in our relations with our parents or family and friends?

2. As part of his humble obedience, Abraham had a great trust in God. Though he and Sarah were very old and had no children, he still believed God when he was told his descendants would be as numerous as the stars. Abraham's vocation was to be the father of a multitude of nations. Think about what God may be calling you to do. What are some ways you can prepare yourself to accept what God wants you to do? Who could you go to for help in discerning your vocation?

3. At World Youth Day in 2003, the following quote was part of a speech given to all the young people that were present: "Homosexuality is not a 'variant' of human sexuality that can be put on an equal footing with heterosexuality. It is the expression of unresolved conflictive tension in a tendency that is separate from sexual identity." What does this mean? How can this quote be related to the CCC excerpts in this chapter that concern homosexuality?

King Melchizedek of Salem Blesses Abraham

"And he blessed him and said, 'Blessed be Abram by God Most High, maker of heaven and earth; and blessed be God Most High, who has delivered your enemies into your hand!'"
(Gn 14:19-20)

FROM THE CATECHISM

60 The people descended from Abraham would be the trustee of the promise made to the patriarchs, the chosen people, called to prepare for that day when God would gather all his children into the unity of the Church (cf. Rom 11: 28; Jn 11: 52; 10: 16). They would be the root on to which the Gentiles would be grafted, once they came to believe (cf. Rom 11: 17-18, 24).

72 God chose Abraham and made a covenant with him and his descendants. By the covenant God formed his people and revealed his law to them through Moses. Through the prophets, he prepared them to accept the salvation destined for all humanity.

145 The Letter to the Hebrews, in its great eulogy of the faith of Israel's ancestors, lays special emphasis on Abraham's faith: "By faith, Abraham obeyed when he was called to go out to a place which he was to receive as an inheritance; and he went out, not knowing where he was to go" (Heb 11: 8; cf. Gn 12: 1-4). By faith, he lived as a stranger and pilgrim in the promised land (cf. Gn 23: 4). By faith, Sarah was given to conceive the son of the promise. And by faith Abraham offered his only son in sacrifice (cf. Heb 11: 17).

150 Faith is first of all a personal adherence of man to God. At the same time, and inseparably, it is a *free assent to the whole truth that God has revealed.* As personal adherence to God and assent to his truth, Christian faith differs from our faith in any human person. It is right and just to entrust oneself wholly to God and to believe absolutely what he says. It would be futile and false to place such faith in a creature (cf. Jer 17: 5-6; Ps 40: 5; 146: 3-4).

1080 From the very beginning God blessed all living beings, especially man and woman. The covenant with Noah and with all living things renewed this blessing of fruitfulness despite man's sin which had brought a curse on the ground. But with Abraham, the divine blessing entered into human history which was moving toward death, to redirect it toward life, toward its source. By the faith of "the father of all believers," who embraced the blessing, the history of salvation is inaugurated.

1819 Christian hope takes up and fulfills the hope of the chosen people which has its origin and model in the *hope of Abraham,* who was blessed abundantly by the promises of God fulfilled in Isaac, and who was purified by the test of the sacrifice (cf. Gn 17: 4-8; 22: 1-18). "Hoping against hope, he believed, and thus became the father of many nations" (Rom 4: 18).

2571 Because Abraham believed in God and walked in his presence and in covenant with him (cf. Gn 15: 6; 17: 1 f.), the patriarch is ready to welcome a mysterious Guest into his tent. Abraham's remarkable hospitality at Mamre foreshadows the annunciation of the true Son of the promise (cf. Gn 18: 1-15; Lk 1: 26-38). After that, once God had confided his plan, Abraham's heart is attuned to his Lord's compassion for men and he dares to intercede for them with bold confidence (cf. Gn 18: 16-33).

Endnotes

1. We use the alternate reading of the Revised Standard Version, given in a footnote. Compare Sir 44: 21.
2. Gn 13: 1.
3. Gn 15: 9.
4. Gn 16: 2.
5. Gn 18: 1-8.
6. Gn 18: 9-15.
7. Gn 18: 16-33.
8. Gn 19: 5.
9. Gn 19: 17.
10. Gn 19: 26.
11. Gn 19: 31.
12. Gn 21: 10.
13. Gn 21: 11-13.
14. 4 Mc 13: 12.

Chapter 6
The Patriarchs

*"Your name shall no more be called Jacob,
but Israel, for you have striven with God and with men,
and have prevailed."*

Genesis 32: 28

Chapter 6

The Patriarchs

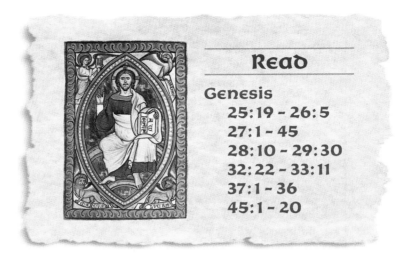

Read

Genesis
- 25:19 – 26:5
- 27:1 – 45
- 28:10 – 29:30
- 32:22 – 33:11
- 37:1 – 36
- 45:1 – 20

Although Abraham had settled permanently in Canaan, he was still a foreigner there. He was living among people who had different customs, spoke with a different accent, and—most of all—worshiped different gods. God had promised the land to his descendants. How horrible it would be if those descendants fell into the revolting idolatry of the Canaanites!

But that was just what might happen if Isaac married one of the local women. That same old problem with the "sons of God" and the "daughters of men" might come up all over again.

Finding A Wife For Isaac

> And Abraham said to his servant, the oldest of his house, who had charge of all that he had, "Put your hand under my thigh, and I will make you swear by the LORD, the God of heaven and of the earth, that you will not take a wife for my son from the daughters of the Canaanites, among whom I dwell, but will go to my country and to my kindred, and take a wife for my son Isaac." (Gn 24:2-4)

All God's promises to Abraham were to be fulfilled though Isaac. The only way to keep Isaac from falling into idolatry, Abraham had decided, was to keep him away from the Canaanites. Abraham's servant therefore went back to Mesopotamia, where Abraham's relatives still lived. Outside the city of Nahor, he stopped by a well.

The Bible is full of scenes at wells. With no running water, the well was a natural gathering place for the whole community. In particular, it was a gathering place for women, who usually did the work of filling up the water jugs and hauling them back to the house. In ancient Eastern society, the well was one of the few places women gathered outside the home, which is why we first meet many of the most important women in the Bible at a well.

Abraham's servant saw the women gathering at the well and prayed to God to guide him. "Let the maiden to whom I shall say, 'Pray, let down your jar that I may drink,' and who shall say, 'Drink, and I will water your camels'—let her be the one whom thou hast appointed for thy servant Isaac."[1]

"...he bowed himself to the earth before the Lord. And the servant brought forth jewelry of silver and gold, and raiment, and gave them to Rebekah;..." (Gn 24: 52-53)

Love at first sight: Isaac meets Rebekah

Just then a beautiful young woman appeared at the well and filled her jar.

"Pray, give me a little water to drink from your jar," Abraham's servant said.

"Drink, my lord," the woman said. Then, when the servant had drunk, she said, "I will draw for your camels also, until they have done drinking."[2]

This was the one!

The young woman was Rebekah, the granddaughter of Nahor, Abraham's brother. Her brother Laban was the head of the household now. When Abraham's servant came to his house, he told Laban how Abraham had prospered, and what his mission was. Hearing the story of the meeting at the well, and seeing the lavish gifts Abraham had sent, Laban had no objection to the proposed match. "The thing comes from the LORD," he said.

But still Rebekah had to agree. She had to make the same decision Abraham had made years before: she had to leave her home and go to a land he had never seen, all on the strength of a promise.

Jacob And Esau

It was love at first sight when Isaac finally met Rebekah. But for a long time, Rebekah was childless. Finally God answered her prayers. She conceived twins—two sons that seemed to be fighting inside her even before they were was born. What was going on? She "went to inquire of the LORD," and this was the answer she got:

> Two nations are in your womb,
> and two peoples, born of you, shall be divided;
> the one shall be stronger than the other,
> the elder shall serve the younger. (Gn 25:23)

They were still struggling when they were born. The first came out red all over, so they named him Esau, which sounded like the word for "red"; the second came out grabbing the first one's heel, so they called him Jacob, which sounded like the Hebrew for "he takes by the heel" or "he supplants." As the boys grew up, Esau (the first-born by only minutes) was his father Isaac's favorite. But Jacob was his mother's favorite, and mothers in the Bible usually manage to have their way.

The first story we hear about them as young men gives us a good idea of their characters.

> Once when Jacob was boiling pottage, Esau came in from the field, and he was famished. And Esau said to Jacob, "Let me eat some of that red pottage, for I am famished!"... Jacob said, "First sell me your birthright." Esau said, "I am about to die, of what use is a birthright to me?" Jacob said, "Swear to me first." So he swore to him, and sold his birthright to Jacob. Then Jacob gave Esau bread and pottage of lentils, and he ate and drank, and rose and went his way. Thus Esau despised his birthright. (Gn 25:29-34)

Esau thought only of what he wanted now; Jacob thought of the long term. Jacob was also willing to take advantage of the present circumstances to get his way. Esau had sworn to give up a great deal: as the first-born, he would have become the head of the family, and he was entitled to a double share of the inheritance. He gave all that up because all he could think about was his stomach.

Still, it was unlikely that their father Isaac would ratify that deal. He would insist on giving the first-born's blessing to Esau. Even after Esau had married two local pagan women who "made life bitter for Isaac and Rebekah,"[3] he was still his father's favorite. But Isaac was old and blind by now, and Rebekah came up with a plan to get that blessing for her favorite son.

Isaac had asked Esau to prepare him some of the venison stew he made so well, then come and receive his blessing. Rebekah overheard, and she quickly told her son to bring in some meat before Esau could come back. Rebekah made a stew like Esau's, then put Esau's clothes on Jacob. Because Esau was very hairy all over his body, Rebekah also made Jacob wear goatskins on the exposed parts of his body that Isaac could feel.

Isaac might be old and blind, but he could still hear. When Jacob came in and said, "I am Esau your first-born," the voice sounded wrong.

> Then Isaac said to Jacob, "Come near, that I may feel you, my son, to know whether you are really my son Esau or not." So Jacob went near to Isaac, who felt him and said, "The voice is Jacob's voice, but the hands are the hands of Esau." And he did not recognize him, because his hands were hairy like his brother Esau's hands; so he blessed him. (Gn 27:21-23)

A blessing was not a light thing. Once it had been given, it could not be retracted. Thinking he was blessing his favorite son Esau, Isaac gave Jacob the blessing Esau would have had:

Let peoples serve you, and nations bow down to you.
Be lord over your brothers, and may your mother's sons bow down to you.
Cursed be every one who curses you,
    and blessed be every one who blesses you. (Gn 27: 29)

When Esau came back, he was understandably disappointed. He had probably forgotten all about selling his birthright to Jacob, and even if he remembered it he had probably never taken that oath very seriously. Isaac, too, was horrified.

> Then Isaac trembled violently, and said, "Who was it then that hunted game and brought it to me, and I ate it all before you came, and I have blessed him?—yes, and he shall be blessed." (Gn 27: 33)

It was too late: the blessing had been given. All that was left for Esau was a prophecy that was not very consoling:

Behold, away from the fatness of the earth shall your dwelling be,
    and away from the dew of heaven on high.
By your sword you shall live,
    and you shall serve your brother;
but when you break loose
    you shall break his yoke from your neck. (Gn 28: 39-40)

The prophecy referred to the future of the two nations, Israel and Edom. Israel would dominate over Edom for a long time, but when Israel declined, Edom would break free.

The Journeys Of Isaac And Rebekah

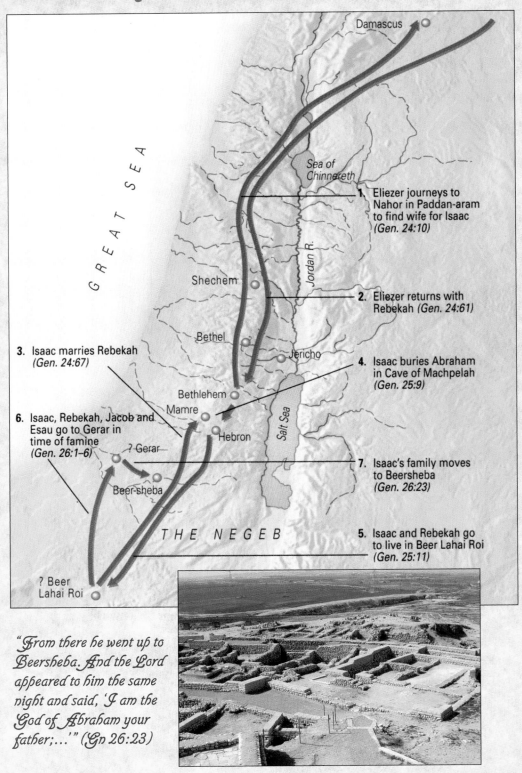

GREAT SEA

Damascus

Sea of Chinnereth

Jordan R.

Shechem

Bethel

Jericho

Bethlehem

Mamre

Hebron

? Gerar

Beer-sheba

Salt Sea

THE NEGEB

? Beer Lahai Roi

1. Eliezer journeys to Nahor in Paddan-aram to find wife for Isaac *(Gen. 24:10)*

2. Eliezer returns with Rebekah *(Gen. 24:61)*

3. Isaac marries Rebekah *(Gen. 24:67)*

4. Isaac buries Abraham in Cave of Machpelah *(Gen. 25:9)*

6. Isaac, Rebekah, Jacob and Esau go to Gerar in time of famine *(Gen. 26:1–6)*

7. Isaac's family moves to Beersheba *(Gen. 26:23)*

5. Isaac and Rebekah go to live in Beer Lahai Roi *(Gen. 25:11)*

"*From there he went up to Beersheba. And the Lord appeared to him the same night and said, 'I am the God of Abraham your father;...'*" *(Gn 26:23)*

Jacob's Ladder

Esau was furious: he wanted to kill Jacob. Rebekah, however, heard of Esau's plot, so she warned Jacob to run away to his uncle Laban until Esau got over his anger. Isaac blessed him and sent him on his way, telling him to find a wife there. "You shall not marry one of the Canaanite women," he told Jacob.[4] Esau's wives had been making Isaac and Rebekah miserable; they wanted Jacob to avoid the same mistake.

Jacob went off toward Haran, where his uncle lived, taking nothing with him but the staff in his hand.[5] Stopping for the night, he lay down with a stone for a pillow and had a strange dream.

> And he dreamed that there was a ladder set up on the earth, and the top of it reached to heaven; and behold, the angels of God were ascending and descending on it! And behold, the LORD stood above it and said, "I am the LORD, the God of Abraham your father and the God of Isaac; the land on which you lie I will give to you and to your descendants; and your descendants shall be like the dust of the earth, and you shall spread abroad to the west and to the east and to the north and to the south; and by you and your descendants shall all the families of the earth be blessed."[6] (Gn 28:12-14)

It was a renewal of the covenant with Abraham. The same promises were there: land, a dynasty, and (most amazing of all) universal blessing through his descendants. When he woke from his vision, Jacob called the place Beth-el: "House of God."

God had chosen to make Jacob, the younger brother, the one who would carry the promise. It was true that he had tricked his older brother out of his birthright, but God does not choose us because we deserve to be chosen. Jacob would be the one whose descendants would receive Abraham's blessing. But first Jacob would have to get a taste of his own medicine.

Jacob And Laban

When Jacob came near Haran, he stopped at a well, and there he saw a beautiful young woman. It was Rachel, his uncle Laban's daughter. He fell in love instantly.

When Jacob met his uncle Laban, there was a joyous family reunion. Jacob stayed for a month, helping Laban tend his flocks. Finally, Laban began to worry that he was taking advantage of Jacob. "Because you are my kinsman, should you therefore serve me for nothing?" he asked Jacob. "Tell me, what shall your wages be?"

Jacob knew right away what he wanted. He wanted Rachel. It was usual for a man to offer a "marriage present"—a large sum of money or the equivalent in property—to the father of his bride. But Jacob had nothing to offer. So he told Laban, "I will serve you seven years for your younger daughter Rachel."[7]

Laban agreed. But he had an older daughter, Leah, who was not quite so beautiful as Rachel. What would he do with her?

Seven years flew by for Jacob: he was so much in love that "they seemed to him but a few days." The wedding was arranged, and Jacob's veiled bride was brought to his dark tent that night.

When he woke up the next morning, Jacob had quite a shock. The woman next to him was Leah, not Rachel! Laban had tricked him! But there was no going back now.

> And in the morning, behold, it was Leah; and Jacob said to Laban, "What is this you have done to me? Did I not serve with you for Rachel? Why then have you deceived me?"
> Laban said, "It is not done in our country, to give the younger before the first-born. Complete the week of this one, and we will give you the other also in return for serving me another seven years." (Gn 29:25-27)

If Jacob wanted Rachel, he would have to work another seven years! He was so much in love that he agreed. At the end of the week of Leah's marriage celebrations, Jacob married Rachel, too, and then settled down to serve Laban for seven more years. Jacob the deceiver had been deceived by his crafty old uncle—and he had become an unwilling polygamist.

Jacob the deceiver had been deceived by his crafty old uncle Laban.

The Journeys Of Jacob And Rachel

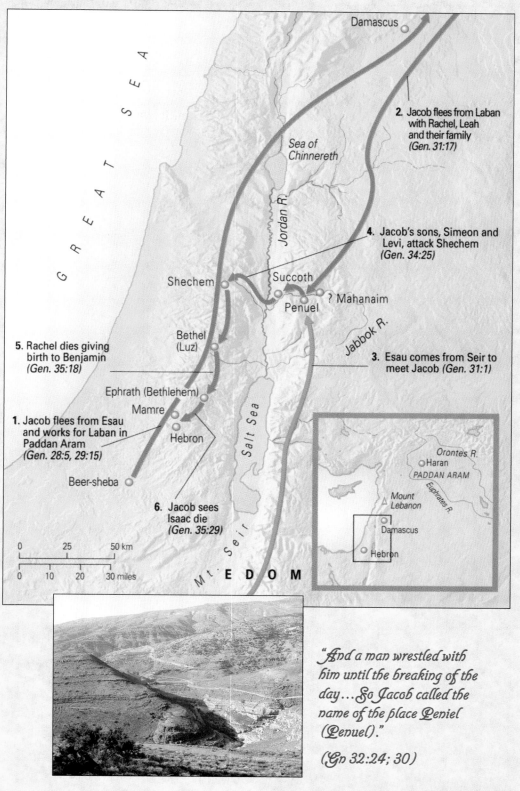

Damascus

G R E A T   S E A

Sea of Chinnereth

Jordan R.

2. Jacob flees from Laban with Rachel, Leah and their family *(Gen. 31:17)*

4. Jacob's sons, Simeon and Levi, attack Shechem *(Gen. 34:25)*

Shechem

Succoth

? Mahanaim

Penuel

Bethel (Luz)

Jabbok R.

5. Rachel dies giving birth to Benjamin *(Gen. 35:18)*

3. Esau comes from Seir to meet Jacob *(Gen. 31:1)*

Ephrath (Bethlehem)

Mamre

Salt Sea

Hebron

1. Jacob flees from Esau and works for Laban in Paddan Aram *(Gen. 28:5, 29:15)*

Beer-sheba

6. Jacob sees Isaac die *(Gen. 35:29)*

| 0 | 25 | 50 km |
| 0 | 10 | 20 | 30 miles |

Mt. Seir

E D O M

Orontes R.

Haran

PADDAN ARAM

Euphrates R.

Mount Lebanon

Damascus

Hebron

"And a man wrestled with him until the breaking of the day…So Jacob called the name of the place Peniel (Penuel)."

(Gn 32:24; 30)

Twelve Sons

Rachel

Leah

Polygamy in the Bible almost always leads to misery. Jacob never loved Leah the way he loved Rachel, and Leah knew it. But Rachel was barren, whereas Leah easily conceived and bore four sons. She named them Reuben, Simeon, Levi, and Judah. (All Jacob's sons would be named by his wives; as far as we know, he left that decision up to them.)

Rachel was miserable because she had no sons. Leah was miserable because Jacob obviously loved Rachel more. Rachel gave her maid to Jacob to bear sons for her (as Sarah had done with Hagar); she bore Dan and Naphthali. So Leah, who had not produced any children for a while, gave her maid to Jacob, and she bore Gad and Asher. Then Leah bore two more sons, Issachar and Zebulun; Rachel ceased to be sterile and finally herself bore a son named Joseph. So far there were eleven sons. The twelfth, Benjamin, would be born years later.

Even after the seven years were up, Laban didn't want to let Jacob go. Jacob finally agreed to stay a few more years in exchange for all the spotted sheep and goats in the flock. For the next few years, Laban and Jacob spent most of their time trying to outwit each other, with Laban trying to make sure all the lambs and kids were born solid-colored and Jacob using selective breeding to make sure all the best animals came out spotted. Jacob came out ahead in the game, and he grew rich with his spotted flock.[8]

At last a vision came to Jacob in a dream: he saw an angel who told him that God (not just selective breeding) was responsible for his prosperity. "Now arise, go forth from this land, and return to the land of your birth."

Jacob therefore made his escape from Laban and headed back toward Canaan. It was a good thing to escape from Laban after about twenty years of serving him, but now Jacob had an old problem to face. He would have to meet his brother Esau.

The Twelve Tribes Of Israel

Jacob fathered twelve sons: Asher, Benjamin, Dan, Gad, Issachar, Joseph, Judah, Levi, Naphtali, Reuben, Simeon, and Zebulun They are the ancestors of the tribes of Israel, and the ones for whom the tribes are named. Joseph is the father of two tribes: Manasseh and Ephraim. The tribes were encamped around four sides of the wilderness Tabernacle. (except the tribe of Levi, which was set apart to serve in the Holy Temple).

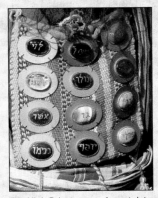

The High Priest wore a breastplate with twelve gems engraved with the names of the Twelve Tribes of Israel.

Eastern Tribes	Southern Tribes	Western Tribes	Northern Tribes
Judah	Reuben	Ephraim	Dan
Issachar	Simeon	Manasseh	Asher
Zebulun	Gad	Benjamin	Naphtali

Wrestling With God: Jacob Named Israel

Jacob sent messengers ahead of him to Esau. They came back with news that frightened Jacob: "We came to your brother Esau, and he is coming to meet you, and four hundred men with him." Esau—the brother who had planned to kill Jacob—was coming to meet him with a small army. Was that good news or bad? Jacob assumed the worst.

Jacob, now a rich man, also had a lot of followers with him. But he didn't want to risk losing everything in a battle with his brother's army. He divided his followers into two groups, thinking that if Esau attacked the first, at least the second would have time to get away. Then he prayed to God. It was something he apparently hadn't done in a while, but his fear led him back to the God of his fathers.

> O God of my father Abraham and God of my father Isaac, O LORD who didst say to me, "Return to your country and to your kindred, and I will do you good," I am not worthy of the least of all the steadfast love which thou hast shown to thy servant, for with only my staff I crossed this Jordan, and now I have become two companies. Deliver me, I pray thee, from the hand of my brother, from the hand of Esau, for I fear him, lest he come and slay us all, the mothers with the children. But thou didst say, "I will do you good, and make your descendants as the sand of the sea, which cannot be numbered for multitude." (Gn 32: 9-12)

After he had prayed, Jacob picked out the best of his flock and sent them with his servants as a present for Esau. Then putting his wives and children as far out of harm's way as he could, he spent the night alone.

There Jacob had his strangest vision yet. A man wrestled with him all night. Neither Jacob nor the mysterious man could win the struggle. Finally dawn began to appear. "Let me go," said the mysterious man, "for day is breaking."

But Jacob had realized that the man was more than just a man.

> But Jacob said to him, "I will not let you go, unless you bless me." And he said to him, "What is your name?" And he said, "Jacob." Then he said, "Your name shall no more be called Jacob, but Israel, for you have striven with God and with men, and have prevailed." (Gn 32: 26-28)

Jacob had been wrestling with the angel of God himself! Receiving a new name was like being created anew, and the angel explains Israel as meaning "He who strives with God." It was an appropriate name for Jacob, and it would be even more appropriate for the nation that would come from his descendants.

God renews his promise to Jacob, the ancestor of the twelve tribes of Israel. Before confronting his elder brother Esau, Jacob wrestles all night with a mysterious figure who refuses to reveal his name, but he blesses him before leaving him at dawn. From this account, the spiritual tradition of the Church has retained the symbol of prayer as a battle of faith and as the triumph of perseverance. (CCC 2573)

The next day, Jacob saw Esau and his whole army coming in the distance. He feared the worst—but he had no need to fear. His prayer had been answered. After twenty years, Esau got over his grudge, and he was delighted to see his younger brother again. They exchanged gifts, enjoyed their reunion for a while, and went their separate ways.

Some time later, God appeared to Jacob again to renew his promise of a new creation.

> And God said to him, Your name is Jacob; no longer shall your name be called Jacob, but Israel shall be your name... I am God Almighty: be fruitful and multiply; a nation and a company of nations shall spring from you. (Gn 35:10-11)

Once again, we see those words "be fruitful and multiply." We saw them before at the original creation (Gn 1:28) and at the new creation after the Flood (Gn 9:1). Here they are again, this time marking the creation of God's people, Israel.

Jacob Seeking Forgiveness of Esau

Joseph's Brothers Sell Him As A Slave

Of all his sons, Joseph was Jacob's favorite. Naturally, his ten elder brothers resented him for that. (Benjamin, the last of Jacob's sons, was still a little boy.) They resented him even more when Jacob gave Joseph a beautiful and expensive robe.[9] Not everyone agrees on the exact meaning of the Hebrew in the story; some say it was a robe with long sleeves, others that it was a full-length tunic. The traditional translation is "a coat of many colors," and that may be right: Egyptian paintings show rich Semitic visitors wearing many-colored coats. What is clear is that it was a very expensive and luxurious item.

The brothers resented him all the more when Joseph told them two dreams he had dreamt.

In the first dream, he saw himself and his brothers binding sheaves of grain in the field; "and lo, my sheaf arose and stood upright; and behold, your sheaves gathered round and bowed down to my sheaf."[10]

It was hard to miss the symbolism of that dream. Joseph expected to rule over his older brothers.

The next dream was even more provoking. "Behold, I have dreamed another dream; and behold, the sun, the moon, and eleven stars were bowing down to me."[11]

Obviously the sun and moon were Joseph's father and mother. Even indulgent old Jacob told his son to keep his dreams to himself.

*"Then they took Joseph's robe, and killed a goat, and dipped the robe in the blood;...
and brought it to their father, and said, 'This we have found; see now whether
it is your son's robe or not.'" (Gn 37: 31–32)*

Joseph's brothers resented Joseph more and more. Finally when they were all together far out in the field, they saw Joseph coming toward them. They decided to kill him. "Here comes this dreamer. Come now, let us kill him and throw him into one of the pits; then we shall say that a wild beast has devoured him, and we shall see what will become of his dreams."[12]

Only Reuben, the eldest, was against the scheme, yet he didn't dare take on the others. Instead, he told them not to bring the guilt of bloodshed on themselves. They could just throw him into a pit. Reuben thought he could come back secretly later and rescue Joseph.

So they did it. But while Reuben was away, they saw a caravan of slave-traders coming toward them. Here was an opportunity to get rid of Joseph and make a profit at the same time. They sold him to the traders. When Reuben came back to the pit to rescue Joseph, the pit was empty. Jacob was left believing his favorite son was dead.

Joseph, meanwhile, ended up in Egypt.

Joseph's Journey To Egypt As A Slave

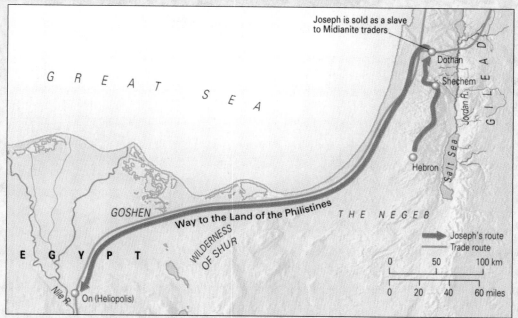

Joseph is sold as a slave to Midianite traders

Dothan

Shechem

GILEAD

Jordan R.

GREAT SEA

Hebron

Salt Sea

GOSHEN

Way to the Land of the Philistines

THE NEGEB

EGYPT

WILDERNESS OF SHUR

Nile R.

On (Heliopolis)

➤ Joseph's route
— Trade route

0   50   100 km

0   20   40   60 miles

Joseph Sold By His Brethren – "Then Midianite traders passed by; and they drew Joseph up and lifted him out of the pit, and sold him to the Ishmaelites for twenty shekels of silver; and they took Joseph to Egypt." (Gn 37: 28)

The Merneptah Stele, an Egyptian text, ca. 1230 B.C. mentions Israel—the first known occurrence of the term outside of the Bible.

121

God Turns Evil Into An Instrument Of Salvation

After years of service, Joseph rose to become the prime minister to the Pharaoh, the king of Egypt. Inspired by God, Joseph was able to predict that seven years of plenty would be followed by seven years of famine. Under his wise government, Egypt stored up so much grain in the years of plenty that the Egyptians had more than enough food during the famine. The rest of the world, however, was starving.

> When Jacob learned that there was grain in Egypt, he said to his sons, "Why do you look at one another?" And he said, "Behold, I have heard that there is grain in Egypt; go down and buy grain for us there, that we may live, and not die." So ten of Joseph's brothers went down to buy grain in Egypt. But Jacob did not send Benjamin, Joseph's brother, with his brothers, for he feared that harm might befall him. (Gn 42:1-4)

Foreigners who wanted to buy grain had to buy it through Pharaoh's chief minister, Zaphenathpaneah. What Jacob's sons did not know was that Zaphenathpaneah was the Egyptian name that Pharaoh had given to their brother Joseph. He recognized them right away: they were older, but they dressed and talked the way he remembered them. There they were, his brothers, bowing down before him — just as the dream had foretold all those years before.

Joseph, on the other hand, was dressed like an Egyptian nobleman and spoke Egyptian through an interpreter. It would probably also have been inexcusably bad etiquette to look directly at the Pharaoh's prime minister.

Joseph did not reveal himself right away. He played some tricks on his brothers, making them suffer a bit for what they had done to him. When he finally did decide to tell them who he was, they were afraid of him. After all, he was the second-most-powerful man in the world. If he wanted to take his revenge, he could. But Joseph reassured them. "And now do not be distressed, or angry with yourselves, because you sold me here; for God sent me before you to preserve life."[13]

God had managed to bring good out of evil. Joseph's brothers had betrayed and sold him, but God had used that betrayal to save the whole family. For that reason, early Christians saw Joseph as a "type" of Christ. Jesus Christ also would be betrayed by his own people, and God would use that betrayal to save the very people who betrayed him.

Joseph correctly interpreted Pharaoh's dreams. After seven years of growth, Egypt and nearby regions experienced a severe famine. But thanks to Joseph's wise counsel and the Pharaoh's foresight, the Egyptian people were prepared.

"So Joseph said to his brothers, 'Come near to me, I pray you.' And they came near. And he said, 'I am your brother, Joseph, whom you sold into Egypt. And now do not be distressed, or angry with yourselves, because you sold me here; for God sent me before you to preserve life.'" (Gn 45: 4-5)

In time we can discover that God in his almighty providence can bring a good from the consequences of an evil, even a moral evil, caused by his creatures: "It was not you", said Joseph to his brothers, "who sent me here, but God... You meant evil against me; but God meant it for good, to bring it about that many people should be kept alive" (Gn 45: 8; 50: 20; cf. Tb 2:12-18 (Vulg.)). From the greatest moral evil ever committed—the rejection and murder of God's only Son, caused by the sins of all men—God, by his grace that "abounded all the more" (cf. Rom 5: 20), brought the greatest of goods: the glorification of Christ and our redemption. But for all that, evil never becomes a good. (CCC 312)

When Jacob heard that Joseph was still alive, he could hardly believe it. But God spoke to him in a vision once again, telling him to go down to Egypt. It was part of God's plan.[14]

So Jacob went down to Egypt, and the whole family—seventy people, counting sons and grandsons—was reunited. Pharaoh gave Joseph's family the best grazing land in the country, and they grew even richer. So, contrary to what we might have expected, the book of Genesis ends, not in the Promised Land of Canaan, but in the foreign land of Egypt.

SUPPLEMENTARY READING

Tertullian, *An Answer to the Jews*, Ch. 10:

Joseph, again, himself was made a figure of Christ in this point alone (to name no more, not to delay my own course), that he suffered persecution at the hands of his brethren, and was sold into Egypt, on account of the favor of God; just as Christ was sold by Israel (and therefore, according to the flesh, by his brethren) when he was betrayed by Judas.

Commentary, Genesis 45: 1-28

The dénouement maintains the dramatic tone typical of the story so far. And now we are given the real reasons behind everything that Joseph, the wise man, has done. Once he makes himself known to his brothers, they interpret his behavior from their own, human, point of view—their fear of his vengeance (cf. v. 3 and later 50: 15). Joseph explains that everything was part of God's plan (cf. vv. 5-13). The generosity of the pharaoh was also a mark of divine mercy, but the greatest mercy of all is that Jacob has found the son he thought he lost (cf. v. 28).

As well as revealing God's mercy, this history shows forth the greatness of Joseph, who, far from harboring rancor or even thinking of vengeance, directs all his actions to getting back his brothers, leading them gradually to repent the sin they committed, forgiving them from the very start and treating them as the brothers they are. Joseph's behavior is a model of how we should treat one another; forgiveness should be ever-present in our relationship with others. Pope John Paul II has written that "Society can become 'ever more human' only when we introduce into all the mutual relationships which form its moral aspect the moment of forgiveness, which is so much of the essence of the Gospel. Forgiveness demonstrates the presence in the world of *the love which is more powerful than sin.* Forgiveness is also the fundamental condition for reconciliation, not only in the relationship of God with man, but also in relationships between people. A world from which forgiveness was eliminated would be nothing but a world of cold and unfeeling justice, in the name of which each person would claim his or her own rights *vis-à-vis* others; the various kinds of selfishness latent in man would transform life and human society into a system of oppression of the weak by the strong, or into an arena of permanent strife between one group and another" (*Dives in misericordia,* 14).

With his father Jacob near death, Joseph brought his two sons, Manasseh and Ephraim to be blessed by their grandfather. Paralleling Jacob's blessing from Isaac, the old man blessed Ephraim, the younger of the two even though Joseph attempted to guide the hand to the head of the elder son, Manasseh.

VOCABULARY

CANAAN

The land God promised to Abraham's descendants. It covered about the same territory as modern Israel. Its inhabitants were idol-worshipers who sacrificed their own children in cult rituals.

EGYPT

The ancient kingdom along the Nile River. During the time of the Patriarchs, Egypt was the wealthiest and most powerful nation on earth.

ESAU

The elder of Isaac and Rebekah's twin sons. The ancestor of the Edomites. He gave up his birthright for a bowl of Jacob's stew.

ISRAEL

The name given to Jacob after he wrestled with God. Also the name of the nation descended from him.

JACOB

The younger of Isaac and Rebekah's twin sons. He fooled his father into giving him the first-born's blessing, becoming Isaac's heir. Through him God renewed the covenant with Abraham's descendants.

JOSEPH

Jacob's favorite among his twelve sons. His envious brothers sold him as a slave, but Joseph rose to become prime minister of Egypt, where he was ultimately able to save his family from starvation.

PATRIARCH

A father who leads a family or tribe. Abraham and his descendants, the founders of Israel, are known as the Patriarchs.

PHARAOH

The title of the king of Egypt.

REBEKAH

Wife of Isaac, mother of Jacob and Esau. She plotted to gain Isaac's blessing for Jacob, her favorite.

STUDY QUESTIONS

1. Where did Isaac's wife Rebekah originate?

2. Who was Laban?

3. What were the blessings given to the first son?

4. For what price did Esau sell his birthright?

5. Why did Isaac bless Jacob instead of Esau?

6. Why did Jacob leave for his Uncle Laban's household?

7. How long did Jacob work for his uncle before he could marry Rachel?

8. How was it that Jacob became an unwilling polygamist?

9. What does the name "Israel" mean, according to the angel?

10. What does the Church say regarding the story of Jacob wrestling the angel?

11. Why did Joseph's brother resent him?

12. Why did Joseph go to Egypt?

13. Who was Zaphenathpaneah?

14. According to the text, how is Joseph considered a "type" of Christ?

15. How can God deal with evil?

PRACTICAL EXERCISES

1. Reread the story found in this chapter where Esau gives up his birthright for some of Jacob's pottage. What does this story reveal about Esau's personality? What does it reveal about Jacob's personality? Many people become weak and fall into a life of sin because they cannot overcome their impulses and try to satisfy every desire. How might you better prepare yourself to be strong the next time you are tempted? What sacraments did Christ give to the Church to aid us?

2. Jacob gained his father's blessing by pretending he was Esau and deceiving his father Isaac. Why do you think God still made him the founder of his chosen nation instead of Esau? What does that say about God's plan and its relationship with fallen humanity?

3. Joseph's brothers committed a terrible sin when they intended to leave Joseph for dead and then sold him into slavery in Egypt. God, however, used the situation to let Joseph assume a place of power in Egypt and eventually save his whole family from starvation. How does this story relate to the story of Noah? How does this story relate to the suffering and death of Jesus Christ?

FROM THE CATECHISM

218 In the course of its history, Israel was able to discover that God had only one reason to reveal himself to them, a single motive for choosing them from among all peoples as his special possession: his sheer gratuitous love (cf. Dt 4:37; 7:8; 10:15). And thanks to the prophets Israel understood that it was again out of love that God never stopped saving them and pardoning their unfaithfulness and sins (cf. Is 43:1-7; Hos 2).

287 The truth about creation is so important for all of human life that God in his tenderness wanted to reveal to his People everything that is salutary to know on the subject. Beyond the natural knowledge that every man can have of the Creator (cf. Acts 17:24-29; Rom 1:19-20), God progressively revealed to Israel the mystery of creation. He who chose the patriarchs, who brought Israel out of Egypt, and who by choosing Israel created and formed it, this same God reveals himself as the One to whom belong all the peoples of the earth, and the whole earth itself; he is the One who alone "made heaven and earth" (cf. Is 43:1; Ps 115:15; 124:8; 134:3).

707 Theophanies (manifestations of God) light up the way of the promise, from the patriarchs to Moses and from Joshua to the visions that inaugurated the missions of the great prophets. Christian tradition has always recognized that God's Word allowed himself to be seen and heard in these theophanies, in which the cloud of the Holy Spirit both revealed him and concealed him in its shadow.

Endnotes

1. Gn 24:14.
2. Gn 24:17-19.
3. Gn 26:34-35.
4. Gn 28:1.
5. See Gn 32:10.
6. We use the alternate reading given in a footnote in the Revised Standard Version.
7. Gn 29:17.
8. Gn 30.
9. Gn 37:3.
10. Gn 37:7.
11. Gn 37:9.
12. Gn 37:19-20.
13. Gn 45:5.
14. Gn 46:2-4.

The Exodus

*It would not be Moses leading the people:
it would be God leading the people through Moses.*

Chapter 7

The Exodus

Read

Exodus
    1:8 – 2:15
    3:1 – 22
    5:1 – 6:1
    11:1 – 12:50
    13:17 – 14:31
    20:1 – 20

The book of Exodus begins where Genesis leaves off. It tells us that, after Joseph died, his family and his brothers' families — starting with that symbolically perfect number of seventy souls — "multiplied and grew exceedingly strong." They formed a big part of the population of northern Egypt. They were rich, too: they owned much of the best land. But that prosperity wouldn't last forever. It was not God's plan that they should remain guests in Egypt, with no homeland of their own.

And as the people of Israel moved toward the land God had promised them, God would establish a new covenant — not with one man, or with one family, or with one tribe, but with the whole nation.

The Birth And Rescue Of Moses

- **A new king in Egypt enslaves the people of Israel.**
- **The Egyptians are ordered to kill every male Israelite child at birth.**
- **Moses escapes and is brought up in the king's court.**

"Now there arose a new king over Egypt, who did not know Joseph." Possibly a palace coup succeeded in overthrowing one pharaoh and his dynasty and replacing it with a new dynasty. In any case, it doesn't mean the new king had never heard of Joseph. It means that this new king refused to have the kind of friendly relations with the people of Israel that his predecessors had.

"Behold," he said to his people, "the people of Israel are too many and too mighty for us. Come, let us deal shrewdly with them, lest they multiply, and, if war befall us, they join our enemies and fight against us and escape from the land."[1] To justify the brutal oppression he was about to introduce, the king appealed to patriotic Egyptians by painting the Israelites as dangerous subversives. It's an old tyrant's trick.

So the Pharaoh (which is what the Egyptians called their kings) enslaved the Israelites, making them work on his building projects. But the people of Israel still multiplied. "And the Egyptians were in dread of the people of Israel."[2]

As part of his program of "dealing shrewdly," Pharaoh decided to kill all the male children of Israel at birth—but not the females. Why not the females? When the females grew up, they would have to marry Egyptians. Then all the good land that the people of Israel owned would go right back into Egyptian hands. It was a wicked plan, but it made a certain diabolical sense.

Of course, the Hebrew midwives would not cooperate, and the people of Israel still multiplied. Some of the children were slaughtered, but one in particular was successfully hidden before being killed. His name was Moses, which the Hebrews interpreted as "brought up out of the water."[3]

Moses Rebels

- **Moses is raised in Pharaoh's court with his own Hebrew mother as nurse.**
- **As a young man, Moses kills an Egyptian for abusing a Hebrew slave.**
- **Fearing for his life, Moses flees Egypt and settles in Midian.**

It is hard not to see the hand of God in the story of Moses' rescue. Pharaoh's daughter found a basket floating in the reeds and took pity on the baby inside. When she asked for a Hebrew nurse, she was led to Moses' own mother—though she never found out the woman's secret identity. "And the child grew, and she brought him to Pharaoh's daughter, and he became her son; and she named him Moses, for she said, Because I drew him out of the water" (Ex 2:10). Moses was raised with all the advantages Pharaoh's palace could offer him. He grew up getting the best clothes, the best education, the best food, the best everything. But his own Hebrew mother was there to teach him the true faith of his ancestors.[4]

As he became a young man, Moses began to notice how badly the people of Israel—his people—were treated.

One day, as he was out walking among the Hebrews, he saw an Egyptian taskmaster beating a Hebrew slave. It must have been an intolerably savage beating. Something snapped in Moses. He killed the Egyptian. At that moment, he branded himself a rebel. He threw away his allegiance to

Pharaoh's court and took his stand with the Hebrews, "choosing rather to share ill-treatment with the People of God than to enjoy the fleeting pleasures of sin."[5]

Still, Moses seems to have had second thoughts. Realizing what he had done, he hid the body and hoped no one would ever find out.[6]

But the next day, he saw two Hebrews fighting. He tried to break up the fight, but the one who had started it had a nasty surprise for him. "Who made you a prince and a judge over us?" he asked Moses sarcastically. "Do you mean to kill me as you killed the Egyptian?"[7]

The secret was out! Fearing for his life, Moses ran away to Midian. He found refuge with a priest named Jethro, and soon he had married the priest's daughter Zipporah. Since they were Midianites, they were descendants of Abraham (see Gn 25:12).

That might have been the end of the story of Moses. He settled down and grew old in Midian, raising livestock with his well-to-do father-in-law and bringing up his own family.

But God had not forgotten the troubles of his people in Egypt, even if Moses had.

Date Of The Exodus

Based on archaeological studies, the Exodus is often dated to the time of the 19th Dynasty of Egyptian pharaohs, in particular the reign of Rameses II, 1292-1290 B.C., and Merneptah, (1212-1204 B.C.)

If the Exodus took place in the 1200's B.C., Seti I, Rameses II, or Merneptah would be the pharaohs who spoke to Moses face-to-face.

The Temple of Rameses II at Abu-Simbel

The Burning Bush: God Reveals His Name To Moses

- **Moses unexpectedly encounters the God of Abraham, Isaac, and Jacob at Sinai.**
- **God orders Moses to go back to Egypt and lead Israel to freedom.**
- **God reveals his sacred Name to Moses.**
- **Knowing God's Name means knowing the truth about God.**

One day Moses, by now eighty years old, had led his sheep and cattle into the wilderness to the side of Mount Horeb, "the mountain of God" as the sacred writer calls it, which is in the wilderness of Sinai. Suddenly he saw a strange sight: a bush was on fire—but although the bush was burning, it was not being burned up. Moses decided to take a closer look. That was when God spoke to him for the first time.

"I am the God of your father, the God of Abraham, the God of Isaac, and the God of Jacob," the voice from the bush told him. Moses naturally covered his face, "for he was afraid to look at God."[8]

God identified himself as the God of Abraham, Isaac, and Jacob. If God was just the God of Abraham, the Midianites and the Ishmaelites could claim him, because both peoples came from Abraham. Even the Egyptians could lay some claim—after all, one of Abraham's wives, the first one to bear him a child, was Hagar, the Egyptian. If God had just said, "Abraham and Isaac," the Edomites, who were descended from Esau, could have claimed him.

Instead, God narrowed down the family lines: Abraham, Isaac, Jacob. This was the God of the people of Israel, God's own covenant family—the people who were now slaves in Egypt.

"I have seen the affliction of my people who are in Egypt," God told Moses. God had a plan for his people: he would bring them to a land of their own, the land he promised to their father Abraham. And then God told Moses the really big news: Moses would be the one to go back to Egypt and free his people.

The last place Moses wanted to go was Egypt. As far as he knew, he was still a wanted criminal there. The task seemed doomed to failure from the start.

"Who am I that I should go to Pharaoh, and bring the sons of Israel out of Egypt?" Moses asked.[9]

"But I will be with you," God reminded him. He promised Moses that he would bring the people of Israel to worship God on the very mountain where they now stood.

Moses still wasn't convinced that he could do it. "If I come to the people of Israel and say to them, 'The God of your fathers has sent me to you,' and they ask me, 'What is his name?' what shall I say to them?"

"I AM WHO I AM," God answered. "Say this to the people of Israel, 'I AM has sent me to you.'"[10] God's name, the sacred truth about God's nature, is "I AM."

Moses was still reluctant. The same pattern appears in Scripture over and over: God chooses a prophet who does not want to be chosen. God's assignments are never easy. But the prophet cannot run away. Moses tried every excuse, but God had an answer for every one. If Moses was worried about his speaking ability, he could ask his brother Aaron—a good public speaker—to help him.

God had chosen Moses for a reason. Moses might not think of himself as a leader, but God would be with him. It would not be Moses leading the people: it would be God leading the people through Moses.

> God revealed himself to his people Israel by making his name known to them. A name expresses a person's essence and identity and the meaning of this person's life. God has a name; he is not an anonymous force. To disclose one's name is to make oneself known to others; in a way it is to hand oneself over by becoming accessible, capable of being known more intimately and addressed personally. (CCC 203)
>
> God revealed himself progressively and under different names to his people, but the revelation that proved to be the fundamental one for both the Old and the New Covenants was the revelation of the divine name to Moses in the theophany of the burning bush, on the threshold of the Exodus and of the covenant on Sinai. (CCC 204)

Sunrise from atop the traditional location of Mount Sinai, Jebel Musa, "the mountain of Moses."

The Message To Pharaoh

- **Israel is God's first-born son, the covenant head of the family of nations.**
- **Israel is called to act as a priest for the other nations.**

God sent Moses to Egypt with a message and a demand, both to be delivered to Pharaoh. The message was this: "Israel is my first-born son."[11]

In other words, Israel is the elder brother of all the nations. Israel will be their covenant head. The other nations are like God's younger children, Israel's younger siblings, but God will make Israel a model for righteousness and wisdom so that nations might learn how to walk in the ways of God—much like Shem, and much like Shem's descendant, Abraham.

The demand was simple and reasonable: let the people of Israel go three days' journey into the desert to offer sacrifice to the Lord. Moses was not to demand their freedom, or even ask Pharaoh to be less hard on them. They just needed a few days for a religious festival. But there was an ominous threat that went with the demand: "If you refuse to let him [Israel] go, behold, I will slay your first-born son."[12] Egypt, God says, could be his child, too—but only by letting God's first-born son Israel go to serve God, so that Egypt would learn how to serve God by watching him. Israel is going to be like a priest. Just as Adam was called to be a priest-king, Israel is called to be a royal priestly nation.

Of course, God knew that Pharaoh would not listen. "And the LORD said to Moses, 'When you go back to Egypt, see that you do before Pharaoh all the miracles which I have put in your power; but I will harden his heart, so that he will not let the people go.'"[13] Because of that, God would bring judgment on the Egyptians. The first-born of Egypt would be killed, and Israel would be led out of slavery toward the Promised Land.

Below Jebel Musa, The Monastery of St. Catherine, built by Justinian ca. 550 A.D., marks the traditional spot where early Christians believed Moses met God at the burning bush. Springs in the area still supply water for Bedouin flocks.

The Plagues

- **The first nine plagues are arranged in three cycles.**
- **Israel is commanded to kill the Egyptian gods as sacrifices.**
- **The plagues, too, are judgments on the Egyptian gods.**

So two old men—Moses at eighty years old and his brother Aaron at eighty-three—went back to Egypt to confront the most powerful king in the world.

> Afterward Moses and Aaron went to Pharaoh and said, "Thus says the LORD, the God of Israel, 'Let my people go, that they may hold a feast to me in the wilderness.'" But Pharaoh said, "Who is the LORD, that I should heed his voice and let Israel go? I do not know the LORD, and moreover I will not let Israel go." Then they said, "The God of the Hebrews has met with us; let us go, we pray, a three days' journey into the wilderness, and sacrifice to the LORD our God, lest he fall upon us with pestilence or with the sword." But the king of Egypt said to them, "Moses and Aaron, why do you take the people away from their work? Get to your burdens." And Pharaoh said, "Behold, the people of the land are now many and you make them rest from their burdens!" (Ex 5: 1-4)

As far as Pharaoh was concerned, the Lord—that is, Yahweh—was just the name of some tribal god he had never heard of. If the Israelites had enough free time to plan elaborate feasts in the wilderness, Pharaoh would give them something to do.

> The same day Pharaoh commanded the taskmasters of the people and their foremen, "You shall no longer give the people straw to make bricks, as heretofore; let them go and gather straw for themselves. But the number of bricks which they made heretofore you shall lay upon them, you shall by no means lessen it; for they are idle; therefore they cry, 'Let us go and offer sacrifice to our God.' Let heavier work be laid upon the men that they may labor at it and pay no regard to lying words." (Ex 5: 6-10)

So the Egyptians made the Israelite slaves work even harder, and of course the Israelites blamed Moses and Aaron.

Because Pharaoh refused to listen, God sent ten plagues to Egypt. We can see them as nine plagues plus one: the last one, the killing of the first-born of Egypt, was the plague that broke even Pharaoh's hard heart.

The sacred writer has arranged the first nine plagues in three cycles of three each. In each cycle, the first two plagues come after a warning, and the third with no warning to Pharaoh at all.

1. Plague of blood (Ex 7: 14-24)	4. Plague of flies (Ex 8: 20-32)	7. Plague of hail (Ex 9: 13-35)	God tells Moses, *"Go to Pharaoh in the morning . . ."*
2. Plague of frogs (Ex 8: 1-15)	5. Plague on Egyptian cattle (Ex 9: 1-7)	8. Plague of locusts (Ex 10: 1-20)	God tells Moses, *"Go in to Pharaoh . . ."*
3. Plague of "gnats" or "lice" (Ex 8: 16-19)	6. Plague of boils (Ex 9: 8-12)	9. Plague of darkness (Ex 10: 21-28)	Moses gives Pharaoh no warning.

Pharaoh shrugged off the first two plagues; his court magicians could create at least something that looked like the same sort of plague. With the plague of gnats (which might have been some sort of mosquito), the magicians threw up their hands and admitted, "This is the finger of God." Pharaoh, however, still wouldn't listen.

With the fourth plague, God made it even more obvious that it was the God of the Israelites who was sending the plague. When the flies came, they covered all of Egypt—except Goshen, where the Israelites lived.

Now Pharaoh was willing to negotiate. Perhaps the Israelites could just take some time off and sacrifice here in Egypt, he suggested. But Moses could not accept those conditions. And his argument is very important, because it tells us not only why God chose these particular plagues, but also why God asked the Israelites to sacrifice animals like cattle, sheep, and goats.

> But Moses said, "It would not be right to do so; for we shall sacrifice to the LORD our God offerings abominable to the Egyptians. If we sacrifice offerings abominable to the Egyptians before their eyes, will they not stone us? We must go three days' journey into the wilderness and sacrifice to the LORD our God as he will command us." (Ex 8: 26-27)

What does Moses mean when he says that the sacrifices will be "abominable to the Egyptians?" He means that the people of Israel would sacrifice the very animals Egyptians worshiped as gods! In fact, another translation of what Moses said is "we shall sacrifice the abominations of the Egyptians to the LORD our God." God's message to his people was clear: Israel had to give up the Egyptian gods and worship the one true God. The animal sacrifices would be a permanent warning against falling back into the idolatry of the Egyptians.

The Seventh Plague of Egypt by William Turner

The plagues, too, were judgments on the gods of Egypt. The Egyptians worshiped the Nile as a god (Hapi); God turned its water to blood. The Egyptians worshiped a bull; God brought a plague on their cattle. The Egyptians worshiped a frog; God sent them so many frogs that they had to shovel them into stinking piles of dead Egyptian gods.

> In return for their foolish and wicked thoughts,
> which led them astray to worship irrational serpents and worthless animals,
> thou didst send upon them a multitude of irrational creatures to punish them,
> that they might learn that one is punished by the very things by which he sins.
> (Wis 11: 15-16)

After each plague, Pharaoh seemed willing to listen to reason. But as soon as Moses prayed to God and the plague was gone, Pharaoh backed out of his deal with Moses and refused to let Israel go into the wilderness.

The Passover

- **The last plague kills every first-born son in Egypt.**
- **The plague skips the houses of the Israelites, marked with the blood of the Passover lamb.**
- **The Passover lamb is a type of Christ, the Lamb of God, whose blood saves us from eternal death.**
- **The Egyptians hurry the Israelites out of Egypt.**

Moses' first message to Pharaoh had carried a grim warning. Israel, the Lord said, was God's first-born son, and "if you refuse to let him go, behold, I will slay your first-born son."[14] The time had come when God would carry out that threat.

The Lord told Moses that he would send the angel of death to kill the first-born sons of Egypt, including the first-born male offspring of all the cattle, sheep, and goats. Once again, by killing the animals, God would symbolically slaughter the gods of Egypt. (In fact, Nm 33: 4 says exactly that: "upon their gods also the LORD executed judgments.")

But God gave the people of Israel a way to save their first-born sons. The Israelites were told to take a lamb without blemish, sacrifice it, spread its blood over their doorposts, and eat it as part of a sacred meal. As the angel of death passed through Egypt, it would pass over their houses, sparing their first-born sons.

The instructions for the ceremonial feast were very specific. The Israelites would eat unleavened bread—bread with no yeast in it—because there would be no time for them to let it rise before Pharaoh himself would throw them out of Egypt. The lamb had to be roasted, not boiled. And the Israelites had to eat their feast with their traveling clothes on.[15] Not only that, but for the rest of time, the children of Israel were to observe a week-long Passover every year, so that they would never forget what God had done for them.

"At midnight the Lord smote all the first-born in the land of Egypt, from the first-born of Pharaoh who sat on his throne to the first-born of the captive who was in the dungeon,..." (Ex 12: 29)

The blood of the Passover lamb was a type of the blood of Christ, who by his blood
saved us from eternal death.

The Passover Lamb As A Type Of Christ

The Passover was more than a deliverance from bondage in Egypt. The blood of the Passover lamb, sprinkled on the doorposts to save the first-born sons of Israel from immediate death, was a type of the blood of Christ, who by his blood saved us from eternal death. By celebrating the Passover every year, the People of God would be preparing themselves to understand the death of the Lamb of God.

As God had told Moses, the angel of death passed *through* Egypt, killing all the first-born sons and the first-born of all the cattle. But wherever the blood of the Passover lamb was sprinkled on the doorposts, the angel of death passed *over* that house.

> And Pharaoh rose up in the night, he, and all his servants, and all the Egyptians; and there was a great cry in Egypt, for there was not a house where one was not dead. And he summoned Moses and Aaron by night, and said, "Rise up, go forth from among my people, both you and the people of Israel; and go, serve the Lord, as you have said. Take your flocks and your herds, as you have said, and be gone; and bless me also!"
>
> And the Egyptians were urgent with the people, to send them out of the land in haste; for they said, "We are all dead men." So the people took their dough before it was leavened, their kneading bowls being bound up in their mantles on their shoulders. (Ex 12:30-33)

Now the Egyptians demanded that the Hebrews leave at once. In the middle of the night, hundreds of thousands of Israelites—who had already packed what they could carry, following Moses' instructions—began their march into the wilderness. God himself led them with a pillar of fire by night and a pillar of cloud by day.

The Route Of The Exodus

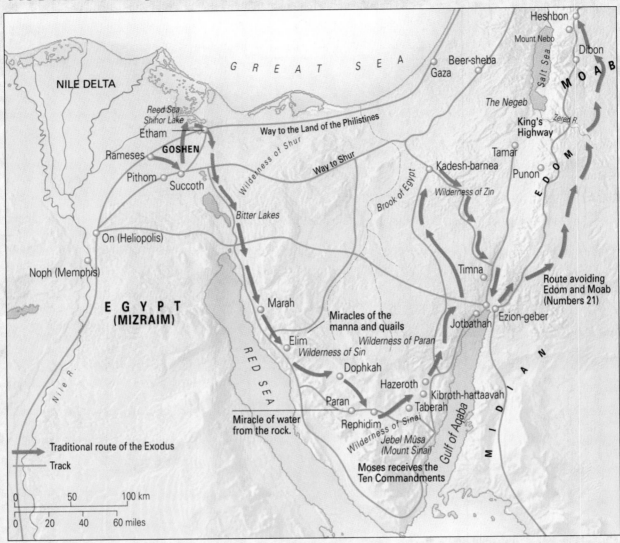

NILE DELTA

GREAT SEA

Reed Sea
Shihor Lake
Etham
GOSHEN
Rameses
Pithom
Succoth

Way to the Land of the Philistines

Wilderness of Shur

Way to Shur

Beer-sheba
Gaza

The Negeb

Mount Nebo

Heshbon
Dibon
Salt Sea
M O A B

Zered R.

King's
Highway

Tamar
Kadesh-barnea
Punon

Wilderness of Zin

Brook of Egypt

E D O M

On (Heliopolis)

Bitter Lakes

Noph (Memphis)

**E G Y P T
(MIZRAIM)**

Nile R.

Marah

Miracles of the
manna and quails

Elim
Wilderness of Sin

RED SEA

Dophkah

Paran

Miracle of water
from the rock.

Rephidim

Hazeroth

Wilderness of Paran

Timna

Jotbathan

Ezion-geber

Route avoiding
Edom and Moab
(Numbers 21)

Kibroth-hattaavah
Taberah

Wilderness of Sinai

Jebel Mûsa
(Mount Sinai)

Gulf of Aqaba

M I D I A N

Moses receives the
Ten Commandments

→ Traditional route of the Exodus

— Track

| 0 | 50 | 100 km |
| 0 | 20 | 40 | 60 miles |

The Wilderness of Paran

Escape From Egypt

- **Pharaoh changes his mind again and chases after the Israelites.**
- **Clearing a path through the sea, God miraculously saves the Israelites from the Egyptian army.**

As soon as the Israelites were packed and gone, Pharaoh had yet another change of heart—his last, as it would turn out. He and his nobles suddenly realized that they had lost all their cheap labor. "What is this we have done, that we have let Israel go from serving us?" they asked one another.[16]

So Pharaoh gathered a formidable army, including horses and chariots, and set out to catch up with the Israelites. The Israelites had reached the Sea of Reeds (which is usually translated as "Red Sea" in English). In front of them was the water; behind them, they saw a horde of Egyptian warriors about to descend on them.

As they would do many times afterward, the people turned against Moses.

> When Pharaoh drew near, the people of Israel lifted up their eyes, and behold, the Egyptians were marching after them; and they were in great fear. And the people of Israel cried out to the LORD; and they said to Moses, "Is it because there are no graves in Egypt that you have taken us away to die in the wilderness? What have you done to us, in bringing us out of Egypt? Is not this what we said to you in Egypt, 'Let us alone and let us serve the Egyptians'? For it would have been better for us to serve the Egyptians than to die in the wilderness." (Ex 14:10-12)

But God told Moses to stretch out his rod toward the sea, and a fearful storm came up. The pillar of fire and cloud moved between the Israelites and the Egyptians, so that neither side could see the other. God sent a strong east wind to blow all night, and it cleared a dry path straight through the water. The Israelites marched straight through the sea on dry land.

When the Egyptians saw what had happened, they were furious. They followed the same path straight into the sea. But their chariots got stuck in the mud. By the time the people of Israel were all safely across, the Egyptians were all bogged own in the middle of the sea.

Then God told Moses to stretch out his rod again. The waters came crashing back over the Egyptians, and Pharaoh and his whole army drowned. Without raising a sword, Israel had defeated Egypt, the mightiest empire in the world. God himself had won the victory. It was a kind of baptism: through the waters of the Red Sea, God had saved the people of Israel from certain death. (See 1 Cor 10:12, where Paul says that "our fathers were all under the cloud, and all passed through the sea, and all were baptized into Moses in the cloud and in the sea.")

The Exodus—Greek for "going out"—was Israel's declaration of independence. From now on, the Israelites would be on their own. But what would they do with their independence? So far they had no land, and no government except God himself through Moses. Israel was not yet a nation.

Inset: Pharaoh Rameses II and his chariot is carved on the wall of his temple at Abu-Simbel.

Spiritual Food In The Wilderness

- **Hungry and thirsty, the Israelites complain to Moses.**
- **God sends them miraculous food and water.**
- **The "bread which the LORD has given" is a type of the Eucharist.**

With no more Egyptians to worry about, the people had time to think about their own bellies again. The Israelites had been driven out of Egypt with no time to pack any food for the journey. In a few days, they were hungry and miserable. Once again, they began to think of their slavery in Egypt as "the good old days." "Would that we had died by the hand of the LORD in the land of Egypt," they grumbled to Moses and Aaron, "when we sat by the fleshpots and ate bread to the full; for you have brought us out into this wilderness to kill this whole assembly with hunger."[17]

But God had a way of dealing with their hunger. "I will rain bread from heaven for you," he told Moses. And the next morning the Israelites found "a fine, flake-like thing, fine as hoarfrost on the ground."[18]

"What is it?" they asked one another.

"It is the bread which the LORD has given you to eat," Moses told them.

So they called the thing "manna," meaning "what-is-it?" As long as Israel wandered in the wilderness, the manna continued to appear on the ground, enough to feed the whole nation.

And when the people complained that they were thirsty ("Why did you bring us up out of Egypt, to kill us and our children and our cattle with thirst?"), God gave them water from a dry rock in the desert.[19]

Once again, Christians can see that God was doing more than taking care of his people's hunger and thirst. The manna was a type of the Eucharist, as Jesus himself would point out:

> So they [the multitude] said to him, "Then what sign do you do, that we may see, and believe you? What work do you perform? Our fathers ate the manna in the wilderness; as it is written, 'He gave them bread from heaven to eat.'"
>
> Jesus then said to them, "Truly, truly, I say to you, it was not Moses who gave you the bread from heaven; my Father gives you the true bread from heaven. For the bread of God is that which comes down from heaven, and gives life to the world."
>
> They said to him, "Lord, give us this bread always."
>
> Jesus said to them, "I am the bread of life; he who comes to me shall not hunger, and he who believes in me shall never thirst." (Jn 6:30-35)

And the rock itself was a type of Christ, who gives us living water to drink—as St. Paul would tell the Corinthians:

> I want you to know, brethren, that our fathers were all under the cloud, and all passed through the sea, and all were baptized into Moses in the cloud and in the sea, and all ate the same supernatural food and all drank the same supernatural drink. For they drank from the supernatural Rock which followed them, and the Rock was Christ. (1 Cor 10:1-4)

The manna was a type of the Eucharist, as Jesus himself would point out.

"This is what the Lord has commanded: 'Gather of it, every man of you, as much as you can eat;...'"
(Ex 16: 16)

The Covenant At Sinai

After three months of wandering, Israel reached the Mountain of God in the wilderness of Sinai—the very same mountain where God had revealed his sacred name to Moses from the burning bush. There Moses went up the mountain alone, and God gave him a message for the whole nation of Israel:

> And Moses went up to God, and the LORD called to him out of the mountain, saying, "Thus you shall say to the house of Jacob, and tell the people of Israel: You have seen what I did to the Egyptians, and how I bore you on eagles' wings and brought you to myself. Now therefore, if you will obey my voice and keep my covenant, you shall be my own possession among all peoples; for all the earth is mine, and you shall be to me a kingdom of priests and a holy nation. These are the words which you shall speak to the children of Israel."

> So Moses came and called the elders of the people, and set before them all these words which the LORD had commanded him. And all the people answered together and said, "All that the LORD has spoken we will do." And Moses reported the words of the people to the LORD. (Ex 19: 3-8)

José de Ribera's *Moses* is represented as the penultimate teacher, instructing his people in the ways of the Lord with patience, but also knowing how difficult it is for them to keep God's commandments.

If the people would obey God's voice, then they would be a nation of priests. What does that mean? It means that God, who made the whole world, had chosen Israel as the nation to bring his word to the rest of the nations. God would have a personal relationship with his people. He would talk to them directly, and he would be their leader and guide. In turn, Israel—as God's first-born—would carry God's message to the rest of the family of nations.

The people purified themselves for three days, and on the third day they saw a thick cloud descend on the mountain. Moses alone entered the cloud, but the whole people heard the voice of God from the cloud. They all heard the conditions of God's covenant with them—the rules we know as the Ten Commandments:

> I am the LORD your God, who brought you out of the land of Egypt, out of the house of bondage.
>
> 1. You shall have no other gods before me. You shall not make for yourself a graven image, or any likeness of anything that is in heaven above, or that is in the earth beneath, or that is in the water under the earth; you shall not bow down to them or serve them; for I the LORD your God am a jealous God, visiting the iniquity of the fathers upon the children to the third and the fourth generation of those who hate me, but showing steadfast love to thousands of those who love me and keep my commandments.
>
> 2. You shall not take the name of the LORD your God in vain; for the LORD will not hold him guiltless who takes his name in vain.
>
> 3. Remember the sabbath day, to keep it holy. Six days you shall labor, and do all your work; but the seventh day is a sabbath to the LORD your God; in it you shall not do any work, you, or your son, or your daughter, your manservant, or your maidservant, or your cattle, or the sojourner who is within your gates; for in six days the LORD made heaven and earth, the sea, and all that is in them, and rested the seventh day; therefore the LORD blessed the sabbath day and hallowed it.
>
> 4. Honor your father and your mother, that your days may be long in the land which the LORD your God gives you.
>
> 5. You shall not kill.
>
> 6. You shall not commit adultery.
>
> 7. You shall not steal.
>
> 8. You shall not bear false witness against your neighbor.
>
> 9-10. You shall not covet your neighbor's house; you shall not covet your neighbor's wife, or his manservant, or his maidservant, or his ox, or his ass, or anything that is your neighbor's. (Ex 20: 2-17)

(The traditional catechetical formula has two commands against coveting: the first against coveting your neighbor's wife, and the second against coveting his property.)

When the people heard the voice of God himself speaking to him, they were so frightened that they begged Moses not to let it happen again. "You speak to us, and we will hear; but let not God speak to us, lest we die."[20]

So Moses went up to speak for the people, and God gave him a more detailed version of the laws by which Israel was to live. Then Moses built an altar, and the people sealed the covenant with a sacrifice. Moses threw half the blood of the sacrifice against the altar. Then he read the book of the covenant to the people, and again they agreed to do everything God had told them to do. Moses sprinkled the other half of the blood on the people, uniting them and God in the same covenant sacrifice. "Behold the blood of the covenant which the LORD has made with you in accordance with all these words."

> In the promise to Abraham and the oath that accompanied it (cf. Heb 6:13), God commits himself but without disclosing his name. He begins to reveal it to Moses and makes it known clearly before the eyes of the whole people when he saves them from the Egyptians: "he has triumphed gloriously" (Ex 15:1; cf. 3:14). From the covenant of Sinai onwards, this people is "his own" and it is to be a "holy (or "consecrated": the same word is used for both in Hebrew) nation" (cf. Ex 19:5-6), because the name of God dwells in it. (CCC 2810)

After that, all the elders of Israel went up to the mountain and saw the glory of the Lord directly, without Moses to stand between them and God. God was keeping his covenant promise: Israel was a nation of priests, speaking directly with God.

The Decalogue And The Natural Law

The Ten Commandments (also called the "Decalogue," literally "ten words") sum up and proclaim God's law. They form an organic unity, outlining in full the requirements for loving both God and neighbor. For example, one cannot honor another person without blessing God his Creator, and one cannot adore God without loving all men, his creatures. In this way, the Decalogue brings man's religious and social life into unity.

The Decalogue involves man's humanity and social existence, and so it also reflects and expresses the natural law. The natural law contains those rules which regulate moral behavior that are available to us through the application of human reason.

Many of the laws of the commandments, such as "Thou shall not kill," can be understood through reason without the help of divine revelation. Many nations at the time of the Exodus, for example, obeyed this commandment because it is understandable that, simply in terms of human experience, killing poses a danger to society. But the commandments of the Decalogue, although accessible to reason, contain a complete and certain understanding of the natural law. The Decalogue is a privileged expression of the natural law because it was made known to us by both divine revelation and human reason.

The Temple In Heaven And On Earth

Now Moses went up the mountain once more, leaving his brother Aaron in charge. For forty days and forty nights he was alone with God. (Here we see that important number forty again, a number we have already seen in the Flood, and one that will appear again more than once.)

This time, God showed Moses the pattern of the Tabernacle, the tent that would serve as a temple for the wandering people of Israel. It was a mirror of the heavenly temple. And its centerpiece would be the Ark of the Covenant, an ornate box in which the tablets with the Law would be stored. That Ark of the Covenant would be God's throne on earth, a shadow of his heavenly throne. The God of all creation, who is present everywhere, would dwell in the midst of his chosen people in a way that made them different from every other nation.

For forty days, God showed Moses visions of heaven itself, as it would be represented on earth in the tabernacle. Moses must have expected that the people would be overjoyed when he came back down to them. God was going to live with them on earth in a way no other people could experience.

But the people of Israel had given up waiting for Moses.

SUPPLEMENTARY READING

Commentary, Exodus 3: 11-12

"But Moses said to God, 'Who am I that I should go to Pharaoh, and bring the sons of Israel out of Egypt?' He said, 'But I will be with you; and this shall be the sign for you, that I have sent you: when you have brought forth the people out of Egypt, you shall serve God upon this mountain.'"

In reply to Moses' first objection about his sheer inability to do what God is asking of him, God assures him that he will be at his side and will protect him—as he will help all who have a difficult mission of salvation (cf. Gn 28: 15; Jos 1: 5; Jer 1: 8). The Blessed Virgin will hear the same words at the Annunciation: "The Lord is with you" (Lk 1: 27).

The sign which God gives Moses is linked to his faith, because it involves both a promise and a command: when they come out of Egypt, Moses and the people will worship God on this very mountain. When this actually happens, Moses will acknowledge the supernatural nature of his mission but, meanwhile, he has to obey faithfully the charge given him by God.

Moses' conversation with the Lord is a beautiful prayer and one worth imitating. By following his example, a Christian can dialogue personally and intimately with the Lord: "We ought to be seriously committed to dealing with God. We cannot take refuge in the anonymous crowd. If interior life doesn't involve personal encounter with God, it doesn't exist—it's as simple as that. There are few things more at odds with Christianity than superficiality. To settle down to routine in our Christian life is to dismiss the possibility of becoming a contemplative soul. God seeks us out, one by one. And we ought to answer him, one by one: 'Here I am, LORD, because you have called me' (1 Kgs 3: 5)" (St. J. Escrivá, *Christ is Passing By*, 174; cf. *Catechism of the Catholic Church*, 2574-5).

Julius Africanus, *Chronography*, frag. 2:

When men multiplied on the earth, the angels of heaven came together with the daughters of men. In some copies I found "the sons of God." What is meant by the Spirit, in my opinion, is that the descendants of Seth are called the sons of God on account of the righteous men and patriarchs who have sprung from him, even down to the Savior Himself; but that the descendants of Cain are named the seed of men, as having nothing divine in them, on account of the wickedness of their race and the inequality of their nature, being a mixed people, and having stirred the indignation of God.

"And Moses deposited the rods before the Lord in the tent of the testimony.

And on the morrow...the rod of Aaron for the house of Levi had sprouted and put forth buds, and produced blossoms,..." (Nm 17: 7–8)

VOCABULARY

AARON
Moses' brother; acted as his spokesman. He founded the priesthood of Israel.

ARK OF THE COVENANT
An ornate box that held the tablets of the Law. It represented God's throne on earth.

DYNASTY
A series of rulers from the same family.

EXODUS
Israel's escape from Egypt; from a Greek word meaning "going out."

HEBREW
The name used by the Egyptians to describe the Israelites and related tribes. The language spoken by these people.

IDOLATRY
The worship of man-made images as though they were gods.

MANNA
The miraculous food that the Israelites ate in the desert. It is a type of the Eucharist.

MIDWIFE
A woman who assists at childbirth. Hebrew midwives defied Pharaoh's command that all male Hebrew children should be killed.

MOSES
The man God chose to lead the Israelites out of Egypt. He was adopted by Pharaoh's daughter and raised in Pharaoh's court, but fled Egypt after rebelling against the Egyptian taskmasters.

"They shall make an ark of acacia wood; two cubits and a half shall be its length, a cubit and a half its breadth, and a cubit and a half its height. And you shall overlay it with pure gold,...And you shall put into the ark the testimony which I shall give you."
(Ex 25: 10–16)

PASSOVER
The saving of the first-born children of Israel when the first-born of the Egyptians were killed. It is the most important event in Israel's history and remembered with an annual feast.

PLAGUE
A disaster that affects a large number of people. The Ten Plagues in Exodus were signs of God's wrath against the Egyptians, and particular judgments against the Egyptians' false gods.

REEDS, SEA OF (RED SEA)
The body of water initially blocking the Israelites' escape from Egypt. It miraculously parted for them, but Pharaoh and his armies were drowned when they pursued.

SINAI
The mountain where Moses received the Law from God.

TABERNACLE
The tent that served as a meeting place and temple for the Israelites while they wandered in the desert. It was designed as a reflection of the temple of heaven.

TEN COMMANDMENTS
The fundamental laws given by God at Sinai. They deal with our relationship with God and each other.

STUDY QUESTIONS

1. Why did the Pharaoh want to kill all the male children of Israel, but not the females?

2. What incident caused Moses to rebel against the Egyptians?

3. Who was Zipporah?

4. How did God identify himself when Moses approached the burning bush?

5. What did this answer indicate?

6. What was Moses' first excuse when God told him he was to go back to Egypt?

7. How was Moses told to identify the God of Israel to the Jewish people?

8. What is the usual response to God's call to prophets in Scripture?

9. What was the first demand Moses was told to make to Pharaoh?

10. How did Pharaoh react to Moses and Aaron's plea to go sacrifice to God?

11. Why would the Israelites not be able to sacrifice to God among the Egyptians?

12. How did God punish the Egyptians for Pharaoh's refusal?

13. Why did the Israelites sprinkle lambs blood on their doors on the night of the Passover?

14. What were the instructions for the ceremonial feast?

15. What else was required?

16. What was the symbolism of the blood?

17. How did God keep the Egyptians from catching the Israelites?

18. How did God succeed in defeating the Egyptians who came after Moses?

19. Of what Sacrament is the manna a type?

20. What is the significance of God choosing the Israelites as a nation of priests?

21. How did Moses seal the covenant between God and Israel after God had given the Ten Commandments?

22. How long was Moses alone on the mountain with God?

23. What did God show Moses?

PRACTICAL EXERCISES

1. The story of Moses offers us another opportunity to analyze how God calls each of us to fulfill a certain part of his plan. God chose Moses to lead the people of Israel out of slavery in Egypt, and Moses was at first unwilling. Read Exodus 4:1-17 and list all of the ways Moses tries to convince God that he would not be able to free Israel. How does God respond? What does this tell us about what God may be calling us to do?

2. The Church states that the Ten Commandments "form an organic unity. To transgress one commandment is to infringe all the others. One cannot honor another person without blessing God his Creator. One cannot adore God without loving all men, his creatures. The Decalogue (the Ten Commandments) brings man's religious and social life into unity" (CCC 2069). What does this teaching mean? Try to come up with other examples of how disobeying one commandment infringes on another.

FROM THE CATECHISM

205 God calls Moses from the midst of a bush that burns without being consumed: "I am the God of your father, the God of Abraham, the God of Isaac, and the God of Jacob" (Ex 3:6). God is the God of the fathers, the One who had called and guided the patriarchs in their wanderings. He is the faithful and compassionate God who remembers them and his promises; he comes to free their descendants from slavery. He is the God who, from beyond space and time, can do this and wills to do it, the God who will put his almighty power to work for this plan.

"I am who I am."

> Moses said to God, "If I come to the people of Israel and say to them, 'The God of your fathers has sent me to you,' and they ask me, 'What is his name?' what shall I say to them?" God said to Moses, "I AM WHO I AM." And he said, "Say this to the people of Israel, 'I Am has sent me to you'...this is my name for ever, and thus I am to be remembered throughout all generations" (Ex 3:13-15).

1334 In the Old Covenant bread and wine were offered in sacrifice among the first fruits of the earth as a sign of grateful acknowledgment to the Creator. But they also received a new significance in the context of the Exodus: the unleavened bread that Israel eats every year at Passover commemorates the haste of the departure that liberated them from Egypt; the remembrance of the manna in the desert will always recall to Israel that it lives by the bread of the Word of God (cf. Dt 8:3) (cf. Ps 104:13-15); their daily bread is the fruit of the promised land, the pledge of God's faithfulness to his promises.

The "cup of blessing" (1 Cor 10:16) (Gn 14:18; cf. *Roman Missal*, EP I [Roman Canon] 95) at the end of the Jewish Passover meal adds to the festive joy of wine an eschatological dimension: the messianic expectation of the rebuilding of Jerusalem. When Jesus instituted the Eucharist, he gave a new and definitive meaning to the blessing of the bread and the cup.

2574 Once the promise begins to be fulfilled (Passover, the Exodus, the gift of the Law, and the ratification of the covenant), the prayer of Moses becomes the most striking example of intercessory prayer, which will be fulfilled in "the one mediator between God and men, the man Christ Jesus" (1 Tm 2:5).

Endnotes

1. Ex 1:9-10.	8. Ex 3:6.	15. Ex 12:1-13.
2. Ex 1:12.	9. Ex 3:11.	16. Ex 14:5.
3. Ex 2:10.	10. Ex 3:14.	17. Ex 16:3.
4. Ex 2:5-10.	11. Ex 4:22.	18. Ex 16:14.
5. Heb 11:25.	12. Ex 4:23.	19. Ex 17:1-7.
6. Ex 2:12.	13. Ex 4:21.	20. Ex 20:19.
7. Ex 2:14.	14. Ex 4:23.	

Jan van Eyck's *Adoration of the Lamb* from The Ghent Altarpiece brings together worshipers from the Old Testament and the New Testament. The lamb on the altar symbolizes the Passover Lamb and Christ the Lamb of God.

The Law

The Laws in Exodus and Leviticus gave the people of Israel a form of government unique in the world.

Chapter 8
The Law

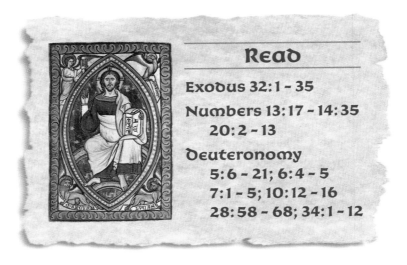

Read

Exodus 32:1 - 35
Numbers 13:17 - 14:35
   20:2 - 13
Deuteronomy
   5:6 - 21; 6:4 - 5
   7:1 - 5; 10:12 - 16
   28:58 - 68; 34:1 - 12

When Moses disappeared for more than a month, the people of Israel did not know what had happened to him. They grew impatient; and as a result of their impatience, they sinned so greatly that they lost much of their special status. Now they would be held to a rigorous code of laws that would constantly remind them how they had sinned.

But that code of laws would not be enough to keep them on the path of holiness. After forty years of wandering in the desert, the Israelites, still rebellious, needed a stronger constitution to hold them together. Moses would have to give them the laws in Deuteronomy, laws that included many concessions to their "hardness of heart." Even those laws would not be enough; Moses prophesied that the people would break them and Israel would fall apart. But he also foresaw a time when God would bring all his people together under a new law, one that would be written in their hearts.

The Old Law is indeed the first stage of the revealed law, and as we will see in the New Testament, the Law of the Gospel fulfills, refines, surpasses, and leads the Old Law to its perfection (Mt 5:17-19). Jesus' Sermon on the Mount, "far from abolishing or devaluing the moral prescriptions of the Old Law, releases their hidden potential and has new demands arise from them: it reveals their entire divine and human truth" (CCC 1968).

The Golden Calf Changes Israel's Relationship With God

- **The people of Israel have Aaron make an idol for them to worship.**
- **The "golden calf" is a fertility god like the ones they knew in Egypt.**
- **Worshiping the golden calf involves not only idolatry but also immoral behavior.**

The Exodus was Israel's declaration of independence. Like the American Declaration of Independence, it did not specify any form of government or any laws. It simply separated them from the government that had controlled them.

As long as they followed Moses' instructions, the Israelites did well. But when Moses was away, the people of Israel quickly fell back into their old habits.

> When the people saw that Moses delayed to come down from the mountain, the people gathered themselves together to Aaron, and said to him, "Up, make us gods, who shall go before us; as for this Moses, the man who brought us up out of the land of Egypt, we do not know what has become of him." And Aaron said to them, "Take off the rings of gold which are in the ears of your wives, your sons, and your daughters, and bring them to me." (Ex 32:1-2)

Perhaps Aaron thought he could make the people stop and think by showing them how expensive their project would be. But the people were not discouraged.

> So all the people took off the rings of gold which were in their ears, and brought them to Aaron. And he received the gold at their hand, and fashioned it with a graving tool, and made a molten calf; and they said, "These are your gods, O Israel, who brought you up out of the land of Egypt!" When Aaron saw this, he built an altar before it; and Aaron made proclamation and said, "Tomorrow shall be a feast to the LORD." And they rose up early on the morrow, and offered burnt offerings and brought peace offerings; and the people sat down to eat and drink, and rose up to play. (Ex 32:3-6)

Egyptian statue of Apis from the 18th Dynasty, ca. 1380 B.C.

Why a "golden calf?" The statue of a bull that Aaron had made represented Apis, an Egyptian fertility god. The bull is a common symbol of strength and power—the Canaanites, too, had a fertility god in the form of a bull. When the sacred author tells us that the people "sat down to eat and drink, and rose up to play," he means they indulged in all kinds of immoral celebrations, just as worshipers of other fertility gods did in that time. Aaron might have been trying to save some appearance of loyalty to God by saying that the statue represented Yahweh, the True God, but the people were in fact worshiping a fertility god like the ones they had known in Egypt.

In other words, the people had completely renounced the covenant they had just made with God, and the moral laws that went with it. They had turned around and gone back to their old Egyptian ways. And they pretended that it was this bull-god who had brought them out of Egypt!

The Institution Of The Priesthood

- **The Israelites' rejection of God causes God to reject them.**
- **Moses pleads for the people.**
- **The tribe of Levi earns its priesthood by attacking idolatry.**

Up on the mountain, Moses had just received the two tablets with the Law written by God's own hand. Now God suddenly brought him some very bad news.

> And the LORD said to Moses, "Go down; for your people, whom you brought up out of the land of Egypt, have corrupted themselves; they have turned aside quickly out of the way which I commanded them; they have made for themselves a molten calf, and have worshiped it and sacrificed to it, and said, 'These are your gods, O Israel, who brought you up out of the land of Egypt!'" (Ex 32:7-8)

God no longer called Israel "my people." Now Israel was "your people." After all, the people had decided they didn't want the Lord for their God. Now God had every right to disown them.

> And the LORD said to Moses, "I have seen this people, and behold, it is a stiff-necked people; now therefore let me alone, that my wrath may burn hot against them and I may consume them; but of you I will make a great nation." (Ex 32:9-10)

God was offering Moses the chance to be a new Abraham. But Moses was supremely selfless. Instead of taking the chance to be the founder of a new nation, he pleaded with God for Israel.

> But Moses besought the LORD his God, and said, "O LORD, why does thy wrath burn hot against thy people, whom thou hast brought forth out of the land of Egypt with great power and with a mighty hand? Why should the Egyptians say, 'With evil intent did he bring them forth, to slay them in the mountains, and to consume them from the face of the earth'? Turn from thy fierce wrath, and repent of this evil against thy people. Remember Abraham, Isaac, and Israel, thy servants, to whom thou didst swear by thine own self, and didst say to them, 'I will multiply your descendants as the stars of heaven, and all this land that I have promised I will give to your descendants, and they shall inherit it for ever.'" And the LORD repented of the evil which he thought to do to his people. (Ex 32:11-14)

After that, Moses went down the mountain and saw things for himself. The celebration was still going on, and it was even worse than Moses had expected. Whatever Moses saw, it made him furious. He was so furious, in fact, that he threw the two stone tablets on the ground and smashed them to bits. Since God had already prepared him for the golden calf, what Moses saw must have been much worse than simple idolatry. But the smashed tablets were a good symbol of the covenant that Israel had broken.

Egypt's Cow goddess, Mehit-Weret, from Tutankhamen's tomb.

"And he took the calf which they had made, and burnt it with fire, and ground it to powder, and scattered it upon the water, and made the people of Israel drink it." (Ex 32: 20)

After demanding an explanation from Aaron, Moses realized that the people were on the road to total destruction.

> And when Moses saw that the people had broken loose (for Aaron had let them break loose, to their shame among their enemies), then Moses stood in the gate of the camp, and said, "Who is on the LORD's side? Come to me." And all the sons of Levi gathered themselves together to him. And he said to them, "Thus says the LORD God of Israel, 'Put every man his sword on his side, and go to and fro from gate to gate throughout the camp, and slay every man his brother, and every man his companion, and every man his neighbor.'" And the sons of Levi did according to the word of Moses; and there fell of the people that day about three thousand men. And Moses said, "Today you have ordained yourselves for the service of the LORD, each one at the cost of his son and of his brother, that he may bestow a blessing upon you this day." (Ex 32: 25-29)

It was certainly a harsh judgment. But by slaughtering the idolaters, the Levites prevented the utter destruction of Israel. The nation would survive.

But now things would be different.

> After Israel's sin, when the people had turned away from God to worship the golden calf, God hears Moses' prayer of intercession and agrees to walk in the midst of an unfaithful people, thus demonstrating his love (cf. Ex 32; 33: 12-17). When Moses asks to see his glory, God responds "I will make all my goodness pass before you, and will proclaim before you my name 'the LORD' [YHWH]" (Ex 33: 18-19). Then the LORD passes before Moses and proclaims, "YHWH, YHWH, a God merciful and gracious, slow to anger, and abounding in steadfast love and faithfulness"; Moses then confesses that the LORD is a forgiving God (Ex 34: 5-6; cf. 34: 9). (CCC 210)

After The Fall

- **By falling into idolatry, Israel loses some of its unique relationship with God**
- **The Levites assume the priesthood that would have belonged to all the people**
- **The laws given after the golden calf are meant to teach humility and holiness**

Israel's sin in worshiping the golden calf was much like the original sin of Adam and Eve. Once again, it destroyed a unique relationship with God.

The original covenant with Israel would have made the whole nation a kingdom of priests. Every father would have been a priest in his own house. Every first-born son would have been dedicated to God. Every family would have known God personally.

But now it was obvious that nothing could take Egyptian idolatry out of Israel. So the Levites became the priestly class, insulating the rest of the people from God. Otherwise, their own sinfulness might literally kill them. Without a mediator, they could never safely approach the absolute holiness of God.

> The chosen people was constituted by God as "a kingdom of priests and a holy nation" (Ex 19:6; cf. Is 61:6). But within the people of Israel, God chose one of the twelve tribes, that of Levi, and set it apart for liturgical service; God himself is its inheritance (cf. Nm 1:48-53; Jos 13:33). A special rite consecrated the beginnings of the priesthood of the Old Covenant. The priests are "appointed to act on behalf of men in relation to God, to offer gifts and sacrifices for sins" (Heb 5:1; cf. Ex 29:1-30; Lv 8). (CCC 1539)

> Instituted to proclaim the Word of God and to restore communion with God by sacrifices and prayer (cf. Mal 2:7-9), this priesthood nevertheless remains powerless to bring about salvation, needing to repeat its sacrifices ceaselessly and being unable to achieve a definitive sanctification, which only the sacrifice of Christ would accomplish (cf. Heb 5:3; 7:27; 10:1-4). (CCC 1540)

Just like Adam and Eve, the Israelites had brought toil and labor on themselves. Now they would have to live by the law. Every aspect of their lives would be bound by rules. These precise regulations would tell them everything from how and what they could eat to how they should wear their beards.

The laws that God gave Israel were different from human laws. They were meant to do more than just keep order. Even though God had brought them out of slavery in Egypt, the people had shown that they were still slaves to Egypt's gods. They were not yet holy enough to bring God's message to the nations.

With laws of ritual purity, God meant to teach his people humility. They would have to live apart from the other nations, so that they would not be infected with false religions. And they would have to make regular sacrifices, each time deliberately slaughtering one of the animals they had worshiped as gods in Egypt. In other words, every day they would have to kill one of their false gods.

These laws might have looked like a punishment, but God was still a loving father to his people. Like a loving father, he did not merely punish his people for what they had done wrong. He gave them laws to help rehabilitate them. In the same way, our own parents would tighten the rules when we got into serious trouble—not because they had stopped loving us, but because they wanted to keep us from getting into trouble again.

Moses went up the mountain once again, and God wrote two new stone tablets to replace the ones that Moses had smashed. God renewed his covenant with his people, emphasizing the prohibitions against worshiping foreign gods.

Heaven On Earth

- **Moses receives instructions for building the Tabernacle.**
- **The design of the Tabernacle is an earthly representation of the heavenly temple.**

The book of Exodus ends with the building of the Tabernacle, the portable temple that would be God's dwelling-place in the midst of his people. When the work was finally finished, all the people watched as God took up residence:

> Then the cloud covered the tent of meeting, and the glory of the LORD filled the tabernacle. And Moses was not able to enter the tent of meeting, because the cloud abode upon it, and the glory of the LORD filled the tabernacle. Throughout all their journeys, whenever the cloud was taken up from over the tabernacle, the people of Israel would go onward; but if the cloud was not taken up, then they did not go onward till the day that it was taken up. For throughout all their journeys the cloud of the LORD was upon the tabernacle by day, and fire was in it by night, in the sight of all the house of Israel. (Ex 40:34-38)

The Cloud of the Lord and the Children of Israel in the Wilderness by Raphael

In the Septuagint, the Greek translation of the Old Testament that the New Testament writers used, verse 35 says that the power of the Lord "overshadowed" the Tabernacle. That same unusual word will come up in Luke 1:35: "The power of the Most High will overshadow you." In Luke, an angel is speaking to Mary, telling her that she is about to become the Mother of God.

The Law

- **The book of Leviticus teaches Israel how to be a holy people.**
- **The deaths of Aaron's sons showed how important it was to follow the rules precisely.**

After Exodus comes a book we call Leviticus, a Latin word meaning "having to do with the Levites." In Hebrew tradition it was known as the Manual for Priests, and that's exactly what it is. Now that the Levites were going to be the mediators between God and Israel, they needed an instruction book. God gave the instructions they needed to Moses in the Tabernacle.

There are many different kinds of laws in Leviticus, but the reason for all of them is the same: to teach Israel how to be a holy people. Leviticus, in fact, is a manual of holiness. By one scholar's count, the word "holiness" occurs eighty-seven times in this one book.

The book starts with the people's relationship with God, giving instructions for sacrifices (Chapter 17) and the consecration of the priests (Chapter 8).

In Chapter 9 the priests begin following the instructions they have received so far. But in Chapter 10, Aaron's sons Nadab and Abihu "offered unholy fire before the Lord, such as he had not commanded them."[1] In other words, they thought they could worship their own way, ignoring the laws God had given them.

The results were fatal. The fire from the Lord's Presence flared up and burned both of them to death. The rules were meant to be taken seriously.

After that short demonstration of what it means to be a holy people under the law, Leviticus goes on to give the rules about what foods the people could eat. The rules are very specific, and they have to do with more than health. Some foods that are perfectly healthy to eat—shellfish and pork, for example—are prohibited. Whenever their neighbors offered them those foods, the Israelites would have to refuse, and that would make them remember that they were different: a holy people who belonged to God.

Some of the laws in Leviticus have to do with relationships between people, but even those are designed to keep them pure and holy. Of course, the people will sometimes break the laws God gives them, so there are instructions for offerings to make atonement for their sins.

The laws in Exodus and Leviticus together gave the people of Israel a form of government unique in the world. They would be a holy people, governed not by kings but by God himself.

Even this manual of holiness, however, was not enough to keep the people faithful. As they would soon prove, their hearts were too hard for the laws God had given them.

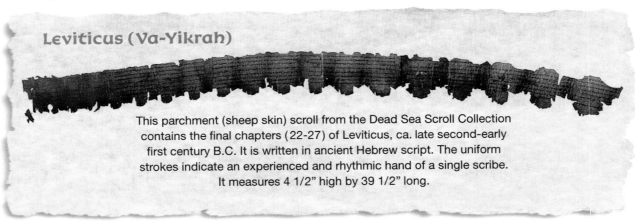

Leviticus (Va-Yikrah)

This parchment (sheep skin) scroll from the Dead Sea Scroll Collection contains the final chapters (22-27) of Leviticus, ca. late second-early first century B.C. It is written in ancient Hebrew script. The uniform strokes indicate an experienced and rhythmic hand of a single scribe. It measures 4 1/2" high by 39 1/2" long.

Wilderness of Zin. In this wilderness, Israel was guilty of murmuring against the LORD (Nm 27:14).

In The Wilderness

- **Spies come back from Canaan with a pessimistic report.**
- **The people despair and rebel.**
- **As punishment for their lack of faith, the rebellious generation will not enter the Promised Land.**
- **Moses loses patience and shares the people's punishment.**

The next book after Leviticus is a history of Israel's failure to live up to the Law. The title in English is Numbers, because it contains a census of all the tribes of Israel. In Hebrew tradition the book is called "In the Wilderness," and that is a good description of its contents. The book tells how Israel spent forty years wandering through the wilderness between Egypt and the Promised Land.

Why forty years? It was not a terribly long journey: about eleven days under normal circumstances (see Dt 1:2). They knew where they were going. Why did it take them forty years to get there?

The answer is simple: they failed to trust God.

When they came near the Promised Land, Moses sent spies to check out the land and bring back a report.[2]

The report they came back with should have been encouraging. The land was "flowing with milk and honey"—every good thing was there. In fact, they brought back a bunch of grapes so huge it took two men to carry it strung up on a pole.[3]

So far it sounded like paradise. "Yet the people who dwell in the land are strong," the spies continued, "and the cities are fortified and very large, and besides we saw the descendants of Anak there."[4] (The descendants of Anak were a tribe of people who seemed frighteningly tall to the Israelites.) Most of the spies believed the task before them was impossible: Israel could never conquer Canaan.

Two of the spies, Caleb and Joshua, were confident that Israel could conquer the land. But the rest of the spies despaired. "We are not able to go up against the people," they said, "for they are stronger than we."[5]

Of course, the people of Israel believed the pessimists. Once again, they turned against Moses. "Would that we had died in the land of Egypt! Or would that we had died in this wilderness! Why does the LORD bring us into this land, to fall by the sword? Our wives and our little ones will become prey; would it not be better for us to go back to Egypt?"[6]

Only Joshua and Caleb had faith in God. "If the LORD delights in us," they said, "he will bring us into this land and give it to us, a land which flows with milk and honey. Only, do not rebel against the LORD; and do not fear the people of the land, for they are bread for us; their protection is removed from them, and the LORD is with us; do not fear them."[7]

Instead of listening to Joshua and Caleb, the people tried to stone them to death. The people had no faith, and God granted their wish to die in the wilderness.

> Say to them, "As I live," says the LORD, "what you have said in my hearing I will do to you: your dead bodies shall fall in this wilderness; and all of your number, numbered from twenty years old and upward, who have murmured against me, not one shall come into the land where I swore that I would make you dwell, except Caleb the son of Jephunneh and Joshua the son of Nun. But your little ones, who you said would become a prey, I will bring in, and they shall know the land which you have despised." (Nm 14: 28-31)

All the people who had wished to die in the wilderness would get their wish. They would spend the next forty years wandering in the wilderness. Only Caleb and Joshua would live long enough to enter the Promised Land.

So for the next forty years, the people wandered in the wilderness. All that time, they grumbled and sometimes openly rebelled. Finally even Moses lost patience with them. Unable to find water, the people yet again grumbled against Moses: "Why have you made us come up out of Egypt, to bring us to this evil place?"[8] God told Moses and Aaron to speak to a rock, and it would give them water. But Moses was angry, and he did not follow God's instructions. "Hear now, you rebels," he shouted to the people; "shall we bring forth water for you out of this rock?"[9] Then he struck the rock twice with his staff.

Water came pouring out of the rock, but God was not pleased with Moses and Aaron. Moses had not done as God said; he had struck the rock in anger, as though he himself were bringing the water out of it, rather than speaking to it and showing that all the power came from God alone. "Because you did not believe in me, to sanctify me in the eyes of the people of Israel, therefore you shall not bring this assembly into the land which I have given them."[10] Moses and Aaron would never set foot in the Promised Land.

The Constitution Of Israel

- **Israel falls into idolatry again at Beth-peor.**
- **In Deuteronomy, Moses gives the people a new constitution for the state of Israel.**
- **Many laws in Deuteronomy make concessions to Israel's hard hearts.**
- **Deuteronomy is also a prophetic road map for Israel's history.**
- **Like the U.S. Constitution, Deuteronomy is amended as times change.**

After forty years, all the people who had refused to go into Canaan were dead. But their children, the next generation, were no better — as they would soon prove.

Coming into the land of Moab, the men of Israel began to associate with the Moabite women. The Moabites invited their new husbands and boyfriends to go worship their god Baal with them. (Some historians believe that the cult of Baal of Peor required women to prostitute themselves at the god's temple, which gives you an idea what kind of "worship" might have been going on.) And so the people of Israel once again forgot all about their covenant with God. They went and sacrificed to Baal of Peor.[11] "While Israel dwelt in Shittim the people began to play the harlot with the daughters of Moab" (Nm 25:1).

Because Phinehas, the grandson of Aaron, was faithful to God, punishing the idolaters, God promised that the office of high priest would always belong to his descendants.[12] But because of their faithlessness, God would have to give the people of Israel a second law.

"Deuteronomy," the title we give to the last book of the Pentateuch, means just that: "Second Law." Instead of laws spoken directly in the voice of God, these laws come in the words of Moses.

You remember that when the United States declared its independence, the new nation tried at first to live under a set of laws called "Articles of Confederation." But the Articles were not strong enough. The United States almost fell apart. The founders of the new country decided they needed a new law to hold the country together: the Constitution of the United States.

It was the same way with Israel. After the Exodus — Israel's declaration of independence — the nation tried to live under the code of laws in Exodus and Leviticus. But it wasn't enough. The nation needed a new constitution, and that constitution is in Deuteronomy. After forty years of rebellions, Moses had figured out what God knew all along: Israel wasn't ready to be a nation of priests. Deuteronomy gave them the constitution they needed to be just another nation-state.

Deuteronomy was also a lower law, a law that made concessions to Israel's hard hearts. For example, Moses now allowed divorce (see Dt 24:1-4). "For your hardness of heart Moses allowed you to divorce your wives," Jesus would explain to the Pharisees, "but from the beginning it was not so."[13] Genocidal warfare now will also be part of the conquest of the Promised Land, and the second law provides for that evil (see Dt 20:16-18). At Baal-peor, the people had proved that they couldn't live side by side with idolaters without turning away from the True God.

The prophet Ezekiel was thinking of the laws in Deuteronomy when he wrote, conveying the word of God, "I gave them statutes that were not good and ordinances by which they could not have life."[14] What does it mean that God gave "statutes that were not good"? It means that, instead of teaching Israel the way to holiness, the lower law takes into account the certainty that Israel will not always be holy. The new laws regulate a people who will certainly fall away from the good laws God gave them before.

Deuteronomy is more than just a constitution; it is also a prophetic road map for Israel. After forty years, Moses had figured out what God always knew: that the people of Israel would always be tempted by foreign gods, and that their weakness would lead to the destruction of the nation. But Moses also knew that God would not let Israel be completely destroyed. The Israelites would lose everything because of their faithlessness, but their loss would turn their hearts back to God.

Finally, just like the United States Constitution, Deuteronomy can be amended. Later, Joshua and Samuel added to the Book of the Law when Israel's circumstances changed. In the case of Deuteronomy, of course, the work of one divinely inspired prophet could be amended only by another divinely inspired prophet. Amendments were made in later centuries, even the Deuteronomic Code under Josiah.

Israel And America

One way of remembering the steps in the founding of Israel is to compare it with the establishment of the United States. Both nations followed similar processes in their emergence as independent nations. This is a simple comparison between the development of two very different nations, and it is only intended to serve as an analogy. Any further comparisons may render a simplistic or incorrect understanding of the history of either nation. But the successive steps shown below offer an easy way to remember Bible History.

United States	Israel
Colonies oppressed by King George III	Tribes oppressed by Pharaoh
Escaped from tyranny through Declaration of Independence	Escaped from tyranny through Exodus
Temporary government under Articles of Confederation	Temporary government under Leviticus
Final form of government in Constitution of the United States	Final form of government in Deuteronomy
States amend the Constitution to deal with new circumstances	God's prophets amend Deuteronomy to deal with new circumstances

King George III

Pharaoh

A Close Look At Deuteronomy

Most of Deuteronomy is written in the words of Moses. It's a series of speeches Moses gave to the Israelites when they had reached the river Jordan. Except for Moses, Joshua, and Caleb, the whole generation that had left Egypt in the Exodus was dead. Just across the river was Canaan, and the time would soon come for them to cross the river and take the land God had promised them. When that happened, they would need the new constitution Moses was about to give them.

Moses begins by summarizing the history of Israel's wanderings in the wilderness. The introduction explains what makes this new law necessary: Israel's continuous rebellion and unfaithfulness.

OUTLINE OF DEUTERONOMY

I.   **Chapters 1-4: Moses' introductory speech.** Almost all the people who had come out of Egypt with Moses were dead. The new generation needs a brief history lesson before Moses can give them the law.

    Chapters 1-3: Historical introduction. Moses reminds the new generation how they came to be where they are, and shows how Israel's history of unfaithfulness makes this law necessary.

    Chapter 4: Reasons for obeying the law.

II. **Chapters 5-11: The Law of Sinai.** Moses restates the most important parts of the law, including the Ten Commandments. He also gives the new generation some historical background, reminding them how God was faithful to their parents but their parents were not faithful to God. Some important highlights:

    Chapter 5: 7-21. The Ten Commandments.

    Chapter 6: 4-5. The Great Commandment. "Hear, O Israel: The LORD our God is one LORD; and you shall love the LORD your God with all your heart, and with all your soul, and with all your might."

    Chapter 7: 1-5. Law of separation from the Canaanites.

    Chapter 9: 7-29. A reminder of the Golden Calf incident.

    Chapter 10: 12-13. What God requires. "And now, O Israel, what does the LORD require of you, but to fear the LORD your God, to walk in all his ways, to love him, to serve the LORD your God with all your heart and with all your soul, and to keep the commandments and statutes of the LORD, which I command you this day for your good?"

III. **Chapters 12-26: The Constitution of Israel.** This is the heart of Deuteronomy, the new law for living "in the land which the LORD, the God of your fathers, has given you to possess, all the days that you live upon the earth."[15]

IV. **Chapter 27: The ratification ceremony.** When Israel reaches the Promised Land, the people will ratify their new constitution in a ceremony that invokes curses on anyone who breaks the law.

V.   **Chapters 28-30: The prophetic road map.** Moses shows Israel what its future history will be. They will forsake the Lord and bring the curses upon themselves, but divine blessing and future restoration will follow.

VI. **Chapters 31-34: The last days of Moses.** Moses leaves Israel his last words in the form of two songs that the people are to remember forever. Then he sees the Promised Land, but only from a distance. He dies, and God himself buries him in a secret grave, to prevent the Israelites from turning the grave of Moses into a site for idolatrous worship of their great prophet.

The Tabernacle In The Wilderness

At Timna Park, in Israel's southern desert, the Negev, a life-size replica of the Biblical Tabernacle has been constructed. The model is accurate in every measurement, proportion and color based upon the Biblical description. (with the exception that precious metals were not used e.g., gold, silver.)

The model, measuring 75 feet by 150 feet is complete with altar, ritual bath, Holy of Holies and other elements mentioned in the Book of Exodus.

It stands near Solomon's Pillars, the impressive russet sandstone formations that have made Timna Park and the Timna copper mines famous throughout the region.

"The length of the court shall be a hundred cubits, the breadth fifty, and the height five cubits, with hangings of fine twined linen and bases of bronze." (Ex 27:18)

The Outer Court: The bronze laver and bronze altar were located in the outer court. The altar was 7.5 feet square and 4.5 feet high, made of acacia wood overlaid with bronze, and had a horn on each corner. The fire on the altar was to be kept burning at all times and the daily sacrifices were offered in the morning and afternoon.

The Altar of Incense: Also known as the "golden altar" or the "inner altar," this three-foot high altar was the location of regular incense offerings. Every morning and evening when tending the light of the menorah, the priests would offer a mixture of frankincense and other aromatic gums. On the Day of Atonement, the high priest would sprinkle blood on the horns of this altar.

"The Holy of Holies" at the temple of Arad, 9th century B.C.

SUPPLEMENTARY READING

Commentary, Introduction to Leviticus § 4

Behind the various sacrifices or offerings, it describes lies a deep conviction that God is the Lord of all creation. Man's physical needs are such that he has recourse to God by means of rites and offerings closely connected with the world on which he depends. Thus, when the people are leading a nomadic existence in the desert, their sacrifice consists of an animal taken from the flock. Later, when they are more typically tillers of the soil, they add further sacrifices and offer agricultural produce, the first-fruits. However, animal offerings continued to have pride of place, on account of the value attaching to animals and the symbolism involved (especially in the sheddings of blood). Sacrifice was the highest act of worship, the best way man could show his feelings towards God—adoration, recognition, gratitude and supplication.

Besides, in all ancient peoples man's religious sense always expressed itself in some form of ceremonial worship.

This explains why, albeit in a way peculiar to it, the chosen people had a system of worship in which it performed certain rites to show that it acknowledged and worshiped the God of Israel. The rules surrounding this worship took shape over time. Initially certain basic rites developed and, alongside them, the requirement that they be performed by a person with a certain authority, someone who would be the people's representative before God. In other words, the need for a priesthood emerged, and for persons to exercise that priesthood, that is, *priests*. In the early stages of the people of Israel, it was the father of the family who performed the liturgy. Once the monarchy was established, this role passed to the king: his role was both royal and priestly. Later still, priestly functions became the preserve of people who had this special role—Eleazar and Zadok, for example, in David's time, and later on Zadok's descendants, the Zadokites, who exercised the high priesthood.

In the Levitical system, the laws concerning *cleanness* (purity) and *holiness* also contain profound teaching which extends much further than the formalism which is apparent at fist sight. We need to see that anything unsuitable for the worship of God was considered to be "unclean." God is pure, beautiful, the source of health and life; and nothing dirty, harmful or dead can gain access to him. "Purity" or cleanness, then, is something external and ritual, but it had very much to do with man's relationship with God. For its part, "holiness" is that inaccessible dwelling place of the mystery of God (cf. CCC 2809); it is just possible to glimpse that holiness through the way God's majesty shines out in the things that he has created an in his interventions in history.

The chosen people had a system of worship in which it performed certain rites to show that it acknowledged and worshiped the God of Israel.

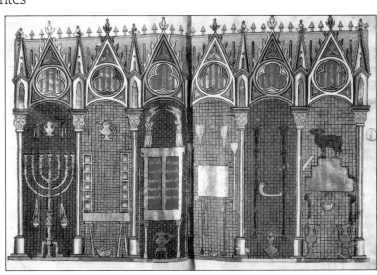

VOCABULARY

CALEB
One of the spies sent to Canaan. Only he and Joshua had faith in God's promise to deliver the land to Israel.

CALF, GOLDEN
An idol made by Aaron when the Israelites demanded it. The people worshiped it as the god that had brought them out of Egypt.

CONSTITUTION
The fundamental law that governs a nation. The law in Deuteronomy would serve as the constitution of the nation of Israel.

DEUTERONOMY
Greek for "second law." The name of the book that contains the laws that would become the constitution of the state of Israel. It also restates many of the important laws given earlier, including the Ten Commandments.

GENOCIDE
The destruction of an entire people. Genocidal warfare was one of the evil consequences of Israel's lack of faith.

JOSHUA
One of the spies sent to Canaan; only he and Caleb had faith in God's promise to deliver the land to Israel. He would be Moses' successor as leader of Israel.

LEVITES
Members of the tribe of Levi, who would be the priests for the rest of Israel.

LEVITICUS
The priestly book containing the laws designed to make Israel a holy people.

PRIEST
A man dedicated to the service of God. Israel was meant to be a nation of priests; but, after the incident of the Golden Calf, the tribe of Levi was chosen for the priesthood.

YHWH
The Name of God in Hebrew, usually rendered Yahweh or Jehovah and translated "LORD" in many English Bible versions. (Hebrew was written with only consonants.)

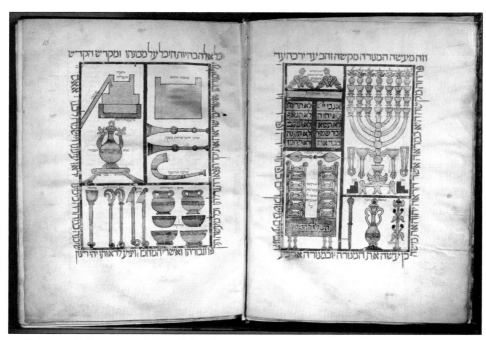

"Now even the first covenant had regulations for worship and an earthly sanctuary. For a tent was prepared, the outer one, in which were the lampstand and the table and the bread of the Presence; it is called the Holy Place." (Heb 9:1-2)

STUDY QUESTIONS

1. Why did Moses make concessions regarding God's law?

2. Where did Aaron get the gold to make the Golden Calf?

3. What Egyptian god did the Golden Calf resemble?

4. What opportunity did God offer Moses when Israel turned away to worship the Golden Calf?

5. Why was Israel spared from God's wrath after worshiping the Golden Calf?

6. What was the symbol of the broken tablets?

7. What were Moses' orders for the Levites who were still loyal to God?

8. Which tribe became the priests of the nation, mediating between God and Israel?

9. Why did God make the Israelites abide by so many new laws after their fall in Exodus?

10. What was the purpose of the laws of ritual purity?

11. Where did the Levites obtain the instructions they needed to write the book of Leviticus?

12. What does Leviticus mean?

13. What was the purpose of the laws God gave to Israel in Leviticus?

14. What did some of the Levitical laws cover?

15. What is the book of Numbers called in the Hebrew tradition?

16. Why didn't Israel go straight into the Promised Land?

17. Who were Caleb and Joshua?

18. What was Israel's punishment for refusing to believe that Canaan could be conquered with God's help?

19. Why was Moses never to be allowed in the Promised Land?

20. What does Deuteronomy mean, literally?

PRACTICAL EXERCISES

1. The Church teaches that while the Levite priesthood of the Old Testament was "instituted to proclaim the Word of God and to restore communion with God by sacrifices and prayer, this priesthood nevertheless remains powerless to bring about salvation, needing to repeat its sacrifices ceaselessly and being unable to achieve a definitive sanctification, which only the sacrifice of Christ would accomplish" (CCC 1540). How are priests in the Church today different from these Levite priests? What is the purpose of the priesthood in the Catholic Church? What are some ways we can take advantage of the help priests have to offer us as we work toward the salvation that has been won for us?

2. The text compares Israel's sin of idolatry with the Golden Calf to the original sin of Adam and Eve because it destroyed a unique relationship with God. Review the first chapter of this book and list as many similarities as you can between both the original sin and Israel's sin and the consequences that followed from them.

3. Why do you think God's love and compassion for his people is so often rejected, even when it means an end to their suffering? How do you think the prophets felt when faced with a disbelieving people? When faced with unbelieving peers, how would you try to help them find faith in God?

FROM THE CATECHISM

62 After the patriarchs, God formed Israel as his people by freeing them from slavery in Egypt. He established with them the covenant of Mount Sinai and, through Moses, gave them his law so that they would recognize him and serve him as the one living and true God, the provident Father and just judge, and so that they would look for the promised Savior (cf. DV 3).

1975 According to Scripture the Law is a fatherly instruction by God which prescribes for man the ways that lead to the promised beatitude, and proscribes the ways of evil.

1981 The Law of Moses contains many truths naturally accessible to reason. God has revealed them because men did not read them in their hearts.

2112 The first commandment condemns *polytheism.* It requires man neither to believe in, nor to venerate, other divinities than the one true God. Scripture constantly recalls this rejection of "idols, [of] silver and gold, the work of men's hands. They have mouths, but do not speak; eyes, but do not see." These empty idols make their worshipers empty: "Those who make them are like them; so are all who trust in them" (Ps 115: 4-5, 8; cf. Is 44: 9-20; Jer 10: 1-16; Dn 14: 1-30; Bar 6; Wis 13: 1-15: 19). God, however, is the "living God" (Jos 3: 10; Ps 42: 3; etc.) who gives life and intervenes in history.

2114 Human life finds its unity in the adoration of the one God. The commandment to worship the Lord alone integrates man and saves him from an endless disintegration. Idolatry is a perversion of man's innate religious sense. An idolater is someone who "transfers his indestructible notion of God to anything other than God" (Origen, *Contra Celsum* 2, 40: PG 11, 861).

2132 The Christian veneration of images is not contrary to the first commandment which proscribes idols. Indeed, "the honor rendered to an image passes to its prototype," and "whoever venerates an image venerates the person portrayed in it" (St. Basil, *De Spiritu Sancto* 18, 45: PG 32, 149C; Council of Nicaea II: DS 601; cf. Council of Trent: DS 1821-1825; Vatican Council II: *Sacrosanctum Concilium* 126; LG 67). The honor paid to sacred images is a "respectful veneration," not the adoration due to God alone:

Religious worship is not directed to images in themselves, considered as mere things, but under their distinctive aspect as images leading us on to God incarnate. The movement toward the image does not terminate in it as image, but tends toward that whose image it is (St. Thomas Aquinas, STh II-II, 81, 3 ad 3).

Endnotes

1. Lv 10: 1.	6. Nm 14: 2-3.	11. Nm 25: 1-3.
2. Nm 13.	7. Nm 14: 8-9.	12. Nm 25: 7-13.
3. Nm 13: 23.	8. Nm 20: 5.	13. Mt 19: 8.
4. Nm 13: 28.	9. Nm 20: 10.	14. Ez 20: 25.
5. Nm 13: 31.	10. Nm 20: 12.	15. Dt 12: 1.

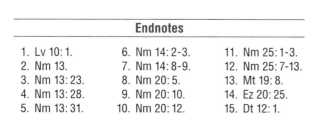

The Rise of The Kingdom

"Arise, anoint him; for this is he,"
God told Samuel. Samuel anointed David,
". . . and the Spirit of the Lord came mightily upon
David from that day forward."

Chapter 9

The Rise of The Kingdom

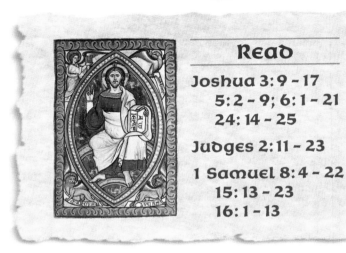

Read

Joshua 3: 9 – 17
    5: 2 – 9; 6: 1 – 21
    24: 14 – 25

Judges 2: 11 – 23

1 Samuel 8: 4 – 22
    15: 13 – 23
    16: 1 – 13

Israel was a nation set apart—a nation governed not by human laws, but by God himself through his prophets. But the attraction of worldly ways would prove too much. Seduced by the religions of the Canaanites, God's people would fall into idolatry and anarchy. At last they would give up on the idea of being a nation set apart. They would want to be governed like every other nation.

It was a direct rejection of God. Yet God would use that rejection to bring about the right conditions for another covenant with his people—a covenant that would partially restore the relationship that Adam's sin had destroyed. It would also pave the way for the New Covenant in Jesus Christ, through which all the people of the earth would be restored to their right relationship with God.

God told Joshua the time had come to cross the river Jordan into Canaan. For Christians, the crossing of the Jordan is another type of baptism.

View over Jericho and the Jordan Valley.

The Conquest Begins

At the age of 120, Moses passed away, leaving his faithful servant Joshua to take over the leadership of Israel. At last it was time to begin the conquest of Canaan.

In spite of Israel's faithlessness, God once again fought for Israel. But it would be a long and bloody struggle. Although the people of Israel would ultimately conquer Canaan, they would never completely drive out their Canaanite enemies. Those Canaanites would be thorns in their sides, constantly tempting God's people away from the true faith and toward the wicked idols of Canaan.

The book of Joshua describes the beginning of the conquest of Canaan. The first target was Jericho.

Some archaeologists call Jericho the oldest city in the world. Settlement there goes back to the Stone Age. In the time of Joshua, Jericho was already thousands of years old.

It was also the strategic key to Palestine, a strong and important city right in the middle of the Promised Land. If Israel could take Jericho, it would be a crushing blow to the Canaanites.

When God told Joshua the time had come to cross the river Jordan into Canaan,[1] Joshua's sensible first step was to send two spies to look over the city. They stayed with a woman named Rahab, described as a "harlot" (which might mean only that she ran an inn). Rahab believed in the God of Israel, and she knew that Israel would conquer. When the king of Jericho found out about the spies, Rahab hid them. Then she made a deal with them: she and her family would be saved when Israel destroyed Jericho, as long as they stayed in their house. A scarlet cord tied in her window would be the sign to the Israelites that Rahab's house was to be left untouched.[2]

After a hair-raising escape through a window, the spies made it back to camp and told Joshua what they had found out: everyone in the land was already afraid of Israel. "Truly the LORD has given all the land into our hands."[3]

The time was right. "Sanctify yourselves," Joshua warned the people, "for tomorrow the LORD will do wonders among you."

Then he told the Levite priests to take up the Ark of the Covenant and walk to the Jordan. As soon as their feet touched the water, the river dried up. Once again, the people walked through the water on dry land. For Christians, the crossing of the Jordan is another type of baptism, in which we, the new Israel, pass through the water to the Promised Land.

Renewing the covenant with God, Joshua had all the men of Israel circumcised. (The generation that grew up in the wilderness had not been circumcised yet.) Then he began the siege of Jericho.

The Israelites did not attack the city in any conventional way. Following God's instructions, they simply marched silently all the way around the city once each day, while priests blew trumpets. For six days they repeated their silent march.

On the seventh day, the people marched around the city not once but seven times. Then the people gave a mighty shout, and the walls came tumbling down by themselves. The army of Israel marched right up over the rubble and destroyed the city.[4]

But they saved Rahab and her family, just as they had promised. Rahab is very important for Christian history: Rahab later married an Israelite, and St. Matthew tells us[5] that she was one of the ancestors of David, and thus ultimately one of the human ancestors of Jesus Christ.

A stone tower in the ancient city of Jericho, ca. 7,000 B.C.
Jericho is the oldest continuously inhabited city in the world dating to 8,000 B.C.

Canaan At The Time Of The Conquest ca. 1406 B.C.

Byblos
Lebo-hamath
Aphekah

HITTITE EMPIRE

Sidon
Damascus
△ Mt. Hermon

Tyre
Laish (Dan)

SIDONIANS (Phoenicians)

Kedesh
BASHAN (Kingdom of Og)

Hazor
Accho
Merom

CANAANITES

Sea of Chinnereth
Ashtaroth

G R E A T   S E A

Dor
Megiddo
Beth-shan
Dothan

Mahanaim

SIHON

CANAANITES

Mount Ebal △
Shechem
Mount Gerizim △

Zaphon
Succoth
Penuel

Jordan R.

AMMON

Joppa

HIVITES

Bethel
Ai
Gilgal
Jericho

AMORITES

Heshbon

Ashdod
Ekron

Jebus (Jerusalem)
Bethlehem

△ Mt. Nebo

JEBUSITES

Medeba

Ashkelon
Eglon
Lachish
Hebron

Gaza
Gerar
Debir

Dibon

KENITES

Salt Sea

Arad

Raphia
Beer-sheba

M O A B

AMALEKITES

Rehoboth

WILDERNESS OF ZIN

Zoar

Brook of Egypt

0   25   50 km
0   10   20   30 miles

Kadesh-barnea

E D O M

Philistine city ◉
Area controlled by Israelites ▨

171

Jericho

Is the story of the conquest of Jericho historically accurate? Although some archaeologists disagree, many see signs of a catastrophic earthquake that toppled the walls of Jericho just about the time Joshua and the Israelites would have been besieging the city. A layer of charred remains tells of a great fire about the same time. ("And they burned the city with fire, and all within it," says Jos 6:24.)

According to some archaeologists, one small section of the city walls seems to have been left standing—a section that had small houses built into it. Now, in the book of Joshua, the house of Rahab "was built into the city wall, so that she dwelt in the wall" (Jos 2:15). The Bible says that Rahab and all her family were spared when Jericho was destroyed. Could that one small section of wall that didn't come down have been Rahab's house?

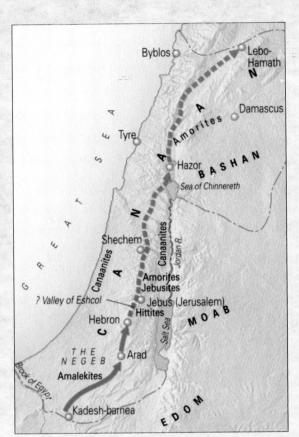

The Route Of The Spies

Jericho ("moon city," a city where the moon god was worshiped) is 17 miles northeast of Jerusalem and 5 miles west of the Jordan. The record conquest of Jericho makes it clear that God gave the city into the hands of the Israelites (Jos 6). The contents of Jericho were burned as a "first fruits" offering in which everything was devoted to the Lord.

Joshua's Covenant With Israel

As long as Joshua was their leader, the people of Israel were mostly faithful to God. They conquered city after city and tribe after tribe of the Canaanites. When he was 110 years old, and he knew that he was dying, Joshua called all the heads of the tribes together at Shechem—the very place where God had promised to give the land to Abraham,[6] and where Joshua (Jos 24:32) was buried.[7] There all the tribes swore to serve God faithfully.

Joshua gave them a chance to back out. He suggested that serving God would be too hard for them. "You cannot serve the LORD; for he is a holy God; he is a jealous God; he will not forgive your transgressions or your sins. If you forsake the LORD and serve foreign gods, then he will turn and do you harm, and consume you, after having done you good."[8]

But the people insisted that they would serve God. "Nay, but we will serve the LORD," they assured him.

> Then Joshua said to the people, "You are witnesses against yourselves that you have chosen the LORD, to serve him." And they said, "We are witnesses." He said, "Then put away the foreign gods which are among you, and incline your heart to the LORD, the God of Israel." And the people said to Joshua, "The LORD our God we will serve, and his voice we will obey." So Joshua made a covenant with the people that day, and made statutes and ordinances for them at Shechem. (Jos 24:22-25)

Then Joshua died. The book of Joshua tells us that all the heads of the tribes who had made that covenant with Joshua were faithful to it. Israel served the True God as long as they were alive.[9]

Once they died, however, Israel began to lapse again.

The ancient remains of the Baal-Berith Temple in Shechem, Samaria. A prominent Biblical city which occupied a strategic position in the pass between Mt. Gerizim and Mt. Ebal. In Rabbinical literature, the idol Baal-berith, which the Jews worshiped after the death of Gideon, was identical, according to the Rabbis, with Baal-zebub, "the ba'al of flies," the god of Ekron (2 Kings 1:2). He was worshiped in the shape of a fly; and so addicted were the Jews to his cult that they would carry an image of him in their pockets, producing it, and kissing it from time to time.

The Right Time To Attack

God promised to send "hornets" before Israel to help drive the Canaanites out of the Promised Land (see Ex 23:28). He kept his promise—not by sending a literal plague of hornets, but by plaguing the Canaanites with civil wars and difficult times.

For a long time before the Israelites arrived, Canaan had been under the influence of Egypt. The Canaanite tribes had been more or less united, and they could count on strong Egyptian armies to defend them.

But by the time Israel was ready to begin the conquest of the Promised Land, Egypt had pulled back. With no great power to keep them in line, the Canaanite cities and tribes started fighting with one another. Instead of uniting against the Israelite invaders, the Canaanites kept up their petty civil wars.

With no united opposition, the Israelites were able to take town after town. They still had to fight for every inch of territory, but the Canaanites' difficulties made the conquest possible. Once again, God had kept his promise to his people.

The Invasion Of Canaan

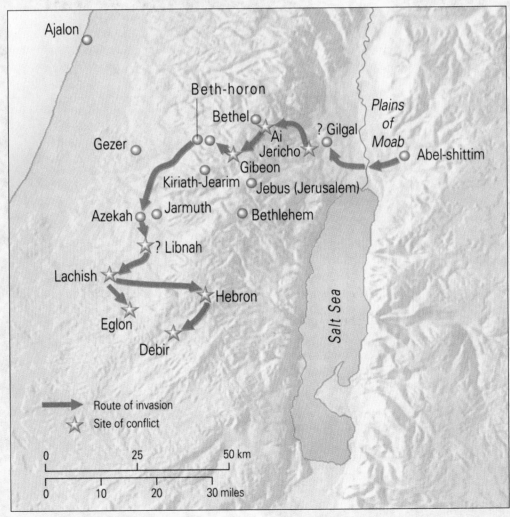

Time-Line Of Early Israel And Her Neighbors

Date	Early Israel	Egypt	Mesopotamia	Asia Minor
3000 B.C.				
		Old Kingdom 29th-23rd centuries **Pyramid Age** 26th-25th centuries	**Early Sumerians** 2800-2360	
2500			**Sargon of Akkad Dynasty** ca. 2360-2180 **Ur III**	
2000	**Abraham leaves Ur**	**Middle Kingdom** 21st-18th centuries **Syria-Palestine**		
1750				
		Hyksos ca. 1720-1550 **New Kingdom** ca. 1570-1310		**Old Hittite Empire** 1740-1460
1500	**Ugaritic Texts** 14th Century	**Amarna Letters** ca. 1400-1350 **Exodus of Hebrews** ca. 1280 (?)		**New Hittite Empire** 1460-1200
1250	**Hebrew Conquest** 1250-1200 **Judges** 1200-1020	**Rameses II** **End of Egyptian Empire** ca. 1100	**Assyria strong under Tiglath-pileser I** 1118-1078	
1000	**Saul** 1020-1000 **David** 1000-961 **Solomon** 961-922		**Ashur-dan II** 934-912	

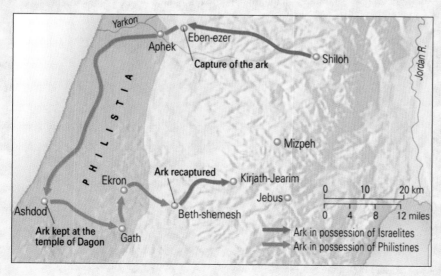

The Capture Of The Ark By The Philistines And The Return Of The Ark To The Israelites

In a battle (ca.1050 B.C.) to protect Shiloh from the threatening Philistines, the Israelites suffered a crushing defeat by the Philistines at Eben-ezer. The Philistines captured the Ark, which the Israelites had brought to the battlefield hoping it would make them victorious. The plagues and calamities that were wrought upon the Philistines by God forced them to return the Ark by ox-cart to Beth-shemesh.

The Judges

After the book of Joshua comes the book of Judges. In Judges we read how, over and over, Israel fell away from God into idolatry—and then into anarchy and even civil war. But at the darkest hours, God raised up "judges"—soldier-prophets who rescued the people of Israel from their enemies. But as soon as they were safe, they forgot about God again, and the cycle started all over.

Why did Israel fall away so easily? The book of Judges gives a simple answer: Israel failed to drive out the Canaanites. It was much easier for the people of Israel just to settle down in the land they had already conquered and ignore the Canaanites who were too hard to conquer. The first chapter of Judges gives a long list of Canaanite tribes and cities that the Israelites left alone.

The Canaanites were city-dwellers, people who built temples of stone and lived in comfortable brick houses. They must have seemed very sophisticated to the nomadic Israelites, who were used to living in tents. Whenever the people of Israel settled close to the Canaanites, the Canaanite civilization always started to attract them. And, of course, the Canaanite religions went with that civilization. Soon the Canaanite cities would be full of Israelites admiring the magnificent temples and their impressive ceremonies.

Meanwhile, Israel was falling apart. The tribes were acting as separate units, not as a unified nation. Once they even fell into a sordid civil war, in which the tribe of Benjamin was nearly exterminated. Disunited and squabbling, the tribes of Israel were easy prey for stronger powers—like the newly arrived Philistines on the coast, who would be Israel's most hated enemies for a very long time. (The name "Palestine" comes from the Philistines who settled there.) God brought them champions to redeem them from their enemies, but all too often the people of Israel would simply turn back to God for a little while and then lapse back into idolatry. Then, as punishment for their sins, God would allow them to fall into the hands of another conqueror.

"And the Lord said to Gideon, 'The people are still too many; take them down to the water and I will test them for you there;'...and the Lord said to Gideon, 'Every one that laps the water with his tongue, as a dog laps, you shall set by himself; likewise every one that kneels down to drink.'" (Jgs 7: 4–5)

The Judges Of Israel:
Deliverers Of Law—Freedom Fighters—Champions

JUDGE	Years of Service	Oppressor	Years of Oppression	Years of Peace	Biblical Reference	Province or Tribe
OTHNIEL		Cushan-Rishathaim Of Mesopotamia	8	40	Judges 3:8-11	Judah
EHUD		Eglon, King of Moab	18	80	Judges 3:12-30	Benjamin
SHAMGAR		Philistines			Judges 3:31	Son of Anath (non-Israelite?)
DEBORAH with BARAK		Canaanites led by King Jabin and Sisera his general	20	40	Judges 4:1-5:31	Deborah-Ephraim Barak-Naphtali
GIDEON		Midianites and Amalekites	7	40	Judges 6:1-8:27	Manasseh
TOLA	23				Judges 10:1-2	Issachar
JAIR				22	Judges 10:3-5	Gilead
JEPHTHAH	6	Ammonites and Philistines	18		Judges 10:6-12:7	Gilead
IBZAN	7				Judges 12:8-10	Bethlehem
ELON	10				Judges 12:11-12	Zebulun
ABDON	8				Judges 12:13-15	Ephraim
SAMSON	20	Philistines	40		Judges 13-16	Dan
SAMUEL	Last of the Judges—First of the Prophets—The "bridge" between judges and kings				1 and 2 Samuel	Benjamin

Mount Tabor and the Jezreel Plain is the site of the defeat of the Canaanite army by Deborah and Barak.

Deborah was the only woman among the judges of Israel. Along with Barak, she defeated the Canaanites, King Jabin and his general, Sisera.

The "Song of Deborah" (Jgs 5) celebrates this victory. This victory allowed the Israelites to settle in the plain without fear of Canaanite attacks for 40 years.

Samuel The King-Maker

Finally Israel was in a state of anarchy. "Every man did what was right in his own eyes," Judges 21:25 tells us. Even the Levite priests of the True God had become mercenaries, making themselves rich on the sacrifices of the poor people of Israel.

The Israelites themselves knew that something radical had to be done to change the situation. Instead of turning humbly back to God, however, they decided they wanted a king. If they had a king to unite them, they thought, he might solve all their problems.

Samuel, the last of the Judges, had been the leader of Israel for a long time. He had won great victories over the Philistines, but in his old age he had made the mistake of setting his sons up to succeed him. It was a mistake because his sons were not like him: they were greedy men who "took bribes and perverted justice."[10]

All the leaders of the Israelites confronted Samuel at his home. "Behold," they said, "you are old and your sons do not walk in your ways; now appoint for us a king to govern us like all the nations."[11]

Samuel was personally insulted. Hadn't he been a good leader? So he prayed, and God answered his prayer.

> And the LORD said to Samuel, "Hearken to the voice of the people in all that they say to you; for they have not rejected you, but they have rejected me from being king over them. According to all the deeds which they have done to me, from the day I brought them up out of Egypt even to this day, forsaking me and serving other gods, so they are also doing to you. Now then, hearken to their voice; only, you shall solemnly warn them, and show them the ways of the king who shall reign over them." (1 Sm 8:7-9)

The people were not rejecting Samuel; they were rejecting the idea of being a nation set apart. They wanted to be like every other nation. It was exactly as Moses had prophesied, and the Book of the Law, Deuteronomy, had provided for this occasion.

So Samuel warned the people what they could expect from a king.

> So Samuel told all the words of the LORD to the people who were asking a king from him. He said, "These will be the ways of the king who will reign over you: he will take your sons and appoint them to his chariots and to be his horsemen, and to run before his chariots; and he will appoint for himself commanders of thousands and commanders of fifties, and some to plow his ground and to reap his harvest, and to make his implements of war and the equipment of his chariots. He will take your daughters to be perfumers and cooks and bakers. He will take the best of your fields and vineyards and olive orchards and give them to his servants. He will take the tenth of your grain and of your vineyards and give it to his officers and to his servants. He will take your menservants and maidservants, and the best of your cattle and your asses, and put them to his work. He will take the tenth of your flocks, and you shall be his slaves. And in that day you will cry out because of your king, whom you have chosen for yourselves; but the LORD will not answer you in that day."

But the people refused to listen to the voice of Samuel; and they said, "No! but we will have a king over us, that we also may be like all the nations, and that our king may govern us and go out before us and fight our battles." (1 Sm 8:10-20)

Samuel told the people exactly what they could expect from a king: taxes, military service, and oppression. But the people insisted. Samuel obeyed their wishes and God's word. He agreed to find a king for them, no matter how much he hated the idea himself. But all his predictions would come true.

On a high hill overlooking Jerusalem from the north is a mosque covering one traditional site of Samuel's tomb. In Arabic it is called Nebi Samwil. A few miles east is Er Ram thought to be ancient Ramah, Samuel's birthplace and home. 1 Sm 25:1 states that Samuel was buried at Ramah. Like many places in Bible lands, exact locations can remain controversial.

Saul, The Anointed One

God led Samuel to a man named Saul from the tiny tribe of Benjamin. Saul certainly looked like a king. He was the handsomest man anyone in Israel had seen, and he was taller by a head than anyone else. Still, he had no idea that he was about to be chosen to rule Israel. Saul had to see Samuel to ask about some lost livestock; imagine his surprise when he found that Samuel had an expensive dinner prepared for him.

Saul must have been even more surprised by what Samuel did next. "Then Samuel took a vial of oil and poured it on his head, and kissed him and said, 'Has not the LORD anointed you to be prince over his people Israel?'"[12]

To "anoint" means to put oil on something as a sign of consecration. The oil was a visible sign that Saul had been chosen by God. Once he was anointed by God's prophet, Saul became the *anointed one*—"messiah" in Hebrew, or "christ" in Greek. That is what "christ" means: the anointed one, someone chosen by God and anointed to be the leader and savior of God's people.

Until this time, only priests had been anointed. But after Saul had been anointed, he began to prophesy. The Spirit of God had come upon him. The people might have rejected God from being king over them, but God was showing them that he would still rule them through their king. Saul would be king not because the people had chosen him, but because God himself had chosen him.

Saul's First Big Mistake

At first, things went very well under the new king. He defeated the Ammonites gloriously, and the people began to congratulate themselves on having made the right choice.

But power quickly went to Saul's head. "If both you and the king who reigns over you will follow the LORD your God, it will be well," Samuel warned the people; "but if you will not hearken to the voice of the LORD, but rebel against the commandment of the LORD, then the hand of the LORD will be against you and your king."[13]

Saul wanted to lead, not follow. He was king now, wasn't he? It was time for him to start showing a little authority.

His new attitude showed itself when a new war began with the Philistines. At first things went well, but then the Philistines put together a huge army at Michmash—"troops like the sand on the seashore in multitude,"[14] the sacred author tells us.

The people of Israel didn't know what to do. Most of them seem to have been certain that the Philistines would win. Many hid out in caves or tombs; many more crossed the Jordan as refugees into neighboring countries. Even the small number—about 600 soldiers—who stayed with Saul were "trembling."[15]

In such desperate straits, the right thing to do was to ask for God's help, and that was what Saul did. Samuel told Saul to wait at Gilgal for seven days, and then Samuel would come and offer sacrifices.

But Samuel was a little bit late. When he didn't show up right on time, even the few remaining loyal soldiers started to wander away. Saul decided to take things into his own hands. He had the sacrifices brought to him and offered them himself.

Just as he finished, Samuel showed up. "What have you done?" Samuel demanded.

Saul tried to explain. "When I saw that the people were scattering from me, and that you did not come within the days appointed, and that the Philistines had mustered at Michmash, I said, 'Now the Philistines will come down upon me at Gilgal, and I have not entreated the favor of the LORD'; so I forced myself, and offered the burnt offering."

The Kingdom of Saul, ca. 1050 B.C.

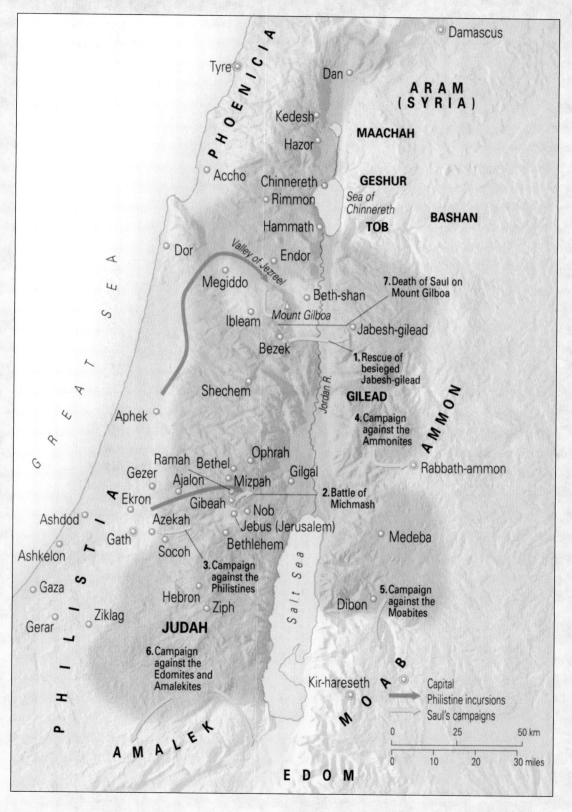

Damascus

Tyre

Dan

**ARAM
(SYRIA)**

Kedesh

MAACHAH

Hazor

Accho

Chinnereth

GESHUR

Rimmon

*Sea of
Chinnereth*

BASHAN

Hammath

TOB

P H O E N I C I A

Dor

Endor

Valley of Jezreel

7. Death of Saul on
Mount Gilboa

Megiddo

Beth-shan

Mount Gilboa

Ibleam

Jabesh-gilead

Bezek

1. Rescue of
besieged
Jabesh-gilead

Shechem

Jordan R.

GILEAD

AMMON

Aphek

4. Campaign
against the
Ammonites

Ophrah

Ramah Bethel

Gezer

Gilgal

Rabbath-ammon

Ajalon

Mizpah

Ekron

Gibeah

Nob

2. Battle of
Michmash

Ashdod

Jebus (Jerusalem)

Azekah

Medeba

Gath

Bethlehem

Ashkelon

Socoh

3. Campaign
against the
Philistines

Salt Sea

Gaza

Hebron Ziph

5. Campaign
against the
Moabites

Dibon

Ziklag

Gerar

JUDAH

6. Campaign
against the
Edomites and
Amalekites

G R E A T   S E A

P H I L I S T I A

A M A L E K

Kir-hareseth

M O A B

Capital

Philistine incursions

Saul's campaigns

0   25   50 km

0   10   20   30 miles

E D O M

181

The answer made some sense: after all, it was a time of crisis. But Saul's answer showed where his heart really was. He offered sacrifices not out of love for God, but rather because he wanted God to do something for him, and thought a sacrifice would be God's price. Saul had crossed an important line—the same line Aaron's sons had crossed when they "offered unholy fire before the LORD" (see Lv 10). He had decided to worship God his way, not God's way. It was the Golden Calf again.

"You have done foolishly," Samuel told Saul; "you have not kept the commandment of the LORD your God, which he commanded you; for now the LORD would have established your kingdom over Israel forever. But now your kingdom shall not continue; the LORD has sought out a man after his own heart; and the LORD has appointed him to be prince over his people, because you have not kept what the LORD commanded you."

Then Samuel turned around and walked away.

Now, Saul was still king. God had not deposed him. But his son would not be king after him: that was his punishment so far. He would not found a dynasty. Instead, some unrelated person would succeed him.

Saul's Second Big Mistake

Saul's next big mistake came when God, through Samuel the prophet, told Israel to destroy Amalek completely. The Amalekites were some of Israel's most dangerous enemies; they had often made horrible and bloody raids on peaceful Israelite towns. God told Saul to destroy everything not only because the Amalekites were evil, but also so that the lure of loot and booty would not become an excuse for making war on Israel's neighbors.

But Saul and his soldiers kept "the best of the sheep and of the oxen and of the fatlings, and the lambs, and all that was good, and would not utterly destroy them; all that was despised and worthless they utterly destroyed."[16] They kept what was valuable and destroyed what was worthless.

God told Samuel what Saul had done, and Samuel, furious, went off to see for himself.

> And Samuel came to Saul, and Saul said to him, "Blessed be you to the LORD; I have performed the commandment of the LORD." And Samuel said, "What then is this bleating of the sheep in my ears, and the lowing of the oxen which I hear?" Saul said, "They have brought them from the Amalekites; for the people spared the best of the sheep and of the oxen, to sacrifice to the LORD your God; and the rest we have utterly destroyed."
> (1 Sm 15:13-15)

Saul can hardly have missed the bitter sarcasm in Samuel's question about the animal noises. He knew he had been caught red-handed, and Samuel did not accept his feeble excuse. "Why did you swoop on the spoil, and do what was evil in the sight of the LORD?"[17] Samuel demanded. Once again Saul tried the excuse that the animals were saved for sacrifices, but Samuel did not believe it. Even if that were true, Saul was missing the point.

> And Samuel said,
> "Has the LORD as great delight in burnt offerings and sacrifices,
>   as in obeying the voice of the LORD?
> Behold, to obey is better than sacrifice,
>   and to hearken than the fat of rams." (1 Sm 15:22)

Saul had been trying to buy God's favor with sacrifices, not with obedience. In doing so, Saul had shown that he was the wrong sort of man to be king, and Samuel pronounced his final sentence:

> Because you have rejected the word of the LORD,
>   He has rejected you from being king. (1 Sm 15:23)

Now at last Saul seemed to grasp that he had done wrong. "I have sinned," he admitted; "for I have transgressed the commandment of the LORD and your words, because I feared the people and obeyed their voice." (Notice that Saul is still trying to lay at least part of the blame on his soldiers, not on himself.) "Now therefore, I pray, pardon my sin, and return with me, that I may worship the LORD." [18]

When Samuel refused and turned to go, Saul grabbed the hem of Samuel's mantle—a traditional gesture of pleading. But Samuel must have been walking away briskly. The mantle tore, leaving Saul kneeling, with a shred of fabric dangling from his hand.

Samuel saw the accident as a powerful symbol. "The LORD has torn the kingdom of Israel from you this day," Samuel declared, "and has given it to a neighbor of yours, who is better than you." [19]

There was Saul's final sentence. For his first offense he had lost his dynasty; now he lost the kingdom itself. In the very next chapter of the book, we read how God sent Samuel to Bethlehem to anoint another king to replace Saul—a young man from the neighboring tribe of Judah who seemed like a very unlikely choice for a king.

The cliffs of Michmash. In 1020 B.C., the Philistines invaded Israel and camped in force at Michmash, threatening King Saul's capital at Gibeah. Jonathan and his armour-bearer surprised the Philistine garrison by climbing across from Geba at a steep place down the valley, and in the panic that followed, Saul defeated the Philistines chasing them back to their own borders.

The Man After God's Own Heart

When God told Samuel to go to the house of Jesse and anoint one of Jesse's sons, Samuel might have expected to find another regal-looking prince like Saul. There were many stately young men among Jesse's large family. But one by one Jesse's sons appeared before Samuel, and no matter how kingly they might have looked, not one of them was God's choice. "Do not look on his appearance or the height of his stature," God told Samuel as Samuel admired Jesse's eldest son, "because I have rejected him; for the LORD sees not as man sees; man looks on the outward appearance, but the LORD looks on the heart."[20]

In fact, the choice turned out to be Jesse's youngest son David. Jesse had not even called David in to meet Samuel. David was a shepherd, and he was out tending the sheep—which was all Jesse thought he was good for. But God saw David's heart "Arise, anoint him; for this is he," God told Samuel. Samuel anointed David, and "the spirit of the LORD came mightily upon David from that day forward."[21]

Then, in the very next verse, we find that "the Spirit of the LORD departed from Saul." There could be only one Messiah, one Anointed One. Although Saul still possessed the kingdom, his special status as the Lord's Anointed was gone. Instead, an evil spirit came to torment him.

Now comes an ironic twist in the story. Saul's ministers decided that music would be good for him. And where would they find a good musician? "Behold," one of them began, "I have seen a son of Jesse the Bethlehemite..."

David—the young shepherd whom Samuel had just anointed to replace Saul—was also the best musician in the kingdom. Completely unaware that David was God's choice to replace him, Saul took David into his court. Whenever the evil spirit came on Saul, David would play his lyre, and Saul felt better. Christian readers will be reminded of how, in the Gospels, evil spirits fled the presence of Jesus Christ, the heir of David's kingdom (see, for example, Luke 4:41, where the demons "knew that he was the Christ"—that is, the Anointed One).

"And David came to Saul, and entered his service. And Saul loved him greatly, and he became his armour-bearer.... And whenever the evil spirit from God was upon Saul, David took the lyre and played it with his hand; so Saul was refreshed,...and the evil spirit departed from him." (1 Sm 16:21-23)

SUPPLEMENTARY READING

Augustine, *City of God*, Book XVII
From Chapter 6

In this way, too, the kingdom of Saul himself, who certainly was reprobated and rejected, was the shadow of a kingdom yet to come which should remain to eternity. For, indeed, the oil with which he was anointed, and from that chrism he is called Christ, is to be taken in a mystical sense, and is to be understood as a great mystery; which David himself venerated so much in him, that he trembled with smitten heart when, being hid in a dark cave, which Saul also entered when pressed by the necessity of nature, he had come secretly behind him and cut off a small piece of his robe, that he might be able to prove how he had spared him when he could have killed him, and might thus remove from his mind the suspicion through which he had vehemently persecuted the holy David, thinking him his enemy. Therefore he was much afraid lest he should be accused of violating so great a mystery in Saul, because he had thus meddled even his clothes. For thus it is written: "And David's heart smote him because he had taken away the skirt of his cloak." But to the men with him, who advised him to destroy Saul thus delivered up into his hands, he saith, "The LORD forbid that I should do this thing to my lord, the LORD's Christ, to lay my hand upon him, because he is the LORD's Christ." Therefore he showed so great reverence to this shadow of what was to come, not for its own sake, but for the sake of what it prefigured. Whence also that which Samuel says to Saul, "Since thou hast not kept my commandment which the LORD commanded thee, whereas now the LORD would have prepared thy kingdom over Israel for ever, yet now thy kingdom shall not continue for thee; and the LORD will seek Him a man after His own heart, and the LORD will command him to be prince over His people, because thou hast not kept that which the LORD commanded thee," is not to be taken as if God had settled that Saul himself should reign for ever, and afterwards, on his sinning, would not keep this promise; nor was He ignorant that he would sin, but He had established his kingdom that it might be a figure of the eternal kingdom. Therefore he added, "Yet now thy kingdom shall not continue *for thee*." Therefore what it signified has stood and shall stand; but it shall not stand for this man, because he himself was not to reign for ever, nor his offspring; so that at least that word "for ever" might seem to be fulfilled through his posterity one to another.

"He (David) said to his men, 'The Lord forbid that I should do this thing to my lord, the Lord's anointed, to put forth my hand against him, seeing he is the Lord's anointed.' So David persuaded his men with these words, and did not permit them to attack Saul."
(1 Sm 24: 6–7)

VOCABULARY

CHRIST
Greek for "messiah." See Messiah.

DAVID
The second king of Israel, a "man after God's own heart." God made a new covenant with all the nations through David.

JERICHO
An ancient and strategically vital city in Canaan, the first major city to be captured by the Israelites.

JORDAN
The river that formed the eastern border of Canaan. Many, including Jesus, were baptized here by St. John the Baptist

JUDGES
Temporary leaders appointed by God to lead the people of Israel when enemies oppressed them.

MANTLE
An outer garment that was also the symbol of the wearer's office.

MESSIAH
Hebrew for "Anointed One," a title of the kings of Israel.

PALESTINE
Another name for the land of Canaan. Named for the Philistines who settled there.

PHILISTINES
A powerful nation that invaded Canaan from the sea and became the most hated enemies of Israel.

RAHAB
A Canaanite woman of Jericho who helped the Israelite spies escape. She later married an Israelite and became one of the human ancestors of Jesus Christ.

SAMUEL
A Levite priest, the last of the Judges, and the man chosen by God to anoint a king for Israel.

SAUL
The first king of Israel, anointed by Samuel. Later rejected by God.

"And David said, 'The Lord who delivered me from the paw of the lion and from the paw of the bear, will deliver me from the hand of this Philistine.' And Saul said to David, 'Go, and the Lord be with you!'"
(1 Sm 17: 37)

STUDY QUESTIONS

1. What was the first target of the Israelites in Canaan?

2. Who succeeded Moses as leader of Israel?

3. With whom did Joshua's spies stay in Canaan?

4. What happened when the Levite priests reached the river Jordan with the Ark?

5. What important ceremony did the Israelites perform before beginning the conquest of Jericho?

6. How did the army of Israel defeat the city of Jericho?

7. Name two important descendants of Rahab.

8. Why did Israel need God to send them "judges"?

9. Why was the tribe of Benjamin nearly exterminated?

10. Why did the people of Israel want a king so badly?

11. What did God tell Samuel was the real reason they desired a king?

12. What did Samuel prophesy about the king who would rule over Israel?

13. What ceremony did Samuel perform to show that Saul had been chosen by God as king of Israel?

14. What does "anointed" mean?

15. What two mistakes did Saul make that cost him his dynasty and his kingdom?

16. Where did God send Samuel to find Saul's successor?

17. Who was chosen by God to succeed Saul as king of Israel?

"... an evil spirit from God rushed upon Saul, and he raved within his house, ... and Saul cast the spear, for he thought, 'I will pin David to the wall.' But David evaded him twice." (1 Sm 18: 10-11)

PRACTICAL EXERCISES

1. The Israelites went about conquering Jericho in a very interesting way. God used this event to show that the conquest of the Promised Land would be a gift from him, and not gained by the merits of Israel or its military prowess. All the people of Israel had to do was to follow God's orders and he led them to victory, even though it seemed the orders were not very oriented toward military strategy. What important lesson is God giving the people of Israel? What gift does God want to give everyone on earth in the same way he gave Israel the Promised Land? How might this affect the way we look at our daily lives and our obedience to God's Word?

2. The most important figures in Israelite history were descended from Rahab, a Canaanite woman of Jericho. What lesson about God's plan are we able to learn from that fact?

3. Saul acted foolishly when he made the sacrifice to God without waiting for Samuel because he was acting with the wrong intention. He offered sacrifices not out of love for God, but rather because he wanted God to do something for him. Because of this, Saul was punished with the loss of his future dynasty. What important lesson does this teach us? What should we be ultimately concerned about in our relationship with God?

4. Of all Jesse's sons, the one picked as the next king of Israel was David. David was the youngest of the sons and a shepherd. Jesse hadn't even called David in to meet Samuel because he didn't think he was good for anything but watching the sheep. God, however, chose David as the next king and told Samuel to anoint him. Reread the section titled "The man after God's own heart." How did God's way of choosing the next Anointed One differ from human ways? What quality did David have that allowed God to make him a great leader?

Endnotes

1. Jos 1:2.	8. Jos 24:19-20.	15. 1 Sm 13:7.
2. Jos 2:18-20.	9. Jos 24:31.	16. 1 Sm 15:9.
3. Jos 2:24.	10. 1 Sm 8:3.	17. 1 Sm 15:19.
4. Jos 6.	11. 1 Sm 8:5.	18. 1 Sm 15:24-25.
5. Mt 1:5.	12. 1 Sm 10:1.	19. 1 Sm 15:27-28.
6. Gn 12:6-7.	13. 1 Sm 12:14-15.	20. 1 Sm 16:7.
7. Gn 50:13.	14. 1 Sm 13:5.	21. 1 Sm 16:12-13.

The Kingdom of David

"His line shall endure for ever,
his throne as long as the sun before me.
Like the moon it shall be established for ever;
it shall stand firm while the skies endure."

Psalm 89: 36–37

Chapter 10

The Kingdom of David

Read

1 Samuel
26:6 – 11

2 Samuel
6:1 – 7:29
11:1 – 12:14

Psalm 89

With Saul dead, David was free to take over the kingdom. But it didn't just fall into his hands. The tribe of Judah followed him, but the northern part of Israel chose to follow Ishbaal, one of Saul's sons.[1] (His name is given as Ishbosheth in 2 Samuel. The word "bosheth" means "shame;" the writer wrote that instead of "baal" so that readers would not have to speak the name of a horrible Canaanite false god.)

Only after a long civil war did David finally wear down Ishbaal's armies. In the end, two of Ishbaal's own generals, seeing that the situation was hopeless, assassinated Ishbaal and brought his head to David. They thought they would get a reward. Instead, David had them executed as murderers, saying they had "slain a righteous man."[2] Unlike most rulers, David could distinguish between the character of Ishbaal and the unfortunate circumstances that made Ishbaal his enemy.

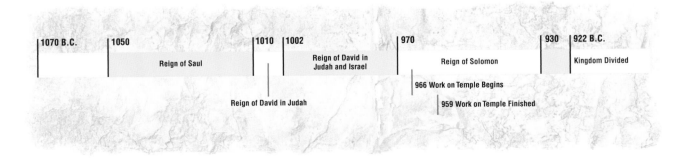

1070 B.C.	1050		1010	1002		970		930	922 B.C.
		Reign of Saul			Reign of David in Judah and Israel		Reign of Solomon		Kingdom Divided
						966 Work on Temple Begins			
				Reign of David in Judah		959 Work on Temple Finished			

Jerusalem, David's New Capital

When the founders of the United States were deciding where to put the capital of the new country, they faced a serious problem. Whatever city they chose, it would make one state seem more important than the others. In the beginning, it was hard to hold the states together, and more regional jealousy was the last thing the new nation needed. So the national government finally decided to build a new city, one that would not be in any state. Even today, the District of Columbia is governed directly by Congress.

David had exactly the same problem. It was hard to hold the twelve tribes together. If David put his capital in his own homeland, Judah, the northern tribes—already rebellious—might think he wanted nothing to do with them. But if David put his capital somewhere in the north, it would seem as though he was turning his back on his faithful followers in Judah.

But there was an ancient city right on the border between Judah and the other tribes, a city that belonged to none of the tribes.

Jerusalem was one of those Canaanite cities that the Israelites had failed to destroy during the conquest. "But the people of Benjamin did not drive out the Jebusites who dwelt in Jerusalem; so the Jebusites have dwelt with the people of Benjamin in Jerusalem to this day," says Judges 1:21. Joshua 15:63 says that *Judah* failed to drive out the Jebusites, and that the Jebusites are still dwelling with the people of Judah. Evidently Jerusalem was right on the border between Judah and Benjamin.

Finishing the job that ought to have been done generations before, David finally attacked the proud and wicked Jebusites. The Jebusites thought Jerusalem could never be taken. They heaped insults on David, telling him that even the blind and the lame in their city could turn back his puny army.[3] So David offered his generals an incentive: "Whoever shall smite the Jebusites first shall be chief and commander."[4] His general Joab made the first strike, so Joab became David's right-hand man—his prime minister, so to speak. We'll hear a lot more about Joab later. David's army drove out the Jebusites, and David immediately made his home in Jerusalem.

From that time on, Jerusalem was David's capital. It even became known as the City of David—a name the old part of the city still bears today. David built up the city, and his new ally King Hiram of Tyre sent Phoenician craftsmen to build a palace for King David. We know from other historical sources that Tyre was just entering a golden age of prosperity under King Hiram, and this would not be the last time in his long reign that Hiram would prove a friend to Israel.

The City of David from the southwest. The earliest city of Jerusalem is the City of David on a smaller hill south of and lower than the Temple Mount. Jerusalem stands high in the Judean hills with no access by sea or river. The ground drops steeply away on all sides except to the north. To the east, between Jerusalem and the Mount of Olives is the Kidron Valley. The Hinnom Valley curves around the city to the south and west. The Central or Tyropoean Valley cuts through the ancient city.

David's Kingdom

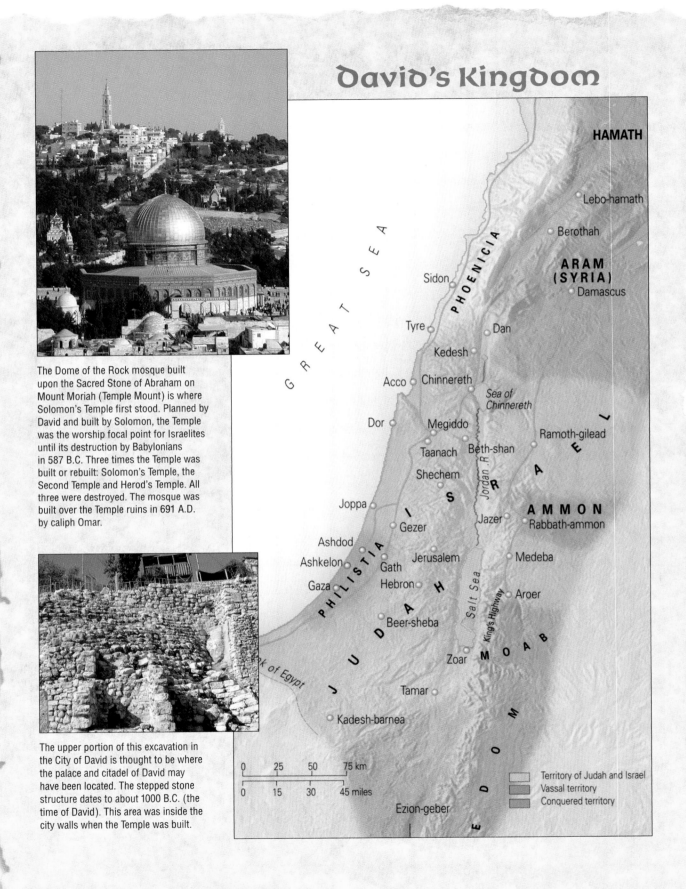

The Dome of the Rock mosque built upon the Sacred Stone of Abraham on Mount Moriah (Temple Mount) is where Solomon's Temple first stood. Planned by David and built by Solomon, the Temple was the worship focal point for Israelites until its destruction by Babylonians in 587 B.C. Three times the Temple was built or rebuilt: Solomon's Temple, the Second Temple and Herod's Temple. All three were destroyed. The mosque was built over the Temple ruins in 691 A.D. by caliph Omar.

The upper portion of this excavation in the City of David is thought to be where the palace and citadel of David may have been located. The stepped stone structure dates to about 1000 B.C. (the time of David). This area was inside the city walls when the Temple was built.

HAMATH

Lebo-hamath

Berothah

ARAM (SYRIA)

Damascus

Sidon

PHOENICIA

GREAT SEA

Tyre

Dan

Kedesh

Acco

Chinnereth

Sea of Chinnereth

Dor

Megiddo

Ramoth-gilead

Taanach

Beth-shan

ISRAEL

Shechem

Jordan R.

AMMON

Joppa

Jazer

Rabbath-ammon

Gezer

Ashdod

Jerusalem

Medeba

Ashkelon

Gath

Gaza

PHILISTIA

Hebron

JUDAH

Aroer

King's Highway

Salt Sea

Beer-sheba

MOAB

Zoar

Brook of Egypt

Tamar

Kadesh-barnea

EDOM

| 0 | 25 | 50 | 75 km |
| 0 | 15 | 30 | 45 miles |

Territory of Judah and Israel
Vassal territory
Conquered territory

Ezion-geber

Bringing The Ark To Jerusalem

Once David had firmly established himself at Jerusalem, he decided to bring the Ark of the Covenant there. That would make Jerusalem not just the political center of Israel, but the religious center as well.

David's first try at bringing the ark was a dismal failure. He brought a brand-new cart to carry it, but the cart rocked back and forth. When one of the procession reached out to steady the ark, he was struck dead on the spot. David was so afraid of God's wrath that he refused to go any farther. He stopped and left the ark in the care of Obed-edom, whose house was nearby.

What went wrong? David had not followed the law. The instructions for carrying the ark were very specific: it had to be borne on the shoulders of Levite priests.[5] And no one could ever touch the ark itself.[6] As the sign of God's presence among his people, it was a holy thing. David himself understood exactly what went wrong: "we did not care for it in the way that is ordained."[7]

David didn't try bringing the ark to Jerusalem again for three months, and he spent those months making preparations. This time, he would do everything right. He prepared a place for the ark and pitched a tent there. He told the Levites who would carry it to sanctify themselves. He arranged for a magnificent procession, with music and sacrifices.[8]

Thy solemn processions are seen, O God,
    the processions of my God, my King, into the sanctuary —
the singers in front, the minstrels last,
    between them maidens playing timbrels... (Ps 68: 24-25)

This time, everything did go right. David himself led the parade, dressed not as a king but as a priest, in a linen ephod. He leaped and danced for joy "with all his might."[9] And when the ark reached its place, David himself offered the sacrifices.

Why was it all right for David to act as a priest? He was not a Levite. When Saul tried offering sacrifices, he was severely punished.

But there was a huge difference between David and Saul. David was a man after God's own heart. Saul's sacrifices were just a business transaction with God. David danced and made offerings out of love and joy, not because he wanted something from God. And God had chosen David for a new covenant that would begin to erase some of the distinctions made by the law.

Saul's daughter Michal, David's wife, understood the difference, too. She watched David from her window and thought he looked ridiculous. When she came out to meet him, she was dripping with sarcasm. "How the king of Israel has honored himself today," she said with a sneer, "uncovering himself before the eyes of his servants' maids, as one of the vulgar fellows shamelessly uncovers himself!"[10]

For Michal, royal dignity was the important thing. She could not understand the sincere love and joy that David had felt. Like Saul, she had never felt it herself.

"I will make merry before the LORD," David told her. "I will make myself yet more contemptible than this, and I will be abased in your eyes; but by the maids of whom you have spoken, by them I shall be held in honor."[11]

The Liturgy Of The Ark

What was that grand procession like when David brought the Ark to Jerusalem? Many scholars believe that the actual liturgy David used is preserved for us in Psalm 24. We can imagine what the scene must have been like.

As the Ark slowly moves toward Jerusalem, hundreds of voices sing a hymn of praise:

> The earth is the LORD's, and the fullness thereof,
>> the world and those who dwell therein;
> for he has founded it upon the seas,
>> and established it upon the rivers.

Then the procession reaches the base of Mount Zion, and the choir sings a new hymn:

> Who shall ascend the hill of the LORD?
>> And who shall stand in his holy place?
> He who has clean hands and a pure heart,
>> who does not lift up his soul to what is false,
>> and does not swear deceitfully.
> He will receive blessing from the LORD,
>> and vindication from the God of his salvation.
> Such is the generation of those who seek him,
>> who seek the face of the God of Jacob.

Now a huge orchestra of every kind of instrument makes a joyful noise,[22] and to the sound of drums and harps and cymbals and lyres, the Ark makes its way up the hill to the gates of the city. Finally, the procession reaches the gate. The music stops, and the choir sings out,

> Lift up your heads, O gates!
>> and be lifted up, O ancient doors!
>>> that the King of glory may come in.

> On cue, the people inside the gates call out,
>> Who is this King of glory?

> From the choir outside comes the answer,
>> The LORD, strong and mighty,
>>> the LORD, mighty in battle!

> Then again the choir sings out,
>> Lift up your heads, O gates!
>>> and be lifted up, O ancient doors!
>>> that the King of glory may come in.

> Once again, the people inside the gates call out,
>> Who is this King of glory?

> From the choir outside comes the answer,
>> The LORD of hosts,
>>> he is the King of glory!

Then the orchestra strikes up again, and to thunderous cheers and shouts of joy, the Ark enters the city, with King David himself leaping and dancing at the head of the procession.

All this is guessing, of course. But it is a well-educated guess. David wrote Psalm 24, and we know from 1 Chronicles 15 that he himself prepared the music for the procession. It is not unreasonable to assume that he wrote the words and music for the occasion himself. Even if Psalm 24 is not exactly the liturgy used on that occasion, it gives us a good idea of the sort of thing David would have written.

The Covenant With David

Now Jerusalem was the political and spiritual capital of Israel, and Israel had become a power to reckon with in the region. David's conquests had built Israel into a small empire. After a while, Jerusalem had grown to reflect the new status of David and Israel. The crowning glory of the city was David's palace, built of cedar wood imported from Lebanon. The City of David had begun to look like an imperial capital.

But the Ark of the Covenant was still in a tent. It was probably a richly decorated tent, but it was still only a tent.

"See now," David said to the prophet Nathan, "I dwell in a house of cedar, but the ark of God dwells in a tent."

Nathan understood what David had in mind right away: a temple, a real building where for the first time the True God could be worshiped as magnificently as the false gods of the Canaanites. "Go, do all that is in your heart," Nathan replied, "for the LORD is with you."[12]

But that night Nathan had a vision from God. "Go and tell my servant David, 'Thus says the LORD: Would you build me a house to dwell in? I have not dwelt in a house since the day I brought up the people of Israel from Egypt to this day…'"[13]

David will not build a temple, God told Nathan. Instead, God had something much more important for him.

> "'…Moreover the LORD declares to you that the LORD will make you a house. When your days are fulfilled and you lie down with your fathers, I will raise up your offspring after you, who shall come forth from your body, and I will establish his kingdom. He shall build a house for my name, and I will establish the throne of his kingdom for ever. I will be his father, and he shall be my son. When he commits iniquity, I will chasten him with the rod of men, with the stripes of the sons of men; but I will not take my steadfast love from him, as I took it from Saul, whom I put away from before you. And your house and your kingdom shall be made sure for ever before me; your throne shall be established forever.'"
> (2 Sm 7: 11-16)

Nathan went to David the next morning and told him everything God had promised. And God was giving David a lot.

- *The Lord will make you a house:* David will be the founder of a **dynasty**.

- *I will establish his kingdom:* The son of David will be ruler of a **kingdom**.

- *He shall build a house for my name:* David's son will build the **temple** that David had planned to build.

- *I will be his father, and he shall be my son:* David's son would be adopted as **God's own son**. This is the first time the idea of divine sonship is applied to one individual. Before this, the whole people of Israel had been called God's first-born son, but no single person had ever been "son of God."

- *I will chasten him…but I will not take my steadfast love from him:* God would **never disown** David's line the way he disowned Saul, no matter how much his descendants might sin. The covenant would be permanent. Like a loving father, God would punish his son, but only for his own good. Nothing could change the father-son relationship.

- *Your throne shall be established for ever:* The dynasty of David would **never end**. Dynasties rise and fall in all other earthly monarchies, but the throne of David would always be occupied by a descendant of David himself.

Even David, one of the great poets of all time, had trouble finding words to express his feelings. He ran to the tent where the Ark was kept, sat down in front of it, and poured out his heart.

Then King David went in and sat before the LORD, and said, "Who am I, O LORD God, and what is my house, that thou hast brought me thus far? And yet this was a small thing in thy eyes, O LORD God; thou hast spoken also of thy servant's house for a great while to come; this is the law for man,[14] O LORD God! And what more can David say to thee? For thou knowest thy servant, O LORD God! Because of thy promise, and according to thy own

heart, thou hast wrought all this greatness, to make thy servant know it. Therefore thou art great, O LORD God; for there is none like thee, and there is no God besides thee, according to all that we have heard with our ears. What other nation on earth is like thy people Israel, whom God went to redeem to be his people, making himself a name, and doing for them great and terrible things, by driving out before his people a nation and its gods? And thou didst establish for thyself thy people Israel to be thy people for ever; and thou, O LORD, didst become their God. And now, O LORD God, confirm for ever the word which thou hast spoken concerning thy servant and concerning his house, and do as thou hast spoken; and thy name will be magnified for ever, saying, 'The LORD of hosts is God over Israel,' and the house of thy servant David will be established before thee. For thou, O LORD of hosts, the God of Israel, hast made this revelation to thy servant, saying, 'I will build you a house'; therefore thy servant has found courage to pray this prayer to thee. And now, O LORD God, thou art God, and thy words are true, and thou hast promised this good thing to thy servant;

now therefore may it please thee to bless the house of thy servant, that it may continue for ever before thee; for thou, O LORD God, hast spoken, and with thy blessing shall the house of thy servant be blessed for ever." (2 Sm 7:18-29)

David is par excellence the king "after God's own heart," the shepherd who prays for his people and prays in their name. His submission to the will of God, his praise, and his repentance, will be a model for the prayer of the people. His prayer, the prayer of God's Anointed, is a faithful adherence to the divine promise and expresses a loving and joyful trust in God, the only King and Lord (cf. 2 Sm 7:18-29). In the Psalms, David, inspired by the Holy Spirit, is the first prophet of Jewish and Christian prayer. The prayer of Christ, the true Messiah and Son of David, will reveal and fulfill the meaning of this prayer. (CCC 2579)

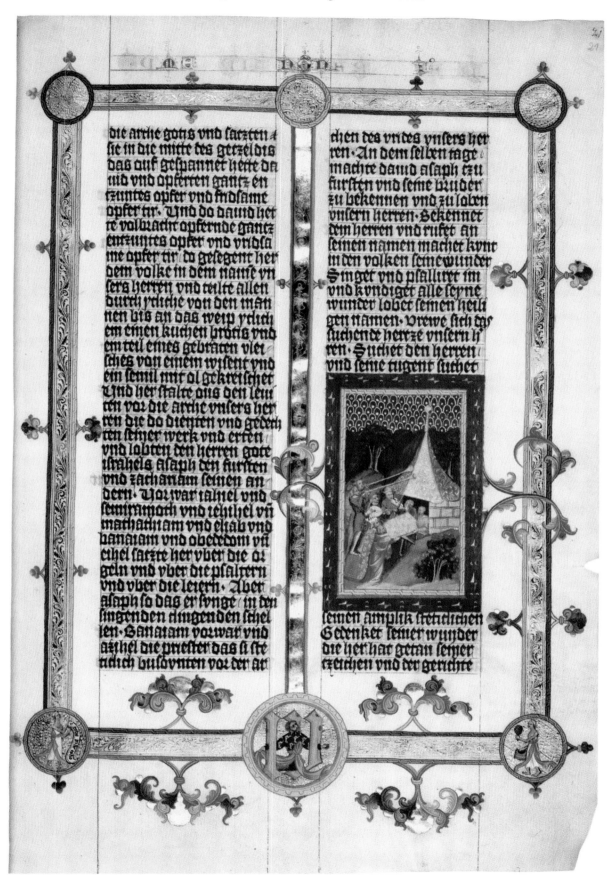

A page from 1 Chronicles shows King David placing the Ark of the Covenant in the Tabernacle.
From The Wenceslas Bible, Prague, ca. 1389-1395

Beyond Sinai To Zion

From the moment David learned of God's covenant with him, Jerusalem replaced Sinai as the center of Israel's religion. At Sinai, God had given the people of Israel a law designed to set them apart from the other nations and keep them separate. Now the time had come for the Israelites to begin the mission that God had always planned for them: to be a nation of priests, leading the other nations of the world to God.

The Sinai Covenant	The Zion Covenant	
Tent: the center of worship is a temporary shelter that can be moved with nomadic tribes	**Temple:** the center of worship is a permanent structure that draws all people to Jerusalem	
National: the covenant is with Israel only	**International:** the covenant reaches to all nations through Israel	
Exclusive: designed to keep the nations out	**Inclusive:** designed to invite the nations in	
Torah: a law designed to keep the Israelites separate from the nations	**Wisdom literature:** a new Torah designed to speak to all mankind	
Sin offering: the most important religious ceremony is an offering to atone for sins	**Todah:** the most important religious ceremony is the thank offering (in Greek, "eucharist") in thanksgiving for God's deliverance	

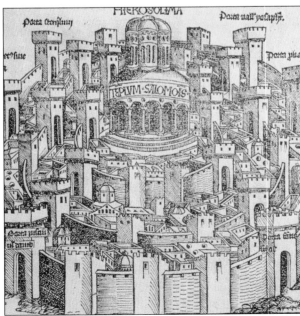

The Davidic Covenant: Seven Primary Features

When we look at how the history of David's dynasty developed, we can point out seven primary features of the Davidic covenant:

1. David's line will have a **kingdom**. A kingdom is more than just a nation. The difference between a kingdom and a nation is like the difference between England and Wales, or the United States and Iowa. And David and his descendants will be more than kings; they will be *great* kings.

> And I will make him the first-born,
>> the highest of the kings of the earth. (Ps 89: 27)

2. The covenant is made with David's whole **dynasty**.

> Moreover the LORD declares to you that the LORD will make you a house [that is, a dynasty]. When your days are fulfilled and you lie down with your fathers, I will raise up your offspring after you, who shall come forth out of your body, and I will establish his kingdom. He shall build a house [that is, the Temple] for my name, and I will establish the throne of his kingdom forever. (2 Sm 7: 11-13)

3. When the son of David is anointed, he is adopted as **God's own son**.

> I will be his father, and he shall be my son. (2 Sm 7: 14)

> I will tell of the decree of the LORD:
> He said to me, "You are my son,
>> today I have begotten you." (Ps 2: 7)

Anointing with oil makes the Son of David "messiah" in Hebrew or "Christ" in Greek—that is, the Anointed One. Psalm 110 calls him a priest as well as king: "You are a priest forever after the order of Melchizedek."[15] (Melchizedek was king and priest in the Jerusalem of Abraham's time.)

4. The covenant is **unlimited** in time and space. David's throne will be everlasting, and "the ends of the earth" (Ps 2: 8; Ps 72: 8) his kingdom's boundaries.

> "...His line shall endure for ever,
>> his throne as long as the sun before me.
> Like the moon it shall be established for ever;
>> it shall stand firm while the skies endure." (Ps 89: 36-37)

> Ask of me, and I will make the nations your heritage,
>> and the ends of the earth your possession. (Ps 2: 8)

> May he have dominion from sea to sea,
>> and from the River to the ends of the earth! (Ps 72: 8)

When Jesus tells his disciples to be his witnesses "in Jerusalem and in all Judea and Samaria and to the end of the earth,"[16] he draws a kind of concentric map of David's kingdom, showing that Jesus is the new heir of the Davidic covenant.

5. Jerusalem becomes the spiritual center of the world. Zion, the central mountain of Jerusalem, eclipses Sinai. Now Zion is the holy mountain of God.

> I have set my king
>> on Zion, my holy hill. (Ps 2: 6)

> For out of Zion shall go forth the law,
>> and the word of the LORD from Jerusalem. (Is 2: 3)

The prophets foretold a time when all nations would flock to Zion (see Is 2). In Sirach 24, Wisdom searches the universe for a resting place, but finally rests at Zion by the commandment of God.

In the New Testament, Zion takes on even more meaning. The Temple would be built on the next hill over, but Zion is where the Upper Room was—the room where Christ's Church was born. And the New Testament writers would speak of a new Mount Zion as a "heavenly Jerusalem"[17] welcoming all believers.

6. The **Temple** is the architectural sign of the Davidic covenant, a building where all people of the earth were invited to worship the God of Israel. It is a place of international family reunion. As we'll see in the next chapter, it was even built by Gentiles: the talented Phoenician artists and craftsmen sent by King Hiram of Tyre.

7. Wisdom is the new law of the Davidic covenant. Solomon, David's son, would be given wisdom to govern. Wisdom literature is to the Davidic covenant what the Pentateuch was to the Mosaic covenant. "Thou hast shown me the law for man," David says in 2 Samuel 7:19.[18] "Law" is "Torah"— the name Jewish tradition gave to the five books of Moses. And "Adam" is used to mean all mankind. In other words, God has revealed to David a Torah for Adam—a law for all mankind. David's son is going to get something more than Moses got: a law for every nation, not just for the people of Israel. We'll read more about that new law in the next chapter of this book.

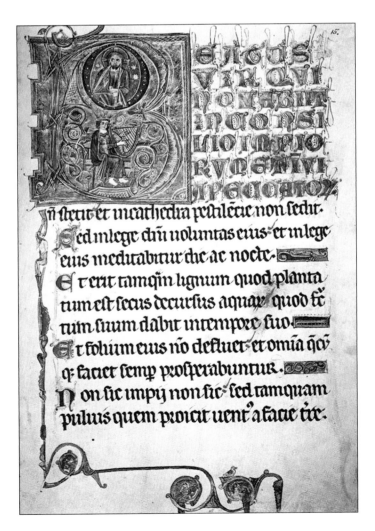

"Blessed is the man who walks not in the counsel of the wicked,..." (Ps 1: 1f.)

An illuminated page from the Psalter of St. Margaret of Hungary, ca.1261, open to Psalm 1. The first initial B of the text is the most beautifully decorated letter in the manuscript showing Christ in the upper half and King David playing his harp in the lower half.

The Davidic Covenant In Psalm 89

Of old thou didst speak in a vision to thy
 faithful one, and say:
"I have set the crown upon one who is mighty,
 I have exalted one chosen from the people.
I have found David, my servant;
 with my holy oil I have anointed him;
so that my hand shall ever abide with him,
 my arm also shall strengthen him.
The enemy shall not outwit him,
 the wicked shall not humble him.
I will crush his foes before him
 and strike down those who hate him.
My faithfulness and my steadfast love shall be with him,
 and in my name shall his horn be exalted.
I will set his hand on the sea
 and his right hand on the rivers.
He shall cry to me, 'Thou art my Father,
 My God, and the Rock of my salvation.'
And I will make him the first-born,
 the highest of the kings of the earth.
My steadfast love I will keep for him for ever,
 and my covenant will stand firm for him.
I will establish his line for ever
 and his throne as the days of the heavens.
If his children forsake my law
 and do not walk according to my ordinances,
if they violate my statutes
 and do not keep my commandments,
then I will punish their transgression with the rod
 and their iniquity with scourges;
but I will not remove from him my steadfast love,
 or be false to my faithfulness.
I will not violate my covenant,
 or alter the word that went forth from my lips.
Once for all I have sworn by my holiness;
 I will not lie to David.
His line shall endure for ever,
 his throne as long as the sun before me.
Like the moon it shall be established for ever;
 it shall stand firm while the skies endure."

(Ps 89: 19-37)

The Davidic Covenant: Three Secondary Features

Besides those seven primary features of the Davidic Covenant, we can also see three secondary features that will become very important under the New Covenant.

1. The **Queen Mother** becomes an important part of the royal government. It starts with King Solomon in 1 Kings 2:19:

> So Bathsheba went to King Solomon, to speak to him on behalf of Adonijah. And the king rose to meet her, and bowed down to her; then he sat on his throne, and had a seat brought for the king's mother; and she sat on his right.

Everyone bows before Solomon, but Solomon bows before his mother. From that point on, the Queen Mother becomes a permanent fixture, a symbol of the continuity of David's royal line. She is also one of the king's most important advisers. Proverbs 31 is identified as the advice of the queen mother of King Lemuel: "The words of Lemuel, king of Massa, which his mother taught him." (One Jewish tradition has it that Lemuel was a pseudonym for Solomon himself, in which case these are really the teachings of Bathsheba.)

Of course, the role of Queen Mother will take on much more meaning in the New Testament, when the heir to the throne of David is Jesus Christ, whose mother is **Mary**.

2. The "**prime minister**" or chief steward becomes a distinct office in the royal government. The king has many servants, but one man is chief among them and stands between the king and his other ministers. Almost two centuries after David, Isaiah prophesied a transition in the royal government in which one prime minister would be replaced by another (see Is 22:15-25). From his prophecy, we can tell that everyone in the kingdom could identify the prime minister: "he shall be a father to the inhabitants of Jerusalem and to the house of Judah."[19]

The sign of the prime minister's office is the *keys of the kingdom.* "And I will place on his shoulder the key of the house of David; he shall open, and none shall shut; and he shall shut, and none shall open."[20] Compare that to Jesus' words to **Peter**: "I will give you the keys of the kingdom of heaven, and whatever you bind on earth shall be bound in heaven, and whatever you loose on earth shall be loosed in heaven."[21]

The Davidic Covenant establishes the *Queen Mother* as a symbol of the continuity of David's royal lineage from Bathsheba to Mary.

3. The **thank offering** or "sacrifice of thanksgiving" becomes the primary liturgy celebrated at Temple, rather than the sin offering.

> Do I eat the flesh of bulls,
> > or drink the blood of goats?
> Offer to God a sacrifice of thanksgiving,
> > and pay your vows to the Most High;
> and call upon me in the day of trouble;
> > I will deliver you, and you shall glorify me. (Ps 50:13-15)

> For thou hast delivered my soul from death,
> > my eyes from tears,
> > my feet from stumbling...
> I will offer to thee the sacrifice of thanksgiving
> > and call on the name of the LORD.
> I will pay my vows to the LORD
> > in the presence of all his people,
> in the courts of the house of the LORD,
> > in your midst, O Jerusalem. (Ps 116:8, 17-19)

The thank offering is unleavened bread and wine freely offered to God in gratitude for deliverance. Ancient Jewish teachers predicted that, when the Messiah came, no other sacrifice would be offered: the thank offering alone would continue.

The word for "thank offering" is "**todah**" in Hebrew, which was later translated as "**eucharistia**" by Greek-speaking Jews.

Summary: The Main Features of the Davidic Covenant

Seven Primary Features:

1. God gives David a **kingdom**.

2. God promises David a **dynasty**.

3. The king becomes **God's adopted son** when he is anointed.

4. The covenant is **unlimited** in time and space.

5. **Jerusalem** is the spiritual center of the world.

6. The **Temple** is the architectural sign of the covenant.

7. **Wisdom** literature is the new Torah.

Three Secondary Features:

1. The **Queen Mother** becomes an important figure.

2. The **prime minister** is a permanent feature of the government.

3. The **thank offering** becomes the primary liturgy celebrated at the Temple.

The Davidic Covenant establishes the *prime minister* to stand between the King and the other ministers. The sign of the office is *the keys of the kingdom.*

SUPPLEMENTARY READING

Augustine, *City of God*, Book XVII

He who thinks this grand promise was fulfilled in Solomon greatly errs; for he attends to the saying, "He shall build me a house," but he does not attend to the saying, "His house shall be faithful, and his kingdom for evermore before me." Let him therefore attend and behold the house of Solomon full of strange women worshiping false gods, and the king himself, aforetime wise, seduced by them, and cast down into the same idolatry: and let him not dare to think that God either promised this falsely, or was unable to foreknow that Solomon and his house would become what they did. But we ought not to be in doubt here, or to see the fulfillment of these things save in Christ our Lord, who was made of the seed of David according to the flesh, lest we should vainly and uselessly look for some other here, like the carnal Jews. For even they understand this much, that the son whom they read of in that place as promised to David was not Solomon; so that, with wonderful blindness to Him who was promised and is now declared with so great manifestation, they say they hope for another. Indeed, even in Solomon there appeared some image of the future event, in that he built the temple, and had peace according to his name (for Solomon means "pacific"), and in the beginning of his reign was wonderfully praiseworthy; but while, as a shadow of Him that should come, he foreshowed Christ our Lord, he did not also in his own person resemble Him. Whence some things concerning him are so written as if they were prophesied of himself, while the Holy Scripture, prophesying even by events, somehow delineates in him the figure of things to come. For, besides the books of divine history, in which his reign is narrated, the 72nd Psalm also is inscribed in the title with his name, in which so many things are said which cannot at all apply to him, but which apply to the Lord Christ with such evident fitness as makes it quite apparent that in the one the figure is in some way shadowed forth, but in the other the truth itself is presented. For it is known within what bounds the kingdom of Solomon was enclosed; and yet in that Psalm, not to speak of other things, we read, "He shall have dominion from sea even to sea, and from the river to the ends of the earth," which we see fulfilled in Christ. Truly he took the beginning of His reigning from the river where John baptized; for, when pointed out by him, He began to be acknowledged by the disciples, who called Him not only Master, but also Lord.

A page from the Duc de Berry's Psalter, 1402, painted by the Flemish artist, Beauneveu. The illustration shows King David on a great throne playing his harp.

VOCABULARY

CHASTEN

To punish for the purpose of correcting. God promised that he would chasten David's successors when they needed it, but never abandon them.

EUCHARIST

Greek for "thank offering." See Thank Offering.

JEBUSITES

The Canaanite inhabitants of Jerusalem, whom the Israelites had not conquered up to the time of David.

JERUSALEM

A Canaanite city conquered by David that became the capital and religious center of Israel.

JOAB

An Israelite general who became David's prime minister by being the first to strike the Jebusites in Jerusalem.

NATHAN

A prophet. One of David's chief advisors.

PRIME MINISTER

A servant of the king who oversees all the affairs of the kingdom; the king's most trusted advisor.

QUEEN MOTHER

The mother of the reigning king. Under David and his successors, the Queen Mother was a very influential figure in the kingdom.

THANK OFFERING

A sacrifice made in thanksgiving for God's deliverance. Under David and his successors, it became the primary liturgy of the Temple.

ZION

The hill on which the oldest part of Jerusalem was built. A poetic name for the city of Jerusalem.

STUDY QUESTIONS

1. Who was Ishbaal?

2. Why did David decide to live in Jerusalem?

3. Why did David fail to bring the Ark of the Covenant into Jerusalem the first time?

4. Why was David able to perform sacrifices and dress like a priest when his predecessor Saul had been punished for sacrificing?

5. Why did David want to build a temple?

6. Who was Nathan?

7. List the six promises God made in his covenant with David.

8. According to point 2579 of the CCC, how was David's prayer a model for the prayer of his people?

9. Study the chart comparing the Sinai covenant and the Zion covenant found in this chapter. List three ways in which the Zion covenant is more universal than the Sinai covenant.

10. List the primary features of the Davidic covenant.

11. List its secondary features.

12. What was the sign of the prime minister's office under the Davidic covenant?

13. What is the Thank offering?

14. What is the difference between a kingdom and a nation?

15. What important New Testament event takes place on Mount Zion?

16. How does this sign help us to recognize Peter as Christ's "prime minister"?

PRACTICAL EXERCISES

1. When David first tried to have the Ark of the Covenant brought to Jerusalem he did not prepare properly and disaster resulted. A man was killed when he disrespectfully reached out to touch the ark. As the sign of God's presence among the chosen people, the ark needed to be treated with a great respect. What sacrament did Jesus Christ give the Church in order that we might have God's presence with us today? Whenever we enter a church or attend Mass, what signs of respect should we show toward our Lord in the Precious Sacrament in the tabernacle or on the altar? What are some ways in which the tabernacle is like the Ark of the Covenant?

2. One of the three secondary features of the Davidic covenant is that the Queen Mother becomes an important part of the royal government. In the New Testament, Jesus is the heir to David's throne and Mary is his Queen Mother. The *Catechism of the Catholic Church* states: "'The Church's devotion to the Blessed Virgin is intrinsic to Christian worship' (Lk 1: 48; Paul VI, MC 56). 'The Church rightly honors the Blessed Virgin with special devotion'" (LG 66) (CCC 971). What are some ways you can increase your devotion to Mary? Find a book of prayers and learn a new prayer to Mary such as "Hail Holy Queen" or the "Memorare."

This miniature of King David praying is from the Gradual of the Archbishop of Esztergom, Hungary, ca. 1520.

Endnotes

1. 2 Sm 2: 8-10.
2. 2 Sm 4: 5-12.
3. 2 Sm 5: 6.
4. 1 Chr 11: 6.
5. Ex 25: 13-15; 1 Chr 15: 15.
6. Nm 4: 15.
7. 1 Chr 15: 13.
8. 1 Chr 15.
9. 2 Sm 6: 14.
10. 2 Sm 6: 20.
11. 2 Sm 6: 21-22.
12. 2 Sm 7: 2-3.
13. 2 Sm 7: 5-6.
14. We have preferred the translators' alternate reading, rather than the hypothetical correction of the Hebrew text.
15. Ps 110: 4.
16. Acts 1: 8.
17. Heb 12: 22.
18. See the footnote reading in the RSV. The translators' preferred reading, "thou... hast shown me future generations," is based on a hypothetical correction of the Hebrew text.
19. Is 22: 21.
20. Is 22: 22.
21. Mt 16: 19.
22. Many scholars believe that the direction "Selah," which appears here in the psalm, indicates an instrumental interlude.

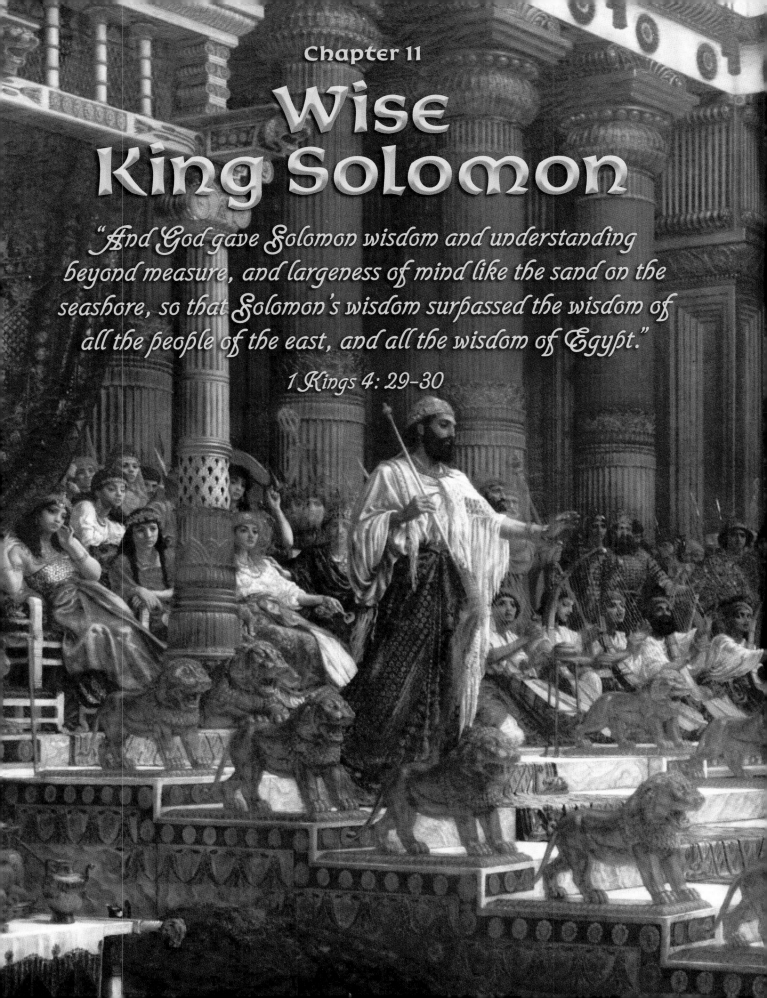

Chapter 11
Wise King Solomon

"And God gave Solomon wisdom and understanding beyond measure, and largeness of mind like the sand on the seashore, so that Solomon's wisdom surpassed the wisdom of all the people of the east, and all the wisdom of Egypt."

1 Kings 4: 29–30

Chapter 11
Wise King Solomon

Read

2 Chronicles
1:1 - 2:6

1 Kings 10:1-10
11:1 - 13

Proverbs 10

After David died and Solomon was firmly established on the throne, God appeared to Solomon in a dream.

> In that night God appeared to Solomon, and said to him, "Ask what I shall give you." And Solomon said to God, "Thou hast shown great and steadfast love to David my father, and hast made me king in his stead. O LORD God, let thy promise to David my father be now fulfilled, for thou hast made me king over a people as many as the dust of the earth. Give me now wisdom and knowledge to go out and come in before these people, for who can rule this thy people, that is so great?" (2 Chr 1: 7-10)

Solomon might have asked for anything: wealth, power, or even revenge on his enemies. Instead, he asked only for the wisdom to govern the people God had set him over as king.

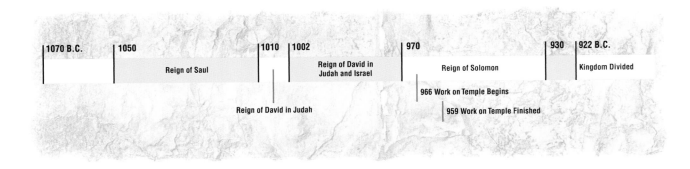

1070 B.C.	1050		1010	1002		970		930	922 B.C.
		Reign of Saul			Reign of David in Judah and Israel		Reign of Solomon		Kingdom Divided
			Reign of David in Judah			966 Work on Temple Begins			
						959 Work on Temple Finished			

God answered Solomon, "Because this was in your heart, and you have not asked for possessions, wealth, honor, or the life of those who hate you, and have not even asked long life, but have asked wisdom and knowledge for yourself that you may rule my people over whom I have made you king, wisdom and knowledge are granted to you. I will also give you riches, possessions, and honor, such as none of the kings had who were before you, and none after you shall have the like." (2 Chr 1:11-12)

God would give Solomon the wisdom he asked for, and also all the good things he didn't ask for. He would be legendary for his wealth and power, but more than anything else he would be the symbol of wisdom for all the ages.

Jerusalem In The Time Of David And Solomon, ca. 1010-930 B.C.

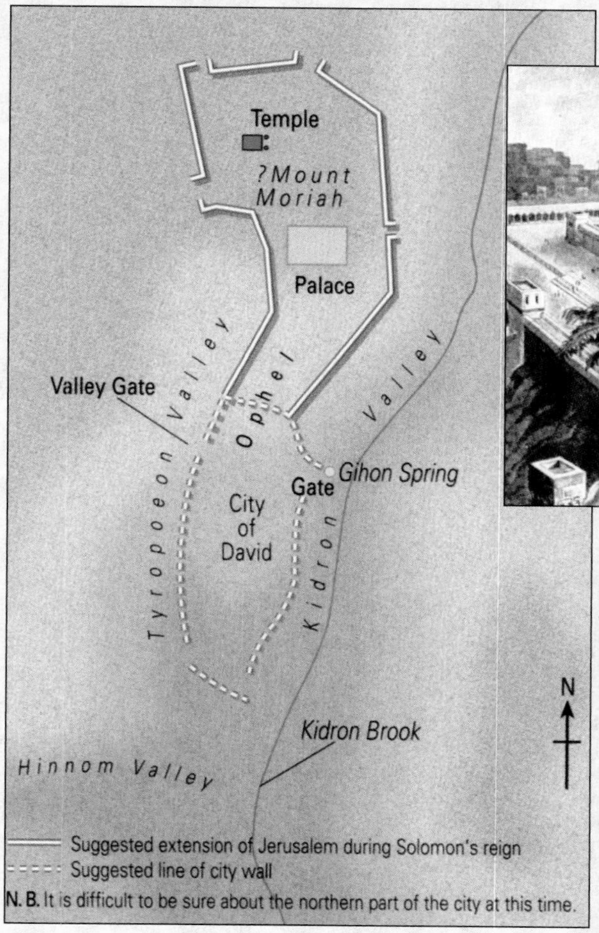

Temple

?Mount Moriah

Palace

Valley Gate

Ophel

Gihon Spring

Gate

City of David

Tyropoeon Valley

Kidron Valley

Kidron Brook

Hinnom Valley

N

——— Suggested extension of Jerusalem during Solomon's reign
------- Suggested line of city wall
N. B. It is difficult to be sure about the northern part of the city at this time.

The Temple Mount, (the location of Araunah's Threshing-floor purchased by David and used by Solomon as the site of the Temple), appears to have been north of the original Zion. It is traditionally associated with Mount Moriah. The Moriah of David's day is the central portion of the eastern hill. The term Zion, initially used to describe the Jebusite fortress to the south, came to be applied to the Temple Mount as well.

Ophel is the name given to the southern extremity of the Temple Mount. South of Ophel was the original Jebusite city of Mount Zion.

Imperial Israel

Solomon's kingdom was an international empire. David's military success had enlarged the borders of Israel considerably, and Solomon's reputation for wisdom and wealth would draw visitors and traders from many nations. "Judah and Israel were as many as the sand by the sea; they ate and drank and were happy."[1]

The new power and wealth of Israel quickly caught the attention of its powerful neighbors.

> Solomon made a marriage alliance with Pharaoh king of Egypt; he took Pharaoh's daughter, and brought her into the city of David, until he had finished building his own house and the house of the LORD and the wall around Jerusalem. (1 Kgs 3:1)

Solomon's marriage to Pharaoh's daughter is almost unique in Egyptian history. Other nations sent their sons and daughters to the court of Pharaoh, but Pharaoh never sent his daughters to a foreign court. Probably Egypt expected Israel to be a great new power, and wanted to share part of the power. Solomon was showing every sign of being an ambitious empire-builder. If a new empire arose between Egypt and Assyria, it would be vitally important for Pharaoh to make sure that the new power was allied with Egypt, not with Assyria.

But Pharaoh's daughter was far from the only marriage alliance Solomon made. We also read that Solomon had 700 wives and 300 concubines. Those are symbolically perfect numbers. They show that Solomon had intermarried with all the nations, that he had in some way extended his dominion to the ends of the earth.

However, polygamy—even on such a grand scale—never comes without a penalty in the Bible. Solomon's harem might have been a symbol of his glory and international stature, but the foreign wives would also lead him away from God who had given him all that glory.

As Solomon's reputation grew, Israel sent traders all over the known world. Solomon also built a substantial navy and made Israel a sea power.

But the international contact that would be most remembered was the visit of the Queen of Sheba. From a faraway land in the south, a land of legendary wealth and splendor, the Queen of Sheba came to see if Solomon was really as wise as people said he was. She probably also had a trading alliance in mind. We read that "she came to test him with hard questions." Asking riddles was a common game among royalty in the Near East, and no one could beat Solomon's answers.

> She came to Jerusalem with a very great retinue, with camels bearing spices, and very much gold, and precious stones; and when she came to Solomon, she told him all that was on her mind. And Solomon answered all her questions; there was nothing hidden from the king which he could not explain to her. (1 Kgs 10:2-3)

Solomon's United Kingdom, ca. 970 B.C.

Solomon was heir to an empire formed largely through the leadership of his father David. Solomon reorganized the kingdom into twelve provinces (1 Kings 4:7-19).

Solomon is said to have ruled from the Euphrates to the border of Egypt (1 Kings 4:21). The Aramaean states as well as Edom and Moab regularly presented tribute to Solomon at Jerusalem.

Solomon's control of Zobah, Damascus, Ammon, Moab and Edom gave him a monopoly of the caravan routes between Arabia and the North.

Solomon's harem of a thousand wives and concubines represented alliances sealed by a marriage (1 Kings 11:1-8).

United kingdom of Israel and Judah
Vassal kingdoms
— — Boundary of Solomon's empire
– – – Boundary of administrative district
⊚ Solomonic fortification or building project

0   25   50 km
0   10   20   30 miles

The Wisdom Of Solomon

The visit of the Queen of Sheba shows us the international invitation of the Davidic Covenant at work. Under Solomon, Israel had grown into a power that all the nations of the world had to reckon with. But the reason for the Davidic kingdom was not creating an earthly empire, but drawing all the world to Zion. Israel never became more than a small empire, but its religion spread to all the nations. Jerusalem never grew to be a great metropolis, but it gave hope to all the world.

It was the wisdom of Solomon that began drawing the nations to God. We see how it worked in the reaction of the Queen of Sheba:

> And she said to the king, "The report was true which I heard in my own land of your affairs and of your wisdom, but I did not believe it until I came and my own eyes had seen it, and, behold, the half was not told me; your wisdom and prosperity surpass the report which I had.... Blessed be the LORD your God, who has delighted in you and set you on the throne of Israel! Because the LORD loved Israel for ever, he has made you king, that you may execute justice and righteousness." (1 Kgs 10: 6-7, 9)

Solomon's power and glory, but most of all his wisdom, led the pagan Queen of Sheba to praise the God of Israel. That was the ultimate purpose of the Davidic kingdom—not to give the people of Israel power and glory (which they didn't deserve any more than we do), but to draw all peoples to God. "And the whole earth sought the presence of Solomon to hear his wisdom, which God had put into his mind."[2]

The wisdom of the Davidic kingdom was expressed in one of the four main classes of Old Testament literature: wisdom literature. Much of the wisdom literature in the Bible is attributed to Solomon; some of it was almost certainly written by him, and some was written by other wise people in the character of Solomon, who was the symbol of all wisdom. That wisdom literature would be the new law for all mankind that God had promised to David.

The book of Proverbs is a good example of wisdom literature. It consists of several collections of wise sayings, some of them Solomon's and some by other wise people—including the only whole chapter in the Bible definitely identified as written by a woman, Proverbs 31.

In Proverbs, scholars find some sections that resemble or even quote from the wisdom literature of other nations. Why would the divinely inspired Hebrew writers quote from the pagan authors of Egypt and Babylon?

First, all wisdom is from God. A true believer never rejects wisdom, no matter where it is found.

But there is an important reason for quoting from the best literature of other nations. Wisdom literature is the new law—the new Torah—of the Davidic covenant. And the whole purpose of the Davidic kingdom is to draw all nations to God. Wisdom literature speaks to the nations in familiar terms, using some of the other nations' favorite proverbs to emphasize the truth that "The fear of the LORD is the beginning of wisdom, and the knowledge of the Holy One is insight" (Prv 9:10).

> And God gave Solomon wisdom and understanding beyond measure, and largeness of mind like the sand on the seashore, so that Solomon's wisdom surpassed the wisdom of all the people of the east, and all the wisdom of Egypt. (1 Kgs 4:29-30)

Solomon's wisdom was greater than the wisdom of Egypt and Babylon, but it was wisdom of the same kind. The wisdom literature of the Davidic kingdom was in the main stream of international philosophy. And because it spoke to the nations in familiar terms, it could lead the main stream of their thought into a new channel. Through their own wisdom traditions, it prepared them to receive the Good News of the Kingdom of God.

Solomon Builds the Temple

Of all Solomon's accomplishments, the one the people of Israel would most remember was the Temple. It was the architectural sign of their covenant with God, the place where God's glory dwelt among them.

David had prepared the way, buying the land for the Temple and providing for much of the Temple liturgy. But it was his son who would supervise the building itself.

Israel had grown suddenly glorious—so suddenly that there were no artists and craftsmen up to the task of building a structure as magnificent as the one Solomon imagined. So he turned to his father David's old friend King Hiram of Tyre, a king who also had a reputation for outstanding wisdom and glory. King Hiram sent materials and the skilled Phoenician craftsmen to work them. Thus the Temple of God, the center of the worship of Israel, was actually built by Gentiles.

It would also be a place of welcome for Gentile worshipers. At the dedication of the Temple, Solomon prayed for his people Israel. But he also prayed for the people of the rest of the world.

> Likewise when a foreigner, who is not of thy people Israel, comes from a far country for thy name's sake (for they shall hear of thy great name, and thy mighty hand, and of thy outstretched arm), when he comes and prays toward this house, hear thou in heaven thy dwelling place, and do according to all for which the foreigner calls to thee; in order that all the peoples of the earth may know thy name and fear thee, as do thy people Israel, and that they may know that this house which I have built is called by thy name. (1 Kgs 8:21-43)

Solomon's prayer is that the Temple will become "a house of prayer for all peoples," as a later prophet would say in Isaiah 56:7.

> The Temple of Jerusalem, the house of prayer that David wanted to build, will be the work of his son, Solomon. The prayer at the dedication of the Temple relies on God's promise and covenant, on the active presence of his name among his People, recalling his mighty deeds at the Exodus (1 Kgs 8:10-61). The king lifts his hands toward heaven and begs the LORD, on his own behalf, on behalf of the entire people, and of the generations yet to come, for the forgiveness of their sins and for their daily needs, so that the nations may know that He is the only God and that the heart of his people may belong wholly and entirely to him. (CCC 2580)

Ancient traditions tell us more of what the people of Israel believed about their Temple. Solomon built the house of God on a rock, an enormous rocky outcropping outside the City of David. The rock was so immense that local legend said it was the gate of Sheol, the underworld—what the Greeks would call Hades. According to that tradition, Solomon's temple sealed off the underworld, and the gates of Hades could not prevail against it.

Tradition also says that the Temple was built on the very spot where Abraham prepared to offer Isaac as a sacrifice.

When the building was finally finished, Solomon assembled all the leaders of Israel and had the priests bring the Ark of the Covenant from the tent to the Temple.

> And when the priests came out of the holy place, a cloud filled the house of the LORD, so that the priests could not stand to minister because of the cloud; for the glory of the LORD filled the house of the LORD. (1 Kgs 8:10-11)

A model of Herod's Temple started in 19 B.C. and completed in 62 A.D. Scholars believe that Herod followed the exact dimensions and instructions for building and furnishing the Temple given to Solomon by the Lord in 1 Kings 6-7.

Building Materials for Solomon's Temple

Cutting down the Cedars of Lebanon

"And so I purpose to build a house for the name of the LORD my God, as the LORD said to David my father,...Now therefore command that cedars of Lebanon be cut for me;..." (1 Kgs 5:5-6)

Today, the last of the Cedars of Lebanon are protected and cherished as a link with the Old Testament and ancient civilizations. The wood was the finest in the Middle East and used by many nations for buildings and sailing vessels. It had an elegant dark-red color, a sweet fragrance, and a durability that made it an ideal building material.

Solomon bought these beautiful trees from King Hiram of Tyre. Ten thousand men were sent to cut the trees and transport them to the sea where they were floated to the port of Joppa, then dragged to Jerusalem to be cut into pillars, beams and wood panels.

Stone for the building probably came from what is known today as King Solomon's Quarry, a deep cavern beneath the Old City of Jerusalem. It extends for hundreds of meters below the surface of the city in the direction of the Temple Mount. The type of stone found in the cave is a white limestone locally known as melech, or "royal" stone.

Because of the cavern's depth, the sound of tools would not have been heard at the construction site of King Solomon's Temple, on the Temple Mount. "When the house was built, it was with stone prepared at the quarry; so that neither hammer nor axe nor any tool of iron was heard in the temple, while it was being built." (1 Kgs 6:7)

Solomon's Pride And Apostasy

Solomon's glory was the talk of the world. But all that glory did not come without a price. It took crushing taxes to pay for Solomon's ambitious building projects, and tens of thousands of Israelites were forced into laboring for their king. People began to grumble that Solomon's glory was only making them miserable. Worse than that, it could even be called unconstitutional. Deuteronomy, the basic law of Israel's government, was very specific about what a king must not do:

> Only he must not multiply horses for himself, or cause the people to return to Egypt to multiply horses, since the LORD has said to you, "You shall never return that way again." And he shall not multiply wives for himself, lest his heart turn away; nor shall he greatly multiply for himself silver and gold. (Dt 17:16-17)

Solomon's stables were the envy of the world; in fact, he lavished so much expense on caring for his horses that tour guides still point out the remains of Solomon's stables today. (Nothing remains of either his Temple or his palace.) With seven hundred wives and three hundred concubines, Solomon could hardly deny that he had multiplied wives for himself. And Solomon's wealth was so legendary that even today the search for King Solomon's lost gold mines is a popular theme in novels and movies.

In fact, Solomon had become exactly the sort of King Samuel had predicted years before:

> So Samuel told all the words of the LORD to the people who were asking a king from him. He said, "These will be the ways of the king who will reign over you: he will take your sons and appoint them to his chariots and to be his horsemen, and to run before his chariots;

and he will appoint for himself commanders of thousands and commanders of fifties, and some to plow his ground and to reap his harvest, and to make his implements of war and the equipment of his chariots. He will take your daughters to be perfumers and cooks and bakers. He will take the best of your fields and vineyards and olive orchards and give them to his servants. He will take the tenth of your grain and of your vineyards and give it to his officers and to his servants. He will take your menservants and maidservants, and the best of your cattle and your asses, and put them to his work. He will take the tenth of your flocks, and you shall be his slaves. And in that day you will cry out because of your king, whom you have chosen for yourselves; but the LORD will not answer you in that day."

But the people refused to listen to the voice of Samuel; and they said, "No! but we will have a king over us, that we also may be like all the nations, and that our king may govern us and go out before us and fight our battles." (1 Sm 8:10-20)

But Solomon's wives were the most unbearable burden. He had married many women from the surrounding nations, the nations God's people had been warned to have nothing to do with.

For when Solomon was old his wives turned away his heart after other gods; and his heart was not wholly true to the LORD his God, as was the heart of David his father. For Solomon went after Ashtoreth the goddess of the Sidonians, and after Milcom the abomination of the Ammonites. So Solomon did what was evil in the sight of the LORD, and did not wholly follow the LORD, as David his father had done. (1 Kgs 11:4-6)

Solomon's wives persuaded him to build temples to their gods in the suburbs of Jerusalem. Instead of drawing the Gentiles to worship the True God, Solomon was drawing his own people to worship foreign gods. Israel would soon pay the price for Solomon's weakness.

The Idol Gods Of Solomon's Wives

Ashtoreth was the goddess of love and fertility. She was worshiped throughout Palestine and other countries. She is thought by some to be Athtar or Ishtar, a universal goddess named after the planet Venus.

Chemosh was the Moabite's national god. Solomon built a shrine for Chemosh which was later destroyed by King Josiah. Chemosh was similar to Molech in attributes and the burnt offering of children.

Molech was the national god of the Ammonites. Children were also sacrificed in his worship.

"Then Solomon built a high place for Chemosh the abomination of Moab, and for Molech the abomination of the Ammonites on the mountain east of Jerusalem. And so he did for all his foreign wives, who burned incense and sacrificed to their gods." (1 Kgs 11:7-8)

Molech the national god of Ammon

SUPPLEMENTARY READING

John Paul II, *Fides et Ratio*

21. For the Old Testament, knowledge is not simply a matter of careful observation of the human being, of the world and of history, but supposes as well an indispensable link with faith and with what has been revealed. These are the challenges which the Chosen People had to confront and to which they had to respond. Pondering this as his situation, biblical man discovered that he could understand himself only as "being in relation"—with himself, with people, with the world and with God. This opening to the mystery, which came to him through Revelation, was for him, in the end, the source of true knowledge. It was this which allowed his reason to enter the realm of the infinite where an understanding for which until then he had not dared to hope became a possibility.

For the sacred author, the task of searching for the truth was not without the strain which comes once the limits of reason are reached. This is what we find, for example, when the Book of Proverbs notes the weariness which comes from the effort to understand the mysterious designs of God (cf. 30:1-6). Yet, for all the toil involved, believers do not surrender. They can continue on their way to the truth because they are certain that God has created them "explorers" (cf. Eccl 1:13), whose mission it is to leave no stone unturned, though the temptation to doubt is always there. Leaning on God, they continue to reach out, always and everywhere, for all that is beautiful, good and true.

22. In the first chapter of his Letter to the Romans, Saint Paul helps us to appreciate better the depth of insight of the Wisdom literature's reflection. Developing a philosophical argument in popular language, the Apostle declares a profound truth: through all that is created the "eyes of the mind" can come to know God. Through the medium of creatures, God stirs in reason an intuition of his "power" and his "divinity" (cf. Rom 1:20). This is to concede to human reason a capacity which seems almost to surpass its natural limitations. Not only is it not restricted to sensory knowledge, from the moment that it can reflect critically upon the data of the senses, but, by discoursing on the data provided by the senses, reason can reach the cause which lies at the origin of all perceptible reality. In philosophical terms, we could say that this important Pauline text affirms the human capacity for metaphysical enquiry.

According to the Apostle, it was part of the original plan of the creation that reason should without difficulty reach beyond the sensory data to the origin of all things: the Creator.

"And Solomon said to God,... 'O Lord God, let thy promise to David my father be now fulfilled, for thou hast made me king over a people as many as the dust of the earth.'"
(2 Chr 1:7-9)

VOCABULARY

APOSTASY
Turning away from the true religion.

ASHTORETH
A pagan fertility goddess worshiped by Solomon in his later years.

GENTILE
A member of any of the nations outside Israel.

MILCOM
One of the many pagan gods worshiped by Solomon in his later years.

PAGAN
One who follows a false religion, worshiping many gods instead of the True God.

SHEBA, QUEEN OF
The queen of a wealthy country to the south. She came to Jerusalem to test Solomon's wisdom, which led her to praise the God of Israel, demonstrating the kingdom's role in leading the nations to the True God.

SHEOL
The Hebrew name for the underworld.

SOLOMON
The son of David who inherited his kingdom and God's covenant. He led Israel to its greatest glory, and was famous for his wisdom.

TEMPLE
The house of God in Jerusalem, which contained the Ark of the Covenant. When the Temple was dedicated, God's glory overshadowed it just as it had done in the Tabernacle. The Temple became the center of worship for Israel.

STUDY QUESTIONS

1. What did Solomon choose when God offered him anything he wished for?

2. With what nation did Solomon make an important and unusual alliance by marriage?

3. How many wives did Solomon have?

4. How many concubines?

5. What did the number of Solomon's wives and concubines indicate?

6. How did Solomon draw other nations to God?

7. What was the ultimate purpose of the Davidic kingdom?

8. Give one reason why the book of Proverbs would contain quotes from other nations' writings.

9. Where did the craftsmen who built the Temple come from?

10. At the dedication of the Temple, who did Solomon pray for?

11. Who was allowed to worship in the Temple?

12. According to legend, what did Solomon's temple accomplish?

13. What did tradition believe about the rock under Solomon's temple?

14. Into what sin did Solomon's wives lead him?

15. Whose prophecy did King Solomon fulfill?

PRACTICAL EXERCISES

1. When God asked Solomon what he wanted from him, all Solomon requested was wisdom enough to rule God's people. In return for his unselfishness, God granted him wisdom and promised him wealth and power beyond any of the other kings of Israel. How did Solomon's wisdom and power bring others to God? How did this spreading of the faith help to fulfill the Davidic covenant? What does God expect us to do with the talents he has given us?

2. Why is it significant that the craftsmen who built the Temple came from a nation outside the chosen people? What does that fact help to reveal about God's purpose for the Temple in the Davidic covenant?

3. Solomon's wealth and power, though they had been instrumental in bringing many different people to God, ended up leading him into sin and idolatry. His many wives convinced him to build pagan temples and ended up turning his heart away from God. Solomon gives us an example of both the great good and the great evil that can come from wealth and power. How would a spirit of poverty have helped Solomon as he wielded his power as king? What are some ways in which we can limit ourselves in earthly possessions? How might this help us stay more focused on God?

The Judgment of Solomon
"Then the king answered and said, 'Give the living child to the first woman, and by no means slay it; she is its mother.'" (1 Kgs 3: 27)

Endnotes

1. 1 Kgs 4: 20.
2. 1 Kgs 11: 24.

The Divided Kingdom

"*I have been very jealous for the Lord, the God of hosts; for the people of Israel have forsaken thy covenant, thrown down thy altars, and slain thy prophets . . . and I, even I only, am left; . . .*"

1 Kings 19: 10

Chapter 12
The Divided Kingdom

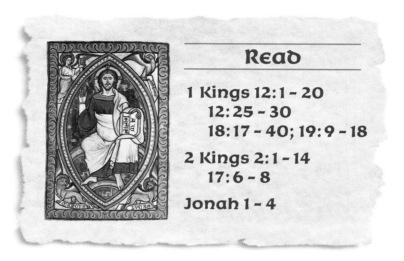

Read

1 Kings 12:1 - 20
12:25 - 30
18:17 - 40; 19:9 - 18

2 Kings 2:1 - 14
17:6 - 8

Jonah 1 - 4

Solomon's reign was Israel's peak of glory. But his taxes and forced labor were making him unpopular with his subjects. Worse yet, his apostasy demanded chastisement from God.

The pride and idolatry of Solomon were the seeds of his empire's undoing. Imperial Israel would never again be a leader among the nations. In fact, the empire itself would not survive Solomon's death.

The Torn Kingdom

One of old king Solomon's top ministers was a young man named Jeroboam.

> And at that time, when Jeroboam went out of Jerusalem, the prophet Abijah the Shilonite found him on the road. Now Abijah had clad himself with a new garment; and the two of them were alone in the open country. Then Abijah laid hold of the new garment that was on him, and tore it into twelve pieces. And he said to Jeroboam, "Take for yourself ten

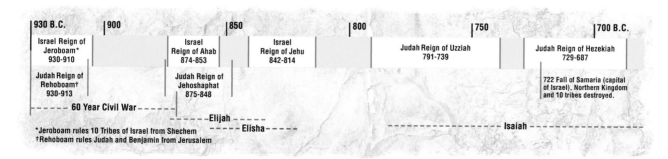

930 B.C.	900		850	800	750	700 B.C.
Israel Reign of Jeroboam* 930-910			Israel Reign of Ahab 874-853	Israel Reign of Jehu 842-814	Judah Reign of Uzziah 791-739	Judah Reign of Hezekiah 729-687
Judah Reign of Rehoboam† 930-913			Judah Reign of Jehoshaphat 875-848			722 Fall of Samaria (capital of Israel), Northern Kingdom and 10 tribes destroyed.

------- 60 Year Civil War ------

----- Elijah -----
----- Elisha -----

-------------------------- Isaiah --------------------------

*Jeroboam rules 10 Tribes of Israel from Shechem
†Rehoboam rules Judah and Benjamin from Jerusalem

pieces, for thus says the LORD, the God of Israel, 'Behold, I am about to tear the kingdom from the hand of Solomon, and will give you ten tribes...because he has forsaken me, and worshiped Ashtoreth the goddess of the Sidonians, Chemosh the god of Moab, and Milcom the god of the Ammonites, and has not walked in my ways, doing what is right in my sight and keeping my statutes and ordinances, as David his father did.'" (1 Kgs 11: 29-33)

When Solomon died, his son Rehoboam was set to succeed him. Rehoboam had grown up in Solomon's magnificent court; he had never known any other life than luxury and idleness.

The people had been suffering under Solomon's policies. Now the elders, with Jeroboam, came to ask Rehoboam if he could take some of the weight off their shoulders. "Your father made our yoke heavy. Now therefore lighten the hard service of your father and his heavy yoke upon us, and we will serve you."[1]

Shechem with Mt. Ebal and Mt. Gerizim. When the kingdom divided, Jeroboam, ruler of the Northern Kingdom, Israel (ten tribes), chose Shechem as his capital. Rehoboam ruled the Southern Kingdom, Judah (Judah and Benjamin), from Jerusalem.

Rehoboam told the elders to come back in three days and he would have an answer for them. Then he turned to the wise old men who had been his father Solomon's counselors. "How do you advise me to answer this people?" he asked them.

"If you will be a servant to this people today and serve them," the wise old men replied, "and speak good words to them when you answer them, then they will be your servants for ever."[2]

That was not really what Rehoboam wanted to hear. He turned to the young men who had grown up with him, the friends who had shared his luxurious and wasted young life at Solomon's court. They told him to take a hard line. So when the elders came back, Rehoboam had this proud answer for them:

"My father made your yoke heavy, but I will add to your yoke; my father chastised you with whips, but I will chastise you with scorpions."[3]

It was exactly the wrong answer. Once again that old rallying cry of rebellion was heard:

> What portion have we in David?
>> We have no inheritance in the son of Jesse.
> To your tents, O Israel!
>> Look now to your own house, David.
>> (1 Kgs 12: 16)

Although Israel had been a united kingdom for more than a century, the tribal traditions were still very important. The large and powerful southern tribe of Judah stayed faithful to its own house of David. But ten tribes rebelled and chose Jeroboam as their king. Aside from Judah, Rehoboam was able to keep control only over the tiny border tribe of Benjamin. Civil war loomed, but at the last minute Rehoboam decided not to try to recover the north. The prophet Shemaiah told him that the division of the kingdom was God's doing, and Rehoboam—perhaps unwilling to risk a war he could never win—backed down.

The kingdom was divided, and it would never be united again.

The Divided Kingdoms Of Israel And Judah, ca. 930 B.C.

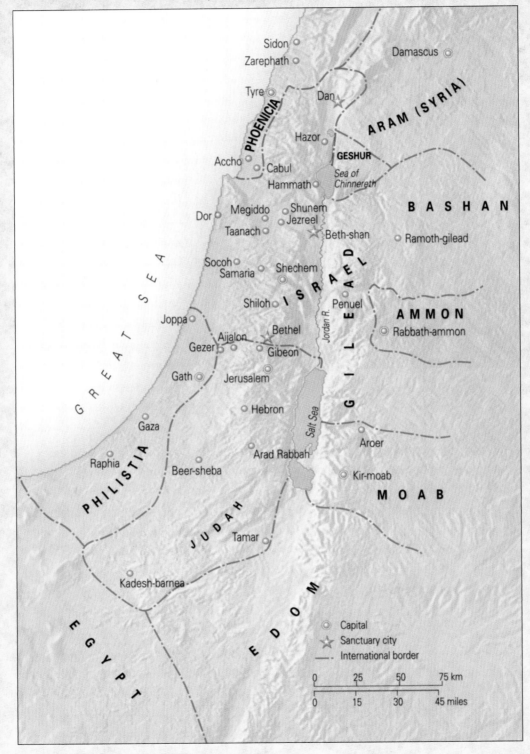

Sidon

Zarephath

Damascus

PHOENICIA

Tyre

Dan

ARAM (SYRIA)

Hazor

GESHUR

Accho

Cabul

Sea of Chinnereth

Hammath

BASHAN

Dor

Megiddo

Shunem

Jezreel

Taanach

Beth-shan

Ramoth-gilead

GREAT SEA

Socoh

Samaria

Shechem

ISRAEL

GILEAD

Shiloh

Penuel

Jordan R.

AMMON

Joppa

Bethel

Rabbath-ammon

Aijalon

Gezer

Gibeon

Gath

Jerusalem

Hebron

Salt Sea

Aroer

Gaza

Kir-moab

Raphia

Arad Rabbah

MOAB

PHILISTIA

Beer-sheba

JUDAH

Tamar

Kadesh-barnea

EDOM

EGYPT

◎ Capital

☆ Sanctuary city

— International border

| 0 | 25 | 50 | 75 km |
| 0 | 15 | 30 | 45 miles |

Back To The Golden Calf

Jeroboam, as the prophet Abijah had made clear, was made king only because it was part of God's plan. But he did not trust God's promises.

> And Jeroboam said in his heart, "Now the kingdom will turn back to the house of David; if the people go up to offer sacrifices in the house of the LORD at Jerusalem, then the heart of this people will turn again to their LORD, to Rehoboam king of Judah, and they will kill me and return to Rehoboam king of Judah." (1 Kgs 12: 26-27)

So instead of trusting in God, Jeroboam made a political decision that would scar the new Kingdom of Israel for centuries.

> So the king took counsel, and made two calves of gold. And he said to the people, "You have gone up to Jerusalem long enough. Behold your gods, O Israel, who brought you up out of the land of Egypt." And he set one in Bethel, and the other he put in Dan. (1 Kgs 12: 28-29)

Israel had gone right back to the Golden Calf! Even the words Jeroboam used were the same words Aaron had used when he dedicated the first Golden Calf in the wilderness (see Ex 32: 4).

God had chosen Jerusalem as the place for his Temple. But Jerusalem was in Judah. To keep the loyalty of his subjects, Jeroboam went back to the sin that had nearly destroyed Israel in the wilderness.

Bull-calf idol from the Ashkelon, a Canaanite city, ca. 2000-1550 B.C.

Good And Bad Kings

Jeroboam's sin set the pattern for the wicked kings of Israel for the rest of its history. From then on, as the books of Kings and Chronicles tell us, both Judah and Israel alternated between good and bad kings.

Good kings, in the sacred authors' way of seeing things, were the ones who reformed worship and led the people back to God. Bad kings introduced foreign gods and sometimes even persecuted true believers.

Both Judah and Israel had their share of bad kings, but Israel had far more bad kings than good. Even the good kings there could never undo the damage Jeroboam had done by setting up golden calves. But at least the golden calves (which were supposed to represent the God of Israel) were better than the horrible Canaanite gods, with their human sacrifices and male and female cult prostitutes.

God did not leave his people without guidance. Prophets rose in Israel and Judah, men and women who were not afraid to denounce the false gods the people were worshiping. It was a dangerous business being a prophet of the True God when the king preferred false gods. Many prophets paid with their lives. But still they spoke out. They couldn't help themselves: God had called them.

King Jeroboam orders the arrest of a prophet. (1 Kgs 13:4)

> If I say, "I will not mention him,
> or speak any more his name,"
> there is in my heart as it were a burning fire
> shut up in my bones,
> and I am weary holding it in,
> and I cannot. (Jer 20:9)

Jonah

In order to understand the literal sense of a biblical text, "it is necessary to understand it according to the literary conventions of the time. When it is a question of a story, the literal sense does not necessarily imply belief that the facts recounted actually took place, for a story need not belong to the genre of history but may be instead a work of imaginative fiction."[4]

The book of Jonah gives us a good idea of how impossible it is to avoid God's call. Jonah was a prophet in the northern kingdom of Israel at a time when the barbaric Assyrians were a constant threat. The story makes its point very clear: that God's mercy overcomes the boundaries of Israel, and that God will be merciful even when his prophets would rather not be.

> Now the word of the LORD came to Jonah the son of Amittai, saying, "Arise, go to Nineveh, that great city, and cry against it; for their wickedness has come up before me." But Jonah rose to flee to Tarshish from the presence of the LORD. He went down to Joppa and found a ship going to Tarshish; so he paid the fare, and went on board, to go with them to Tarshish, away from the presence of the LORD. (Jon 1:1-3)

The last thing Jonah wanted to do was go east to Nineveh, the wicked capital of the hateful Assyrians, and tell them to repent. Like any good Israelite patriot, Jonah wanted to see Nineveh wiped off the face of the earth. He was not a coward: he simply hated the Assyrians, as any good Israelite did, and he wanted them to be destroyed.

So he set off toward Tarshish, which was probably in Spain. It was as far as he could possibly go in the opposite direction. Jonah had a limited opinion of God; he thought he could somehow run away from God's sphere of influence.

But that, of course, is not possible. God sent a "mighty tempest" to toss the ship. The sailors thought they were all going to die; they prayed to their idols, but the storm just got worse. Jonah finally admitted that it was his fault: he had disobeyed God. He made the sailors toss him into the sea, and the tempest stopped immediately.

But God still had plans for Jonah. A great fish swallowed up Jonah and saved his life. For three days he was in the belly of the fish, as good as dead—in fact Jonah says he was in the belly of Sheol, the place of the dead. Then God spoke to the fish, and the fish spit Jonah out onto the land. It was as though he had risen from the dead.

God had not given up on Jonah.

Then the word of the LORD came to Jonah the second time, saying, "Arise, go to Nineveh, that great city, and proclaim to it the message that I tell you." So Jonah arose and went to Nineveh, according to the word of the LORD. (Jon 3:1-3)

This time Jonah had learned his lesson. He went to Nineveh and proclaimed to the people what God had told him to say: "Yet forty days, and Nineveh shall be overthrown!"

Forty days is the symbolic time for serious repentance. God was giving the people of Nineveh time to repent in earnest. And they did. The king made everyone fast and put on sackcloth and ashes, traditional signs of repentance. Even the animals were dressed in sackcloth.

> When God saw what they did, how they turned from their evil way, God repented of the
> evil which he had said he would do to them; and he did not do it. (Jon 3:10)

Jonah's message had had the effect it was supposed to have. And that was exactly what Jonah had been afraid of.

> But it displeased Jonah exceedingly, and he was angry. And he prayed to the LORD, and
> said, "I pray thee, LORD, is not this what I said when I was yet in my own country? That is
> why I made haste to flee to Tarshish; for I knew that thou art a gracious God and merciful,
> slow to anger, and abounding in steadfast love, and repentant of evil. Therefore now, O
> LORD, take my life from me, I beseech thee, for it is better for me to die than to live." And
> the LORD said, "Do you do well to be angry?" (Jon 4:1-4)

Jonah had no answer for that question. Instead, he went out into the hot desert east of the city to sulk.

So God gave him an object lesson. By God's command, a tall plant with big, shady leaves grew over Jonah's head and shaded him from the burning sun. "So Jonah was exceedingly glad because of the plant." But the next day, God sent a worm to eat the base of the plant, and it withered away. The sun beat down on Jonah again, and again he sulked. He just wanted to die.

> But God said to Jonah, "Do you do well to be angry for the plant?" And he said, "I do well to be angry, angry enough to die." And the LORD said, "You pity the plant, for which you did not labor, nor did you make it grow, which came into being in a night, and perished in a night. And should I not pity Nineveh, that great city, in which there are more than a hundred and twenty thousand persons who do not know their right hand from their left, and also much cattle?" (Jon 4: 9-11)

The book ends on that rhetorical question, but we know the answer. The people of Nineveh are worth much more than Jonah's plant. Jonah should not have been angry when God decided to be merciful.

The book of Jonah shows what a prophet had to go through. He had to forget about his own opinions and wants and go where God sent him to say what God told him to say. It was never easy.

Of course, there were false prophets, too. They usually had easy lives. They told the king what he wanted to hear, and the king gave them a good living in return. They lived in ease and comfort, right up to the time when God brought on the judgment that his true prophets had warned of.

Jezebel relentlessly tried to replace the true God with Baal and other pagan deities. Accused of sorcery, she died a brutal death. (2 Kgs 9: 30-37)

Elijah And Jezebel

Of all the wicked kings of Israel, the one most remembered is Ahab—and he is remembered not so much for what he did as for the woman he married. She was a Sidonian princess, an enthusiastic worshiper of the Phoenician god Baal. Her name was Jezebel.

Jezebel persuaded her husband to worship Baal, too. Ahab had a temple of Baal put up in Samaria, the capital of the northern kingdom of Israel. He also set up sacred poles for pagan fertility rites. "Ahab did more to provoke the LORD, the God of Israel, to anger than all the kings of Israel who were before him," says the author of 1 Kings.

Jezebel was not content just to have her god's temple in Samaria. She persecuted the prophets of the true God. The persecution was so terrible that a hundred of the prophets hid in a cave, fed by one of Ahab's ministers who still loved the true God.

To respond to one of the worst of all kings, God sent one of the greatest of all prophets. This is the first we hear of him:

> Now Elijah the Tishbite, of Tishbe in Gilead, said to Ahab, "As the LORD the God of Israel lives, before whom I stand, there shall be neither dew nor rain these years, except by my word." (1 Kgs 17: 1)

The first thing we hear of Elijah—whose name means "The Lord is my God"—is that he was able to stop the rain by his prayer. It would be a convincing demonstration of the power of the True God. But it only made Ahab hate Elijah the more.

Elijah often demonstrated the power of God by miracles. On the run from Jezebel's assassins, he stopped at the house of a poor widow in Zarephath. He asked for something to eat; she told him she had only enough meal and oil for one cake. Because of the drought, a famine had spread over the

land; the widow and her son were about to die of starvation. But Elijah promised her that the meal and oil would last for the duration of the drought, and the widow had plenty from that day on. When the widow's son sickened and died, Elijah's prayer raised him again.[5]

But Elijah's most famous miracle was the contest on Mount Carmel. Elijah challenged 450 prophets of Baal to prove that their god was not real.

The rules were simple. Each side would build an altar and prepare a sacrifice. But no one would light a fire. The real god would send fire down from heaven to light the sacrifice himself. There hadn't been any storms since Elijah shut off the rain, so there was no chance of a random lightning strike.

A huge crowd gathered around to watch the contest. The 450 prophets of Baal went first. From morning till noon they prayed to Baal, but nothing happened. They danced and shouted, but nothing happened. They cut themselves to ribbons and let their blood spill all over the altar, but nothing happened.

Meanwhile, Elijah, the only prophet of God who was brave enough to show his face, stood by and made fun of them. "Cry aloud," he shouted, "for he is a god; either he is musing, or he has gone aside" (which probably was a euphemism for "he had to go to the bathroom"), "or he is on a journey, or perhaps he is asleep and must be wakened."[6]

The prophets of Baal kept shouting and dancing and bleeding till the middle of the afternoon, but nothing happened. Finally Elijah took his turn. He built an altar and prepared the sacrifice; then, to add to the drama of the demonstration, he had the sacrifice soaked with water three times until the whole altar was awash. Then he prayed to God:

> O Lord, God of Abraham, Isaac, and Israel, let it be known this day
> that I am your servant, and that I have done all these things at thy word.
> Answer me, O Lord, answer me, that this people may know that thou,
> O Lord, art God, and that thou hast turned their hearts back. (1 Kgs 18:36-37)

When Elijah had prayed, fire came down from heaven, and the whole altar was incinerated, stones and all. The people were convinced: they fell on their faces shouting, "The Lord, he is God; the Lord, he is God." Then the angry mob, Elijah at their head, killed all the prophets of Baal.

> Elijah is the "father" of the prophets, "the generation of those who seek him, who seek the face of the God of Jacob" (Ps 24:6). Elijah's name, "The Lord is my God," foretells the people's cry in response to his prayer on Mount Carmel (1 Kgs 18:39). St. James refers to Elijah in order to encourage us to pray: "The prayer of the righteous is powerful and effective" (Jas 5:16b-18). (CCC 2582)

Now Elijah told Ahab to eat and drink, for rain was coming. A tiny cloud appeared on the horizon; it grew and grew until at last it was a huge storm that watered the whole land.

Baal, the false god of weather and harvest
worshiped by Ahab and Jezebel.

Above: Elijah raises the widow's son from the dead.

Elijah At Sinai

It looked like a complete triumph for Elijah. But Jezebel was still the real power in the land, and she was not pleased that her god's prophets had been killed. She sent a message telling Elijah he would die like them the next day. Elijah did the only sensible thing: he ran for his life.[7]

Hiding out in the desert, Elijah prayed to God to take away his life. But God still had plans for him. Twice an angel brought him food to eat. "Arise and eat," the angel said, "else the journey will be too great for you." And on the strength of that heavenly food he went forty days and forty nights to Horeb, the mountain in Sinai where Moses had also spent forty days and forty nights. There he saw a vision of God.

> And behold, the LORD passed by, and a great and strong wind rent the mountains, and broke in pieces the rocks before the LORD, but the LORD was not in the wind; and after the wind an earthquake, but the LORD was not in the earthquake; and after the earthquake a fire, but the LORD was not in the fire; and after the fire a still small voice. And when Elijah heard it, he wrapped his face in his mantle and went out and stood at the entrance of the cave. (1 Kgs 19:11-13)

To people who were used to thinking of God in terms of fire and earthquakes and mighty wind, this revelation was something new. God was all-powerful, but the truth about God was in that "still small voice" that Elijah listened to, not in all the fireworks.

> After Elijah had learned mercy during his retreat at the Wadi Cherith, he teaches the widow of Zarephath to believe in The Word of God and confirms her faith by his urgent prayer: God brings the widow's child back to life (cf. 1 Kgs 17:7-24).

> The sacrifice on Mount Carmel is a decisive test for the faith of the People of God. In response to Elijah's plea, "Answer me, O LORD, answer me," the LORD's fire consumes the holocaust, at the time of the evening oblation. The Eastern liturgies repeat Elijah's plea in the Eucharistic *epiclesis*.

> Finally, taking the desert road that leads to the place where the living and true God reveals himself to his people, Elijah, like Moses before him, hides "in a cleft of he rock" until the mysterious presence of God has passed by (cf. 1 Kgs 19:1-14; cf. Ex 33:19-23). But only on the mountain of the Transfiguration will Moses and Elijah behold the unveiled face of him whom they sought; "the light of the knowledge of the glory of God [shines] in the face of Christ," crucified and risen (2 Cor 4:6; cf. Lk 9:30-35). (CCC 2583)

Above: Elijah's Basin with ancient Cyprus trees below the summit of Jebel Musa (Mt. Horeb, Mt. Sinai) where Elijah heard the "still, small voice."

The Journeys Of Elijah And Elisha

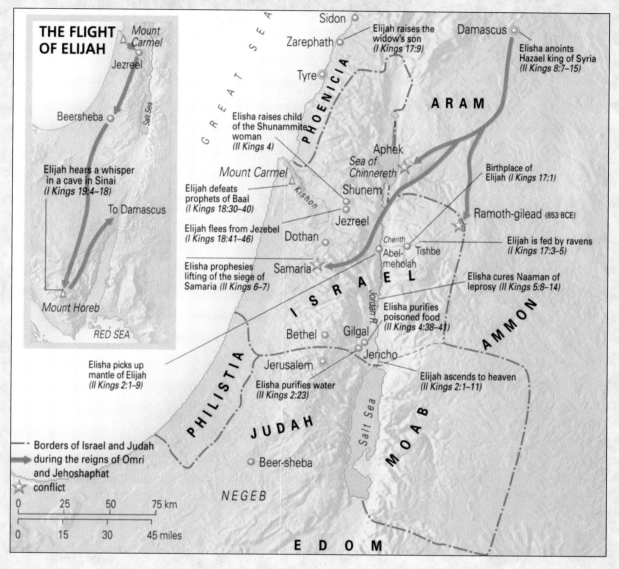

THE FLIGHT OF ELIJAH

Mount Carmel

Jezreel

Beersheba

Salt Sea

Elijah hears a whisper in a cave in Sinai
(I Kings 19:4–18)

To Damascus

Mount Horeb

RED SEA

Sidon

Zarephath

Elijah raises the widow's son
(I Kings 17:9)

Damascus

Elisha anoints Hazael king of Syria
(II Kings 8:7–15)

Tyre

PHOENICIA

ARAM

GREAT SEA

Elisha raises child of the Shunammite woman
(II Kings 4)

Aphek

Sea of Chinnereth

Mount Carmel

Kishon

Shunem

Elijah defeats prophets of Baal
(I Kings 18:30–40)

Jezreel

Birthplace of Elijah (I Kings 17:1)

Ramoth-gilead (853 BCE)

Elijah flees from Jezebel
(I Kings 18:41–46)

Dothan

Cherith

Abel-meholah

Tishbe

Elijah is fed by ravens
(I Kings 17:3–5)

ISRAEL

Elisha prophesies lifting of the siege of Samaria (II Kings 6–7)

Samaria

Elisha cures Naaman of leprosy (II Kings 5:8–14)

Jordan R.

Elisha purifies poisoned food
(II Kings 4:38–41)

AMMON

Bethel

Gilgal

Elisha picks up mantle of Elijah
(II Kings 2:1–9)

Jerusalem

Jericho

Elisha purifies water
(II Kings 2:23)

Elijah ascends to heaven
(II Kings 2:1–11)

PHILISTIA

JUDAH

Salt Sea

MOAB

- - Borders of Israel and Judah
➤ during the reigns of Omri and Jehoshaphat
★ conflict

Beer-sheba

NEGEB

| 0 | 25 | 50 | 75 km |
| 0 | 15 | 30 | 45 miles |

EDOM

Elijah hid from Ahab after he had declared a drought upon the apostate Ahab and his kingdom. 1 Kings 17: 4-6 tells us the LORD ordered ravens to feed Elijah morning and evening by the brook Cherith until it dried up. The raven seems like an odd choice to carry out God's mission because the raven is listed as an unclean animal in Mosaic law. But the books of Job and Psalms mention the raven as a creature under God's care (Job 38: 41; Ps 147: 9). Noah also used the services of a raven, sending one from the ark (Gn 8: 6-7). Because it was strong enough to fly until the waters receded, it did not return to Noah.

"My father, my father! the chariots of Israel and its horsemen!" (2 Kgs 2: 12)

Elijah And Elisha

At Horeb, God told Elijah to anoint a new prophet to take his place: Elisha. On his way back, Elijah found Elisha plowing the field. He tossed his mantle over Elisha, showing that Elisha would take over his prophetic call. Elisha took a hasty leave of his people and followed.

Elijah continued his ministry for several more years, with Elisha following him as a sort of apprentice prophet.

But eventually a time came when both prophets knew that Elijah was about to be taken away. In fact, all the prophets of God knew it.[8] Three times Elijah gave Elisha the chance to stay behind, but Elisha replied, "As the LORD lives, and as you yourself live, I will not leave you."[9]

When they came to the Jordan, Elijah struck the water with his mantle, and a dry path appeared through the river—a very Moses-like miracle from a prophet who had also spent forty days and nights at Sinai. The two prophets crossed the river, and on the other side Elijah finally mentioned what was on both their minds.

> When they had crossed, Elijah said to Elisha, "Ask what I shall do for you, before I am taken from you." And Elisha said, "I pray you, let me inherit a double share of your spirit." And he said, "You have asked a hard thing; yet, if you see me as I am being taken from you, it shall be so; but if you do not see me, it shall not be so." (2 Kgs 2: 9-10)

A "double share" was the inheritance of a first-born son. Elisha was asking to be made Elijah's heir and successor. The thing he asked for wasn't a privilege by most standards: Elijah had spent most of his life under threat of death from the wicked kings of Israel. But it was what a prophet would ask for if his only motive was a burning love for the Lord.

> And as they still went on and talked, behold, a chariot of fire and horses of fire separated the two of them. And Elijah went up by a whirlwind into heaven. And Elisha saw it and he cried, "My father, my father! the chariots of Israel and its horsemen!" And he saw him no more. (2 Kgs 2: 11-12)

Then Elisha tore his own clothes and put on Elijah's mantle. On his way back from the amazing vision of Elijah being taken up into heaven, Elisha again came to the Jordan. "Where is the LORD, the God of Elijah?" he said. And he struck the water with the mantle. Once again, a dry path appeared.

Elisha had indeed inherited Elijah's spirit. We see the confirmation in the miracles done through Elisha: dividing the Jordan, making oil last indefinitely,[10] and raising a young man from the dead[11]—all things Elijah had done.

The Assyrian Threat

But even with prophets like Elijah and Elisha to call them back to God, the people of Israel still went after false gods. Judah, too, had many idol-worshipers, but Israel—in spite of a few outbursts of reform—never really came back to the true worship of God.

Meanwhile, an ominous threat from the northeast was growing more ominous all the time. The Assyrians were rapidly expanding their empire, and it could not be long before they set their sights on Israel.

All conquest was horrible and bloody in ancient times. but the Assyrians were more than usually horrible. Their art and literature shows a real delight in war and killing, as though massacre were the national sport.

Conquest was an Assyrian king's chief glory. At the king's coronation, the pagan priest solemnly informed the new king of what the gods expected from him: "Expand your territory!" It was the king's religious duty to conquer.

For Israel, the most dreadful thing about the Assyrians was their cruel policy of resettlement as insurance against rebellion. The Assyrians would uproot the whole population of a conquered province and send everyone off to live in some foreign land, or even scatter them throughout their empire. They hoped that uprooted refugees would have neither the resources nor the spirit to rebel against the empire.

The capital of Assyria was Nineveh, an enormous city of hundreds of thousands of people. The city was richer than anyone could imagine, swollen with loot pillaged from all over the known world. To the people of Israel and Judah, who lived in constant fear of Assyrian attack, Nineveh was the symbol of everything that was evil in the world—as we saw in the story of Jonah.

The Assyrian reliefs found lining the walls of Sennacherib's palace in Nineveh depict the siege on Lachish and are the only visual data illustrating the siege and its consequences. Many panels of the relief show either the killing of captives or the exile of families from the city. In one scene, the Lachishites are shown impaled on the Assyrian's sharp stakes. The Assyrians used a form of psychological warfare. They raped, murdered and mutilated many of the inhabitants to set an example for the other cities in the area which rarely needed much more encouragement to surrender.

The End Of Israel

Hoshea, the last king of Israel, tried to play the Assyrians off against the Egyptians. It was a big mistake.

After losing a battle with the Assyrians, Hoshea had been forced to pay annual tribute to Nineveh. But one year the tribute didn't arrive. The Assyrian king, Shalamaneser, found out that Hoshea had been sending messengers to Egypt, suggesting a secret alliance that would help Israel break free of Assyria.

The last thing the Assyrians wanted was an Egyptian foothold in Israel. Shalamaneser came down with a huge army and besieged Samaria, the capital of Israel. For three years the city held out, but at last it fell. The Assyrians carried off everyone they could find and resettled them—all the leading citizens of Israel, more than 27,000 of them according to Assyrian records.

> And this was so, because the people of Israel had sinned against the LORD their God, who had brought them out of the land of Egypt from under the hand of Pharaoh king of Egypt, and had feared other gods and walked in the customs of the nations whom the LORD drove out before the people of Israel, and in the customs which the kings of Israel had introduced.... Yet the LORD warned Israel and Judah by every prophet and every seer, saying, "Turn from your evil ways and keep my commandments and my statutes, in accordance with all the law which I commanded your fathers, and which I sent to you by my servants the prophets." But they would not listen, but were stubborn, as their fathers had been, who did not believe in the LORD their God. (2 Kgs 17: 7-8, 13-14)

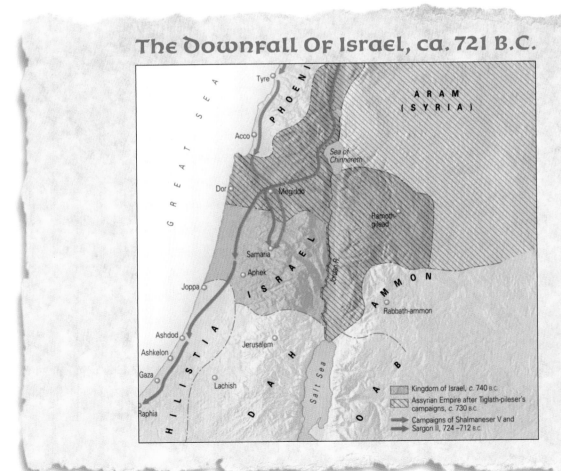

The Downfall Of Israel, ca. 721 B.C.

SUPPLEMENTARY READING

Augustine, *City of God*, Book XVII

But Jeroboam king of Israel, with perverse mind, not believing in God, whom he had proved true in promising and giving him the kingdom, was afraid lest, by coming to the temple of God which was in Jerusalem, where, according to the divine law, that whole nation was to come in order to sacrifice, the people should be seduced from him, and return to David's line as the seed royal; and set up idolatry in his kingdom, and with horrible impiety beguiled the people, ensnaring them to the worship of idols with himself. Yet God did not altogether cease to reprove by the prophets, not only that king, but also his successors and imitators in his impiety, and the people too. For there the great and illustrious prophet Elijah and Elisha his disciple arose, who also did many wonderful works. Even there, when Elijah said, "O Lord, they have slain Thy prophets, they have digged down Thine altars; and I am left alone, and they seek my life," it was answered that seven thousand men were there who had not bowed the knee to Baal.

So also in the kingdom of Judah pertaining to Jerusalem prophets were not lacking even in the times of succeeding kings, just as it pleased God to send them, either for the prediction of what was needful, or for correction of sin and instruction in righteousness; for there, too, although far less than in Israel, kings arose who grievously offended God by their impieties, and, along with their people, who were like them, were smitten with moderate scourges. The no small merits of the pious kings there are praised indeed. But we read that in Israel the kings were, some more, others less, yet all wicked. Each part, therefore, as the divine providence either ordered or permitted, was both lifted up by prosperity and weighed down by adversity of various kinds; and it was afflicted not only by foreign, but also by civil wars with each other, in order that by certain existing causes the mercy or anger of God might be manifested; until, by His growing indignation, that whole nation was by the conquering Chaldeans not only overthrown in its abode, but also for the most part transported to the lands of the Assyrians,—first, that part of the thirteen tribes [counting the two half-tribes of Ephraim and Manasseh] called Israel, but afterwards Judah also, when Jerusalem and that most noble temple was cast down,—in which lands it rested seventy years in captivity. Being after that time sent forth thence, they rebuilt the overthrown temple.

"And he lay down and slept under a broom tree; and behold, an angel touched him, and said to him, 'Arise and eat.'" (1 Kgs 19:5)

VOCABULARY

ABIJAH

A prophet who announced to Jeroboam that God would give him ten of the twelve tribes of Israel.

AHAB

The wicked king of Israel. Led by his Phoenician wife Jezebel, he established the cult of Baal and persecuted the worshipers of the True God.

ASSYRIA

A bloody and wicked empire that terrorized the whole Middle East and constantly threatened both Israel and Judah. Eventually the Assyrians destroyed Israel and scattered its people.

BETHEL

The southern of the two centers of worship in the northern kingdom of Israel where Jeroboam set up golden calves for the people to worship.

DAN

The northern of the two centers of worship in the northern kingdom of Israel where Jeroboam set up golden calves for the people to worship.

ELIJAH

The great prophet who challenged the pagan rulers of Israel. He was taken up to heaven in a fiery chariot.

ELISHA

Elijah's devoted disciple, who continued his mentor's mission in Israel.

ISRAEL

Originally the whole kingdom of the twelve tribes of Israel, but after Solomon's time refers to the northern of the two kingdoms into which Solomon's kingdom was divided. The Assyrians scattered Israel, yet the prophets promised that all twelve tribes would eventually be brought together at the coming of the Messiah.

JEROBOAM

A minister of Solomon who led the revolt against his son Rehoboam. Jeroboam became the first king of the new northern kingdom of Israel.

JEZEBEL

The wicked queen of Israel who persecuted the prophets of the True God. She was a Phoenician, and she was fanatically devoted to the Phoenician god Baal.

JONAH

An unwilling prophet sent to preach repentance to Nineveh. He spent three days as good as dead in the belly of a great fish. Jesus Christ referred to "the sign of Jonah" as a type of his own death and resurrection.

JUDAH

The name used for the southern of the two kingdoms into which Israel was divided after Solomon. Judah kept Jerusalem as its capital and remained loyal to David's line.

NINEVEH

The capital of the Assyrian Empire. See Assyria and Jonah.

REHOBOAM

Solomon's son and heir. His pride caused all but two of the twelve tribes to rebel against him.

TARSHISH

A far-off place, possibly in Spain, to which Jonah planned to escape from his mission to Nineveh.

STUDY QUESTIONS

1. What were the seeds of undoing for the empire of Solomon?

2. Who succeeded Solomon?

3. What favor did the people ask of Rehoboam when he succeeded his father Solomon?

4. What did Rehoboam's wise old men advise him?

5. What was Rehoboam's response and what did it cause?

6. What happened in the rebellion?

7. According to Abijah's prophecy, why was the northern part of the kingdom taken from Solomon's son?

8. How did Jeroboam try to keep the tribes under his control from turning back to Jerusalem?

9. How did God guide his people in times of bad kings?

10. What is the point of the book of Jonah?

11. Why was Jonah on a boat to Tarshish?

12. How long was Jonah in the belly of the fish?

13. What effect did Jonah's preaching have on Nineveh?

14. Why was Jonah angry when Nineveh repented?

15. Describe two miracles God worked through Elijah.

16. What did Elijah do when Jezebel threatened his life?

17. Where did Elijah have his vision of God?

18. What did Elisha ask of Elijah?

19. What signs indicated he had inherited Elijah's spirit?

20. Who was Hoshea?

21. How long did it take for the Assyrian king to take over the city of Samaria?

Elisha's Well. This is one of the predella pictures of the altarpiece made for the Carmelite Church in Siena. The painting depicts a rocky landscape on Mount Carmel, in the foreground is the well which according to tradition was opened up by Prophet Elisha. Scenes from the life of Carmelite hermits are represented both beside the well and in the background.

PRACTICAL EXERCISES

1. Rehoboam refused to listen to the wise old men when they told him to be merciful to the people of Israel. Instead, he listened only to his malformed friends because they told him what he wanted to hear. In the end, he decided he wanted to appear even more powerful than his father, Solomon, and so increased the burden on the people. What deadly sin is this an example of? Explain your choice. What else was wrong with Rehoboam's decision and its effects on the people?

2. During the reigns of bad kings in Israel, many prophets rose up to defend the true God and turn the people away from worshiping idols. Jeremiah wrote about being called by God to be one of these prophets: "If I say, 'I will not mention him, or speak any more his name,' there is in my heart as it were a burning fire shut up in my bones, and I am weary holding it in, and I cannot" (Jer 20:9). Do you think that Jeremiah was forced to be a prophet and could not help it? What other possible explanation could there be for this quote?

3. Reread the section on Jonah and Nineveh. What can we learn about our world today from the story of Jonah's change of heart regarding the people of Nineveh? Do we have enemies to whom we should be bringing the word of God, rather than hoping for their destruction? Think of examples in your own life. How does this lesson affect the way you treat your enemies, or even the way you think about them?

4. A large crowd of people became convinced that the Lord is God when Elijah asked God to send fire from heaven to light his sacrifice. Analyze Elijah's prayer: "O LORD, God of Abraham, Isaac, and Israel, let it be known this day that I am your servant, and that I have done all these things at thy word. Answer me, O LORD, that this people may know that thou, O LORD, art God, and that thou hast turned their hearts back" (1 Kgs 18:36-37). What is Elijah's overall attitude in the prayer? How does he start it and how does it end? What is the purpose of the prayer and what were Elijah's intentions?

5. Reread the section on Elijah at Sinai. Elijah's vision of God started not with a powerful presence but with a "still small voice." How does this revelation tie in with the idea that God has given us complete freedom to choose whether or not to accept his will? How does this revelation help us in our search to know God's will?

Endnotes

1. 1 Kgs 12:4.	4. Pontifical Biblical Commission,	5. 1 Kgs 17:8-24.	9. 2 Kgs 2:2, 2:4, 2:6.
2. 1 Kgs 12:7.	The Interpretation of the Bible	6. 1 Kgs 18:27.	10. 2 Kgs 4:1-7.
3. 1 Kgs 12:12.	in the Church, 79.	7. 1 Kgs 19:1-3.	11. 2 Kgs 4:32-37.
		8. 2 Kgs 2:3.	

Conquest And Exile

"Behold, the days are coming, says the Lord, when I will make a new covenant with the house of Israel and the house of Judah, not like the old covenant which I made with their fathers when I took them by the hand to bring them out of the land of Egypt, a covenant which they broke,..."

Jeremiah 31: 31-32

Chapter 13

Conquest And Exile

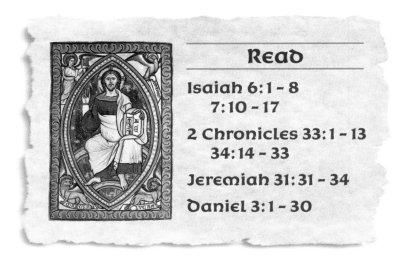

Read

Isaiah 6:1 - 8
    7:10 - 17

2 Chronicles 33:1 - 13
    34:14 - 33

Jeremiah 31:31 - 34

Daniel 3:1 - 30

With the Assyrian conquest, the story of the northern kingdom of Israel came to an end. Some of the poor farmers were probably left in the land, but all the leading citizens were gone, and the tribal structure of most of the northern ten tribes was dissolved. Only Zebulun and Naphtali, which had been conquered by the Assyrians earlier, remained in their homeland, the rural province of Galilee.

To make sure Israel would never be a problem again, the Assyrians brought people from faraway corners of their empire to resettle the empty cities of central Israel. The new settlers brought their own gods, but after a while (and a few attacks by roaming lions) they decided to learn the worship of the God of Israel, supposing he was a territorial deity who had to be appeased.

These new settlers gradually intermarried with the remainder of the Israelite population that had been left behind by the Assyrians. The combined population worshiped God, but also continued to worship foreign gods from all over the Assyrian empire. Because they had settled in the towns around Samaria, they were called Samaritans.

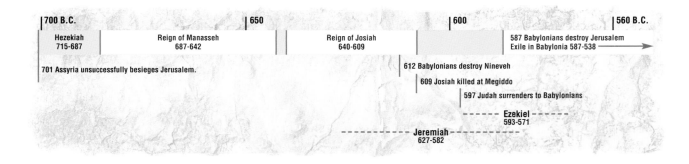

700 B.C.	650	600	560 B.C.
Hezekiah 715-687	Reign of Manasseh 687-642	Reign of Josiah 640-609	587 Babylonians destroy Jerusalem Exile in Babylonia 587-538
701 Assyria unsuccessfully besieges Jerusalem.		612 Babylonians destroy Nineveh	
		609 Josiah killed at Megiddo	
		597 Judah surrenders to Babylonians	
		Ezekiel 593-571	
	Jeremiah 627-582		

The Great Prophet Isaiah

Now all that was left of the old kingdom of David was Judah, which included the large tribe of Judah, the little tribe of Benjamin, and the Levites who had not lived in Israel. Judah was spared the Assyrian conquest. While Israel was coming to an inglorious end, Judah was going through a temporary rebirth under the good king Hezekiah. Hezekiah was determined to do what was right in the sight of God. And for his guide, he had one of the greatest of all the prophets: Isaiah the son of Amoz.

Hezekiah was a serious reformer. He pulled down the pagan altars and sacred poles. He tore down the high places where people worshiped God the wrong way. He destroyed the bronze serpent Moses had made in the wilderness, because the faithless people had even begun to worship that as a god.[1]

Isaiah, Hezekiah's spiritual guide, had been a prophet through the reigns of Uzziah, Jotham, and Ahaz, during whose reigns the people of Judah were progressively seduced by the evil practices of the Canaanites. Uzziah was a worshiper of the True God, but his pride made him try to take over the priests' functions as well. Jotham also worshiped the True God, but he allowed many of the people to slip into idolatry. Manasseh was a pagan; he even burned his own son as an offering to one of the horrible Canaanite idols.

Against that background, Isaiah was sent to call Judah to repentance, and to warn of the destruction to come if Judah did not repent.

> Come now, let us reason together,
>   says the LORD:
> though your sins are like scarlet,
>   they shall be as white as snow;
> though they are red like crimson,
>   they shall become like wool.
> If you are willing and obedient,
>   you shall eat the good of the land;
> but if you refuse and rebel,
>   you shall be devoured by the sword:
> for the mouth of the LORD has spoken.
>   (Is 1:18-20)

But Isaiah was not only a prophet of doom. Even when things looked darkest, Isaiah looked forward to a time when Jerusalem would be not just the capital of Judah, but also the spiritual capital of the world.

> It shall come to pass in the later days
>   that the mountain of the house
> of the LORD shall be established as the
>   highest of the mountains,
> and shall be raised above the hills;
>   and all the nations shall flow to it,
> and many peoples shall come, and say:
>   "Come, let us go up to the mountain of the
> LORD, to the house of the God of Jacob;
>   that he may teach us his ways
>   and that we may walk in his paths."
> For out of Zion shall go forth the law,
>   and the word of the LORD from Jerusalem.
>   (Is 2:2-3)

Many scholars today think that the book of Isaiah, as we have it, is compiled from the writings of three or possibly more prophets. In that case, the first part (chapters 1-39) is mostly the work of Isaiah himself; while the remaining material was compiled later on by those responsible for collecting prophecies attributed to Isaiah, especially for the sake of the exiles living in foreign lands. But the whole book has been put together by a talented editor, and the same themes run all through it.

Of course the idea of repentance, and the judgment that will come unless Judah repents, is one of the main themes of Isaiah's prophecy. But even that judgment cannot cancel God's unconditional promises to David. God will chasten his people, but in spite of that punishment a time will come when the most impossible-sounding promises will all come true. A remnant of Judah—the remnant that has been truly faithful to God—will return to establish a new kingdom in Jerusalem. In fact, that idea was so important to Isaiah that he named his first child A-Remnant-Shall-Return.[2]

Though it might seem impossible, the Davidic kingdom would be restored more glorious than ever before. The line of David, son of Jesse, might seem to be chopped down like a dead tree, but in that time to come, the ideal ruler—the Lord's Anointed, the Messiah or Christ—would rule Israel with ideal righteousness.

> There shall come forth a shoot from the stump of Jesse,
>   and a branch shall grow out of his roots.
> And the Spirit of the LORD shall rest upon him,
>   the spirit of wisdom and understanding,
>   the spirit of counsel and might,
>   the spirit of knowledge and the fear of the LORD ...
>
> In that day the root of Jesse shall stand as an ensign to the peoples; him shall the nations
>   seek, and his dwellings shall be glorious.
> In that day the LORD will extend his hand yet a second time to recover the remnant which
>   is left of his people, from Assyria, from Egypt, from Pathros, from Ethiopia, from
>   Elam, from Shinar, from Hamath, and from the coastlands of the sea. (Is 11: 1-2, 10-11)

It already seemed like an impossible promise: all the faithful of Israel, even the tribes dispersed by the Assyrians, would be reunited under the Lord's Anointed. In the dark times to come, it would seem even more impossible.

Not all the tribes of the north had disappeared. Unlike the rest of the northern tribes, Zebulun and Naphtali had never been completely deported. In the last years of the northern kingdom, Assyria had conquered their land, separating it from the kingdom of Israel. Most of the poor farmers who lived there were left when the rest of Israel was dismembered and taken away.

Those stragglers were still there in the land called Galilee, where they were ignored by Jews and Gentiles alike. Yet Isaiah predicted something unimaginably great for them:

> But there will be no gloom for her that was in anguish. In the former time he brought into
> contempt the land of Zebulun and the land of Naphtali, but in the later time he will make
> glorious the way of the sea, the land beyond the Jordan, Galilee of the nations.
>
> The people who walked in darkness have seen a great light;
>   those who dwelt in a land of deep darkness,
>   on them has light shined....
> For to us a child is born,
>   to us a son is given;
> and the government will be upon his shoulder,
>   and his name will be called
> "Wonderful Counselor, Mighty God,
>   Everlasting Father, Prince of Peace." (Is 9: 1-3, 8)

"...the spirit of wisdom and understanding, the spirit of counsel and might, the spirit of knowledge and the fear of the Lord..." (Is 11: 2)

The people of Judah who heard Isaiah's prophecy would not have been surprised to hear the Galileans called "people who walked in darkness." But they might have doubted whether the Galileans would ever see a great light. Galilee would be made glorious? Galileans were poor farmers, not great leaders. It was one of Isaiah's more unlikely-sounding prophecies.

In the reign of Ahaz, the wicked pagan king, the Assyrians attacked Jerusalem, and it looked like the end for Judah. But God sent Isaiah with a message for Ahaz.

> "Ask a sign of the LORD your God; let it be deep as Sheol or high as heaven." But Ahaz said, "I will not ask, and I will not put the LORD to the test." And he [Isaiah] said, "Hear then, O house of David! Is it too little for you to weary men, that you weary my God also? Therefore the LORD himself shall give you a sign. Behold, a young woman shall conceive and bear a son, and shall call his name Immanuel [that is, God-Is-With-Us]. He shall eat curds and honey when he knows how to refuse the evil and choose the good. For before the child knows how to refuse the evil and choose the good, the land before whose two kings are in dread will be deserted." (Is 7:10-16)

When a son was born to Ahaz, it seemed like the beginning of the fulfillment of the promise. And by the time little Hezekiah was walking around, the siege of Jerusalem had been lifted.

But even Hezekiah, the great reformer, was not the ideal ruler God had promised. After his reign, things rapidly got worse for Judah. The faithful remnant began to understand that the real fulfillment of God's promise was still to come.

The word translated "young woman" in "a young woman shall conceive" can also mean "virgin," and it was translated as "virgin" in the Septuagint, the Greek translation of the Scriptures made about 250 years before the time of Jesus Christ. Reading this prophecy, the faithful people who were still looking for the Lord's Anointed expected him to be born of a virgin.

With God's Help, King Hezekiah Defends Jerusalem, 701 B.C.

On this cylinder, Assyrian King Sennacherib boasts that he captured 46 of Hezekiah's cities and besieged Jerusalem, shutting Hezekiah up in his capital city "like a bird in a cage."

But Hezekiah had prepared Jerusalem for a long siege by digging an underground tunnel through 1,750 feet of solid rock to bring fresh water from the Gihon spring into the city. Hezekiah prayed for help, and God answered by destroying 185,000 Assyrian soldiers. "For I will defend this city to save it, for my own sake and for the sake of my servant David." (2 Kgs 18:13-19)

The Wicked King Manasseh

When Hezekiah died, his son Manasseh succeeded him. It would be hard to imagine a greater contrast between father and son. Hezekiah had pulled down the high places; Manasseh built them up again. Hezekiah had thrown out all the foreign idols; Manasseh brought them back. Manasseh defiled the very Temple of God with pagan altars and images. He even burned his own sons as an offering to the horrible pagan gods. He massacred innocent citizens in his own capital of Jerusalem, persecuting the worshipers of God and turning the true religion into an underground cult. An ancient tradition says that one of his victims was Isaiah the prophet, whom he had cut in two with a saw.

No king of Judah had ever been so purely wicked. Judgment came on him swiftly: Assyrians came down and attacked Jerusalem, carrying off Manasseh in chains.

But then something almost like a miracle happened.

> And when he was in distress he entreated the favor of the LORD his God and humbled himself greatly before the God of his fathers. He prayed to him, and God received his entreaty and heard his supplication and brought him again to Jerusalem into his kingdom. Then Manasseh knew that the LORD was God.
> (2 Chr 33:12-13)

Much later, an unknown writer imagined what Manasseh's prayer in captivity must have been like. The Prayer of Manasseh is considered canonical by some Eastern churches:

The Kidron Valley, north of Jerusalem, was an important place of burial and contains many rock-cut tombs. The reforming kings, such as Hezekiah and Josiah, used the valley as a place to destroy pagan idols and altars. They were burned or ground to a powder.

> ...For the sins I have committed are more in number than the sand of the sea;
>> my transgressions are multiplied, O LORD, they are multiplied!
> I am unworthy to look up and see the height of heaven because of the multitude
>> of my iniquities.
> I am weighted down with an iron fetter, so that I am rejected because of my sins,
>> and I have no relief;
> for I have provoked your wrath and done what is evil in your sight,
>> setting up abominations and multiplying offenses.
> And now I bend the knee of my heart, beseeching you for your kindness.
> I have sinned, O LORD, I have sinned, and I know my transgressions.
>> (Prayer of Manasseh 9-12)

Manasseh was completely changed when he came back to Jerusalem. He took away all the pagan altars and threw out all the foreign cults. He made sacrifices of thanksgiving in the Temple. He lived to reign longer than any other king of Israel and Judah.

The Great Reform

Judah had a brief return to paganism under Amon, the son of Manasseh. But when he was assassinated, the people made Josiah, Amon's son, king. Josiah would be remembered as the great reformer, the king who brought Judah back—at least temporarily—to the statutes and commandments of God.

One day when the priests were going through the Temple archives, one of them came across an old scroll. It had apparently been hidden away, perhaps to keep it safe from Manasseh's soldiers during the worst part of the persecution.

The priests brought it to the king, and the king had it read to him.

When he heard what was in the book, he tore his clothes. The priests had found the Book of the Law—the book we call Deuteronomy. It had been hidden and forgotten when the priests of the True God were being massacred in the streets. And there, for the first time in his life, Josiah heard the curses pronounced on Israel for disobeying the Law.

"Go," the king told the priests, "inquire of the LORD for me, and for the people, and for all Judah, concerning the words of this book that has been found; for great is the wrath of the LORD that is kindled against us, because our fathers have not obeyed the words of this book, to do according to all that is written concerning us."[3]

The priests went to a prophetess named Huldah, and she gave them the bad news.

> Thus says the LORD, the God of Israel: "Tell the man who sent you to me, Thus says the LORD, Behold, I will bring evil upon this place and upon its inhabitants, all the words of the book which the king of Judah has read. Because they have forsaken me and have burned incense to other gods, that they might provoke me to anger with all the work of their hands, therefore my wrath will be kindled against this place, and it will not be quenched. But as to the king of Judah, who sent you to inquire of the LORD, thus shall you say to him, Thus says the LORD, the God of Israel: Regarding the words which you have heard, because your heart was penitent, and you humbled yourself before the LORD...you shall be gathered to your grave in peace, and your eyes shall not see the evil which I will bring upon this place." (2 Kgs 22:15-20)

Josiah gathered the people together and read the Book of the Law to them. Together they swore to keep all the commandments of God. Then Josiah had all the altars to false gods burned, and defiled the site where Molech-worshipers had killed their own children. He expelled all the cult prostitutes.

He tore down the high places where people had worshiped God incorrectly. And he did all this in spite of the fact that doom had already been pronounced on Judah. Josiah had decided to do what was right, even if there could be no immediate benefit.

When Josiah became king in 640 B.C., Hinnom Valley had many pagan shrines. He tore them down and instituted sweeping reforms throughout the land.

Josiah was killed in battle by Pharaoh Necho of Egypt in 608 B.C.

Jeremiah Sees The End Of The World

After Josiah, Judah went downhill fast. Josiah's sons were all worthless, leading Judah back to paganism. God's judgment was quick. One by one, the sons of Josiah were carried away by more powerful kings.

First the Egyptian pharaoh made Judah a tributary and carried off Jehoahaz, making his brother Jehoiakim king in his place. Then Nebuchadnezzar, king of Babylon, came and carried the second brother away to Babylon, along with the best furnishings from the Temple, leaving Jehoiakim's eight-year-old son as a puppet king. But only three months later Nebuchadnezzar decided to take the little boy off to Babylon, too, along with what was left in the Temple and all the best soldiers and craftsmen in Jerusalem. He left the last of Josiah's sons, Zedekiah, to rule as Nebuchadnezzar's vassal.

In spite of all the bad news, there was no repentance. And even as Jerusalem suffered one raid after another, there were flattering false prophets willing to tell the king of the moment that prosperity was just around the corner.

It wasn't easy being a true prophet in those dark times. The news was all bad, and bad news wasn't what people wanted to hear. The great prophet Jeremiah was imprisoned, beaten by thugs, thrown down a well, and repeatedly threatened with death. Yet Jeremiah's stubbornness was the best witness to the truth of his prophecies. Even the worthless Zedekiah consulted Jeremiah in secret.

Zedekiah had decided to rebel against Nebuchadnezzar, relying on help from Egypt. It was precisely the same mistake the last king of Israel, Hoshea, had made a century and a half before. Even though his flattering court prophets promised him that Egypt would save Judah, Zedekiah secretly sent for Jeremiah to find out the truth about his chances of success against Nebuchadnezzar. Jeremiah told him Egypt would do him no good. God had already determined the fate of Jerusalem.

> Thus says the LORD, Do not deceive yourselves, saying, "The Chaldeans will surely stay away from us," for they will not stay away. For even if you should defeat the whole army of Chaldeans who are fighting against you, and there remained of them only wounded men, every man in his tent, they would rise up and burn this city with fire. (Jer 37: 9-10)

Jeremiah was a powerful figure in spite of his unpopularity; he was known for giving prophecies against the reigning authority, and yet the king felt compelled to consult him rather than a more compliant prophet. Jeremiah had the truth, and the king and the people recognized it, even when they didn't want to.

The truth was a terrible thing in those days. Jeremiah told the people of Judah that there would soon be destruction so terrible, so total, that words could hardly describe it. Only a practical demonstration could get the point across.

Thus said the LORD, "Go buy a potter's earthen flask, and take some of the elders of the people and some of the senior priests, and go out to the valley of the son of Hinnom at the entry of the Potsherd Gate, and proclaim there the words that I tell you. You shall say, 'Hear the word of the LORD, O kings of Judah and people of Jerusalem…Behold, I am bringing such evil on this place that the ears of every one who hears of it will tingle.…And in this place I will make void the plans of Judah and Jerusalem, and will cause their people to fall by the sword before their enemies, and by the hand of those who seek their life. I will give their dead bodies to the birds of the air and to the beasts of the earth. And I will make this city a horror, a thing to be hissed at; every one who passes by it will be horrified and will hiss because of all its disasters. And I will make them eat the flesh of their sons and their daughters, and every one shall eat the flesh of his neighbor in the siege and in the distress, with which their enemies and those who seek their life afflict them.'

"Then you shall break the flask in the sight of the men who go with you, and shall say to them, 'Thus says the LORD of hosts: So will I break this people and this city, as one breaks a potter's vessel, so that it can never be mended.…'" (Jer 19:1-3, 7-11)

In his search for words to describe the horror to come, Jeremiah reached all the way back to the beginning of time. Genesis 1 describes how the earth was waste and void before creation began, and God's first act was to create light. Now, in Jeremiah's vision,

I looked on the earth, and lo, it was waste and void;
    and to the heavens, and they had no light.
I looked on the mountains, and lo, they were quaking,
    and all the hills moved to and fro.
I looked, and lo, there was no man,
    and all the birds of the air had fled.
I looked, and lo, the fruitful land was a desert,
    and all its cities were laid in ruins before the LORD,
    before his fierce anger.
    (Jer 4:23-26)

The destruction would be so complete that all the work of creation would be undone.

The Fall Of Judah To Nebuchadnezzar and the Babylonians

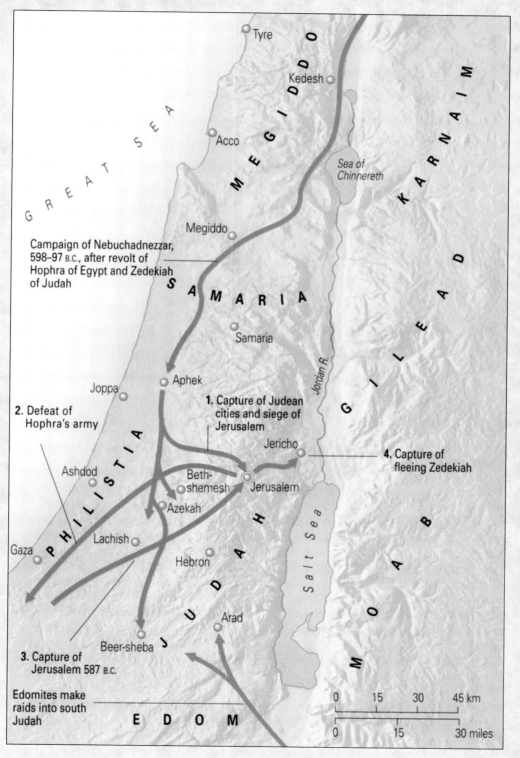

Campaign of Nebuchadnezzar, 598–97 B.C., after revolt of Hophra of Egypt and Zedekiah of Judah

GREAT SEA

Tyre

Kedesh

MEGIDDO

KARNAIM

Acco

Sea of Chinnereth

Megiddo

SAMARIA

Samaria

GILEAD

Jordan R.

Joppa

Aphek

1. Capture of Judean cities and siege of Jerusalem

Jericho

4. Capture of fleeing Zedekiah

2. Defeat of Hophra's army

PHILISTIA

Ashdod

Beth-shemesh

Jerusalem

Salt Sea

MOAB

Azekah

Gaza

Lachish

JUDAH

Hebron

Arad

3. Capture of Jerusalem 587 B.C.

Beer-sheba

Edomites make raids into south Judah

EDOM

| 0 | 15 | 30 | 45 km |
| 0 | | 15 | 30 miles |

The Impossible Promise

Yet creation will not be entirely undone. As with the Flood, God will preserve a remnant, and creation will begin anew. All the disasters of the previous centuries will be reversed, and Israel will be brought back together under the ideal Davidic king.

> Then I will gather the remnant of my flock out of all the countries where I have driven them, and I will bring them back to their fold, and they will be fruitful and multiply. I will set shepherds over them who will care for them, and they shall fear no more, nor be dismayed, neither shall any be missing, says the LORD.

> Behold, the days are coming, says the LORD, when I will raise up for David a righteous Branch, and he shall reign as king and deal wisely, and shall execute justice and righteousness in the land. In his days Judah will be saved, and Israel will dwell securely. And this is the name by which he will be called: "The LORD is our righteousness."
> (Jer 23: 3-6)

This time the people of God will not be united by the covenant of the Law or even by the covenant with David, but by a new covenant.

> "Behold, the days are coming, says the LORD, when I will make a new covenant with the house of Israel and the house of Judah, not like the old covenant which I made with their fathers when I took them by the hand to bring them out of the land of Egypt, a covenant which they broke, though I was their husband, says the LORD. But this is the covenant which I will make with the house of Israel after those days, says the LORD: I will put my law within them, and I will write it upon their hearts; and I will be their God, and they shall be my people. And no longer shall each man teach his neighbor and each his brother, saying, 'Know the LORD,' for they shall all know me, from the least of them to the greatest, says the LORD; for I will forgive their iniquity, and I will remember their sin no more."
> (Jer 31: 31-34)

Israel has been an unfaithful wife, but her sins will be forgiven. The prophets often spoke of Israel's "adultery" in chasing after false gods. Yet the promise was always that God would redeem his unfaithful bride. Many of the prophets used the same metaphor. Hosea, in fact, saw his own marriage as a mirror of the relationship between God and his people. Hosea's wife was unfaithful to him, leaving him and their children to run after other lovers, until she finally ended up as a common slave. Yet Hosea still loved her.

> And the LORD said to me, "Go again, love a woman who is beloved of a paramour and is an adulteress; even as the LORD loves the people of Israel, through they turn to other gods and love cakes of raisins." [Cakes of raisins were part of Canaanite pagan worship.] So I bought her for fifteen shekels of silver and a homer and a lethech of barley. (Hos 3:1-2)

No matter how unfaithful she had been, Hosea redeemed his wife when she had sunk into slavery and degradation. God would do the same for his people: Israel would sink into slavery and degradation, but God would still love her and pay the price to redeem her from slavery.

Ezekiel, who lived at the same time as Jeremiah, made the same amazing promise. Like Jeremiah, he foresaw terrible destruction ahead. But no matter how terrible the destruction might seem, in the more distant future God would redeem his people.

> For I will take you from the nations, and gather you from all the countries, and bring you into your own land. I will sprinkle clean water upon you, and you shall be clean from all your uncleannesses, and from all your idols I will cleanse you. A new heart I will give you, and a new spirit I will put within you; and I will take out of your flesh the heart of stone

"Behold, O Lord, for I am in distress, my soul is in tumult, my heart is wrung within me, because I have been very rebellious." (Lam 1: 20)

and give you a heart of flesh. And I will put my spirit within you, and cause you to walk in my statutes and be careful to observe my ordinances. You shall dwell in the land which I gave to your fathers; and you shall be my people, and I will be your God. (Ez 36: 24-28)

The terrible punishment to come was not revenge, but the chastening discipline of a loving Father. And the redemption to come after that would not come because Israel deserved it, but purely because of God's love.

Then you will remember your evil ways, and your deeds that were not good; and you will loathe yourselves for your iniquities and your abominable deeds. It is not for your sake that I will act, says the LORD God; let that be known to you. Be ashamed and confounded for your ways, O Israel. (Ez 36: 31-32)

Through the prophets, God forms his people in the hope of salvation, in the expectation of a new and everlasting Covenant intended for all, to be written on their hearts (cf. Is 2: 2-4; Jer 31: 31-34; Heb 10: 16). The prophets proclaim a radical redemption of the People of God, purification from all their infidelities, a salvation which will include all the nations (cf. Ez 36; Is 49: 5-6; 53: 11). Above all, the poor and humble of the LORD will bear this hope. Such holy women as Sarah, Rebecca, Rachel, Miriam, Deborah, Hannah, Judith, and Esther kept alive the hope of Israel's salvation. The purest figure among them is Mary (cf. Zep 2: 3; Lk 1: 38). (CCC 64)

The Exodus Reversed

When the destruction finally came, it must have seemed as terrible as Jeremiah had predicted. It's hard for us to imagine how destructive war could be in the ancient world. Even though the weapons were primitive by our standards, armies of tens or hundreds of thousands of soldiers could destroy whole provinces so thoroughly that creation really did seem to be undone. For safety, the people might retreat behind the walls of the chief city. Then the enemy would lay siege to the city, and soon the people inside would find themselves starving.

When Nebuchadnezzar finally took Jerusalem, he decided he'd had enough of that rebellious city. He burned down the Temple, the king's palace, and every important house in the city. He took most of the important citizens away to Babylon, leaving a governor to supervise the ones who were left. Jeremiah the prophet was also left with them. According to 2 Maccabees, he managed to hide the Ark of the Covenant when Nebuchadnezzar was making off with the rest of the loot from Jerusalem. The story said that the Ark would not be found again until all the people of Israel were brought back together.

> It was also in the writing that the prophet [Jeremiah], having received an oracle, ordered that the tent and the ark should follow with him, and that he went out to the mountain where Moses had gone up and had seen the inheritance of God. And Jeremiah came and found a cave, and he brought there the tent and the ark and the altar of incense, and he sealed up the entrance. Some of those who followed him came up to mark the way, but could not find it. When Jeremiah learned of it, he rebuked them and declared: "The place shall be unknown until God gathers his people together again and shows his mercy. And then the LORD will disclose these things, and the glory of the LORD and the cloud will appear, as they were shown in the case of Moses, and as Solomon asked that the place should be specially consecrated." (2 Mc 2:4-8)

Even then the rebellious spirit of Judah was not quite stamped out. Rebels murdered the governor and all his Jewish followers. The Jews who were left were sure the Babylonians would retaliate, so they made plans to flee to Egypt. Jeremiah warned them not to go, but they accused him of being in league with the Babylonians and went anyway—dragging Jeremiah with them against his will.

So the remnant of Judah went back into exile in Egypt—the ultimate curse that had been predicted in the Book of the Law.

> And the LORD will bring you back in ships to Egypt, a journey which I promised that you should never make again; and there you shall offer yourselves for sale to your enemies as male and female slaves, but no man will buy you. (Dt 28:68)

The Babylonian Empire After The Destruction Of Jerusalem

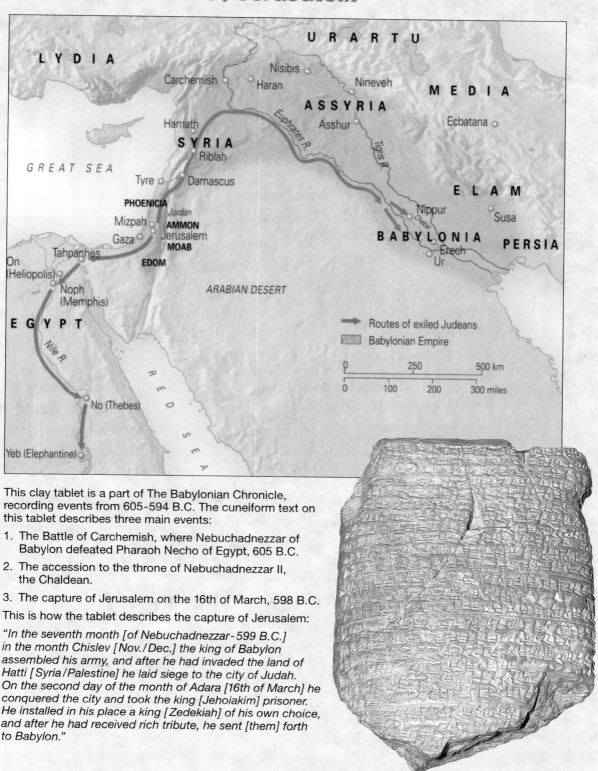

This clay tablet is a part of The Babylonian Chronicle, recording events from 605-594 B.C. The cuneiform text on this tablet describes three main events:

1. The Battle of Carchemish, where Nebuchadnezzar of Babylon defeated Pharaoh Necho of Egypt, 605 B.C.

2. The accession to the throne of Nebuchadnezzar II, the Chaldean.

3. The capture of Jerusalem on the 16th of March, 598 B.C.

This is how the tablet describes the capture of Jerusalem:

"In the seventh month [of Nebuchadnezzar-599 B.C.] in the month Chislev [Nov./Dec.] the king of Babylon assembled his army, and after he had invaded the land of Hatti [Syria/Palestine] he laid siege to the city of Judah. On the second day of the month of Adara [16th of March] he conquered the city and took the king [Jehoiakim] prisoner. He installed in his place a king [Zedekiah] of his own choice, and after he had received rich tribute, he sent [them] forth to Babylon."

253

The Babylonian Exile

By the waters of Babylon,
   there we sat down and wept,
   when we remembered Zion.
On the willows there
   we hung up our lyres.
For there our captors
   required of us songs,
and our tormentors, mirth, saying,
   "Sing us one of the songs of Zion!"

How shall we sing the LORD's song
   in a foreign land?
If I forget you, O Jerusalem,
   let my right hand wither!
Let my tongue cleave to the roof
   of my mouth,
   if I do not remember you,
if I do not set Jerusalem
   above my highest joy!
(Ps 137:1-6)

Jerusalem had meant everything to the people of Judah. It was the beautiful city, the holy city, God's chosen dwelling out of all the earth. Now the city was burned, and the Promised Land had been taken away. The Temple was gone. How could worship even continue without the Temple?

Babylon was a huge city, a place where Nebuchadnezzar sat among immense palaces and temples and ruled the world, and a place where all the vices of the world were collected in one spot. It was magnificent and terrible and completely foreign.

A dragon from the great Ishtar Gate, part of the lavish redevelopment of Babylon by Nebuchadnezzar II.

We can hardly imagine the pain of exile for the people of Judah who had been carried away far to the east. Yet a strange thing was happening. Deprived of everything they had owned, they found themselves remembering God. Surrounded by glorious monuments of paganism, they were beginning to understand the value of what they had lost. They began to remember that they were the chosen people of God.

The result was a flowering of Jewish culture that no one would have expected. Many of the books of the Old Testament were edited in their final forms during the Babylonian Exile. It's a common saying that history is written by the winners. But the case of the Jews is the stunning exception to that rule. Thrown out of their homes, carried away to foreign slavery, they wrote the history of how their people lost everything. And they knew why they had lost, too: they had been unfaithful to their God.

"And he said to me, 'Son of man, go, get you to the house of Israel, and speak with my words to them. For you are not sent to a people of foreign speech and a hard language, but to the house of Israel.'" (Ez 3: 4-5)

The Prophet Ezekiel was among the Jews deported from Jerusalem to Babylon in 597 B.C. He lived among the captives near the river Chebar. After the destruction of Jerusalem, God used Ezekiel to convey a message of hope and future restoration to the exiles. Ezekiel's portrayal of God as a Good Shepherd who would restore His flock (Ez 34: 11-31) foreshadows the New Testament motif of Christ as the Good Shepherd (Jn 10). In this painting of Ezekiel's vision, Raphael uses the symbols of the New Testament Evangelists: angel, lion, ox, eagle—Matthew, Mark, Luke, John.

Daniel: Heroic Stories Of The Exile

The book of Daniel tells some memorable stories about faithful Jews in the Babylonian Exile, and how they stayed faithful to the True God even when all the powers of paganism were brought against them. Daniel himself was legendary for his wisdom, and he earned a very high position in the Babylonian court. The book begins with Daniel and three other young men of noble Jewish families being picked out to be trained as servants to the king. Daniel refused to break the Jewish dietary laws by eating the king's rich food, eating only vegetables and water. Probably it was the only way he could be sure not to eat meat cooked with the blood or any of the other things faithful Jews had to avoid. Already we see how hard it was to stay faithful to God in a foreign land.

Next comes the story of Nebuchadnezzar's dream, and how Daniel interpreted it. The king had called his wise men and demanded that they not only interpret his dream, but also tell him what it was. "Let the king tell his servants the dream," they answered, "and we will show its interpretation." But that answer didn't satisfy Nebuchadnezzar, who decided to kill all the wise men—including Daniel. Daniel, however, prayed to God, and God showed him what the king had dreamed.

Nebuchadnezzar dreamed that he saw an enormous statue.

1. The head was gold;
2. the breast and arms silver;
3. the belly and thighs bronze;
4. the legs iron; the feet partly iron and partly clay.
5. Then a rock was cut from a mountain by no human hand, and it struck the statue and broke it in pieces. The stone then became a great mountain and filled the whole earth.

Daniel was able to interpret the dream, too:

1. The golden head was Nebuchadnezzar, the greatest of all earthly kings.
2. After him would come a kingdom inferior to Nebuchadnezzar's, as silver is inferior to gold.
3. After that would come a kingdom inferior to the second, as bronze is inferior to silver.
4. Then a fourth kingdom would arise that would crush the first three, as iron breaks everything. But the kingdom would be partly strong and partly brittle, like potter's clay.
5. Finally, God himself would set up a final kingdom which would never be destroyed, but—like the rock—would fill the whole earth.

In other words, Nebuchadnezzar's dream was an outline of future history. Naturally, Nebuchadnezzar was impressed with Daniel's ability to tell him his dream and interpret it, and Daniel became one of Nebuchadnezzar's top ministers.[4]

Daniel tried to tell Nebuchadnezzar that it was God, not Daniel, who was the source of all wisdom. But Nebuchadnezzar didn't grasp the distinction between the True God and false gods. The next story we hear is the famous story of Shadrach, Meshach, and Abednego in the fiery furnace. Nebuchadnezzar had decreed that everyone should bow before a huge idol he had set up, but the three young men—Daniel's companions, who had been brought up in the Babylonian court with him—refused to bow. The penalty was being tossed into a fiery furnace. But when the young men were thrown in, something amazing happened.

Then Nebuchadnezzar was astonished and rose up in haste. He said to his counselors, "Did we not cast three men bound into the fire?" They answered the king, "True, O king." He answered, "But I see four men loose, walking in the midst of the fire, and they are not hurt; and the appearance of the fourth is like a son of the gods." (Dn 3: 24-25)

Sure enough, the three young men came out of the furnace unhurt. "Blessed be the God of Shadrach, Meshach, and Abednego," said Nebuchadnezzar, "who has sent his angel and delivered his servants, who trusted him, and set at nought the king's command, and yielded up their bodies rather than serve and worship any god except their own God."[5]

Stories like these encouraged the Jews to be faithful to their own God for the half-century they were exiled in Babylon. Though they lived in the capital of the pagan world, the Jews kept their distinct identity and culture. And they never forgot Jerusalem.

The forgetting of the Law and the infidelity to the covenant end in death: it is the Exile, apparently the failure of the promises, which is in fact the mysterious fidelity of the Savior God and the beginning of a promised restoration, but according to the Spirit. The People of God had to suffer this purification (cf. Lk 24: 26). In God's plan, the Exile already stands in the shadow of the Cross, and the Remnant of the poor that returns from the Exile is one of the most transparent prefigurations of the Church. (CCC 710)

SUPPLEMENTARY READING

Commentary, *Introduction to Chronicles § 4*

4. The Books of Chronicles in the Light of the New Testament

The books of Chronicles end with the divine decree to rebuild the temple of Jerusalem and send the exiles home (cf. 2 Chr 36: 22-23). By the time these books were redacted (the fourth century B.C.), that decree had been put into effect, and the people once again were dwelling in the promised land and worshiping God in the temple in the manner laid down by David, according to these books. The people and its priests are now, therefore, the "successors" of David, and in the temple and its liturgy they discover their true identity and the guarantee of divine protection. Chronicles, therefore, does not make it quite clear that this was a temporary situation and one that would remain so until the Messiah came, the successor of David; although the attention focused on David might seem to imply that outcome. Instead, this history gives the impression that God's Covenant with David is already being fulfilled, just as it was in the case of those successors of David who were faithful to God. In this sense one must say that there is no dimension of messianic hope in 1 and 2 Chronicles.

However, these books do mark an important stage in the unfolding of divine Revelation which will reach its climax in the New Testament. Perhaps more strongly than anywhere else in the Old Testament, they evidence awareness of the presence of God among his people through the temple of Jerusalem and the institutions connected with it, and the continuity of that presence as long as due worship is offered there. In this sense 1 and 2 Chronicles prepare the way for the Revelation of the New Testament, according to which God has become truly present in the midst of his people and all mankind through the incarnation of his Son Jesus Christ. The teaching contained in Chronicles gives us a better grasp of Jesus' zeal for the temple (cf. Mt 21: 12-17) and of how he could even identify himself with the temple by describing himself as the definitive dwelling place of God among men (cf. Mt 12: 6; Jn 2: 21). The physical death of Jesus (cf. Jn 2: 18-22), a true sacrifice and an act of worship to the Father, "presaged the destruction of the Temple, which would manifest the dawning of a new age in the history of salvation: 'The hour is coming when neither on this mountain nor in Jerusalem will you worship the Father' (Jn 4: 21; cf. Jn 4: 23-24; Mt 27: 51; Heb 9: 11, Acts 21: 22)" (CCC 586). Jesus, then, is the new David who provides in himself the place where people—not just the Jews, but all mankind—truly meet God.

"Then Ebed-melech the Ethiopian said to Jeremiah, 'Put the rags and clothes between your armpits and the ropes.' Jeremiah did so. Then they drew Jeremiah up with ropes and lifted him out of the cistern. And Jeremiah remained in the court of the guard." (Jer 38: 10-13)

VOCABULARY

BABYLON

The great imperial city to which the conquered people of Judah were taken as captives by Nebuchadnezzar.

DANIEL

A great prophet who rose during the Exile. He defied many attempts to force him to worship the pagan gods of Babylon, and in his visions he foresaw the end of Nebuchadnezzar's kingdom.

EXILE

The time the people of Judah spent as captives in Babylon.

GALILEE

A district of Israel whose population was not deported with the rest of the kingdom.

HEZEKIAH

The reforming king of Judah who temporarily returned Judah to the pure worship of God.

ISAIAH

The great prophet who guided the reforms of Hezekiah. His prophecies often refer to the coming of the Messiah.

JEREMIAH

A great prophet who stood up to official persecution to bring God's word to the people of Judah. He saw his people being carried off to captivity in Babylon captivity, but he predicted that God would gather the remnant of his flock from the four corners of the world. He also foresaw a time when God would make a "new covenant" with his people.

JOSIAH

A reforming king of Judah who returned the people to the worship of the True God. During his reign the Book of the Law was found in the Temple, where it might have been hidden during Manasseh's persecutions.

MANASSEH

A king of Judah who destroyed all his father Hezekiah's reforms and persecuted the worshipers of the True God. After many disasters, he repented and turned back to God.

MESSIAH

"Anointed One." The ideal future king of Israel promised by God through the prophets. The Greek translation is "christ."

NAPHTALI

One of the northern tribes in Galilee not deported with the rest of Israel.

NEBUCHADNEZZAR

King of Babylon who finally conquered Judah and carried the best families off to exile in Babylon.

REMNANT

In Isaiah, the small number out of all God's people who will return to Jerusalem after the coming exile. The idea was so important to Isaiah that he named one of his children A-Remnant-Shall-Return.

ZEBULUN

One of the northern tribes in Galilee not deported with the rest of Israel.

A tablet known as The Siloam Inscription, dating from 700 B.C., was discovered in Hezekiah's Tunnel. It marked the point where the two groups of tunnellers, who had started at each end, met in the middle. The inscription describes the drama of the meeting: *"On the day of the piercing through, the stone-cutters struck through each to meet his fellow, axe against axe. Then ran the water from the spring to the pool..."*

STUDY QUESTIONS

1. Who were the Samaritans?

2. Who was Hezekiah?

3. Why did Hezekiah destroy Moses' bronze serpent?

4. What is the main theme of Isaiah's prophecy?

5. According to Isaiah, what unlikely place would be made glorious "in the later time"?

6. How did King Manasseh begin his reign?

7. What happened when Manasseh was taken away by the Assyrians?

8. Who was known as the great reformer?

9. What important discovery did the priests make during Josiah's reign?

10. How did Josiah react when he found out Judah was to be punished by God?

11. Who was Zedekiah?

12. Where did the remnant of Judah flee after the leading citizens had been deported to Babylon?

13. When were many books of the Old Testament edited in their final forms?

14. What happened to Shadrach, Meshach, and Abednego?

PRACTICAL EXERCISES

1. Manasseh became king after his father, the good king Hezekiah, died. Manasseh was a wicked king and quickly reversed all the reforms his father had set in place. He set up pagan altars, defiled the Temple of God, and even persecuted God's faithful. When the Assyrians attacked, why did Manasseh finally turn to God? How did God respond? What sacrament can this story be related to? How does this story show how that sacrament is of great importance?

2. Reread the section explaining Nebuchadnezzar's dream about the statue. One interpretation of this story relates the statue's feet to a person who has many strengths and talents but does not trust in God. In this interpretation, what would the iron represent? What would the brittle clay represent? There are many people who are very successful in life while at the same time denying the importance of living God's will. How could this story serve as a warning to them?

3. With difficulty, Daniel committed himself to abstain from the rich foods of the king, eating only foods that did not violate the Jewish dietary laws. This was especially difficult to do because he was in a foreign land under pressure to follow their popular beliefs and practices. Describe a time in your life when you were challenged to live up to your religious beliefs and how you handled the situation.

Endnotes

1. 2 Kgs 18: 4.
2. Is 7: 3.
3. 2 Kgs 22: 13.
4. Dn 2.
5. Dn 3: 28.

A Remnant Returns

"Then I said to them, 'You see the trouble we are in, how Jerusalem lies in ruins with its gates burned. Come let us build the wall of Jerusalem, . . .'"

Nehemiah 2: 17

Chapter 14

A Remnant Returns

Read

Daniel 5:1 - 30

Isaiah 45:1 - 4

Ezra 1:1 - 7

Nehemiah 8:1 - 12

Malachi 1:6 - 14

Nebuchadnezzar was one of the great conquerors in history. But his empire was never governed very well, and his successors did not have Nebuchadnezzar's military genius. It took a surprisingly short time — about a generation — for the Babylonian empire to fall from world domination to the brink of destruction.

Belshazzar's Feast

Belshazzar was the son of the reigning Babylonian king, but the king had gone off to fight foreign wars and left Belshazzar in charge to rule as king in his place. From the account in Daniel, we can guess that Belshazzar was a poor regent. From sources outside the Bible, we know that the Persian army was advancing on Babylon. All the pagan idols from surrounding towns had been brought into Babylon for safekeeping. Piece by piece, the Babylonian empire was falling apart. Yet here was Belshazzar having a feast for a thousand of his closest friends, inviting them to eat and drink from the best silver — namely, the silver that had been looted from the Temple at Jerusalem.

> Then they brought in the golden and silver vessels which had been taken out of the temple, out of the house of God in Jerusalem; and the king and his lords, his wives, and his concubines drank from them. They drank wine, and praised the gods of gold and silver, bronze, iron, wood, and stone.

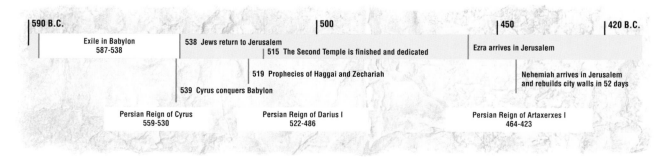

590 B.C.		500		450	420 B.C.
	Exile in Babylon 587-538	538 Jews return to Jerusalem	515 The Second Temple is finished and dedicated	Ezra arrives in Jerusalem	
			519 Prophecies of Haggai and Zechariah		Nehemiah arrives in Jerusalem and rebuilds city walls in 52 days
		539 Cyrus conquers Babylon			
	Persian Reign of Cyrus 559-530		Persian Reign of Darius I 522-486	Persian Reign of Artaxerxes I 464-423	

> Immediately the fingers of a man's hand appeared and wrote on the plaster of the wall of the king's palace, opposite the lampstand; and the king saw the hand as it wrote. Then the king's color changed, and his thoughts alarmed him; his limbs gave way and his knees knocked together. (Dn 5: 3-6)

No one could read the writing. The king offered a huge reward to any of his astrologers and magicians who could read it, but they all shrugged. Then the queen remembered Daniel, who had been so good at interpreting dreams back in the days of Nebuchadnezzar.

When Daniel came in, Belshazzar offered to make him prime minister if he could interpret the writing on the wall. Daniel refused the reward right away: he knew it would do him no good. Belshazzar would be gone soon.

The writing, Daniel explained, came from the Most High God. Nebuchadnezzar had learned his lesson, Daniel told Belshazzar, reminding him of Nebuchadnezzar's years of madness.

> And you his son, Belshazzar, have not humbled your heart, though you knew all this, but you have lifted up yourself against the LORD of heaven; and the vessels of his house have been brought in before you, and you and your lords, your wives, and your concubines have drunk wine from them; and you have praised the gods of silver and gold, of bronze, iron, wood, and stone, which do not see or hear or know, but the God in whose hand is your breath, and whose are all your ways, you have not honored.
>
> Then from his presence the hand was sent, and this writing was inscribed. And this is the writing that was inscribed: MENE, MENE, TEKEL, and PARSIN. This is the interpretation of the matter: MENE, God has numbered the days of your kingdom and brought it to an end; TEKEL, you have been weighed in the balance and found wanting; PERES [the singular of PARSIN], your kingdom is divided and given to the Medes and Persians. (Dn 5: 22-28)

Belshazzar gave Daniel a purple robe and gold chain and declared him third ruler of the kingdom, in spite of Daniel's refusal. But that night Belshazzar was killed, and Babylon passed into the hands of the Medes and Persians.

Cyrus The Messiah

Babylon fell without a fight. There was no long siege, no wholesale destruction, no massacre. The Persians simply marched in and took over everything in an orderly fashion. Cyrus, the Persian king, took no delight in bloodshed. He won his empire by war, but he kept it by inspiring loyalty in his subjects. All the conquered peoples were allowed to keep their own customs and worship in their own ways. After the oppressive policies of Babylon, Persian rule seemed like a breath of freedom.

To the Jews in exile, Cyrus was more than another conqueror. He was a liberator. In the very first year of his reign, he issued a decree that allowed any Jew who wished to go to return to Jerusalem.

> Thus says Cyrus king of Persia: The LORD, the God of heaven, has given me all the kingdoms of the earth, and he has charged me to build him a house at Jerusalem, which is in Judah. Whoever is among you of all his people, may his God be with him, and let him go up to Jerusalem, which is in Judah, and rebuild the house of the LORD, the God of Israel— he is the God who is in Jerusalem; and let each survivor, in whatever place he sojourns, be assisted by the men of his place with silver and gold, with goods and with beasts, besides freewill offerings for the house of God which is in Jerusalem. (Ezr 1: 2-4)

The exile was over, at least for anyone who wanted to return. The benevolent Cyrus did not force all the Jews to return; he simply gave permission to anyone who wished to go back to Jerusalem. Not only that, but he took responsibility for rebuilding the Temple of God! Cyrus was more than a liberator; he was the conqueror chosen by God to restore God's people. In fact, he was the Lord's Anointed—a title that had never before been given to anyone but an Israelite.

> I am the LORD ... who says of Cyrus, "He is my shepherd,
>   and he shall fulfill all my purpose;"
> saying of Jerusalem, "She shall be built,"
>   and of the temple, "Your foundation shall be laid."
> Thus says the LORD to his anointed, to Cyrus ... (Is 44: 24, 28-45: 1)

The monumental tomb of King Cyrus II at Pasargadae in south-central Iran.

"O man, whoever you are and wherever you come from, for I know that you will come— I am Cyrus, son of Cambyses, who founded the Empire of the Persians and was king of the East. Do not grudge me this spot of earth which covers my body."

A Persian gold coin from the time of Cyrus II or Darius I.

Rulers of the Persian Empire B.C.

Cyrus II (the Great)	550-529
Cambyses II	529-522
Darius I	522-486
Xeres I	486-465
Artaxerxes I	465-425
Xerxes II	425-424
Darius II	423-404
Artaxerxes II	404-359
Artaxerxes III	359-338
Arses	338-336
Darius III	336-330

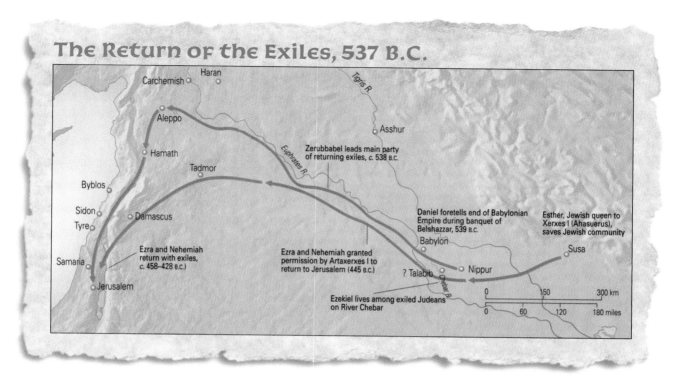

The Return of the Exiles, 537 B.C.

Map labels:

Haran
Carchemish
Tigris R.
Aleppo
Asshur
Hamath
Euphrates R.
Zerubbabel leads main party of returning exiles, c. 538 B.C.
Tadmor
Byblos
Sidon
Damascus
Tyre
Daniel foretells end of Babylonian Empire during banquet of Belshazzar, 539 B.C.
Esther, Jewish queen to Xerxes I (Ahasuerus), saves Jewish community
Babylon
Susa
Samaria
Ezra and Nehemiah return with exiles, c. 458–428 B.C.)
Ezra and Nehemiah granted permission by Artaxerxes I to return to Jerusalem (445 B.C.)
? Talabib
Nippur
Chebar R.
Jerusalem
Ezekiel lives among exiled Judeans on River Chebar

0   150   300 km
0   60   120   180 miles

Beginning The New Jerusalem

A remnant returned to Jerusalem. Many—probably most—of the Jews stayed in Babylon. This business of moving back to the burnt-out towns of Judah was a difficult enterprise. It was hard to see how the returning exiles could make it work. But the ones who went back were full of enthusiasm. They were determined to have a new Jerusalem with a new Temple.

> In spite of the holy Law that again and again their Holy God gives them—"You shall be holy, for I the LORD your God am holy"—and although the LORD shows patience for the sake of his name, the people turn away from the Holy One of Israel and profane his name among the nations (Ez 20: 9, 14, 22, 39; cf. Lv 19: 2). For this reason the just ones of the old covenant, the poor survivors returned from exile, and the prophets burned with passion for the name. (CCC 2811)

The Jerusalem they found was a wreck. Nothing had been done to it for half a century. The great houses were still ruins, and the Temple was still a charred open space.

After they had settled in the towns and in Jerusalem, the returning exiles came together to lay the foundations for a new Temple. But it quickly became clear that it would be nothing like Solomon's original. They had neither the money nor the resources to build anything nearly so magnificent.

> And all the people shouted with a great shout, when they praised the LORD, because the foundation of the house of the LORD was laid. But many of the priests and Levites and heads of fathers' houses, old men who had seen the first house, wept with a loud voice when they saw the foundation of this house being laid, though many shouted aloud for joy; so that the people could not distinguish the sound of the joyful shout from the sound of the people's weeping, for the people shouted with a great shout, and the sound was heard afar. (Ezr 3: 11-13)

It is not surprising that the people had mixed reactions. Some of the people who had seen the first Temple must have realized at that moment that there would be no real restoration. They would have a Temple, but it would be a pale thing compared with the first one. And the Ark of the Covenant would not be there. The Holy of Holies would just be an empty space.

Trouble With The Samaritans

Even that diminished Temple was hard to build. Cyrus had given the command to build it, but "the adversaries of Judah and Benjamin" did everything they could to stop it. Those were the Samaritans, who at first tried to join with the returned exiles in building the Temple. But the Samaritans of those days were pagans: they worshiped the True God, but only as one of the many gods they worshiped.

The Jews who came back were very much aware that their troubles had all come on them because they had been unfaithful to God in the same way as the Samaritans. They kept their distance, and rejected the offer of help. Knowing that mixing with pagans had got them into trouble in the first place, the returned Jews kept themselves as separate as they could from the local women.

The Samaritans were offended. They started a campaign to stop the building, using the vast Persian bureaucracy against the people in Jerusalem.

Like any large government, the Persian empire was full of major and minor officials who controlled things like budgets and building permits. Most of the officials were easy to bribe. When bribing local officials failed, the Samaritans sent a letter to the king himself. The new king, Artaxerxes, was not familiar with the edict of Cyrus permitting the Temple to be built. The Samaritans accused the Jews of planning to rebuild Jerusalem's defenses and then rebel against Persia. Artaxerxes had a search made in the great Persian government archives and found that Jerusalem did indeed have a history of rebelling against its overlords. He ordered building to cease.

For years the project sat half-finished, a constant embarrassment to the city. Even more embarrassing was the way prosperous men of Jerusalem were building splendid new houses for themselves, while the Temple was still a half-built ruin.

The deadlock was finally broken by the enthusiasm of some of the prophets, notably Haggai and Zechariah. Haggai brought a forceful message to the rich men in their splendid houses:

> Thus says the LORD of hosts: This people say the time has not yet come to build the house of the LORD.... Is it a time for you yourselves to dwell in your paneled houses, while this house lies in ruins?... Go up to the hills and bring wood and build the house, that I may take pleasure in it and that I may appear in my glory, says the LORD. (Hg 1: 2, 4, 8)

Spurred on by the prophets, the Jewish remnant began to rebuild the Temple without waiting for permission from Persia. When local officials demanded to know where they got permission to build, the Jews pointed to the original edict from Cyrus.

The new Persian king, Darius, had another search made of the archives, and the decree of Cyrus was found. It was a principle of Persian law that a king's decree could never be revoked, not even by the king himself. The building was allowed to continue, and Darius himself paid for the work out of the taxes from the province that included Jerusalem.

At the summit of Mount Gerizim are the ruins of a Samaritan temple. The Samaritan community, which today only numbers in the hundreds, still carries out its traditional Passover sacrifices on this mountain.

Ezra prays: "But now for a brief moment favor has been shown by the Lord our God, to leave us a remnant, and to give us a secure hold within his holy place,…" (Ezr 9:8)

Ezra The Scribe

The Temple was finished, and the people celebrated the Passover with joy and thanksgiving. But they were still a tiny remnant of the Jews who had been deported, and they were surrounded by powerful enemies. How would they make their little colony a success?

A certain priest and scribe named Ezra was in favor with the Persian king, who put him in charge of the official Persian subsidy for the Temple, and gave him authority to appoint judges and magistrates in Judah. Ezra's dream was to restore a purified Israel in the Promised Land. But when he got to Jerusalem, he found that the priests and leaders of the people had been marrying pagan women from among the surrounding people. It looked as though the cycle of infidelity was beginning all over again.

By prayers and arguments and his very forceful personality, Ezra persuaded the people to put away their foreign wives. To Ezra, it was a matter of life or death. The whole success of the restoration depended on keeping Israel free from pagan entanglements.

Ezra quickly became the moral leader of the Jews. He was the one who taught them the Law. He edited the Hebrew Scriptures, and his edition of the Torah became the standard version. He had the Law read to the people in a great assembly—with interpreters to translate it, since most of the common people now spoke Aramaic, a language closely related to Hebrew that was the standard language throughout the Middle East.[1]

With Ezra as the spiritual leader, the rest of the responsibility fell on Nehemiah, who shared Ezra's dream of a pure Israel restored. Nehemiah persuaded the Persian king to make him governor in Jerusalem, and he set about restoring the city's defenses to protect against attacks by the surrounding Samaritans. Although Nehemiah could legally have taken a large salary for his position, he took nothing and paid for his expenses out of his own pocket.

What God Really Wants

Nehemiah's good example was necessary because many of the rich citizens of Jerusalem were making themselves richer by cheating the poor. Having escaped slavery in Babylon, some of the poor Jews were now forced to sell themselves back into slavery to pay off the rich loan sharks.

Pagan worship was no longer the main problem facing Jerusalem. The main problem was hypocrisy. Rich men bought and sold their neighbors, then went to make a small offering to God at the Temple, as though that made everything all right.

Even the sacrifices they offered were often taken from the worthless animals of their flocks. The prophet Malachi brought an angry message to the hypocrites who profaned the altar with worthless sacrifices: "When you offer blind animals in sacrifice, is that no evil? And when you offer those that are lame or sick, is that no evil? Present that to your governor; will he be pleased with you or show you favor?"

But even perfect sacrifices were not what God really desired from his people. Righteousness was what God wanted. Would God be pleased with the sacrifice of a rich man who had just sold his poor neighbor into slavery?

> Thus says the LORD of hosts: Render true judgments, show kindness and mercy each to his brother, do not oppress the widow, the fatherless, the sojourner, or the poor; and let none of you devise evil against his brother in his heart. (Zec 7: 9-10)

These were the things God really wanted from his people. But it was so much easier for them to sin a lot and sacrifice a little.

The prophet Malachi announces the theme of salvation:

"...*Veniet ad templum sanctum suum dominator dominus quem vos queritis, et angelum testamenti quem vos vultis...*"

"...*the Lord whom you seek will suddenly come to his temple; the messenger of the covenant in whom you delight,...*"

(*Mal 3: 1*)

The Promise Unfulfilled

Jerusalem was restored, and the Temple was a center of worship again. A remnant of God's people were back in the Promised Land.

But God had promised much more than that.

> "Behold, at that time I will deal with all your oppressors.
> And I will save the lame and gather the outcast,
>   and I will change their shame into praise and renown in all the earth.
> At that time I will bring you home, at the time when I gather you together;
>   yea, I will make you renowned and praised among all the peoples of the earth,
> when I restore your fortunes before your eyes," says the LORD.
>   (Zep 3:19-20)

A few of the people had been brought back. But they were hardly renowned and praised among all the peoples of the earth. They were barely surviving, a little colony of Jews surrounded by enemies.

> Your gates shall be open continually;
>   day and night they shall not be shut;
> that men may bring to you the wealth of
>   nations, with their kings led in procession.
>   (Is 60:11)

The gates of Jerusalem were closed fast at night to protect against raids from the countryside, and the kings who were not enemies simply ignored the place.

It became clearer and clearer that the glorious promises had not been fulfilled yet. And it seemed impossible that they would ever be fulfilled. Jerusalem was to be mistress of the nations; instead it was a little provincial town. God's glory would fill the Temple; instead, the Temple was a pale imitation of the original, with an empty space at its heart. David's line would rule forever; instead, Judah was just a small part of the Persian province called Beyond the River.

Yet the prophets still promised that all those glorious things would happen. The restoration of the Jewish remnant was only the beginning. The ideal Davidic king, the Anointed One, would still come.

Rejoice heart and soul, daughter of Zion! Shout for joy, daughter of Jerusalem!
Look, your king is approaching, he is vindicated and victorious,
humble and riding on a donkey, on a colt, the foal of a donkey.
(Zec 9:9, New Jerusalem Bible)

SUPPLEMENTARY READING

Commentary, Introduction to Ezra and Nehemiah § 3-4

3. Message

While the city walls and the temple were being rebuilt, the national and religious life of the Jewish people also underwent reorganization. In this context it was important that they should be aware of the links between old and new institutions. The altar and the house of God were built on the same site as before (cf. Ezr 3:3; 6:7). The sacred vessels that the returned exiles brought back to Jerusalem were the same ones as Nebuchadnezzar had taken to Babylon as plunder (Ezr 5:14). The priests and the other personnel involved in the liturgy were descendants of the men who had had these functions prior to the exile (Ezr 2:36-63; Neh 7:39-65).

This continuity between the new and the old is something that these books are at pains to point out, for it bears witness to the fact that God guides the course of salvation history, providing new answers to fit changed circumstances, but ensuring that the link with the people's origins is never weakened.

4. The Books of Ezra and Nehemiah in the Light of the New Testament

Within the canon of Holy Scripture, the books of Ezra and Nehemiah, as well as recording

God's dealings with his people on the return from exile, also show the inspired writer's understanding of God and of the chosen people, and the sort of teachings he wanted to get across to his contemporaries. In this sense, Ezra-Nehemiah evidences a particular point in Old Testament revelation; contrary to what the Jewish canon of the Bible might lead us to think (for it ends with these books and Chronicles), that revelation was ongoing and it is to be found in later Jewish (and also canonical) books, such as 1 Maccabees or Wisdom, and it reaches its climax in the book of the New Testament. From this perspective, Ezra-Nehemiah should be seen and read as dealing with a preparatory and transitory stage of revelation prior to the New Testament. Preparatory, because both books allow us to see to a considerable extent (but not entirely, because there were other tendencies in Judaism not reflected here) the religious circumstances and mentality of the Jewish people, centered on obedience to the Law, in the period in which Jesus lived and the Church came into being. Transitory, in so far as the teachings in Ezra-Nehemiah about the Law being the only way to draw down the mercy of God, and about segregation from Gentiles as a way to protect the identity of the Jewish people, will undergo profound changes in the New Testament. For, according to the New Testament, although the Law still holds, God's mercy reaches man, all mankind, be they Jews or not, through Jesus Christ, the Messiah; the identity of the Church, the new people of God, is not a function of segregation from Gentiles: it derives from the fidelity and holiness of its members in the midst of the world.

Ezra-Nehemiah should be seen and read as dealing with a preparatory and transitory stage of revelation prior to the New Testament.

VOCABULARY

ARAMAIC

A language closely related to Hebrew that was spoken throughout the Middle East. After the Exile, most Jews probably spoke Aramaic as their everyday language.

BELSHAZZAR

The last king of Babylon. He lost the kingdom to the Medes and Persians.

BEYOND THE RIVER

The Persian name for the province that included Judah.

CYRUS

The Persian king who conquered Babylon and allowed the Jews to return to Jerusalem.

EZRA

A priest who led the returned exiles in Jerusalem, and who put together the standard edition of the Old Testament scriptures.

HOLY OF HOLIES

The inner sanctuary of the Temple. In the rebuilt Temple, it was empty; the Ark of the Covenant had been hidden.

JEW

Originally a member of the tribe of Judah, but used from the Exile on to refer to any inhabitant of the old territory of Judah, including the remnants of the tribes of Benjamin and Levi. In a religious sense, it came to mean anyone who was committed to the Temple, including those who were scattered through other parts of the world.

NEHEMIAH

A wealthy Jew who persuaded the Persian king to make him governor of the province that included Jerusalem. He rebuilt the city's defenses.

PERSIA

The great empire that conquered Babylon and freed the Jews from exile. The Persians allowed their subjects to keep their own customs, and the Jews prospered under Persian rule.

SAMARITANS

The mixed population that inhabited the old territory of Israel during the Exile. They were hostile to the returning exiles.

STUDY QUESTIONS

1. Who was Belshazzar?

2. Where did the gold and silver drinking vessels used at Belshazzar's feast originate?

3. What occurred during Belshazzar's feast?

4. What did Daniel explain to Belshazzar that the writing on the wall meant?

5. What army was advancing on Babylon?

6. What important edict did Cyrus issue in the first year of his reign?

7. What surprising title is given to Cyrus in the book of Isaiah?

8. According to CCC 2811, what is the failure of the Israelites?

9. Why did the people have mixed reactions toward rebuilding the Temple?

10. What group opposed the rebuilding of the Temple?

11. How was Artaxerxes convinced to order the Jews to stop building the Temple?

12. What was the prophet Ezra's dream?

13. Who edited the standard version of the Torah after the return from exile?

14. Why was Ezra so adamant about the people not taking pagan wives?

15. How much did Nehemiah take for his salary as governor?

16. What did God desire from the Israelites at the time of Zechariah?

PRACTICAL EXERCISES

1. Belshazzar used the silver from the Temple of God to entertain his wives and concubines at his feast. This was an example of sacrilege: the sin of violating or profaning something sacred. As a result of this sacrilege, God delivered the writing on the wall foretelling the fall of Belshazzar's kingdom. What are some ways in which people still show a lack of respect for sacred things today? At Mass, when we receive our Lord in the Blessed Sacrament, it is especially important to show our respect. What are some ways we can show more respect for God in our dress and behavior when we receive Holy Communion?

2. Ezra was very effective in addressing the priests and leaders of the people about their pagan wives. He knew that pagan wives would lead the priests and leaders away from God and that the rest of Israel would follow. Ezra made sure that he was preaching what God wanted him to by prayer and listening to God's word. How did knowing God's word help to make him such a forceful teacher? The truth is a powerful weapon. List some ways in which you can learn more about the truth. Who might be in need of knowing this truth? How could you help them?

3. In the Old Testament, a great amount of importance was given to the many laws which needed to be followed in order to be faithful. Unfortunately, many people acted only to fulfill these laws and forgot about the importance of their intentions and their love for God. This resulted in many hypocrites who followed the rules minimally and acted against God's law outside of their religious lives. What are some examples of hypocrisy in today's society? How can this topic relate to Catholic politicians and their belief in the dignity of life? How can this relate to Catholics and their belief in the Holy Eucharist?

FROM THE CATECHISM

1081 The divine blessings were made manifest in astonishing and saving events: the birth of Isaac, the escape from Egypt (Passover and Exodus), the gift of the promised land, the election of David, the presence of God in the Temple, the purifying exile, and return of a "small remnant." The Law, the Prophets, and the Psalms, interwoven in the liturgy of the Chosen People, recall these divine blessings and at the same time respond to them with blessings of praise and thanksgiving.

"Immediately the fingers of a man's hand appeared and wrote on the plaster of the wall of the king's palace, opposite the lampstand; and the king saw the hand as it wrote." (Dn 5:5)

Endnote

1. Neh 8:8.

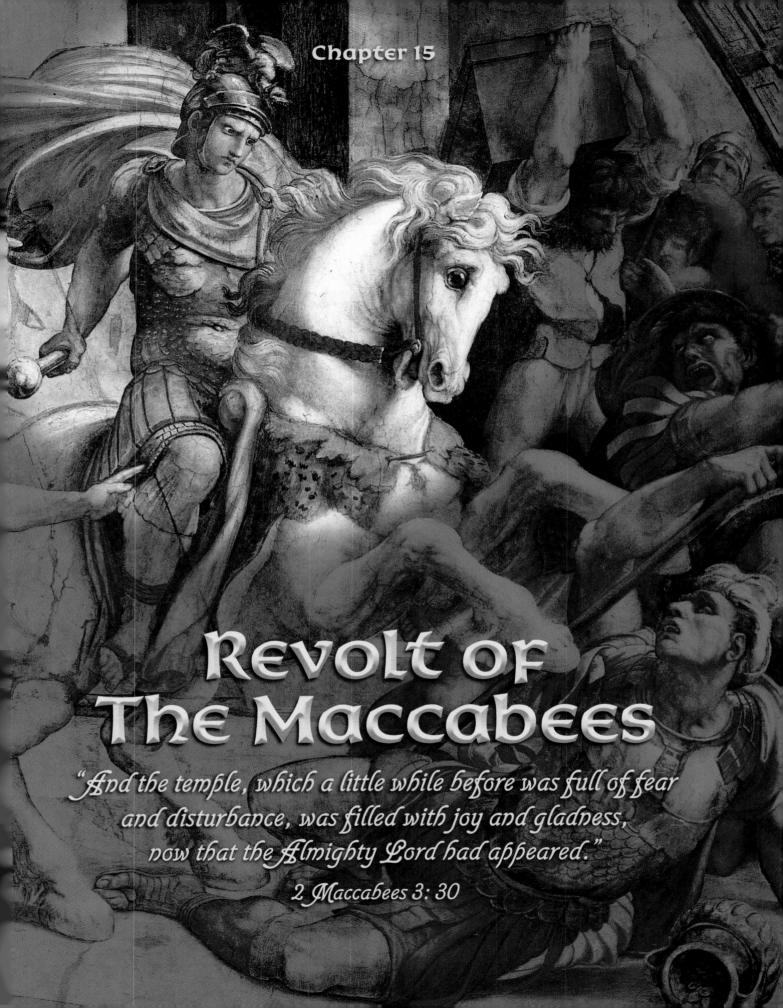

Revolt of The Maccabees

"And the temple, which a little while before was full of fear and disturbance, was filled with joy and gladness, now that the Almighty Lord had appeared."

2 Maccabees 3: 30

Chapter 15

Revolt of The Maccabees

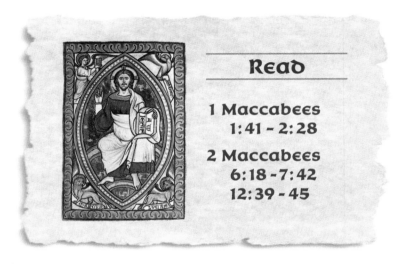

Read

**1 Maccabees
1:41 – 2:28**

**2 Maccabees
6:18 – 7:42
12:39 - 45**

Persian rule was good for the faithful remnant of Israel. The Persians encouraged local populations to keep their own customs, and (as we saw earlier) the Persian kings even gave generous subsidies to the Temple in Jerusalem.

Jews throughout the rest of the Empire prospered, too. Jewish merchants settled everywhere the Persians went, and Persian kings put a high value on Jewish advisors.

But the Persian Empire could not last forever. Its end was sudden and catastrophic.

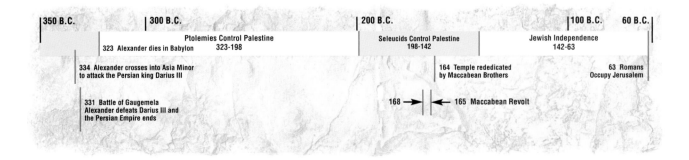

350 B.C.	300 B.C.		200 B.C.		100 B.C.	60 B.C.
	Ptolemies Control Palestine 323-198		Seleucids Control Palestine 198-142		Jewish Independence 142-63	
	323 Alexander dies in Babylon					
	334 Alexander crosses into Asia Minor to attack the Persian king Darius III		164 Temple rededicated by Maccabean Brothers		63 Romans Occupy Jerusalem	
	331 Battle of Gaugemela Alexander defeats Darius III and the Persian Empire ends		168 → ← 165 Maccabean Revolt			

Only One World To Conquer

Over in Greece, a handful of cities had grown rich by trading throughout the Mediterranean. Greek culture also flourished: poets, philosophers, sculptors, and playwrights created masterpieces of art and literature that are still models for us today. And even though the Greek cities were always warring against each other, they managed to band together long enough to keep the Persians from expanding westward.

Philip of Macedon finally brought most of Greece under his rule by a combination of war, diplomacy, and cheating. It was a spectacular achievement, considering the fierce independence of the Greek cities.

But Philip's son Alexander had much bigger ideas. With lightning speed he conquered Egypt and the whole Persian Empire. He got as far as India, the end of the known world—and he conquered that, too. Then, according to one favorite story, he broke down and wept because there were no more worlds to conquer.

The world was "Hellenized" overnight. (The Greeks called themselves "Hellenes," so the Hellenized civilization after Alexander is known as "Hellenistic" to historians.) Everywhere, Greek had become the language of commerce. Greek ideas of art permanently changed sculpture and painting even as far away as India, and the whole eastern Mediterranean sprouted Greek temples and libraries. Everyone who wanted to be up to date started dressing and acting like a Greek.

This silver coin is a tetradrachm minted in 314-310 B.C. by Ptolemy I Soter, Satrap and King of Egypt (323-285 B.C.). It depicts Alexander the Great wearing an elephant's scalp and the coiled ram's horn of Ammon, an Egyptian deity. A tetradrachm was worth four drachmas, a Greek monetary unit.

Marble sculpture of Alexander the Great 3rd century B.C.

The Entry of Alexander into Babylon by Charles Le Brun. Alexander defeated the Persians in 333 B.C.

Conquests Of Alexander The Great, ca. 336-323 B.C.

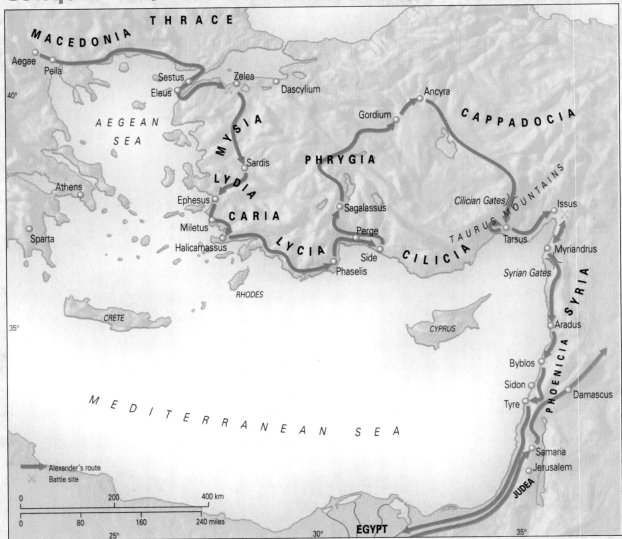

Alexander died of fever in Babylon at the age of 33 in 323 B.C. His conquests were divided up among five of his generals. By 312 B.C. after years of struggle, two emerged as the leading powers in the Near East, Ptolemy controlled Egypt and Seleucus controlled the old Babylonian empire. Palestine lay between the two powers and changed hands several times until the Seleucid ruler Antiochus III Megas won control in 199 B.C. He was followed by Seleucus IV Philopator 187-175 B.C. then Antiochus IV Epiphanes 175-164 B.C. who provoked the Maccabean Revolt.

Ruins of the Temple of Artemis (a Greek goddess of the hunt and twin of Apollo) in the Hellenistic city of Gerasa (modern Jerash, Jordan) one of a league of ten cities east of the Jordan river known as the Decapolis.

Ptolemy I Soter 323-285 B.C. resettled many Jews in Alexandria, Egypt. Under Ptolemy II Philadelphus 285-246 B.C., the Scriptures were translated into Greek. This work is known as the Septuagint because it was translated by seventy (Latin septuaginta) scholars brought to Egypt by Ptolemy II to serve the needs of the Greek-speaking Jewish community.

Jerusalem In The Middle

Alexander himself died very young, leaving no successor. After many civil wars, his empire was divided three ways, with one ruler in Greece, one in Egypt, and one occupying about the territory of the old Persian Empire.

The Greek rulers in Egypt were the Ptolemies, of whom the most famous would be the last, Cleopatra. The Seleucids ruled the old Persian Empire, including Syria.

As usual, Palestine was caught in the middle. At first it belonged to the Ptolemies; then the Seleucids conquered it. Just as had happened with Babylon and Egypt, and before that with Assyria and Egypt, there were factions supporting each side in Jerusalem, and sometimes people who thought they were clever enough to play one empire off against another. There was also a "Hellenizing" faction, especially among the rich and powerful, who were attracted by Greek civilization, and didn't mind if a few pagan gods went with it.

Faithful Jews were deeply offended when they saw fashionable young men wearing Greek hats and going to Greek festivals. But until the reign of the Seleucid king Antiochus IV, at least the Jews who wanted to could worship the True God in peace.

Antiochus IV called himself Epiphanes—Greek for "God Manifest." He thought more highly of himself than many of his subjects did. They called him Epimanes—Greek for "Out of His Mind." He was just crazy enough to think of himself as a god, and brutal enough that no one dared to speak against him to his face. Even his most debauched courtiers were thoroughly embarrassed by his behavior. They could hardly bear to watch when the exalted king of the world's greatest empire stood up on the stage in the public theater to perform lewd dances.

It was Antiochus' greatest ambition to make his whole vast empire Greek. Greek culture—and Greek religion—would be brought to every province. Local customs would have to give way to a uniformly Hellenized state.

Under Antiochus' empire, the Jewish high priest was also the secular ruler of his people. It was a powerful position, and Antiochus sold it to the highest bidder, regardless of qualifications. The winning bidder offered Antiochus 440 talents of silver. It was literally tons of money—about sixteen tons, to be precise.

Now that the high priesthood was in the hands of the rich Hellenists, the young men of the best families adopted Greek customs and forgot about the Law of Moses. Even the priests joined the fun, neglecting the sacrifices so they could go to the arena and watch wrestling.[1] The high priest himself sent some of the Temple revenue off to buy sacrifices to Hercules.[2]

The Final Desecration

Greeks often saw local deities as alternate manifestations of their own gods, so it made perfect sense to Antiochus to Hellenize the worship of his Jewish subjects. The Temple of God in Jerusalem was made the temple of Olympian Zeus. The temple of the Samaritans on Mt. Gerizim was made a temple of Zeus-Friend-of-Strangers.[3]

Far more than the name changed. Antiochus and his followers introduced Greek styles of worship at the Temple. Greek worship was full of immoralities that shocked the faithful remnant of Israel.

> Harsh and utterly grievous was the onslaught of evil. For the temple was filled with debauchery and reveling by the Gentiles, who dallied with harlots and had intercourse with women within the sacred precincts, and besides brought in things for sacrifice that were unfit. The altar was covered with abominable offerings which were forbidden by the

laws. A man could neither keep the Sabbath, nor observe the feasts of his fathers, nor so much as confess himself to be a Jew. (2 Mc 6:3-5)

Anyone who openly practiced Judaism—which is what the Jews began to call their religion, to distinguish it from "Hellenism"—was in mortal danger. Antiochus insisted that everyone must take part in the pagan sacrifices. That meant not only eating food sacrificed to idols, but also eating things like pork that were forbidden to Jews who followed the Law of Moses.

Still many of the remnant of faithful Israel defied Antiochus, even when the king resorted to murder and torture to make his point. Mothers who had their children circumcised were killed with their children. Old men died for refusing to eat unclean meats. Antiochus topped off his campaign of terror by desecrating the Temple itself, filling it with harlots and offering unclean sacrifices on the altar.

> God revealed the resurrection of the dead to his people progressively. Hope in the bodily resurrection of the dead established itself as a consequence intrinsic to faith in God as creator of the whole man, soul and body. The creator of heaven and earth is also the one who faithfully maintains his covenant with Abraham and his posterity. It was in this double perspective that faith in the resurrection came to be expressed. In their trials, the Maccabean martyrs confessed:
>
> The King of the universe will raise us up to an everlasting renewal of life, because we have died for his laws (2 Mc 7:9). One cannot but choose to die at the hands of men and to cherish the hope that God gives of being raised again by him (2 Mc 7:14; cf. 7:29; Dn 12:1-13). (CCC 992)

Amazing Success Of The Maccabees

At first the resistance was individual and unorganized. But soon one family became the standard-bearers for the revolt. An old priest named Mattathias and his five sons retreated to the countryside and started organizing the resistance. It was an obviously hopeless effort; they could never succeed against the power of the world's greatest empire. The only reason for resisting was that it was better to die than to be unfaithful to God.

Yet against all odds the revolt did succeed. Trusting in God, the sons of Mattathias began to take back bits and pieces of territory. Judas Maccabeus, the most talented soldier among them, gained amazing victories against the pagan armies. Within three years, the faithful Jews were able to purify and rededicate the Temple. Jewish families still celebrate that event as the festival of Hanukkah.

When Judas died, the victories continued under his brothers. The pagan kings were forced to come to terms with the Maccabees, as Judas and his brothers were called. Soon they controlled most of Judah. From there they pressed their successes outward, until they had actually conquered most of the territory of David's kingdom. They made alliances with Sparta and with Rome, a rising power in the west. The Greek kings were forced to admit what had already in fact happened: Israel was now an independent power. About 125 years before the birth of Christ, an independent Israel had finally been restored.

Was this the fulfillment of all the prophecies? It certainly must have looked that way to many faithful Jews. Israel was whole again, and the shackles of the oppressors had been thrown off. All that was needed to complete the fulfillment was a king of David's line, a branch from the stump of Jesse.

The Hasmonean Kingdom, ca. 165-37 B.C.

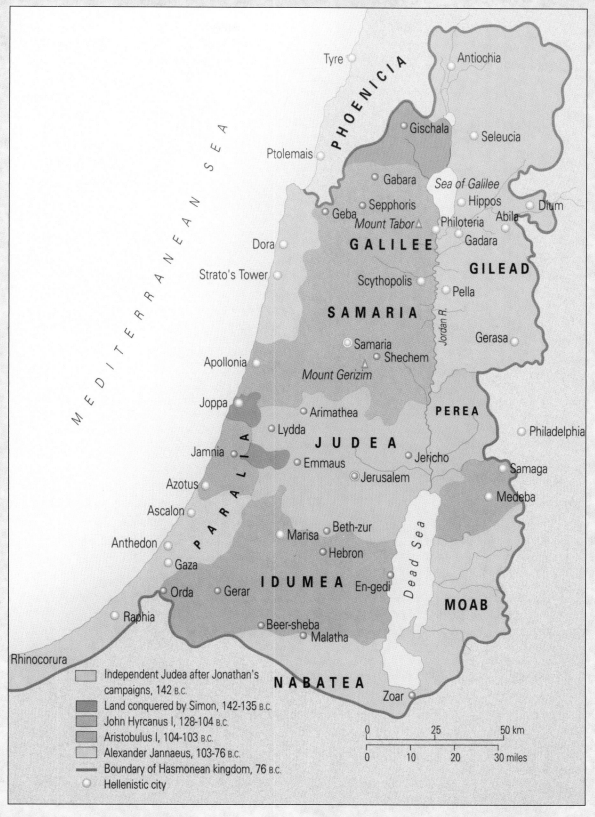

Tyre

PHOENICIA

Antiochia

Gischala

Seleucia

Ptolemais

Gabara

Sea of Galilee

Hippos

Dium

Geba

Sepphoris

Philoteria

Abila

MEDITERRANEAN SEA

Mount Tabor △

Gadara

Dora

GALILEE

GILEAD

Strato's Tower

Scythopolis

Pella

SAMARIA

Jordan R.

Samaria

Gerasa

Apollonia

Shechem

Mount Gerizim

Joppa

Arimathea

PEREA

Lydda

Philadelphia

Jamnia

PARALIA

JUDEA

Jericho

Emmaus

Samaga

Azotus

Jerusalem

Ascalon

Dead Sea

Medeba

Anthedon

Marisa

Beth-zur

Gaza

Hebron

Orda

Gerar

IDUMEA

En-gedi

MOAB

Raphia

Beer-sheba

Malatha

Rhinocorura

NABATEA

Zoar

Independent Judea after Jonathan's campaigns, 142 B.C.

Land conquered by Simon, 142-135 B.C.

John Hyrcanus I, 128-104 B.C.

Aristobulus I, 104-103 B.C.

Alexander Jannaeus, 103-76 B.C.

Boundary of Hasmonean kingdom, 76 B.C.

○ Hellenistic city

0   25   50 km

0   10   20   30 miles

Maccabees Family Tree

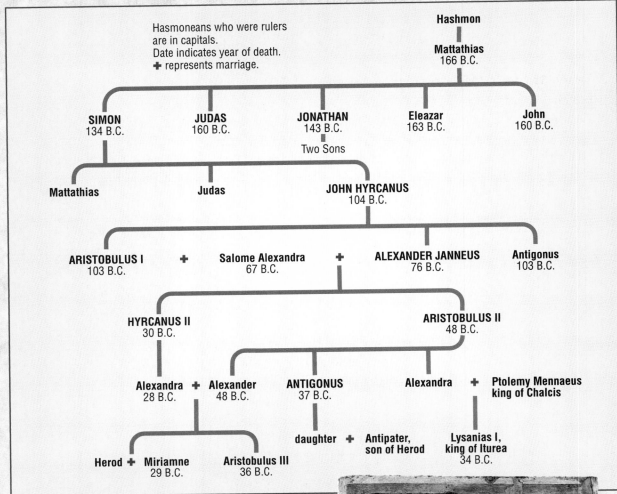

Hasmoneans who were rulers are in capitals.
Date indicates year of death.
✚ represents marriage.

Hashmon

Mattathias
166 B.C.

SIMON
134 B.C.

JUDAS
160 B.C.

JONATHAN
143 B.C.
Two Sons

Eleazar
163 B.C.

John
160 B.C.

Mattathias

Judas

JOHN HYRCANUS
104 B.C.

ARISTOBULUS I
103 B.C.
✚
Salome Alexandra
67 B.C.
✚
ALEXANDER JANNEUS
76 B.C.

Antigonus
103 B.C.

HYRCANUS II
30 B.C.

ARISTOBULUS II
48 B.C.

Alexandra
28 B.C.
✚
Alexander
48 B.C.

ANTIGONUS
37 B.C.

Alexandra
✚
Ptolemy Mennaeus
king of Chalcis

Herod ✚ Miriamne
29 B.C.

Aristobulus III
36 B.C.

daughter ✚ Antipater,
son of Herod

Lysanias I,
king of Iturea
34 B.C.

Full independence was achieved under the last Maccabee brother, Simon Hasmoneus. Named for Simon, this period is called the Hasmonean Period. The Jews began to date contracts and agreements from 142 B.C.

"In the first year of Simon the great high priest and commander and leader of the Jews." (1 Mc 13: 42)

This icon's inscription is "The Holy Seven Maccabees." Next to each portrait is the saint's name. The seven young saints and the elder Eleazar hold rolled-up scrolls rather than more traditional martyr's crosses.

A Hasmonean coin from Mattathias Antigonos, 40-37 B.C. Traces of a Greek inscription surround the seven-branched Menorah. This coin is unusual because Jewish religious law forbade the Menorah image to be used in art.

What The Jews Believed

The two books of the Maccabees are valuable as history, but they are just as valuable for what they tell us about Jewish beliefs. Written only about a century before the birth of Jesus Christ, they give us a glimpse of Jewish life just before the Incarnation.

1. "Israel" is the faithful remnant.

For the authors of the books of Maccabees, the name "Israel" does not mean everyone of Jewish descent. It means the people who were faithful to God—often a small minority.

> And he [Antiochus Epiphanes] appointed inspectors over all the people and commanded the cities of Judah to offer sacrifice, city by city. Many of the people, every one who forsook the law, joined them, and they did evil in the land; they drove Israel into hiding in every place of refuge they had. (1 Mc 1: 51-53)

Many of the people of Judah offered the sacrifices, but "Israel" went into hiding. The author is making a clear distinction: only the people who refused to forsake the law can be called "Israel."

This is exactly the meaning of "Israel" that St. Paul often used in the New Testament.

> For not all who are descended from Israel belong to Israel, and not all are children of Abraham because they are his descendants . . . it is not the children of the flesh who are the children of God, but the children of the promise are reckoned as descendants. (Rom 9: 6-8)

"Israel" meant all the people who were faithful to God. But because the New Covenant extended God's kingdom to all the nations, every person from every race is now called to enter into the Family of God, with no distinction between Jewish and Gentile.

> There is neither Jew nor Greek, there is neither slave nor free; there is neither male nor female; for you are all one in Christ Jesus. And if you are Christ's, then you are Abraham's offspring, heirs according to the promise. (Gal 3: 28-29)

"Israel" is a foreshadowing of the Church.

2. The saints who die will rise again to an eternal reward.

By the time the books of Maccabees were written, many Jews believed in the resurrection of the dead. (Not everyone believed: even in the time of Jesus, the Sadducees still denied the resurrection.) After we die, we expect to be judged by God.

> For even if for the present I should avoid the punishment of men, yet whether I live or die I shall not escape the hands of the Almighty. (2 Mc 6: 26)

Those who have been faithful to God's commandments will have everlasting life as their reward.

> And when he was at his last breath, he said, "You accursed wretch, you dismiss us from this present life, but the King of the universe will raise us up to an everlasting renewal of life, because we have died for his laws." (2 Mc 7: 9)

This eternal life would be a resurrection of the *body*, as Christians still confess in the Apostles' Creed.

> When it was demanded, he quickly put forth his tongue and courageously stretched forth his hands, and said nobly, "I got these from Heaven, and because of his laws I disdain them, and from him I hope to get them back again." (2 Mc 7: 12)

But the wicked would have no share in this eternal reward.

> And when he was near death he said, "One cannot but choose to die at the hands of men and to cherish the hope that God gives of being raised again by him. But for you there will be no resurrection to life!" (2 Mc 7: 14)

3. Martyrdom is preferable to apostasy.

Because God's saints expect to receive eternal life as their reward, it is far better to lose this life than to turn away from God. Apostasy—the sin of turning away from the worship of the True God—is never worth while, no matter how tempting tyrants may try to make it look. When we compare the shortness of this life to eternity, nothing that happens to us on earth is worth giving up our chance at everlasting life.

> As a result the king himself and those with him were astonished at the young man's spirit, for he regarded his sufferings as nothing. (2 Mc 7:12)

> For our brothers after enduring a brief suffering have drunk of everflowing life under God's covenant; but you, by the judgment of God, will receive just punishment for your arrogance. (2 Mc 7:36)

> Scripture bears witness to faith in creation "out of nothing" as a truth full of promise and hope. Thus the mother of seven sons encourages them for martyrdom:

>> I do not know how you came into being in my womb. It was not I who gave you life and breath, nor I who set in order the elements within each of you. Therefore the Creator of the world, who shaped the beginning of man and devised the origin of all things, will in his mercy give life and breath back to you again, since you now forget yourselves for the sake of his laws...Look at the heaven and the earth and see everything that is in them, and recognize that God did not make them out of things that existed. Thus also mankind comes into being (2 Mc 7:22-23, 28). (CCC 297)

4. God judges his people as a father judges his children.

The people of God may suffer from time to time, but these sufferings come because Israel needs discipline, not because God wants revenge.

> For we are suffering because of our own sins. And if our living LORD is angry for a little while, to rebuke and discipline us, he will again be reconciled with his own servants. (2 Mc 7:32-33)

5. It is good and wise to pray for the dead.

When Judas Maccabeus found that some of his soldiers had died with pagan amulets, he prayed to God to forgive their sin. Although they were dead, he didn't regard their state after death as a closed issue.

> Then under the tunic of every one of the dead soldiers they found sacred tokens of the idols of Jamnia, which the law forbids the Jews to wear. And it became clear to them that this was why these men had fallen. So they all blessed the ways of the LORD, the righteous Judge, who reveals the things that are hidden; and they turned to prayer, beseeching that the sin which had been committed might be wholly blotted out...He [Judas] also took up a collection, man by man, to the amount of two thousand drachmas of silver, and sent it to Jerusalem to provide for a sin offering. In doing this he acted very well and honorably, taking account of the resurrection. For if he were not expecting that those who had fallen would rise again, it would have been superstitious and foolish to pray for the dead. But if he was looking for the splendid reward that is laid up for those who fall asleep in godliness, it was a holy and pious thought. Therefore he made atonement for the dead, that they might be delivered from their sin. (2 Mc 12:40-45)

Because of his firm belief in the resurrection, Judas did what he could to make atonement for the sin of the soldiers who died. That entails a belief that the dead can still be helped by our prayers, which is the basis for the Christian doctrine of Purgatory.

This teaching is also based on the practice of prayer for the dead, already mentioned in Sacred Scripture: "Therefore [Judas Maccabeus] made atonement for the dead, that they might be delivered from their sin" (2 Mc 12: 46). From the beginning the Church has honored the memory of the dead and offered prayers in suffrage for them, above all the Eucharistic sacrifice, so that, thus purified, they may attain the beatific vision of God (cf. Council of Lyons II (1274): DS 856). The Church also commends almsgiving, indulgences, and works of penance undertaken on behalf of the dead:

> Let us help and commemorate them. If Job's sons were purified by their father's sacrifice, why would we doubt that our offerings for the dead bring them some consolation? Let us not hesitate to help those who have died and to offer our prayers for them.[4] (CCC 1032)

Judas Maccabeus And The Story Of Hanukkah

Hanukkah is a Hebrew word meaning "dedication." It is also spelled Chanuka, Chanukah or Hannukah.

In 167 B.C., Antiochus IV ordered an altar to Zeus erected in the Jewish Temple. After the successful revolt against the Seleucid monarchy by the Maccabees, the Temple was liberated, cleansed and rededicated in 164 B.C.

The festival of Hanukkah was instituted by Judas Maccabeus and his brothers to celebrate this rededication of the Temple (1 Mc 4: 59). Judas ordered the Temple to be cleansed, a new altar to be built in place of the polluted one, and new holy vessels to be made. When the fire had been rekindled upon the altar and the lamps of the candlestick lit, the dedication of the altar was celebrated for eight days amid sacrifices and songs (1 Mc 4: 36).

Some historians believe that the reason for the eight day celebration was that the first Hanukkah was a belated celebration of the festival of Sukkot, the Feast of Tabernacles (2 Mc 1: 9; 10: 6). During the revolt, the Jews were not able to celebrate Sukkot properly. Sukkot also lasts for eight days, and was a holiday in which the lighting of lamps played a prominent part during the Second Temple period. Lights were also kindled in the household, and the popular name of the festival was "Festival of Lights."

SUPPLEMENTARY READING

Clement of Alexandria: *Miscellanies,* Book IV

Chapter 9: Christ's Sayings Respecting Martyrdom.

On martyrdom the Lord hath spoken explicitly, and what is written in different places we bring together. "But I say unto you, Whosoever shall confess in Me before men, the Son of man also shall confess before the angels of God; but whosoever shall deny Me before men, him will I deny before the angels." "Whosoever shall be ashamed of Me or of My words in this adulterous and sinful generation, of him shall the Son of man also be ashamed when He cometh in the glory of His Father with His angels. Whosoever therefore shall confess in Me before men, him will I also confess before my Father in heaven." "And when they bring you before synagogues, and rulers, and powers, think not: beforehand how ye shall make your defense, or what ye shall say. For the Holy Spirit shall teach you in the same hour what ye must say."

❖ ❖ ❖

But if the Spirit of the Father testifies in us, how can we be any more hypocrites, who are said to bear testimony with the voice alone? But it will be given to some, if expedient, to make a defense, that by their witness and confession all may be benefited—those in the Church being confirmed, and those of the heathen who have devoted themselves to the search after salvation wondering and being led to the faith; and the rest seized with amazement. So that confession is by all means necessary. For it is in our power. But to make a defense for our faith is not universally necessary. For that does not depend on us. "But he that endureth to the end shall be saved." For who of those who are wise would not choose to reign in God, and even to serve? So some "confess that they know God," according to the apostle; "but in works they deny Him, being abominable and disobedient, and to every good work reprobate." And these, though they confess nothing but this, will have done at the end one good work. Their witness, then, appears to be the cleansing away of sins with glory. For instance, the Shepherd says: "You will escape the energy of the wild beast, if your heart become pure and blameless." Also the Lord Himself says: "Satan hath desired to sift you; but I have prayed."

"For there appeared to them a magnificently caparisoned horse, with a rider of frightening mien, and it rushed furiously at Heliodorus and struck him with its front hoofs." (2 Mc 3: 25)

VOCABULARY

ALEXANDER THE GREAT

The Greek conqueror who spread his empire as far as India. Despite the empire's breakup after his death, Alexander's conquests spread Greek culture throughout the known world.

ANTIOCHUS IV ("EPIPHANES")

The Seleucid king who tried to force Hellenism, including Greek religion, on his Jewish subjects.

GERIZIM

The mountain on which the Samaritans had their temple to God.

HELLENISM

The fashion of adopting Greek culture and ideas, popular all over the Middle East after Alexander's conquests.

JUDAISM

The practice of traditional Jewish religion, defined in opposition to "Hellenism."

JUDAS MACCABEUS

The Jewish general who led the revolt against Antiochus IV.

MACCABEES

The collective name of Judas Maccabeus and his brothers, leaders of the Jewish revolt against Antiochus IV.

MARTYR

One who dies for the sake of faith in God. Greek for "witness."

MATTATHIAS

A priest who touched off the Jewish revolt against Antiochus IV. He was the father of Judas Maccabeus.

PURGATORY

A state of final purification after death and before entrance into heaven for those who died in God's friendship but were only imperfectly purified. God's people knew their prayers were efficacious for the dead even in the time of the Maccabees.

RESURRECTION

The time when the faithful people who have died will come back to eternal life. "All the dead will rise, those who have done good to the resurrection of life and those who have done evil to the resurrection of judgment" (CCC 998).

SELEUCIDS

The Greek rulers of the eastern part of Alexander's empire. Their territory included Palestine.

Greek columns in the Hellenized city Gerasa, Jordan.

STUDY QUESTIONS

1. What does "Hellenized" mean?

2. Who were the Greek rulers in Egypt?

3. What notorious king began the persecution of Jews who refused to convert to Greek forms of worship?

4. What did Antiochus IV do to the Jewish and Samaritan temples?

5. Why would a revelation like that described in CCC 992 be important during times of persecution?

6. What position did Antiochus IV sell to the highest bidder?

7. What loyal priest led the resistance to the persecution?

8. Which of that priest's sons became famous for his military victories?

9. What does the Jewish Feast of Hanukkah celebrate?

10. According to 1 Maccabees, who deserves the name of "Israel"?

11. What truths can be determined from the Books of Maccabees?

12. What is apostasy?

13. Why is it good and wise to pray for the dead?

PRACTICAL EXERCISES

1. In the story of the Maccabees, Antiochus puts all seven brothers to death when they refuse to turn from God. Read 2 Maccabees 7: 20-30. Discuss the mother's fortitude when facing the death of her sons. How does the youngest son respond to Antiochus' offers? In the end, the mother dies along with her seven sons. How can this story of fortitude and love for God be an inspiration to us? When might we need the same sort of fortitude?

2. God's promise of eternal life in heaven was one of the great sources of strength for the Maccabees and the rest of the martyrs. God created humans with the sole purpose of serving him and being with him forever in heaven. Heaven is our end. It is the only place where we can be truly fulfilled and truly happy. What do you know about heaven? What will it be like to see God there? Can we know anything about heaven without God revealing it to us?

3. Because Judas Maccabeus had a firm belief in the resurrection, he prayed for his soldiers who had died wearing the pagan amulets. The Church dedicates the month of November, which starts with All Saints Day and All Souls Day, to praying for the deceased. How do our prayers for people after their deaths offer them any help? Why do we believe it is necessary to pray for the dead?

Endnotes

1. 2 Mc 4: 12-15.
2. 2 Mc 4: 19.
3. 2 Mc 6: 2.
4. St. John Chrysostom, Hom. in 1 Cor. 41,
   5: PG 61, 361; cf. Job 1: 5.

The World of The New Testament

"'The land of Zebulun and the land of Naphtali, toward the sea, across the Jordan, Galilee of the Gentiles—the people who sat in darkness have seen a great light,...'"

Matthew 4: 15–16

Chapter 16

The World of The New Testament

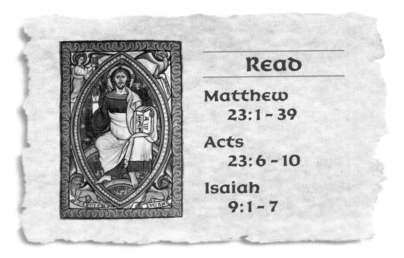

Read

Matthew
23:1 – 39

Acts
23:6 – 10

Isaiah
9:1 – 7

The amazing successes of the Maccabees revealed the power of God. Once again there was an independent Israel, with Jerusalem as its capital. The Temple had been purified, and the worship of the True God could go on again as it was prescribed in the Law of Moses. The high priest was also the secular ruler of his people, so once again the state and the church became one.

The Prophecies Fulfilled?

When John Hyrcanus became high priest, he decided to take the next step. He would purify the whole country of pagan influences. He gave everyone in the country a choice: be circumcised or leave. Being circumcised, of course, meant taking on the whole Law of Moses, with all its rituals and requirements. The country was "Judaized"—made Jewish—almost overnight. To

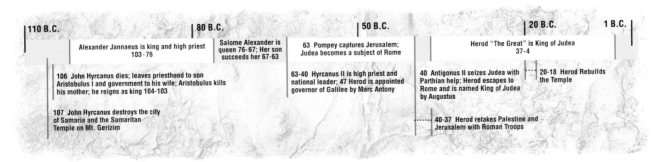

110 B.C. | 80 B.C. | 50 B.C. | 20 B.C. | 1 B.C.

Alexander Jannaeus is king and high priest 103-76

Salome Alexander is queen 76-67; Her son succeeds her 67-63

63 Pompey captures Jerusalem; Judea becomes a subject of Rome

Herod "The Great" is King of Judea 37-4

106 John Hyrcanus dies; leaves priesthood to son Aristobulus I and government to his wife; Aristobulus kills his mother; he reigns as king 104-103

63-40 Hyrcanus II is high priest and national leader; 47 Herod is appointed governor of Galilee by Marc Antony

40 Antigonus II seizes Judea with Parthian help; Herod escapes to Rome and is named King of Judea by Augustus

20-18 Herod Rebuilds the Temple

107 John Hyrcanus destroys the city of Samaria and the Samaritan Temple on Mt. Gerizim

40-37 Herod retakes Palestine and Jerusalem with Roman Troops

make sure God was worshiped in the right way, Hyrcanus also destroyed the temple of the Samaritans on Mount Gerizim—an act that earned the undying hatred of the Samaritans.

As a military leader, Hyrcanus conquered almost all the territories that had belonged to the Davidic kingdom. The amazing restoration was continuing: now Israel's territory was intact again. It looked as though all the promises of the prophets were coming true.

There was only one more logical step, and the successor of Hyrcanus took it. In the year 106 B.C., John Hyrcanus died, and Aristobulus assumed the office of high priest. Then he did what many people had been waiting for: he proclaimed himself king.

Now, it seemed, the promises of the prophets had been fulfilled. Israel was whole again, and a king reigned in Jerusalem.

But one thing was completely wrong. It was not a king of the line of David: Aristobulus and his successors were Levites. The prophets had all promised that the Lord's Anointed would be from the tribe of Judah and the descendants of David.

The united Israel was no easier to maintain than it had been in Rehoboam's time. Within a very short time, Israel became deeply divided between two powerful parties that had grown up: the Pharisees and the Sadducees.

The Pharisees

How could the Jews be faithful to God when Judea was a small province of a huge pagan empire? There was more than one way to answer that question. One group of prominent scholars decided that the best way to stay faithful was to build a wall around themselves and keep out the Gentiles. They were called "the separated," which is "Perushim" in Hebrew, from which we get "Pharisees."

For the Pharisees, the only way for Jews to be faithful was to keep themselves pure. The Law alone wasn't enough: the Pharisees taught that even ordinary Jewish families should imitate the complicated and ritualistic purity of the priests in Jerusalem. They legislated more and more customs and oral traditions, adding rituals like cleansing their hands before meals. (They washed their hands not to get rid of dirt, but to get rid of any chance of ritual defilement.)

Of course, the Pharisees refused to associate with Gentiles. Even entering a Gentile's house would defile a Jew, they taught. To distinguish themselves from Gentiles, they emphasized and exaggerated their distinctly Jewish customs.

There were good reasons for the Pharisees to believe what they believed. Anyone who knew the history of Israel could see how associating with pagans had led to trouble. But the Pharisees made the Law an intolerable burden. As time went on, they emphasized the external signs of separation more and more. Among them there were those who exaggerated the details of Jewish national dress, wearing big phylacteries (boxes with verses of Scripture that pious Jews wore when praying) and conspicuous fringes (the fringes that the law of Moses commands in Nm 15:38). They made sure everyone was keeping the Sabbath by the strictest possible interpretation. They also enforced a strict interpretation of the dietary laws. At the same time, though, they were perfectly capable of evading the spirit of the law when it suited them, inventing interpretations that helped them cheat the poor or even their own parents.

> They bind heavy burdens, hard to bear, and lay them on men's shoulders; but they themselves will not move them with their finger. They do all their deeds to be seen by men; for they make their phylacteries broad and their fringes long, and they love the place of honor at feasts and the best seats in the synagogues, and salutations in the market places, and being called rabbi by men. (Jesus Christ in Mt 23:4-7)

Judaism In New Testament Times

According to the Jewish historian Josephus, "The Jews… had three philosophies…that of the Essenes, that of the Sadducees, and thirdly, that of the group called the Pharisees" (*Jewish Antiquities* XVIII,11).

The Pharisees emphasized the external signs of separation from the Gentiles. Among them were those who exaggerated the details of Jewish national dress, wearing phylacteries (boxes containing verses of Scripture) on their foreheads and fringes that the law of Moses commands in Nm 15: 38.

The Pharisees were the forerunners of the rabbis. By applying written Torah to daily life, the Pharisees made practicing the faith possible in places far from the city.

The Sadducees were the party of political power. First under the Maccabees, then under the Romans. A council called the Sanhedrin made decisions regarding the day-to-day governing of Judah. While the Pharisees had some position in the Sanhedrin, the Sadducees were its dominant membership.

A group of religious Judeans protested the combining of the kingship and the high priesthood by the Maccabees. They believed that the Temple under the Sadducees had become hopelessly corrupt, so they moved out of Jerusalem and established a small community at Qumran, in the desert beside the Dead Sea. Their writings (the Dead Sea Scrolls discovered in the 1940's) reveal a community that saw themselves as pure and righteous, in comparison to the tainted Sadducees and (probably) the Pharisees. There is a theory that St. John the Baptist was an Essene.

A group known as Zealots also functioned in the first century A.D. in Judea. They may have ignited the uprising of 66 A.D. similar to the Maccabee's revolution some 230 years earlier.

By the time of Jesus, the Pharisees were a very powerful sect. Many of the Jews accepted that the Pharisees were as righteous as they claimed to be. But many of the poor resented the heavy burdens of ritual that the Pharisees laid on them.

The Pharisees had come up with a successful answer to the question of how the Jewish religion could survive in a Gentile empire, but it was an answer that depended on rejecting the Gentiles completely. They had to forget or reject the promise of the Davidic covenant and of the prophets: that Jerusalem would be a center of worship for all nations, not just the Jews. When Jesus came and began to fulfill that promise by drawing the Gentiles to God, the Pharisees immediately recognized that he was preaching a religion that was inclusive, not exclusive. They hated him for that.

The Sadducees

On the other side of almost every question were the Sadducees. They were the heirs of Zadok, Solomon's priest, who were supposed to have been the priests forever in Jerusalem. They thought that the best way for the Jewish religion to survive was by cooperating with the Gentiles. Although the Pharisees were revered by the Jewish public, the Sadducees were the ones who had the most power in the government. Naturally, the Pharisees hated them.

The Sadducees had very different ideas of religion from the Pharisees. For the Sadducees, only the books of Moses—Genesis, Exodus, Leviticus, Numbers, Deuteronomy—were canonical Scripture. They did not believe in any life after death, or in any kind of resurrection from the dead. They did not believe in angels or spirits. Since they rejected everything except the Torah, the Sadducees naturally rejected all the Pharisees' traditional interpretations of and additions to the Law.

> The Pharisees and many of the Lord's contemporaries hoped for the resurrection. Jesus teaches it firmly. To the Sadducees who deny it he answers, "Is not this why you are wrong, that you know neither the scriptures nor the power of God?" (Mk 12: 24; cf. Jn 11: 24; Acts 23: 6). Faith in the resurrection rests on faith in God who "is not God of the dead, but of the living" (Mk 12: 27). (CCC 993)

After The Maccabees

The freedom gained under the Maccabees could not last forever. Even if Israel had been united, the great empires of the world would hardly have left such a strategically important place alone. But Israel was not united. It was split into warring parties, and the internal dissent was a wedge that outsiders were very willing to make use of.

Even the kings contributed to the disunity. More than once the throne was disputed by rival family members, which again led to civil war and chaos.

So when Rome, the new superpower in the Mediterranean, expanded into Palestine, Judea fell without much of a fight. At first the Jewish kings kept their throne as

The Ark of the Covenant image carved on a stone from an ancient synagogue in Capernaum.

Roman tributaries. But in the year 40 B.C., an ambitious and ruthless thug, Herod the Great, managed to persuade the Romans to give him the throne of Judea. He established himself on the throne by besieging Jerusalem (with a Roman army of 60,000 to back him up) and massacring many of the residents. That set the tone for his long reign, a bloody tyranny that would inflame the anti-Roman hatred of much of the population.

Herod The Great

By almost any standard, Herod was insane. He murdered three of his own sons in such horrible ways that one Roman general said he would rather be Herod's pig than Herod's son. But Herod was a crafty lunatic who knew how to grasp power and keep it. And the Romans cared little for how many people he murdered, as long as he kept the tribute flowing into Rome on schedule. Just to make sure, though, Herod sent lavish gifts to prominent Romans to keep himself in favor with them.

Herod was not even Jewish, but he did his best to look like a Davidic king. Although he was an Edomite, he spread the story that he was actually a Jew returned from the Exile. He rebuilt the Temple in Jerusalem on a magnificent scale. He had multiple wives, just like Solomon. He also was careful to subsidize the Temple priests generously, which meant that most of the influential priests supported him.

Herod might have been ruthless, but he knew how to spend money. He was a talented architect (or he took credit for the work of other talented architects) who built magnificent palaces, fortresses, and public buildings all over his kingdom.

His greatest work was his new Temple, which by all accounts was more glorious even than Solomon's. It was such a spectacle that pilgrims came from all over the known world just to see it. (In Acts 8, for example, we read of a wealthy court official who had come all the way from Ethiopia.) While they were there, they spent their money in Jerusalem, which helped keep the economy healthy.

In fact, the combination of Roman peace, worldwide trade, and Herod's expensive building programs brought on an economic boom like nothing Israel had seen before. It must have seemed to many Jews that the prophets' promises had finally been fulfilled. Herod was a bloody tyrant, but when had God insisted on perfection? Even David was an adulterer. Israel was united and rich, the Temple was more glorious than ever, and people from all the nations were coming to see Jerusalem. Perhaps Herod was the promised Messiah. He would be known as Herod "the Great"—not because he was universally admired, but because his reign was so prosperous in comparison with the reigns of his successors.

When Herod the Great died, the Romans split his kingdom four ways among his surviving sons. In Greek, the split kingdom was called the "Tetrarchy," which means "rule of four." Herod Antipas, one of Herod the Great's sons, ruled over Galilee during the ministry of Jesus Christ.

Worshipers at the Western Wall, also called the Wailing Wall, a surviving outer courtyard wall of Herod's Temple. The Western Wall continues to have a powerful hold on the devotion of Jews from all over the world. For centuries, millions have come as tourists and pilgrims to touch the Wall with their hands, leave written prayers in its crevices, and feel the sanctity that emanates from it.

The Herods' Family Tree

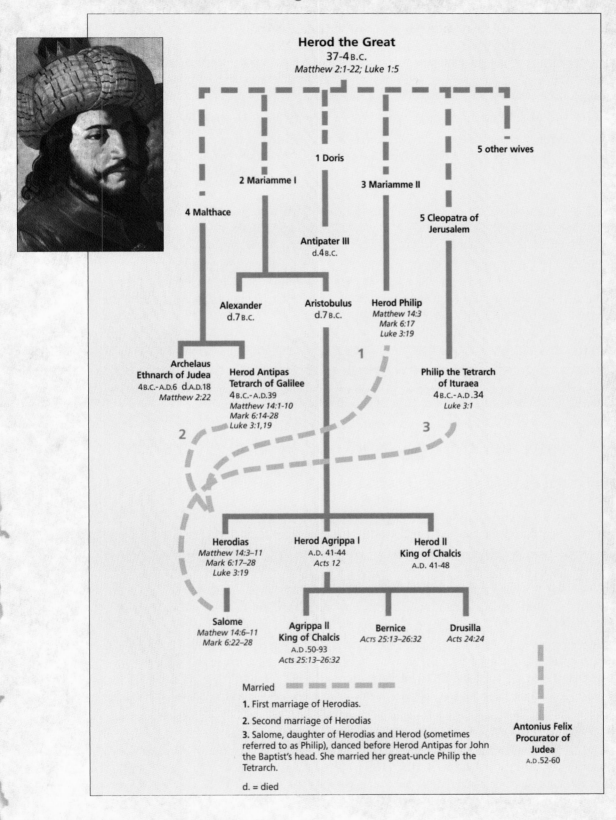

Herod the Great
37-4 B.C.
Matthew 2:1-22; Luke 1:5

1 Doris

2 Mariamme I

3 Mariamme II

5 Cleopatra of Jerusalem

5 other wives

4 Malthace

Antipater III
d.4 B.C.

Alexander
d.7 B.C.

Aristobulus
d.7 B.C.

Herod Philip
Matthew 14:3
Mark 6:17
Luke 3:19

Archelaus
Ethnarch of Judea
4 B.C.-A.D.6 d.A.D.18
Matthew 2:22

Herod Antipas
Tetrarch of Galilee
4 B.C.-A.D.39
Matthew 14:1-10
Mark 6:14-28
Luke 3:1,19

Philip the Tetrarch
of Ituraea
4 B.C.-A.D.34
Luke 3:1

1

2

3

Herodias
Matthew 14:3–11
Mark 6:17–28
Luke 3:19

Herod Agrippa I
A.D. 41-44
Acts 12

Herod II
King of Chalcis
A.D. 41-48

Salome
Mathew 14:6–11
Mark 6:22–28

Agrippa II
King of Chalcis
A.D.50-93
Acts 25:13–26:32

Bernice
Acts 25:13–26:32

Drusilla
Acts 24:24

Married ▬ ▬ ▬ ▬ ▬ ▬ ▬

1. First marriage of Herodias.

2. Second marriage of Herodias

3. Salome, daughter of Herodias and Herod (sometimes referred to as Philip), danced before Herod Antipas for John the Baptist's head. She married her great-uncle Philip the Tetrarch.

Antonius Felix
Procurator of
Judea
A.D.52-60

d. = died

When The Time Had Fully Come

By the end of Herod's reign, many of the Jews were still expecting the Messiah, but many others were convinced that Herod's temple represented the divine fulfillment of prophecy. The squabbling parties were still squabbling, and occasional terrorist raids disrupted the tranquility of the province, but Herod's iron fist—backed up by Rome, the world's greatest power—managed to keep order most of the time.

This was the world in which the Christ was born. The Messiah came, signifying the fullness of time.

> But when the time had fully come, God sent forth his Son, born of woman, born under the law, to redeem those who were under the law, so that we might receive adoption as sons. (Gal 4: 4-5)

Why had the time "fully come" for the Incarnation? For one thing, the political state of the world was remarkably stable. After decades of destructive wars, a large part of the civilized world was under the control of one great world-empire: Rome. The "Roman peace" (*pax Romana* in Latin, the language of Rome) was just beginning when Jesus was born, and it would last for hundreds of years.

When Caesar Augustus defeated Pompey and Mark Anthony, he became sole ruler of most of the known world, and he began an era of relative peace that would last for centuries. By the time the Christian Church began to spread, it was possible to travel from Britain to Arabia without ever leaving the boundaries of the Empire.

In many ways travel was easier in the Roman Empire at that time than it is in the same area now. We can get from one place to another faster; but the Romans had no borders to cross, no checkpoints to worry about, no currency conversions to calculate. From Spain to Palestine, from Britain to Africa, it was all one great Empire, with the same currency and the same laws. But although the Roman Empire was politically stable, its religion was crumbling into irrelevance.

Religion In The Roman Empire

Roman religion was very businesslike. If you performed the right ceremonies, for the right gods, at the right times, with the right words, then you expected that the gods would be happy with you. And if the gods were happy with you, then everything would go well in your life. Any deeper involvement with the gods was only superstition to the Romans.

As long as people kept the peace and followed a few simple rules, the Romans allowed them to worship any gods they liked. In fact, the Romans themselves often paid tribute to the local gods of the people they conquered. Augustus, who was emperor when Jesus was born, had sacrifices offered for himself at the Temple in Jerusalem. For him, the God of the Jews was just one more local god to be appeased.

Many philosophers did not believe in the traditional Roman or Greek gods at all. Some thought that there were gods, but they were too far above us to care about human affairs. Many others believed in a single first cause: they came to monotheism (the belief in only one God) by pure reason. Without God's own revelation, they could never know God, even though they knew he existed. But the philosophers helped prepare the way for God's revelation when it came through Jesus Christ.

> Man's faculties make him capable of coming to a knowledge of the existence of a personal God. But for man to be able to enter into real intimacy with him, God willed both to reveal himself to man and to give him the grace of being able to welcome this revelation in faith. The proofs of God's existence, however, can predispose one to faith and help one to see that faith is not opposed to reason. (CCC 35)

Herod's Sons Inherit His Kingdom: The "Tetrarchy"

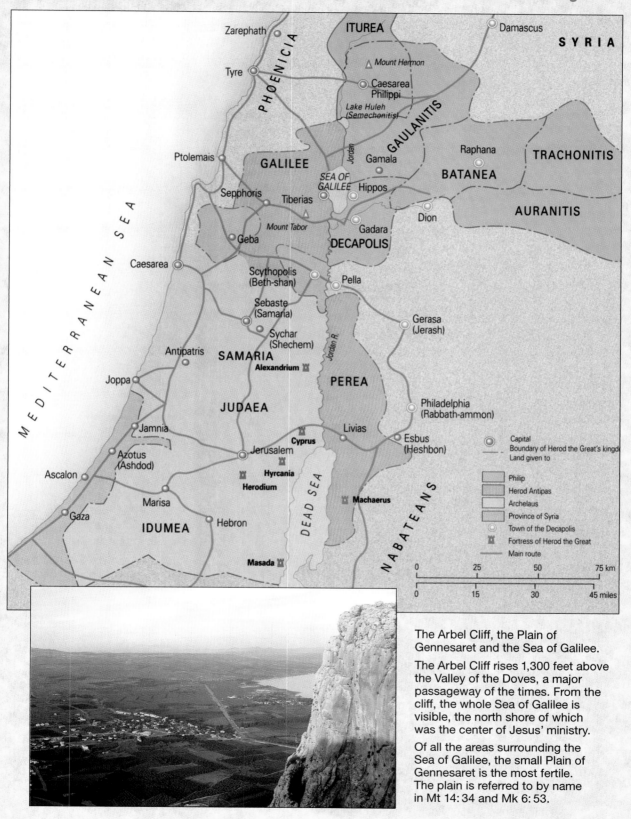

The Arbel Cliff, the Plain of Gennesaret and the Sea of Galilee.

The Arbel Cliff rises 1,300 feet above the Valley of the Doves, a major passageway of the times. From the cliff, the whole Sea of Galilee is visible, the north shore of which was the center of Jesus' ministry.

Of all the areas surrounding the Sea of Galilee, the small Plain of Gennesaret is the most fertile. The plain is referred to by name in Mt 14: 34 and Mk 6: 53.

295

All over the Empire, people were searching for answers to the most important questions: How can I have eternal life? How can I be free from sin? How can I know God? These were questions for which Roman religion had no answers.

So people turned to other religions, especially to religions from the East. The city of Rome itself was soon cluttered with temples to foreign gods. Isis came from Egypt, Mithra from Persia, and even the God of Abraham from Palestine.

Many educated Romans looked down on all these new religions as superstitious nonsense. *"Credat Judaeus"*—"A Jew might believe it"—was how the poet Horace described something he thought was entirely unbelievable. But most educated Romans did not believe in the Roman gods, either. And even educated Romans had an inborn need to know God.

The Spread Of The Jewish Religion

- **Jewish neighborhoods appeared in every town of the Roman Empire.**
- **The Hebrew Scriptures were translated into Greek, the common language of the eastern Empire.**
- **Our Liturgy of the Word comes from the ancient synagogue liturgy.**

The dispersion of the Jews also prepared the way for the coming of the Christ. Remember that only a small remnant had come back to Jerusalem after the Exile. Many of the Jews were doing very well in Babylon or in Egypt. They saw no reason to abandon their homes and businesses to go back to the home of their ancestors. They stayed. Later, when Alexander conquered the East, they spread all over his empire. Alexandria in Egypt became second only to Jerusalem as a center of Jewish culture.

When the Romans took over, Jewish merchants continued to settle everywhere, until there was hardly a town in the Roman Empire without a Jewish neighborhood. One historian calculates that Jews made up 7% of the population of the Empire—a very significant minority. We know that, at the time of Christ, the city of Rome itself had about 10,000 Jewish men, not counting women and children. Alexandria, the second city of the Empire, was probably at least a quarter Jewish.

Even though some of these far-flung Jews forgot their native language, they never forgot the Scriptures. By the time of Jesus, the complete Old Testament had been translated into Greek, the language almost everyone spoke in the eastern half of the Roman Empire. The Greek version was called the Septuagint, from the Greek word for seventy, because seventy scholars worked on it. When the New Testament quotes from the Old Testament, it is usually in the words of the Septuagint.

Synagogues first appeared during the Exile, when the faithful people of God could no longer get to the Temple in Jerusalem to make their sacrifices. Even after the exiles returned and rebuilt the Temple, the far-flung communities of the faithful kept up their synagogues, just as we keep up our parish churches.

When the faithful met every week, their service was very much like our Liturgy of the Word, the first part of our Mass. They heard a reading from the Law—the first five books of the Old Testament. Then they heard a reading from the Prophets, in which they heard God's promise to send a Messiah to free them from their bondage and restore the kingdom of Israel. After that, a speaker might give what we would call a homily.

Christians have kept that old synagogue liturgy, but with this important difference: we proclaim that the Messiah has already come. When Jesus told the congregation at Nazareth that they had seen the Scriptures fulfilled that day (see Lk 4:16-21), he marked the change from Old Testament worship to Christian worship.

The Roman Empire, 14 A.D.

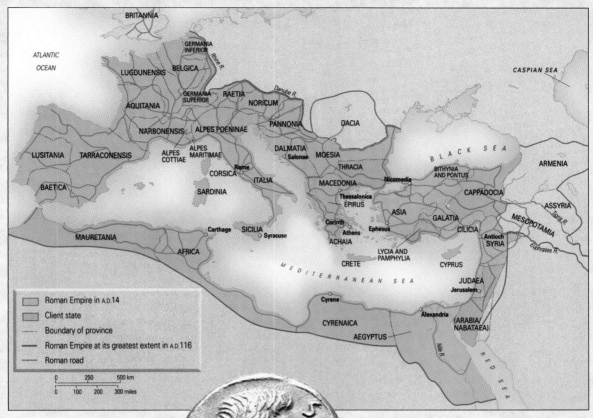

Roman Empire in A.D.14
Client state
Boundary of province
Roman Empire at its greatest extent in A.D.116
Roman road

0   250   500 km
0 100 200 300 miles

Caesar Augustus 63 B.C.-14 A.D. was the first Roman ruler to put his image on official Roman coinage. Known in his earlier life as Gaius Julius Caesar Octavianus, he was named the first "Augustus" (revered one) by the Roman Senate on January 16, 27 B.C. He was the first Roman Emperor and ruled as an autocrat for forty years. He ended a century of civil wars and gave Rome an era of peace, prosperity, and imperial greatness.

Mithras was the most widely venerated god in the Roman Empire at the time of Christ. Mithras was important to the Roman legions, due to Mithraism's strong emphasis on honor and courage. Mithras is shown slaying the constellation bull symbol Taurus. Mithraism was practiced in the Roman Empire from the 1st century B.C. to the 5th century A.D.

Proselytes Of The Gate

- **Judaism appealed to many Gentiles in the Roman Empire.**
- **"Proselytes of the Gate" were Gentile converts who were not circumcised.**
- **These proselytes of the Gate knew enough of the Scriptures to recognize Jesus as the Christ.**

Because Romans all over the Empire were constantly searching for new religions, many of them turned to the Jews. Judaism became another of the fashionable Eastern religions popular among all classes of people in the Empire.

To be a full member of the Jewish community, you had to be circumcised and obey all the dietary laws. But there was an intermediate step. You could be attached to the Jewish community without being fully Jewish. These intermediate people were called "proselytes of the Gate." They went to worship at the synagogues, and they learned all about the Hebrew Scriptures. Although they weren't full members of the Jewish community, they expected to have some share in the future kingdom when the Christ came.

When the early Christians started to spread the Good News, they made many converts in the Jewish communities everywhere. But they made even more converts among the proselytes of the Gate. Wherever the apostles went, they found pockets of God-fearing Gentiles who knew the Scriptures and understood how Jesus Christ fulfilled them. Then those Gentiles would take the Good News back to their families and friends and make more converts. No wonder the Gospel spread so fast!

See Acts 13:16-41 for a good example of how St. Paul preached a sermon to both Jews and proselytes. He addresses them as "Men of Israel, and you that fear God" (Acts 13:16), and "Brethren, sons of the family of Abraham, and those among you that fear God." In other words, there are two groups in his audience: Jews and God-fearing Gentiles. He expects both to know the stories of the Exodus, Saul, and David. In the end, many of the Gentiles "were glad and glorified the word of God." If they had not understood all of Paul's allusions to the Scriptures, they never would have understood his message.

Judea And Galilee

- **Judea, the southern part of Palestine, was settled by exiles returning from Babylon.**
- **Some Jewish settlers also moved into Galilee in the north.**
- **Rome left Palestine under the rule of the Herods.**

Palestine was part of that great Roman Empire in the time of Jesus, and it was one of the more troublesome parts. It was full of rebels who were always trying to start a revolution against the Romans. Sometimes one of those rebels would claim to be the Christ, and then the Romans would have to send in the legions to put down the disturbance.

When the Jewish remnant had returned from exile in Babylon, they had settled around Jerusalem, roughly in the old territory of the kingdom of Judah. The Romans called that area Judea, and its inhabitants were Judeans, or Jews as we would call them.

Some Jewish settlers also moved into Galilee, the land that had been the northern part of the kingdom of Israel. Galilee was already inhabited by Israelites, descendants of the tribes of Zebulun and Naphtali, which had not been deported with the rest of Israel. It was a pleasant land of small towns and poor, honest farmers. The Jews in Jerusalem thought of Galileans as no better than peasants. When Jews from all over came to Jerusalem for religious festivals, you could always tell the Galileans by their accent.

As they often did, the Romans left local kings nominally in charge, although the indigenous people had to answer to a Roman governor. When Jesus was born, the king in charge was Herod "the Great," who would murder every infant under two in Bethlehem in an attempt to kill Jesus.

Capernaum is on the north side of the Sea of Galilee. After leaving Nazareth, Jesus made it the home of his ministry (Mt 4: 12-16). A fourth century synagogue of white limestone stands in Capernaum. The foundation of this synagogue is constructed of black basaltic stone, probably dating to the first century synagogue built by the Roman centurion who was stationed here (Lk 7: 5). At the request of this centurion and encouraged by the synagogue elders, Jesus healed the centurion's servant.

The Samaritans

- **The Samaritans were a mixed population who worshiped God in a different way from the Jews**
- **Jews refused to have any dealings with Samaritans**
- **Jesus shocked his contemporaries by speaking to Samaritans**

Between Judea and Galilee was Samaria, where the Samaritans lived.

Throughout the Gospels, we hear about the Samaritans. We can tell that most Jews didn't like them. In John 4:9, a Samaritan woman is astonished that Jesus will even speak to her: "The Samaritan woman said to him, 'How is it that you, a Jew, ask a drink of me, a woman of Samaria?' For Jews have no dealings with Samaritans."

Who were these Samaritans, and why did the Jews hate them?

When the Assyrians carried off the northern tribes of Israel, they probably left behind some of the poorer population. We know that the Assyrians resettled other exiles from all over their empire in Israel (see 2 Kgs 17:24), and those people began to worship the God of Israel alongside their own gods (2 Kgs 17:25-41). They probably intermarried with the Israelite stragglers left behind.

There were also poor farmers left behind when Judah was carried off to Babylon (2 Kgs 25:12), and those may have mixed with the already mixed Samaritan population.

The Samaritans of Jesus' time, like the Samaritans today, worshiped the one true God, but in a different way.

Only the five books of Moses are considered Scripture by the Samaritans. They don't accept any of the historical books, wisdom literature, or prophecy. Instead of worshiping at the Temple in Jerusalem, they worship on Mount Gerizim, near the present city of Nablus in the Palestinian West Bank. (See Jn 4:20, where the Samaritan woman tells Jesus, "Our fathers worshiped on this mountain, and you [meaning the Jews] say that in Jerusalem is the place to worship.") They believe that their holy mountain has a better claim than Mount Zion, since it was a worship site long before King David conquered Jerusalem (see Dt 27:12).

To the Jews of Jesus' time, the Samaritans were hated heretics who defied God's word as spoken through his prophets. Even talking to a Samaritan would taint a proper Jew with the Samaritan heresy. It was shocking when Jesus spoke to Samaritans as though they were human beings.

Today there are at most a few hundred Samaritans left. For more than two thousand years they have kept their traditions, in spite of everything that has happened in Palestine. But even now they are a persecuted minority, and the last Samaritans may die out in the near future.

Modern-day Samaritans celebrating Passover on Mt. Gerizim.

SUPPLEMENTARY READING

Josephus, *Antiquities of the Jews*, from Book 18

3. Now, for the Pharisees, they live simply, and despise delicacies in diet; and they follow the conduct of reason; and what that prescribes to them as good for them they do; and they think they ought earnestly to strive to observe reason's dictates for practice. They also pay a respect to such as are in years; nor are they so bold as to contradict them in any thing which they have introduced; and when they determine that all things are done by fate, they do not take away the freedom from men of acting as they think fit; since their notion is, that it hath pleased God to make a temperament, whereby what he wills is done, but so that the will of man can act virtuously or viciously. They also believe that souls have an immortal rigor in them, and that under the earth there will be rewards or punishments, according as they have lived virtuously or viciously in this life; and the latter are to be detained in an everlasting prison, but that the former shall have power to revive and live again; on account of which doctrines they are able greatly to persuade the body of the people; and whatsoever they do about Divine worship, prayers, and sacrifices, they perform them according to their direction; insomuch that the cities give great attestations to them on account of their entire virtuous conduct, both in the actions of their lives and their discourses also.

Commentary, *The New Testament*

The entire New Testament tells us about Jesus Christ, revealing him to be "the Son of God made man, the Father's one, perfect and unsurpassable Word" (CCC 65). That is why reading the New Testament is a very good way to get to know Jesus. The Gospels tell us what "Jesus, the Son of God, while he lived among men, really did and taught" (Vatican II, DV, 19). The other books, "in accordance with the wise design of God, firmly establish those matters which concern Christ the Lord, formulate more and more precisely his authentic teaching, preach the saving power of Christ's divine work, recount the beginnings and wonderful spread of the Church, and foretell its glorious consummation" (ibid., 20). This means that, by reading and reflecting on the books of the New Testament, Christians find a compass for their life's journey: the Gospels bear true witness to Jesus' life on earth and provide Christians with their Model; the letters help them to see what Christ's person and work mean for them today and for their Christian life; and the book of Revelation and other eschatological passages in the New Testament give them strength and encouragement to cope with difficulties and to keep alive their hope in ultimate victory.

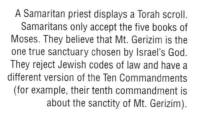

A Samaritan priest displays a Torah scroll. Samaritans only accept the five books of Moses. They believe that Mt. Gerizim is the one true sanctuary chosen by Israel's God. They reject Jewish codes of law and have a different version of the Ten Commandments (for example, their tenth commandment is about the sanctity of Mt. Gerizim).

VOCABULARY

ARISTOBULUS
The Jewish high priest who declared himself king in Jerusalem. He was a Levite, not a descendant of David.

GALILEE
The land that had been the northern part of ancient Israel, on the western shore of the Sea of Galilee.

HEROD THE GREAT
A wickedly ambitious king who took over the government of Palestine with the support of the Romans. He was an Edomite, but he portrayed himself as a Jew returned from exile.

HYRCANUS, JOHN
The Jewish high priest who conquered almost all the territory of the ancient Davidic kingdom and "Judaized" the whole country.

PHARISEES
A Jewish sect that believed in keeping separate from the Gentiles. They followed the Law of Moses strictly and added many traditional interpretations and regulations of their own.

PROSELYTES OF THE GATE
Gentiles who worshiped the True God and knew the Jewish Scriptures, but were not circumcised and did not keep the whole Law of Moses.

SADDUCEES
A Jewish sect that believed in accommodating Judaism to modern life. They held most of the positions of power in the priesthood. Sadducees did not believe in the resurrection and denied the existence of angels and spirits.

TETRARCHY
The division of Herod the Great's kingdom among his four sons.

The largest building stone. A large course of stones is visible beneath the Western Wall of Herod's Temple. The master course consists of four stones, the largest of which weighs 570 tons and is 44 feet long, 10 feet high and 12-16 feet deep. These are the largest stones ever quarried by man. No stone this size exists in Greece or in Egypt (the largest stone in the great pyramid weighs 11 tons). It is an engineering mystery how they were quarried and moved into position. These stones can be viewed in the archeological tunnels that have been opened in the past few years.

STUDY QUESTIONS

1. Which high priest successfully conquered all the Kingdom of Israel's former territory?

2. What choice did he offer all the non-Jewish residents in his territory?

3. Why was circumcision so important?

4. Which high priest declared himself king?

5. From what tribe did the new king come?

6. Which group of scholars decided it would be best to separate themselves from the Gentiles?

7. Which Jewish sect encouraged all Jews to imitate the ritual purity of the priests in Jerusalem?

8. Which Jewish sect denied any kind of resurrection of the body?

9. How did the Sadducees plan to ensure the Jewish religion would survive?

10. What did the Sadducees believe?

11. How did Herod establish his rule in Jerusalem?

12. Why was Herod called "the Great"?

13. What were the effects of the Roman Peace?

14. How did the Romans deal with local religions?

15. What does *"Credat Judaeus"* mean?

16. How did Jewish people outside Jerusalem worship?

17. Who were the Proselytes of the Gate?

18. Who were the Samaritans?

19. Where did the remnant from Babylon settle after the return?

20. What was the Septuagint?

21. Why did synagogues first appear?

22. How did the Samaritans worship?

PRACTICAL EXERCISES

1. The Pharisees were a group of Jewish believers who appear often in the New Testament. Though the Gospels only mention the Pharisees when they are at odds with Christ, there were many laudable teachings of the Pharisees in the Old Law. What were some of the teachings of the Pharisees that led to their opposition to Christ? What were some of their habits that Christ spoke out against? What are some habits that people have today that can be related to the faults of the Pharisees?

2. Since God exists outside of time, he is able to see all things at once. The past, the present and the future are all right in front of him, always. Why do you think that God chose to send his son to save us when he did? Why was that moment chosen as the "fullness of time?" Was it because we needed it? Was it because that was when God's word would be spread the fastest, and the most people would believe?

3. How did the Jewish and Christian religions differ from other religions within the Roman world? Do you think this had an effect on their acceptance in the Roman world? Did believing in one God necessarily interfere with the Roman state?

FROM THE CATECHISM

2 So that this call should resound throughout the world, Christ sent forth the apostles he had chosen, commissioning them to proclaim the gospel: "Go therefore and make disciples of all nations, baptizing them in the name of the Father and of the Son and of the Holy Spirit, teaching them to observe all that I have commanded you; and lo, I am with you always, to the close of the age" (Mt 28: 18-20). Strengthened by this mission, the apostles "went forth and preached everywhere, while the Lord worked with them and confirmed the message by the signs that attended it" (Mk 16: 20).

156 What moves us to believe is not the fact that revealed truths appear as true and intelligible in the light of our natural reason: we believe "because of the authority of God himself who reveals them, who can neither deceive nor be deceived" (*Dei Filius* 3: DS 3008). So "that the submission of our faith might nevertheless be in accordance with reason, God willed that external proofs of his Revelation should be joined to the internal helps of the Holy Spirit" (*Dei Filius* 3: DS 3009). Thus the miracles of Christ and the saints, prophecies, the Church's growth and holiness, and her fruitfulness and stability "are the most certain signs of divine Revelation, adapted to the intelligence of all;" they are "motives of credibility" (*motiva credibilitatis*), which show that the assent of faith is "by no means a blind impulse of the mind" (*Dei Filius* 3: DS 3008-10; cf. Mk 16: 20; Heb 2: 4).

422 "But when the time had fully come, God sent forth his Son, born of a woman, born under the law, to redeem those who were under the law, so that we might receive adoption as sons" (Gal 4: 4-5). This is "the gospel of Jesus Christ, the Son of God" (Mk 1: 1): God has visited his people. He has fulfilled the promise he made to Abraham and his descendants. He acted far beyond all expectation—he has sent his own "beloved Son" (Mk 1: 11; cf. Lk 1: 55, 68).

588 Jesus scandalized the Pharisees by eating with tax collectors and sinners as familiarly as with themselves (cf. Lk 5: 30; 7: 36; 11: 37; 14: 1). Against those among them "who trusted in themselves that they were righteous and despised others," Jesus affirmed: "I have not come to call the righteous, but sinners to repentance" (Lk 18: 9; 5: 32; cf. Jn 7: 49; 9: 34). He went further by proclaiming before the Pharisees that, since sin is universal, those who pretend not to need salvation are blind to themselves (cf. Jn 8: 33-36; 9: 40-41).

791 The body's unity does not do away with the diversity of its members: "In the building up of Christ's Body there is engaged a diversity of members and functions. There is only one Spirit who, according to his own richness and the needs of the ministries, gives his different gifts for the welfare of the Church" (LG 7 § 3). The unity of the Mystical Body produces and stimulates charity among the faithful: "From this it follows that if one member suffers anything, all the members suffer with him, and if one member is honored, all the members together rejoice" (LG 7 § 3; cf. 1 Cor 12: 26). Finally, the unity of the Mystical Body triumphs over all human divisions: "For as many of you as were baptized into Christ have put on Christ. There is neither Jew nor Greek, there is neither slave nor free, there is neither male nor female; for you are all one in Christ Jesus" (Gal 3: 27-28).

1349 The *Liturgy of the Word* includes "the writings of the prophets," that is, the Old Testament, and "the memoirs of the apostles" (their letters and the Gospels). After the homily, which is an exhortation to accept this Word as what it truly is, the Word of God (cf. 1 Thes 2: 13) (cf. DV 21), and to put it into practice, come the intercessions for all men, according to the Apostle's words: "I urge that supplications, prayers, intercessions, and thanksgivings be made for all men, for kings, and all who are in high positions" (1 Tm 2: 1-2) (cf. Lk 24: 13-35).

The New Testament

*Each Evangelist emphasizes different details,
because each one is writing for a different audience.*

Chapter 17

The New Testament

Read

Luke 1:1 - 4

Acts 1:1 - 5

Hebrews
9:1 - 10:10

Revelation
21:1 - 8

Behold, the days are coming, says the LORD, when I will make a new covenant with the house of Israel and the house of Judah, not like the covenant which I made with their fathers when I took them by the hand to bring them out of the land of Egypt, my covenant which they broke, though I was their husband, says the LORD. But this is the covenant which I will make with the house of Israel after those days, says the LORD: I will put my law within them, and I will write it upon their hearts; and I will be their God, and they shall be my people. And no longer shall each man teach his neighbor and each his brother, saying, "Know the LORD," for they shall all know me, from the least of them to the greatest, says the LORD; for I will forgive their iniquity, and I will remember their sin no more. (Jer 31: 31-34)

The New Testament does not replace the Old Testament: it fulfills the Old Testament.

St. Augustine said that the New Testament is hidden in the Old, and the Old is revealed in the New. Without the New Testament, the Old Testament is just a collection of tragic stories and unfulfilled promises. But when we see the Old Testament in the light of the New Testament, we can see that the Old Testament is the story of the gradual unfolding of God's plan of salvation—the plan that reaches its climax with the death and resurrection of Jesus Christ.

> The Old Law is a *preparation for the Gospel.* "The Law is a pedagogy and a prophecy of things to come."[1] It prophesies and presages the work of liberation from sin which will be fulfilled in Christ; it provides the New Testament with images, "types," and symbols for expressing the life according to the Spirit. (CCC 1964)

How The New Testament Is Organized

The books of the New Testament can be put into the same classes as the books of the Old Testament.

1. **Law: the Four Gospels.** In the Old Testament, the five books of Moses give the old law and the story of the founding of Israel. In the same way, the four Gospels give us the New Law and the story of the founding of the Church, which is the new Israel.

2. **History: the Acts of the Apostles.** Just as the Old Testament, beginning in Joshua, gives us the history of Israel from the death of Moses, so the Acts of the Apostles gives us the history of the early Church from the ascension of Jesus Christ.

3. **Wisdom: the Epistles.** The letters written by the Apostles tell us how to live as Christians.

4. **Prophecy: the Revelation to John.** John brings us the word of the Lord in symbols and images often recalling those used in the Old Testament prophets.

The New Law: The Four Gospels

- **All four Gospels tell the same story.**
- **Each Gospel writer tells it from a different point of view.**
- **The first three Gospels are called "synoptic" because their points of view are similar.**

When we look at the four Gospels, we can see that they all tell the same story. But they tell it from different points of view. Each Evangelist (as the Gospel writers are called, from the Latin *evangelium*) emphasizes different details, because each one is writing for a different audience.

But of the four Gospels, John's is the one that is *most* different. In fact, John tells the story so differently that Matthew, Mark, and Luke are often called the "synoptic" Gospels, from a Greek word that means "seeing together." Compared with the Gospel according to John, the first three Gospels share a similar viewpoint.

Scholars have suggested many ways in which the three "synoptic" Gospels could be related. The most popular suggestion has been that Mark's Gospel was the first of the three, and that Matthew and Luke both used Mark as one of their sources. In addition, the scholars suggest, there was a collection of Jesus' sayings, which scholars call "Q," from which Matthew and Luke took much of their material. We must remember, however, that all these suggestions are speculations. No one has ever seen a copy of "Q," and scholars can only guess what might have been in it, if it ever existed at all.

No matter how the Gospels were written and what sources they used, we know that they are all true. They supplement but never contradict one another. Together, they tell us not only what Jesus did and said, but also who he was.

Matthew

- **Jewish Christians were the main audience for Matthew's Gospel.**
- **Matthew emphasizes Jesus as the true heir of David's kingdom.**

Although most scholars believe that Matthew's Gospel was partly based on the Gospel according to Mark, some believe that it may have been the earliest of the four Gospels. Traditionally, the Church has taught that this Gospel was written by Matthew, also called Levi, a tax collector who walked away from his desk in the collections office to follow Jesus.

> As Jesus passed on from there, he saw a man called Matthew sitting at the tax office; and he said to him, "Follow me." And he rose and followed him. (Mt 9: 9)

Matthew's Gospel was written mostly for Jews, so to Matthew, the most important thing is to show how Jesus fulfilled their expectations of the Messiah. As we have already seen, he begins his Gospel with an artful genealogy designed to show how Jesus is the ideal successor of David. Over and over again, Matthew uses Old Testament scripture to remind us that Jesus is the Son of David, the Christ, the Anointed One who had been promised by all the prophets.

Of all the Gospel writers, Matthew is the one who most lets Jesus speak for himself. The famous Sermon on the Mount, for example, takes up three whole chapters, in which Matthew never interrupts with his own words: he simply reports what Jesus said.

" '...For I came not to call the righteous, but sinners.' " (Mt 9: 13)

Mark

- **Roman Christians were Mark's main audience.**
- **Mark emphasizes Jesus as leader of a new Exodus.**
- **Peter was Mark's main source for the story of Jesus' life.**
- **Many scholars believe that Mark's Gospel was the earliest of the four.**

John Mark was a disciple of Peter who followed Peter to Rome and later (according to tradition) went to Egypt. He was very close to Peter; Peter calls him "my son Mark" at the end of his first letter (1 Pt 5:13).

Mark wrote his Gospel based on the stories Peter had told him. The main audience was probably the Gentile Christians in Rome. One tradition has it that Peter was so pleased with Mark's work that he had copies of Mark's Gospel made for all the churches.

Of the four Gospels, Mark's is the shortest, and many scholars believe it was the earliest. Many also believe that Matthew and Luke used it as a source for writing their own Gospels, and it is true that certain passages appear word for word in all three of the "synoptic" Gospels.

Mark's Gospel tells the story of Jesus' life in a straightforward way. Although he includes many of the words of Jesus, Mark is more interested in what Jesus did. Throughout, we see Jesus leading us— the new Israel—on a new Exodus.

Mark includes one odd little story that none of the other Gospels tell. After Jesus had been arrested, the authorities led him off to the high priest.

> And a young man followed him, with nothing but a linen cloth about his body; and they seized him, but he left the linen cloth and ran away naked. (Mk 14:51-52)

Why does Mark report this embarrassing little incident? Most scholars believe that the naked young man was Mark himself, who added this little story to remind people who knew him that he was an eyewitness to some of the events.

Mark's favorite word is "immediately"—he uses it more than forty times—and his Gospel runs along at a brisk pace. Reading Mark's Gospel straight through at one sitting is easy, and it's a good way to understand how exciting the Good News must have been to the earliest believers.

"And he said, 'With what can we compare the kingdom of God,…? It is like a grain of mustard seed, which, when sown upon the ground, is the smallest of all the seeds on earth; yet when it…grows up…puts forth large branches, so that the birds of the air can make nests in its shade.'" (Mk 4:30-32)

Luke

- **Gentile Christians were Luke's main audience.**
- **Luke includes details of Jesus' conception and birth not found anywhere else.**
- **Jesus' own Mother may have been Luke's source for those details.**

St. Paul calls Luke "the beloved physician," and we know from the Acts of the Apostles (which Luke also wrote) that Luke spent a lot of time traveling with Paul and the others. From his own writing, we can tell that Luke was a well-educated man who had mastered all the literary techniques of the best writers of the day. He wrote mainly to Gentile converts, so he emphasizes Jesus' ministry to all nations.

When Luke wrote his Gospel, "many" other narrations of Jesus' life had already been written. So why did Luke write another one?

He probably had two reasons.

First, he emphasizes that he wants to give an "orderly account." That probably means Luke, with his literary education, thought the other accounts of Jesus' life were not written in the best order. We don't know whether Luke's version is strictly chronological, but we do know that Luke was a careful historian who made sure to give his readers the proper historical setting for each story.

Second, he had information that none of the other Gospel writers had, especially about Jesus' conception and birth. Of the four Gospels, only Luke gives us the familiar stories of the Annunciation, the baby in the manger, the visit of the shepherds, and Jesus' teaching in the Temple when he was twelve years old.

Where did Luke get his stories about the conception, birth, and infancy of Jesus? Many great Christian teachers have believed that this information came from Mary, the mother of Jesus.

> But Mary kept all these things, pondering them in her heart. (Lk 2:19)
>
> ...and his mother kept all these things in her heart. (Lk 2:51)

Who but Mary could have told him the things she kept in her heart? Luke might have made these remarks to explain why his Gospel contained information not found in the many other accounts of Jesus' life. We know that Luke was with the Apostles at the same time as Mary. If he had decided to write an orderly account of Jesus' life, it would have been natural for him to ask her what happened at the beginning.

> The Gospel according to St. Luke emphasizes the action of the Holy Spirit and the meaning of prayer in Christ's ministry. Jesus prays *before* the decisive moments of his mission: before his Father's witness to him during his baptism and Transfiguration, and before his own fulfillment of the Father's plan of love by his Passion (cf. Lk 3:21; 9:28; 22:41-44). He also prays before the decisive moments involving the mission of his apostles: at his election and call of the Twelve, before Peter's confession of him as "the Christ of God," and again that the faith of the chief of the Apostles may not fail when tempted (cf. Lk 6:12; 9:18-20; 22:32). Jesus' prayer before the events of salvation that the Father has asked him to fulfill is a humble and trusting commitment of his human will to the loving will of the Father. (CCC 2600)

John

- **John emphasizes Jesus as the Word of God Incarnate.**
- **John also stresses our new creation in Christ.**
- **John's Gospel fills in details left out of the other three Gospels.**
- **The family relationship of the Trinity is revealed most completely in John.**

The Gospel of John itself tells us that it was written by "the disciple whom Jesus loved," Jesus' best friend John. Tradition tells us that John lived to be very old, and most scholars believe that his Gospel was the last of the four to be written.

To John, the most important thing is to remind his readers that Jesus Christ was truly God Incarnate, the Word of God who had existed with God from the beginning.

John's Gospel was probably written mostly for Jewish Christians, since it is filled with allusions to Old Testament events and symbols that only Jewish readers would have understood.

"So Jesus again said to them, 'Truly, truly, I say to you, I am the door of the sheep....
I am the good shepherd. The good shepherd lays down his life for the sheep.'" (Jn 10: 7–11)

History: The Acts Of The Apostles

St. Luke wrote this book as a sequel to his Gospel. He gives us our only reliable history of the early Church. Archaeologists and historians have confirmed that Luke was an extraordinarily careful historian. Every detail of his narrative that can possibly be verified has turned out to be exactly right.

Luke himself was an eyewitness to many of the events he describes. For large portions of the book, he switches from "they" to "we"—indicating that he himself was traveling with the Apostles. His account of the shipwreck at Malta (Acts 27) is famous as one of the most vivid and accurate descriptions of navigation in ancient history.

The Gangitis River near Philippi, Greece is thought to be the river where Lydia was baptized by Paul.

"We remained in this city some days; and on the sabbath day we went outside the gate to the riverside, where we supposed there was a place of prayer; and we...spoke to the women who had come together. One...was a woman named Lydia,...who was a worshiper of God. The Lord opened her heart to give heed to what was said by Paul." (Acts 16: 12–14)

Wisdom: The Epistles

As the Church spread, the Apostles wrote letters to the churches they had founded. Some of the letters addressed specific problems that came up, such as incorrect teachings. Others were more general, and some were addressed to the whole Church at large. All of them address problems that faced Christians as they tried to live holy lives in a secular world.

By far the largest part of this new wisdom literature was written by St. Paul, whose conversion from persecutor to Apostle dramatically changed the course of history. Paul was an intelligent and well-educated Roman citizen, Jewish by birth, whose background gave him both a thorough knowledge of the Scriptures and a good grasp of popular trends in pagan philosophy. He was able to draw on both sources to fulfill his mission of spreading the Gospel to the Gentiles.

The letters of Paul are arranged together in the New Testament, roughly in order from longest to shortest. Most of them are written to churches in various cities of the Roman Empire:

Romans

1 Corinthians

2 Corinthians

Galatians

Ephesians

Philippians

Colossians

1 Thessalonians

2 Thessalonians

Four of St. Paul's letters are written to individuals:

1 Timothy

2 Timothy

Titus

Philemon

The letters to Titus and Timothy give advice to Christian leaders who worked with Paul. The letter to Philemon asks a particular favor: Philemon's slave Onesimos had run away, but Paul had converted him to Christianity, and now he asks that Philemon take Onesimos back as a brother. It was a dangerous thing Onesimos was doing, going back to his master, since Philemon had the legal right to punish him with death if he wanted. But since the letter was kept and passed around in the early Church, we can guess that Philemon did what Paul wanted. Early Church history knows a bishop named Onesimos, who may well have been Philemon's former slave, freed by his master and accepted as a brother Christian.

Hebrews. The author of Hebrews does not give us his name. One ancient tradition says it was Paul, but many modern scholars think it was written by one of Paul's disciples. It shows how the Old Testament is fulfilled in the life of Jesus Christ. It is one of the most important tools we have for understanding the connection between the Old Testament and the New.

The "catholic epistles" ("catholic" meaning "universal") are addressed to the whole Church.

James tells Christians to be "Doers of the word, and not merely hearers." The letter gives some of the best advice for Christians living together.

1 Peter helps Christians live their faith in a hostile world. **2 Peter** warns against false teachers and reminds us of the promised return of Christ.

The three letters of **John** warn against false spirits and teachers who lead the Church astray, and remind us that our first duty as Christians is to love.

Jude again warns against false teachers, and against those who would divide the Church.

Prophecy: The Revelation

The Revelation, traditionally attributed to the apostle John, is a vision of the things to come that is both terrifying and comforting. Since it speaks in symbols, it is sometimes hard to understand, and not everyone agrees on the interpretation of it. But the main message is that, in spite of many tribulations to come, God will preserve all his people and bring them into the Heavenly Jerusalem, where all their tears will be wiped away.

"After this I looked, and lo, in heaven an open door!... At once I was in the Spirit, and lo, a throne stood in heaven,... Round the throne were twenty-four thrones, and seated... were twenty-four elders,... and before the throne burn seven torches of fire,..." (Rv 4: 1-5)

SUPPLEMENTARY READING

Jerome, *Against Jovinian*, 1:26

Matthew as though he were writing of a man begins thus: "The book of the genealogy of Jesus Christ, the son of David, the son of Abraham;" Luke begins with the priesthood of Zechariah; Mark with a prophecy of the prophets Malachi and Isaiah. The first has the face of a man, on account of the genealogical table; the second, the face of a calf, on account of the priesthood; the third, the face of a lion, on account of the voice of one crying in the desert, "Prepare the way of the Lord, make His paths straight." But John like an eagle, soars aloft, and reaches the Father Himself, and says, "In the beginning was the Word, and the Word was with God, and the Word was God. The same was in the beginning with God," and so on.

Jerome, *On Illustrious Men*, 1

Simon Peter, the son of John, from the village of Bethsaida in the province of Galilee, brother of Andrew the apostle, and himself chief of the apostles, after having been bishop of the church of Antioch and having preached to the Dispersion—the believers in circumcision, in Pontus, Galatia, Cappadocia, Asia and Bithynia—pushed on to Rome in the second year of Claudius to overthrow Simon Magus, and held the sacerdotal chair there for twenty-five years until the last, that is the fourteenth, year of Nero. At his hands he received the crown of martyrdom being nailed to the cross with his head towards the ground and his feet raised high, asserting that he was unworthy to be crucified in the same manner as his Lord.... Buried at Rome in the Vatican near the triumphal way, he is venerated by the whole world.

Jerome, *On Illustrious Men*, 8

Mark, the disciple and interpreter of Peter wrote a short Gospel at the request of the brethren at Rome embodying what he had heard Peter tell. When Peter had heard this, he approved it and published it to the churches to be read by his authority as Clement in the sixth book of his *Hypotyposes* and Papias, bishop of Hierapolis, record. Peter also mentions this Mark in his first epistle, figuratively indicating Rome under the name of Babylon: "She who is in Babylon elect together with you salutes you and so does Mark my son" (1 Pt 5:13). So, taking the Gospel which he himself composed, he went to Egypt and first preaching Christ at Alexandria, he formed a church so admirable in doctrine and continence of living that he constrained all followers of Christ to his example.... He died in the eighth year of Nero and was buried at Alexandria, Annianus succeeding him.

The four Gospels give us the New Law and the story of the founding of the Church, which is the new Israel.

VOCABULARY

ANNUNCIATION

The visit of the angel Gabriel to Mary to tell her that she would be the mother of the Messiah. The story of the Annunciation is found in Luke.

APOSTLE

One who is sent. The Twelve Apostles were chosen by Jesus Christ to spread his message throughout the world; they are the foundation upon which the Church is built. The word "apostle" is used to describe the Twelve and St. Paul.

CATHOLIC

Universal. The Catholic Epistles are the epistles written to the whole Church.

EPISTLE

Letter. Much of the New Testament consists of epistles written to individuals, to whole congregations, or to the Church as a whole.

GOSPEL

Good News. Specifically, a book that tells the Good News. The four Gospels were written by Matthew, Mark, Luke, and John.

PEDAGOGUE

A slave who acted as a private tutor for the master's children. Until the children reached adulthood, the pedagogue had absolute authority over them. According to St. Paul, the Law of Moses acted as our pedagogue until the coming of Christ.

Q

A hypothetical collection of Jesus' sayings that many scholars think was used by the Gospel writers. No one knows for certain whether the document ever existed; all the evidence for it comes from scholarly analysis of the Gospels.

SYNOPTIC GOSPELS

Matthew, Mark, and Luke. They are called "synoptic" (Greek for "seeing together") because they have a similar point of view when contrasted with the Gospel of John.

A page from the *Book of Kells* depicts the four Evangelists identified by their symbols. Matthew's symbol is a man because his gospel emphasizes Christ's humanity and opens with his genealogy. Mark's symbol is a lion because it opens with the command "Prepare the way of the Lord." Luke's symbol is a bull because his gospel speaks of priestly duties and temple sacrifices. John's gospel is symbolized by an eagle because of the lofty language in the opening verses.

STUDY QUESTIONS

1. Briefly describe the relationship between the Old Testament and the New Testament.

2. What is the Old Testament?

3. What are the similarities between the divisions of the Old and New Testaments?

4. Why are the writers of the New Testament called evangelists?

5. Why are the Gospels of Matthew, Mark, and Luke called synoptic?

6. Who was the main audience for Matthew's Gospel?

7. Which Gospel represents the tradition taught by Peter?

8. Who was Mark's main audience?

9. How does he relate his Gospel?

10. Who was Luke's audience?

11. Name two reasons why Luke wrote his Gospel.

12. Name four stories from Jesus' early life that can only be found in the Gospel of Luke.

13. How could Luke have known about those stories of Jesus' early life?

14. What does the Gospel of Luke emphasize?

15. What was John's main goal in writing his Gospel?

16. Who were most likely John's main audience?

17. Which book gives us a reliable history of the early Church?

18. Who wrote the Acts of the Apostles?

19. Who wrote the bulk of the Epistles in the New Testament?

20. Which of the Epistles are called "Catholic Epistles"?

21. Why are they called "Catholic"?

PRACTICAL EXERCISES

1. The stories we have about Jesus' life are gathered from the Gospels of Matthew, Mark, Luke, and John. What are the advantages of having four different Gospels to tell the same story? What if there had only been one Gospel to recount each story? Would the writings be more or less believable? Would we have a better understanding of what happened or of what God intended?

2. Personal letters (epistles) are rare in the Old Testament, but they make up more than half of the New Testament. Why do you think personal letters are so appropriate for spreading the Word of God? What should be a main priority in all of our closest relationships with our family and friends?

3. In everyday life we come across opportunities to help other people realize who God is. If someone were to ask you who Jesus was and what he taught, how would you respond? Briefly give an account of Jesus' most important teachings and actions in the New Testament.

FROM THE CATECHISM

124 "The Word of God, which is the power of God for salvation to everyone who has faith, is set forth and displays its power in a most wonderful way in the writings of the New Testament" (DV 17; cf. Rom 1:16) which hand on the ultimate truth of God's Revelation. Their central object is Jesus Christ, God's incarnate Son: his acts, teachings, Passion and glorification, and his Church's beginnings under the Spirit's guidance (cf. DV 20)

140 The unity of the two Testaments proceeds from the unity of God's plan and his Revelation. The Old Testament prepares for the New and the New Testament fulfills the Old; the two shed light on each other; both are true Word of God.

214 God, "He who is," revealed himself to Israel as the one "abounding in steadfast love and faithfulness" (Ex 34:6). These two terms express summarily the riches of the divine name. In all his works God displays not only his kindness, goodness, grace, and steadfast love, but also his trustworthiness, constancy, faithfulness, and truth. "I give thanks to your name for your steadfast love and your faithfulness" (Ps 138:2; cf. Ps 85:11). He is the Truth, for "God is light and in him there is no darkness"; "God is love," as the apostle John teaches (1 Jn 1:5; 4:8).

515 The Gospels were written by men who were among the first to have the faith (cf. Mk 1:1; Jn 21:24) and wanted to share it with others. Having known in faith who Jesus is, they could see and make others see the traces of his mystery in all his earthly life. From the swaddling clothes of his birth to the vinegar of his Passion and the shroud of his Resurrection, everything in Jesus' life was a sign of his mystery (cf. Lk 2:7; Mt 27:48; Jn 20:7). His deeds, miracles and words all revealed that "in him the whole fullness of deity dwells bodily" (Col 2:9). His humanity appeared as "sacrament," that is, the sign and instrument, of his divinity and of the salvation he brings: what was visible in his earthly life leads to the invisible mystery of his divine sonship and redemptive mission.

1967 The Law of the Gospel "fulfills," refines, surpasses, and leads the Old Law to its perfection (cf. Mt 5:17-19). In the Beatitudes, the New Law *fulfills the divine promises* by elevating and orienting them toward the "kingdom of heaven." It is addressed to those open to accepting this new hope with faith—the poor, the humble, the afflicted, the pure of heart, those persecuted on account of Christ—and so marks out the surprising ways of the Kingdom.

2640 St. Luke in his Gospel often expresses wonder and praise at the marvels of Christ and in his *Acts of the Apostles* stresses them as actions of the Holy Spirit: the community of Jerusalem, the invalid healed by Peter and John, the crowd that gives glory to God for that, and the pagans of Pisidia who "were glad and glorified the word of God" (Acts 2:47; 3:9; 4:21; 13:48).

Endnote

1. St. Irenaeus, *Adv. haeres.* 4, 15, 1: PG 7/1, 1012.

The Incarnation

"Do not be afraid, Mary, for you have found favor with God. And behold, you will conceive in your womb and bear a son, and you shall call his name Jesus."

Luke 1:30-31

Chapter 18

The Incarnation

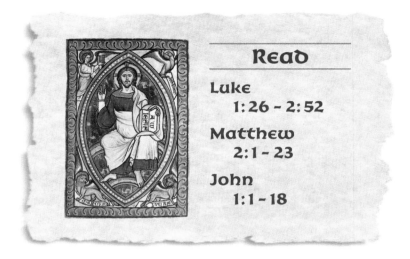

Read

Luke
1:26 – 2:52

Matthew
2:1 – 23

John
1:1 – 18

> In the beginning was the Word, and the Word was with God, and the Word was God.... And the Word became flesh and dwelt among us, full of grace and truth; we have beheld his glory, glory as of the only Son from the Father. (Jn 1:1, 14)

The Gospel according to John begins with an amazing truth: The Word of God, God the Son, who existed before creation and by which everything in the universe was created, became human and lived with us.

We find the same idea in St. Paul's letter to the Colossians:

> ...for in him all things were created, in heaven and on earth, visible and invisible, whether thrones or dominions or principalities or authorities—all things were created through him and for him. (Col 1:16-17)

God became flesh. That is literally the central event in history. We call it the Incarnation—from the Latin that simply means "becoming flesh"—and we date everything in history according to whether it happened before or after the Incarnation.

Jesus Christ was the Son of God, who had existed from eternity. But Jesus was also a man, born at a particular time in history and killed thirty-three or so years later outside Jerusalem in the Roman province of Judea. Jesus was both true God and true man.

10 B.C.	5 B.C.	1 B.C.	1 A.D.	5 A.D.	10 A.D.
13 - 4 Herod descends into madness	6 Jesus is born	3 Holy Family returns to Nazareth from Egypt			6 Jesus in Jerusalem for Passover

8 Mary and Joseph are betrothed; Gabriel visits Zechariah announcing son for Elizabeth

5 Herod orders all male infants in Bethlehem killed; Joseph takes Holy Family to Egypt

4 In Rome, Augustus names Tiberius his heir

6 Jesus remains at the Temple for three days participating in lively discussions with Temple elders

4 Herod dies; 4 B.C.- 39 A.D. Herod Antipas rules Galilee

7 Gabriel appears to Mary announcing birth of Jesus; John is born to Elizabeth

5 Saul is born to a devout Jewish family in Tarsus, Greece

Allegory of the Old and New Testaments

"For the law was given through Moses; grace and truth came through Jesus Christ. No one has ever seen God; the only Son . . . has made him known." (Jn 1: 17–18)

Those two inseparable natures are the heart of the mystery of the Incarnation.

Taking up St. John's expression, "The Word became flesh" (Jn 1:14), the Church calls "Incarnation" the fact that the Son of God assumed a human nature in order to accomplish our salvation in it. In a hymn cited by St. Paul, the Church sings the mystery of the Incarnation:

Have this mind among yourselves, which is yours in Christ Jesus, who, though he was in the form of God, did not count equality with God a thing to be grasped, but emptied himself, taking the form of a servant, being born in the likeness of men. And being found in human form he humbled himself and became obedient unto death, even death on a cross (Phil 2: 5-8; cf. LH, Saturday, Canticle at Evening Prayer). (CCC 461)

The *Letter to the Hebrews* refers to the same mystery:

Consequently, when Christ came into the world, he said, "Sacrifices and offerings you have not desired, but a body have you prepared for me; in burnt offerings and sin offerings you have taken no pleasure. Then I said, 'Lo, I have come to do your will, O God'" (Heb 10: 5-7, citing Ps 40: 6-8 ([7-9] LXX)). (CCC 462)

Belief in the true Incarnation of the Son of God is the distinctive sign of Christian faith: "By this you know the Spirit of God: every spirit which confesses that Jesus Christ has come in the flesh is of God'" (1 Jn 4: 2). Such is the joyous conviction of the Church from her beginning whenever she sings "the mystery of our religion": "He was manifested in the flesh" (1 Tm 3: 16). (CCC 463)

The Son Of David

- **The New Testament begins by showing how Jesus descended from David and Abraham.**
- **Matthew uses literary art to show that Jesus is the perfect Son of David.**
- **For Matthew, the Exile ends with the coming of Jesus.**

John emphasizes that Jesus was the Son of God, who existed at the beginning of creation. But the human nature of Jesus Christ is just as important. The whole New Testament begins with the genealogy of Jesus Christ, "the son of David, the son of Abraham."

The genealogy in Matthew is more than just the reference material it appears to be. It is also a work of subtle literary art—an art that probably would have been much more striking to its original audience than it is to us.

Matthew introduces his genealogy with these words:

> The book of the genealogy of Jesus Christ...[1]

In the Septuagint—the Greek translation of the Old Testament used everywhere in Matthew's time—Genesis 5:1 begins its summary of Adam's descendants with these words:

> This is the book of the genealogy of Adam.[2]

Matthew is deliberately using *exactly the same words* to show that the story that begins with Adam (Greek, anthropon) ends with Jesus Christ.

If we compare Matthew's list of names closely with the Old Testament, we discover that Matthew has sometimes compressed generations. Why? He is using his literary art to show us an important truth about Jesus. The genealogy itself shows us that Jesus descended from David. But Matthew makes it clear that Jesus is more than just any descendant of David: he is the *perfect* or ideal descendant of David.

> So all the generations from Abraham to David were fourteen generations, and from David to the deportation to Babylon were fourteen generations, and from the deportation to Babylon to Christ were fourteen generations.[3]

Matthew has arranged the names in three groups of fourteen. Three, you remember, is a symbolically perfect number. And fourteen is twice seven. Seven is another symbolically perfect number, so fourteen is symbolically a *doubly* perfect number.

But Matthew's choice of fourteen is even more deeply symbolic than that. Hebrew uses letters to represent numbers, just the way the Romans did. In Roman numerals, for example, V represents five and X represents ten. In Hebrew numerals the letter *daleth* (D) represented 4, and the letter *vav* (V) represented 6.

Because letters also represented numbers, you could add up the letters in a Hebrew name and get a number. And people often did that, seeing a mysterious symbolic value in the numbers that went with various names.

Since there were no vowels in Hebrew, the name David was spelled with the letters for DVD. Add up the letters in David's name—**4 + 6 + 4**—and you get fourteen.

Fourteen, fourteen, fourteen: by repeating the number of David's name a perfect three times, Matthew is showing us that Jesus is the ideal heir of David, the true Anointed One who inherits all the promises God made in the Davidic Covenant.

Family Of David

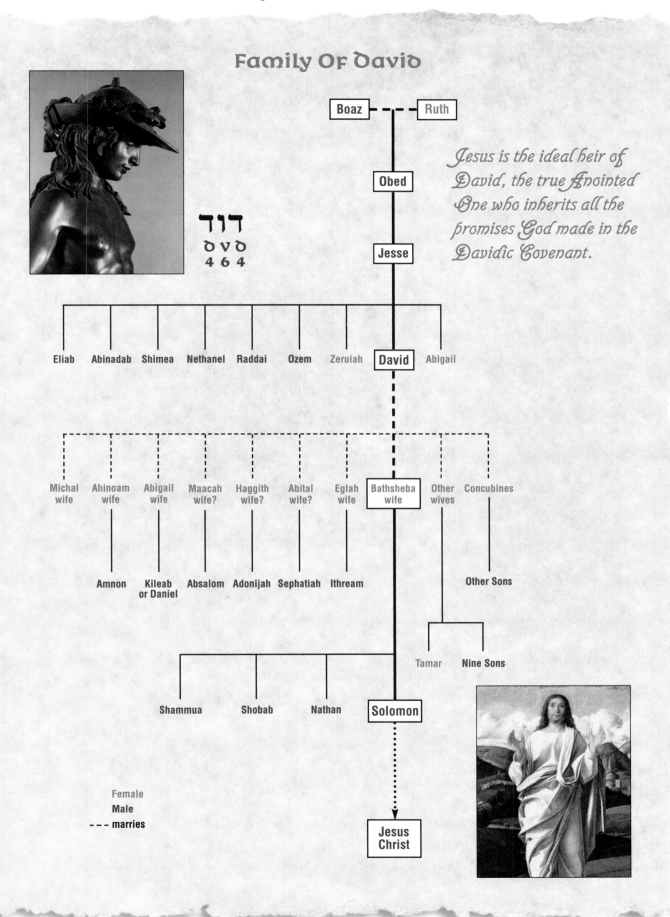

Jesus is the ideal heir of David, the true Anointed One who inherits all the promises God made in the Davidic Covenant.

דוד
δ∨δ
4 6 4

Boaz - - - Ruth

Obed

Jesse

Eliab   Abinadab   Shimea   Nethanel   Raddai   Ozem   Zeruiah   **David**   Abigail

Michal wife   Ahinoam wife   Abigail wife   Maacah wife?   Haggith wife?   Abital wife?   Eglah wife   Bathsheba wife   Other wives   Concubines

Amnon   Kileab or Daniel   Absalom   Adonijah   Sephatiah   Ithream   Other Sons

Tamar   Nine Sons

Shammua   Shobab   Nathan   Solomon

Jesus Christ

Female
Male
- - - marries

Now notice how Matthew divides the history of Israel. There are three important events that sum up history for Matthew:

1. **The covenant with Abraham;**
2. **The covenant with David;**
3. **The deportation to Babylon.**

The first two both involve promises that would not be fulfilled until Christ: all the people of the earth would be blessed through Abraham, and David's descendants would be set over all the kings of the earth.

The third, the deportation to Babylon, seemed to mean the end of the first two promises. Although a small remnant later returned to Jerusalem, the exile had never really ended. Many of the Jews stayed in Babylon, or in Egypt and other places where they had gone to escape Nebuchadnezzar. More important, there had never again been a king of David's line on the throne in Jerusalem. Except for a brief period under the Maccabees, Israel was always a province of some foreign empire.

The exile ends only with the coming of Jesus, who draws all people together in the Kingdom of God.

Hail Mary

Only St. Luke gives us the familiar stories of the Annunciation and the birth of Jesus. He probably heard the stories from Mary herself; he would have spent quite a bit of time with her when he was staying with the apostles.

Mary was a young woman engaged to be married to a carpenter. In Jewish custom, an engagement like that was considered equivalent to a marriage: although the couple did not live together until after the marriage ceremony, it took a legal divorce to break the engagement.

Mary first learned that she would be more than a carpenter's wife when the angel Gabriel appeared to her. As always, the appearance of an angel was a frightening thing, and Gabriel had to tell her not to be afraid.

> And he came to her and said, "Hail, full of grace, the Lord is with you!" But she was greatly troubled at the saying, and considered in her mind what sort of greeting this might be. And the angel said to her, "Do not be afraid, Mary, for you have found favor with God. And behold, you will conceive in your womb and bear a son, and you shall call his name Jesus.
>
> He will be great, and will be called the Son of the Most High;
> and the Lord God will give to him the throne of his father David,
> and he will reign over the house of Jacob for ever;
> and of his kingdom there will be no end."
>
> And Mary said to the angel, "How can this be, since I have no husband?" And the angel said to her,
>
> "The Holy Spirit will come upon you,
> and the power of the Most High will overshadow you;
> therefore the child to be born will be called holy,
> the Son of God...."
> (Lk 1: 28-35)

The word for "overshadow" is a very unusual one in Greek, one that is rarely used in the New Testament, when God's glory is revealed (e.g., the Transfiguration of Jesus). But it would have reminded Luke's Greek readers of a place in the Old Testament where the same word appears:

"Just as the rising of the sun is foretold in the heavens by the morning star, so the incarnation of the Son of God,…is preceded by the immaculate conception of the Virgin Mary."

—Prayer of the Holy Father, Pope John Paul II

"The most Blessed Virgin Mary was, from the first moment of her conception, by a singular grace and privilege of almighty God and by virtue of the merits of Jesus Christ, Savior of the human race, preserved immune from all stain of original sin." (CCC 491)

Then the cloud covered the tent of meeting, and the glory of the LORD filled the tabernacle. And Moses was not able to enter the tent of meeting, because the cloud abode upon it, and the glory of the LORD filled the tabernacle. (Ex 40:34-35)

The word for "abode upon" is translated "overshadowed" in the Greek version that Luke knew. The Holy Spirit would "overshadow" Mary in the same way that the cloud "overshadowed" the Tabernacle once the Ark of the Covenant had been put in it.

Mary's response is what makes her the model for all the faithful people of God:

Behold, I am the handmaid of the Lord; let it be to me according to your word. (Lk 1:38)

Mary's submission to God's will contrasts with Israel's long history of rebellion. As the mother of the Lord's Anointed, Mary had been kept "full of grace" from her birth, free from the taint of sin that caused Israel to wander so many times from the right path. She remained a virgin before, during, and after the birth of her Son.

> To become the mother of the Savior, Mary "was enriched by God with gifts appropriate to such a role" (LG 56). The angel Gabriel at the moment of the annunciation salutes her as "full of grace" (Lk 1:28). In fact, in order for Mary to be able to give the free assent of her faith to the announcement of her vocation, it was necessary that she be wholly borne by God's grace. (CCC 490)

> Through the centuries the Church has become ever more aware that Mary, "full of grace" through God (Lk 1:28), was redeemed from the moment of her conception. That is what the dogma of the Immaculate Conception confesses, as Pope Pius IX proclaimed in 1854:

>> The most Blessed Virgin Mary was, from the first moment of her conception, by a singular grace and privilege of almighty God and by virtue of the merits of Jesus Christ, Savior of the human race, preserved immune from all stain of original sin (Pius IX, *Ineffabilis Deus,* 1854: DS 2803). (CCC 491)

> The "splendor of an entirely unique holiness" by which Mary is "enriched from the first instant of her conception" comes wholly from Christ: she is "redeemed, in a more exalted fashion, by reason of the merits of her Son" (LG 53, 56). The Father blessed Mary more

> than any other created person "in Christ with every spiritual blessing in the heavenly places" and chose her "in Christ before the foundation of the world, to be holy and blameless before him in love" (cf. Eph 1:3-4). (CCC 492)

> The Fathers of the Eastern tradition call the Mother of God "the All-Holy" (*Panagia*), and celebrate her as "free from any stain of sin, as though fashioned by the Holy Spirit and formed as a new creature" (LG 56). By the grace of God Mary remained free of every personal sin her whole life long. (CCC 493)

When Luke tells the story of Mary's visit to her cousin Elizabeth, who also was pregnant with a son who would be named John, he uses more suggestive language to point out Mary as the new Ark of the Covenant. The details Luke gives us remind us of David bringing the Ark of the Covenant up to Jerusalem.

David Brings The Ark	Mary Visits Elizabeth	
"David arose and went" to bring up the ark. (2 Sm 6:2)	"Mary arose and went" to visit Elizabeth. (Lk 1:39)	
David said, "How can the ark of the LORD come to me?" (2 Sm 6:9)	Elizabeth said, "And why is this granted me, that the mother of my Lord should come to me?" (Lk 1:43)	
David was "leaping and dancing before the LORD." (2 Sm 6:16)	"The babe in my womb leaped for joy." (Lk 1:44)	
"And the ark of the LORD remained in the house of Obededom the Gittite three months." (2 Sm 6:11)	"And Mary remained with her about three months." (Lk 1:56)	

The Birth Of Jesus

Luke is very careful to give us the exact historical setting for Jesus' birth.

- **It was in the reign of Caesar Augustus,**
- **when Quirinius was governor of Syria,**
- **Augustus decreed that "all the world should be enrolled."**

Since so much time has passed since then, modern historians are not sure exactly when those three things came together, or what being "enrolled" meant (it might have been a census for taxation or an oath of loyalty). But Luke's original audience would have known. It would have been a signal to them that Luke was being very careful to get the historical details right.

Joseph lived in Nazareth, but he had to go back to his native city of Bethlehem—the ancient town where David had been born—to be properly enrolled. Bethlehem was a small town, but it was ancient and famous as the birthplace of David the king. The prophet Micah had also suggested that it had a distinguished future ahead of it:

> But you, O Bethlehem Ephratha,
> who are little to be among the clans of Judah,
> from you shall come forth for me
> one who is to be ruler in Israel,
> whose origin is from of old,
> from ancient days. (Mi 5: 2)

The ancient city of Bethlehem today.

Even though Mary was almost ready to give birth, she and Joseph made the trip from Galilee down past Jerusalem to Bethlehem. Once they got there, they found that everyone else was making the same kind of trip. There was no room for them in the inn, and they had to be put up in a stable. When Mary's son was born, the only safe place to lay the baby down was in a feeding trough.

It must have seemed an ordinary event to all the people in Bethlehem. Most of them were probably too busy with enrollment business to notice a baby in a manger. But in the fields outside the town, a group of shepherds had an astonishing visit from an angel.

> And in that region there were shepherds out in the field, keeping watch over their flock by night. And an angel of the Lord appeared to them, and the glory of the Lord shone around them, and they were filled with fear. And the angel said to them, "Be not afraid; for behold, I bring you good news of a great joy which will come to all the people; for to you is born this day in the city of David a Savior, who is Christ the Lord." (Lk 2: 8-11)

By the titles the angels had used, the shepherds knew right away that the Messiah had been born. He was

- **a Savior, who would rescue his people from bondage**
- **the Christ, the Anointed One, the promised successor to David**
- **the Lord, the one who sits at God's right hand.**

Anyone who knew the Scriptures would have known that the child who bore those titles was the long-expected Messiah.

Shepherds were more or less outcasts. Most religious Jews avoided them. But David himself had been a shepherd in those same fields outside Bethlehem. Now the arrival of the Son of David was announced first to shepherds.

"'And this will be a sign for you: you will find a babe wrapped in swaddling cloths and lying in a manger.'" (Lk 2: 12)

The Journeys Of Jesus: Nativity To Baptism

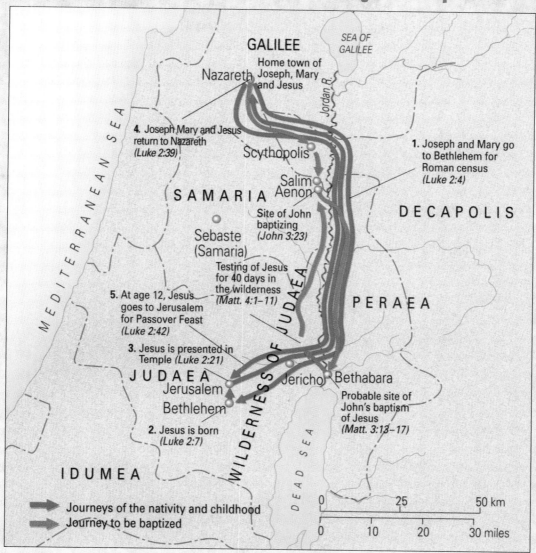

GALILEE

SEA OF GALILEE

Nazareth — Home town of Joseph, Mary and Jesus

4. Joseph Mary and Jesus return to Nazareth (*Luke 2:39*)

Scythopolis

1. Joseph and Mary go to Bethlehem for Roman census (*Luke 2:4*)

Salim Aenon

Site of John baptizing (*John 3:23*)

SAMARIA

DECAPOLIS

Sebaste (Samaria)

Testing of Jesus for 40 days in the wilderness (*Matt. 4:1–11*)

5. At age 12, Jesus goes to Jerusalem for Passover Feast (*Luke 2:42*)

3. Jesus is presented in Temple (*Luke 2:21*)

PERAEA

WILDERNESS OF JUDAEA

JUDAEA

Jerusalem

Jericho

Bethabara

Probable site of John's baptism of Jesus (*Matt. 3:13–17*)

Bethlehem

2. Jesus is born (*Luke 2:7*)

IDUMEA

MEDITERRANEAN SEA

Jordan R.

DEAD SEA

→ Journeys of the nativity and childhood
→ Journey to be baptized

0 — 25 — 50 km
0 — 10 — 20 — 30 miles

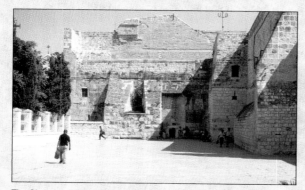

The Church of the Nativity in Bethlehem was originally built in the 4th century by Emperor Constantine to mark the birthplace of Jesus. It was destroyed in 529 A.D. and rebuilt by Justinian ca. 550. In 614 it was spared from destruction by Persians who had burned every church in Bethlehem. They recognized the images of their ancestors, the Magi, above the entrance and allowed the church to stand.

It is possible that a whole clan of the line of David from the exiled tribe of Judah returned from Babylon about 100 B.C. and established the town of Nazareth. Archaeological research suggests that at the time of Jesus, the population of Nazareth was about 120-150. Jesus described the citizens of Nazareth as being "...his own kin, and in his own house." (Mk 6:4)

Nunc Dimittis

Forty days after his birth, Jesus was presented in the Temple as the Law specified.

> Now there was a man in Jerusalem, whose name was Simeon, and this man was righteous and devout, looking for the consolation of Israel, and the Holy Spirit was upon him. And it had been revealed to him by the Holy Spirit that he should not see death before he had seen the Lord's Christ. And inspired by the Spirit he came into the temple, and when the parents brought in the child Jesus, to do for him according to the custom of the law, he took him up in his arms and blessed God and said,
>
> "Lord, now let your servant depart in peace,
>   according to your word;
> for my eyes have seen your salvation
> which you have prepared in the presence of all peoples,
> a light for revelation to the Gentiles,
> and for glory to your people Israel."
> (Lk 2: 25-32)

You may recognize Simeon's words from the Christian liturgy as the "nunc dimittis." It is Latin for "now dismiss". Inspired by the Spirit, Simeon recognized the Christ, and he prophesied the fulfillment of the promises made to the Son of David: glory to Israel, and salvation for all nations. A prophetess named Anna recognized him, too, "and spoke of him to all who were looking for the redemption of Jerusalem."[4]

In spite of the material prosperity, the glorious new Temple, and the apparent restoration of Israel under Herod, there were still faithful people who were "looking for the redemption of Jerusalem." They saw in Jesus the real Anointed One. But Simeon also saw that his arrival would tear Israel in half.

Simeon's Prophecy To Mary
by Rembrandt

> And his father and his mother marveled at what was said about him; and Simeon blessed them and said to Mary his mother,
>
> "Behold, this child is set for the fall and rising of many in Israel,
> and for a sign that is spoken against
> (and a sword will pierce through your own soul also),
> that thoughts of many hearts may be revealed."
> (Lk 2: 33-35)

The Epiphany

One day Herod, the king, received some distinguished visitors: three wise men from the East. They may well have been astrologers from Persia. "Where is he who has been born king of the Jews?" they asked. "For we have seen his star in the East, and have come to worship him."

Can there be a new king of the Jews? Herod knew his Scriptures well enough to suspect the truth. He called the priests and scribes together and asked them where the Christ was to be born. They told him Bethlehem was the place, quoting Micah's prophecy.

Herod, like any tyrant, was nervous about any new claimant to the throne. He was especially nervous about this one, perhaps because he remembered Balak's prophecy that "a star shall come forth out of Jacob," at which time "Edom shall be dispossessed." Herod was an Edomite.

> Then Herod summoned the wise men secretly and ascertained from them what time the star appeared; and he sent them to Bethlehem, saying, "Go and search diligently for the child, that I too may come and worship him." (Mt 2:7-8)

Worship wasn't really what was on Herod's mind, but the wise men had the information they came for. They set off for Bethlehem, and the star led them straight to Jesus. They bowed before him and gave him their expensive gifts: gold, frankincense, and myrrh. Gold and frankincense, Isaiah had said, would be brought by all the nations to the God of Israel:

> And nations shall come to your light,
>   and kings to the brightness of your rising....
> They shall bring gold and frankincense,
>   and shall proclaim the praise of the Lord. (Is 60:3, 6)

Myrrh is an aromatic spice added to the holy oil used to anoint the priests of Israel (Ex 30:23). Together, the gifts suggested that the child Jesus was God, king, and priest. Since myrrh was also used to anoint a dead body for burial, it also suggested Jesus' ultimate sacrifice on the cross.

> The *Epiphany* is the manifestation of Jesus as Messiah of Israel, Son of God and Savior of the world. The great feast of Epiphany celebrates the adoration of Jesus by the wise men (*magi*) from the East, together with his baptism in the Jordan and the wedding feast at Cana in Galilee (Mt 2:1; cf. LH, Epiphany, Evening Prayer II, Antiphon at the Canticle of Mary). In the magi, representatives of the neighboring pagan religions, the Gospel sees the first-fruits of the nations (cf. Mt 2:2; Nm 24:17-19; Rv 22:16), who welcome the good news of salvation through the Incarnation. The magi's coming to Jerusalem in order to pay homage to the king of the Jews shows that they seek in Israel, in the messianic light of the star of David, the one who will be king of the nations. Their coming means that pagans can discover Jesus and worship him as Son of God and Savior of the world only by turning towards the Jews and receiving from them the messianic promise as contained in the Old Testament (cf. Jn 4:22; Mt 2:4-6). The Epiphany shows that "the full number of the nations" now takes its "place in the family of the patriarchs," and acquires *Israelitica dignitas* (St. Leo the Great, *Sermo 3 in epiphania Domini* 1-3, 5: PL 54, 242; LH, Epiphany, OR; Roman Missal, Easter Vigil 26, Prayer after the third reading) (are made "worthy of the heritage of Israel"). (CCC 528)

The Holy Innocents

The three wise men didn't go back to Herod. A dream warned them not to see him again, so they left by a different route. By the time Herod figured out what had happened, they were long gone.

Joseph also had a dream.

> Now when they had departed, behold, an angel of the Lord appeared to Joseph in a dream and said, "Rise, take the child and his mother, and flee to Egypt, and remain there till I tell you; for Herod is about to search for the child to destroy him." (Mt 2:13)

So Joseph and Mary took Jesus to Egypt. There were large Jewish populations in Alexandria and Elephantine and perhaps other Egyptian cities, and Egypt was also part of the same big Roman Empire. The travelers would not have attracted much attention. But they would be safe from the madness of Herod.

With no way to find the child he thought might be the Christ, Herod went into one of his towering rages. He could have had a search made, but that would take time and effort. He decided on a simpler strategy.

> Then Herod, when he saw that he had been tricked by the wise men, was in a furious rage, and he sent and killed all the male children in Bethlehem and in all that region who were two years old or under, according to the time which he had ascertained from the wise men. (Mt 2:3)

By most standards it was a lunatic act of rage, but Herod had murdered three of his own sons, not to mention his wife—supposedly his favorite wife. Herod was used to murdering others to get his way. There was a certain insane logic to Herod's act, just as there had been a certain insane logic to Pharaoh's decision to kill all the Hebrew male children when Moses was born. Like Moses, Jesus had escaped wholesale slaughter of innocent children by a cruel but powerful tyrant. Matthew is beginning to show us that Jesus is *a prophet like Moses.*

The Flight Into Egypt

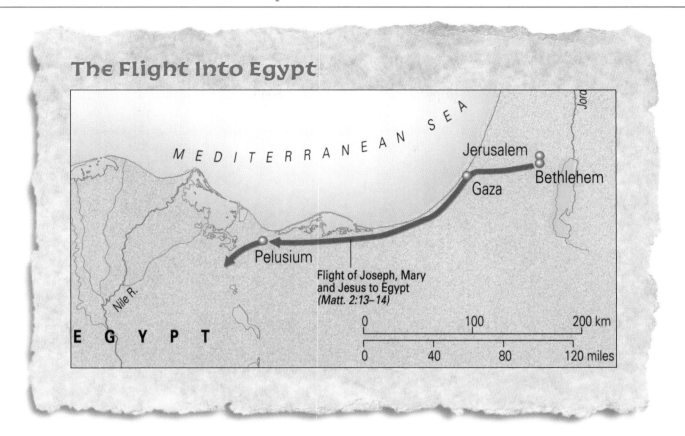

Flight of Joseph, Mary and Jesus to Egypt (Matt. 2:13–14)

Teaching The Teachers

Not long afterward, Herod died, and Joseph and Mary were able to bring Jesus back to their home in Nazareth. From then on we know almost nothing about Jesus until he was an adult. All the Gospels skip from his infancy to the time when he was about thirty years old—all, that is, except Luke.

Luke has one isolated story from the time when Jesus was twelve years old. Because he tells it from Mary and Joseph's point of view, he probably heard it from Mary herself.

The whole family had gone with a big group of their friends and relatives to Jerusalem to celebrate the Passover. When they were going back to Nazareth, Mary and Joseph assumed Jesus was with some of the rest of the party; after all, they were all people he had grown up with, and it was natural for people in a small town like Nazareth to look after each other's children. But a day out of Jerusalem they finally discovered that Jesus was missing. They ran back to Jerusalem in a panic, and in the crowded city they looked everywhere for Jesus for three days.

> After three days they found him in the temple, sitting among the teachers, listening to them and asking them questions; and all who heard him were amazed at his understanding and his answers. And when they saw him they were astonished; and his mother said to him, "Son, why have you treated us so? Behold, your father and I have been looking for you anxiously." And he said to them, "How is it that you sought me? Did you not know that I must be in my father's house?" And they did not understand the saying which he spoke to them. And he went down with them and came to Nazareth, and was obedient to them; and his mother kept all these things in her heart. (Lk 2:46-51)

The *finding of Jesus in the temple* is the only event that breaks the silence of the Gospels about the hidden years of Jesus (cf. Lk 2:41-52). Here Jesus lets us catch a glimpse of the

mystery of his total consecration to a mission that flows from his divine sonship: "Did you not know that I must be about my Father's work?" (Lk 2: 49 alt.). Mary and Joseph did not understand these words, but they accepted them in faith. Mary "kept all these things in her heart" during the years Jesus remained hidden in the silence of an ordinary life. (CCC 534)

Even at twelve, Jesus was a master of the Scriptures, astonishing the world's greatest Scripture scholars with his knowledge and wisdom. But he was also a human little boy who had worried his mother sick. For three days she thought she had lost him forever; only on the third day did she find him again, alive and well.

After that, Luke has only one thing more to say about the young Jesus:

And Jesus increased in wisdom and in stature, and in favor with God and man. (Lk 2: 52)

During the greater part of his life Jesus shared the condition of the vast majority of human beings: a daily life spent without evident greatness, a life of manual labor. His religious life was that of a Jew obedient to the law of God (cf. Gal 4: 4), a life in the community. From this whole period it is revealed to us that Jesus was "obedient" to his parents and that he "increased in wisdom and in stature, and in favor with God and man" (Lk 2: 51-52). (CCC 531)

The obedience of Christ in the daily routine of his hidden life was already inaugurating his work of restoring what the disobedience of Adam had destroyed (cf. Rom 5: 19). (CCC 532)

That is a mystery of the Incarnation: God made flesh, Jesus the Christ, chose to go through all the stages of growth—physical and intellectual—that the rest of us pass through. He passed through childhood and adolescence before he finally became a man, fully human like us. But this man was also God.

SUPPLEMENTARY READING

John Paul II: *Redemptoris Mater*

7. "Blessed be the God and Father of our Lord Jesus Christ, who has blessed us in Christ with every spiritual blessing in the heavenly places" (Eph 1: 3). These words of the Letter to the Ephesians reveal the eternal design of God the Father, his plan of man's salvation in Christ. It is a universal plan, which concerns all men and women created in the image and likeness of God (cf. Gn 1: 26). Just as all are included in the creative work of God "in the beginning," so all are eternally included in the divine plan of salvation, which is to be completely revealed, in the "fullness of time," with the final coming of Christ. In fact, the God who is the "Father of our Lord Jesus Christ"—these are the next words of the same Letter—"chose us in him before the foundation of the world, that we should be holy and blameless before him. He destined us in love to be his sons through Jesus Christ, according to the purpose of his will, to the praise of his glorious grace, which he freely bestowed on us in the Beloved. In him we have redemption through his blood, the forgiveness of our trespasses, according to the riches of his grace" (Eph 1: 4-7).

The divine plan of salvation—which was fully revealed to us with the coming of Christ—is eternal. And according to the teaching contained in the Letter just quoted and in other Pauline Letters (cf. Col 1: 12-14; Rom 3: 24; Gal 3: 13; 2 Cor 5: 18-29), it is also eternally linked to Christ. It includes everyone, but it reserves a special place for the "woman" who is the Mother of him to whom the Father has entrusted the work of salvation. As the Second Vatican Council says, "she is already prophetically foreshadowed in that promise made to our first parents after their fall into sin"—according to the Book of Genesis (cf. 3: 15). "Likewise she is the Virgin who is to conceive and bear a son, whose name will be called Emmanuel"—according to the words of Isaiah (cf. 7: 14). In this way the Old Testament prepares that "fullness of time" when God "sent forth his Son, born of woman...so that we might receive adoption as sons." The coming into the world of the Son of God is an event recorded in the first chapters of the Gospels according to Luke and Matthew.

8. Mary is definitively introduced into the mystery of Christ through this event: the Annunciation by the angel. This takes place at Nazareth, within the concrete circumstances of the history of Israel, the people which first received God's promises.

"Hail, full of grace, the Lord is with you!" (Lk 1: 28)

VOCABULARY

ANNA
A prophetess who recognized the Messiah when Jesus was presented at the Temple.

AUGUSTUS
The first Roman emperor. After many years of civil war, he established peace throughout the Mediterranean.

BETHLEHEM
The city where Jesus Christ was born. It was the ancestral home of David, which is why Joseph being of the house of David had to go there to be "enrolled."

CAESAR
A title used by all the Roman emperors. When a New Testament writer mentions "Caesar," he means the emperor who was reigning at the time.

EPIPHANY
The manifestation of Jesus as the Christ. The feast of Epiphany celebrates the adoration of the Christ child by the royal visitors from the east.

HAIL MARY
The words with which the angel Gabriel greeted Mary at the Annunciation: "Hail, full of grace, the Lord is with thee."

IMMACULATE CONCEPTION
Mary was conceived without the stain of original sin.

INCARNATION
The coming of God in human form. Latin for "becoming flesh."

JESUS CHRIST
The long-promised Anointed One, God the Son in human form. Jesus was true God and true man. His human nature was not merely an appearance, but God on earth.

SIMEON
A priest who recognized the Christ child when Jesus was presented at the Temple.

SON OF DAVID
A title that belongs not only to Solomon but also to Jesus Christ as the promised heir of the Davidic kingdom.

"And he rose and took the child and his mother by night, and departed to Egypt, and remained there until the death of Herod. This was to fulfil what the Lord had spoken by the prophet, 'Out of Egypt have I called my son.'" (Mt 2: 14–15)

STUDY QUESTIONS

1. What does it mean that Jesus was both true God and true man?

2. What truth is at the heart of the mystery of the Incarnation?

3. Why does Matthew's Gospel begin with a listing of the genealogy of Jesus?

4. What is Matthew demonstrating by compressing the genealogy of Jesus numerically?

5. What are the three important events that Matthew uses to sum up the history of Israel?

6. When does the Babylonian exile end?

7. How does the angel address Mary when he comes to announce that she will bear a child?

8. According to CCC 491, what is the teaching of the Immaculate Conception?

9. According to CCC 492, how is Mary blessed?

10. What was Bethlehem known for?

11. What three titles did the angels use to describe the child Jesus to the shepherds?

12. What did these titles indicate?

13. What prophet and what prophetess recognized Jesus as the Christ when he was presented in the Temple?

14. What did the gifts of the Magi indicate?

15. What does the feast of the Epiphany celebrate?

16. What does the coming of the Magi indicate?

17. Who were the Holy Innocents?

18. How did Jesus escape the massacre of the Holy Innocents?

PRACTICAL EXERCISES

1. The Incarnation is a core mystery of the Christian faith. Why is it considered the central event of human history? How does the Incarnation relate to the sin of Adam and Eve? Why is the sacrifice of Christ on the cross of greater value than any Old Testament sacrifices?

2. What was Matthew's purpose in citing Old Testament prophecies regarding the Messiah? What connection does Jesus have to David and Abraham? Why is this important to Matthew's Jewish listeners?

3. What is Luke's purpose in drawing a parallel between the Ark of the Covenant and Mary's visit to Elizabeth? In what sense is Mary a tabernacle?

The Grotto of the Nativity has the greatest religious significance in the Church of the Nativity in Bethlehem. The marble altar was built over the traditional site of Jesus' birth. A fourteen-point silver star is embedded in the white marble. The fifteen silver lamps represent different Christian communities: six belong to Greek Orthodox, four to Catholics, and five to Armenian Orthodox.

FROM THE CATECHISM

470 Because "human nature was assumed, not absorbed" (GS 22 § 2), in the mysterious union of the Incarnation, the Church was led over the course of centuries to confess the full reality of Christ's human soul, with its operations of intellect and will, and of his human body. In parallel fashion, she had to recall on each occasion that Christ's human nature belongs, as his own, to the divine person of the Son of God, who assumed it. Everything that Christ is and does in this nature derives from "one of the Trinity." The Son of God therefore communicates to his humanity his own personal mode of existence in the Trinity. In his soul as in his body, Christ thus expresses humanly the divine ways of the Trinity (cf. Jn 14: 9-10):

> The Son of God...worked with human hands; he thought with a human mind. He acted with a human will, and with a human heart he loved. Born of the Virgin Mary, he has truly been made one of us, like to us in all things except sin (GS 22 § 2).

488 "God sent forth his Son," but to prepare a body for him (Gal 4: 4; Heb 10: 5), he wanted the free co-operation of a creature. For this, from all eternity God chose for the mother of his Son a daughter of Israel, a young Jewish woman of Nazareth in Galilee, "a virgin betrothed to a man whose name was Joseph, of the house of David; and the virgin's name was Mary" (Lk 1: 26-27):

> The Father of mercies willed that the Incarnation should be preceded by assent on the part of the predestined mother, so that just as a woman had a share in the coming of death, so also should a woman contribute to the coming of life (LG 56; cf. ibid. 61).

503 Mary's virginity manifests God's absolute initiative in the Incarnation. Jesus has only God as Father. "He was never estranged from the Father because of the human nature which he assumed...He is naturally Son of the Father as to his divinity and naturally son of his mother as to his humanity, but properly Son of the Father in both natures" (Council of Friuli (796): DS 619; cf. Lk 2: 48-49).

606 The Son of God, who came down "from heaven, not to do [his] own will, but the will of him who sent [him]" (Jn 6: 38), said on coming into the world, "Lo, I have come to do your will, O God." "And by that will we have been sanctified through the offering of the body of Jesus Christ once for all" (Heb 10: 5-10). From the first moment of his Incarnation the Son embraces the Father's plan of divine salvation in his redemptive mission: "My food is to do the will of him who sent me, and to accomplish his work" (Jn 4: 34). The sacrifice of Jesus "for the sins of the whole world" (1 Jn 2: 2) expresses his loving communion with the Father. "The Father loves me, because I lay down my life," said the Lord, "[for] I do as the Father has commanded me, so that the world may know that I love the Father" (Jn 10: 17; 14: 31).

2674 Mary gave her consent in faith at the Annunciation and maintained it without hesitation at the foot of the Cross. Ever since, her motherhood has extended to the brothers and sisters of her Son "who still journey on earth surrounded by dangers and difficulties" (LG 62). Jesus, the only mediator, is the way of our prayer; Mary, his mother and ours, is wholly transparent to him: she "shows the way" *(hodigitria)*, and is herself "the Sign" of the way, according to the traditional iconography of East and West.

Endnotes

1. Mt 1: 1. 3. Mt 1: 17.
2. Gn 5: 1. 4. Lk 2: 38.

What Jesus Did

"Jesus said to her, 'Every one who drinks of this water will thirst again, but whoever drinks of the water that I shall give him will never thirst; the water that I shall give him will become in him a spring of water welling up to eternal life.'"

John 4: 13-14

Chapter 19

What Jesus Did

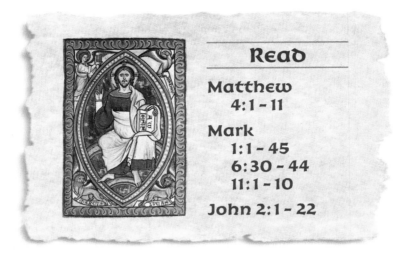

Read

Matthew
4:1 - 11

Mark
1:1 - 45
6:30 - 44
11:1 - 10

John 2:1 - 22

When Peter, the head of the apostles, came to preach the Gospel in the house of a Gentile for the first time, he gave a quick summary of the truth about Jesus.

You know the word which he sent to Israel, preaching good news of peace by Jesus Christ (he is Lord of all), the word which was proclaimed throughout all Judea, beginning from Galilee after the baptism which John preached: how God anointed Jesus of Nazareth with the Holy Spirit and with power; how he went about doing good and healing all that were oppressed by the devil, for God was with him. And we are witnesses of all that he did both in the country of the Jews and in Jerusalem. They put him to death by hanging him on a tree; but God raised him on the third day and made him manifest; not to all the people, but to us who were chosen by God as witnesses, who ate and drank with him after he rose from the dead. And he commanded us to preach to the people, and to testify that he is the one ordained by God to be judge of the living and the dead. To him all the prophets bear witness that every one who believes in him receives forgiveness of sins through his name. (Acts 10: 36-43)

We know who Jesus was: he was the Son of David, the Anointed One who had been promised by the prophets, and the Word of God, God made flesh, born in a human body but eternally begotten of the Father.

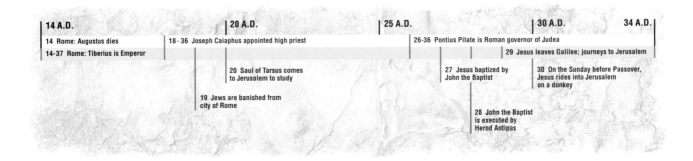

14 A.D.	20 A.D.	25 A.D.	30 A.D.	34 A.D.
14 Rome: Augustus dies	18-36 Joseph Caiaphus appointed high priest		26-36 Pontius Pilate is Roman governor of Judea	
14-37 Rome: Tiberius is Emperor			29 Jesus leaves Galilee; journeys to Jerusalem	
	20 Saul of Tarsus comes to Jerusalem to study		27 Jesus baptized by John the Baptist	30 On the Sunday before Passover, Jesus rides into Jerusalem on a donkey
	19 Jews are banished from city of Rome		28 John the Baptist is executed by Herod Antipas	

Now we need to know what he did. Jesus had a very specific mission during his short life on earth. His life was the perfect fulfillment of all the promises in the Old Testament. Peter's summary gives us the basic outline that everyone who tells the story of Jesus follows.

The four Gospels tell the story of Jesus' life in different ways. Since they were written to tell us the truth about who Jesus was, they do not always put the events of his life in historical order. Instead, sometimes the Gospel writers arranged the stories in the way that best explained the truth they were trying to express. Sometimes that means the same stories appear in different places in different Gospels. The basic outline is always the same, but the details are not always in the same order.

John The Baptist Makes Straight The Way

Matthew 3:1-12; Mark 1:2-8; Luke 3:1-20; John 1:6-8; 1:19-28

- **John the Baptist was a Levite.**
- **Hundreds came to John to confess their sins.**
- **His ministry fulfilled the prophecy that Elijah would return and "turn the hearts" of the people.**

In all four Gospels, the story of Jesus' ministry begins the same way: with the story of the man who prepared the way.

John the Baptist was a Levite, a member of the priestly tribe. He was also a cousin of Jesus, older by only a few months.

The Gospel writers tell us exactly what John looked like:

> Now John was clothed with camel's hair, and had a leather belt around his waist, and ate locusts and wild honey. (Mk 1:6)

Back in 2 Kings, when King Ahaziah's messengers met a man along the road who insulted the king, the king asked them what the man looked like.

> He said to them, "What kind of man was he who came to meet you and told you these things?" They answered him, "He wore a garment of haircloth, with a girdle of leather about his loins." And he said, "It is Elijah the Tishbite." (2 Kgs 1: 7-8)

The prophet Elijah was instantly recognizable by what he wore. John the Baptist dressed exactly the same way as Elijah.

John had a simple message: "Repent, for the kingdom of heaven is at hand." People from all over Judea came to confess their sins to him and be baptized in the Jordan as a sign of their repentance. Often, John would rebuke the people who came with strong words — "You brood of vipers! Who warned you to flee from the wrath to come?" But they still came to him by the hundreds. John became so popular that the government started to worry about him.

Why would the government worry about a prophet in the wilderness? After all, what harm could there be in people repenting of their sins?

The answer is in what the people thought of when they heard the words "kingdom of heaven." That could mean only one thing: the Christ was coming. And many Judeans expected that the Christ (the Messiah, the Anointed One) would overthrow the current corrupt government and rule as a perfect earthly king. Naturally, that idea worried the members of the current corrupt government.

John himself preached that he was only a forerunner. Priests and Levites came from Jerusalem to ask him the question on everyone's mind: "Are you the Christ?"

"I am not the Christ," John answered. Well then, who was he? Was he Elijah? Was he the "prophet like me" that Moses had promised (Dt 18: 15)? No, John answered: "I am the voice of one crying in the wilderness, 'Make straight the way of the Lord,' as the prophet Isaiah said."[1]

"Then why are you baptizing, if you are not the Christ, nor Elijah, nor the prophet?" the priests asked.

"I baptize with water," John answered, "but among you stands one whom you do not know, even he who comes after me, the thong of whose sandal I am not worthy to untie."[2]

The last words of the last prophet in the Old Testament promise that Elijah will return.

> Behold, I will send you Elijah the prophet before the great and terrible day of the Lord comes. And he will turn the hearts of fathers to their children and the hearts of children to their fathers, lest I come and smite the land with a curse. (Mal 4: 5)

Earlier generations interpreted that to mean that Elijah himself would literally come back from the dead before the Christ arrived. Jesus Christ would interpret that promise typologically when his disciples asked him about it:

> He replied, "Elijah does come, and he is to restore all things; but I tell you that Elijah has already come, and they did not know him, but did to him whatever they pleased. So also the Son of man will suffer at their hands." Then the disciples understood that he was speaking to them of John the Baptist. (Mt 17: 11-13)

John the Baptist's ministry fulfilled Malachi's prophecy: a prophet like Elijah (remember that John even looked like Elijah) came and turned the hearts of the people, so that huge crowds came to confess their sins and repent.

> John the Baptist is "more than a prophet" (Lk 7: 26). In him, the Holy Spirit concludes his speaking through the prophets. John completes the cycle of prophets begun by Elijah (cf. Mt 11: 13-14). He proclaims the imminence of the consolation of Israel; he is the "voice" of the Consoler who is coming (Jn 1: 23; cf. Is 40: 1-3). As the Spirit of truth will also do, John "came to bear witness to the light" (Jn 1: 7; cf. Jn 15: 26; 5: 35). In John's sight, the Spirit thus brings to completion the careful search of the prophets and fulfills the longing of the angels (cf. 1 Pt 1: 10-12). "He on whom you see the Spirit descend and remain, this is he who baptizes with the Holy Spirit. And I have seen and have borne witness that this is the Son of God....Behold, the Lamb of God" (Jn 1: 33-36). (CCC 719)

Jesus Baptized

Matthew 3: 13-17; Mark 1: 9-11; Luke 3: 21-22

(John 1: 32-34 leaves out the baptism, but tells what John the Baptist saw when Jesus was baptized)

- **Jesus' baptism by John identified Jesus with us sinners.**
- **As a Levite and prophet, John anointed Jesus for his ministry.**
- **The Spirit came to Jesus as it had to the kings of Israel when they were anointed.**

One day when John was baptizing in the Jordan, a man came who was different from the rest.

> Then Jesus came from Galilee to the Jordan to John, to be baptized by him. John would have prevented him, saying, "I need to be baptized by you, and do you come to me?" But Jesus answered him, "Let it be so now, for thus it is fitting for us to fulfill all righteousness." Then he consented. (Mt 3: 13-15)

Why did Jesus want to be baptized by John? What did he mean by "it is fitting to fulfill all righteousness?"

First of all, although Jesus was sinless himself, it was fitting for him to be identified with us, the sinful human race. He freely chose to go through everything sinners would have to go through.

We should also remember that John the Baptist was a Levite and a prophet. Jesus was the Son of David, the heir to David's kingdom. David and all the kings after him were anointed by Levites; a Levite would also baptize Jesus.

> And when Jesus was baptized, he went up immediately from the water, and behold, the heavens were opened and he saw the Spirit of God descending on him like a dove, and alighting on him; and behold, a voice from heaven, saying, "This is my beloved Son, with whom I am well pleased." (Mt 3: 16-17)

The dove reminds us of the dove that Noah sent out after the Flood. Like the Flood, Baptism is a new creation. We also

recall the kings of Israel who were anointed by Levitical priests. When Saul was anointed, "the spirit of God came mightily upon him" (1 Sm 10:10). When David was anointed, "the Spirit of the LORD came mightily upon David from that day forward" (1 Sm 16:13). The Gospel writers are showing us that Jesus himself was the perfect Anointed One.

The setting, too, reminds us of famous events in the Old Testament. Joshua—whose name is the same as "Jesus" in Hebrew—crossed the Jordan to bring Israel into the Promised Land. In the same way, the Israelites had crossed the Red Sea on their way to Sinai.

> The baptism of Jesus is on his part the acceptance and inauguration of his mission as God's suffering Servant. He allows himself to be numbered among sinners; he is already "the Lamb of God, who takes away the sin of the world" (Jn 1:29; cf. Is 53:12). Already he is anticipating the "baptism" of his bloody death (cf. Mk 10:38; Lk 12:50). Already he is coming to "fulfill all righteousness," that is, he is submitting himself entirely to his Father's will: out of love he consents to this baptism of death for the remission of our sins (Mt 3:15; cf. 26:39). The Father's voice responds to the Son's acceptance, proclaiming his entire delight in his Son (cf. Lk 3:22; Is 42:1). The Spirit whom Jesus possessed in fullness from his conception comes to "rest on him" (Jn 1:32-33; cf. Is 11:2). Jesus will be the source of the Spirit for all mankind. At his baptism "the heavens were opened" (Mt 3:16)—the heavens that Adam's sin had closed—and the waters were sanctified by the descent of Jesus and the Spirit, a prelude to the new creation. (CCC 536)

The Temptation In The Wilderness
Matthew 4: 1-11; Mark 1: 12-13; Luke 4: 1-13

- **Jesus prepares for his ministry by fasting in the wilderness.**
- **The symbolic number forty recalls the fasts of Moses and Elijah and the wanderings of Israel in the wilderness.**
- **Jesus overcomes the temptations that Adam and Israel could not resist.**

Before his ministry began, though, Jesus prepared for it by fasting in the wilderness for forty days—the same time Elijah (1 Kgs 19:8) and Moses (Ex 24:18) had spent fasting in the wilderness of Sinai, the number of years Israel had spent wandering in the wilderness before entering the Promised Land (Dt 1:3), the number of days and nights of rain it took to engulf the world in the Flood (Gn 7:12) so it could be newly created.

During his fast, while he was still in the wilderness, Jesus was tempted by the devil. The word "tempted" means "tested"; Jesus could not have sinned, since he was God incarnate. But it was fitting for Jesus, the perfect man, to face the temptations that had caused all other humans to sin. And the devil wanted to find out whether Jesus was really the Son of God.

Now, the devil knew that Jesus was truly human. After a long fast, he was painfully hungry. So the devil attacked him first through his stomach.

> And the tempter came and said to him, "If you are the Son of God, command these stones to become loaves of bread." But he answered, "It is written,
>
> 'Man shall not live by bread alone,
>   but by every word that proceeds from the mouth of God.'" (Mt 4:3-4)

The devil was trying to make Jesus turn away from the path of suffering and think about himself. But Jesus replied by quoting Scripture (Dt 8:3), reminding the devil that God's plan is far more important than human hunger.

So the devil tried another tactic.

> Then the devil took him to the holy city, and set him on the pinnacle of the temple, and said to him, "If you are the Son of God, throw yourself down; for it is written,
>
> 'He will give his angels charge of you,' and
> 'On their hands they will bear you up,
> lest you strike your foot against a stone.'"
> Jesus said to him, "Again it is written,
> 'You shall not tempt the Lord your God.'" (Mt 4: 5-7)

This time the devil himself was quoting Scripture! (The devil quotes from Ps 91: 1-12; Jesus answers with Dt 6: 16.) If Jesus was the Son of God, the devil said, then it should be no trouble to prove it. But when Jesus refused that temptation, the devil tried once more.

> And the devil took him up, and showed him all the kingdoms of the world in a moment of time, and said to him, "To you I will give all this authority and their glory; for it has been delivered to me, and I give it to whom I will. If you, then, will worship me, it shall all be yours." (Lk 4: 5-7)

This was the most important test of all. Jesus had the opportunity to be the kind of Christ most Judeans expected: a glorious king who would conquer the world. He could rule Israel and all the Gentiles with justice and mercy, and he would never have to suffer on the cross. He could be "like God," as the devil had told Adam and Eve. But the price the devil asked was that Jesus should worship him.

> Then Jesus said to him, "Begone, Satan! for it is written,
>
> 'You shall worship the Lord your God
> and him alone shall you serve.'"
> (Mt 4: 10)

After that, the devil gave up—although Luke adds that he left only "until an opportune time."[3] The devil never stops fighting against the Kingdom of Heaven; he is always watching for his opportunity.

As the new Adam, Jesus had overcome the temptation that the first Adam had been unable to resist. As the King of Israel, Jesus had repeated the trial of Israel in the wilderness, but had overcome the temptation to worship false gods.

> Jesus' temptation reveals the way in which the Son of God is Messiah, contrary to the way Satan proposes to him and the way men wish to attribute to him (cf. Mt 16: 21-23). This is why Christ vanquished the Tempter *for us*: "For we have not a high priest who is unable to sympathize with our weaknesses, but one who in every respect has been tested as we are, yet without sinning."[4] By the solemn forty days of *Lent* the Church unites herself each year to the mystery of Jesus in the desert. (CCC 540)

Water Into Wine

Jesus' first miracle almost seems frivolous. In most of the miracle stories we remember, Jesus healed someone who had been suffering miserably for years, or even raised someone from the dead. But in this case the only problem was that a wedding party had run out of wine.

On the third day there was a marriage at Cana in Galilee, and the mother of Jesus was there; Jesus also was invited to the marriage, with his disciples. When the wine failed, the mother of Jesus said to him, "They have no wine." And Jesus said to her, "O woman, what have you to do with me? My hour has not yet come." His mother said to the servants, "Do whatever he tells you." Now six stone jars were standing there, for the Jewish rites of purification, each holding twenty or thirty gallons. Jesus said to them, "Fill the jars with water." And they filled them up to the brim. He said to them, "Now draw some out, and take it to the steward of the feast." So they took it. When the steward of the feast tasted the water now become wine, and did not know where it came from (though the servants who had drawn the water knew), the steward of the feast called the bridegroom and said to him, "Every man serves the good wine first; and when men have drunk freely, then the poor wine; but you have kept the good wine until now." This, the first of his signs, Jesus did at Cana in Galilee, and manifested his glory; and his disciples believed in him. (Jn 2:1-11)

Why would Jesus choose this occasion to be the first time he "manifested his glory"? It was a nice thing to do for the young married couple, but we can be sure that John, the Gospel writer, means to say more than that.

Why did Jesus say "My hour has not yet come"? The idea of wine must have provoked that enigmatic statement. Although he consents to help the bridegroom here, the time for Jesus to provide wine is really when his "hour" comes. The "hour" is the time of Jesus' suffering on the cross; we commemorate that suffering in the Eucharist, where the wine becomes the blood of Christ.

> The Gospel reveals to us how Mary prays and intercedes in faith. At Cana (cf. Jn 2:1-12), the mother of Jesus asks her son for the needs of a wedding feast; this is the sign of another feast—that of the wedding of the Lamb where he gives his body and blood at the request of the Church, his Bride. It is at the hour of the New Covenant, at the foot of the cross (cf. Jn 19:25-27), that Mary is heard as the Woman, the new Eve, the true "Mother of all the living." (CCC 2618)

Cleansing The Temple

John 2:13 - 36

According to John, Jesus began his public ministry with what must have looked like an outburst of bad temper to the priests and elders of Jerusalem. But the poor of the city knew exactly why Jesus was angry.

> And he entered the temple and began to drive out those who sold and those who bought in the temple, and he overturned the tables of the money-changers and the seats of those who sold pigeons; and he would not allow anyone to carry anything through the temple. And he taught, and said to them, "Is it not written, 'My house shall be called a house of prayer for all the nations'? But you have made it a den of robbers." (Mk 11:15-17)

If the chief priests had not already seen Jesus as their enemy, they certainly did after this episode. But "all the multitude was astonished at his teaching," Mark reports. The ordinary poor believers must have felt the same way Jesus felt about the money-changers and pigeon-sellers.

What the vendors were selling was religion. For one thing, faithful Jews had to pay their Temple tax. But although the people of Judea used Roman money for much of their business, the Temple tax could be paid only in Temple currency. The "money-changers" would do the currency exchange—keeping a healthy percentage for themselves, of course.

Jewish religion also required animal sacrifices at certain times. It was hard for pilgrims to bring sacrificial animals with them over long distances, so the animal sellers helpfully offered to sell them the animals on the spot—at inflated prices.

So Temple worship had become big business. For Jesus, though, there was an even worse desecration. The Temple was a series of concentric courts. The outermost court, the Court of the Gentiles, was supposed to be a place where people of all nations could come to worship the True God. When Jesus said, "Is it not written, 'My house shall be called a house of prayer for all the nations'?" he was quoting Isaiah 56:7. Isaiah foresaw a time when all nations, not just Israel, would come to the Temple to worship:

> And the foreigners who join themselves to the LORD,
> to minister to him, to love the name of the LORD,
> and to be his servants,
> every one who keeps the sabbath, and does not profane it,

and holds fast my covenant—
these I will bring to my holy mountain,
and make them joyful in my house of prayer;
their burnt offerings and their sacrifices
will be accepted on my altar;
for my house shall be called a house of prayer
for all peoples.
(Is 56:6-7)

The Court of the Gentiles was supposed to be the place where "foreigners who join themselves to the LORD" could offer their worship. Instead, it had been turned into a noisy street market, cluttered up with vendors' stalls and filled with the sound of hawkers' cries and clanking coins.

John places the cleansing of the Temple near the beginning of Jesus' ministry; other Gospel writers place it near the end. Perhaps Jesus did it more than once, or perhaps the Gospel writers were simply arranging events topically. By starting Jesus' ministry with this story, John points out that Jesus is bringing a New Covenant. The old institutional religion had turned into big business, a series of formal observances that mainly benefited the rich. Jesus announced the coming of a new age, in which the spirit of the law, not the letter, would be the important thing.

View of the Sea of Galilee and the Mt. of Beatitudes in spring.

The Land Of Zebulun And Naphtali

Except for the visit to Jerusalem mentioned in John, most of Jesus' early ministry was in Galilee. He might have chosen Galilee in part because Judea was a dangerous place: John the Baptist had just been arrested for speaking out against the immoral life of Herod, the son of Herod the Great. But Matthew recognized the fulfillment of Isaiah's prophecy:

> Now when he heard that John had been arrested, he withdrew into Galilee; and leaving Nazareth he went and dwelt in Capernaum by the sea, in the territory of Zebulun and Naphtali, that what was spoken by the prophet Isaiah might be fulfilled:
>
> > The land of Zebulun and Naphtali,
> > toward the sea, across the Jordan,
> > Galilee of the Gentiles—
> > the people who sat in darkness
> > have seen a great light,
> > and for those who sat in the region and shadow of death,
> > light has dawned.
>
> (Mt 4:12-16)

Jesus made Capernaum, a town on the Sea of Galilee, his headquarters. Capernaum was right on the border of Zebulun and Naphtali.

Jesus' Galilean Ministry

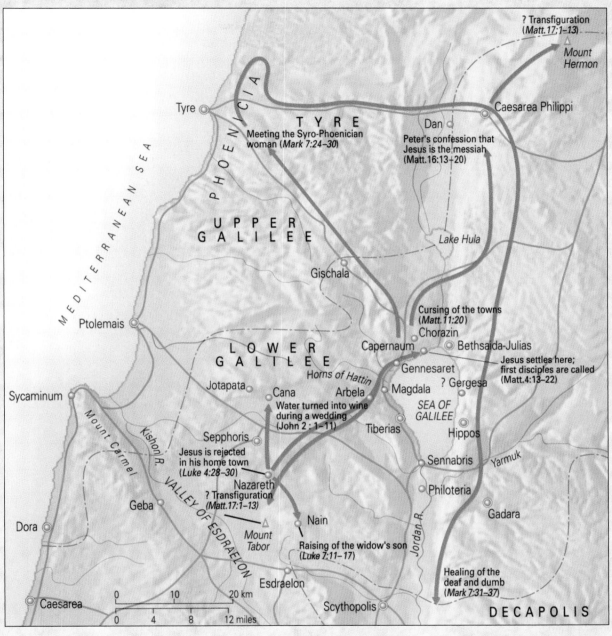

? Transfiguration
(*Matt. 17:1–13*)

△ Mount
Hermon

Tyre

T Y R E

Meeting the Syro-Phoenician
woman (*Mark 7:24–30*)

Dan

Caesarea Philippi

Peter's confession that
Jesus is the messiah
(Matt.16:13+20)

P H O E N I C I A

M E D I T E R R A N E A N   S E A

U P P E R
G A L I L E E

Lake Hula

Gischala

Ptolemais

Cursing of the towns
(*Matt.11:20*)

Chorazin

L O W E R
G A L I L E E

Capernaum

Bethsaida-Julias

Jesus settles here;
first disciples are called
(Matt.4:13–22)

Gennesaret

Horns of Hattin

? Gergesa

Sycaminum

Jotapata

Cana

Arbela

Magdala

SEA OF
GALILEE

Water turned into wine
during a wedding
(John 2 : 1–11)

Tiberias

Hippos

Mount Carmel

Kishon R.

Sepphoris

Jesus is rejected
in his home town
(*Luke 4:28–30*)

Sennabris

Yarmuk

Nazareth

Philoteria

? Transfiguration
(*Matt.17:1–13*)

Geba

VALLEY OF ESDRAELON

△
Mount
Tabor

Nain

Gadara

Jordan R.

Dora

Raising of the widow's son
(*Luke 7:11–17*)

Esdraelon

Healing of the
deaf and dumb
(*Mark 7:31–37*)

0		10		20 km

0	4	8	12 miles

Caesarea

Scythopolis

D E C A P O L I S

Capernaum area
viewed from the
southeast.

Healing The Sick

From Capernaum Jesus traveled throughout the region, preaching and doing good. The word spread quickly that Jesus was healing the sick. Mark tells us that his fame caused him some trouble. After healing a leper, Jesus asked the man not to say anything to anyone.

> But he went out and began to talk freely about it, and to spread the news, so that Jesus could no longer openly enter a town, but was out in the country; and people came to him from every quarter. (Mk 1: 45)

The miraculous healings began to make some people suspect that Jesus was the promised Son of David. In the time of the Messiah, according to Isaiah, Zion would be restored and the sick would be healed.

> And no inhabitant will say, "I am sick;"
> the people who dwell there will be forgiven their iniquity.(Is 33: 24)

> The man of the Old Testament lives his sickness in the presence of God. It is before God that he laments his illness, and it is of God, Master of life and death, that he implores healing (cf. Pss 6: 3; 38; Is 38). Illness becomes a way to conversion; God's forgiveness initiates the healing (cf. Pss 32: 5; 38: 5; 39: 9, 12; 107: 20; cf. Mk 2: 5-12). It is the experience of Israel that illness is mysteriously linked to sin and evil, and that faithfulness to God according to his law restores life: "For I am the Lord, your healer" (Ex 15: 26). The prophet intuits that suffering can also have a redemptive meaning for the sins of others (cf. Is 53: 11). Finally Isaiah announces that God will usher in a time for Zion when he will pardon every offense and heal every illness (cf. Is 33: 24). (CCC 1502)

Miraculous healings were one of the things the faithful People of God expected to see as signs of the true Son of David, the Christ. As Isaiah shows, sickness was thought to be bound up with sin. It was the sinfulness of the people that brought on their sickness. The forgiveness of sins would come with healing.

> And when he returned to Capernaum after some days, it was reported that he was at home. And many were gathered together, so that there was no longer room for them, not even about the door; and he was preaching the word to them. And they came, bringing to him a paralytic carried by four men. And when they could not get near him because of the crowd, they removed the roof above him; and when they had made an opening, they let down the pallet on which the paralytic lay. And when Jesus saw their faith, he said to the paralytic, "My son, your sins are forgiven." (Mk 2: 1-5)

How could Jesus say "your sins are forgiven"? Only God could forgive sins, and only the priests at the Temple in Jerusalem could declare sins forgiven.

> Now some of the scribes were sitting there, questioning in their hearts, "Why does this man speak like this? It is blasphemy! Who can forgive sins but God alone?" And immediately Jesus, perceiving in his spirit that they questioned like this within themselves, said to them, "Which is easier, to say to the paralytic, 'Your sins are forgiven,' or to say, 'Rise, take up your pallet and walk'? But that you may know that the Son of man has authority on earth to forgive sins"—he said to the paralytic—"I say to you, rise, take up your pallet and go home." And he rose, and immediately took up the pallet and went out before them all; so that they were all amazed and glorified God, saying, "We never saw anything like it." (Mk 2: 6-12)

Jesus claimed the authority to forgive sins! No wonder the scribes called him a blasphemer. He was making himself equal to God!

Who Sinned?

While ordinary people seem to have understood who Jesus was, the greatest Scripture scholars of the age failed to understand. Matthew brings home that point by telling the story of two blind men who understood who Jesus was.

> And as Jesus passed on from there, two blind men followed him, crying aloud, "Have mercy on us, Son of David." When he entered the house, the blind men came to him; and Jesus said to them, "Do you believe that I am able to do this?" They said to him, "Yes, Lord." Then he touched their eyes, saying, "According to your faith let it be done to you." And their eyes were opened. (Mt 9:27-30)

The eyes of the two blind men did not see, but their hearts could "see" the truth about Jesus: he was the promised Son of David, the Lord's Anointed. The scribes and Pharisees, whose eyes worked well enough, were blind to that spiritual truth.

Although Jesus often pronounced forgiveness of sins as part of his healing, he was careful to point out that sin was not always the cause of sickness.

> As he passed by, he saw a man blind from his birth. And his disciples asked him, "Rabbi, who sinned, this man or his parents, that he was born blind?" Jesus answered, "It was not that this man sinned, or his parents, but that the works of God might be made manifest in him." (Jn 9:1-3)

When Jesus healed that man, though, the Pharisees still insisted that the man was "born in utter sin." It was the Pharisees who were really blind and really sinners. Even when they saw God working in Jesus, they refused to believe it.

Casting Out Demons

Jesus also cast out many demons in his ministry.

> Satan or the devil and the other demons are fallen angels who have freely refused to serve God and his plan. Their choice against God is definitive. They try to associate man in their revolt against God. (CCC 414)

His power over demons ought to have shown everyone who he was. The demons themselves recognized him at once, but many of the Pharisees and other leaders of the people were too stubborn to do that. Once again, it was the ordinary people who recognized who Jesus was long before the leaders did.

> And immediately there was in their synagogue a man with an unclean spirit, and he cried out, "What have you to do with us, Jesus of Nazareth? I know who you are, the Holy One of God." But Jesus rebuked him, saying, "Be silent, and come out of him!" And the unclean spirit, convulsing him and crying with a loud voice, came out of him. And they were all amazed, so that they questioned among themselves, saying, "What is this? A new teaching! With authority he commands even the unclean spirits, and they obey him."
> (Mk 1: 23-27)

Jesus simply spoke, and the demon could not resist his command. That ought to have been enough to show who Jesus was. Yet the scholars of the day could convince themselves that Jesus cast out demons by demonic power.

> And the scribes who came down from Jerusalem said, "He is possessed by Beelzebul, and by the prince of demons he casts out demons. And he [Jesus] called them to him and said to them in parables, "How can Satan cast out Satan? If a kingdom is divided against itself, that kingdom cannot stand. And if a house is divided against itself, that house cannot stand. And if Satan has risen up against himself and is divided, he cannot stand, but is coming to an end. But no one can enter a strong man's house and plunder his goods, unless he first binds the strong man; then indeed he may plunder his house." (Mk 3: 22-27)

Jesus' answer must have left them wondering even more. They could easily understand his parable of a robber binding a strong man. But when the strong man was Satan, who could be strong enough to bind him?

Eating With Sinners

Jesus' social life was also a source of disgust and surprise to the Pharisees and their followers. A good Pharisee kept himself from even casual contact with "sinners"—that is, people who did not follow the Law, as interpreted by the Pharisees. Yet Jesus could be found, day after day, visiting the outcasts and even the Gentiles and having dinner with them.

In fact, one of Jesus' most devoted followers was a tax collector named Levi or Matthew—the author, tradition tells us, of the Gospel bearing his name. Tax collectors were hated throughout the Roman world, because they were usually extortionists. When the Romans contracted with a local tax collector, they cared only that the right amount got back to Rome. The way to get rich at it was to collect more than the Romans required and keep the extra money. Even an honest tax collector would be hated by many in Judea and Galilee, since he represented the Gentile conquerors who ruled the Promised Land. The more fanatical Jews insisted that it was wrong for a Jew even to pay his Roman taxes. If anyone was a "sinner," certainly it was the hated tax collector.

So when Jesus stopped at the tax office and said to the man behind the desk, "Follow me," many people were surprised. They were even more surprised when he went to dinner at the man's house—a dinner attended by all his friends from the tax office.

> And as he sat at table in the house, behold, many tax collectors and sinners came and sat down with Jesus and his disciples. And when the Pharisees saw this, they said to his disciples, "Why does your teacher eat with tax collectors and sinners?" But when he heard it he said, "Those who are well have no need for a physician, but those who are sick. Go and learn what this means, 'I desire mercy, and not sacrifice.' For I came not to call the righteous, but sinners." (Mt 9:10-13)

Women And Samaritans

Even more shocking was the way Jesus talked to women and Samaritans. A well-bred man did not talk to women in public, and no Jew would speak to a Samaritan.

Luke especially emphasizes Jesus' ministry to Samaritans, and only Luke includes Jesus' parable of the Good Samaritan (see the next chapter of this book). For Luke, the only Gentile among the Gospel writers, it was important to show that Jesus extended his ministry beyond the Jews. But the Samaritan ministry has another significance as well. Samaritans were descended from the mixture of the remnant of Israel with foreigners imported by the Assyrians. By bringing the Good News to Samaritans, Jesus fulfills the promises that the whole kingdom of Israel would be restored.

Unlike other teachers, Jesus treated women as human beings with minds and hearts. Naturally, women followed him in great numbers. Some of his most faithful followers were women, and it was one of those women to whom he first revealed himself after his resurrection.

The Twelve

Jesus had hundreds of followers, but he entrusted his ministry to twelve in particular. That number twelve is not an accident: it is the same number as the number of tribes in Israel, and the prophets had proclaimed that the Messiah would restore the kingdom of Israel, bringing all the tribes back together under his rule. Jesus' twelve "apostles"—a Greek word that means "ones who are sent"— not only went with him throughout his ministry, but (more importantly) would be the leaders of his Church, the new Israel.

You might have expected Jesus to choose distinguished leaders of the people for those twelve vital positions. Instead, most of them came from the lower classes. When he did choose one who was close to the ruling class, it was Matthew—a tax collector, whose job made him universally hated among the Jews. The apostles were an unlikely group to lead a spiritual revolution.

Like many Jews, some of the Apostles had two names—a Jewish name, by which they were known to family and friends, and a Greek or Roman name, which was useful in business in the Gentile world. Sometimes different writers use one name or the other, but the list of apostles is really the same:

Simon Peter	Thomas
Andrew	Matthew (or Levi)
James	James, son of Alphaeus
John	Judas (or Thaddaeus), son of James
Philip	Simon "the Zealot"
Bartholomew (or Nathanael)	Judas Iscariot

Jesus' Journey To Jerusalem

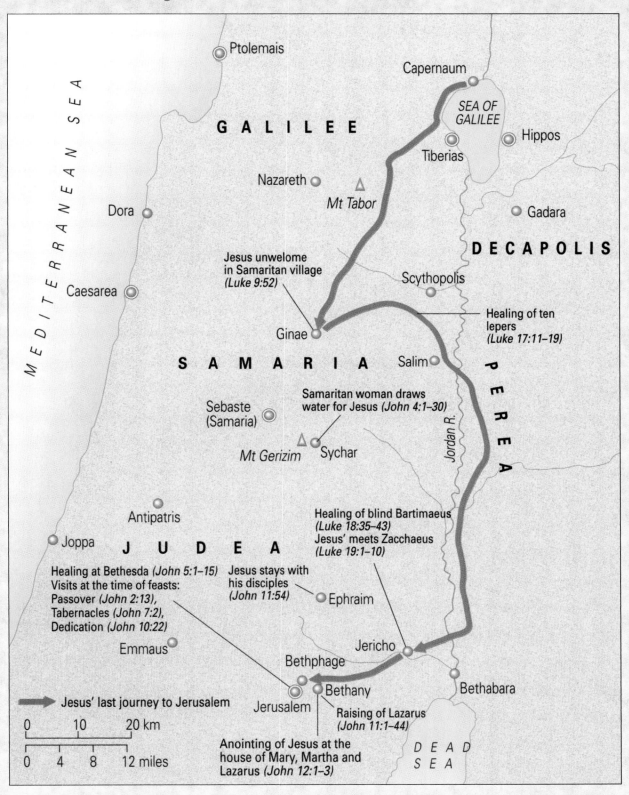

Ptolemais

Capernaum

SEA OF GALILEE

G A L I L E E

Hippos

Tiberias

Nazareth

△ *Mt Tabor*

Gadara

Dora

D E C A P O L I S

Jesus unwelome
in Samaritan village
(Luke 9:52)

Scythopolis

Caesarea

Healing of ten
lepers
(Luke 17:11–19)

Ginae

S A M A R I A

Salim

Samaritan woman draws
water for Jesus *(John 4:1–30)*

P E R E A

Sebaste
(Samaria)

△

Jordan R.

Mt Gerizim   Sychar

Antipatris

Healing of blind Bartimaeus
(Luke 18:35–43)
Jesus' meets Zacchaeus
(Luke 19:1–10)

Joppa   **J U D E A**

Healing at Bethesda *(John 5:1–15)*
Visits at the time of feasts:
Passover *(John 2:13),*
Tabernacles *(John 7:2),*
Dedication *(John 10:22)*

Jesus stays with
his disciples
(John 11:54)

Ephraim

Emmaus

Jericho

Bethphage

Jesus' last journey to Jerusalem

Bethany

Bethabara

0   10   20 km

Jerusalem

Raising of Lazarus
(John 11:1–44)

0   4   8   12 miles

Anointing of Jesus at the
house of Mary, Martha and
Lazarus *(John 12:1–3)*

*D E A D
S E A*

Hosanna To The Son Of David

After three years of public ministry, Jesus knew it was time to face the suffering that awaited him in Jerusalem. He knew that the authorities there were planning to kill him.

But the ordinary people of Jerusalem had heard the news about Jesus, and they were ready to welcome him as the Son of David, the Messiah.

> And many spread their garments on the road, and others spread leafy branches which they had cut from the fields. And those who went before and those who followed cried out, "Hosanna! Blessed is he who comes in the name of the Lord! Blessed is the kingdom of our father David that is coming! Hosanna in the highest!" (Mk 11:8-10)

> How will Jerusalem welcome her Messiah? Although Jesus had always refused popular attempts to make him king, he chooses the time and prepares the details for his messianic entry into the city of "his father David" (Lk 1:32; cf. Mt 21:1-11; Jn 6:15). Acclaimed as son of David, as the one who brings salvation (*Hosanna* means "Save!" or "Give salvation!"), the "King of glory" enters his City "riding on an ass" (Ps 24:7-10; Zec 9:9). Jesus conquers the Daughter of Zion, a figure of his Church, neither by ruse nor by violence, but by the humility that bears witness to the truth (cf. Jn 18:37). And so the subjects of his kingdom on that day are children and God's poor, who acclaim him as had the angels when they announced him to the shepherds (cf. Mt 21:15-16; cf. Ps 8:3; Lk 19:38; 2:14). Their acclamation, "Blessed be he who comes in the name of the LORD" (cf. Ps 118:26), is taken up by the Church in the *"Sanctus"* of the Eucharistic liturgy that introduces the memorial of the Lord's Passover. (CCC 559)

And how did Jesus ride through those crowds? Not in a chariot, or on a litter, or on a white horse, the way a king might be expected to ride. He was riding on a colt, the foal of a donkey. It was a triumph—but it was the incongruous triumph that Zechariah had prophesied:

> Rejoice heart and soul, daughter of Zion!
> Shout for joy, daughter of Jerusalem!
> Look, your king is approaching,
> he is vindicated and victorious,
> humble and riding on a donkey,
> on a colt, the foal of a donkey.
> (Zec 9:9, New Jerusalem Bible)

The triumph would not last long. Within a week, the rejoicing would be turned to mourning, and the promised Kingdom of David would appear to be lost forever.

SUPPLEMENTARY READING

John Paul II: *Dives in misericordia*

Before His own townspeople, in Nazareth, Christ refers to the words of the prophet Isaiah: "The Spirit of the Lord is upon me, because he has anointed me to preach good news to the poor. He has sent me to proclaim release to the captives and recovering of sight to the blind, to set at liberty those who are oppressed, to proclaim the acceptable year of the Lord." These phrases, according to Luke, are His first messianic declaration. They are followed by the actions and words known through the Gospel. By these actions and words Christ makes the Father present among men. It is very significant that the people in question are especially the poor, those without means of subsistence, those deprived of their freedom, the blind who cannot see the beauty of creation, those living with broken hearts, or suffering from social injustice, and finally sinners. It is especially for these last that the Messiah becomes a particularly clear sign of God who is love, a sign of the Father. In this visible sign the people of our own time, just like the people then, can see the Father.

It is significant that, when the messengers sent by John the Baptist came to Jesus to ask Him: "Are you he who is to come, or shall we look for another?" He answered by referring to the same testimony with which He had begun His teaching at Nazareth: "Go and tell John what it is that you have seen and heard: the blind receive their sight, the lame walk, lepers are cleansed, and the deaf hear, the dead are raised up, the poor have good news preached to them." He then ended with the words: "And blessed is he who takes no offense at me."

Especially through His lifestyle and through His actions, Jesus revealed that love is present in the world in which we live—an effective love, a love that addresses itself to man and embraces everything that makes up his humanity. This love makes itself particularly noticed in contact with suffering, injustice and poverty—in contact with the whole historical "human condition," which in various ways manifests man's limitation and frailty, both physical and moral. It is precisely the mode and sphere in which love manifests itself that in biblical language is called "mercy."

Christ, then, reveals God who is Father, who is "love," as St. John will express it in his first letter; Christ reveals God as "rich in mercy," as we read in St. Paul. This truth is not just the subject of a teaching; it is a reality made present to us by Christ.

"*As he walked by the Sea of Galilee, he saw two brothers, Simon who is called Peter and Andrew his brother, casting a net into the sea;...And he said to them, 'Follow me, and I will make you fishers of men.'*" (*Mt* 4: 18-19)

VOCABULARY

BAPTIZE

To wash ceremonially. The baptism of John the Baptist was an external sign of repentance. The sacrament washes away the stain of original sin.

CAPERNAUM

A town on the Sea of Galilee that became Jesus' home during his Galilean ministry.

COURT OF THE GENTILES

The outer court of the Temple in Jerusalem where Gentiles were permitted. In the time of Jesus, it was cluttered up with money-changers and vendors.

DEMON

One of the fallen angels who rebelled against God. Jesus Christ's power over demons was one of the signs of his divinity.

FAST

To go without food. Fasting is an ancient religious practice that denies the wants of the body in order to strengthen the spirit.

JOHN THE BAPTIST

A cousin of Jesus, older by six months. His baptizing and preaching in the wilderness prepared the way for Jesus.

LAMB OF GOD

A title given not only to the Passover sacrifice at the Exodus but also to Jesus Christ as the perfect sacrifice "who takes away the sins of the world."

LEPER

Someone who suffers from leprosy, a serious skin disease.

MONEY-CHANGERS

Businessmen who exchanged the ordinary Roman coins used in everyday business to the special Temple coinage used to pay the Temple tax. They notoriously took a certain percentage for themselves.

PILGRIM

Someone who makes a journey for religious reasons. Jewish pilgrims from all over the world came to Jerusalem to worship at the Temple.

TEMPT

To test, usually by offering something forbidden. The devil offered Jesus food, divine protection, and earthly glory at the price of worshiping Satan.

TWELVE, THE

The Twelve Apostles whom Jesus chose to help him in his ministry. Twelve is also the number of tribes of Israel.

"And taking the five loaves and the two fish he looked up to heaven, and blessed, and broke the loaves, and gave them to the disciples to set before the people; and he divided the two fish among them all. And they ate and were satisfied." (Mk 6: 41-42)

STUDY QUESTIONS

1. What Old Testament prophet did John the Baptist resemble, especially in the way he dressed?

2. From what tribe did John the Baptist come?

3. What was John the Baptist's message?

4. Why did Jesus want to be baptized by John?

5. How many days did Jesus stay in the wilderness?

6. What was the third temptation the devil presented Jesus with in the desert?

7. According to John, what was Jesus' first public miracle?

8. What is John's point in including the cleansing of the Temple story at the beginning of Jesus' ministry?

9. Why did the scribes call Jesus a blasphemer when he was curing the paralytic?

10. Why would a man get sick, according to the Jews?

11. What profession did Matthew follow before becoming Jesus' disciple?

12. Whose prophecy did Jesus fulfill when he entered Jerusalem on a donkey?

PRACTICAL EXERCISES

1. The mission God gave the Israelites was to believe in the one God and keep the covenant. List the similarities and differences between the Old Covenant and the New Covenant given by Jesus. How did Jesus' life bear witness to these differences? Why did he choose twelve apostles?

2. How did Jesus' dealings with tax collectors, prostitutes, and Samaritans signify a radical change in the notion of basic human worth and forgiveness?

3. After reading the Scriptures, the Jewish people were expecting Elijah himself to precede the Messiah, but God sent John the Baptist. Though John the Baptist resembled Elijah very closely, he was still not Elijah himself. What does this tell us about a strictly literal interpretation of the Bible?

FROM THE CATECHISM

517 Christ's whole life is a mystery of *redemption*. Redemption comes to us above all through the blood of his cross (cf. Eph 1:7; Col 1:13-14; 1 Pt 1:18-19), but this mystery is at work throughout Christ's entire life:

—already in his Incarnation through which by becoming poor he enriches us with his poverty (cf. 2 Cor 8:9);

—in his hidden life which by his submission atones for our disobedience (cf. Lk 2:51);

—in his word which purifies its hearers (cf. Jn 15:3);

—in his healings and exorcisms by which "he took our infirmities and bore our diseases" (Mt 8:17; cf. Is 53:4);

—and in his Resurrection by which he justifies us (cf. Rom 4:25).

551 From the beginning of his public life Jesus chose certain men, twelve in number, to be with him and to participate in his mission (cf. Mk 3:13-19). He gives the Twelve a share in his authority and "sent them out to preach the kingdom of God and to heal" (Lk 9:2). They remain associated for ever with Christ's kingdom, for through them he directs the Church:

> As my Father appointed a kingdom for me, so do I appoint for you that you may eat and drink at my table in my kingdom, and sit on thrones judging the twelve tribes of Israel (Lk 22:29-30).

566 The temptation in the desert shows Jesus, the humble Messiah, who triumphs over Satan by his total adherence to the plan of salvation willed by the Father.

574 From the beginning of Jesus' public ministry, certain Pharisees and partisans of Herod together with priests and scribes agreed together to destroy him (cf. Mk 3:6; 14:1). Because of certain acts of his expelling demons, forgiving sins, healing on the sabbath day, his novel interpretation of the precepts of the Law regarding purity, and his familiarity with tax collectors and public sinners (cf. Mt 12:24; Mk 2:7, 14-17; 3:1-6; 7:14-23)—some ill-intentioned persons suspected Jesus of demonic possession (cf. Mk 3:22; Jn 8:48; 10:20). He is accused of blasphemy and false prophecy, religious crimes which the Law punished with death by stoning (cf. Mk 2:7; Jn 5:18; Jn 7:12; 7:52; 8:59; 10:31, 33).

1505 Moved by so much suffering Christ not only allows himself to be touched by the sick, but he makes their miseries his own: "He took our infirmities and bore our diseases" (Mt 8:17; cf. Is 53:4) (Lk 6:19; cf. Mk 1:41; 3:10; 6:56). But he did not heal all the sick. His healings were signs of the coming of the Kingdom of God. They announced a more radical healing: the victory over sin and death through his Passover. On the cross Christ took upon himself the whole weight of evil and took away the "sin of the world" (Jn 1:29; cf. Is 53:4-6) (Mt 8:17; cf. Is 53:4), of which illness is only a consequence. By his passion and death on the cross Christ has given a new meaning to suffering: it can henceforth configure us to him and unite us with his redemptive Passion.

Endnotes

1. Jn 1:19-23.
2. Jn 1:24-27.
3. Lk 4:13.
4. Heb 4:15.

What Jesus Taught

"'Teacher, do you not care if we perish?'...he awoke and rebuked
the wind,...and the wind ceased, and there was a great calm...
And they were filled with awe,...'Who then is this,
that even wind and sea obey him?'"

Mark 4: 38–41

Chapter 20

What Jesus Taught

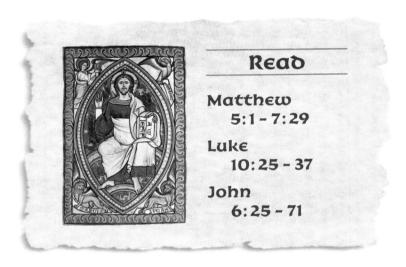

Read

Matthew
5:1 - 7:29

Luke
10:25 - 37

John
6:25 - 71

When Jesus taught, people had strong reactions. Some believed him and gave up everything they had to follow him. Others picked up stones and tried to kill him. But no one could ignore what Jesus was saying. Temple guards sent out to arrest him came back without him, shaking their heads. "No man ever spoke like this man!"[1]

Sometimes what Jesus said was so difficult to accept that even many of his followers gave up on him. But the ones who stayed recognized that Jesus was more than just a provocative teacher. He had the truth. "Lord, to whom shall we go? You have the words of eternal life, and we have believed, and have come to know, that you are the Holy One of God."[2]

Teaching With Authority

Jesus seemed to be a rabbi—a Jewish teacher well educated in the Scriptures. Yet he taught "with authority," as everyone who heard him remarked.

An ordinary rabbi interpreted Scripture by quoting well-known teachers of the past, then offering his own suggested interpretation. But Jesus simply declared the truth. When he quoted Scripture, he gave an interpretation that didn't admit of debate. To the poor in spirit, Jesus seemed to be a fountain of comforting truth. To the traditional teachers and intellectuals, he seemed to be an arrogant impostor. But everyone agreed: "No man ever spoke like this man!"[3]

Parables

Jesus often used "parables" to teach important ideas. A parable is a story or example based on a life experience that illustrates a principle. Most of Jesus' parables were simple stories or comparisons. But some of them are hard to understand, because the principles they illustrate are hard to understand. And often the parables that seem to be simplest reveal deeper meanings and surprising associations when we look at them carefully.

Here is an example of one of Jesus' simplest parables:

> Every one then who hears these words of mine and does them will be like a wise man who built his house upon a rock; and the rain fell, and the floods came, and the winds blew and beat upon that house, but it did not fall, because it had been founded on the rock. And every one who hears these words of mine and does not do them will be like a foolish man who built his house upon the sand; and the rain fell, and the floods came, and the winds blew and beat against that house, and it fell; and great was the fall of it. (Mt 7:24-27)

The first layer of meaning is easy to understand. If you do what Jesus says, you will be secure; otherwise, you will be washed away.

But even this short parable reveals more layers of meaning when we look deeper into it. For example, the words "wise man" would instantly remind Jesus' first audience of King Solomon, the man to whom all wisdom was attributed. And did Solomon build a house? Yes, he did: he built the Lord's house—that is, the Temple in Jerusalem. And the Lord's house was built on a famous rock, the Foundation Stone. (Today, a beautiful mosque called the Dome of the Rock, built on that same Foundation Stone, stands on the site of the Temple.) The rock was enormous: local legend had it that the great rock was the gate of the underworld itself—the place of the dead, which the Greeks called "Hades"—sealed off by God's holy Temple.

So Solomon, the wise man, built the Lord's House upon a rock. Later in the same Gospel, we come across Peter's Great Confession: "You are the Christ, the Son of the living God."[4] Jesus' response should remind us of the parable of the wise builder:

> And Jesus answered him, "Blessed are you, Simon Bar-Jona! For flesh and blood has not revealed this to you, but my Father who is in heaven. And I tell you, you are Peter, and on this rock [petra in Greek] I will build my church, and the gates of Hades shall not prevail against it." (Mt 16:17-18)[5]

When we remember the parable of the wise builder, we understand why Jesus is building his church on a "rock"—that is, on Peter. And when we know that the people who first heard that parable would have thought right away of Solomon's Temple, built on the Foundation Stone, we understand more of what Jesus is telling us. Solomon, the son of David and the Anointed One, built the Temple

Above: The Sacred Rock of Abraham is the centerpiece of the mosque known as the Dome of the Rock.

on a rock and sealed off the gates of Hades. Jesus, the last Son of David and the perfect Anointed One, will build his church on a rock and seal off the gates of Hades. The Church, the whole community of believers, will replace Solomon's Temple.

Now we see how much we can learn from one little parable—one that takes up only four verses in Matthew.

> Jesus' invitation to enter his kingdom comes in the form of *parables*, a characteristic feature of his teaching (cf. Mk 4:33-34). Through his parables he invites people to the feast of the kingdom, but he also asks for a radical choice: to gain the kingdom, one must give everything (cf. Mt 13:44-45; 22:1-14). Words are not enough, deeds are required (cf. Mt 21:28-32). The parables are like mirrors for man: will he be hard soil or good earth for the word? (cf. Mt 13:3-9). What use has he made of the talents he has received? (cf. Mt 25:14-30). Jesus and the presence of the kingdom in this world are secretly at the heart of the parables. One must enter the kingdom, that is, become a disciple of Christ, in order to "know the secrets of the kingdom of heaven" (Mt 13:11). For those who stay "outside," everything remains enigmatic (Mk 4:11; cf. Mt 13:10-15). (CCC 546)

The Kingdom Of God Is At Hand

The first thing we hear from Jesus in Mark's Gospel is this: "The time is fulfilled, and the kingdom of God is at hand; repent, and believe in the gospel."[6]

That was the theme of everything Jesus taught. The rest of his teachings told us what the Kingdom of God was like, and how to live in it.

To what is the Kingdom of God comparable? In the Kingdom, we obey the spirit of the law, not merely the letter. We act out of love, not obligation. The last shall be first, and the first shall be last. We can never deserve the marvelous reward God has in store for us, but he gives it to us because of his own love for us. The way to the Kingdom is through Jesus Christ. And it is our duty to show everyone the way.

These are easy teachings to hear, but very difficult to understand. Jesus used parables, striking paradoxes, and the example of his own life to help us see what the Kingdom really means.

The Parable of the Blind Leading the Blind - Mt 15:14

"'And if a blind man leads a blind man, both will fall into a pit.'"

Plucking Grain on the Sabbath

"On a sabbath, while he was going through the grainfields, his disciples plucked and ate some ears of grain,....But some Pharisees said, 'Why are you doing what is not lawful to do on the sabbath?'... And he said to them, 'The Son of man is lord of the sabbath.'" (Lk 6: 1-5)

Born From Above

While Jesus was still in Jerusalem, a certain prominent Pharisee named Nicodemus came to him in secret at night. Most of the Pharisees already hated Jesus, but Nicodemus just couldn't dismiss Jesus the way the other Pharisees had done.

"Rabbi," he said, "we know that you are a teacher from God, for no one can do these signs that you do, unless God were with him."

"Rabbi" was the way a student would address a teacher. Nicodemus was talking to Jesus as if he were prepared to be one of Jesus' disciples.

> Jesus answered him, "Truly, truly, I say to you, unless one is born anew, he cannot see the kingdom of God." (Jn 3: 3)

The word translated "anew" can mean either "again" or "from above." Nicodemus takes it the first way, and that creates a strange image in his head.

> Nicodemus said to him, "How can a man be born when he is old? Can he enter a second time into his mother's womb and be born?" Jesus answered, "Truly, truly, I say to you, unless one is born of water and the Spirit, he cannot enter the kingdom of God." (Jn 3: 4-5)

In baptism, we are born "from above" with water and the Holy Spirit. Nicodemus had difficulty understanding what Jesus said at first, but Jesus' words stuck with him. He later would defend Jesus when the rest of the Jerusalem establishment was trying to get rid of him, and finally he had the courage to stand up and identify himself as a disciple of Jesus after Jesus had been executed (see the next chapter of this book).

The Letter Of The Law Is Not Enough

Over and over, Jesus repeats the message of the Old Testament prophets: God desires mercy, not sacrifice. (See Hos 6:6)

Obeying the letter of the Law isn't enough. The Law was meant to teach us holiness, but the Law of Moses made concessions to our hardness of heart. For example, Moses allowed divorce. But they were concessions, not recommendations.

To be holy, we must obey the spirit of the Law, not the letter. This is what it means that Jesus "fulfills the Law."

> From the *Sermon on the Mount* onwards, Jesus insists on *conversion of heart:* reconciliation with one's brother before presenting an offering on the altar, love of enemies, and prayer for persecutors, prayer to the Father in secret, not heaping up empty phrases, prayerful forgiveness from the depths of the heart, purity of heart, and seeking the Kingdom before all else (cf. Mt 5:23-24, 44-45; 6:7, 14-15, 21, 25, 33). This filial conversion is entirely directed to the Father. (CCC 2608)

Once a lawyer—someone who knew all about the traditional Old Testament Law and all the developments of it—stood up to ask Jesus, "Teacher, what shall I do to inherit eternal life?"

Jesus knew he was being tested, but he turned the test around and asked the lawyer what he thought. Surprisingly, the lawyer came up with the right answer: "You shall love the Lord your God with all your heart, and with all your soul, and with all your strength, and with all your mind; and your neighbor as yourself."

Jesus says elsewhere that those two statements sum up the whole Old Testament; see Mark 12:28-34. "You have answered right," he said; "do this, and you will live."

But the lawyer had one more question: "And who is my neighbor?" He wanted a definitive answer, one that would tell him exactly which of the people around him he had to love and which he was allowed to ignore. He wanted to obey the law to the letter and no more.

In reply, Jesus told a story that every Christian remembers—one that showed perfectly the difference between the letter and the spirit of the Law.

A man was going down from Jerusalem to Jericho, and he fell among robbers, who stripped him and beat him, and departed, leaving him half dead. Now by chance a priest was going down that road; and when he saw him he passed by on the other side. So likewise a Levite, when he came to the place and saw him, passed by on the other side. But a Samaritan, as he journeyed, came to where he was; and when he saw him, he had compassion, and went to him and bound up his wounds, pouring on oil and wine; then he set him on his own beast and brought him to an inn, and took care of him. And the next day he took out two denarii and gave them to the innkeeper, saying, "Take care of him; and whatever more you spend, I will repay you when I come back." Which of these three, do you think, proved neighbor to the man who fell among the robbers? (Lk 10:30-36)

Rabbis sat on the "Seat of Moses" to teach. This Seat of Moses is from the fourth century synagogue in Chorazin, Galilee. Chorazin is "upbraided" by Jesus in Mt 11: 21. "Woe to you, Chorazin!"

The priest and the Levite were people who knew the Law of Moses backwards and forwards. The man by the side of the road looked dead, and touching a dead body would make a Jew ritually impure. That would be dreadfully inconvenient for someone who was out on a business trip. So they walked around the body.

But the Samaritan understood more than the letter of the law. He showed mercy, not mere compliance with the rules. As the prophet Micah had said:

> Will the LORD be pleased with thousands of rams,
>   with ten thousands of rivers of oil?...
> He has showed you, O man, what is good;
>   and what does the LORD require of you
> but to do justice, and to love kindness,
>   and to walk humbly with your God?
> (Mi 6: 7-8)

The lawyer gave the obvious answer to Jesus' question of which was the neighbor:

> He said, "The one who showed mercy on him." And Jesus said to him, "Go and do likewise." (Lk 10: 37)

The Last Shall Be First

It's easy to see why Jesus had so many followers among the poor and outcast. He taught over and over that, in the Kingdom of God, the last shall be first.

> Blessed are the poor in spirit, for theirs is the kingdom of heaven.
> Blessed are those who mourn, for they shall be comforted.
> Blessed are the meek, for they shall inherit the earth....
> Blessed are those who are persecuted for righteousness' sake, for theirs is the
> kingdom of heaven.
> Blessed are you when men revile you and persecute you and utter all kinds of evil against
> you falsely on my account. Rejoice and be glad, for your reward is great in heaven, for
> so men persecuted the prophets who were before you.
> (Mt 5: 3-5, 10-11)

> The Beatitudes take up and fulfill God's promises from Abraham on by ordering them to the kingdom of Heaven. They respond to the desire for happiness that God has placed in the human heart. (CCC 1725)

Jesus often repeated the same message. The people who are lowest in this world's view will be highest in the kingdom of heaven. The glory of the People of God is nothing like the glory of the rulers of this earth.

> You know that the rulers of the Gentiles lord it over them, and their great men exercise authority over them. It shall not be so among you; but whoever would be great among you must be your servant, and whoever would be first among you must be your slave; even as the Son of man came not to be served but to serve, and to give his life as a ransom for many. (Mt 20: 25-28)

We see here how Jesus fulfills the Old Law by elevating and orienting it toward the "kingdom of heaven." He addresses those open to accepting new hope with faith—the poor, the humble, the afflicted, the pure of heart, those persecuted on account of Christ—and so marks out the surprising ways of the Kingdom. The Catechism teaches us:

> The New Law is called a *law of love* because it makes us act out of the love infused by the Holy Spirit, rather than from fear; a *law of grace*, because it confers the strength of grace to act, by means of faith and the sacraments; a *law of freedom*, because it sets us free from the ritual and juridical observances of the Old Law, inclines us to act spontaneously by the prompting of charity and, finally, lets us pass from the condition of a servant who "does not know what his master is doing" to that of a friend of Christ—"For all that I have heard from my Father I have made known to you"—or even to the status of son and heir (Jn 15: 15; cf. Jas 1: 25; 2: 12; Gal 4: 1-7, 21-31; Rom 8: 15). (CCC 1972)

The Beatitudes respond to the desire for happiness that God has placed in the human heart.

The Church of the Sermon sits atop a traditional location of the Sermon on the Mount. This hill is in Tabigha, south of Capernaum. The Horns of Hattin, west of Capernaum, is another region also considered to be a possible location for the "Blessed" Sermon.

The First Shall Be Last

On the other hand, the people who are attached to worldly things have the least chance at the Kingdom of Heaven.

> But woe to you that are rich, for you have received your consolation.
> Woe to you that are full now, for you shall hunger.
> Woe to you that laugh now, for you shall mourn and weep.
> Woe to you, when all men speak well of you, for so their fathers did to the false prophets.
> (Lk 6: 24-26)

If you have your rewards in this life, you're likely to neglect the greater rewards of the next life. When a rich young man asked Jesus how to get into the Kingdom of Heaven, Jesus told him to keep the commandments.

> The young man said to him, "All these I have observed; what do I still lack?" Jesus said to him, "If you would be perfect, go, sell what you possess and give to the poor, and you will have treasure in heaven; and come, follow me." When the young man heard this he went away sorrowful; for he had great possessions.

> And Jesus said to his disciples, "Truly I say to you, it will be hard for a rich man to enter the kingdom of heaven. Again I tell you, it is easier for a camel to go through the eye of a needle than for a rich man to enter the kingdom of God." (Mt 19: 20-24)

Still, things aren't hopeless even for the rich and respected. God's mercy is great.

> When the disciples heard this they were greatly astonished, saying, "Who then can be saved?" But Jesus looked at them and said to them, "With men this is impossible, but with God all things are possible." (Mt 19:25-26)

Parable of the Workers at the Eleventh Hour - Mt 20: 1-16

"So the last will be first, and the first last." (v. 16)

Love Your Enemies

For most of us, the hardest teaching of Jesus to practice is one of the simplest: Love your enemies.

> But I say to you that hear, Love your enemies, do good to those that hate you, bless those who curse you, pray for those who abuse you. To him who strikes you on the cheek, offer the other cheek also; and from him who takes away your cloak do not withhold your coat as well....
>
> If you love those who love you, what credit is that to you? For even sinners love those who love them. And if you do good to those who do good to you, what credit is that to you? For even sinners do the same.... But love your enemies, and do good, and lend, expecting nothing in return; and your reward will be great, and you will be sons of the Most High, for he is kind to the ungrateful and the selfish. Be merciful, even as your Father is merciful. (Lk 6: 27-29, 32-33, 35-36)

There is no limit to the number of times Christians should show mercy. Peter thought he was being remarkably generous when he asked Jesus, "Lord, how often shall my brother sin against me, and I forgive him? As many as seven times?" But Jesus answered, "I do not say to you seven times, but seventy times seven."[7] In other words, an unlimited number. Jesus also turns the revenge ethic of Lamech on its head:

> "...I have slain a man for wounding me,
>   a young man for striking me.
> If Cain is avenged sevenfold,
>   truly Lamech seventy-seven-fold." (Gn 4: 24)

In the Septuagint, "seventy-seven-fold" is translated "seventy times seven." Forgiveness as unlimited as the evil of the world is unlimited: that is what Jesus demands of us.

> Deliberate *hatred* is contrary to charity. Hatred of the neighbor is a sin when one deliberately wishes him evil. Hatred of the neighbor is a grave sin when one deliberately desires him grave harm. "But I say to you, Love your enemies and pray for those who persecute you, so that you may be sons of your Father who is in heaven" (Mt 5: 44-45). (CCC 2303)

God's Grace Is Undeserved

"Be merciful, even as your father is merciful." That was how Jesus told us to treat even our enemies. God is more merciful to us than we could ever deserve.

Jesus told several parables to illustrate how unlimited and undeserved God's mercy is. These are simple stories, but even today many people have trouble accepting them.

For example, in the story of the Prodigal Son, one of a rich man's two sons takes his father's money, runs away from home, and spends it all in wild living. When he begins to starve he comes to his senses, and he decides to go back and offer himself as a servant to his father, so he would at least have something to eat.

Now, the young man deserved nothing good from his father. He had wasted all his money, and now he was paying the price.

> But the father said to his servants, "Bring quickly the best robe, and put it on him; and put a ring on his hand, and shoes on his feet; and bring the fatted calf and kill it, and let us eat and make merry; for this my son was dead, and is alive again; he was lost, and is found." And they began to make merry. (Lk 15: 22-24)

Meanwhile the other brother had stayed with his father and faithfully served him the whole time. He certainly deserved good treatment. Why was his father giving all this attention to the worthless son who had wasted all his money?

"Behold, these many years I have served you, and I never disobeyed your command; yet you never gave me a kid, that I might make merry with my friends. But when this son of yours came, who has devoured your living with harlots, you killed for him the fatted calf!" (Lk 15: 29-30)

It was a normal human response. And yet nothing had been taken away from the good brother. He had always enjoyed the good things of his father's house. "Son, you are always with me, and all that is mine is yours," his father told him.

We must overcome that normal human desire for strict justice in order to understand God's grace and his mercy. And we also need to learn that we are every bit as undeserving of grace and mercy as anyone else. God gives us his grace not because we deserve it, but because he loves us the way a father loves his children, even when those children don't do the right things.

The New Law is the grace of the Holy Spirit received by faith in Christ, operating through charity. It finds expression above all in the Lord's Sermon on the Mount and uses the sacraments to communicate grace to us. (CCC 1983)

Parable of the Prodigal Son - Lk 15: 11-32

Pray Without Ceasing

Because our Father in heaven is merciful without limit, our prayers really are heard and answered. Jesus himself gave us a model for our prayers.

> Our father in heaven,
> Hallowed be your name.
> Your kingdom come.
> Your will be done,
> On earth as it is in heaven.
> Give us this day our daily bread;
> And forgive us our trespasses,
> As we also have forgiven those who trespass against us;
> And lead us not into temptation, but deliver us from evil.
> (Mt 6: 9-13)

First we give glory to God and ask that his will be carried out in all circumstances. Then we ask for what we need. The prayer is simple and humble. We pray not to be seen praying, but to ask for God's mercy.

Our lives should be filled with prayer. Even an ordinary person finds it easier to give in when a friend or neighbor keeps asking for something over and over. How can we doubt, then, that God will give us what we need?

Jesus Is The Bread Of Life

Jesus' most important teaching was the one that was hardest to understand. He told a crowd in a synagogue in Capernaum,

> I am the bread of life; he who comes to me shall not hunger, and he who believes in me shall never thirst. (Jn 6: 35)

Was Jesus speaking in metaphors? It was hard for the crowds to understand what Jesus meant. But he repeated himself, becoming more and more specific.

> I am the living bread which came down from heaven; if any one eats of this bread, he will live for ever; and the bread which I shall give for the life of the world is my flesh. (Jn 6: 51)

Now the crowds were amazed, and probably disgusted. Jesus expected them to eat him? They weren't cannibals! But Jesus persisted.

> Truly, truly, I say to you, unless you eat the flesh of the Son of man and drink his blood, you have no life in you; he who eats my flesh and drinks my blood has eternal life, and I will raise him up at the last day. For my flesh is food indeed, and my blood is drink indeed. He who eats my flesh and drinks my blood abides in me, and I in him. As the living Father sent me, and I live because of the Father; so he who eats me will live because of me. This is the bread which came down from heaven, not such as the fathers ate and died; he who eats this bread will live forever. (Jn 6: 53-58)

It was shocking enough to cost him many of his disciples. It was even more shocking because the word we translate "eats" was an especially vivid one. There could be no mistake about what Jesus meant; it was like saying "he who munches on my body."

When Jesus saw that many of his followers had left him, he turned to the Twelve.

> Jesus said to the Twelve, "Will you also go away?" Simon Peter answered him, "Lord, to whom shall we go? You have the words of eternal life; and we have believed, and have come to know, that you are the Holy One of God." (Jn 6:67-69)

Peter and the rest had faith to stay with Jesus even though they had a hard time understanding this difficult teaching. Only at their last meal together, which we know as the Last Supper, would the full meaning of it be revealed to them. Jesus had made his triumphal entry into Jerusalem in time to celebrate the Passover. As they ate the Passover meal, Jesus showed them what it would mean to eat his body and drink his blood.

> And as they were eating, he took bread, and blessed, and broke it, and gave it to them, and said, "Take; this is my body." And he took a cup, and when he had given thanks he gave it to them, and they all drank of it. And he said to them, "This is my blood of the covenant, which is poured out for many." (Mk 14:22-24)

When we consider what Jesus had said in that synagogue in Capernaum, we understand that the bread and wine were more than symbols. He had been very careful to show that his disciples would be eating his true body and drinking his true blood—even though it meant losing a lot of his followers. When we celebrate the Eucharist today, the bread really becomes the body of Christ, and the wine really becomes his blood.

> Jesus said: "I am the living bread that came down from heaven; if any one eats of this bread, he will live for ever;...he who eats my flesh and drinks my blood has eternal life and... abides in me, and I in him" (Jn 6:51, 54, 56). (CCC 1406)

> The Eucharist is the heart and the summit of the Church's life, for in it Christ associates his Church and all her members with his sacrifice of praise and thanksgiving offered once for all on the cross to his Father; by this sacrifice he pours out the graces of salvation on his Body which is the Church. (CCC 1407)

"Take; this is my body." (Mk 14:22)

SUPPLEMENTARY READING

John XXIII, *Paenitentiam Agere*

5. Now we have only to open the sacred books of the Old and New Testament to be assured of one thing: it was never God's will to reveal Himself in any solemn encounter with mortal men — to speak in human terms — without first calling them to prayer and penance. Indeed, Moses refused to give the Hebrews the tables of the Law until they had expiated their crime of idolatry and ingratitude.

6. So too the Prophets; they never wearied of exhorting the Israelites to make their prayers acceptable to God, their supreme Overlord, by offering them in a penitential spirit. Otherwise they would bring about their own exclusion from the plan of divine Providence, according to which God Himself was to be the King of His chosen people.

7. The most deeply impressive of these prophetic utterances is surely that warning of Joel which is constantly ringing in our ears in the course of the Lenten liturgy: "Now therefore, says the LORD, Be converted to me with all your heart, in fasting and in weeping and in mourning. And rend your hearts and not your garments … Between the porch and the altar the priests, the LORD's ministers, shall weep and say: Spare, O LORD, spare thy people, and give not thy inheritance to reproach, that the heathen should rule over them."

8. Nor did these calls to penance cease when the Son of God became incarnate. On the contrary, they became even more insistent. At the very outset of his preaching, John the Baptist proclaimed: "Do penance, for the kingdom of heaven is at hand." And Jesus inaugurated His saving mission in the same way. He did not begin by revealing the principal truths of the faith. First He insisted that the soul must repent of every trace of sin that could render it impervious to the message of eternal salvation: "From that time Jesus began to preach and to say, Do penance, for the kingdom of heaven is at hand."

9. He was even more vehement than were the Prophets in His demands that those who listened to Him should undergo a complete change of heart and submit in perfect sincerity to all the laws of the Supreme God. "For behold," He said "the kingdom of God is within you."

10. Indeed, penance is that counterforce which keeps the forces of concupiscence in check and repels them. In the words of Christ Himself, "the kingdom of heaven has been enduring violent assault, and the violent have been seizing it by force."

Parable of the Lost Coin - Lk 15: 8-10

"'Or what woman, having ten silver coins, if she loses one coin, does not light a lamp and sweep the house and seek diligently until she finds it?… Just so, I tell you, there is joy before the angels of God over one sinner who repents.'"

VOCABULARY

HADES

Greek for the world of the dead. Similar to "Sheol" in Hebrew.

NICODEMUS

An influential Pharisee who came by night to hear Jesus' teachings. He defended Jesus when the other Pharisees attacked him, and finally became an open disciple of Jesus after the Crucifixion.

OUR FATHER

The prayer Jesus taught his disciples; also called the Lord's Prayer.

PARABLE

A story or example based on a familiar experience that illustrates a principle. It uses familiar ideas to explain unfamiliar ideas.

PARADOX

An apparent contradiction that is really true. Jesus used paradoxes like "the first shall be last" to show how different the Kingdom of Heaven would be from the state of things on earth.

PETER

One of Jesus' disciples, who became the leader of the Twelve and of the Church. Named Simon, Jesus gave him the name Peter, which means "Rock."

PRODIGAL

Wasteful. In the story of the Prodigal Son, a young man wastes his entire inheritance and has to return to his father with nothing.

RABBI

In the Old Testament, it referred to a holder of an office. A rabbi was a teacher of the Jewish Scriptures. It was the name disciples used for their teacher.

SYNAGOGUE

A Jewish house of meeting. Sacrifices could be offered only at the Temple in Jerusalem, but Jews all over the world went to local synagogues to worship and to hear the Scriptures read and interpreted.

STUDY QUESTIONS

1. What is a rabbi?
2. What is a parable?
3. What famous "house" did Solomon build on a rock?
4. On what "rock" did Jesus build his Church?
5. Who is the last Son of David?
6. Who will replace the Solomon's Temple?
7. What is the first thing we learn from St. Mark's Gospel?
8. Who was Nicodemus?
9. How does the Law enable us to become holy?
10. Which two commandments, according to Jesus, sum up the whole Old Testament?

11. What did the Good Samaritan understand that was above the letter of the Law?
12. Why is it harder for people who are attached to worldly things to enter heaven?
13. What is the limitation on Christian mercy?
14. How did Jesus turn the revenge ethic of Lamech on its head?
15. What two things do we accomplish when we pray the Lord's Prayer?
16. What was Jesus referring to when he said "I am the bread of life; he who comes to me shall not hunger, and he who believes in me shall never thirst."?
17. When do the apostles finally realize what it would mean to eat Jesus' body and drink his blood?

PRACTICAL EXERCISES

1. Christ's parables comprise an invitation to the Kingdom of Heaven. Explain how his parables call for action on the part of believers. In all of his parables those who behave correctly are rewarded while those who do not encounter insurmountable difficulties. What does this tell us about good works? How does actively living your faith compare to merely professing it?

2. Jesus said, "The kingdom of God is at hand." Was he simply referring to the time when he was on earth? What signs do you see of his kingdom on earth?

3. What is the difference between the letter of the law and the spirit of the law? Which is more important? Which is easier to live?

4. Jesus came to complete and fulfill the law of the Old Testament. Only through imitating the immense love of Christ can we participate in the fullness of the law. Judging from the parable of the Good Samaritan, what does it mean to love your neighbor? How is this love different from the love we often hear about in movies or on TV? Why is such love possible only through the grace of God?

FROM THE CATECHISM

581 The Jewish people and their spiritual leaders viewed Jesus as a rabbi (cf. Jn 11:28; 3:2; Mt 22:23-24, 34-36). He often argued within the framework of rabbinical interpretation of the Law (cf. Mt 12:5; 9:12; Mk 2:23-27; Lk 6:6-9; Jn 7:22-23). Yet Jesus could not help but offend the teachers of the Law, for he was not content to propose his interpretation alongside theirs but taught the people "as one who had authority, and not as their scribes" (Mt 7:28-29). In Jesus, the same Word of God that had resounded on Mount Sinai to give the written Law to Moses, made itself heard anew on the Mount of the Beatitudes (cf. Mt 5:1). Jesus did not abolish the Law but fulfilled it by giving its ultimate interpretation in a divine way: "You have heard that it was said to the men of old...But I say to you..." (Mt 5:33-34). With this same divine authority, he disavowed certain human traditions of the Pharisees that were "making void the word of God" (Mk 7:13; cf. 3:8).

1384 The Lord addresses an invitation to us, urging us to receive him in the sacrament of the Eucharist: "Truly, I say to you, unless you eat the flesh of the Son of man and drink his blood, you have no life in you" (Jn 6:53).

1717 The Beatitudes depict the countenance of Jesus Christ and portray his charity. They express the vocation of the faithful associated with the glory of his Passion and Resurrection; they shed light on the actions and attitudes characteristic of the Christian life; they are the paradoxical promises that sustain hope in the midst of tribulations; they proclaim the blessings and rewards already secured, however dimly, for Christ's disciples; they have begun in the lives of the Virgin Mary and all the saints.

Endnotes

1. Jn 7:46.
2. Jn 6:68-69.
3. Jn 7:46.
4. Mt 16:16.
5. For this illustration, we have used the literal rendering "the gates of Hades," given in a footnote in the Revised Standard Version.
6. Mk 1:15.
7. Mt 18:21-22.

The Cup of Consummation

*"Abba, Father, all things are possible to you;
remove this cup from me; yet not what I will, but what you will."*

Mark 14: 36

Chapter 21

The Cup of Consummation

Read

Matthew
26:17 - 56

John
18:25 - 19:30

Psalm 22

It was no accident that the Last Supper was a Passover meal. Jesus is the perfect Passover Lamb. Everything that happened after that meal will be clearer to us when we understand how the Passover was celebrated, and what was unusual about the way Jesus celebrated it.

By celebrating the Last Supper with his apostles in the course of the Passover meal, Jesus gave the Jewish Passover its definitive meaning. Jesus' passing over to his father by his death and Resurrection, the new Passover, is anticipated in the Supper and celebrated in the Eucharist, which fulfills the Jewish Passover and anticipates the final Passover of the Church in the glory of the kingdom. (CCC 1340)

The Missing Cup

In the time of Jesus, the Passover was celebrated with four "cups": that is, the guests drank wine four times.

1. After a solemn blessing, the first cup was drunk, followed by bitter herbs that symbolized the bitterness of captivity in Egypt.

2. Then someone read the Passover story from Exodus 12, Psalm 113 (the "Little Hallel") was sung, and the second cup was drunk.

3. Then came the main meal of lamb and unleavened bread, after which the third cup, the "cup of blessing," was drunk.

4. Finally, Psalms 114-118 (the "Great Hallel") were sung, and the Passover came to its climax when the fourth cup, the "cup of consummation," was drunk.

"I tell you I shall not drink again of the fruit of the vine until that day..." (Mt 26: 29)

This is the way Jesus and his disciples would have been celebrating the Passover. And it seems to have gone just as the disciples expected until the main meal. Then Jesus did something that was hard for them to understand at the time:

> Now as they were eating, Jesus took bread, and blessed, and broke it, and gave it to the disciples and said, "Take, eat; this is my body." And he took a cup, and when he had given thanks he gave it to them, saying, "Drink of it, all of you; for this is my blood of the covenant, which is poured out for many for the forgiveness of sins. I tell you I shall not drink again of the fruit of the vine until that day when I drink it new with you in my Father's kingdom." (Mt 26: 26-29)

Here was the third cup, the "cup of blessing," but Jesus said that the bread and wine were his body and blood. What could he mean by that? "Blood of the covenant" was a quotation from Exodus 24: 8, a passage that all the disciples would have recognized: it referred to the ratification of the covenant between God and Israel. Jesus talks as though he's introducing a new covenant, one that will be ratified with his own blood.

Next in the liturgy was the singing of a hymn, and then should come the "cup of consummation." But Jesus said that he would not drink wine again, so we read that "when they had sung a hymn, they went out to the Mount of Olives."[1] Any reader who knew what the Passover was like would have been shocked and amazed. They had abandoned their Passover before the most important part! Jesus left the Passover before it was finished. For some reason, he had decided that it was not yet time to drink the "cup of consummation."

Not all the disciples went with Jesus, though. One of them had left early: Judas Iscariot was on his way through the darkness to the chief priests.

In Gethsemane

On the Mount of Olives, Jesus told his disciples what was about to happen.

> And Jesus said to them, "You will all fall away; for it is written, 'I will strike the shepherd, and the sheep will be scattered.' But after I am raised up, I will go before you to Galilee." Peter said to him, "Even though they all fall away, I will not." And Jesus said to him, "Truly, I say to you, this very night, before the cock crows twice, you will deny me three times." But he said vehemently, "If I must die with you, I will not deny you." And they all said the same. (Mk 14: 27-31)

Then Jesus took them to a place called Gethsemane (which means "olive press"), where he told them to wait while he went off to pray. But he took aside Peter, James, and John—his closest friends, the same disciples who had seen his Transfiguration.

> And he said to them, "My soul is very sorrowful, even unto death; remain here, and watch." And going a little farther, he fell on the ground and prayed that, if it were possible, the hour might pass from him. And he said, "Abba, Father, all things are possible to you; remove this cup from me; yet not what I will, but what you will." (Mk 14: 35-36)

That word "cup" should catch our attention. Jesus had cut the Passover short before it was finished. He still had one cup to drink—the "cup of consummation." Now he was praying to his Father ("Abba" is a familiar Aramaic word for "Father") to take away "this cup."

> The cup of the New Covenant, which Jesus anticipated when he offered himself at the Last Supper, is afterwards accepted by him from his Father's hands in his agony in the garden at Gethsemani (cf. Mt 26: 42; Lk 22: 20), making himself "obedient unto death." Jesus prays: "My Father, if it be possible, let this cup pass from me..." (Phil 2: 8; Mt 26: 39; cf. Heb 5: 7-8). Thus he expresses the horror that death represented for his human nature. Like ours, his human nature is destined for eternal life; but unlike ours, it is perfectly exempt from sin, the cause of death (cf. Rom 5: 12; Heb 4: 15). Above all, his human nature has been assumed by the divine person of the "Author of life," the "Living One" (cf. Acts 3: 15; Rv 1: 17; Jn 1: 4; 5: 26). By accepting in his human will that the Father's will be done, he accepts his death as redemptive, for "he himself bore our sins in his body on the tree" (1 Pt 2: 24; cf. Mt 26: 42). (CCC 612)

When Jesus came back to his three friends, they were all asleep. It was very late, and they had eaten a big meal. Jesus woke them up and went off to pray again, and again he came back to find them asleep.

The third time he found them asleep, he said, "Are you still sleeping and taking your rest? It is enough; the hour has come; the Son of man is betrayed into the hands of sinners. Rise, let us be going; see, my betrayer is at hand."[2]

"Behold, the hour is at hand, and the Son of man is betrayed into the hands of sinners." (Mt 26: 45)

*"Again, for the second time, he went away and prayed,
'My father, if this cannot pass unless I drink it, thy will be done.'" (Mt 26: 42)*

"And he came up to Jesus at once and said, 'Hail, Master!' And he kissed him."
(Mt 26: 49)

Jesus Arrested In Gethsemane

Immediately Judas appeared, leading a band of soldiers with swords and clubs to Gethsemane. "The one I shall kiss is the man," Judas had told them; "seize him and lead him away safely."[3] Judas greeted the Master with a kiss—the ordinary way a disciple would greet his master. But there was no disguising what he was doing.

The soldiers had come expecting a fight. But there was no battle—only one incident. The disciples asked, "Lord, shall we strike with the sword?" Peter, who always let his heart run away with him, did not wait for an answer. He struck at the high priest's slave, cutting off his ear. But Jesus said, "Put your sword into its sheath; shall I not drink the chalice which the Father has given me?"[4] And he touched the slave's ear and healed him.[5] It would be his last miraculous healing on earth. Jesus was ready to drink the fourth cup.

Then Jesus went peacefully with the soldiers. Peter followed at a distance, and so did John.

They took Jesus to Annas, who was the father-in-law of the current high priest. Annas had been deposed by the Romans years before, but most Jews still considered him the rightful high priest. His son-in-law Caiaphas seems to have deferred to Annas, allowing him to interrogate Jesus first.[6]

"'This man was with Jesus of Nazareth.' And again he denied it with an oath, 'I do not know the man.'" (Mt 26: 71-72)

Peter's Denial

Meanwhile, the soldiers and servants who had brought Jesus waited outside for their instructions. Since it was a chilly night, they built a fire to warm themselves. John noticed specifically that Peter was warming himself beside a "charcoal fire"—a term that occurs only one other place in the New Testament, as we'll soon see.[7] Peter, too, stood outside and waited where he could see the interrogation from a distance, hoping no one would recognize him.

One of the maids recognized Peter in the light of the fire. "You also were with the Nazarene, Jesus," she said. Peter reacted immediately: "I neither know nor understand what you mean." A little while later someone else recognized him, and Peter gave the same response. Then a third one picked him out by his Galilean accent: "Certainly you are one of them, for you are a Galilean." Then Peter swore he didn't know Jesus. Immediately he heard the cock crow, and he saw Jesus turn and look at him. He remembered what Jesus had said: "Before the cock crows today, you will deny me three times."

"And he went out and wept bitterly," the Gospel writers tell us.[8] He must have felt that he, too, had betrayed Jesus. But unlike Judas, he was capable of true repentance. Judas, as we'll soon see, would react with anger and despair; Peter wept out of love. He would have a chance to restore himself.

Blasphemy!

Annas sent Jesus off to the house of his son-in-law Caiaphas,[9] where the Sanhedrin had gathered in an emergency session. The leaders in Jerusalem must have considered Jesus an extraordinary threat if they gathered in the middle of the night to condemn him.

They were taking no chances. They bribed false witnesses to lie about Jesus, but even the bribed witnesses' stories didn't agree. Finally the high priest put a direct question to Jesus: "Are you the Christ, the Son of the Blessed?"

Jesus answered, "I am; and you will see the Son of man sitting at the right hand of Power, and coming with the clouds of heaven."

"'He has uttered blasphemy. Why do we still need witnesses?'" (Mt 26: 65)

That was what Caiaphas wanted to hear. He tore his robes — a gesture of furious protest, and also an explicit violation of the Law of Moses. ("The priest who is chief among his brethren, upon whose head the anointing oil is poured, and who has been consecrated to wear the garments, shall not let the hair of his head hang loose, nor rend his clothes," says Lv 21: 10.) In his desperate eagerness to condemn the innocent Jesus, the high priest himself disregarded the laws he accused Jesus of breaking.

"Why do we still need witnesses?" Caiaphas demanded. "You have heard his blasphemy. What is your decision?"[10]

Caiaphas had a point. Jesus' calling himself the Son of God would certainly be blasphemy — unless it were true. The Sanhedrin condemned Jesus to death.

> Now the men who were holding Jesus mocked him and beat him; they also blindfolded him and asked him, "Prophesy! Who is it that struck you?" And they spoke many other words against him, reviling him. (Lk 22: 63-64)

The Sanhedrin had sentenced Jesus to death, but there was one problem. Under Roman rule, the Jewish leaders had no authority to carry out a death sentence. They could judge in religious matters, but only the Roman governor could impose a death sentence.

So the Roman governor would have to be persuaded to have Jesus killed. As soon as the morning came, the Sanhedrin sent Jesus off to be tried by the governor, Pontius Pilate.

"'I have sinned in betraying innocent blood.' They said, 'What is that to us?'"
(Mt 27: 4)

Judas Repents

Meanwhile, Judas began to have second thoughts. When he betrayed his Master, he might not have believed that the authorities would actually kill Jesus.

> When Judas, his betrayer, saw that he was condemned, he repented and brought back the thirty pieces of silver to the chief priests and the elders, saying, "I have sinned in betraying innocent blood." They said, "What is that to us? See to it yourself." And throwing down the pieces of silver in the temple, he departed; and he went and hanged himself. (Mt 27: 3-5)

Although Judas "repented," he still failed to understand what Jesus had been trying to teach him. If he had understood, he would not have fallen into despair. He would have known that he could ask for Jesus' forgiveness even when Jesus was on the cross, and Jesus would forgive him.

> But the chief priests, taking the pieces of silver, said, "It is not lawful to put them into the treasury, since they are blood money." So they took counsel, and bought with them the potter's field, to bury strangers in. Therefore that field has been called the Field of Blood to this day. (Mt 27: 6-7)

An ancient tradition says that Judas was buried in the valley of Hinnom or Topheth, on the exact spot where Jeremiah had smashed a pot:

> Then you shall break the flask in the sight of the men who go with you, and shall say to them, "Thus says the LORD of hosts: So will I break this people and this city, as one breaks a potter's vessel, so that it can never be mended. Men shall bury in Topheth because there will be no place else to bury." (Jer 19: 10-11)

Pilate Examines Jesus

What could Jesus be charged with that would provoke Pilate to execute him? The Sanhedrin could think of only one thing: he said he was King of the Jews. Pilate would see that as a threat to start yet another Jewish insurrection. "We found this man perverting our nation, and forbidding us to give tribute to Caesar, and saying that he himself is Christ a king,"[11] the Sanhedrin told Pilate. The part about forbidding them to give tribute to Caesar was a lie, but it was the sort of charge they needed if Pilate was to be persuaded that Jesus was a danger to Rome.

Pilate wanted nothing to do with the case. "Take him yourselves and judge him by your own law," he told the Jerusalem leaders. But they reminded him, "It is not lawful for us to put any man to death." And death was what they wanted.

So Pilate interrogated Jesus.

> Pilate entered the praetorium again and called Jesus, and said to him, "Are you the King of the Jews?" Jesus answered, "Do you say this of your own accord, or did others say it to you about me?" Pilate answered, "Am I a Jew? Your own nation and the chief priests have handed you over to me; what have you done?" Jesus answered, "My kingship is not of this world; if my kingship were of this world, my servants would fight, that I might not be handed over to the Jews; but my kingship is not of this world." Pilate said to him, "So you are a king?" Jesus answered, "You say that I am a king. For this I was born, and for this I have come into the world, to bear witness to the truth. Every one who is of the truth hears my voice." Pilate said to him, "What is truth?" (Jn 18: 3-38)

As far as Pilate could tell, Jesus was a harmless philosopher. "I find no crime in this man," he told the crowd.

But the crowd was insistent. "He stirs up the people, teaching throughout all Judea, from Galilee even to this place."

Was Jesus a Galilean? Galilee was King Herod's jurisdiction. So Pilate sent Jesus over to Herod Antipas, who happened to be in Jerusalem at the time. Herod Antipas — the son of the wicked King Herod who had killed the Holy Innocents in Bethlehem — questioned him for a while, but Jesus refused to answer. So Herod and his soldiers, thinking they were having a great joke, put Jesus in kingly clothes and sent him right back to Pilate.

Crucify Him!

Pilate brought the Sanhedrin together again. "You brought me this man as one who was perverting the people," he said; "and after examining him before you, behold, I did not find this man guilty of any of your charges against him; neither did Herod, for he sent him back to us. Behold, nothing deserving death has been done by him; I will therefore chasten him and release him."[12]

That was not what the crowd wanted to hear. There were indignant shouts.

"I find no crime in him," Pilate told the assembled crowd again. "But you have a custom that I should release one man for you at the Passover; will you have me release for you the King of the Jews?"[13]

"And when they had mocked him, they stripped him of the robe, and put his own clothes on him, and led him away to crucify him." (Mt 27: 31)

The crowd had been primed to demand nothing less than Jesus' death. "Not this man," they shouted, "but Barabbas!"[14]

Barabbas was exactly the sort of terrorist fanatic the crowd accused Jesus of being. He "had committed murder in the insurrection," Mark tells us. In Aramaic, his name meant "son of the father." Instead of the Son of the Father, whose kingdom was not of this world, the crowd demanded the release of a robber and murderer who was the opposite of Jesus.

Pilate sent Jesus off to be scourged, hoping that would appease the crowd. A scourge was a particularly horrible kind of whip designed to tear the skin. If the torturer was overly enthusiastic, the victim could die from the injuries. But Jesus did not die. He was weak but still standing when they were through with him. The soldiers, deciding to have a little more fun with him, made a crown out of thorns and stuck it on his head; then they found a purple robe (purple was the color of royalty) and put it on him. They took turns striking him while shouting "Hail, King of the Jews!"

At last Pilate brought Jesus back out to the crowd. "See," he said, "I am bringing him out to you, that you may know that I find no crime in him."

But all the chief priests and officers shouted, "Crucify him!"[15]

Still Pilate seemed unwilling to send Jesus off to die. The chief priests had to play their trump card. "If you release this man, you are not Caesar's friend," they told Pilate; "everyone who makes himself a king sets himself against Caesar."[16]

The threat was not hard to see behind the veil. If Pilate let Jesus go, word would get back to Rome that Pilate had been allowing open rebellion in his province. The governor would have to answer to the Caesar, the Roman emperor, and Caesar would not be pleased.

> In her Magisterial teaching of the faith and in the witness of her saints, the Church has never forgotten that "sinners were the authors and the ministers of all the sufferings that the divine Redeemer endured" (*Roman Catechism* I, 5, 11; cf. Heb 12:3). Taking into account the fact that our sins affect Christ himself (cf. Mt 25:45; Acts 9:4-5), the Church does not hesitate to impute to Christians the gravest responsibility for the torments inflicted upon Jesus, a responsibility with which they have all too often burdened the Jews alone:
>
>> We must regard as guilty all those who continue to relapse into their sins. Since our sins made the Lord Christ suffer the torment of the cross, those who plunge themselves into disorders and crimes crucify the Son of God anew in their hearts (for he is in them) and hold him up to contempt. And it can be seen that our crime in this case is greater in us than in the Jews. As for them, according to the witness of the Apostle, "None of the rulers of this age understood this; for if they had, they would not have crucified the Lord of glory." We, however, profess to know him. And when we deny him by our deeds, we in some way seem to lay violent hands on him.[17]
>
>> Nor did demons crucify him; it is you who have crucified him and crucify him still, when you delight in your vices and sins.[18] (CCC 598)

Jesus Crucified

When Jesus started on the way, he was carrying his own cross.[19] He had been weakened by the scourging, and he was probably physically incapable of carrying the cross all the way.

So the soldiers took hold of an innocent passer-by, Simon of Cyrene, and made him carry the cross. Legally, a Roman soldier could press a native into service to carry baggage for a distance of one Roman mile. (Jesus referred to that law in the Sermon on the Mount when he said, "if any one forces you to go one mile, go with him two miles."[20])

"So they took Jesus, and he went out, bearing his own cross, to the place called the place of a skull, which is called in Hebrew Golgotha." (Jn 19: 17)

Many of the women who had been Jesus' disciples followed him, mourning.

> But Jesus turning to them said, "Daughters of Jerusalem, do not weep for me, but weep for yourselves and for your children. For behold, the days are coming when they will say, 'Blessed are the barren, and the wombs that never bore, and the breasts that never gave suck!' Then they will begin to say to the mountains, 'Fall on us,' and to the hills, 'Cover us.' For if they do this when the wood is green, what will happen when it is dry?" (Lk 23: 28-31)

When they came to Golgotha, the place of crucifixion, someone offered Jesus wine mixed with myrrh—a painkiller meant to reduce his suffering a little. Jesus refused to take it. He would not lessen the pain he had to suffer.

So Jesus was nailed to the cross like the worst of common criminals, and two of the worst of common criminals were crucified with him, one on either side. Even as he was suffering the horrible agony of nails being driven through his hands and feet, Jesus still found the strength to say, "Father, forgive them; for they know not what they do."

> Pilate also wrote a title and put it on the cross; it read, "Jesus of Nazareth, the King of the Jews." Many of the Jews read this title, for the place where Jesus was crucified was near the city; and it was written in Hebrew, in Latin, and in Greek. The chief priests of the Jews then said to Pilate, "Do not write, 'The King of the Jews,' but, 'This man said, I am King of the Jews.'" Pilate answered, "What I have written I have written." (Jn 19: 19-22)

Today, the letters **INRI** appear on Christian crosses and in church decorations. Those are the initials of Pilate's Latin inscription: *Iesus Nazarenus Rex Iudeorum* which is *Jesus of Nazareth, the King of the Jews.*

The soldiers, meanwhile, were dividing up Jesus' meager property. They each took some of his clothes. But when they came to his tunic, they discovered that it was made all of one piece, with no seams, just like the sacred tunic that a Jewish high priest wore. It seemed a shame to tear it in pieces. So they cast lots for it, which is to say they flipped a coin or rolled the dice.

Some of the bystanders shook their heads and mocked him. "He saved others; let him save himself, if he is the Christ of God, his Chosen One!"

One of the thieves also mocked Jesus the same way.

> But the other rebuked him, saying, "Do you not fear God, since you are under the same sentence of condemnation? And we indeed justly; for we are receiving the due reward of our deeds; but this man has done nothing wrong." And he said to him, "Truly, I say to you, today you will be with me in Paradise." (Lk 23: 40-43)

Behold, Your Mother

Crucifixion was a long and horrible death; the victim had plenty of time to realize he was dying and think about the end that was coming. Jesus had one important piece of earthly business to take care of.

> When Jesus saw his mother, and the disciple whom he loved standing near, he said to his mother, "Woman, behold, your son!" Then he said to the disciple, "Behold, your mother!" And from that hour the disciple took her to his own home. (Jn 19: 26-27)

In ancient Judea, a widow with no sons had no way to support herself. Jesus made his best friend responsible for Mary because Mary had no other sons to take that responsibility.

Because John, who tells this story, deliberately keeps his name a secret to the end, he invites us to see ourselves as "the disciple whom Jesus loved." Every beloved follower of Jesus has Mary for a mother and Jesus for a brother, with God himself for our father.

The Last Cup

> And when the sixth hour had come, there was darkness over the whole land until the ninth hour. And at the ninth hour Jesus cried with a loud voice, "Eloi, Eloi, lama sabachthani?" which means, "My God, my God, why have you forsaken me?" (Mk 15: 33-34)

Some of the onlookers who did not hear correctly, or who did not know Aramaic, thought he was calling for Elijah. But in fact Jesus was reciting the first line of Psalm 22, which in hindsight seems to be a perfect description of everything Jesus suffered. (See the sidebar *The Crucifixion Psalm.*)

> Jesus did not experience reprobation as if he himself had sinned (cf. Jn 8: 46). But in the redeeming love that always united him to the Father, he assumed us in the state of our waywardness of sin, to the point that he could say in our name from the cross: "My God, my God, why have you forsaken me?" (Mk 15: 34; Ps 22: 2; cf. Jn 8: 29). Having thus established him in solidarity with us sinners, God "did not spare his own Son but gave him up for us all," so that we might be "reconciled to God by the death of his Son" (Rom 8: 32; 5: 10) (CCC 603)

"Eloi, Eloi, lama sabachthani?"

As Jesus came close to the end, one of the onlookers offered him a sponge of sour wine on a branch of hyssop[21]—the same herb that was used for sprinkling the blood of the Passover lamb in Exodus 12:22.

After he had drunk the vinegar, Jesus said, "It is finished." It was the last cup of the Passover, the Cup of Consummation—the one Jesus had sworn not to drink until the time had come. Jesus had drunk the chalice which his father had given him, "and he bowed his head and gave up his spirit."[22]

> And the curtain of the temple was torn in two, from top to bottom. And when the centurion, who stood facing him, saw that he thus breathed his last, he said, "Truly this man was the Son of God!" (Mk 15:38-39)

The curtain physically separated the people from the dwelling-place of God. At the moment of Jesus' death, that separation ended. If it was the outer curtain, then the tearing also prefigured the end of the world of the Old Covenant: the outer curtain was decorated with pictures representing the whole creation.

The Sabbath was fast approaching (the Jewish day began at sunset). The crucified criminals would have to be buried before then, since no work could be done on the Sabbath.

> Since it was the day of Preparation, in order to prevent the bodies from remaining on the cross on the Sabbath (for that Sabbath was a high day), the Jews asked Pilate that their legs might be broken, and that they might be taken away. (Jn 19:31)

Breaking the legs of the criminals was actually a mercy; it made them die quicker, which was all they could hope for. But Jesus was already dead. When the soldiers came to him, they saw that he was dead, so they did not break his legs. ("You shall not break a bone of it," says Exodus 12:46, giving instructions for preparing the Passover lamb.)

> But one of the soldiers pierced his side with a spear, and at once there came out blood and water. (Jn 19:34)

In the time of Jesus, wine was mixed with water before it could be drunk. The Church still keeps up that custom in preparing the wine for the Eucharist.

After Jesus' crucifixion, Christ, his human soul still united to his divine person, went down to the realm of the dead. Early Apostolic preaching regarding Christ's decent into hell taught us that Jesus, like all men, experienced death, but he descended there as Savior, proclaiming the Good News to the imprisoned spirits (1 Pet 3:18-19). The descent into hell brings the Gospel message of salvation to complete fulfillment, and this is the last phase of Jesus' messianic mission. During this time after his death and before his resurrection, Jesus spread his redemptive work to all men of all times and all places. There he opened heaven's gates for the just who had gone before him.

Pontius Pilate

Every time we say the Creed, we remember that Jesus "was crucified under Pontius Pilate." But the Gospel writers paint Pilate as more than a simple villain. St. John, especially, shows him as a complex character who believes Jesus is innocent but lacks the courage to act on what he believes. The chief priests and the anti-Jesus faction take advantage of his cowardice by playing on his fear of his Roman superiors (see Jn 19:12: "If you release this man, you are no friend of Caesar.")

Pilate had no respect at all for the traditions and customs of his Jewish subjects, but he lived in constant fear of riots. That taught the people of Judea a simple lesson: if you want to get something out of Pilate, all you have to do is threaten a riot. If he had had respect for his subjects' traditions, but had shown courage against the mobs, he might have been an ideal governor. As it was, it didn't take long for the Romans to realize they had the wrong man for the job. A few years after the trial of Jesus, Pilate was recalled in disgrace. One tradition says he killed himself rather than return to Rome as a failure.

But there is an alternate ending to the story. In some Asian churches, the tradition grew up that Pilate was haunted by guilt after Jesus' death. He tried to kill himself, but was repeatedly saved by divine intervention. At last he came to believe, was baptized a Christian, and died a saint.

The Ecce Homo Basilica. One of three Ecce Homo Arches along the Via Dolorosa, the traditional route by which Jesus went from Pilate's hall of judgment to Calvary.

The Crucifixion Psalm

As Jesus hung dying on the cross, he cried out with a loud voice, *"Eloi, Eloi, lama sabachthani?"*

Some of the bystanders who couldn't hear too clearly thought he was calling for Elijah. But the disciples who heard him knew that he was reciting the first line of Psalm 22. When they remembered the rest of Psalm 22, they realized that it was a perfect description of the suffering Jesus had endured.

Yet Psalm 22 ends in triumph. Although the psalmist seems to accuse God of forsaking him, he ends with a hymn of praise for God's certain deliverance. There on the cross, when he seemed to be defeated and dying, Jesus was looking forward to his triumphant victory over death.

My God, my God, why hast thou forsaken me?
    Why art thou so far from helping me, from the words of my groaning?
O my God, I cry by day, but thou dost not answer;
    and by night, but find no rest.

Yet thou art holy,
    enthroned on the praises of Israel.
In thee our fathers trusted;
    they trusted, and thou didst deliver them.
To thee they cried, and were saved;
    in thee they trusted, and were not disappointed.

But I am a worm, and no man;
    scorned by men, and despised by the people.
All who see me mock at me,
    they make mouths at me, they wag their heads;
"He committed his cause to the LORD; let him
      deliver him,
    let him rescue him, for he delights in him!"

Yet thou art he who took me from the womb;
    thou didst keep me safe upon my mother's
      breast.
Upon thee was I cast from my birth;
    and since my mother bore me thou hast
      been my God.
Be not far from me;
    for trouble is near, and there is none to help.

Many bulls encompass me,
    strong bulls of Bashan surround me;
they open wide their mouths at me,
    like a ravening and roaring lion.

I am poured out like water,
    and all my bones are out of joint;
my heart is like wax,
    it is melted within my breast;
my strength is dried up like a potsherd,
    and my tongue cleaves to my jaws;
    thou dost lay me in the dust of death.

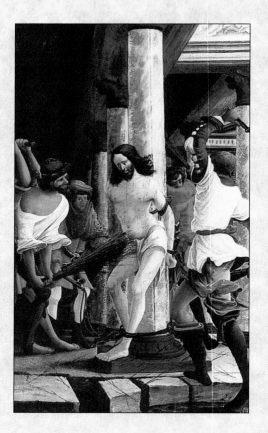

Yea, dogs are round about me,
    a company of evildoers encircle me;
    they have pierced my hands and feet—
I can count all my bones—
    they stare and gloat over me;
They divide my garments among them,
    and for my raiment they cast lots.

But thou, O Lord, be not far off!
    O thou my help, hasten to my aid!
Deliver my soul from the sword,
    my life from the power of the dog!
Save me from the mouth of the lion,
    my afflicted soul from the horns of the
        wild oxen!

I will tell of thy name to my brethren;
    in the midst of the congregation I will
        praise thee:
You who fear the Lord, praise him!
    all you sons of Jacob, glorify him,
    and stand in awe of him, all you sons of
        Israel!
For he has not despised or abhorred
    the affliction of the afflicted;
and he has not hid his face from him,
    but has heard, when he cried up to him.

From thee comes my praise in the great
        congregation;
    my vows I will pay before those who
        fear him.
The afflicted shall eat and be satisfied;
    those who seek him shall praise the Lord!
    May your hearts live forever!

All the ends of the earth shall remember
    and turn to the Lord;
and all the families of the nations
    shall worship before him.
For dominion belongs to the Lord,
    and he rules over the nations.

Yea, to him shall all the proud of the earth bow down;
    before him shall bow all who go down to the dust,
    and he who cannot keep himself alive.
Posterity shall serve him;
    men shall tell of the Lord to the coming generation,
and proclaim his deliverance to a people yet unborn,
    that he has wrought it.

The Jews

Throughout the Passion narrative in St. John's Gospel, Jesus' opponents are described as "the Jews." Sometimes later readers concluded that the Jews as a race or a nation bore the guilt of crucifying Jesus.

Of course, a more careful reading of the Gospel would prevent that misunderstanding. Jesus was a Jew. John, who wrote it, was a Jew. Almost all the earliest Christians were Jews. Probably most of the people who first read the Gospel of John were Jews.

Some commentators say that John was using the term "Jews" to mean simply the Jewish authorities. But the first readers would have heard more than that. Later Gentile readers might read about "the Jews" in John's Gospel and say, "They crucified Christ." But St. John's first readers, Jews themselves, would read the same Gospel and say, "We crucified Christ." Some would argue the term "Jews" would refer to all of those who have rejected Christ throughout the centuries as distinct from those of Jewish blood.

Jewish children praying at the Western Wall.

Later, we'll read about St. Peter's first sermon after Christ's resurrection. On the day of Pentecost, he told a crowd of thousands of Jews of all nations,

> Men of Israel, hear these words: Jesus of Nazareth, a man attested to you by God with mighty works and wonders and signs which God did through him in your midst, as you yourselves know—this Jesus, delivered up according to the definite plan and foreknowledge of God, you crucified and killed by the hands of lawless men. (Acts 2:22-23)

Peter's message to his audience is unmistakable: *you* crucified Jesus.

As a result of Peter's sermon, about 3,000 people—probably some of the same crowd that had shouted "Crucify him!"—believed and were baptized. The people who had the most to be forgiven were the ones who most welcomed the gospel of forgiveness.

The same should be true for us today. When we read the Gospel, we should remember that all of us are sinners, and all of us bear the guilt of crucifying the Son of God.

> The historical complexity of Jesus' trial is apparent in the Gospel accounts. The personal sin of the participants (Judas, the Sanhedrin, Pilate) is known to God alone. Hence we cannot lay responsibility for the trial on the Jews in Jerusalem as a whole, despite the outcry of a manipulated crowd and the global reproaches contained in the apostles' calls to conversion after Pentecost (cf. Mk 15:11; Acts 2:23, 36; 3:13-14; 4:10; 5:30; 7:52; 10:39; 13:27-28; 1 Thes 2:14-15). Jesus himself, in forgiving them on the cross, and Peter in following suit, both accept "the ignorance" of the Jews of Jerusalem and even of their leaders (cf. Lk 23:34; Acts 3:17). Still less can we extend responsibility to other Jews of different times and places, based merely on the crowd's cry: "His blood be on us and on our children!" a formula for ratifying a judicial sentence (Mt 27:25; cf. Acts 5:28; 18:6). As the Church declared at the Second Vatican Council:
>
> > ...[N]either all Jews indiscriminately at that time, nor Jews today, can be charged with the crimes committed during his Passion...[T]he Jews should not be spoken of as rejected or accursed as if this followed from holy Scripture.[23] (CCC 597)

In 2000, Pope John Paul II prayed at the Western Wall asking God's forgiveness for the suffering Christians have caused Jews.

SUPPLEMENTARY READING

John Paul II, *Ecclesia de Eucharistia*

A causal influence of the Eucharist is present at the Church's very origins. The Evangelists specify that it was the Twelve, the Apostles, who gathered with Jesus at the Last Supper (cf. Mt 26:20; Mk 14:17; Lk 22:14). This is a detail of notable importance, for the Apostles "were both the seeds of the new Israel and the beginning of the sacred hierarchy." By offering them his body and his blood as food, Christ mysteriously involved them in the sacrifice which would be completed later on Calvary. By analogy with the Covenant of Mount Sinai, sealed by sacrifice and the sprinkling of blood, the actions and words of Jesus at the Last Supper laid the foundations of the new messianic community, the People of the New Covenant.

The Apostles, by accepting in the Upper Room Jesus' invitation: "Take, eat," "Drink of it, all of you" (Mt 26:26-27), entered for the first time into sacramental communion with him. From that time forward, until the end of the age, the Church is built up through sacramental communion with the Son of God who was sacrificed for our sake: "Do this is remembrance of me ... Do this, as often as you drink it, in remembrance of me" (1 Cor 11: 24-25; cf. Lk 22:19).

22. Incorporation into Christ, which is brought about by Baptism, is constantly renewed and consolidated by sharing in the Eucharistic Sacrifice, especially by that full sharing which takes place in sacramental communion. We can say not only that *each of us receives Christ,* but also that *Christ receives each of us.* He enters into friendship with us: "You are my friends" (Jn 15:14). Indeed, it is because of him that we have life: "He who eats me will live because of me" (Jn 6:57). Eucharistic communion brings about in a sublime way the mutual "abiding" of Christ and each of his followers: "Abide in me, and I in you" (Jn 15:4).

By its union with Christ, the People of the New Covenant, far from closing in upon itself, becomes a "sacrament" for humanity, a sign and instrument of the salvation achieved by Christ, the light of the world and the salt of the earth (cf. Mt 5:13-16), for the redemption of all. The Church's mission stands in continuity with the mission of Christ: "As the Father has sent me, even so I send you" (Jn 20:21). From the perpetuation of the sacrifice of the Cross and her communion with the body and blood of Christ in the Eucharist, the Church draws the spiritual power needed to carry out her mission. The Eucharist thus appears as both *the source* and *the summit* of all evangelization, since its goal is the communion of mankind with Christ and in him with the Father and the Holy Spirit.

The Eucharist is both the source and the summit of all evangelization.

VOCABULARY

ANNAS

The former high priest. He was deposed by the Romans but still considered the true high priest by many Jews.

BLASPHEMY

The crime of insulting God or of claiming Godlike attributes. Jesus was accused of blasphemy for identifying himself as the Son of God and Christ.

CAIAPHAS

The reigning high priest who had been appointed by the Roman government.

CALVARY

See Golgotha

CRUCIFIXION

A form of execution used by the Romans in which the victim is nailed to a wooden cross and left to die slowly.

CUP OF CONSUMMATION

The last cup in the Passover ceremony. At the Last Supper, Jesus ended the meal before the Cup of Consummation; his death on the Cross was to be the consummation of his Passover sacrifice.

GETHSEMANE

Means "olive press." A garden outside Jerusalem where Jesus went to pray after the Last Supper. He was betrayed and arrested there by a band of soldiers.

GOLGOTHA

A hill outside Jerusalem where Jesus was crucified. The name means "place of the skull."

JUDAS ISCARIOT

One of the Twelve. He betrayed Jesus to the authorities.

LAST SUPPER

The Passover meal that Jesus and his disciples celebrated before his arrest. Jesus instituted the Eucharist at the Last Supper.

NAZARENE

Someone from the town of Nazareth. This is how a placard identified Jesus on the cross.

PONTIUS PILATE

The Roman governor of Judea. Although he found Jesus guilty of nothing, he sentenced him to death by crucifixion.

PRAETORIUM

The center of Roman government in a province.

SANHEDRIN

The Jewish governing council. Its responsibilities were mainly religious; the Romans had taken over its governmental functions.

SIMON OF CYRENE

The man who was forced to help carry Jesus' cross to Golgotha.

STUDY QUESTIONS

1. When Passover was celebrated, what four "cups" were drunk?

2. What psalms were sung during the meal?

3. What did the phrase "blood of the covenant" indicate?

4. What important part of the Passover celebration did Jesus leave out at the Last Supper?

5. Where did Jesus go with the Apostles after the Last Supper?

6. What "cup" is Jesus referring to when he is praying at Gethsemane?

7. By what sign did Judas identify Jesus to the soldiers who had come to arrest him?

8. Who was Annas?

9. How many times did Peter deny that he knew Jesus?

10. What is the difference between the weeping of Judas and St. Peter?

11. What was the charge used to condemn Jesus?

12. Why did the Sanhedrin not kill Jesus right away?

13. What did the chief priests do with the money Judas threw back at them after Jesus had been betrayed?

14. What did the Sanhedrin accuse Jesus of in order to get Pilate to execute him?

15. Who did the crowd want freed instead of Jesus?

16. What does CCC 598 tell us?

17. What two people carried Jesus' cross to Golgotha?

18. What title did Pilate have placed on the cross?

19. Which disciple did Jesus choose to care for his mother?

20. When did Jesus drink the Cup of Consummation?

PRACTICAL EXERCISES

1. St. Peter's denial of Christ is an oft-quoted part of the gospels. Though it is easy to recognize Peter's weakness in denying Christ, often overlooked is the amount of courage it took him to go to the courtyard in the first place. Do you think you would have had the nerve to go? What do you think was going through Peter's mind when he decided to take the risk?

2. Jesus' death and resurrection changed the whole history of mankind. What do you think would be the conditions prevalent in the world if Jesus had not suffered for us? Would we be living as the Old Testament pagans did?

3. St. Thomas Aquinas believed that blasphemy was a greater sin than murder. What do you think were his reasons for saying this? Is blasphemy a serious problem today?

FROM THE CATECHISM

596 The religious authorities in Jerusalem were not unanimous about what stance to take towards Jesus (cf. Jn 9:16; Jn 10:19). The Pharisees threatened to excommunicate his followers (cf. Jn 9:22). To those who feared that "everyone will believe in him, and the Romans will come and destroy both our holy place and our nation," the high priest Caiaphas replied by prophesying: "It is expedient for you that one man should die for the people, and that the whole nation should not perish" (Jn 11:48-50). The Sanhedrin, having declared Jesus deserving of death as a blasphemer but having lost the right to put anyone to death, hands him over to the Romans, accusing him of political revolt, a charge that puts him in the same category as Barabbas who had been accused of sedition (cf. Mt 26:66; Jn 18:31; Lk 23:2, 19). The high priests also threatened Pilate politically so that he would condemn Jesus to death (cf. Jn 19:12, 15, 21).

611 The Eucharist that Christ institutes at that moment will be the memorial of his sacrifice (1 Cor 11:25). Jesus includes the apostles in his own offering and bids them perpetuate it (cf. Lk 22:19). By doing so, the Lord institutes his apostles as priests of the New Covenant: "For their sakes I sanctify myself, so that they also may be sanctified in truth (Jn 17:19; cf. Council of Trent: DS 1752; 1764)."

1009 *Death is transformed by Christ.* Jesus, the Son of God, also himself suffered the death that is part of the human condition. Yet, despite his anguish as he faced death, he accepted it in an act of complete and free submission to his Father's will (cf. Mk 14:

33-34; Heb 5:7-8). The obedience of Jesus has transformed the curse of death into a blessing (cf. Rom 5:19-21).

1365 Because it is the memorial of Christ's Passover, the Eucharist is also a sacrifice. The sacrificial character of the Eucharist is manifested in the very words of institution: "This is my body which is given for you" and "This cup which is poured out for you is the New Covenant in my blood" (Lk 22:19-20). In the Eucharist Christ gives us the very body which he gave up for us on the cross, the very blood which he "poured out for many for the forgiveness of sins" (Mt 26:28).

1851 It is precisely in the Passion, when the mercy of Christ is about to vanquish it, that sin most clearly manifests its violence and its many forms: unbelief, murderous hatred, shunning and mockery by the leaders and the people, Pilate's cowardice and the cruelty of the soldiers, Judas' betrayal—so bitter to Jesus, Peter's denial and the disciples' flight. However, at the very hour of darkness, the hour of the prince of this world (cf. Jn 14:30), the sacrifice of Christ secretly becomes the source from which the forgiveness of our sins will pour forth inexhaustibly.

2471 Before Pilate, Christ proclaims that he "has come into the world, to bear witness to the truth" (Jn 18:37). The Christian is not to "be ashamed then of testifying to our Lord" (2 Tm 1:8). In situations that require witness to the faith, the Christian must profess it without equivocation, after the example of St. Paul before his judges. We must keep "a clear conscience toward God and toward men" (Acts 24:16).

Endnotes

1. Mk 14:26.	8. Mt 26:75; Lk 22:62.	14. Jn 18:40.	19. Jn 19:17.
2. Mk 14:41-42.	9. Jn 18:24.	15. Jn 19:1-6.	20. Mt 5:41.
3. Mk 14:44.	10. Mk 14:61-64.	16. Jn 19:12.	21. Jn 19:29.
4. Jn 18:11.	11. Lk 23:2.	17. Roman Catechism I, 5, 11;	22. Jn 19:30.
5. Lk 22:53.	12. Lk 23:14-16.	cf. Heb 6:6; 1 Cor 2:8.	23. Nostra Aetate 4.
6. Jn 18:12-14; 19-23.	13. Jn 18:38-39.	18. St. Francis of Assisi,	
7. Jn 18:18.		*Admonitio* 5, 3.	

The Resurrection

"And now I am no more in the world, but they are in the world, and I am coming to thee. Holy Father, keep them in thy name,...'"

John 17: 11

Chapter 22

The Resurrection

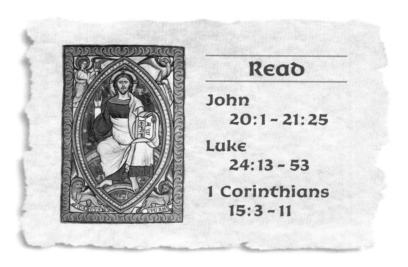

Read

John
20:1 – 21:25

Luke
24:13 – 53

1 Corinthians
15:3 – 11

Ordinarily, the bodies of crucified criminals would be dumped in a public burial ground. But one of Jesus' wealthy followers, Joseph of Arimathea, was bold enough to risk his position in the Sanhedrin by asking Pilate for Jesus' body. Nicodemus, too, the well-known Pharisee who had come to see Jesus by night, brought myrrh and aloes for a traditional Jewish burial. Everything had to be done before the Sabbath began to avoid defilement. Jesus' body was quickly wrapped in linen and laid in a new tomb donated by Joseph of Arimathea.

Joseph was a rich man, and the tomb he donated was worthy of a royal burial. It was probably dug into the rock in the side of a hill. The gate to the tomb was a big disk-shaped stone, so big that it took more than one strong man to move it.

Meanwhile, the chief priests were still afraid of what the followers of Jesus might do. They had at last begun to understand some of what Jesus taught, though they did not believe it. They asked Pilate to post a Roman guard at the tomb to make sure no one came and stole the body. He told them to get their own guard, which they did.

"'Do not be amazed; you seek Jesus of Nazareth, who was crucified.
He has risen, he is not here; see the place where they laid him.'"
(Mk 16: 6)

"'Rabboni!'.... Jesus said to her, 'Do not hold me, for I have not yet ascended to the Father;...'" (Jn 20: 16-17)

The Women Who Met The Risen Lord

Jesus had been buried so hastily that there had not been time to embalm his body correctly. When the Sabbath was over, some of the women who had followed him decided to do this one last honor for their beloved master.

> And when the Sabbath was past, Mary Magdalene, and Mary the mother of James, and Salome, brought spices, so that they might go and anoint him. And very early on the first day of the week, they went to the tomb when the sun had risen. And they were saying to one another, "Who will roll away the stone for us from the door of the tomb?" And looking up, they saw that the stone was rolled back; for it was very large. And entering the tomb, they saw a young man sitting on the right side, dressed in a white robe; and they were amazed. And he said to them, "Do not be amazed; you seek Jesus of Nazareth, who was crucified. He has risen, he is not here; see the place where they laid him. But go, tell his disciples and Peter that he is going before you to Galilee; there you will see him, as he told you." (Mk 16:1-7)

Mary Magdalene ran back to Simon and John, and told them, "They have taken the Lord out of the tomb, and we do not know where they have laid him."[1] Peter and John ran to the tomb; John got there first, but he waited for Peter to go in. All they found was Jesus' burial clothes. They went away puzzled.

> But Mary stood weeping outside the tomb, and as she wept she stooped to look into the tomb; and she saw two angels in white, sitting where the body of Jesus had lain, one at the head and one at the feet. They said to her, "Woman, why are you weeping?" She said to them, "Because they have taken away my Lord, and I do not know where they have laid

him." Saying this, she turned round and saw Jesus standing, but she did not know that it was Jesus. Jesus said to her, "Woman, why are you weeping? Whom do you seek?" Supposing him to be the gardener, she said to him, "Sir, if you have carried him away, tell me where you have laid him, and I will take him away." Jesus said to her, "Mary." She turned and said to him in Hebrew, "Rabboni!" (which means Teacher). Jesus said to her, "Do not hold me, for I have not yet ascended to the Father; but go to my brethren and say to them, I am ascending to my Father and your Father, to my God and your God." Mary Magdalene went and said to the disciples, "I have seen the Lord;" and she told them that he had said these things to her. (Jn 20:11-18)

According to Luke, "these words seemed to them an idle tale." They could not believe that Mary had really seen the Lord alive.

Mary Magdalene and the holy women who came to finish anointing the body of Jesus, which had been buried in haste because the Sabbath began on the evening of Good Friday, were the first to encounter the Risen One (Mk 16:1; Lk 24:1; Jn 19:31, 42). Thus the women were the first messengers of Christ's Resurrection for the apostles themselves (cf. Lk 24:9-10; Mt 28:9-10; Jn 20:11-18). They were the next to whom Jesus appears: first Peter, then the Twelve. Peter had been called to strengthen the faith of his brothers (cf. 1 Cor 15:5; Lk 22:31-32), and so sees the Risen One before them; it is on the basis of his testimony that the community exclaims: "The Lord has risen indeed, and has appeared to Simon!" (Lk 24:34, 36). (CCC 641)

The Road To Emmaus: Jesus Revealed In The Eucharist

But two of Jesus' other followers had some business in a little village called Emmaus, a few hours' walk from Jerusalem. Naturally, while they walked they were talking about what had happened in the past few days.

While they were talking and discussing together, Jesus himself drew near and went with them. But their eyes were kept from recognizing him. And he said to them, "What is this conversation which you are holding with each other as you walk?" And they stood still, looking sad. Then one of them, named Cleopas, answered him, "Are you the only visitor to Jerusalem who does not know the things that have happened there in these days?" (Lk 24:15-18)

The two disciples went on to tell the story of the last few days—including the odd tale they had heard from Mary Magdalene and the other women.

And he said to them, "O foolish men, and slow of heart to believe all that the prophets
have spoken! Was it not necessary that the Christ should suffer these things and enter into
his glory?" And beginning with Moses and all the prophets, he interpreted to them in all
the scriptures the things concerning himself. (Lk 24:15-17)

What Jesus taught them was the same thing we have been learning in this book—how all of history
led up to the death and resurrection of the Christ.

They had quite some time to spend talking as they walked on their way, and it was nearly sunset
by the time they reached Emmaus. The two disciples invited the stranger to stay with them and
have dinner.

When he was at table with them, he took the bread and blessed and broke it, and gave it
to them. And their eyes were opened and they recognized him; and he vanished out of
their sight. (Lk 24:30-31)

It was in the breaking of bread that they recognized Jesus. Luke uses the same words he used in
describing the Last Supper. The two disciples ran back to Jerusalem and found the apostles, telling
them everything they had seen, "and how he was known to them in the breaking of the bread."[2]

"...he took the bread and blessed and broke it, and gave it to them. And their eyes were opened and they
recognized him;...'Did not our hearts burn within us while he talked to us...?'" (Lk 24:30-32)

The Power To Forgive And Retain Sins

Ten of the eleven remaining apostles were all huddled in a locked room that evening (they were still afraid of what the Jewish authorities might do to them). Suddenly Jesus was standing among them, saying "Peace be with you."

> When he had said this, he showed them his hands and his side. Then the disciples were glad when they saw the Lord. Jesus said to them again, "Peace be with you. As the father has sent me, even so I send you." And when he had said this, he breathed on them, and said to them, "Receive the Holy Spirit. If you forgive the sins of any, they are forgiven. If you retain the sins of any, they are retained." (Jn 20: 20-23)

Only God had the power to forgive sins—a power that was manifest in Jesus, God the Son. Now Jesus was giving his power to the apostles. He held nothing back from them; he was giving them the same authority he himself had.

> Since Christ entrusted to his apostles the ministry of reconciliation (cf. Jn 20: 23; 2 Cor 5: 18), bishops who are their successors, and priests, the bishops' collaborators, continue to exercise this ministry. Indeed bishops and priests, by virtue of the sacrament of Holy Orders, have the power to forgive all sins "in the name of the Father, and of the Son, and of the Holy Spirit." (CCC 1461)

Doubting Thomas

But one of the apostles was missing. Thomas had not been there when Jesus appeared, and he refused to believe the story he heard. "Unless I see in his hands the print of his nails, and place my finger in the mark of the nails, and place my hand in his side, I will not believe."

A week later, the disciples were gathered in the same place. This time Thomas was with them.

> The doors were shut, but Jesus came and stood among them, and said, "Peace be with you." Then he said to Thomas, "Put your finger here, and see my hands; and put out your hand, and place it in my side; do not be faithless, but believing." Thomas answered him, "My Lord and my God." Jesus said to him, "You have believed because you have seen me. Blessed are those who have not seen and yet believe." (Jn 20: 26-29)

Tradition tells us that Thomas became the greatest traveler of all the apostles, taking the Good News as far as India. Tradition also gives us a fascinating detail about Thomas. The very earliest Christians did not use a cross as a symbol of their faith, but Thomas always kept a plain wooden cross with him wherever he went. It must have reminded him of what he had learned in that one blinding moment: that Jesus Christ really had died, and really had risen from the dead.

Back To Galilee

After he had given them the power to forgive and retain sins, Jesus' disciples followed the instructions they had been given to go back to Galilee.

"Why Galilee?" we might ask. Certainly it was a question most Jews in Jerusalem would have asked. Jerusalem was the center of the Jewish world; Galilee was a backwater. But the prophets had foretold the restoration of the whole kingdom of Israel, not just Judah. And Isaiah's prophecy had picked out Galilee as the place where that restoration would begin.

The land of Zebulun and
   Naphtali,
toward the sea, across the
   Jordan,
Galilee of the Gentiles—
the people who sat in darkness
have seen a great light,
and for those who sat in the
   region and shadow of death,
light has dawned.

(Isaiah's prophecy as quoted
in Mt 4:13-16)

There, by the Sea of Galilee, Peter, John, and several other disciples went back to fishing. After a night of no luck at all, they saw a stranger calling to them from the beach. When he heard that they had caught no fish, the stranger told them to cast the net on the other side of the boat. Since they were willing to try anything, they did as he said, and they could hardly lift the net for the weight of the fish they caught. John understood then who the stranger was: "It is the Lord!"[3]

Peter jumped into the water and swam to shore, leaving the rest of the apostles to haul in the load of fish. They found 153 fish in the net—a symbolic number: Greek philosophers identified 153 different kinds of fish in the world, so the apostles would be sent by our Lord to preach to every nation in the world.

Peter's Redemption

When they reached the shore, Jesus had a fire ready—a "charcoal fire," John tells us. That term occurs only one other place in the New Testament: in John's account of Peter's triple denial. Now Jesus is setting up the same situation, giving Peter a chance to redeem himself.

> When they had finished breakfast, Jesus said to Simon Peter, "Simon, son of John, do you love me more than these?" He said to him, "Yes, Lord, you know that I love you." He said to him, "Feed my lambs." A second time he said to him, "Simon, son of John, do you love me?" He said to him, "Yes, Lord, you know that I love you." He said to him, "Tend my sheep." He said to him the third time, "Simon, son of John, do you love me?" Peter was grieved because he said to him the third time, "Do you love me?" And he said to him, "Lord, you know everything; you know that I love you." Jesus said to him, "Feed my sheep." (Jn 21:15-17)

Three times Peter had denied Jesus in front of a charcoal fire; now Jesus had given him a chance to undo that denial three times. Jesus in return gave Peter the care over his "lambs," all the believers everywhere. As he had declared before, Christ would build his Church on Peter.

The Resurrection and Ascension of Jesus

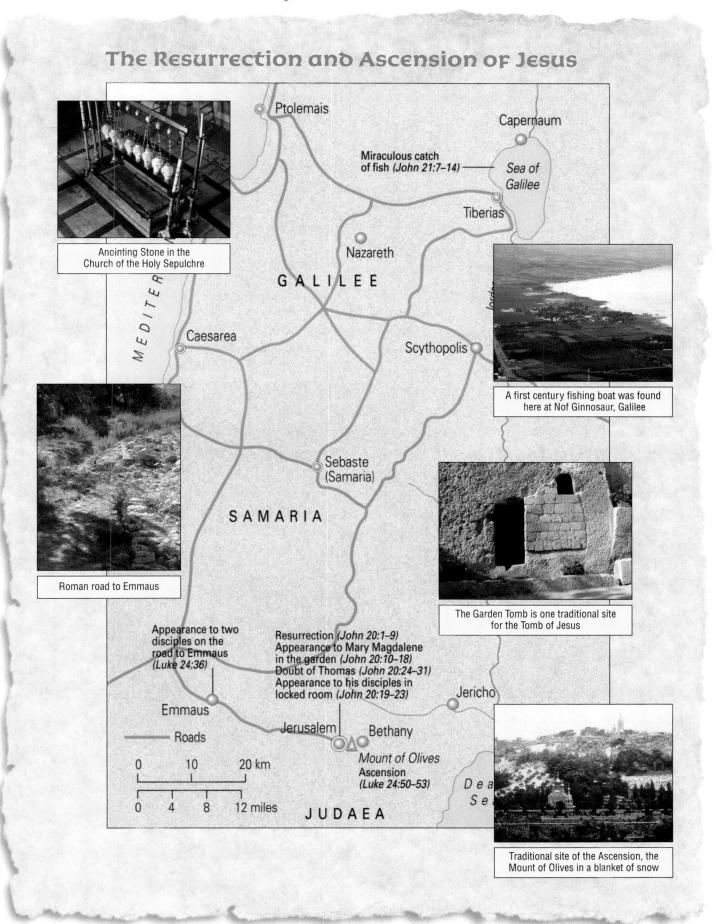

Anointing Stone in the
Church of the Holy Sepulchre

Ptolemais

Capernaum

Miraculous catch
of fish *(John 21:7–14)*

*Sea of
Galilee*

Tiberias

Nazareth

GALILEE

MEDITER

Caesarea

Scythopolis

A first century fishing boat was found
here at Nof Ginnosaur, Galilee

Sebaste
(Samaria)

SAMARIA

The Garden Tomb is one traditional site
for the Tomb of Jesus

Roman road to Emmaus

Appearance to two
disciples on the
road to Emmaus
(Luke 24:36)

Resurrection *(John 20:1–9)*
Appearance to Mary Magdalene
in the garden *(John 20:10–18)*
Doubt of Thomas *(John 20:24–31)*
Appearance to his disciples in
locked room *(John 20:19–23)*

Jericho

Emmaus

Jerusalem

Bethany

Roads

Mount of Olives
Ascension
(Luke 24:50–53)

*Dea
Se*

0   10   20 km

0   4   8   12 miles

JUDAEA

Traditional site of the Ascension, the
Mount of Olives in a blanket of snow

413

SUPPLEMENTARY READING

Athenagoras the Athenian: *On the Resurrection of the Dead*

It behooves, therefore, those who disbelieve or doubt concerning the resurrection, to form their opinion on the subject, not from any view they have hastily adopted, and from what is acceptable to profligate men, but either to assign the origin of men to no cause (a notion which is very easily refuted), or, ascribing the cause of all things to God, to keep steadily in view the principle involved in this article of belief, and from this to demonstrate that the resurrection is utterly unworthy of credit. This they will succeed in, if they are able to show that it is either impossible for God, or contrary to His will, to unite and gather together again bodies that are dead, or even entirely dissolved into their elements, so as to constitute the same persons. If they cannot do this, let them cease from this godless disbelief, and from this blasphemy against sacred things: for, that they do not speak the truth when they say that it is impossible, or not in accordance with the divine will, will clearly appear from what I am about to say.

A thing is in strictness of language considered impossible to a person, when it is of such a kind that he either does not know what is to be done, or has not sufficient power for the proper doing of the thing known. For he who is ignorant of anything that requires to be done, is utterly unable either to attempt or to do what he is ignorant of; and he, too, who knows ever so well what has to be done, and by what means, and how, but either has no power at all to do the thing known, or not power sufficient, will not even make the attempt, if he be wise and consider his powers; and if he did attempt it without due consideration, he would not accomplish his purpose.

But it is not possible for God to be ignorant, either of the nature of the bodies that are to be raised, as regards both the members entire and the particles of which they consist, or whither each of the dissolved particles passes, and what part of the elements has received that which is dissolved and has passed into that with which it has affinity, although to men it may appear quite impossible that what has again combined according to its nature with the universe should be separable from it again.

Just inside the edicule in the Church of the Holy Sepulchre is the small Chapel of the Angel with a small door which gives access to the stone Tomb of Jesus.

VOCABULARY

CLEOPAS

One of the followers of Jesus who met him on the road to Emmaus.

EMMAUS

A small village a few hours away from Jerusalem. After his Resurrection, two of Jesus' followers met him on the road to Emmaus, but did not recognize him until he broke bread with them.

JOSEPH OF ARIMATHEA

An influential member of the Sanhedrin who buried Jesus' body in his own tomb.

MARY MAGDALENE

One of the women who followed Jesus. She was the first person to have seen the risen Lord.

RECONCILIATION

The sacrament by which Christ forgives sins. Jesus gave his Apostles—who passed it on to their successors down to this day—the power to forgive and retain sins.

RESURRECTION

Jesus' coming to life again on the third day. There were many witnesses who saw the risen Jesus.

THOMAS

One of the Twelve. He was not present when Jesus appeared to the rest. He refused to believe Jesus had risen unless he could see for himself. He became a zealous missionary, traveling to India.

STUDY QUESTIONS

1. Who donated the tomb Jesus was buried in?

2. Who were the first messengers of Christ's Resurrection?

3. Who brought the news of the Resurrection to the apostles?

4. Who went to the tomb to check out the report?

5. What did Jesus do that made him recognizable to the disciples who had met him on the way to Emmaus?

6. What sacrament did Jesus grant the apostles the authority to minister when he first appeared to them after the Resurrection?

7. What did Jesus do before authorizing the apostles to minister Reconciliation?

8. How does Jesus respond when Thomas recognizes him as "Lord and God"?

9. Where did the apostle Thomas do his ministry?

10. Where did Jesus' disciples go when they left Jerusalem?

11. Where did the prophet Isaiah foretell the restoration would begin?

12. Why was it symbolic that the apostles caught 153 fish when they cast their nets where Jesus told them to?

13. What is the symbolism of the charcoal fire?

14. On the shore of the Sea of Galilee, what important question did Jesus ask Peter three times and why ask it?

PRACTICAL EXERCISES

1. "*Easter* is not simply one feast among others, but the 'Feast of feasts,' the 'Solemnity of solemnities,' just as the Eucharist is the 'Sacrament of sacraments' (the Great Sacrament). St. Athanasius calls Easter 'the Great Sunday' (St. Athanasius (ad 329) *ep. fest.* 1: PG 24, 1366) and the Eastern Churches call Holy Week 'the Great Week.' The mystery of the Resurrection, in which Christ crushed death, permeates with its powerful energy our old time, until all is subjected to him" (CCC 1169). What does this quote mean? Why does it make sense that Easter is celebrated as the most important day of the Church year?

2. The two disciples on the road to Emmaus did not know why Jesus had died on the cross or that he had been resurrected. All they knew was that their master had died and his body had disappeared. When they spoke to Jesus, he explained how all the scriptures led up to his death and resurrection for the forgiveness of our sins. The two disciples finally recognized Christ in the breaking of the bread, and understood all that had happened. Though we may not understand everything that is happening in the world or why God allows certain events, it is important to accept what God permits, both good and bad. What are some things happening in the world that seem to have no good purpose? How can the Gospels, prayer, and the Eucharist help us to understand the world as these two disciples did?

3. Thomas was skeptical when he first heard about Jesus' appearance after his passion and death. He did not believe based on the words of the other apostles alone. God did more than just offer Thomas the grace to believe, he let him touch his wounds as definitive proof. Was Thomas' doubting a sin? What do we all need from God in order to believe in and to know him?

FROM THE CATECHISM

153 When St. Peter confessed that Jesus is the Christ, the Son of the living God, Jesus declared to him that this revelation did not come "from flesh and blood," but from "my Father who is in heaven" (Mt 16:17, cf. Gal 1:15; Mt 11:25). *Faith is a gift of God, a supernatural virtue infused by him.* "Before this faith can be exercised, man must have the grace of God to move and assist him; he must have the interior helps of the Holy Spirit, who moves the heart and converts it to God, who opens the eyes of the mind and 'makes it easy for all to accept and believe the truth'" (DV 5; cf. DS 377; 3010).

434 Jesus' Resurrection glorifies the name of the Savior God, for from that time on it is the name of Jesus that fully manifests the supreme power of the "name which is above every name" (Phil 2:9-10; cf. Jn 12:28). The evil spirits fear his name; in his name his disciples perform miracles, for the Father grants all they ask in this name (cf. Acts 16: 16-18; 19:13-16; Mk 16:17; Jn 15:16).

644 Even when faced with the reality of the risen Jesus the disciples are still doubtful, so impossible did the thing seem: they thought they were seeing a ghost. "In their joy they were still disbelieving and still wondering" (Lk 24:38-41). Thomas will also experience the test of doubt and St. Matthew relates that during the risen Lord's last appearance in Galilee "some doubted" (cf. Jn 20:24-27; Mt 28:17). Therefore the hypothesis that the Resurrection was produced by the apostles' faith (or credulity) will not hold up. On the contrary their faith in the Resurrection was born, under the action of divine grace, from their direct experience of the reality of the risen Jesus.

Endnotes

1. Jn 20:2.
2. Lk 24:35.
3. Jn 21:7.

Jesus Fulfills The Old Testament

"And we bring you the good news that what God promised to the fathers, this he has fulfilled to us their children by raising Jesus;...'Thou art my son, today I have begotten thee.'"

Paul's Sermon at Antioch – Acts 13: 32-33

Chapter 23

Jesus Fulfills The Old Testament

Read

Acts
   7:1 – 60
   13:16 – 43

2 Corinthians
   3:7 – 18

But he was wounded for our transgressions,
   he was bruised for our iniquities;
upon him was the chastisement that made us whole,
   and with his stripes we are healed.
All we like sheep have gone astray;
   we have turned every one to his own way;
and the LORD has laid on him
   the iniquity of us all.

He was oppressed, and he was afflicted,
   yet he opened not his mouth;
like a lamb that is led to the slaughter,
   and like a sheep that before its shearers is dumb,
   so he opened not his mouth.
By oppression and judgment he was taken away;
   and as for his generation, who considered
that he was cut of out of the land of the living,
   stricken for the transgression of my people?
And they made his grave with the wicked,
   and with a rich man in his death,
although he had done no violence,
   and there was no deceit in his mouth.

...he poured out his soul to death
   and was numbered with the transgressors;
yet he bore the sin of many,
   and made intercession for the transgressors.

Most Christians will hear this poem as a summary of what the Church believes about Jesus. Some might therefore be surprised to learn that it was written hundreds of years before the time of Jesus, in the Old Testament book of Isaiah (chapter 53).

Fulfilling The Law And The Prophets

- **The Old Testament cannot be understood without the New Testament.**
- **Jesus Christ lifts the veil from the Old Testament so we can see its full meaning.**
- **The promises of the five Old Testament covenants are perfectly fulfilled in Christ.**

When Jesus said that he had come to "fulfill" the Law and the Prophets (see Mt 5:17), most of his hearers probably thought of the long-anticipated restoration of the Davidic kingdom. Only later did Jesus' disciples understand how the Scriptures they knew had prepared them to understand the real truth about Jesus. He would fulfill all those promises in the Scriptures, but he would fulfill them by suffering and dying, as Isaiah had prophesied.

> And taking the twelve, he said to them, "Behold, we are going up to Jerusalem, and everything that is written of the Son of man by the prophets will be accomplished. For he will be delivered to the Gentiles, and will be mocked and shamefully treated and spit upon; they will scourge him and kill him, and on the third day he will rise." But they understood none of these things; this saying was hid from them, and they did not grasp what was said. (Lk 18:31-34)

Although Jesus did what he could to prepare them for what was to come, the disciples really understood it all only in hindsight.

But once they did understand, they could see how perfectly Jesus fulfilled all the promises and prophecies of the Old Testament. In fact, when the Apostles preached to Jewish audiences, their theme was always the same: how all the things the Scriptures had taught them to expect were fulfilled in Jesus Christ.

> And we bring you the good news that what God promised to the fathers, this he has fulfilled to us their children in raising Jesus; as also it is written in the second psalm,
> "Thou art my Son,
> today I have begotten thee."
> (St. Paul in Acts 13:32-33)

Just as he did for his disciples, Jesus Christ lifts the veil from the Old Testament for us, so that we can understand the full meaning of what we only partly understood before. Moses wore a veil after he came down from Sinai because the people were afraid to look at his glowing face. St. Paul tells us that those who read the Old Testament without the New are still blocked from seeing what Moses really meant: "for to this day, when they read the old covenant, that same veil remains unlifted, because only in Christ is it taken away. Yes, to this day, whenever Moses is read a veil lies over their minds; but when a man turns to the Lord the veil is removed."[1]

Jesus perfectly fulfills the promises of every one of the five covenants in the Old Testament:

1. With **Adam**, because Jesus restores our relationship with God that was broken by Adam's sin;

2. With **Noah**, because the waters no longer destroy but rather redeem us;

3. With **Abraham**, because through Jesus (Abraham's descendant) all people of the world are blessed;

4. With **Moses**, because the righteousness demanded by the Law is given to us in Jesus Christ;

5. With **David**, because Jesus, the Son of David, is Lord of all the nations.

The Church Before Jesus

- **From the beginning, God had a plan to save us.**

- **God told his people about that plan long before Jesus was born.**

- **The early Church Fathers called Abraham, David, and other faithful people "Christians" because they expected the coming of the Christ.**

The word "Church" (Latin *ecclesia*, from the Greek *ek-ka-lein*, to "call out of ") means a convocation or an assembly. It designates the assemblies of the people, usually for a religious purpose (cf. Acts 19:39). *Ekklesia* is used frequently in the Greek Old Testament for the assembly of the Chosen People before God, above all for their assembly on Mount Sinai where Israel received the Law and was established by God as his holy people (cf. Ex 19). By calling itself "Church," the first community of Christian believers recognized itself as heir to that assembly. In the Church, God is "calling together" his people from all the ends of the earth. The equivalent Greek term *Kyriake*, from which the English word *Church* and the German *Kirche* are derived, means "what belongs to the Lord." (CCC 751)

In fact, the history of the Church really begins with Creation. In the beginning, when God created us in his image, he meant for us to live happily with him forever. When we disobeyed him, that did not change the plan. But it did mean that we would have to be saved from ourselves.

Because we disobey God, we deserve death. All of us, even the greatest saints, are sinners. But God does not want a single one of us to be lost. Although we deserve death, God was willing to pay any price to bring us back to him. As soon as Eve and Adam sinned, God already had a plan to save us. That plan was to send his only Son to die in our place.

Even in Old Testament times, the people of God knew about God's plan. Most of them did not understand it very well, but the prophets had told them what would happen. All through the Old Testament, the prophets speak of a time when God's Anointed One will come to save his people. One reason Jesus' message spread so quickly was that the whole Jewish world was expecting a Messiah.

In fact, the early Church Fathers insisted that faithful people like Abraham, David, and the prophets could correctly be called Christians, because they expected God's Anointed One, the Christ.

"All these," said the historian Eusebius, "whose righteousness won them commendation, going back from Abraham himself to the first man, might be described as Christians in fact if not in name, without departing far from the truth. . . . Obviously we must regard the religion proclaimed in recent years to all nations through Christ's teaching as none other than the first, most ancient, and most primitive of all religions, discovered by Abraham and his followers, God's beloved."

1. Jesus Fulfills The Covenant With Adam

- **The human family was created in the beginning as an image of the perfect love of the Trinity.**
- **Early Christians pointed out that the Gospel was first told to Adam and Eve.**

But in fact Christ has been raised from the dead, the first fruits of those who have fallen asleep. For as by a man came death, by a man has come also the resurrection of the dead. For as in Adam all die, so also in Christ shall all be made alive. (1 Cor 15: 20-22)

Adam	Jesus, the New Adam
Adam was "the son of God." (Mt 1: 1)	Jesus was the only-begotten Son of God.
Adam was tempted by the devil, and fell.	Jesus was tempted by the devil, but resisted.
Adam disobeyed God.	Jesus was perfectly obedient, even to death.
Adam brought sin and death to all humanity.	Jesus saved all humanity from sin and death.
Adam lost our place in paradise.	Jesus restores our place in paradise.

Jesus is conceived by the Holy Spirit in the Virgin Mary's womb because he is the New Adam, who inaugurates the new creation: "The first man was from the earth, a man of dust; the second man is from heaven" (1 Cor 15: 45, 47). From his conception, Christ's humanity is filled with the Holy Spirit, for God "gives him the Spirit without measure" (Jn 3: 34). From "his fullness" as the head of redeemed humanity "we have all received, grace upon grace" (Jn 1: 16; cf. Col 1: 18). (CCC 504)

"Let us make man in our image, after our likeness," God says in Genesis 1: 26. If there is only one God, who is "us"?

Some scholars would say that "us" refers to ancient mythology in which God was only the chief of a court of heavenly beings. Others would say that the plural is a "plural of majesty," a feature of Hebrew grammar similar to the way the Queen of England refers to herself as "we."

But many early Christians saw it as an expression of the Trinity. We are created in the image of God, and because God is three Persons, God's nature is social. "So God created man in his own image, in the image of God he created him; male and female he created them. And God blessed them, and God said to them, 'Be fruitful and multiply…'"[2]

Not just the individual person is created in the image of God. "Male and female he created them." The human family—father, mother, children—is the image of God's perfect love—Father, Son, and Holy Spirit.

As we know, however, sin corrupted that perfect image of God. But from the beginning, God had a plan to save his creatures from sin and death. Christian readers can see that he revealed that plan to Adam and Eve as soon as they confessed their sin. Genesis 3: 15 is God's curse on the serpent:

> I will put enmity between you and the woman,
> and between your seed and her seed;
> he shall bruise your head,
> and you shall bruise his heel.

Elsewhere in Scripture, the word "seed" usually refers to the offspring of a man. The "seed" of a woman could be only one man in history: Jesus Christ, who was born of a woman but was not the seed of a man. The serpent was an apparition of Satan, who will be defeated by Christ ("bruise your head" could be more literally translated "crush your head"), but only at the price of Christ's own crucifixion, when his heel would be nailed to the cross.

The early Christians called this verse the "Protoevangelium," which is Latin for "first Gospel." The first people to hear the Good News about Jesus Christ were Adam and Eve.

> After his fall, man was not abandoned by God. On the contrary, God calls him and in a mysterious way heralds the coming victory over evil and his restoration from his fall (cf. Gn 3:9, 15). This passage in Genesis is called the *Protoevangelium* ("first gospel"): the first announcement of the Messiah and Redeemer, of a battle between the serpent and the Woman, and of the final victory of a descendant of hers. (CCC 410)

2. Jesus Fulfills The Covenant With Noah

- **Noah's flood was a new creation.**
- **The Flood was a type of our own new creation in baptism.**

The early Christians always kept the connection between baptism and the Flood in mind. In the early days of the Church, new converts were baptized at Easter. The season of Lent was a time for the "catechumens" (as they called converts who were learning their catechism) to do penance and learn about the truths of their newfound faith. And Lent, as you know, lasts forty days and forty nights—exactly the time it took the Flood to reduce the earth to nothing but water. In other words, the catechumens spent forty days and forty nights destroying their old worlds so they could be newly created in the waters of baptism.

Creation	The Flood (a new creation)	Baptism (our own new creation)
	Forty days and forty nights of rain prepare for a new creation.	Forty days and forty nights of fasting and penance prepare for our new creation.
Creation begins with nothing but water.	The new creation begins with nothing but water.	Our new creation begins with nothing but water.
God's Spirit moves across the waters.	God's Spirit moves across the waters.	God's Spirit comes to us with the water.
God tells the first people to "be fruitful and multiply and fill the earth."	God tells Noah and his family to "be fruitful and multiply and fill the earth."	God tells us to "make disciples of all nations." In other words, to fill the earth with Christians.

3. Jesus Fulfills The Covenant With Abraham

- **God promised Abraham that all people would be blessed through him.**
- **The promise of universal blessing was fulfilled in Jesus Christ.**
- **By faith in Christ, we all become heirs of the promise to Abraham.**

Now the LORD said to Abram, "Go from your country and your kindred and your father's house to the land that I will show you. And I will make of you a great nation, and I will bless you, and make your name great, so that you will be a blessing. I will bless those who bless you, and him who curses you I will curse; and in you all the families of the earth will be blessed."[3] (Gn 12:1-3)

"All the families of the earth will be blessed"—that promise of universal blessing was the most incredible promise God made to Abram (soon to be known as Abraham). And it was not fulfilled until the coming of Jesus Christ.

Some of the promise to Abraham is already fulfilled in the Old Testament. Abraham's descendants did become a great nation. And in some ways, Israel was always a blessing to the rest of the nations. As long as a faithful remnant kept alive the knowledge of the True God, the word of God could come to the nations.

God's promises are often fulfilled in an ascending spiral. That universal blessing promised to Abraham went much further than the nation of Israel. Every single family on earth would be blessed through Abraham. Only with the resurrection of Jesus Christ was that promise fulfilled. The death and resurrection of Christ freed all people of all nations from bondage to sin.

4. Jesus Fulfills The Covenant With Moses

"The LORD your God will raise up for you a prophet like me from among you,"[4] Moses told his people in the wilderness. Yet the end of Deuteronomy tells us that no prophet like Moses had yet appeared. "And there has not arisen a prophet since in Israel like Moses, whom the LORD knew face to face," says Deuteronomy 34:10.

Not until Jesus Christ did another prophet like Moses arise. And the Gospel writers constantly remind us just how much like Moses Jesus was:

Moses	Jesus, the New Moses
Born in the reign of a ruthless pharaoh.	Born in the reign of the ruthless Herod.
Escaped when Pharaoh ordered all the male children of the Hebrews killed.	Escaped when Herod ordered all the male children of Bethlehem killed.
Exiled in Midian before his ministry.	Exiled in Egypt before his ministry.
Passed through the waters of the Red Sea.	Passed through the waters of the Jordan in baptism.
Tested in the wilderness 40 years.	Tested in the wilderness 40 days.
Fasted for 40 days and nights at Sinai.	Fasted for 40 days and nights in the wilderness.
First sign: changed water into blood.	First sign: changed water into wine, later wine into blood.
Brought the Law down from a mountain.	Taught the New Law from a mountain.
Gave Israel manna and water in the wilderness.	Gave all people true heavenly food and spiritual drink.
Led Israel out of bondage in Egypt.	Led all people out of bondage of sin and death.

The New Exodus

The Passover looked *forward* as well as backward: backward to the deliverance from bondage in Egypt, forward to the coming deliverance brought by the Messiah.

The Rabbinic tradition held that the Messiah would come on Passover night.

Jesus instituted the Eucharist on Passover night. In the Eucharist, the Messiah comes to us.

> At the Last Supper the Lord himself directed his disciples' attention toward the fulfillment of the Passover in the kingdom of God: "I tell you I shall not drink again of this fruit of the vine until that day when I drink it new with you in my Father's kingdom" (Mt 16:29; cf. Lk 22:18; Mk 14:25). Whenever the Church celebrates the Eucharist she remembers this

promise and turns her gaze "to him who is to come." In her prayer she calls for his coming: *"Marana tha!"* "Come, Lord Jesus!"(Rv 1: 4; 22: 20; 1 Cor 16: 22). "May your grace come and this world pass away!" (*Didache* 10: 6: SCh 248, 180). (CCC 1403)

Jesus the Passover Lamb

Passover Lamb	Jesus, the Lamb of God
The lamb must be without blemish (Ex 12: 5).	Jesus was without sin.
The lambs were slaughtered by the priests beginning at the sixth hour on the day of Preparation.	Jesus was handed over to be crucified at "about the sixth hour" on the day of Preparation (Jn 19: 14-16).
No bones of the lamb could be broken (Ex 12: 46).	Jesus' bones were not broken, although soldiers broke the bones of other crucified criminals (Jn 19: 32-33).
A branch of hyssop was used for sprinkling the blood of the lamb (Ex 12: 22).	The sponge of vinegar was given to Jesus on a branch of hyssop (Jn 19: 29).
The high priest wore a holy linen tunic when making the sacrifice (Lv 16: 4).	Jesus, our High Priest, wore a seamless linen tunic before his crucifixion.

5. Jesus Fulfills The Covenant With David

The Church is the new Kingdom of Israel, and Jesus is its King. The relationship of the Church to David's kingdom is so important that it will have a chapter of its own later in this book. Jesus, as head of the Church, is the King of the new Israel, which is no longer a nation or an ethnic group but rather the community of all the faithful everywhere. The *international* aspect of the Davidic covenant—the promise that the Son of David would be Lord of all the nations—is perfectly fulfilled in Jesus.

The Son of David would also build the Temple, as Solomon did. But Jesus spoke of his own body as a temple—a Temple that exists not just in Jerusalem, but everywhere believers gather to celebrate the Eucharist.

Finally, the kingdom of the Son of David was to be everlasting. Only in Jesus, the perfect Son of David, does this promise find its complete fulfillment.

The New Testament gives Jesus four titles that refer specifically to the Davidic covenant:

Son of David. Jesus was a direct descendant of David "according to the flesh" (that is, through his human ancestors). He inherits all the things promised to the Son of David (see Ps 89: 19-37).

King of Israel. Although Pilate called Jesus "King of the Jews" ironically, Jesus acknowledged that the title really did belong to him, though not in the way some of the Jews expected (see Jn 18: 33-37). Jesus is King of the New Israel, which is the Church.

Christ or Messiah ("Anointed One"). The kings of the line of David were anointed with oil to signify that they were God's chosen leaders on earth. Jesus was anointed with the Holy Spirit at his baptism.

Son of God. When he was anointed, the Davidic king was adopted as "Son of God" (see 2 Sm 7:14). That foreshadowed the coming of Jesus Christ, the true only-begotten Son of God.

The prophecies cited in the New Testament as predicting the death and resurrection of Jesus were originally understood as referring to the restoration of Israel (see Hos 6:2). The resurrection of Jesus in body and our union with that body in Baptism effect the restoration of Israel and the nations.

In Jesus' time, many Jews expected that the promised restoration would look like the kingdom of Solomon. They did not take into account God's love for his whole creation. The restored Israel would be more than just a kingdom at the eastern end of the Mediterranean. It would be a glorious new kingdom of righteousness, one that ruled over the whole world. Israel would be restored as the Church of Christ.

Son of David (Old Kings of Israel)	Son of David (Jesus Christ)
Descended from David.	Descended from David.
Anointed by Levites.	Baptized by John, a Levite.
Ruler of an international empire.	Lord of all the nations.
Paid homage by foreign princes.	Paid homage by the Magi.
Builds the Temple.	Rebuilds the temple of his body.
Promised an everlasting kingdom.	Receives a truly everlasting kingdom.

SUPPLEMENTARY READING

Irenaeus, Against Heresies, 4:26:1

If anyone, therefore, reads the Scriptures with attention, he will find in them an account of Christ, and a foreshadowing of the new calling. For Christ is the treasure which was hid in the field (cf. Mt 13:44), that is, in this world (for "the field is the world" [Mt 13:38]); but the treasure hid in the Scriptures is Christ, since He was pointed out by means of types and parables. Hence His human nature could not be understood, prior to the consummation of those things which had been predicted, that is, the advent of Christ. And therefore it was said to Daniel the prophet: "Shut up the words, and seal the book even to the time of consummation, until many learn, and knowledge be completed. For at that time, when the dispersion shall be accomplished, they shall know all these things" (Dn 12:4, 7). But Jeremiah also says, "In the last days they shall understand these things" (Jer 23:20). For every prophecy, before its fulfillment, is to men full of enigmas and ambiguities. But when the time has arrived, and the prediction has come to pass, then the prophecies have a clear and certain exposition. And for this reason, indeed, when at this present time the law is read to the Jews, it is like a fable; for they do not possess the explanation of all things pertaining to the advent of the Son of God, which took place in human nature; but when it is read by the Christians, it is a treasure, hid indeed in a field, but brought to light by the cross of Christ, and explained, both enriching the understanding of men, and showing forth the wisdom of God, and declaring His dispensations with regard to man, and forming the kingdom of Christ beforehand, and preaching by anticipation the inheritance of the holy Jerusalem, and proclaiming beforehand that the man who loves God shall arrive at such excellency as even to see God, and hear His word, and from the hearing of His discourse be glorified to such an extent, that others cannot behold the glory of his countenance, as was said by Daniel: "Those who do understand, shall shine as the brightness of the firmament, and many of the righteous as the stars for ever and ever" (Dn 12:3). Thus, then, I have shown it to be, if any one read the Scriptures. For thus it was that the Lord discoursed with the disciples after His resurrection from the dead, proving to them from the Scriptures themselves "that Christ must suffer, and enter into His glory, and that remission of sins should be preached in His name throughout all the world" (Lk 24:26, 47). And the disciple will be perfected, and rendered like the householder, "who brings forth from his treasure things new and old" (Mt 13:52).

VOCABULARY

CATECHUMEN
One who is learning in preparation for baptism to gain entry to the Church.

CHRISTIAN
One who believes Jesus is the Christ, the Anointed One of God. The Church Fathers sometimes spoke of Abraham, David, and other faithful people of the Old Testament as Christians because they believed in the future coming of the Christ.

CONVERT
One who has changed to a new religion.

LAW AND THE PROPHETS
The Old Testament Scriptures. Jesus said that he had come to fulfill the Law and the Prophets.

RABBINIC
Having to do with the Rabbis, the leaders of Judaism.

TRINITY
God the Father, God the Son, and God the Holy Spirit. The Trinity refers to three persons but one God.

STUDY QUESTIONS

1. What did Jesus mean when he said he came to "fulfill the law" and the prophets?

2. What was always the theme of the apostles' sermons to Jewish audiences?

3. How does Jesus fulfill the covenants God made in the Old Testament?

4. According to CCC 751, what does the Greek term *Kyriake* mean?

5. When does the history of the Church begin?

6. Why did Jesus' message spread so quickly?

7. How was the human family created in the beginning?

8. List four ways in which Jesus made up for Adam's fault?

9. Why did the early Church Fathers insist that faithful people like Abraham, David, and the prophets be called Christians?

10. What does *Protoevangelium* mean?

11. Who were the first to hear the Good News about Jesus Christ?

12. In the early Church, at what festival were new converts usually baptized?

13. How long did the converts spend preparing for their baptism?

14. How does Jesus fulfill the covenant with Abraham?

15. Name ways in which Jesus represented the "new Moses."

16. What does "Maranatha" mean?

17. Name three ways in which Jesus, as the Lamb of God, represents the Passover lamb.

18. Name four titles given to Jesus that refer specifically to the Davidic covenant.

PRACTICAL EXERCISES

1. The Bible uses the word 'veiled' to indicate things which can be perceived only incompletely. What have you learned in this course which lifted the "veil" for you? Have you found out you were mistaken about some things you thought were true?

2. Some of the greatest saints were once great sinners. What can be learned from their change of heart? What do you think was the primary cause of their change?

3. It is easy to look at idolatry in the Old Testament and laugh at those who worshiped animals. Is idolatry a problem today? Make a list of things which people tend to put before God in their lives. Can giving so much importance to these things be considered idolatry?

FROM THE CATECHISM

359 "In reality it is only in the mystery of the Word made flesh that the mystery of man truly becomes clear" (GS 22 § 1).

> St. Paul tells us that the human race takes its origin from two men: Adam and Christ...The first man, Adam, he says, became a living soul, the last Adam a life-giving spirit. The first Adam was made by the last Adam, from whom he also received his soul, to give him life...The second Adam stamped his image on the first Adam when he created him. That is why he took on himself the role and the name of the first Adam, in order that he might not lose what he had made in his own image. The first Adam, the last Adam: the first had a beginning, the last knows no end. The last Adam is indeed the first; as he himself says: "I am the first and the last" (St. Peter Chrysologus, *Sermo* 117; PL 52, 520-521).

388 With the progress of Revelation, the reality of sin is also illuminated. Although to some extent the People of God in the Old Testament had tried to understand the pathos of the human condition in the light of the history of the fall narrated in Genesis, they could not grasp this story's ultimate meaning, which is revealed only in the light of the death and Resurrection of Jesus Christ (cf. Rom 5: 12-21). We must know Christ as the source of grace in order to know Adam as the source of sin. The Spirit-Paraclete, sent by the risen Christ, came to "convict the world concerning sin" (Jn 16: 8), by revealing him who is its Redeemer.

539 The evangelists indicate the salvific meaning of this mysterious event: Jesus is the new Adam who remained faithful just where the first Adam had given in to temptation. Jesus fulfills Israel's vocation perfectly: in contrast to those who had once provoked God during forty years in the desert, Christ reveals himself as God's Servant, totally obedient to the divine will. In this, Jesus is the devil's conqueror: he "binds the strong man" to take back his plunder (cf. Ps 95: 10; Mk 3: 27). Jesus' victory over the tempter in the desert anticipates victory at the Passion, the supreme act of obedience of his filial love for the Father.

601 The Scriptures had foretold this divine plan of salvation through the putting to death of "the righteous one, my Servant" as a mystery of universal redemption, that is,

FROM THE CATECHISM continued

as the ransom that would free men from the slavery of sin (Is 53:11; cf. 53:12; Jn 8:34-36; Acts 3:14). Citing a confession of faith that he himself had "received," St. Paul professes that "Christ died for our sins in accordance with the scriptures" (1 Cor 15:3; cf. also Acts 3:18; 7:52; 13:29; 26:22-23). In particular Jesus' redemptive death fulfills Isaiah's prophecy of the suffering Servant (cf. Is 53:7-8 and Acts 8:32-35). Indeed Jesus himself explained the meaning of his life and death in the light of God's suffering Servant (cf. Mt 20:28). After his Resurrection he gave this interpretation of the Scriptures to the disciples at Emmaus, and then to the apostles (cf. Lk 24:25-27, 44-45).

608 After agreeing to baptize him along with the sinners, John the Baptist looked at Jesus and pointed him out as the "Lamb of God, who takes away the sin of the world" (Jn 1:29; cf.

Lk 3:21; Mt 3:14-15; Jn 1:36). By doing so, he reveals that Jesus is at the same time the suffering Servant who silently allows himself to be led to the slaughter and who bears the sin of the multitudes, and also the Paschal Lamb, the symbol of Israel's redemption at the first Passover (Is 53:7, 12; cf. Jer 11:19; Ex 12:3-14; Jn 19:36; 1 Cor 5:7). Christ's whole life expresses his mission: "to serve, and to give his life as a ransom for many" (Mk 10:45).

652 Christ's Resurrection is the fulfillment of the promises both of the Old Testament and of Jesus himself during his earthly life (cf. Mt 28:6; Mk 16:7; Lk 24:6-7, 26-27, 44-48). The phrase "in accordance with the Scriptures" (cf. 1 Cor 15:3-4; cf. the Nicene Creed) indicates that Christ's Resurrection fulfilled these predictions.

"Then he led them out as far as Bethany, and lifting up his hands he blessed them. While he blessed them, he parted from them and was carried up into heaven."
(Lk 24:50-51)

Endnotes

1. 2 Cor 3:14-16.
2. Gn 1:27-28.
3. We used the alternate reading given in a footnote in the Revised Standard Version.
4. Dt 18:15.

Chapter 24
The Birth of The Church

"And suddenly a sound came from heaven like the rush of a mighty wind, and it filled all the house where they were sitting. And there appeared to them tongues as of fire, distributed and resting on each one of them."

Acts 2: 2-3

Chapter 24

The Birth of The Church

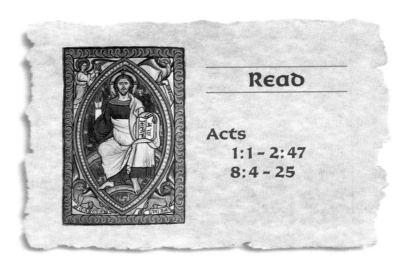

Read

Acts
1:1 – 2:47
8:4 – 25

Jesus had died and risen from the dead. He had appeared to many of his faithful friends and disciples. Everything had happened as he predicted it would. But one promise from before the beginning of his ministry had not yet been fulfilled.

When John the Baptist was baptizing crowds in the Jordan, he told them to expect a different kind of baptism from the one who would come after him. "I baptize you with water, but he who is mightier than I is coming, the thong of whose sandals I am not worthy to untie; he will baptize you with the Holy Spirit and with fire."[1]

Where was this baptism with the Holy Spirit and with fire?

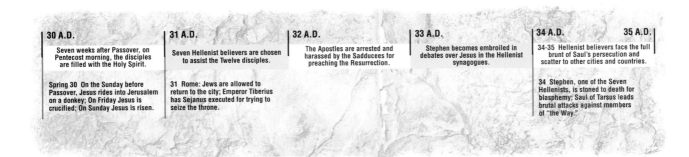

30 A.D.	31 A.D.	32 A.D.	33 A.D.	34 A.D.	35 A.D.
Seven weeks after Passover, on Pentecost morning, the disciples are filled with the Holy Spirit.	Seven Hellenist believers are chosen to assist the Twelve disciples.	The Apostles are arrested and harassed by the Sadducees for preaching the Resurrection.	Stephen becomes embroiled in debates over Jesus in the Hellenist synagogues.	34-35 Hellenist believers face the full brunt of Saul's persecution and scatter to other cities and countries.	
Spring 30 On the Sunday before Passover, Jesus rides into Jerusalem on a donkey; On Friday Jesus is crucified; On Sunday Jesus is risen.	31 Rome: Jews are allowed to return to the city; Emperor Tiberius has Sejanus executed for trying to seize the throne.			34 Stephen, one of the Seven Hellenists, is stoned to death for blasphemy; Saul of Tarsus leads brutal attacks against members of "the Way."	

Restoring The Kingdom

For forty days after his resurrection, Jesus continued to teach his disciples, "speaking of the kingdom of God."[2]

That word "kingdom" was the key to his teaching. Just as Jesus had spent forty days preparing for his ministry, now he was giving the Twelve forty days to prepare for their ministry. That ministry would be nothing less than restoring the only kingdom God had ever endorsed: the kingdom of David.

> And while staying with them he charged them not to depart from Jerusalem, but to wait for the promise of the Father, which, he said, "you heard from me, for John baptized with water, but before many days you shall be baptized with the Holy Spirit." (Acts 1: 4-5)

The baptism with the Holy Spirit was yet to come. Until then, the apostles should stay in Jerusalem. Jerusalem, of course, was David's capital, and all the Old Testament prophets promised that it would once again be the capital of the kingdom—a new, greater kingdom, which would invite all the nations to worship God.

> And many nations shall join themselves to the LORD in that day, and shall be my people; and I will dwell in the midst of you, and you shall know that the LORD of hosts has sent me to you. And the LORD will inherit Judah as his portion in the holy land, and will again choose Jerusalem. (Zec 2: 11-12)

The book of Acts does not tell us exactly what Jesus said during most of those forty days. But by the end of that time, the apostles knew enough to ask the right question:

> So when they had come together, they asked him, "Lord, will you at this time restore the kingdom to Israel?" He said to them, "It is not for you to know times or seasons which the Father has fixed by his own authority. But you shall receive power when the Holy Spirit has come upon you; and you shall be my witnesses in Jerusalem and in all Judea and Samaria and to the end of the earth." (Acts 1: 6-8)

Jesus has just drawn a verbal map of the Davidic kingdom: the center at Jerusalem, then Judea (the part that was left after the division of Israel and Judah), Samaria (the rest of the lost kingdom of Israel), and the end of the earth (all the Gentile nations).

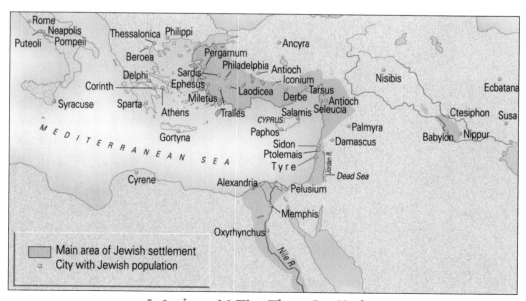

Judaism At The Time Of Christ

Christ, high priest and unique mediator, has made of the Church "a kingdom, priests for his God and Father" (Rv 1:6; cf. Rv 5:9-10; 1 Pt 2:5, 9). The whole community of believers is, as such, priestly. The faithful exercise their baptismal priesthood through their participation, each according to his own vocation, in Christ's mission as priest, prophet, and king. Through the sacraments of Baptism and Confirmation the faithful are "consecrated to be...a holy priesthood" (LG 10 § 1). (CCC 1546)

That was the last thing Jesus said to the apostles on earth. "And when he had said this, as they were looking on, he was lifted up, and a cloud took him out of their sight."[3] Mark adds that he "sat down at the right hand of God."[4] The right hand of a king was a place of honor.

Jesus had left the apostles with their last orders: that they should wait for the coming of the Holy Spirit, then restore the Davidic kingdom. Then Jesus himself was immediately enthroned "at the right hand of God"—the place of the Anointed One, the Son of David, the Son of God, according to Psalm 110:

The LORD says to my lord, "Sit at my right hand,
    till I make your enemies your footstool."
(Ps 110:1)

The apostles are to restore the kingdom, and Jesus Christ sits enthroned as King. The ascension is a royal enthronement, not just a disappearance. Reigning from heaven, Jesus the King leaves his royal ministers on earth to handle the earthly affairs of the kingdom.

The Election Of Matthias

Jesus' last orders showed the order of the restoration: first Israel must be restored, then the kingdom extended to the rest of the world.

The twelve apostles were symbolic heads of the twelve tribes of Israel, reunited under them. But there were only eleven apostles. Judas, the betrayer, was dead.

In those first days, the apostles had made their headquarters in the Upper Room—that same large room where Jesus had celebrated the Last Supper. There the apostles, Mary the mother of Jesus, the women who had followed Jesus, and other believers gathered every day to pray. Although the community was small, there were some believers who had followed Jesus from the beginning.

Peter, the leader on earth now that Jesus had ascended, decided that the restoration would have to begin by choosing a replacement for Judas.

In those days Peter stood up among the brethren (the company of persons was in all about a hundred and twenty) and said, "Brethren, the Scripture had to be fulfilled, which the Holy Spirit spoke beforehand by the mouth of David, concerning Judas who was guide to those who arrested Jesus....For it is written in the book of Psalms,

'Let his habitation be desolate,
    and let there be no one to live in it,'
and
    'His office let another take.'

So one of the men who have accompanied us during all the time that the Lord Jesus went in and out among us, beginning from the baptism of John until the day when he was taken up from us—one of these men must become with us a witness to his resurrection."
(Acts 1:15-16, 20-22)

As Peter had decided, the disciples decided to choose one man to replace Judas. They narrowed the choice down to two, and chose between them by lot, praying that the Lord would show which one he had chosen. The lot fell on Matthias, who became the twelfth apostle. Once again, Jesus' college of royal ministers on earth was complete.

In Greek, the word translated "office" ("His *office* let another take") is *episkope*, the word from which we get the English word "episcopacy," which is related to the word "bishop." Another translation (from Challoner's Douay Bible) of Peter's quotation is "And his bishopric let another take." The bishoprics of the Twelve, who "constitute a single apostolic college" (CCC 880) have continued in unbroken succession to the bishops of today. Every Catholic bishop is, by his *office*, a successor to the apostles.

> The bishops, established by "the Holy Spirit, succeed the apostles. They are the visible source and foundation of unity in their own particular churches" (LG 23). (CCC 938)

The Upper Room

On Mt. Zion, in the Old City, Christian pilgrims visit this room known as the Cenacle or Room of the Last Supper. The lower floor is a synagogue housing a cenotaph (empty tomb) worshiped by Jews as the Tomb of David. Although the room is a Crusader era basilica, the structure has traces of Roman era masonry and is traditionally identified as the site of the "Upper Room" of the Eucharist and the Pentecost.

The Seven Deacons of Acts 6: 1-7

"Now in these days when the disciples were increasing in number, the Hellenists [Greek-speaking Jews] murmured against the Hebrews [Aramaic-speaking Jews] because their widows were neglected in the daily distribution [of food]. And the twelve summoned the body of the disciples and said, 'It is not right that we should give up preaching the word of God to serve tables....pick out from among you seven men of good repute, full of the spirit and of wisdom,...and they chose...'"

Stephen
Philip
Prochorus (Procurus, Apostle John's scribe)
Nicanor
Timon
Parmenas
Nicolaus (Nicolas)

Pentecost

The apostles, now with Matthias, continued to wait and pray until the feast of Pentecost. Fifty days after the Passover ("Pentecost" comes from the Greek word for "fifty"), Pentecost was a feast on which the Jews celebrated the giving of the Law to Moses on Sinai. Faithful Jews from all over the world came to Jerusalem for the celebration. The apostles were all gathered together, too.

> When the day of Pentecost had come, they were all together in one place. And suddenly a sound came from heaven like the rush of a mighty wind, and it filled all the house where they were sitting. And there appeared to them tongues as of fire, distributed and resting on each one of them. And they were all filled with the Holy Spirit and began to speak in other tongues, as the Spirit gave them utterance. (Acts 2:1-4)

This at last was the baptism "with the Holy Spirit and with fire" that John the Baptist had predicted. And it happened just when Jerusalem was filled with worshipers from all over the world.

> Now there were dwelling in Jerusalem Jews, devout men from every nation under heaven. And at this sound the multitude came together, and they were bewildered, because each one heard them speaking in his own language. And they were amazed and wondered, saying, "Are not all these who are speaking Galileans? And how is it that we hear, each of us in his own native language?"... But others mocking said, "They are filled with new wine." (Acts 2:5-13)

As leader of the Twelve, Peter stood up and addressed the crowd. They were not drunk, he told them: after all, it was still the middle of the morning. Instead, this was the fulfillment of the prophecies. Joel had told us this would happen in the last days: the Spirit of God would be poured out on everyone.

The pouring out of the Spirit on Mary and the Apostles at Pentecost is a significant development in the relationship between God and man. God made covenants with men throughout the ages in order to bind the human and the divine. Jesus Christ, being both fully human and fully divine, perfectly completed this relationship by establishing the New Covenant. But what remained unanswered at the time of His Ascension was the way in which this relationship would continue until Christ's return. At Pentecost we receive the answer.

Jesus promised his Apostles that he would not leave them, and at Pentecost, God shows that He does not forget his promises. The Holy Spirit was given to the Apostles in order to establish Christ's Church on earth, and since the Holy Spirit is present in the Church since this very first Pentecost, the Church remains the principal means through which Christ is present in the world. The Church continues Christ's mission on earth, and in this way, she is a sacrament of salvation—the sign and instrument of the communion of God and men.

Peter's Authority

Like Jesus, Peter taught with authority. His subject was the restoration of the kingdom: Jesus, Peter said, fulfilled the promise God made to restore the kingdom of David. Later, we will study his sermon in more detail, when we look at how the Church continues the Davidic kingdom. Right now it is most important to notice how Peter has inherited the teaching authority of Jesus.

> Now when they had heard this they were cut to the heart, and said to Peter and the rest of the apostles, "Brethren, what shall we do?" And Peter said to them, "Repent, and be baptized every one of you in the name of Jesus Christ for the forgiveness of your sins, and you shall receive the gift of the Holy Spirit." (Acts 2: 37-38)

When the people ask what to do, Peter—like Jesus before him—has the answer. About three thousand believed and were baptized that day, Luke tells us. "And they held steadfastly to the apostles' teaching and fellowship, to the breaking of the bread and to the prayers."

"…at that gate of the Temple which is called Beautiful to ask alms of those who entered…" (Acts 3: 2)

Already, less than two months after the Resurrection, there was a church of about three thousand Christians in Jerusalem. They celebrated the Eucharist, listened to the teaching of the apostles, and shared everything they owned, so that no one was rich or poor among them.

They also continued to worship at the Temple. One day a lame beggar at the Temple gate asked Peter for some change.

> But Peter said, "I have no silver and gold, but I give you what I have: in the name of Jesus Christ of Nazareth, rise and walk." And he took him by the right hand and raised him up, and immediately his feet and ankles were made strong. (Acts 3: 6-7)

Peter received the power to heal from Jesus, too. Jesus had held nothing back from his apostles. Seeing the crowds gathering around him, Peter once again taught them the Good News—this time right at the gate of the Temple.

The chief priests and other authorities had the apostles arrested. It was too late, of course: by the end of the day there were about five thousand Christians in Jerusalem.

They were brought before the Sanhedrin and, the apostles once again answered through Peter.

> And when they had set them in their midst, they inquired, "By what power or by what name did you do this?" Then Peter, filled with the Holy Spirit, said to them, "Rulers of the people and elders, if we are being examined today concerning a good deed done to a cripple, by what means this man has been healed, be it known to you all, and to all the people of Israel, that by the name of Jesus Christ of Nazareth, whom you crucified, whom God raised from the dead, by him this man is standing before you well." (Acts 4: 7-10)

The chief priests knew that Peter and John were "uneducated, common men," but here was an ordinary fisherman assuming the authority to teach the teachers! Yet they could do nothing against the apostles. The man who had been healed was standing right beside them on his own two feet. Thousands of people had seen him. If the authorities arrested the Twelve, there might be a riot; so they let them go with a warning.

Throughout these early days of the Church, we see that the power and authority of Jesus to heal and to teach have been given completely to the apostles. Peter is always their leader. When one couple tried to cheat the Church, it was Peter who pronounced God's sentence on them (see Acts 5: 1-11).

The apostles all worked miracles and taught the people, but it was Peter—by their common consent—who made the important decisions.

> The Kingdom of heaven was inaugurated on earth by Christ. "This kingdom shone out before men in the word, in the works and in the presence of Christ" (LG 5). The Church is the seed and beginning of this kingdom. Her keys are entrusted to Peter. (CCC 567)

The Martyrdom Of Stephen

As time went on, the Apostles came to be quite popular in Jerusalem. Just as they had done with Jesus, the crowds lined up just to see them, or to bring their sick for Peter to heal.

The Temple authorities had thought they would stamp out the Jesus sect by killing Jesus, but Luke tells us (Acts 5:13) that "great numbers of men and women" were joining the movement (which they called "the Way") all the time.

The high priest and the Sadducees finally threw the Apostles in jail, but the Apostles miraculously escaped. Brought before the Sanhedrin (without force, Luke tells us, for fear of starting a riot), they refused to stop teaching in Jesus' name.

Baffled by the Apostles' stubbornness, the court had them whipped and released with orders to stop preaching—orders the Apostles immediately disregarded.

"But he, full of the Holy Spirit, gazed into the heaven and saw the glory of God, and Jesus standing at the right hand of God;..." (Acts 7: 55)

Finally Stephen, a convert who had been making a reputation both by his teaching and by his miracles, offended some powerful people by out-arguing them at a public debate (Acts 6: 9-10). They had their revenge by accusing him of blasphemy.

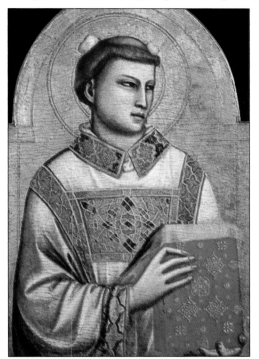

"And Stephen, full of grace and power, did great wonders and signs among the people." (Acts 6: 8)

When he was given a chance to defend himself, Stephen made a long speech which is recorded in Acts 7. He told the court how the coming of the Christ had been predicted all the way through the Old Testament. Then he went on to provide the court with all the evidence it needed against him. "Behold, I see the heavens opened, and the Son of man standing at the right hand of God."

That was it. It was blasphemy. The court turned into a mob. Without even bothering to convict him, they rushed Stephen out of the city and stoned him after they placed their garments at the foot of a man named Saul. Two years after the Resurrection, Stephen had become the first Christian martyr.

That incident gave the authorities the excuse they needed. They determined to wipe out the Jesus cult by any means necessary. Saul himself headed a brutal squad of temple guards who burst suddenly into Christians' homes and hauled whole families off to prison (Acts 8: 3).

At first, the persecution seemed to be working. Christians fled from Jerusalem until only the Apostles themselves were left. But they didn't lose their faith. Instead of destroying the Jesus cult, the persecution spread it all over Judea and Samaria, and even farther to nearby cities like Damascus.

What The Early Christian Community Was Like

From the beginning, the Eucharist was what set the Christians apart as Christians. The first Christians went to the Temple every day, and then celebrated the Eucharist in their homes. They knew they had been given an important new truth about God's plan of salvation, but they didn't believe they were starting a new religion.

As the Good News spread beyond Jerusalem, Christians still thought of themselves as followers of the Jewish religion. The Apostles always went to the synagogue every Sabbath, and Christians were still going to synagogues almost half a century after Jesus' resurrection. Only after the destruction of the Temple did the Jewish leaders finally expel the Christians.

So the early Christians worshiped in two ways: by going to the Synagogue every Sabbath, and then on the first day of the week, Sunday, by meeting in private homes to celebrate the Eucharist. Long after they were banned from the synagogues, Christians still kept the Eucharist as a separate, private worship for the baptized only.

Our Mass today still preserves the memory of those earliest times. The Liturgy of the Word—the first part of the Mass—comes from the old synagogue liturgy. The Eucharist—the second part of our Mass—comes from the old Temple liturgy of the thank offering and the Passover. In the Christian Mass, the liturgies of the synagogue and the Temple are united.

SUPPLEMENTARY READING

John Chrysostom, *Homily on Acts no. 7*

"Now when they heard these words, they were pricked in their heart, and said unto Peter and to the rest of the Apostles, Men and brethren, what shall we do?"

Do you see what a great thing gentleness is? More than any vehemence, it pricks our hearts, inflicts a keener wound. For as in the case of bodies which have become callous the man that strikes upon them does not affect the sense so powerfully, but if he first mollify them and make them tender, then he pierces them effectually; so in this instance also, it is necessary first to mollify. But that which softens, is not wrath, not vehement accusation, not personal abuse; it is gentleness. The former indeed rather aggravate the callousness, this last alone removes it.

If then you are desirous to reprove any delinquent, approach him with all possible mildness. For see here; he gently reminds them of the outrages they have committed, adding no comment; he declares the gift of God, he goes on to speak of the grace which bore testimony to the event, and so draws out his discourse to a still greater length. So they stood in awe of the gentleness of Peter, in that he, speaking to men who had crucified his Master, and breathed murder against himself and his companions, discoursed to them in the character of an affectionate father and teacher. Not merely were they persuaded; they even condemned themselves, they came to a sense of their past behavior. For he gave no room for their anger to be roused, and darken their judgment, but by means of humility he dispersed, as it were, the mist and darkness of their indignation, and then pointed out to them the daring outrage they had committed. For so it is; when we say of ourselves that we are injured, the opposite party endeavor to prove that they have not done the injury; but when we say, we have not been injured, but have rather done the wrong, the others take the contrary line.

If, therefore, you wish to place your enemy in the wrong, beware of accusing him; nay, plead for him, he will be sure to find himself guilty. There is a natural spirit of opposition in man.

Such was the conduct of Peter. He did not accuse them harshly; on the contrary, he almost endeavored to plead for them, as far as was possible. And this was the very reason that he penetrated into their souls.

VOCABULARY

BISHOP

The Greek word means, literally, "overseer." A successor of the apostles as a teacher, leader, and shepherd of the Church.

HOLY SPIRIT

The third person of the Trinity. Jesus promised his followers the Holy Spirit to guide and protect them after he ascended to his Father. That promise was fulfilled ten days later at Pentecost. God the Holy Spirit continues to guide and protect the Church today.

MASS

The Church's most important liturgy. From the Latin *"Ite missa est"* at the end of the Mass.

MATTHIAS

The disciple chosen to replace Judas as one of the Twelve.

MINISTER

A servant; in particular, the servant of a king.

PENTECOST

A Jewish festival, fifty days after Passover, celebrating the giving of the Law to Moses at Sinai. Also the birthday of the Church. On the Pentecost after Jesus' resurrection, the Holy Spirit descended on the Twelve and Mary.

STEPHEN

The first Christian martyr. A popular deacon whose death marked the first wave of persecution against Christians.

UPPER ROOM

The room where Jesus celebrated the Last Supper. The locked gathering place for the first Christians before Pentecost. One of the first Christian churches.

"Then they cast him out of the city and stoned him; and the witnesses laid down their garments at the feet of a young man named Saul....he knelt down and cried with a loud voice, 'Lord, do not hold this sin against them.'" (Acts 7: 58)

STUDY QUESTIONS

1. What mission did Jesus give the apostles?

2. How large is the Kingdom?

3. What were the apostles waiting for after Jesus ascended into heaven?

4. Who called the disciples to replace Judas?

5. Who was chosen to fill Judas' place as the twelfth apostle?

6. Who are the successors of the apostles today?

7. What historical event did the Jews celebrate at Pentecost?

8. Why were Jews from many different nations able to hear the apostles in their own languages?

9. How did some of the Jewish people react when they found out the apostles were speaking so many different languages?

10. Which apostle acted as leader of the Twelve?

11. What miracle did Peter work at the gates of the Temple?

12. What was St. Stephen accused of after out-arguing his adversaries?

13. What was the outcome of St. Stephen's trial?

14. Who persecuted the Jewish people who became Christian?

15. How did early Christians worship?

16. How do the parts of the Mass reflect the way the early Christians worshiped?

PRACTICAL EXERCISES

1. On the feast of Pentecost, the twelve apostles were baptized in fire and the Holy Spirit. Why is this event seen as the birth of the Church? At this point, who was the Church made up of? What was so important about the Twelve receiving the gift of the Holy Spirit?

2. Christ left the apostles with a mission to restore the kingdom of Israel and then extend it to the end of the world. As representatives of the twelve united tribes of Israel, it was important that the eleven apostles choose someone to replace Judas, who had betrayed Jesus and then taken his own life. Why was it important that Peter was the one who decided to choose another apostle? How does this decision display his role as the Vicar of Christ? Who is the present day successor of Peter and heir to all the authority Christ gave him?

3. "But they could not withstand the wisdom and the Spirit with which he spoke" (Acts 6:10). Before and during his martyrdom, St. Stephen, the first martyr, was filled with the Holy Spirit. How could the early Church be sure of this fact? How would God's grace and the Holy Spirit have been present in Stephen's preaching and his address to the Sanhedrin? How would Stephen's strength in the face of martyrdom have been a sign of the Holy Spirit's presence?

FROM THE CATECHISM

553 Jesus entrusted a specific authority to Peter: "I will give you the keys of the kingdom of heaven, and whatever you bind on earth shall be bound in heaven, and whatever you loose on earth shall be loosed in heaven" (Mt 16: 19). The "power of the keys" designates authority to govern the house of God, which is the Church. Jesus, the Good Shepherd, confirmed this mandate after his Resurrection: "Feed my sheep" (Jn 21: 15-17; cf. 10: 11). The power to "bind and loose" connotes the authority to absolve sins, to pronounce doctrinal judgments, and to make disciplinary decisions in the Church. Jesus entrusted this authority to the Church through the ministry of the apostles (cf. Mt 18: 18) and in particular through the ministry of Peter, the only one to whom he specifically entrusted the keys of the kingdom.

738 Thus the Church's mission is not an addition to that of Christ and the Holy Spirit, but is its sacrament: in her whole being and in all her members, the Church is sent to announce, bear witness, make present, and spread the mystery of the communion of the Holy Trinity:

> All of us who have received one and the same Spirit, that is, the Holy Spirit, are in a sense blended together with one another and with God. For if Christ, together with the Father's and his own Spirit, comes to dwell in each of us, though we are many, still the Spirit is one and undivided. He binds together the spirits of each and every one of us,...and makes all appear as one in him. For just as the power of Christ's sacred flesh unites those in whom it dwells into one body, I think that in the same way the one and undivided Spirit of God, who dwells in all, leads all into spiritual unity (St. Cyril of Alexandria, *In Jo. ev.*, 11, 11: PG 74, 561).

763 It was the Son's task to accomplish the Father's plan of salvation in the fullness of time. Its accomplishment was the reason for his being sent (cf. LG 3; *Ad gentes* 3). "The Lord Jesus inaugurated his Church by preaching the Good News, that is, the coming of the Reign of God, promised over the ages in the scriptures" (LG 5). To fulfill the Father's will, Christ ushered in the Kingdom of heaven on earth. The Church "is the Reign of Christ already present in mystery" (LG 3).

1345 As early as the second century we have the witness of St. Justin Martyr for the basic lines of the order of the Eucharistic celebration. They have stayed the same until our own day for all the great liturgical families. St. Justin wrote to the pagan emperor Antoninus Pius (138-161) around the year 155, explaining what Christians did:

— On the day we call the day of the sun, all who dwell in the city or country gather in the same place.

— The memoirs of the apostles and the writings of the prophets are read, as much as time permits.

— When the reader has finished, he who presides over those gathered admonishes and challenges them to imitate these beautiful things.

— Then we all rise together and offer prayers* for ourselves...and for all others, wherever they may be, so that we may be found righteous by our life and actions, and faithful to the commandments, so as to obtain eternal salvation.

— When the prayers are concluded we exchange the kiss.

— Then someone brings bread and a cup of water and wine mixed together to him who presides over the brethren.

— He takes them and offers praise and glory to the Father of the universe, through the name of the Son and of the Holy Spirit and for a considerable time he gives thanks (in Greek: *eucharistian*) that we have been judged worthy of these gifts.

— When he has concluded the prayers and thanksgivings, all present give voice to an acclamation by saying: 'Amen.'

FROM THE CATECHISM continued

—When he who presides has given thanks and the people have responded, those whom we call deacons give to those present the "eucharisted" bread, wine and water and take them to those who are absent (St. Justin, *Apol.* 1, 65-67: PG 6, 428-429; the text from before the asterisk [*] is from chap. 67).

1346 The liturgy of the Eucharist unfolds according to a fundamental structure which has been preserved throughout the centuries down to our own day. It displays two great parts that form a fundamental unity:

—the gathering, the liturgy of the Word, with readings, homily and general intercessions;

—the liturgy of the Eucharist, with the presentation of the bread and wine, the consecratory thanksgiving, and communion.

The liturgy of the Word and liturgy of the Eucharist together form "one single act of worship" (*Sacrosanctum Concilium* 56); the Eucharistic table set for us is the table both of the Word of God and of the Body of the Lord (cf. DV 21).

1831 The seven *gifts* of the Holy Spirit are wisdom, understanding, counsel, fortitude, knowledge, piety, and fear of the Lord. They belong in their fullness to Christ, Son of David (cf. Is 11:1-2). They complete and perfect the virtues of those who receive them. They make the faithful docile in readily obeying divine inspirations.

> Let your good spirit lead me on a level path (Ps 143:10).

> For all who are led by the Spirit of God are sons of God.... If children, then heirs, heirs of God and fellow heirs with Christ (Rom 8:14, 17).

1832 The *fruits* of the Spirit are perfections that the Holy Spirit forms in us as the first fruits of eternal glory. The tradition of the Church lists twelve of them: "charity, joy, peace, patience, kindness, goodness, generosity, gentleness, faithfulness, modesty, self-control, chastity" (Gal 5:22-23 [Vulg.]).

2473 *Martyrdom* is the supreme witness given to the truth of the faith: it means bearing witness even unto death. The martyr bears witness to Christ who died and rose, to whom he is united by charity. He bears witness to the truth of the faith and of Christian doctrine. He endures death through an act of fortitude. "Let me become the food of the beasts, through whom it will be given me to reach God" (St. Ignatius of Antioch, *Ad Rom.* 4, 1: SCh 10, 110).

2624 In the first community of Jerusalem, believers "devoted themselves to the apostles' teaching and fellowship, to the breaking of bread, and the prayers" (Acts 2:42). This sequence is characteristic of the Church's prayer: founded on the apostolic faith; authenticated by charity; nourished in the Eucharist.

St. Stephen's Gate, also called the Lions' Gate, on the east side of the city wall is identified by Christians as the site near the traditional place of St. Stephen's martyrdom. There are also two churches built in Jerusalem as memorials to Stephen.

Endnotes

1. Lk 3:16.
2. Acts 1:3.
3. Acts 1:9.
4. Mk 16:19.

Reaching Out To All Nations

"And he fell to the ground and heard a voice saying to him, 'Saul, Saul, why do you persecute me?' And he said, 'Who are you, Lord?' And he said, 'I am Jesus, whom you are persecuting; but rise…and you will be told what to do.'"

Acts 3: 4–6

Chapter 25

Reaching Out To All Nations

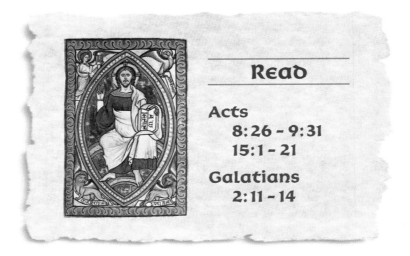

Read

Acts
   8:26 – 9:31
   15:1 – 21

Galatians
   2:11 – 14

Philip Baptizes The Ethiopian

So far the apostles had put all their effort into preaching the Gospel to the Jews and the Samaritans. But Jesus had sent them out to all nations.

> But an angel of the Lord said to Philip, "Rise and go toward the south to the road that goes down from Jerusalem to Gaza." This is a desert road. And he rose and went. And behold, an Ethiopian, a eunuch, a minister of Candace, the queen of the Ethiopians, in charge of all her treasure, had come to Jerusalem to worship and was returning; seated in his chariot, he was reading the prophet Isaiah. (Acts 8:26-28)

Ethiopia was a civilized and wealthy country in Africa. At the time it was governed by a line of queens (Candace seems to have been their title rather than their name), and those queens were capable enough leaders that even the Romans could never conquer Ethiopia. An ancient (but probably not reliable) Ethiopian tradition said that Ethiopian rulers were descended from the union of King Solomon and the Queen of Sheba.

35 A.D.

40 A.D.

45 A.D.

50 A.D.

35 Saul has a vision of Jesus on the road to Damascus and is converted

38-46 Paul, the converted Saul, preaches in Cilicia and Syria

52 The Apostolic Council of Jerusalem is convened to discuss the acceptance of Gentiles

35 Philip, one of the Seven, converts an Ethiopian who carries the faith to Africa; Peter baptizes Cornelius a Roman Centurion in Caesarea

41-44 Herod Agrippa rules over Palestine supporting Jewish unrest with the Christian movement

Rome: 37-41 Caligula is Emperor
41-54 Claudius is Emperor
43-84 Romans conquer Britain

37 The name "Christian" is first used in Antioch to describe believers

43-44 Herod Agrippa arrests and beheads Apostle James the Greater, son of Zebedee. He was the brother of John the Evangelist and was present at the Transfiguration with John and Peter and in the Garden of Gethsemane while Jesus prayed.

There were many Jews among the Ethiopians (as we know from Is 11:11), and the queen's treasurer must have heard about their religion from them. This eunuch was a man of very high position. He was important enough to ride in a chariot on the long trip from Ethiopia to Jerusalem and back. (The "chariot" was actually a large carriage, big enough to hold at least two passengers and a driver.) Even so, because he was a eunuch he could never be either a Jew or a proselyte (see Deuteronomy 23:1). But he may have been reading Isaiah because Isaiah promised a place in the Kingdom even to eunuchs:

> For thus says the LORD:
> "To the eunuchs who keep my Sabbaths,
>   who choose the things that please me
>   and hold fast my covenant,
> I will give in my house and within my walls
>   a monument and a name
>   better than sons and daughters.
> I will give them an everlasting name
>   which shall not be cut off."
> (Is 56:4-5)

In those days, people often read aloud even when they were alone, so Philip could hear what the Ethiopian was reading.

> And the Spirit said to Philip, "Go up and join this chariot." So Philip ran to him, and heard him reading Isaiah the prophet, and asked, "Do you understand what you are reading?" And he said, "How can I, unless someone guides me?" And he invited Philip to come up and sit with him. Now the passage of the scripture which he was reading was this:
>
> > As a sheep led to the slaughter
> >   or a lamb before its shearer is dumb,
> >   so he opens not his mouth.
> > In his humiliation justice was denied him.
> > Who can describe his generation?
> > For his life is taken up from the earth.
>
> And the eunuch said to Philip, "About whom, pray, does the prophet say this, about himself or about some one else?" Then Philip opened his mouth, and beginning with this scripture he told him the good news of Jesus.
> (Acts 8:29-35)

Showing how Jesus fulfilled the Scriptures was always the early Christians' most effective argument.

> And as they went along the road they came to some water, and the eunuch said, "See, here is water! What is to prevent my being baptized?" (Acts 8:36)

Now Philip had a decision to make. Was there anything to prevent the Ethiopian from becoming a Christian? If being a Christian meant first being a Jew, then there *was* something to prevent it: a eunuch could not become a Jew. But Philip had been led by an angel and guided by the Spirit. Surely this must be the will of God.

> And he commanded the chariot to stop, and they both went down into the water, Philip and the eunuch, and he baptized him. (Acts 8:38)

This was the first time a Gentile had been baptized as a Christian. And it was symbolically appropriate that it was an Ethiopian. To the Romans, Ethiopia represented the farthest point of the known world—"the end of the earth," in fact. And Philip had been led to the Ethiopian by the Holy Spirit. It was a sign the Apostles could hardly ignore. The Good News was not just for the Jews; it really was for all nations. The preaching of the Gospel to the whole world had begun.

Early Spread Of "The Good News"

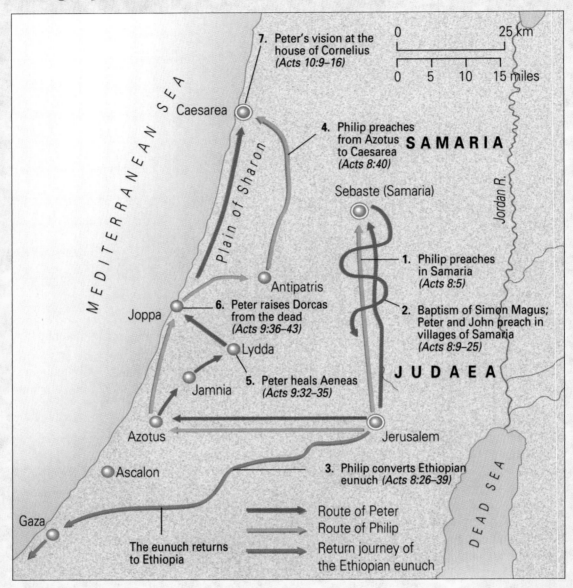

7. Peter's vision at the house of Cornelius (Acts 10:9–16)

4. Philip preaches from Azotus to Caesarea (Acts 8:40)

SAMARIA

Caesarea

Sebaste (Samaria)

1. Philip preaches in Samaria (Acts 8:5)

2. Baptism of Simon Magus; Peter and John preach in villages of Samaria (Acts 8:9–25)

Antipatris

6. Peter raises Dorcas from the dead (Acts 9:36–43)

Joppa

Lydda

Jamnia

5. Peter heals Aeneas (Acts 9:32–35)

JUDAEA

Azotus

Jerusalem

Ascalon

3. Philip converts Ethiopian eunuch (Acts 8:26–39)

Gaza

The eunuch returns to Ethiopia

→ Route of Peter
→ Route of Philip
→ Return journey of the Ethiopian eunuch

MEDITERRANEAN SEA

Plain of Sharon

Jordan R.

DEAD SEA

The ruins of Herod's palace in Caesarea which in New Testament times was the capital of the Roman province of Judea and named in honor of Caesar Augustus.

The city of Joppa, now called Jaffa, was the only harbor between Mt. Carmel and Egypt in Old Testament times and today is contiguous with Tel Aviv, the largest city in Israel.

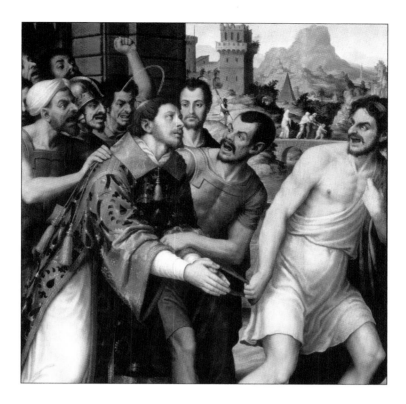

Saul The Persecutor

Meanwhile, it was becoming less and less safe to be a Christian in Jerusalem. After the death of Stephen, the authorities decided to try to stamp out the Jesus cult once and for all. Leading the charge against the Christians was a fanatical Pharisee named Saul—the man who had approved Stephen's execution.

Saul was born in Tarsus, a seaport at the northeastern corner of the Mediterranean in Cilicia. It was "no mean city," as he would remember later—one of the most important centers of learning in the Roman Empire. Although he was raised as a Jew, his father was a Roman citizen, a much-envied privilege that made life a lot easier for the people who possessed it. Saul inherited the Roman citizenship.

After his early years of education in Tarsus, Saul went to Jerusalem to study under Gamaliel, one of the most famous of the Pharisees. Saul ended up with the best of both educations: an amazingly thorough knowledge of the Hebrew Scriptures along with a complete training in Greek literature and philosophy.

He might have intended to become a rabbi, but usually a young man learned some sort of business as well. Saul learned to make tents. There was always a market for tent cloth in the eastern part of the Roman Empire, and it was a trade that would support Saul even at the height of his fame as a traveling missionary.

Saul was an awkward young man—not very tall, and not very good-looking. He was not a very good speaker, either. But he was fanatically devoted to the Law of Moses, and his zeal earned him a high position among the Jewish authorities. Though he was still a young man, we hear that it was Saul who led the squads of Temple guards during the first big persecution of Christians in Jerusalem. "But Saul laid waste the church," Luke tells us, "and entering house after house, he dragged off men and women and committed them to prison."[1]

Saul's Conversion

Hearing that there were followers of Jesus even in Damascus, Saul decided to go there and root them out. But Jesus Christ had a different plan for him.

> Now as he journeyed he approached Damascus, and suddenly a light from heaven flashed about him. And he fell to the ground and heard a voice saying to him, "Saul, Saul, why do you persecute me?" And he said, "Who are you, Lord?" And he said, "I am Jesus, whom you are persecuting; but rise and enter the city, and you will be told what you are to do." The men who were traveling with him stood speechless, hearing the voice but seeing no one. Saul arose from the ground; and when his eyes were opened, he could see nothing; so they led him by the hand and brought him to Damascus. (Acts 9:3-8)

When he reached Damascus, Saul was blind, disoriented, and Christian.

The Christians in Damascus wanted nothing to do with him. Jesus sent a man named Ananias to Saul, but Ananias, Luke tells us (Acts 9:13-14), argued with Jesus himself, pointing out what a dangerous man this Saul was. But Ananias did go, and Saul was cured of his blindness and baptized. He stayed in Damascus for a while, and the astounded Jews and Christians there heard Saul, the head of the Jerusalem temple guards who had come to haul all the Christians back in chains, preaching in the synagogues that Jesus is the Son of God.

Some time after that he went off to Arabia for a while,[2] but soon he was back in Damascus. He spoke so boldly that he started getting death threats. Finally his life was in so much danger that he had to escape over the city wall in a basket.

Unwelcome in Damascus, Saul decided it was time to go back to Jerusalem and meet the Twelve for the first time.

Remember that Saul had been the leader of the first big persecution in Jerusalem. It was hard for the Christian community in Jerusalem to believe that Saul was on their side now. Most of the Christians had run away after Stephen was killed; the Apostles who remained remembered Stephen's death vividly. Now they were supposed to believe that Saul had changed his ways completely.

Of all the Christians in Jerusalem, only Barnabas was willing to take a chance on Saul at first. Satisfied that Saul was telling the truth, Barnabas brought him back to the Apostles and made them listen to Saul's story.

Once they were persuaded that Saul really was a Christian, the Apostles thanked God for sending them such a powerful ally and joyfully welcomed him into the Way, as they called the religion Christ had taught them.

Are Christians Jews?

Would the people of the whole world have to become Jews before they could become Christians? Would they have to be circumcised and follow the whole Law of Moses? Peter learned the answer just before he met Cornelius, a Roman commander who was one of the "Proselytes of the Gate"—a Gentile who worshiped the True God but had not been circumcised. Cornelius had been told in a vision from God to send for Peter. He immediately sent two servants to Joppa, where Peter was staying at the time.

> The next day, as they were on their journey and coming near the city, Peter went up on the housetop to pray, about the sixth hour. And he became hungry and desired something to eat; but while they were preparing it, he fell into a trance and saw the heaven opened, and something descending like a great sheet, let down by four corners upon the earth. In it were all kinds of animals and reptiles and birds of the air. And there came a voice to him, "Rise, Peter; kill and eat." But Peter said, "No, Lord; for I have never eaten anything that is common or unclean." And the voice came to him again a second time, "What God has cleansed, you must not call unclean." This happened three times, and the thing was taken up at once to heaven. (Acts 10: 9-16)

Shortly after that, at the home of Cornelius, the Holy Spirit came to a crowd listening to Peter's preaching—Jews and Gentiles alike. "Can anyone forbid these people to be baptized," Peter asked, "since they have received the Holy Spirit, too?"[3]

The answer was obvious. All the believers who had gathered at the house of Cornelius were baptized—Jews and Gentiles alike.

The Council Of Jerusalem

Saul took on the job of preaching the Gospel to the Gentiles, and he made thousands of converts. But that old question came up again: Did Christians have to be Jews first?

Antioch, a city in Syria, was the first great center of the Church outside Jerusalem. Some of the followers of Jesus had fled there after the death of Stephen. It was the third-largest city in the Empire. Only Rome itself and Alexandria were larger.

Paul and Barnabas had great success in bringing the Good News to the Gentiles there. For a year they preached, and they gained such a reputation that, in about the year 41, the Greek-speaking inhabitants of the city came up with a new name for their followers. They called them Christians. Until then, the converts had simply said that they followed "the Way."

Everything was going well until some inspectors came from Jerusalem. Paul says they were sent by James (Gal 2:12), but we know that James had not given them authority for what they started to teach (Acts 15:24). They told the new Gentile converts that they could not be saved unless they were circumcised and followed the Law of Moses. They said it with such conviction and authority that even Peter was shaken.

"Before certain men came from James," Paul remembered later, "he [Peter] ate with the Gentiles; but when they came he drew back and separated himself, fearing the circumcision party." (See Gal 2:12.) It was the same old Peter we remember from the Gospels—the Peter who said he would never deny Christ and then denied Christ three times.

Paul confronted Peter directly. "I said to Cephas before them all, 'If you, though a Jew, live like a Gentile and not like a Jew, how can you compel the Gentiles to live like Jews?'"[4]

Finally, in the year 49 or 50, the Apostles decided to call a general convention in Jerusalem to decide the matter. Paul came to argue his side; numerous converts from among the Pharisees were there to argue for circumcision. At the head of the table sat James the Just, a close relative of Jesus and the head of the Church in Jerusalem. He was known to everyone as the most devoted follower of the Law in the city. He never cut his beard; he was a strict vegetarian, going far beyond the dietary requirements of the Law; he was also authorized to wear the linen robes of a Jewish priest. For a devout Jew, James represented the ideal. One reason so many of the Pharisees had converted was that they saw James the Just following the law so completely.

Now here was James the Just sitting at the meeting that would determine how the Gentiles would be treated. Things looked bad for Paul's side.

The debate went on and on without a decision. Finally Peter stood up to speak. We can imagine how the room went suddenly quiet. What would Peter say? Possibly the Pharisees had heard how Paul had embarrassed him in front of half of Antioch; they might have expected Peter to take his revenge.

"My brothers," Peter said,

> you remember how quite a while ago God chose me to bring the Good News to the Gentiles. And you remember how God, who knows our hearts, sent the Holy Spirit to them the same way he did to us, making no distinction between us and them, purifying their hearts by faith. So why should we tempt God by putting a yoke on their necks that neither our ancestors nor we were able to bear? No, we believe that it is through the grace of the Lord Jesus Christ that we shall be saved, as they will. (Acts 15:7-11)

The whole crowd was silent. Peter had come out decisively for Paul's side. James himself directed that a letter should be sent to the Church in Antioch, informing them that his representatives had spoken without his authorization, and that Gentiles would not have to be circumcised. For the time being, he asked them to abstain from food offered to idols and to follow a few dietary restrictions, but otherwise they were free from the burden of the Law.

This famous meeting, described by Luke in Acts 15, was the first council of the whole Church. We know it today as the Council of Jerusalem.

> "At all times and in every race, anyone who fears God and does what is right has been acceptable to him. He has, however, willed to make men holy and save them, not as individuals without any bond or link between them, but rather to make them into a people who might acknowledge him and serve him in holiness. He therefore chose the Israelite race to be his own people and established a covenant with it. He gradually instructed this people.... All these things, however, happened as a preparation for and figure of that new and perfect covenant which was to be ratified in Christ...the New Covenant in his blood; he called together a race made up of Jews and Gentiles which would be one, not according to the flesh, but in the Spirit."[5] (CCC 781)

SUPPLEMENTARY READING

John Chrysostom, *Homily on Acts no. 7*

Observe the wisdom of Philip: he did not accuse him, not say, "I know these things exactly," did not pay court to him, and say, "Blessed art thou that readest." But mark his speech, how far it is from harshness alike and from adulation; the speech rather of a kind and friendly man. "Understandest thou what thou readest?" (Acts 5: 30.) For it was needful that he should himself ask, himself have a longing desire. He plainly intimates, that he knows that the other knew nothing: and says, "Understandest thou what thou readest?" at the same time he shows him that great was the treasure that lay therein.

It tells well also, that the eunuch looked not to the outward appearance (of the man), said not, "Who art thou?" did not chide, not give himself airs, not say that he did know. On the contrary, he confesses his ignorance: wherefore also he learns. He shows his hurt to the physician: sees at a glance, that he both knows the matter, and is willing to teach. Look how free he is from haughtiness; the outward appearance announced nothing splendid. So desirous was he of learning, and gave heed to his words; and that saying, "He that seeketh, findeth," (Mt 7: 8) was fulfilled in him.

"And," it says, "he besought Philip, that he would come up and sit with him." (Acts 5: 31.)

Do you mark the eagerness, the longing desire? But should any say he ought to have waited for Philip (to speak), (the answer is), he does not know what is the matter: he could not in the least tell what the other was going to say to him, but supposed merely that he was about to receive some (lesson of) prophecy. And moreover, this was more respectful, that he did not draw him into his chariot, but besought him. "And Philip," we have read, "ran to him, and heard him reading;" even the fact of his running, showed that he wished to say (something).

"And the place," it says, "of the Scripture which he read was this: As a sheep He was led to the slaughter." (Acts 5: 32) And this circumstance, also, is a token of his elevated mind, that he had in hand this prophet, who is more sublime than all others. Philip does not relate matters to him just as it might happen, but quietly: nay, does not say anything until he is questioned. Both in the former instance he prayed him, and so he does now, saying, "I pray thee of whom speaketh the prophet this?" That he should at all know either that the Prophets speak in different ways about different persons, or that they speak of themselves in another person — the question betokens a very thoughtful mind.

Herod's harbor in Caesarea was possibly the first port built in the open sea without the protection of bays and peninsulas. Two enormous, parallel breakwaters were built out from the coast into the sea.

VOCABULARY

ANTIOCH
A great metropolis in Syria. The second center of Christianity after Jerusalem. The name "Christian" was first used in Antioch.

CANDACE
The name of a line of queens who ruled Ethiopia.

CEPHAS
Aramaic for "Peter" or "rock."

COUNCIL OF JERUSALEM
A meeting of Church leaders. There it was decided Gentile converts to Christianity did not have to keep the whole Law of Moses.

DAMASCUS
An ancient city in Syria. Paul was on his way to arrest Christians there when he encountered Christ.

ETHIOPIA
An ancient civilization in eastern Africa. The first Gentile baptized as a Christian was an Ethiopian.

EUNUCH
A man who has been castrated. In some ancient kingdoms, the highest positions in the government went to eunuchs.

GAMALIEL
A famous Pharisee who was Paul's teacher. Gamaliel argued before the Sanhedrin that the Christians should be left alone.

JAMES
A brother (that is, close relative) of Jesus who became the leader of the Church in Jerusalem. James was famous for keeping the whole Law of Moses faithfully.

PAUL
The leader of persecutions against Christians. He was chosen by Christ to be an apostle.

PHILIP
The first Christian to baptize a Gentile. The Holy Spirit led him to an Ethiopian court official who had been reading the prophet Isaiah.

PROSELYTES OF THE GATE
Gentiles who worshiped the True God and knew the Jewish Scriptures, but who were not circumcised and did not keep the Law of Moses.

SAUL OF TARSUS
The Jewish name of St. Paul.

The Altarpiece of St. Philip and St. James from the Cathedral of Huesca, Spain

STUDY QUESTIONS

1. Where did the eunuch baptized by St. Philip originate?

2. Why could that Gentile have never been accepted as a Jewish convert?

3. What Jewish prophet promised a place for eunuchs in the Kingdom?

4. Who is the first baptized gentile Christian reported in the Bible?

5. What was the significance of this Baptism?

6. Who was the fanatical Pharisee who wished to stamp out Christianity?

7. What did Luke mean when he said "but Saul laid waste the church"?

8. Where was Saul going when Jesus Christ appeared to him?

9. Who was Ananias?

10. Where did St. Paul go when he left Damascus?

11. How did Peter know that the crowd at Cornelius' home should be baptized, Jews and Gentiles alike?

12. What was the first great center of Christianity outside Jerusalem?

13. Where were the followers of Jesus Christ first called Christians?

14. What important question did the Council of Jerusalem decide?

15. When was the Council called?

16. What was this Council called?

17. Who was James the Just?

18. What was the Council's decision?

PRACTICAL EXERCISES

1. The conversion of the Ethiopian eunuch and his baptism by Philip offer us an opportunity to reflect on how we live our faith. The Ethiopian had faith in God but could not become a Jew because he was a eunuch. He asked to be baptized without hesitating once he had learned about how God's plan had been fulfilled through Jesus. In the same way, we should not hesitate to make changes in our lives so that we might be closer to God and his will. How can we constantly try to change our lives with regard to prayer, to the sacraments, or to learning more about our faith?

2. Saul, a devout Pharisee, led many persecutions against the earliest Christians. Though he was persecuting the Church, he believed that he was doing what God wanted him to and protecting the Jewish faith. Like any good person, Saul had an open mind to God's will and was trying to learn what God wanted of him. For these reasons, Saul was prepared for God to convert him to the Christian faith. Why is it so important to live your faith and keep your mind open to God's will? How might this come into play in deciding your vocation?

3. Why was the question of circumcision so important? What do you think might have happened to the Church if the matter had been decided the other way?

FROM THE CATECHISM

3 Those who with God's help have welcomed Christ's call and freely responded to it are urged on by love of Christ to proclaim the Good News everywhere in the world. This treasure, received from the apostles, has been faithfully guarded by their successors. All Christ's faithful are called to hand it on from generation to generation, by professing the faith, by living it in fraternal sharing, and by celebrating it in liturgy and prayer (cf. Acts 2: 42).

856 The missionary task implies a *respectful dialogue* with those who do not yet accept the Gospel (cf. *RMiss* 55). Believers can profit from this dialogue by learning to appreciate better "those elements of truth and grace which are found among peoples, and which are, as it were, a secret presence of God" (*Ad gentes* 9). They proclaim the Good News to those who do not know it, in order to consolidate, complete, and raise up the truth and the goodness that God has distributed among men and nations, and to purify them from error and evil "for the glory of God, the confusion of the demon, and the happiness of man" (*Ad gentes* 9).

1086 "Accordingly, just as Christ was sent by the Father so also he sent the apostles, filled with the Holy Spirit. This he did so that they might preach the Gospel to every creature and proclaim that the Son of God by his death and resurrection had freed us from the power of Satan and from death and brought us into the Kingdom of his Father. But he also willed that the work of salvation which they preached should be set in train through the sacrifice and sacraments, around which the entire liturgical life revolves" (*Sacrosanctum Concilium* 6).

1122 Christ sent his apostles so that "repentance and forgiveness of sins should be preached in his name to all nations" (Lk 24: 47). "Go therefore and make disciples of all nations, baptizing them in the name of the Father and of the Son and of the Holy Spirit" (Mt 28: 19). The mission to baptize, and so the sacramental mission, is implied in the mission to evangelize, because the sacrament is prepared for by *the word of God and by the faith* which is assent to this word:

> The People of God is formed into one in the first place by the Word of the living God.... The preaching of the Word is required for the sacramental ministry itself, since the sacraments are sacraments of faith, drawing their origin and nourishment from the Word (*Presbyterorum ordinis* 4 § 1, 2).

2527 "The Good News of Christ continually renews the life and culture of fallen man; it combats and removes the error and evil which flow from the ever-present attraction of sin. It never ceases to purify and elevate the morality of peoples. It takes the spiritual qualities and endowments of every age and nation, and with supernatural riches it causes them to blossom, as it were, from within; it fortifies, completes, and restores them in Christ" (GS 58 § 4).

Endnotes

1. Acts 8: 3.
2. Gal 1: 17-18.
3. Acts 10: 47.
4. Gal 2: 14.
5. LG 9; cf. Acts 10: 35; 1 Cor 11: 25.

Chapter 26
Paul, An Apostle

"*For so the Lord has commanded us, saying,
'I have set you to be a light for the Gentiles, that you may
bring salvation to the uttermost parts of the earth.'*"

Acts 13: 47

Chapter 26

Paul, An Apostle

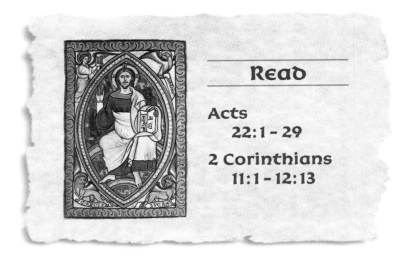

Read

Acts
22:1 - 29

2 Corinthians
11:1 - 12:13

When the early Christians introduced their faith, they told many stories of miracles. But there were two miracles that seemed most astonishing.

The first was that Jesus, who had been dead, was really raised from the dead and had been seen alive by hundreds of people.

The second was that Saul, the most fanatical persecutor of the Christians, had become their most successful apostle.

Under his Roman name, Paul, he is responsible for almost half the books of the New Testament. Yet he had also been responsible for the sufferings of unknown numbers of Christian martyrs.

"The saying is sure and worthy of full acceptance, that Christ Jesus came into the world to save sinners," Paul wrote to his good friend Timothy. "And I am the foremost of sinners; but I received mercy for this reason, that in me, as the foremost, Jesus Christ might display his perfect patience for an example to those who were to believe in him for eternal life."[1]

50 A.D.

50-51 Paul works in Corinth with Silas

52-55 Paul works with churches in Ephesus

55 A.D.

57-59 Paul is imprisoned in Caesarea

60 A.D.

60-62 Paul is under house arrest in Rome

62 (or 64)* Paul is beheaded by Nero

65 A.D.

Rome: 54 Claudius is poisoned by his wife, Agrippina.

54-68 Nero is Emperor.

64 Fire ravages Rome for nine days. Nero blames Christians which institutes first official persecutions

54 Paul writes I Corinthians to answer questions from a Corinth church about marriage, pagan sacrifices and other topics.

56 Paul is arrested in Jerusalem; Roman officials transfer him to Caesarea to protect him from death threats.

62 Ananus, the high priest, orders James the Just to be stoned to death.

64 Rome burns for nine days. Christians are blamed by Nero.

*The exact date of Paul's death, how and where, is a subject of scholarly debate.

Peter And Paul In Acts

In the time of the apostles, it was common for Jews to have a Roman name as well. For example, the author of the second Gospel was called John (Jewish) and Mark (Roman). Saul, too, had a Roman name, and Luke begins to refer to him as Paul when the Good News begins to spread throughout the Roman world (see Acts 13:9).

In the Acts of the Apostles, Luke works hard to show us that Paul has the same authority as the original Twelve. Some scholars think that Luke's main purpose in Acts was to show that Paul was a real apostle. Throughout the Acts of the Apostles, Paul's ministry parallels Peter's in significant ways.

Peter	Paul
First sermon announces the fulfillment of the Davidic covenant. (Acts 2: 14-36)	First sermon announces the fulfillment of the Davidic covenant. (Acts 13: 16-41)
Reprimands Simon the Magician. (Acts 8: 9-24)	Reprimands Bar-Jesus the magician. (Acts 13: 6-12)
Heals the lame. (Acts 3: 1-10)	Heals the lame. (Acts 14: 8-10)
Refuses to be worshiped as a god by Cornelius. (Acts 10: 24-26)	Refuses to be worshiped as a god by the people of Lystra. (Acts 14: 8-18)
Rescued from prison by a miracle. (Acts 12: 6-11)	Rescued from prison by a miracle. (Acts 16: 25-34)
Becomes famous for healings, so that the sick hope to be touched by his shadow. (Acts 5: 15-16)	Becomes famous for healings, so that the sick are healed by handkerchiefs or aprons that touched him. (Acts 19: 1-12)
Raises Tabitha from the dead. (Acts 9: 36-42)	Raises Eutychus from the dead. (Acts 20: 7-12)

Over and over again, God shows his power through Paul in the same way as through Peter. None of the early Christians doubted that Peter was a true apostle. Luke shows us that we must believe Paul for the same reasons.

Apostle To The Gentiles

Jesus chose Paul for a specific mission: to bring the Gospel to the Gentiles. No one could have been better qualified:

- **Paul's classical education had taught him to speak to the Greeks and Romans in their own terms.**
- **That education also gave him a thorough grounding in logic, which he used to make important distinctions in Christian doctrine.**
- **His intense study of the Hebrew Scriptures gave him the tools to refute any argument Jewish authorities might bring against him.**
- **His Roman citizenship kept him safe from the plots of anti-Christian conspirators (for an example, see Acts 23: 27).**

Paul understood that the New Covenant was in every way the fulfillment of the Old Covenant. It was natural that it should be preached first to the Jews, the people of the Old Covenant. But the Good News was for all people.

> And Paul and Barnabas spoke out boldly, saying, "It was necessary that the word of God should be spoken first to you [the Jews in Pisidia]. Since you thrust it from you, and judge yourselves unworthy of eternal life, behold, we turn to the Gentiles. For the Lord has commanded us, saying,
> 'I have set you to be a light to the Gentiles,
> that you may bring salvation to the uttermost parts of the earth.'"
> (Acts 13: 46-47)

Although the Gospel was preached first to the Jews, the New Covenant really erased every distinction between people.

> There is neither Jew nor Greek, there is neither slave nor free, there is neither male nor female; for you are all one in Christ Jesus. (Gal 3:28)

As we saw, it was Paul who insisted that the Gentiles did not need to be circumcised and follow the Law of Moses. Yet Paul also had his friend Timothy circumcised to avoid scandalizing the Jews.[2] Although the New Covenant made him free from the Law of Moses, Paul was always willing to sacrifice that freedom if it meant that he could help people see past their prejudice to the Good News of Christ.

> For though I am free from all men, I have made myself a slave to all, that I might win the more. To the Jews I became as a Jew, in order to win Jews; to those under the law I became as one under the law—though not being myself under the law—that I might win those under the law. To those outside the law I became as one outside the law—not being without law toward God but under the law of Christ—that I might win those outside the law. To the weak I became weak, that I might win the weak. I have become all things to all men, that I might by all means save some. I do it all for the sake of the gospel, that I may share in its blessings. (1 Cor 9:19-23)

The Law Was Our Custodian

- **Roman sons were guided by "custodians" until adulthood.**
- **The Law of Moses was our custodian.**
- **When Christ came, we were freed from the authority of the custodian.**

Before the Council of Jerusalem, some Christians thought that the followers of Christ would have to follow the whole Law of Moses. But Paul insisted—and the Church, guided by Peter, agreed—that Gentiles could not be held responsible for the Law. The New Covenant made us free from the Law.

So what was the purpose of the Law in the first place?

Paul explains that the Law of Moses was like a "custodian" or tutor. In Roman times, well-to-do parents would have a private *pedagogue* (Greek for "child-leader") or custodian for their son. The pedagogue was a slave, but the father gave him absolute authority over the son. But when the son grew up and became an adult, the pedagogue had no more authority over him. As an adult, he was subject only to his father.

The Law of Moses, Paul says, was our pedagogue. With the coming of Christ, we grew up into faith.

Now before faith came, we were confined under the law, kept under restraint until faith should be revealed. So that the law was our custodian until Christ came, that we might be justified by faith. But now that faith has come, we are no longer under a custodian; for in Christ Jesus you are all sons of God, through faith....

I mean that the heir, as long as he is a child, is no better than a slave, though he is owner of all the estate; but he is under guardians and trustees until the date set by the father....So through God you are no longer a slave but a son, and if a son then an heir. (Gal 3:23-26; 4:1-2, 7)

Being Christian means being free from the Law, which bound us only until Christ came. Now we are subject only to God directly.

This divine pedagogy appears especially in the gift of the Law (cf. Ex 19-20; Dt 1-11; 29-30). God gave the Law as a "pedagogue" to lead his people towards Christ (Gal 3:24). But the Law's powerlessness to save man deprived of the divine "likeness," along with the growing awareness of sin that it imparts (cf. Rom 3:20), enkindles a desire for the Holy Spirit. The lamentations of the Psalms bear witness to this. (CCC 708)

Sin Brings Death Through The Law

What then shall we say? That the law is sin? By no means. Yet, if it had not been for the law, I should not have known sin. I should not have known what it is to covet if the law had not said, "You shall not covet." But sin, finding opportunity in the commandment, wrought in me all kinds of covetousness. Apart from the law sin lies dead. I was once alive apart from the law, but when the commandment came, sin revived and I died; the very commandment which promised life proved to be death in me. For sin, finding opportunity in the commandment, deceived me and by it killed me. So the law is holy, and the commandment is holy and just and good. (Rom 7:7-12)

Nothing is wrong with the Law: the fault is in our own sin. Sin manages to change our good intentions to evil actions. It's like an addiction: we want to give it up, but no matter how hard we try we fall back into our old habit.

I do not understand my own actions. For I do not do what I want, but I do the very thing I hate. Now if I do what I do not want, I agree that the law is good. So then it is no longer I that do it, but sin which dwells within me....So I find it to be a law that when I want to do right, evil lies close at hand. (Rom 7:15-17, 21)

We all sin, even though we know what is right, and even though most of us actually want to do what is right. When we do sin, the law condemns us. It condemns us in our own conscience, even when no one else knows what we have done. Because no one can keep from sinning against the Law, everyone is condemned by the Law.

For no human being will be justified in his sight by works of the law since through the law comes knowledge of sin. (Rom 3:20)

"Justified" means made right with God, clean from sin and worthy to receive God's promises. We can never earn that justification through the Law, because the law is what tells us we are sinners.

"For sin, finding opportunity in the commandment, deceived me and by it killed me. So the law is holy, and the commandment is holy and just and good."
(Rom 7: 11-12)

St. Paul's Doctrine Of Justification

But if the Law of Moses could not make us righteous—that is, worthy of God's promises—then what could?

Paul's answer is that only God himself could do it. We can't earn righteousness, but God gives it to us as a gift. The sacrifice of Jesus Christ atoned for all our sins.

> Justification has been merited for us by the Passion of Christ. It is granted us through Baptism. It conforms us to the righteousness of God, who justifies us. It has for its goal the glory of God and of Christ, and the gift of eternal life. It is the most excellent work of God's mercy. (CCC 2020)

Through God's grace, which we did nothing to deserve, we are given the righteousness we could never earn through the Law. Adam's sin *dis-graced* us all: it removed God's grace from us. Jesus Christ atoned for us all: by his death and resurrection he restored us to our place as children of God.

> Then as one man's trespass led to condemnation for all men, so one man's act of righteousness leads to acquittal and life for all men. For as by one man's disobedience many were made sinners, so by one man's obedience many will be made righteous. Law came in, to increase the trespass; but where sin increased, grace abounded all the more; so that, as sin reigned in death, grace also might reign through righteousness to eternal life through Jesus Christ our Lord. (Rom 5: 18-21)

Without God's gift of righteousness, we are slaves to the cycle of sin and death. We try to obey the Law, we fail, and the Law condemns us. But with God's grace—the help God gives us, which we could never deserve—we can break free from that cycle, through our faith in Jesus Christ and the sacrifice he made for us.

> There is therefore no condemnation for those who are in Christ Jesus. For the law of the Spirit of life in Christ Jesus has set me free from the law of sin and death. For God has done what the law, weakened by the flesh, could not do: sending his own son in the likeness of sinful flesh and for sin, he condemned sin in the flesh, in order that the just requirement of the law might be fulfilled in us, who walk not according to the flesh but according to the Spirit. (Rom 8:1-4)

But why did Jesus have to die? The answer is that God is perfect. Perfect justice demands that the penalty for sin be paid. But we are all sinners: as Psalm 14:3 says, "there is none that does good, no, not one."

Under the Old Covenant, someone who had broken the law would make a sin offering. Under the New Covenant, Jesus Christ himself is our sin offering.

> For there is no distinction; since all have sinned and fall short of the glory of God, they are justified by his grace as a gift, through the redemption which is in Christ Jesus, whom God put forward as an expiation by his blood, to be received by faith. This was to show God's righteousness, because in his divine forbearance he had passed over former sins; it was to prove at the present time that he himself is righteous and that he justifies him who has faith in Jesus. (Rom 3:22-26)

Paul tells us that we are "justified by faith apart from works of the law."[3] The essence of "justification" is divine sonship, which is freely given by the Spirit in baptism.

> Our justification comes from the grace of God. Grace is *favor*, the *free and undeserved help* that God gives us to respond to his call to become children of God, adoptive sons, partakers of the divine nature and of eternal life (cf. Jn 1:12-18; 17:3; Rom 8:14-17; 2 Pt 1:3-4). (CCC 1996)

> Grace is a *participation in the life of God.* It introduces us into the intimacy of Trinitarian life: by Baptism the Christian participates in the grace of Christ, the Head of his Body. As an "adopted son" he can henceforth call God "Father," in union with the only Son. He receives the life of the Spirit who breathes charity into him and who forms the Church. (CCC 1997)

We can never earn the right to be part of God's family, not even by perfect obedience. It must be a free gift from God. Paul says that following the Law of Moses—the rituals and observances that set Israel apart as a nation—can never justify us. Indeed, history shows that the Law could never bring holiness to Israel. Israelites and Gentiles alike can be justified by their faith in Jesus Christ without following the Law of Moses.

> According to Christian tradition, the Law is holy, spiritual, and good (cf. Rom 7:12, 14, 16), yet still imperfect. Like a tutor (cf. Gal 3:24) it shows what must be done, but does not of itself give the strength, the grace of the Spirit, to fulfill it. Because of sin, which it cannot remove, it remains a law of bondage. According to St. Paul, its special function is to denounce and *disclose sin,* which constitutes a "law of concupiscence" in the human heart (cf. Rom 7). However, the Law remains the first stage on the way to the kingdom. It prepares and disposes the chosen people and each Christian for conversion and faith in the Savior God. It provides a teaching which endures for ever, like the Word of God. (CCC 1963)

Paul does *not* mean that good works count for nothing. Some early Christians might have misinterpreted him, thinking that good works were unnecessary because they had faith. A letter from St. James set them straight.

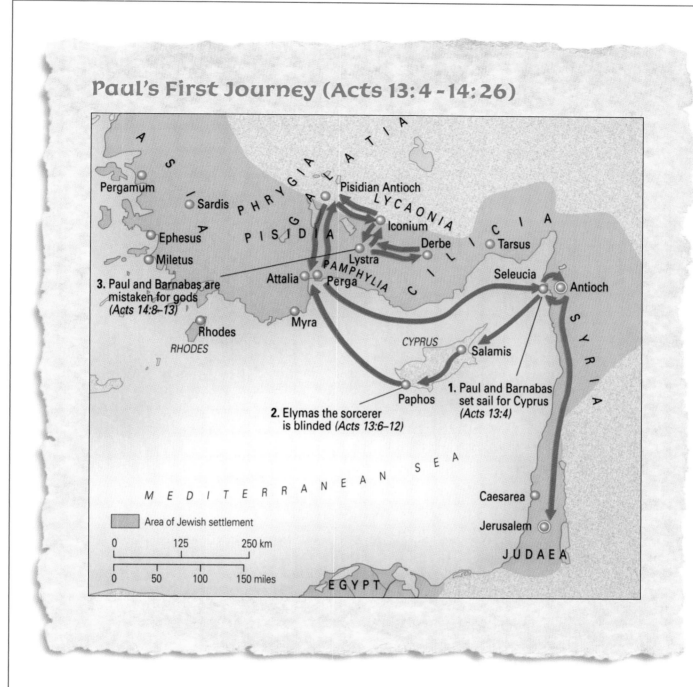

Paul's First Journey (Acts 13:4 - 14:26)

3. Paul and Barnabas are mistaken for gods (Acts 14:8–13)

2. Elymas the sorcerer is blinded (Acts 13:6–12)

1. Paul and Barnabas set sail for Cyprus (Acts 13:4)

Area of Jewish settlement

0   125   250 km

0   50   100   150 miles

What does it profit, my brethren, if a man says he has faith but has not works? Can his faith save him? If a brother or sister is ill-clad and in lack of daily food, and one of you says to them, "Go in peace, be warmed and filled," without giving them the things needed for the body, what does it profit? So faith by itself, if it has no works, is dead.

But some one will say, "You have faith and I have works." Show me your faith apart from your works, and I by my works will show you my faith. (Jas 2:14-18)

Membership in God's family comes to us as a free gift. Once we are members of the family, however, we are expected to abide by the terms of the family covenant—including all the good works Jesus commanded. That does not mean that our good works can buy our way into the family; instead, because God freely gave us membership in his family, we are held to a higher standard.

St. Paul's Travels

Paul's travels took him through much of the Roman Empire. In Asia Minor, in Greece, and in Rome itself, he preached the Gospel, founded new churches, and encouraged churches that had been founded by other apostles. According to one ancient tradition, he even went as far as Spain.

> Three times I have been shipwrecked; a night and a day I have been adrift at sea; on frequent journeys, in danger from rivers, danger from robbers, danger from my own people, danger from Gentiles, danger in the city, danger in the wilderness, danger from false brethren; in toil and hardship, through many a sleepless night, in hunger and thirst, often without food, in cold and exposure. (2 Cor 11: 25-27)

Eventually, though, he ended up in Rome. He was sent there as a prisoner. It was one of those occasions when his Roman citizenship helped him out: he had the legal right to appeal to the Emperor in Rome.

Of course, an appeal like that could take a long time. Meanwhile, Paul was a prisoner, but not badly treated. He was allowed to have visits from his friends, like the physician Luke, who wrote down

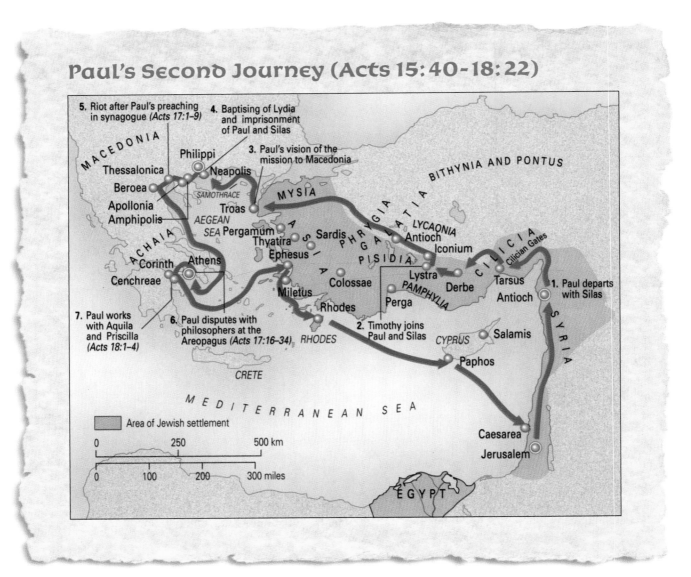

Paul's Second Journey (Acts 15:40-18:22)

5. Riot after Paul's preaching in synagogue *(Acts 17:1–9)*

4. Baptising of Lydia and imprisonment of Paul and Silas

3. Paul's vision of the mission to Macedonia

7. Paul works with Aquila and Priscilla *(Acts 18:1–4)*

6. Paul disputes with philosophers at the Areopagus *(Acts 17:16–34)*

2. Timothy joins Paul and Silas

1. Paul departs with Silas

Area of Jewish settlement

0   250   500 km

0   100   200   300 miles

Paul's story in the Acts of the Apostles. He was also allowed to send letters to friends and to churches he had founded.

Luke's story in Acts ends with Paul in Rome. He had reached the heart of the Roman Empire, carrying out Jesus' orders to take the Gospel to the ends of the earth. He might have been re-leased and arrested again later, or he might have spent the rest of his life a prisoner in Rome.

The tradition of the Church is sure, however, that he eventually died in Rome during Nero's persecution. An ancient tradition says that he died on the same day as St. Peter. Peter was crucified; Paul, as a Roman citizen, was spared that torture. His head was cut off with a sword, which is why you see St. Paul holding a sword in many pictures of him: it reminds us of how he died for the faith.

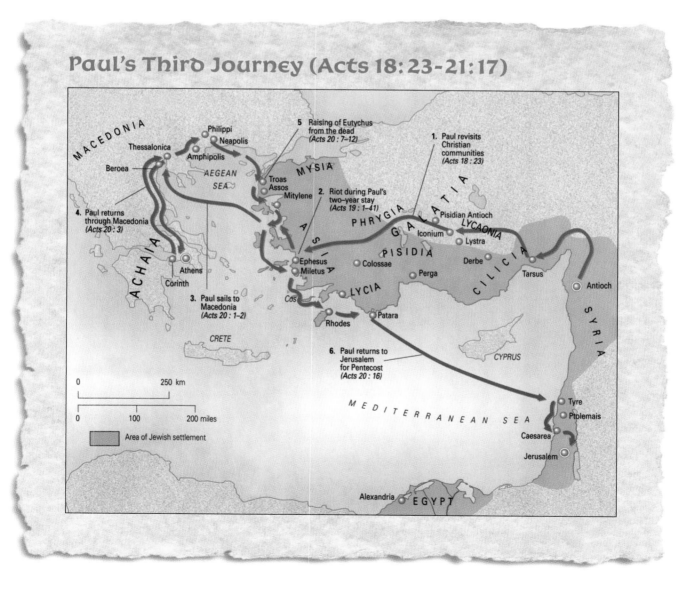

Paul's Third Journey (Acts 18:23-21:17)

Paul's Journey To Rome (Acts 21:26-28:31)

5. Paul awaits trial before Caesar

Rome
ITALIA
Puteoli
ADRIATIC SEA
AEGEAN SEA
Rhegium
SICILIA
Syracuse
Athens
Cnidus
CILICIA
Tarsus
PAMPHYLIA
LYCIA
Myra
Antioch
MALTA
Fair Havens
Phoenix
CRETE
RHODES
CYPRUS
SYRIA
Salmone
4. Shipwrecked on Malta (Acts 28)
CAUDA
Lasea
Sidon
2. Trials before Felix and Festus; Paul appeals to Caesar (Acts 24, 25)
3. Strong winds make navigation difficult (Acts 27)
Caesarea
Antipatris
MEDITERRANEAN SEA
Jerusalem
1. Paul arrested (Acts 21:33)
Alexandria
SYRTIS
EGYPT

0   250   500 km
0 100 200 300 miles

Area of Jewish settlement

"After we had escaped [from the shipwreck], we then learned that the island was called Malta....Paul had gathered a bundle of sticks and put them on the fire, when a viper came out...and fastened on his hand....He... shook off the creature into the fire and suffered no harm... [the natives] said that he was a god." (Acts 28:1-6)

The sword that Paul carries in many paintings and sculptures of him reminds us of how he died for his faith.

SUPPLEMENTARY READING

The heretic Marcion had argued that the God of the New Testament was a different God from the God of the Old Testament. Tertullian refutes that argument: no one had ever doubted that Paul was preaching the same God that the Jews had always worshiped.

Tertullian, *Against Marcion*, ch. 21.

Now if it was with the view of preaching a new god that he [Paul] was eager to abrogate the law of the old God, how is it that he prescribes no rule about the new god, but solely about the old law, if it be not because faith in the Creator was still to continue, and His law alone was to come to an end?—just as the Psalmist had declared: "Let us break their bands asunder, and cast away their cords from us. Why do the heathen rage, and the people imagine a vain thing? The kings of the earth stand up, and the rulers take counsel together against the Lord, and against His Anointed."

And, indeed, if another god were preached by Paul, there could be no doubt about the law, whether it were to be kept or not, because of course it would not belong to the new lord, the enemy of the law. The very newness and difference of the god would take away not only all question about the old and alien law,

but even all mention of it. But the whole question, as it then stood, was this, that although the God of the law was the same as was preached in Christ, yet there was a disparagement of His law. Permanent still, therefore, stood faith in the Creator and in His Christ; manner of life and discipline alone fluctuated. Some disputed about eating idol sacrifices, others about the veiled dress of women, others again about marriage and divorce, and some even about the hope of the resurrection; but about God no one disputed.

Now, if this question also had entered into dispute, surely it would be found in the apostle, and that too as a great and vital point. No doubt, after the time of the apostles, the truth respecting the belief of God suffered corruption, but it is equally certain that during the life of the apostles their teaching on this great article did not suffer at all; so that no other teaching will have the right of being received as apostolic than that which is at the present day proclaimed in the churches of apostolic foundation. You will, however, find no church of apostolic origin but such as reposes its Christian faith in the Creator.

A first century Artemis idol from the Ephesus Museum.

The Great Theatre of Ephesus and the Appian Way. On the westward part of Paul's third journey, Paul spent three years in Ephesus. In this time, Paul brought many to Christ. In Acts 19: 23-41, Demetrius, an Ephesian silversmith whose trade in silver Artemis idols had been jeopardized by Paul's preaching, organized a protest of silversmiths and craftsmen at this great theater which seats twenty-five thousand people. Paul was rescued from a potential riot by Alexander, a town clerk, who assured the Ephesians that Paul and his companions were "neither sacrilegious nor blasphemers." Alexander told the silversmiths to take up any complaint against Paul with the courts and avoid a dangerous riot.

VOCABULARY

ASIA
A part of the Roman Empire corresponding roughly to Turkey. Today known as Asia Minor. Paul founded many churches there.

BARNABAS
A Christian missionary who was Paul's companion in some of his travels. He introduced Paul to the apostles in Jerusalem.

CUSTODIAN
A tutor or pedagogue: someone placed in charge of a child until the child reaches maturity.

JUSTIFICATION
Being made right with God. It is a free and undeserved gift God gives us through the sacrifice of Jesus Christ.

NERO
The wicked (and probably insane) emperor who began the first Roman persecution of the Christians.

ROME
The capital of the Roman Empire, and the greatest city of the ancient world. Peter—the first pope—and Paul died there on the same day after having organized the Church.

SPAIN
The western most province of the Roman Empire. James and perhaps Paul traveled there in their journeys.

TIMOTHY
A friend of Paul to whom he addressed two letters.

An altar dedicated to Sts. Peter and Paul in a prison cell in Mamertine (Mamertinum) Prison in Rome, the prison which held Peter and Paul during his second imprisonment.

STUDY QUESTIONS

1. What two miracles did early Christians deem most astonishing?

2. Why did Paul consider himself an example of Jesus Christ's perfect patience?

3. How does Luke use the Acts to show us that we must believe Paul had the same authority as the original twelve apostles?

4. For what specific mission did Christ chose Paul?

5. What qualified him for this role?

6. What did the New Covenant erase?

7. What was the purpose of the Law if it was only to be discarded when Christ came?

8. How can we achieve righteousness?

9. Why did Jesus have to die?

10. What happens if we do not achieve righteousness?

11. What does Christian tradition say regarding the Law?

12. Does faith make good works unnecessary?

13. Where did St. Paul travel?

14. Where was St. Paul at the end of Luke's story?

15. What does Church Tradition tell us about the end of Paul's life?

PRACTICAL EXERCISES

1. Paul was a well educated man. His studies in Greek and Roman thought, logic, and Hebrew scripture allowed him to be prepared to defend the faith in any situation. Paul also had great faith and was able to perform many of the miracles which Peter also performed as head of the Church. Paul disagreed with Peter on different occasions in matters concerning the Church, but he always ended up submitting to Peter's judgment, though Peter was an uneducated Galilean. Why was Paul so subservient to Peter? What is so important about Peter's position as head of the Church on earth?

2. Why does Paul call himself "the foremost of sinners"? Do you think this label is appropriate? Explain.

3. Church tradition holds that Paul was beheaded in Rome because of his faith. It was only his Roman citizenship that saved him from death on a cross. Why do you think Roman citizens were not allowed to be crucified? What was so terrible about the death our Lord endured for us?

St. Paul holds his sword of martyrdom outside St. Paul's Church in Rome.

FROM THE CATECHISM

32 The *world:* starting from movement, becoming, contingency, and the world's order and beauty, one can come to a knowledge of God as the origin and the end of the universe.

As St. Paul says of the Gentiles: For what can be known about God is plain to them, because God has shown it to them. Ever since the creation of the world his invisible nature, namely, his eternal power and deity, has been clearly perceived in the things that have been made (Rom 1:19-20; cf. Acts 14:15, 17; 17:27-28; Wis 13:1-9).

And St. Augustine issues this challenge: Question the beauty of the earth, question the beauty of the sea, question the beauty of the air distending and diffusing itself, question the beauty of the sky... question all these realities. All respond: "See, we are beautiful." Their beauty is a profession [*confessio*]. These beauties are subject to change. Who made them if not the Beautiful One [*Pulcher*] who is not subject to change? (St. Augustine, *Sermo* 241, 2: PL 38, 1134)

442 Similarly Paul will write, regarding his conversion on the road to Damascus, "When he who had set me apart before I was born, and had called me through his grace, was pleased to reveal his Son to me, in order that I might preach him among the Gentiles..." (Gal 1:15-16). "And in the synagogues immediately [Paul] proclaimed Jesus, saying, 'He is the Son of God'" (Acts 9:20).

639 The mystery of Christ's resurrection is a real event, with manifestations that were historically verified, as the New Testament bears witness. In about A.D. 56 St. Paul could already write to the Corinthians: "I delivered to you as of first importance what I also received, that Christ died for our sins in accordance with the scriptures, and that he was buried, that he was raised on the third day in accordance with the scriptures, and that he appeared to Cephas, then to the Twelve..." (1 Cor 15:3-4). The Apostle speaks here of the living tradition of the Resurrection which he had learned after his conversion at the gates of Damascus (cf. Acts 9:3-18).

1385 To respond to this invitation we must *prepare ourselves* for so great and so holy a moment. St. Paul urges us to examine our conscience: "Whoever, therefore, eats the bread or drinks the cup of the Lord in an unworthy manner will be guilty of profaning the body and blood of the Lord. Let a man examine himself, and so eat of the bread and drink of the cup. For any one who eats and drinks without discerning the body eats and drinks judgment upon himself" (1 Cor 11:27-29). Anyone conscious of a grave sin must receive the sacrament of Reconciliation before coming to communion.

Endnotes

1. 1 Tm 1:15-16.
2. Acts 16:3.
3. Rom 3:28.

The ruins of the bema or platform in Corinth where Gallio judged Paul. (Acts 18:5-17)

The New Kingdom

"The kingdom aims at transforming human relationships; it grows gradually as people slowly learn to love, forgive and serve one another. Jesus sums up the whole Law, focusing it on the commandment of love."

John Paul II

Chapter 27

The New Kingdom

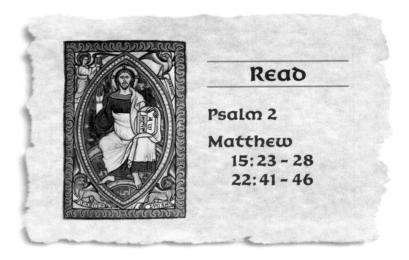

Read

Psalm 2

Matthew
15: 23 - 28
22: 41 - 46

When Jacob was dying, he called all his sons together and gave them a prophetic blessing (see Gn 49). When he came to Judah, he made this prophecy:

> The scepter shall not depart from Judah,
> nor the ruler's staff from between his feet,
> until he comes to whom it belongs;
> and to him shall be the obedience of the peoples. (Gn 49: 10)

Jacob was promising Judah something more than rule over the rest of Jacob's sons. The "scepter"—the symbol of royal power—would belong to Judah until some descendant of Judah came to whom the scepter "belonged." Then not just Israel, but "the peoples"—all the nations—would obey him.

King David came from the tribe of Judah. Jesus Christ's human ancestors came from the line of David, and Jesus inherited David's throne. David ruled over just a small empire in the Middle East, but Christ's reign is unlimited. "The obedience of the peoples" belongs to him.

When the angel Gabriel came to tell Mary that she would bear a child, he told her exactly who this child would be:

> He will be great, and will be called the Son of the Most High;
> and the Lord God will give to him the throne of his father David,
> and he will reign over the house of Jacob forever;
> and of his kingdom there will be no end.
> (Lk 1: 32-33)

The words Gabriel used are a summary of the Davidic covenant. Remember the promises God made to David (see 2 Sm 7): "I will raise up your offspring after you…I will establish the throne of his kingdom forever…your throne shall be established forever." These were the same promises God made to Mary.

The meaning would be clear to any faithful Jew. Mary's son will be the Son of David, the Anointed One (that is, the Messiah or Christ), heir to the throne of David and to all the promises that went with it. But Jesus would turn out to be a different sort of king. Through Jesus would be fulfilled not only the promises to David, but also—finally—the promise to Abraham that all the people of the world would be blessed through him.

The Son Of David

- **As "Son of David," Jesus inherits all the promises of the Davidic covenant.**
- **Matthew shows that the new Israel includes Gentile believers.**

As you remember, the whole New Testament begins with the genealogy of Jesus Christ, "the son of David, the son of Abraham."

For Matthew, the most important thing to know about Jesus was that he was the climax of God's plan of salvation. Jesus Christ fulfilled all the promises God had made to Abraham and to David. As we saw earlier, Matthew uses his literary art to show that Jesus is the ideal successor of David. Jesus is the Anointed One, the Son of David, who inherits all the promises in the Davidic covenant. In fact, Jesus is called "Son of David" at least eight times in Matthew's Gospel.

Why is that title "Son of David" so important to Matthew? The reason is that the Kingdom of Heaven has replaced the Kingdom of Israel. Matthew needs to show his Jewish audience that the prophecies in the Scriptures all point to Jesus. For Jews of that time, the prophecies in the Scriptures all pointed to the Son of David, the Anointed One (Messiah or Christ) who would restore the kingdom of Israel. Matthew's readers need to understand that the prophecies promised something much greater than a new king at the eastern end of the Mediterranean. The Son of David is Lord of all the nations, and all his followers the whole world over make up the new Kingdom of Israel.

Matthew illustrates that new understanding of the kingdom with a story—one that must immediately have struck his Jewish audience:

> And behold, a Canaanite woman from that region came out and cried, "Have mercy on me, O Lord, Son of David; my daughter is severely possessed by a demon." (Mt 15: 22)

This woman was a Syro-Phoenician (according to the same story in Mark), a descendant of the Canaanites who lived in the Promised Land before the conquest. The Canaanites were supposed to have been exterminated during the conquest of the Promised Land, but the Israelites failed to displace them. Instead, the Israelites were often seduced into worshiping the horrible Canaanite idols, which demanded human sacrifice and ritual prostitution. Canaanites were the most hated enemies of Israel, and the very symbols of why it was important for Jews to separate themselves from the Gentiles. But this Canaanite calls Jesus "Lord, Son of David"!

Jesus tests her faith by adopting the traditional Jewish attitude toward Canaanites:

> But he did not answer her a word. And his disciples came and begged him, saying, "Send her away, for she is crying after us." He answered, "I was sent only to the lost sheep of the house of Israel." But she came and knelt before him, saying, "Lord, help me." And he answered, "It is not fair to take the children's bread and throw it to the dogs." She said, "Yes, Lord, yet even the dogs eat the crumbs that fall from their master's table." Then Jesus answered her, "O woman, great is your faith! Be it done for you as you desire." And her daughter was cured instantly. (Mt 15: 23-28)

An ordinary Jewish reader would have seen the shocking message of this story at once: the blessings of the new Kingdom are for the Gentiles, too—even for the Canaanites! And the Canaanite woman recognizes Jesus as "Son of David," and recognizes the Son of David as her "Lord." None of Jesus' own disciples had yet recognized him as the Anointed One. A little while later, Peter was the first to make the connection:

> Now when Jesus came into the district of Caesarea Philippi, he asked his disciples. "Who do men say that the Son of man is?" And they said, "Some say John the Baptist, others say Elijah, and others Jeremiah or one of the prophets." He said to them, "But who do you say that I am?" Simon Peter replied, "You are the Christ, the Son of the living God." (Mt 16: 13-16)

When Peter calls Jesus "the Christ, the Son of the living God," he acknowledges that Jesus is heir to the titles that belong to the throne of David:

- **Anointed One (*Christ or Messiah*)**

- **Son of God (see 2 Sm 7: 14)**

In other words, Jesus is legitimate king, heir to David's throne and the Davidic covenant.

"…'Yes, Lord, yet even the dogs eat the crumbs that fall from their master's table.' Then Jesus answered her, 'O woman, great is your faith! Be it done for you as you desire.'" (Mt 15: 27–28)

"He said to them, 'How is it then that David, inspired by the Spirit, calls him Lord,...'" (Mt 22: 43)

The Riddle: How Can David's Son Be David's Lord?

- **Jesus asked the Pharisees a question they couldn't answer: How can David's son be David's Lord?**
- **Peter's first sermon shows how Jesus fulfills the promises God made to David.**
- **Jesus, Peter says, is the Anointed One, heir to David's throne.**
- **Finally, Peter answers the riddle that stumped the Pharisees.**

After the Pharisees had tried for a while to trap Jesus with questions, Jesus himself turned around and asked them a question they couldn't answer:

Now when the Pharisees were gathered together, Jesus asked them a question, saying, "What do you think of the Christ? Whose son is he?" They said to him, "The son of David." He said to them, "How is it then that David, inspired by the Spirit, calls him Lord, saying,

'The Lord said to my Lord,

Sit at my right hand,

till I put thy enemies under thy feet'?

If David thus calls him Lord, how is he his son?" And no one was able to answer him a word, nor from that day did any one dare to ask him any more questions. (Mt 22: 41-46)

The Pharisees obviously recognized this psalm as referring to the Christ, the Anointed One — in other words, the Son of David. Otherwise, they could have just refused to admit that the psalm had anything to do with the Christ, and they would not have been unable to answer Jesus.

This same saying of Jesus shows up in all three synoptic Gospels: Matthew 22:41-46, Mark 12:35-37, Luke 20:41-44. Since the saying appears in two different settings, Jesus probably said it more than once. He obviously thought it was an important question for the people to think about.

But no one ever answers it in any of the Gospels. Even the Twelve could not answer it until after Jesus' death and resurrection. Then, on the day of Pentecost, Peter was inspired by the Holy Spirit, and he gave a sermon that answered Jesus' riddle.

Peter's sermon is recorded in the Acts of the Apostles, Luke's sequel to his Gospel. His audience were Jews "from every nation under heaven" in Jerusalem. When they heard the Apostles speaking in every language, some of them thought the men were simply drunk. Peter had to speak to an audience that included some of the very same people who had shouted "Crucify him!" when Pilate wanted to let Jesus go. They were also people who expected very little from Galileans. The only way Peter could overcome the crowd's hostility was by showing them that everything they already knew about the Scriptures pointed to Jesus.

1. Peter's sermon begins by explaining what the people are seeing right now — the coming of the Holy Spirit. This very event, he says, was foretold by the prophet Joel.

Men of Judea and all who dwell in Jerusalem, let this be known to you, and give ear to my words. For these men are not drunk, as you suppose, since it is only the third hour of the day; but this is what was spoken by the prophet Joel:

"And in the last days it shall be, God declares,
that I will pour out my Spirit upon all flesh,
and your sons and your daughters shall prophesy,
and your young men shall see visions,
and your old men shall dream dreams;
yea, and on my menservants and my maidservants
    in those days
I will pour out my Spirit; and they shall prophesy.
And I will show wonders in the heaven above
and signs on the earth beneath,
blood, and fire, and vapor of smoke;
the sun shall be turned to darkness
and the moon to blood,
before the day of the Lord comes,
the great and manifest day.
And it shall be that whoever calls on the name of the
    Lord shall be saved."
(Acts 2:14-21)

By quoting Joel, Peter tells the Jews where they are in history: the last days, the days when the Christ, the Anointed One, has already come.

2. Next, Peter reminds his listeners of the miracles worked by Jesus. Many in his audience must have seen some of those miracles themselves. These miracles, Peter tells them, were signs from God that should have told them who Jesus was:

> Men of Israel, hear these words: Jesus of Nazareth, a man attested to you by God with mighty works and wonders and signs which God did through him in your midst, as you yourselves know. (Acts 2:22)

3. Then Peter tells them something amazing: Jesus' crucifixion, which must have seemed like the end of his movement, was actually part of God's plan:

> This Jesus, delivered up according to the definite plan and foreknowledge of God, you crucified and killed by the hands of lawless men. But God raised him up, having loosed the pangs of death, because it was not possible for him to be held by it. (Acts 2:23-24)

4. Who was this miraculous man, then? Peter reminds them of what David said in Psalm 16:

> For David says concerning him,
> "I saw the Lord always before me,
> for he is at my right hand that I may not be shaken;
> therefore my heart was glad, and my tongue rejoiced;
> moreover my flesh will dwell in hope.
> For thou wilt not abandon my soul to Hades,
> nor let thy Holy One see corruption.
> Thou hast made known to me the ways of life;
> thou wilt make me full of gladness with thy presence."
> Brethren, I may say to you confidently of the patriarch David that he both died and was buried, and his tomb is with us to this day. (Acts 2:25-29)

David died, and his body saw corruption. Therefore, he cannot be talking about himself in this psalm.

5. Instead, David was an inspired prophet who was speaking of the Christ, the Anointed One, his descendant who one day would succeed to his throne, and in whom God's promise to David would be fulfilled.

Being therefore a prophet, and knowing that God had sworn with an oath to him that he would set one of his descendants on his throne, he foresaw and spoke of the resurrection of the Christ, that he was not abandoned to Hades, nor did his flesh see corruption. (Acts 2:30-31)

6. So Jesus was the Christ, the Anointed One prophesied by David, who would inherit the throne of David and the kingdom of Israel. As David prophesied, Jesus was not abandoned to Hades:

> This Jesus God raised up, and of that we all are witnesses.
> (Acts 2:32)

7. Now at last Peter can reveal the answer to Jesus' riddle—the riddle that puzzled and silenced even the Pharisees. David calls his son "my Lord" because the Son of David is also the Son of God, who lives and reigns at the right hand of God the Father.

> Being therefore exalted at the right hand of God, and having received from the father the promise of the Holy Spirit, he has poured out this which you see and hear. For David did not ascend into the heavens; but he himself says,
>
> > "The Lord said to my Lord, Sit at my right hand,
> > Till I make thy enemies a stool for thy feet."
>
> Let all the house of Israel therefore know assuredly that God has made him both Lord and Christ, this Jesus whom you crucified. (Acts 2:33-36)

The Church Perfectly Fulfills The Davidic Covenant

- **The new Israel is the community of all believers — the Church.**
- **We can see all the features of the Davidic covenant in the new Israel.**

If Jesus is the Son of David, that means he is king of Israel. But not Israel the small state at the eastern end of the Mediterranean: Jesus is king of a new Israel. The ascending spiral of fulfillment has made all the nations God's own people. Therefore, the new Israel is the community of all the people of God — in other words, the Church.

You may remember that we pointed out seven primary features and three secondary features of the Davidic covenant (see chapter 10). All those features take on new meaning in the Church, the new Kingdom.

The Davidic Covenant: Seven Primary Features

1. David's line would have a great **kingdom**, and David's son would be "the highest of the kings of the earth" (Ps 89:27).

    As **King** of the new Israel, Jesus, the Son of David, is Lord of all the nations.

2. The covenant was made with David's whole **dynasty**. God promised David that his descendants' throne would be established forever (2 Sm 7:13).

    As the last and perfect **Son of David**, Jesus rules over the new Israel forever.

3. When the son of David was anointed, he was adopted as **God's own son**. Anointing with oil made the Son of David "messiah" in Hebrew or "Christ" in Greek — that is, the Anointed One. Psalm 110 calls him a priest as well as king: "You are a priest forever after the order of Melchizedek."[1]

    Jesus, the only-begotten **Son of God**, was anointed at his baptism and in his sacrifice became our High Priest:

    ...where Jesus has gone as a forerunner on our behalf, having become a high priest forever after the order of Melchizedek. (Heb 6:20)

4. The covenant was **unlimited** in time and space. David's throne would be everlasting, and "the ends of the earth" (Ps 2:8; Ps 72:8) his kingdom's boundaries.

    Jesus' kingdom is **forever** and **for all people**. As we pointed out before, when Jesus tells his disciples to be his witnesses "in Jerusalem and in all Judea and Samaria and to the end of the earth,"[2] he's drawing a kind of concentric map of David's kingdom, showing that Jesus is the new heir of the Davidic covenant.

5. **Jerusalem** became the spiritual center of the world. Zion, the central mountain of Jerusalem, eclipsed Sinai and became the holy mountain of God.

    The **heavenly Jerusalem** replaces the earthly Jerusalem as the spiritual center of the Kingdom. The prophets foretold a time when all nations would flock to Zion (see Is 2). In the new Kingdom, that promise is fulfilled.

Then I saw a new heaven and a new earth; for the first heaven and the first earth had passed away, and the sea was no more. And I saw the holy city, new Jerusalem, coming down out of heaven from God, prepared as a bride for her husband; and I heard a great voice from the throne saying, "Behold, the dwelling of God is with men." (Rv 21:1-3)

Remember that Zion is where the Upper Room was—the room where Christ's Church was born.

6. The **Temple** was the architectural sign of the Davidic covenant, a building where all people of the earth were invited to worship the God of Israel.

God himself is the temple in the new Kingdom, and all nations will worship his glory.

And I saw no temple in the city, for its temple is the Lord God Almighty and the Lamb...and the kings of the earth shall bring their glory into it, and its gates shall never be shut by day—and there shall be no night there; they shall bring into it the glory and the honor of the nations. (Rv 21:22, 24-25)

7. **Wisdom** was the new law of the Davidic covenant—a law for all mankind.

The New Law makes no distinction between Jews and non-Jews. It is truly and perfectly a Law for all mankind.

There is neither Jew nor Greek, there is neither slave nor free, there is neither male nor female; for you are all one in Christ Jesus. (Gal 3:28)

The epistles of Paul and the other Apostles are the wisdom literature of the new Israel. As with the wisdom literature of the Old Testament, they tell us how to live godly lives in an ungodly world.

Above: *King David Standing Between Wisdom and Prophecy*

The Davidic Covenant: Three Secondary Features

The three secondary features of the Davidic covenant take on a new importance in the life of the Christian Church.

1. The **Queen Mother** became an important part of the royal government.

> **Mary**, Mother of God, takes the role of the Queen Mother in the new Kingdom. As with the Queen Mothers in Judah, she has a position of great influence and power in the royal government.

2. The "**prime minister**" or chief steward became a distinct office in the royal government. The sign of the prime minister's office was the keys of the kingdom. "And I will place on his shoulder the key of the house of David; he shall open, and none shall shut; and he shall shut, and none shall open."[3]

> In Revelation 3:7, Christ calls himself "the holy one, the true one, who has the key of David, who opens and no one shall shut, who shuts and no one opens." Jesus entrusted the keys of the kingdom to

Peter: "I will give you the keys of the kingdom of heaven, and whatever you bind on earth shall be bound in heaven, and whatever you loose on earth shall be loosed in heaven."[4] Peter became Jesus' prime minister; and as with the old Davidic kingdom, the office continues under his successors, the popes.

3. The **thank offering** or "sacrifice of thanksgiving" became the primary liturgy celebrated at Temple, rather than the sin offering. The thank offering was unleavened bread and wine freely offered to God in gratitude for deliverance. Ancient Jewish teachers predicted that, when the Messiah came, no other sacrifice would be offered: the thank offering alone would continue. The word for "thank offering" in Hebrew, *todah*, was often translated by ancient Jewish scholars (like Philo) with the Greek word, "eucharistia," which resonates with the language of Jesus and the early Church.

> The Eucharist is the sacrament of the Church in which the bread and wine become the true Body and blood of Christ, who delivers us from sin and death.

> The Eucharist is the heart and summit of the Church's life, for in it Christ associates his Church and all her members with his sacrifice of praise and thanksgiving offered once and for all on the cross to his Father; by this sacrifice he pours out the graces of salvation on his body which is the Church. (CCC 1407)

Ancient Jewish teachers predicted that, when the Messiah came, no other sacrifice would be offered: the thank offering alone would continue.

SUPPLEMENTARY READING

John Paul II: *Redemptoris missio*

The kingdom of God is meant for all mankind, and all people are called to become members of it. To emphasize this fact, Jesus drew especially near to those on the margins of society, and showed them special favor in announcing the Good News. At the beginning of his ministry he proclaimed that he was "anointed...to preach good news to the poor" (Lk 4:18). To all who are victims of rejection and contempt Jesus declares: "Blessed are you poor" (Lk 6:20). What is more, he enables such individuals to experience liberation even now, by being close to them, going to eat in their homes (cf. Lk 5:30; 15:2), treating them as equals and friends (cf. Lk 7:34), and making them feel loved by God, thus revealing his tender care for the needy and for sinners (cf. Lk 15:1-32).

> The liberation and salvation brought by the kingdom of God come to the human person both in his physical and spiritual dimensions. Two gestures are character-istic of Jesus' mission: healing and forgiving. Jesus' many healings clearly show his great compassion in the face of human distress, but they also signify that in the kingdom there will no longer be sickness or suffering, and that his mission, from the very beginning, is meant to free people from these evils. In Jesus' eyes, healings are also a sign of spiritual salvation, namely liberation from sin. By performing acts of healing, he invites people to faith, conversion and the desire for forgiveness (cf. Lk 5:24). Once there is faith, healing is an encouragement to go further: it leads to salvation (cf. Lk 18: 42-43). The acts of liberation from demonic possession—the supreme evil and symbol of sin and rebellion against God—are signs that indeed "the kingdom of God has come upon you" (Mt 12:28).

15. The kingdom aims at transforming human relationships; it grows gradually as people slowly learn to love, forgive and serve one another. Jesus sums up the whole Law, focusing it on the commandment of love (cf. Mt 22:34-40; Lk 10:25-28). Before leaving his disciples, he gives them a "new com-mandment": "Love one another; even as I have loved you" (Jn 13:34; cf. 15:12). Jesus' love for the world finds its highest expression in the gift of his life for mankind (cf. Jn 15:13), which manifests the love which the Father has for the world (cf. Jn 3:16). The kingdom's nature, therefore, is one of communion among all human beings—with one another and with God.

The kingdom is the concern of everyone: individuals, society, and the world. Working for the kingdom means acknowledging and promoting God's activity, which is present in human history and transforms it. Building the kingdom means working for liberation from evil in all its forms.

Christ Pantocrator and King David, an illuminated initial from the Bible of Charles V of France

VOCABULARY

JOEL

A prophet. He predicted a time when God would pour out his Spirit upon all flesh. St. Peter told the crowds at Pentecost that what was predicted had come to pass.

KEYS OF THE KINGDOM

The power to bind and loose given by Christ to St. Peter and his successors. The badge of office of the prime ministers of the Davidic kingdom.

NEW ISRAEL

The Church, made up of all the faithful people of God. All the promises the prophets made for Israel are fulfilled in the Church.

POPE

The bishop of Rome. The direct successor of St. Peter. The vicar of Christ on earth and visible head of the Church.

SCEPTER

A staff symbolizing royal power.

SYRO-PHOENICIAN

A resident of the area north of Israel; a descendant of the ancient Canaanites.

STUDY QUESTIONS

1. What did Jacob mean when he told his sons the scepter would not depart from Judah?

2. What did Gabrial's words to Mary summarize?

3. What was the most important point Matthew intended to prove?

4. What title is given to Jesus Christ at least eight times in Matthew's Gospel?

5. Why does Matthew stress the importance of this title so much?

6. What point does the story of the Canaanite woman help get across?

7. Who was the first apostle to recognize Jesus as the Messiah?

8. How did Jesus stump the Pharisees regarding the Christ as the Son of David?

9. Where do we find the answer to the question Jesus asked the Pharisees?

10. What is indicated by St. Peter's quotation from Joel?

11. What is the answer to this question?

12. What is the new Israel?

13. List the new meanings to the Davidic covenant.

14. List three other ways the secondary features of the Davidic covenant take on new meaning in the Church.

15. What takes the place of the "sacrifice of thanksgiving" in the new kingdom?

PRACTICAL EXERCISES

1. "There is neither Jew nor Greek, there is neither slave nor free, there is neither male nor female; for you are all one in Christ Jesus" (Gal 3: 28). What is the meaning of this quote? Though the Church teaches that all people "enjoy an equal dignity" (CCC 1934) because of Christ's sacrifice, it also tells us that between men "differences appear tied to age, physical abilities, intellectual or moral aptitudes, the benefits derived from social commerce, and the distribution of wealth (cf. GS 29 § 2). The 'talents' are not distributed equally" (cf. Mt 25: 14-30; Lk 19: 11-27) (CCC 1936). How can these two teachings be reconciled?

2. In spite of our failures God keeps his covenant with us. Are there any permanent covenants today? Give an example. Do you think God forgives those who break permanent covenants?

3. America is a country without a king. The founders believed that submitting to the king's authority infringed on their freedom to rule themselves. Do you think that submitting to the absolute authority Jesus Christ the King makes it difficult for some Americans to accept Christianity?

FROM THE CATECHISM

439 Many Jews and even certain Gentiles who shared their hope recognized in Jesus the fundamental attributes of the messianic "Son of David," promised by God to Israel (cf. Mt 2: 2; 9: 27; 12: 23; 15: 22; 20: 30; 21: 9, 15). Jesus accepted his rightful title of Messiah, though with some reserve because it was understood by some of his contemporaries in too human a sense, as essentially political (cf. Jn 4: 25-26; 6: 15; 11: 27; Mt 22: 41-46; Lk 24: 21).

592 Jesus did not abolish the Law of Sinai, but rather fulfilled it (cf. Mt 5: 17-19) with such perfection (cf. Jn 8: 46) that he revealed its ultimate meaning (cf. Mt 5: 33) and redeemed the transgressions against it (cf. Heb 9: 15).

668 "Christ died and lived again, that he might be Lord both of the dead and of the living" (Rom 14: 9). Christ's Ascension into heaven signifies his participation, in his humanity, in God's power and authority. Jesus Christ is Lord: he possesses all power in heaven and on earth. He is "far above all rule and authority and power and dominion," for the Father "has put all things under his feet" (Eph 1: 20-22). Christ is Lord of the cosmos and of history. In him human history and indeed all creation are "set forth" and transcendently fulfilled (Eph 1: 10; cf. Eph 4: 10; 1 Cor 15: 24, 27-28).

Endnotes

1. Ps 110: 4.
2. Acts 1: 8.
3. Is 22: 22.
4. Mt 16: 19.

Chapter 28
The Catholic Church in Scripture

The New Testament already speaks of bishops, priests, and deacons. The hierarchy of the Church was developed when the Twelve were still alive. They used it to pass down their authority and their traditions, so that the Church would continue on the course Jesus Christ had set for it.

Chapter 28

The Catholic Church in Scripture

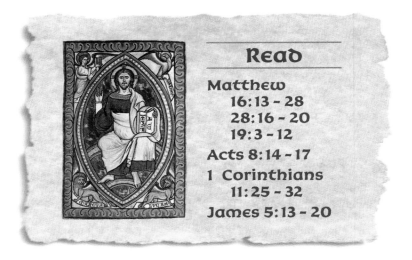

Read

Matthew
   16:13 – 28
   28:16 – 20
   19:3 – 12

Acts 8:14 – 17

1 Corinthians
   11:25 – 32

James 5:13 – 20

A kingdom needs a certain organization, or it will fall apart. The Kingdom of God on earth had to last until the end of time, so Jesus Christ promised to guide and protect it. He also left it with a certain organization that would carry it through even the most difficult periods.

Organization Of The Church

The organization of the Catholic Church is not an invention of the Middle Ages. We can see it already at work in the New Testament, and the roots of it go back to Jesus himself.

When Jesus began his ministry, he chose twelve "apostles"—Greek for "messengers"—to help him spread the Good News. He entrusted his Church to them, and he made Peter their leader. In turn, the Twelve chose others among their followers to help them and continue their mission.

The New Testament already speaks of bishops, priests, and deacons. The hierarchy of the Church was developed when the Twelve were still alive. They used it to pass down their authority and their traditions, so that the Church would continue on the course Jesus Christ had set for it.

The bishops of the Church, as successors of the apostles with the Pope as their head, form a single "college" (CCC 880). They continue to lead the church in an unbroken chain that leads straight back to the Twelve.

> The Lord Jesus endowed his community with a structure that will remain until the Kingdom is fully achieved. Before all else there is the choice of the Twelve with Peter as their head (cf. Mk 3:14-15). Representing the twelve tribes of Israel, they are the foundation stones of the new Jerusalem (cf. Mt 19:28; Lk 22:30; Rv 21:12-14). The Twelve and the other disciples share in Christ's mission and his power, but also in his lot (cf. Mk 6:7; Lk 10:1-2; Mt 10:25; Jn 15:20). By all his actions, Christ prepares and builds his Church. (CCC 765)

The Primacy Of Peter

The head of the apostles was Peter. Jesus himself made Peter their leader when Peter recognized Jesus as the Son of God.

> And Jesus answered him, "Blessed are you, Simon Bar-Jona! For flesh and blood has not revealed this to you, but my Father who is in heaven. And I tell you, you are Peter, and on this rock [*petra* in Greek] I will build my church, and the gates of Hades shall not prevail against it." (Mt 16:17-18) [1]

As soon as Jesus ascended into heaven, Peter began to act as the leader of the Church. The rest of the apostles never questioned his authority, even though before Jesus' death and resurrection they had all been vying for the position of "greatest in the Kingdom of Heaven."

- Peter was the one who decided that the apostles must replace Judas with Matthias.
- Peter was the one who spoke for the apostles at Pentecost.
- Peter was the one who defended the Christians before the Sanhedrin.
- Peter was the one who made the decision against circumcision at the Council of Jerusalem.
- Peter was the one who founded the church in Rome, the capital of the civilized world.

Paul the Apostle accepted wholeheartedly the position of Peter as first of the apostles without any hesitation.

Today, the successor of Peter, the Pope, continues to lead and defend the Church as first among the bishops, the successors of the apostles.

St. Peter's Throne by Bernini in St. Peter's Basilica, the Vatican, Rome

Councils Of The Whole Church

When the Church faced its first important question of doctrine—whether Gentiles must be circumcised—the apostles met in Jerusalem to decide it. There was much debate, but ultimately the decision of the Church was expressed through Peter.

The Church still refers important questions to a council of the whole Church. (The most recent one was the Second Vatican Council in the early 1960s.) Bishops meet and debate the questions before them, and ultimately the decision of the whole Church is expressed through the successor of Peter, the Pope.

The first council of the Church was the Council of Jerusalem, at which the apostles and leaders of the young Church debated the question of circumcision. There was "much debate," Luke tells us in Acts 15:7. All the opinions of all the leaders of the Church were heard. But in the end, it was Peter, the leader, who pronounced the verdict of the whole Church. The decision of the council was written down and sent to the Christians in Antioch, where the question had come up.

Sacraments

Sacraments are efficacious signs of God's grace instituted by Jesus Christ and entrusted to the Church.[2]

> "Adhering to the teaching of the Holy Scriptures, to the apostolic traditions, and to the consensus...of the Fathers," we profess that "the sacraments of the new law were...all instituted by Jesus Christ our Lord." (CCC 1114)

We can find the beginnings of all of them in Scripture, and their significance is ultimately bound up in the Paschal Mystery, that is, Christ's work of redemption accomplished principally by his Passion, death, Resurrection, and glorious Ascension. The Paschal Mystery is celebrated and made present in the liturgy of the Church, and its saving effects are communicated through the sacraments (CCC 1076), especially the Eucharist, which renews the paschal sacrifice of Christ as the sacrifice offered by the Church (CCC 571, 1362-1372). There are seven sacraments:

1. Baptism
2. Confirmation
3. Eucharist
4. Penance (or Reconciliation)
5. Anointing of the Sick
6. Holy Orders
7. Matrimony

Jesus' words and actions during his hidden life and public ministry were already salvific, for they anticipated the power of his Paschal mystery. They announced and prepared what he was going to give the Church when all was accomplished. The mysteries of Christ's life are the foundations of what he would henceforth dispense in the sacraments, through the ministers of his Church, for "what was visible in our Savior has passed over into his mysteries" (St. Leo the Great, Sermo. 74, 2: PL 54, 398). (CCC 1115)

Sacraments are "powers that comes forth" from the Body of Christ (cf. Lk 5:17; 6:19; 8:46), which is ever-living and life-giving. They are actions of the Holy Spirit at work in his Body, the Church. They are "the masterworks of God" in the new and everlasting covenant. (CCC 1116)

Baptism

Baptism is a new birth in water and the Spirit.

> Jesus answered, "Truly, truly, I say to you, unless one is born of water and the Spirit, he cannot enter the kingdom of God." (Jn 3:5)

The Church teaches that baptism is necessary for salvation. Jesus himself commanded his apostles to baptize:

> All authority in heaven and on earth has been given to me. Go therefore and make disciples of all nations, baptizing them in the name of the Father and of the Son and of the Holy Spirit, teaching them to observe all that I have commanded you; and behold, I am with you always, to the close of the age. (Mt 28:18-20)

Normally a priest or deacon performs baptisms. But because baptism is so important, in an emergency any person, even a non-baptized person, with the required intention, can baptize by using the Trinitarian baptismal formula.

Confirmation

The Church has more than one tradition for the sacrament of Confirmation. In the eastern churches, confirmation usually happens at the same time as baptism. The priest administers the sacrament, using oil consecrated by the local bishop or the patriarch. In western churches, Confirmation usually comes later in life, and it is administered by the bishop himself.

We see the same difference in the book of Acts. When the apostles baptized a convert, they laid their hands on the new believer:

> On hearing this, they were baptized in the name of the Lord Jesus. And when Paul had laid his hands upon them, the Holy Spirit came on them; and they spoke with tongues and prophesied. (Acts 19:5-6)

But when the apostles were not present, other believers baptized the converts. Then the apostles confirmed the baptism when they were in the area.

> Now when the apostles at Jerusalem heard that Samaria had received the word of God, they sent to them Peter and John, who came down and prayed for them that they might receive the Holy Spirit; for it had not yet fallen on any of them, but they had only been baptized in the name of the Lord Jesus. Then they laid their hands on them and they received the Holy Spirit. (Acts 8:14-17)

From these two accounts, we can see that confirmation completes baptism. The confirmand receives that out-pouring of the Holy Spirit that happened to the apostles at Pentecost. And it is the apostles — and their successors, the bishops — who are responsible for the administration of this sacrament. Although ordinary priests administer the rite of confirmation in the eastern churches, the link with the apostles is still kept up by the oil specially consecrated by the bishop for confirmations.

> In the first centuries Confirmation generally comprised one single celebration with Baptism, forming with it a "double sacrament," according to the expression of St. Cyprian. Among other reasons, the multiplication of infant baptisms all through the year, the increase of rural parishes, and the growth of dioceses often prevented the bishop from being present at all baptismal celebrations. In the West the desire to reserve the completion of Baptism to the bishop caused the temporal separation of the two sacraments. The East has kept them united, so that Confirmation is conferred by the priest who baptizes. But he can do so only with the "myron" consecrated by a bishop (cf. CCEO, can. 695 § 1; 696 § 1). (CCC 1290)

Eucharist

Jesus instituted the Eucharist at the Last Supper.

> Now as they were eating, Jesus took bread, and blessed, and broke it, and gave it to the disciples and said, "Take, eat; this is my body." And he took a cup, and when he had given thanks he gave it to them, saying, "Drink of it, all of you; for this is my blood of the covenant, which is poured out for many for the forgiveness of sins. I tell you I shall not drink again of the fruit of the vine until that day when I drink it new with you in my Father's kingdom." (Mt 26: 26-29)

The Eucharist is a sacrifice of thanksgiving, in which the sacrifice of Christ on the cross is perpetually re-presented. Christ himself offers the sacrifice; the priests are Christ's ministers through whom all the faithful take part in the Eucharistic sacrifice; "they offer the divine victim to God and offer themselves along with him."[3]

Jesus himself taught that the consecrated bread and wine are really, not just symbolically, his body and blood.

> Truly, truly, I say to you, unless you eat the flesh of the Son of man and drink his blood, you have no life in you; he who eats my flesh and drinks my blood has eternal life, and I will raise him up at the last day. For my flesh is food indeed, and my blood is drink indeed. He who eats my flesh and drinks my blood abides in me, and I in him. As the living Father sent me, and I live because of the Father; so he who eats me will live because of me. This is the bread which came down from heaven, not such as the fathers ate and died; he who eats this bread will live forever. (Jn 6: 53-58)

This doctrine, that the bread and wine change into the true body and blood of Jesus Christ, is called *transubstantiation* — which is a Latin word that simply means the true being of the bread and wine becomes the true being of Jesus Christ, really present on the altar.

Penance

As Christians, we know that we are sinners. Although baptism washes away our sins, it does not make us perfect. We still sin, even after baptism, and we still need forgiveness for those sins.

After he rose from the dead, Jesus spent his remaining time on earth preparing his apostles to lead his Church. Part of that preparation was giving them all his power and authority, holding nothing back — including the authority to forgive sins.

> And when he had said this, he breathed on them, and said to them, "Receive the holy Spirit. If you forgive the sins of any, they are forgiven; if you retain the sins of any, they are retained." (Jn 20: 22-23)

Venial sin harms our relationship with God while mortal sin breaks that communion. The only way to restore that communion when it is broken is through God's forgiveness. And all we have to do to receive that forgiveness is to confess our sins honestly with contrition and ask that they be forgiven.

> Therefore confess your sins to one another, and pray for one another, that you may be healed. (Jas 5: 16)

Because Jesus gave his apostles the authority to forgive and retain sins, the Church uses that power to bring Christians back into a right relationship with God. Only a priest who has received the authority from the Church can pronounce the forgiveness of sins in Christ's name.

Anointing Of The Sick

Is any among you sick? Let him call for the elders of the church, and let them pray over him, anointing him with oil in the name of the Lord; and the prayer of faith will save the sick man, and the Lord will raise him up; and if he has committed sins, he will be forgiven. (Jas 5:14-15)

Jesus Christ left his healing power to his disciples, and anointing with oil was always part of the healing ritual.

And they cast out many demons, and anointed with oil many that were sick and healed them. (Mk 6:13)

The Church continues to exercise that healing power today by anointing the sick through the ministry of a priest. Nevertheless, we must remember that physical healing is not always part of God's plan. Even St. Paul, who was famous for healings and even raised a man from the dead, was not healed when he prayed to be rid of the "thorn" that tormented him. Instead, Christ gave him this answer to his prayers: "My grace is sufficient for you, for my power is made perfect in weakness."[4]

When our prayers for healing seem not to be answered, we should remember that suffering for Christ is a privilege. Through the sacrament of Anointing of the Sick, our sufferings share in the suffering of Jesus on the cross. When we are near death, the sacrament prepares us to face that final struggle with strength and grace.

Holy Orders

Some Christian men are called to dedicate their lives more completely to the service of Christ's Church. The sacrament of Holy Orders consecrates a man for service in the sacramental governing order of the Church.

There are three levels of ordained ministry in the Church: deacon, priest, and bishop.

Bishop comes from a Greek word meaning "supervisor."

Priest comes from a Greek word meaning "elder."

Deacon comes from a Greek word meaning "helper."

The beginnings of all three degrees of service can already be seen in the New Testament.

Stephen, the first Christian martyr, is chosen to be one of the first "deacons."

James, as we just read, advises the sick to "call for the elders of the Church." The word translated "elders" is the word in Greek from which the English "priests" is derived.

In 1 Timothy 3, Paul describes the job of a bishop as caring for God's Church.

In the sacrament of Holy Orders, the bishop lays his hands on the "ordinand" (the person receiving the sacrament) and prays that God will pour out his Holy Spirit, with the gifts of the Spirit that will be needed for the ordinand's ministry. The ordained priest is enabled to act in the person of Christ, the head, shepherd and bridegroom of his Church.

> The sacrament of Holy Orders is conferred by the laying on of hands followed by a solemn prayer of consecration asking God to grant the ordinand the graces of the Holy Spirit required for his ministry. Ordination imprints an indelible sacramental character. (CCC 1597)

Matrimony

> So God created man in his own image, in the image of God he created him; male and female he created them. (Gn 1: 27)

From the beginning of creation, human beings were created male and female. Their mission was to "be fruitful and multiply, and fill the earth."

In the story of Adam and Eve, God brings the animals to Adam one by one, but none of them is a suitable companion. Finally woman is created from the same stuff as man, and Adam recognizes that she is the same as he is: "This at last is bone of my bones and flesh of my flesh..."[5]

Then the sacred author explains:

> Therefore a man leaves his father and mother and cleaves to his wife, and they become one flesh. (Gn 2: 24)

Marriage—the union of a man and a woman—is part of the original creation. And at the other end of the Bible, we find heaven described as a wedding banquet:

> Hallelujah! For the Lord our God the Almighty reigns.
> Let us rejoice and exult and give him the glory,
> for the marriage of the Lamb has come,
> and his Bride has made herself ready...[6]

When Jesus Christ began his ministry, his first public miracle was changing water into wine at a wedding feast. By joining the celebration, Christ showed not only that marriage is good but that he will be present in it.

In marriage, a man and a woman "become one flesh," and that union is meant to be permanent. Although the Law of Moses made provision for divorce, Jesus Christ reminded us that "from the beginning it was not so."

> "By reason of their state in life and of their order, [Christian spouses] have their own special gifts in the People of God" (LG 11 § 2). This grace proper to the sacrament of Matrimony is intended to perfect the couple's love and to strengthen their indissoluble unity. By this grace they "help one another to attain holiness in their married life and in welcoming and educating their children" (LG 11 § 2; cf. LG 41). (CCC 1641)

> *Christ is the source of this grace.* "Just as of old God encountered his people with a covenant of love and fidelity, so our Savior, the spouse of the Church, now encounters Christian spouses through the sacrament of Matrimony" (GS 48 § 2). Christ dwells with them, gives them the strength to take up their crosses and so follow him, to rise again after they have fallen, to forgive one another, to bear one another's burdens, to "be subject to one another out of reverence for Christ" (Eph 5: 21; cf. Gal 6: 2), and to love one another with supernatural, tender, and fruitful love. In the joys of their love and family life he gives them here on earth a foretaste of the wedding feast of the Lamb:

> > How can I ever express the happiness of a marriage joined by the Church, strengthened by an offering, sealed by a blessing, announced by angels, and ratified by the Father?...How wonderful the bond between two believers, now one in hope, one in desire, one in discipline, one in the same service! They are both children of one Father and servants of the same Master, undivided in spirit and flesh, truly two in one flesh. Where the flesh is one, one also is the spirit.[7] (CCC 1642)

SUPPLEMENTARY READING

Tertullian: *Prescription Against Heresies*

Chapter 21: All Doctrine True Which Comes Through the Church from the Apostles, Who Were Taught by God Through Christ. All Opinion Which Has No Such Divine Origin and Apostolic Tradition to Show, Is Ipso Facto False.

From this, therefore, do we draw up our rule. Since the Lord Jesus Christ sent the apostles to preach, (our rule is) that no others ought to be received as preachers than those whom Christ appointed; for "no man knoweth the Father save the Son, and he to whomsoever the Son will reveal Him." Nor does the Son seem to have revealed Him to any other than the apostles, whom He sent forth to preach — that, of course, which He revealed to them. Now, what that was which they preached — in other words, what it was which Christ revealed to them — can, as I must here likewise prescribe, properly be proved in no other way than by those very churches which the apostles rounded in person, by declaring the gospel to them directly themselves, both *viva voce*, as the phrase is, and subsequently by their epistles. If, then, these things are so, it is in the same degree manifest that all doctrine which agrees with the apostolic churches — those moulds and original sources of the faith must be reckoned for truth, as undoubtedly containing that which the (said) churches received from the apostles, the apostles from Christ, Christ from God. Whereas all doctrine must be prejudged as false which savors of contrariety to the truth of the churches and apostles of Christ and God. It remains, then, that we demonstrate whether this doctrine of ours, of which we have now given the rule, has its origin in the tradition of the apostles, and whether all other *doctrines* do not *ipso facto* proceed from falsehood. We hold communion with the apostolic churches because our doctrine is in no respect different *from theirs*. This is our witness of truth.

Tertullian, *On Baptism*, ch. 8:

For just as, after the waters of the deluge, by which the old iniquity was purged — after the baptism, so to say, of the world — a *dove* was the herald which announced to the earth the assuagement of celestial wrath, when she had been sent her way out of the ark, and had returned with the olive-branch, a sign which even among the nations is the fore-token of *peace;* so by the self-same law of heavenly effect, to earth — that is, to our flesh — as it emerges from the font, after its old sins flies the *dove* of the Holy Spirit, bringing us the peace of God, sent out from the heavens where is the Church, the typified ark.

In marriage, a man and a woman "become one flesh," and that union is meant to be permanent.

VOCABULARY

ANOINTING OF THE SICK

One of the seven sacraments. It heals and forgives sins.

BAPTISM

One of the seven sacraments. It washed away the guilt associated with Original Sin.

CONFIRMATION

One of the seven sacraments. It conveys the outpouring of the Holy Spirit that was given to the apostles at Pentecost.

COUNCIL

A meeting of Church leaders. The Council of Jerusalem described in Acts is the Scriptural prototype of a council of the whole Church. The most recent ecumenical council was the Second Vatican Council.

DEACON

A man who is ordained to assist the mission of the Church. From the Greek for "helper."

EUCHARIST

One of the seven sacraments. It is the body, blood, soul, and divinity of Jesus Christ.

HOLY ORDERS

One of the seven sacraments. It ordains a man to a life of serving the Church.

MARRIAGE.

See Matrimony.

MATRIMONY

One of the seven sacraments. It binds a man and woman in a lifelong covenant.

MIDDLE AGES

In the West, the period between the end of the Roman Empire and the beginning of the Renaissance. The Church was frequently the only force that preserved order.

PASCHAL MYSTERY

Christ's work of redemption accomplished principally by his Passion, death, Resurrection, and glorious Ascension, whereby, "dying he destroyed our death, rising he restored our life" (CCC 1067; cf. 654). The Paschal Mystery is celebrated and made present in the liturgy of the Church, and its saving effects are communicated through the sacraments, especially the Eucharist, which renews the paschal sacrifice of Christ as the sacrifice offered by the Church (CCC 571, 1362-1372).

PRIMACY

The highest rank. The Acts of the Apostles shows the "primacy" of St. Peter, that is, it shows he had the highest rank among the apostles.

RECONCILIATION

One of the seven sacraments. It forgives the guilt associated with sins.

SACRAMENT

An outward sign instituted by Jesus Christ to confer the grace indicated by the sign.

Through the sacrament of Anointing of the Sick, our sufferings share in the suffering of Jesus on the cross.

STUDY QUESTIONS

1. Who is at the roots of the Church's organization?

2. When was the Hierarchy of the Church developed?

3. Whom do the twelve apostles represent?

4. When did Christ make St. Peter the head of the apostles?

5. When did St. Peter begin to act as leader of the Church?

6. What does the word "apostle" mean?

7. What is the purpose of Church Councils?

8. What was the first council of the whole Church?

9. What is a sacrament?

10. Who instituted the sacraments?

11. Name the seven sacraments.

12. What sacrament does Confirmation complete?

13. What does the confirmand receive?

14. Who offers the sacrifice of the Eucharist?

15. What is *transubstantiation*?

16. Where does the Sacrament of the Anointing of the Sick have its roots?

17. Name the three levels of ordained ministry in the Church.

18. How is marriage a part of the original creation?

19. What is the union of marriage?

20. What is the special gift of Matrimony?

PRACTICAL EXERCISES

1. "In this sacrament, the sinner, placing himself before the merciful judgment of God, *anticipates* in a certain way the *judgment* to which he will be subjected at the end of his earthly life. For it is now, in this life, that we are offered the choice between life and death, and it is only by the road of conversion that we can enter the Kingdom, from which one is excluded by grave sin" (cf. 1 Cor 5:11; Gal 5:19-21; Rv 22:15) (CCC 1470).
This quote is referring to the sacrament of Penance. What main point is the quote trying to get across? How are we to stay on the road of conversion?

2. Scripture teaches us that the sacrament of Confirmation brings the gifts of the Holy Spirit, just as the Spirit came to the apostles at Pentecost. If you have been confirmed, what have you done with those gifts since your Confirmation? If you haven't been confirmed yet, how have you used the gifts God has given you to prepare yourself for Confirmation and your life of service to him?

3. There are people who do not believe in *transubstantiation*. If challenged, how would you defend your belief in the complete and true Divine Presence in the Eucharist, instead of only symbolic body and blood?

FROM THE CATECHISM

552 Simon Peter holds the first place in the college of the Twelve (cf. Mk 3:16; 9:2; Lk 24:34; 1 Cor 15:5); Jesus entrusted a unique mission to him. Through a revelation from the Father, Peter had confessed: "You are the Christ, the Son of the living God." Our Lord then declared to him: "You are Peter, and on this rock I will build my Church, and the gates of Hades will not prevail against it" (Mt 16:18). Christ, the "living Stone" (1 Pt 2:4), thus assures his Church, built on Peter, of victory over the powers of death. Because of the faith he confessed Peter will remain the unshakable rock of the Church. His mission will be to keep this faith from every lapse and to strengthen his brothers in it (cf. Lk 22:32).

756 "Often, too, the Church is called the *building* of God. The Lord compared himself to the stone which the builders rejected, but which was made into the cornerstone. On this foundation the Church is built by the apostles and from it the Church receives solidity and unity. This edifice has many names to describe it: the house of God in which his *family* dwells; the household of God in the Spirit; the dwelling-place of God among men; and, especially, the holy *temple*. This temple, symbolized in places of worship built out of stone, is praised by the Fathers and, not without reason, is compared in the liturgy to the Holy City, the New Jerusalem. As living stones we here on earth are built into it. It is this holy city that is seen by John as it comes down out of heaven from God when the world is made anew, prepared like a bride adorned for her husband" (LG 6; cf. 1 Cor 3:9; Mt 21:42 and parallels; Acts 4:11; 1 Pt 2:7; Ps 118:22; 1 Cor 3:11; 1 Tm 3:15; Eph 2:19-22; Rv 21:3; 1 Pt 2:5; Rv 21:1-2).

769 "The Church…will receive its perfection only in the glory of heaven," (LG 48) at the time of Christ's glorious return. Until that day, "the Church progresses on her pilgrimage amidst this world's persecutions and God's consolations" (St. Augustine, *De civ. Dei*, 18, 51: PL 41, 614; cf. LG 8). Here below she knows that she is in exile far from the Lord, and longs for the full coming of the Kingdom, when she will "be united in glory with her king" (LG 5; cf. 6; 2 Cor 5:6). The Church, and through her the world, will not be perfected in glory without great trials. Only then will "all the just from the time of Adam, 'from Abel, the just one, to the last of the elect,'… be gathered together in the universal Church in the Father's presence" (LG 2).

816 "The sole Church of Christ [is that] which our Savior, after his Resurrection, entrusted to Peter's pastoral care, commissioning him and the other apostles to extend and rule it….This Church, constituted and organized as a society in the present world, subsists in (*subsistit in*) the Catholic Church, which is governed by the successor of Peter and by the bishops in communion with him" (LG 8 § 2).

> The Second Vatican Council's *Decree on Ecumenism* explains: "For it is through Christ's Catholic Church alone, which is the universal help toward salvation, that the fullness of the means of salvation can be obtained. It was to the apostolic college alone, of which Peter is the head, that we believe that our Lord entrusted all the blessings of the New Covenant, in order to establish on earth the one Body of Christ into which all those should be fully incorporated who belong in any way to the People of God" (*Unitatis redintegratio* 3 § 55).

819 "Furthermore, many elements of sanctification and of truth" (LG 8 § 2) are found outside the visible confines of the Catholic Church: "the written Word of God; the life of grace; faith, hope, and charity, with the other interior gifts of the Holy Spirit, as well as visible elements" (*Unitatis redintegratio* 3 § 2; cf. LG 15). Christ's Spirit uses these Churches and ecclesial communities as means of salvation, whose power derives from the fullness of grace and truth that Christ has entrusted to the Catholic Church. All these

FROM THE CATECHISM continued

blessings come from Christ and lead to him, (cf. *Unitatis redintegratio* 3) and are in themselves calls to "Catholic unity" (cf. LG 8).

1076 The Church was made manifest to the world on the day of Pentecost by the outpouring of the Holy Spirit. The gift of the Spirit ushers in a new era in the "dispensation of the mystery" the age of the Church, during which Christ manifests, makes present, and communicates his work of salvation through the liturgy of his Church, "until he comes" (1 Cor 11:26). In this age of the Church Christ now lives and acts in and with his Church, in a new way appropriate to this new age. He acts through the sacraments in what the common Tradition of the East and the West calls "the sacramental economy"; this is the communication (or "dispensation") of the fruits of Christ's Paschal mystery in the celebration of the Church's "sacramental" liturgy.

1084 "Seated at the right hand of the Father" and pouring out the Holy Spirit on his Body which is the Church, Christ now acts through the sacraments he instituted to communicate his grace. The sacraments are perceptible signs (words and actions) accessible to our human nature. By the action of Christ and the power of the Holy Spirit they make present efficaciously the grace that they signify.

1088 "To accomplish so great a work"—the dispensation or communication of his work of salvation—"Christ is always present in his Church, especially in her liturgical celebrations. He is present in the Sacrifice of the Mass not only in the person of his minister, 'the same now offering, through the ministry of priests, who formerly offered himself on the cross,' but especially in the Eucharistic species. By his power he is present in the sacraments so that when anybody baptizes, it is really Christ himself who baptizes. He is present in his word since it is he himself who speaks when the holy Scriptures are read in the Church. Lastly, he is present when the Church prays and sings, for he has promised 'where two or three are gathered together in my name there am I in the midst of them'" (*Sacrosanctum Concilium* 7; Mt 18:20).

The Baptism of St. Francis

Endnotes

1. For this illustration, we have used the literal rendering "the gates of Hades," given in a footnote in the Revised Standard Version.

2. Glossary in the *Catechism of the Catholic Church.*
3. LG 11.
4. 2 Cor 12:9.

5. Gn 2:23.
6. Rv 19:6-7.
7. Tertullian, *Ad uxorem.* 2, 8, 6-7: PL 1, 1412-1413; cf. FC 13.

The End of History

"'Fear not, I am the first and the last, and the living one. I died, and behold I am alive for evermore, and I have the keys of Death and Hades. Now write what you see, what is and what is to take place hereafter.'"

Revelation 1: 17–19

Chapter 29

The End of History

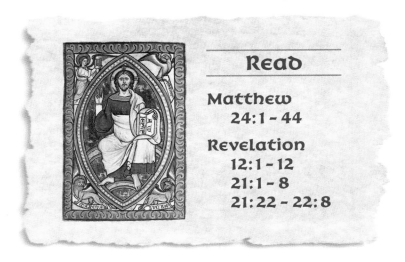

Read

Matthew
24:1 - 44

Revelation
12:1 - 12
21:1 - 8
21:22 - 22:8

In all the books of the New Testament, it often seems that the earliest Christians were expecting the end of the world to come very soon—within their own lifetimes, in fact.

What Jesus Taught About The End Of History

"Truly, I say to you, there are some standing here who will not taste death before they see the Son of man coming in his kingdom," Jesus says in Matthew 16:28. And later, in the middle of a long discourse on the "tribulation" to come, Jesus tells his disciples, "Truly, I say to you, this generation will not pass away till all these things take place."[1]

As it turned out, the earliest Christians were right. The earth itself was not destroyed entirely, but the whole world of the Old Covenant came to a sudden and catastrophic end.

60 A.D.	70 A.D.	80 A.D.	90 A.D.	100 A.D.
63-64 Peter is crucified upside down by Nero	69 Gospel of Mark is written	75 Letter to the Hebrews is written	85-90 Gospels of Matthew and Luke, and Acts are written	90-95 Gospel of John is completed	95 John is exiled to Patmos; writes his revelations

66 Jewish revolt against Roman Procurator Florus' sadistic tyranny is sparked in Caesarea and spreads quickly throughout Judea

73 Jewish defenders of the fortress of Masada commit suicide rather than surrender to the Roman Legions

Rome: 54-68 Nero is Emperor
68 Nero commits suicide
69-79 Vespasian is Emperor
79-81 Titus is Emperor
80 The Colosseum is dedicated by Titus
81-96 Domitian is Emperor
98-117 Trajan is Emperor

93 Josephus writes "Jewish Antiquities" which chronicles Biblical and post-Biblical Jewish events and history

70 Romans led by Titus sack and burn Jerusalem

95 The "Didache" is written; a guide to church order

But because God's promises are often fulfilled in ever-increasing ways throughout history, we can also see the end of the world of the Old Covenant as a preview of the end of our world. For Christians, the end of the world is a promise, not a threat. For the persecutors and the unjust, and for all who look for their reward in this world, the end of the world is a terrible prospect. But Christians look forward to the return of the glorious Christ who will come at the end of time to judge the living and the dead. Then, he will reveal the secret disposition of hearts and will render to each man according to his works and according to his acceptance or refusal of grace. It will be the time of the new heaven and the new earth, where pain and trouble will be no more, and where we will all live in eternal joy with God the Father and our brother Jesus Christ.

Some Christians suppose that they can use the Revelation to John and other prophecies to predict exactly the course of future earthly events. People who think they can tell when the world will end or what will happen in the course of human history tread on very dangerous ground.

> The Antichrist's deception already begins to take shape in the world every time the claim is made to realize within history that messianic hope which can only be realized beyond history through the eschatological judgment. The Church has rejected even modified forms of this falsification of the kingdom to come under the name of millenarianism (cf. DS 3839), especially the "intrinsically perverse" political form of a secular messianism (Pius XI, *Divini Redemptoris*, condemning the "false mysticism" of this "counterfeit of the redemption of the lowly"; cf. GS 20-21). (CCC 676)

The book of Revelation is full of strange visions and symbols, and at first glance it seems hard to understand. But a few keys will open it up. And the first of those keys is an understanding of the historical setting of Revelation.

The End Of The Old Covenant

- **A Judean revolt against Rome led to civil war.**
- **The Christians of Jerusalem fled to the mountains and were saved.**
- **Jerusalem fell in 70 A.D., and the Temple was destroyed.**
- **With the Temple went the whole world of the Old Covenant.**

The end of the world began in 67 A.D., when the mad emperor Nero sent a wicked wastrel named Florus to be governor of Judea. Florus celebrated the beginning of his term by massacring hundreds of innocent people in Jerusalem. Soon the province was on the verge of open revolt.

Florus believed that floggings and massacres were the way to keep order. Some people began to suspect that Florus was deliberately trying to provoke a revolt. Whether he wanted it or not, Florus soon had a revolt on his hands—a revolt with all the horrors of a civil war. Judean fanatics murdered anyone suspected of collaborating with the Romans. The Romans retaliated by murdering anyone suspected of being a Judean fanatic. The cities were filled with dead bodies.

For a while, the Judean side had the upper hand. They managed to defeat the Romans in important battles. So the Romans sent Vespasian, their best general, to put down the Jewish revolt. He was remarkably successful; but before he could finish the job, Nero had committed suicide. Vespasian was proclaimed Emperor by the army, and he had to run back to Rome. He left the Judean problem in the hands of his son Titus.

Meanwhile, the early Christian community in Jerusalem had remembered Jesus' advice: "So when you see the desolating sacrilege spoken of by the prophet Daniel, standing in the holy place...then let those who are in Judea flee to the mountains."[2] (Daniel's prophecy warns that "Forces from him

The Sack of the Temple of Jerusalem by Titus' Troops by Poussin

shall appear and profane the temple and fortress, and shall take away the continual burnt offering. And they shall set up the abomination that makes desolate."³) Early historians also say that the leaders of the Church in Jerusalem had been warned by the Holy Spirit to leave the city. So the Christians of Jerusalem moved to a little town called Pella, in the mountains across the Jordan, before the war began. From there they could watch the end of the world.

When the Romans eventually besieged Jerusalem, the people there suffered horrors we can hardly imagine. Jerusalem was already a crowded city. Now it was jammed with many times its normal population, as refugees fled into the city for protection from the Romans. They were all starving, killing each other for scraps of food, and even resorting to cannibalism. They died by the thousands every day; there were too many to bury. Titus, himself, seeing the mounds of corpses thrown into the valleys outside the city, was horrified, and called his gods to witness that he was not to blame.

At last the city was taken in the year 70. More than a million Judeans had died in battle or in the famine. Most of the rest were sold as slaves or thrown to the lions in the arena. It was the worst disaster that had ever happened to Jerusalem, a city that was used to disasters. The whole city was destroyed—all but a few straggly houses and the little building where the Upper Room was, the room where Jesus had celebrated the Last Supper.

But what made the destruction of Jerusalem the end of the world was this: the Temple, the architectural sign of the Old Covenant, was destroyed, never to be rebuilt—just as Jesus had predicted. The world of the Old Covenant was gone.

All that happened when many of Jesus' original followers were still alive. They must have remembered what Jesus had told them: "Truly, I say to you, this generation will not pass away till all these things take place. Heaven and earth will pass away, but my words will not pass away."⁴

In the Greek, the word "generation" refers to a period of about forty years. The destruction of Jerusalem and the Temple happened almost exactly forty years after Jesus' prediction.

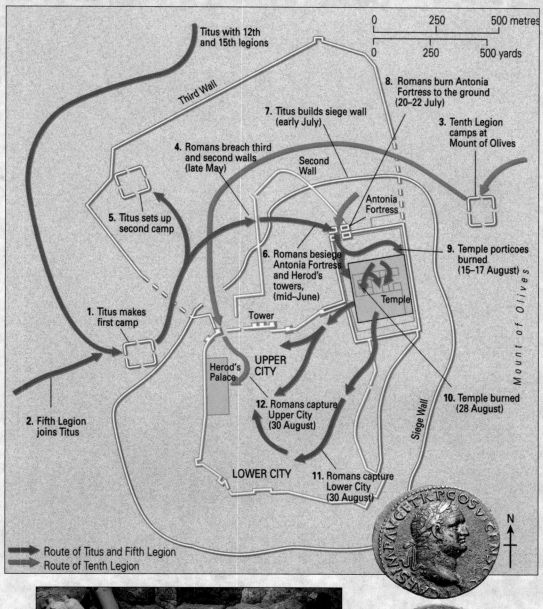

The Siege of Jerusalem 70 A.D.

Titus with 12th and 15th legions

Third Wall

8. Romans burn Antonia Fortress to the ground (20–22 July)

7. Titus builds siege wall (early July)

3. Tenth Legion camps at Mount of Olives

4. Romans breach third and second walls (late May)

Second Wall

5. Titus sets up second camp

Antonia Fortress

6. Romans besiege Antonia Fortress and Herod's towers, (mid-June)

9. Temple porticoes burned (15–17 August)

Temple

1. Titus makes first camp

Tower

2. Fifth Legion joins Titus

Herod's Palace

UPPER CITY

12. Romans capture Upper City (30 August)

10. Temple burned (28 August)

Siege Wall

Mount of Olives

LOWER CITY

11. Romans capture Lower City (30 August)

N

0   250   500 metres
0   250   500 yards

→ Route of Titus and Fifth Legion
→ Route of Tenth Legion

"The Burnt House" is a seven room residence excavated by archaeologists in Jerusalem. Burned to the ground in 70 A.D. by the Romans, this house belonged to a member of the priestly caste.

"JUDAEA CAPTA"
This coin, minted in 77 A.D., commemorates Titus' destruction of Jerusalem. One side shows Titus as Caesar and the reverse shows a female slave with the words "Captive Judea."

507

Apostle John was banished to the island of Patmos by Emperor Domitian in 95 A.D. On this island, John wrote the last book of the New Testament.

The Vision Of The Heavenly Liturgy

- **The Mass is literally heaven on earth.**
- **The book of Revelation follows the pattern of the Mass.**

The second key that opens up Revelation for us is the Mass, or the Divine Liturgy as Eastern Christians call it. John's vision is a vision of the heavenly liturgy, and the liturgy we celebrate here on earth is part of that heavenly liturgy.

> Liturgy is an "action" of the *whole Christ (Christus totus)*. Those who even now celebrate it without signs are already in the heavenly liturgy, where celebration is wholly communion and feast. (CCC 1136)

John describes the heavenly liturgy in terms of things we can see, hear, smell, feel, and taste. Until we reach heaven ourselves, the real truth of the heavenly liturgy is far beyond our comprehension. But John's vision and the liturgy we celebrate in church both give us a way of understanding it in terms of things we already know.

The structure of Revelation is very much like the structure of the Mass we celebrate in church.

There are two parts to our Mass. The first part, called the Liturgy of the Word, includes the Scripture readings and the homily. The second part, the Eucharist, is where we receive the Body and Blood of Christ. That division comes from the earliest tradition of the Christian Church.

In the same way, Revelation falls into two parts, with the division almost exactly in the middle:

Revelation 1: 1 to 11: 18: **Readings of letters to the seven churches (a call to repentance).** **The scroll sealed with seven seals.**	**The Liturgy of the Word**
Revelation 11: 19 to 22: 21: **Pouring out of the chalices.** **The marriage supper of the Lamb.**	**The Eucharist**

In other words, the whole book itself is like a Mass, and everything that happens in it—even the destruction, the plagues, and the battles—is somehow part of the liturgy.

> The *Revelation* of "what must soon take place," the *Apocalypse*, is borne along by the songs of the heavenly liturgy (cf. Rv 4:8-11; 5:9-14; 7:10-12) but also by the intercession of the "witnesses" (martyrs) (Rv 6:10). The prophets and the saints, all those who were slain on earth for their witness to Jesus, the vast throng of those who, having come through the great tribulation, have gone before us into the Kingdom, all sing the praise and glory of him who sits on the throne, and of the Lamb (cf. Rv 18:24; 19:1-8). In communion with them, the Church on earth also sings these songs with faith in the midst of trial. By means of petition and intercession, faith hopes against all hope and gives thanks to the "Father of lights," from whom "every perfect gift" comes down (Jas 1:17). Thus faith is pure praise. (CCC 2642)

The Liturgy Of The Word

Revelation begins with a vision of heaven. "I was in the Spirit on the Lord's day," John says, "and I heard behind me a loud voice like a trumpet saying, 'Write what you see in a book and send it to the seven churches,…'"[5] The Lord's day is Sunday. John saw his vision on the day when Christians everywhere were celebrating the Divine Liturgy.

> Then I turned to see the voice that was speaking to me, and on turning I saw seven golden lampstands, and in the midst of the lampstands one like a son of man, clothed with a long robe and with a golden girdle round his breast; his head and his hair were white as white wool, white as snow; his eyes were like a flame of fire, his feet were like burnished bronze, refined as in a furnace, and his voice was like the sound of many waters; in his right hand he held seven stars, from his mouth issued a sharp two-edged sword, and his face was like the sun shining in full strength. (Rv 1:12-16)

"One like a son of man" means one who looked human, but "Son of man" was also the way Christ had always referred to himself during his ministry. It echoes Daniel 7:13-14, in which "one like a son of man" is given power to rule all the nations forever. As the figure himself explained, this is Jesus Christ in his heavenly glory.

John's vision was terrifying, and we aren't surprised at his reaction: "When I saw him, I fell at his feet as though dead." But the man in the vision told John not to be afraid:

> Fear not, I am the first and the last, and the living one; I died, and behold I am alive for evermore, and I have the keys of Death and Hades. Now write what you see, what is and what is to take place hereafter. As for the mystery of the seven stars which you saw in my right hand, and the seven golden lampstands, the seven stars are the angels of the seven churches and the seven lampstands are the seven churches. (Rv 1:17-20)

Then Christ dictated seven letters, one to each of the seven churches. The letters reflect what was going on in those churches at the time. But seven is also a symbolically complete number—the most important number in Revelation, especially, where almost everything seems to come in sevens. So the letters must also be addressed to the whole Church. They call the churches to turn back to Christ, and promise that heaven will protect all the faithful who repent.

So this whole first section is a call to repentance, very much like the Penitential Rite that begins our Mass. It ends with one of the best-known images of Christ:

> Behold, I stand at the door and knock; if any one hears my voice and opens the door, I will come in to him and eat with him, and he with me. (Rv 3:20)

"Then I turned to see the voice that was speaking to me, and on turning I saw seven golden lampstands, and in the midst of the lampstands one like a son of man,…"
(Rv 1: 12–13)

Jesus Christ comes to every one of us. But we have to open the door for him ourselves.

With that preparation, John is ready for the next part of his vision.

> After this I looked, and lo, in heaven an open door! And the first voice, which I had heard speaking to me like a trumpet, said, "Come up hither, and I will show you what must take place after this." (Rv 4:1)

Now John sees a vision of heaven, and God is enthroned with all the heavenly beings forever worshiping him. Every detail would have reminded the original hearers of the Temple in Jerusalem. The words they sing sound very familiar to anyone who goes to Mass regularly:

> Holy, holy, holy, is the Lord God Almighty,
> who was and is and is to come! (Rv 4:8)

> Worthy art thou, our Lord and God,
> to receive glory and honor and power,
> for thou didst create all things,
> and by thy will they existed and were created. (Rv 4:11)

Next John sees a scroll sealed with seven seals. No one on earth or in heaven is able to open the scroll, but then John hears that the Lion of Judah (a symbol of Christ) has been found worthy to open it. But instead of a lion, what he sees is a lamb—a lamb that appears to have been slaughtered for a sacrifice. Yet the scroll is given to the lamb. Somehow the Lion of Judah is a lamb! The heavenly host sings words that once again sound very familiar:

> Worthy is the Lamb who was slain, to receive power and wealth and wisdom and might
> and honor and glory and blessing! (Rv 5:12)

Now the Lamb begins to open the seven seals on the scroll. With the opening of the first come four riders on four horses. The first one rides out to conquer; the other three bring war, famine, and death. These are the things the people of Judea suffered in the Jewish War, as the revolt against Rome was called.

As each of the remaining seals is opened, frightening portents appear in earth and heaven. The people of the earth hide in the caves and mountains and tremble.

But God will not leave his people unprotected. Before any harm can come to the earth, all the true people of God—a perfect 12,000 from each of the scattered tribes of Israel—will be marked on their foreheads with the seal of the servants of God. The vision recalls Ezekiel 9, in which Ezekiel is prophesying the destruction of Jerusalem.

> And the LORD said to him, "Go through the city, through Jerusalem, and put a mark on the foreheads of the men who sigh and groan over all the abominations that are committed in it." (Ez 9:4)

Those people with the mark on their foreheads would be saved when destruction came to Jerusalem. The word translated "mark" is the Hebrew word *tau*, a letter of the Hebrew alphabet which is shaped like a cross. When Christians are baptized, they receive the mark of the cross on their foreheads.

In the historic context of Revelation, those 144,000 are the Jewish Christians who fled to the mountains across the Jordan. The comforting message John has for them is that, no matter how many disasters befall Judea, they will not be harmed. The message is also for us: the perfect number 144,000 means that not one of us has been left out. All the faithful baptized Christians will be saved.

Finally, the seventh seal is broken, and there is silence in heaven. Then seven angels blow seven trumpets, and with each of the first six trumpets another plague is released over the earth. The plagues recall the plagues that Egypt suffered before the Exodus. And just like Pharaoh, the wicked people who have suffered the plagues refuse to repent.

The ruins of Pella. Christians fled to this small town and escaped the Roman massacre in Jerusalem.

All this emphasis on the scrolls must remind us of the Liturgy of the Word in which the Word of God is proclaimed to the people, even though the first half of Revelation is filled with plagues. After the last of the plagues, an angel declares, "The kingdom of the world has become the kingdom of our Lord and of his Christ, and he shall reign for ever and ever."

The Heavenly Eucharist

> Then God's temple in heaven was opened, and the ark of his covenant was seen within his temple; and there were flashes of lightning, voices, peals of thunder, an earthquake, and heavy hail. (Rv 11:19)

It is hard for us to imagine how shocking this vision—right in the middle of the book—must have been to the people who first heard it. The Ark of the Covenant appeared! It had been missing since the exile, and everyone knew that it would not reappear until all Israel was gathered together again.

> It was also in the writing that the prophet [Jeremiah], having received an oracle, ordered that the tent and the ark should follow with him, and that he went out to the mountain where Moses had gone up and had seen the inheritance of God. And Jeremiah came and found a cave, and he brought there the tent and the ark and the altar of incense, and he sealed up the entrance. Some of those who followed him came up to mark the way, but could not find it. When Jeremiah learned of it, he rebuked them and declared: "The place shall be unknown until God gathers his people together again and shows his mercy. And then the Lord will disclose these things, and the glory of the Lord and the cloud will appear, as they were shown in the case of Moses, and as Solomon asked that the place should be specially consecrated." (2 Mc 2:4-8)

Here it was in John's vision: the Ark of the Covenant, and "the glory of the Lord and the cloud." From that we should know instantly that this is the time when "God gathers his people together again and shows his mercy."

The appearance of the Ark, then, would have grabbed the attention of John's audience and filled their minds with visions of the lost Ark of the Covenant. Then immediately we hear:

> And a great portent appeared in heaven, a woman clothed with the sun, with the moon under her feet, and on her head a crown of twelve stars; she was with child and she cried out in her pangs of birth, in anguish for delivery. (Rv 12:1-2)

We were expecting—almost begging for—more about the Ark of the Covenant. But instead we get a "woman clothed with the sun."

> And another portent appeared in heaven: behold a great red dragon, with seven heads and ten horns, and seven diadems upon his heads. His tail swept down a third of the stars of heaven, and cast them to the earth. And the dragon stood before the woman who was about to bear a child, that he might devour her child when she brought it forth; she brought forth a male child, one who is to rule all the nations with a rod of iron, but her child was caught up to God and to his throne, and the woman fled into the wilderness, where she has a place prepared by God, in which to be nourished for one thousand two hundred and sixty days. (Rv 12: 3-6)

The woman's child will rule the nations, and he is taken up to the throne of God. The "rod of iron" comes from Psalm 2: 9, one of the psalms most often quoted as a prophecy of the Messiah.

> I will tell of the decree of the LORD:
> He said to me, "You are my son,
>   today I have begotten you.
> Ask of me, and I will make the nations your heritage,
>   and the ends of the earth your possession.
> You shall break them with a rod of iron,
>   and dash them in pieces like a potter's vessel."
> (Ps 2: 7-9)

The child is the Messiah, the Christ, the Anointed One. If the child is Christ, then his mother must be Mary. But the crown of twelve stars also identifies her as something more. There are twelve tribes of Israel, and twelve apostles to rule them. The woman is the Church—that is, God's faithful people throughout history, from whom the Christ came under the Old Covenant, and whom God protects in the wilderness of Pella under the New Covenant.

"Now war arose in heaven, Michael and his angels fighting against the dragon; and the dragon and his angels fought, but they were defeated..." (Rv 12: 7-8)

But what happened to the Ark of the Covenant? Why isn't John saying more about it?

The Ark of the Covenant contained the Word of God on stone—the law given to Moses on Sinai. Christ is the Word of God in flesh, as we know from the beginning of John's Gospel. The Ark of the Covenant also contained some of the bread from heaven, the manna, that kept the Israelites alive in the wilderness. Christ is the Bread of Life. Finally, the ark held Aaron's rod. Christ rules the nations with a rod of iron.

The Word, the bread, the rod: those are the things that the Ark holds. In other words, the woman who bore the Christ is herself the Ark of the Covenant! That's why John doesn't mention the Ark again: he's showing us the Ark personified. John has come to the same conclusion Luke did at the beginning of his Gospel. Mary is the Ark of the New Covenant.

But the woman here, who represents Mary, also represents the faithful people of God throughout the ages, the Church before and after the Incarnation. The Church—the faithful of Israel—brings forth the Christ, and then Christ protects her from harm. The Church is also the Ark of the New Covenant. The woman is attacked by a dragon, but the woman is protected in the wilderness—just as the early Church in Jerusalem was protected in the wilderness while the world of the Old Covenant was being destroyed. The Dragon represents Satan.

What we are witnessing is the undoing of sin itself. The serpent—that horrible ancient dragon—tempted Eve and Adam, and they were conquered by temptation. But the woman and her son—the new Eve and the new Adam—overcome the dragon. Adam and Eve were formed without sin; the woman and her son also were formed without sin. Sin attacked humanity through the woman; sin is overcome through the woman's consent. Adam and Eve brought a curse on all humanity; the new Adam and the new Eve bring a blessing on all humanity. The woman's child is the promised seed who would at last crush the serpent's head.

The Beasts

> And I saw a beast rising out of the sea, with ten horns and seven heads, with ten diadems upon its horns and a blasphemous name upon its heads....One of its heads seemed to have a mortal wound, but its mortal wound was healed, and the whole earth followed the beast with wonder. (Rv 13:1, 3)

The horns are symbols of power, and the diadems are symbols of royal authority. The beast would have reminded John's first readers of the Roman Empire, or of the dynasty of Herods who infested Palestine. But it also represents any corrupt government, persecuting the followers of the Word.

The people of the earth worship the beast, or the dragon (Satan) who gives the beast his power—just as people do today when they decide to compromise their faith to get on the government's good side.

The second beast is even more disturbing.

> Then I saw another beast which rose out of the earth; it had two horns like a lamb and it spoke like a dragon. It exercises all the authority of the first beast in its presence, and makes the earth and its inhabitants worship the first beast, whose mortal wound was healed. It works great signs, even making fire come down from heaven to earth in the sight of men...This calls for wisdom: let him who has understanding reckon the number of the beast, for it is a human number, its number is six hundred and sixty-six. (Rv 13:11-13, 18)

Many interpretations have been given for that number. Some point out that the name Nero Caesar, spelled in Hebrew, adds up to 666 (in the same way that we saw David added up to 14). Others point out that Solomon brought in 666 talents of gold a year, so that the beast would represent the corruption of the kingdom of Israel.

For almost two thousand years, Christians have been seeing current world leaders in the descriptions of the beasts. Was one of the beasts Napoleon, Bismarck, Hitler, or Stalin? The answer is yes: although the symbols had meaning for the particular time in which John lived, they also have universal significance. Whenever we see corrupt government leading the people astray, we see the beasts working for their master, Satan.

The New Jerusalem

If Revelation were filled with nothing but plagues and tribulations, we would feel hopeless. But the real message of Revelation is consolation and hope. Though Christians suffer plagues and tribulations, we know that the end is triumph for Christ and his Church.

> Then I saw a new heaven and a new earth; for the first heaven and the first earth had passed away, and the sea was no more. And I saw the holy city, new Jerusalem, coming down out of heaven from God, prepared as a bride adorned for her husband; and I heard a great voice from the throne saying, "Behold, the dwelling of God is with men. He will dwell with them, and they shall be his people, and God himself will be with them; he will wipe away every tear from their eyes, and death shall be no more, neither shall there be mourning nor crying nor pain any more, for the former things have passed away."
>
> And he who sat upon the throne said, "Behold, I make all things new." (Rv 21: 1-5)

At the end of time, the faithful people of God will dwell with him in the new Jerusalem, and the old world of sin and death will be replaced by a new world where we live in joy and worship forever. It will be a great marriage feast, with Christ as the Bridegroom and the Church, the new Jerusalem, as the Bride.

> And I saw no temple in the city, for its temple is the Lord God the Almighty. And the city has no need of sun or moon to shine upon it, for the glory of God is its light, and its lamp is the Lamb. By its light shall the nations walk; and the kings of the earth shall bring their glory into it, and its gates shall never be shut by day—and there shall be no night there; they shall bring into it the glory and the honor of the nations. (Rv 21: 22-26)

At last all the promises of the prophets are fulfilled. Jerusalem is the light of the nations, and all the kings of the earth bring their glory into it.

But we don't really have to wait for the end of time. All through the book, John has shown us that the worship in heaven is the same as the worship on earth. When we are at Mass, we really are in the new Jerusalem, participating in the heavenly liturgy. That's true whether we worship in a great cathedral with stained glass or in a dim basement with fluorescent lights, whether the priest is a great preacher or a monotonous bore, whether the music is inspiring or insipid. The Mass is heaven on earth.

The Warning And The Promise

> The children of our holy mother the Church rightly hope for *the grace of final perseverance and the recompense* of God their Father for the good works accomplished with his grace in communion with Jesus (cf. Council of Trent (1547): DS 1576). Keeping the same rule of life, believers share the "blessed hope" of those whom the divine mercy gathers into the "holy city, the new Jerusalem, coming down out of heaven from God, prepared as a bride adorned for her husband" (Rv 21: 2). (CCC 2016)

What do we know about the end of our world?

First, we know from Christ himself that it is impossible to know when it will happen. For two thousand years, Christians have tried to set a date for the end of the world. When the date has come and gone, the world is still here. That is exactly what we should have expected from what Jesus told his disciples:

> But of that day and hour no one knows, not even the angels of heaven, nor the Son, but the Father only. (Mt 24: 36)

An icon of the Last Judgment. In Latin, the *Dies irae*, the "Day of Wrath"; in Russian, the *Strashnyj sud*, the "terrifying judgment."

> Watch, therefore, for you do not know on what day your Lord is coming. But know this, that if the householder had known in what part of the night the thief was coming, he would have watched and would not have let his house be broken into. Therefore you also must be ready; for the Son of man is coming at an hour you do not expect. (Mt 24:42-44)

> Watch, therefore, for you know neither the day nor the hour. (Mt 25:13)

> Do not marvel at this; for the hour is coming when all who are in the tombs will hear his voice and come forth, those who have done good, to the resurrection of life, and those who have done evil, to the resurrection of judgment. (Jn 5:28-29)

The disciples would not know exactly when Jerusalem would be destroyed, and we do not know when the end of our world will come.

We do know, however, that Revelation is a warning as well as a promise. The defeat of Jerusalem was not something for Christians to celebrate. It was an example for them to fear.

If we needed any more warning, we can look at the list of "the seven churches that are in Asia":

1. **Ephesus**
2. **Smyrna**
3. **Pergamum**
4. **Thyatira**
5. **Sardis**
6. **Philadelphia**
7. **Laodicea**

Those were all cities in the Roman province of Asia. Some, like Ephesus (to which Paul wrote his letter to the Ephesians) were great and prosperous cities that already had large Christian communities. Others were smaller towns where the Church was struggling to get on its feet.

John had warnings from Christ to give to those churches: "Remember then from what you have fallen, repent and do the works you did at first. If not, I will come to you and remove your lampstand from its place, unless you repent."[6] We know from Revelation 1:20 that the seven lampstands in heaven represented the seven churches.

The warning is clear: unless they repented, the Church itself would disappear from Ephesus—just as the Temple was destroyed in Jerusalem.

Not one of those seven churches in Asia is left today. The entire province is part of Turkey now. Since the late Middle Ages, that whole area has been under Muslim rulers, who conquered it in a long series of bloody wars that left most of the cities desolate. In the 1920's, the last of the Greek Christians were expelled from Turkey, except for a small pocket in Constantinople, and since then all the churches mentioned in Revelation have been extinct.

So that list of churches is itself a warning to us. If we turn away from our faith, if we refuse to turn back to Christ, we can suffer the same catastrophe that came to Jerusalem.

Revelation is a warning as well as a promise. We can be sure that God invites his faithful people to the marriage supper of the Lamb. But will we be among the faithful who accept the invitation?

> Behold, I am coming soon, bringing my recompense, to repay every one for what he has done. I am the Alpha and the Omega, the first and the last, the beginning and the end. (Rv 22:12-13)

Christian Churches and Communities 100 A.D.

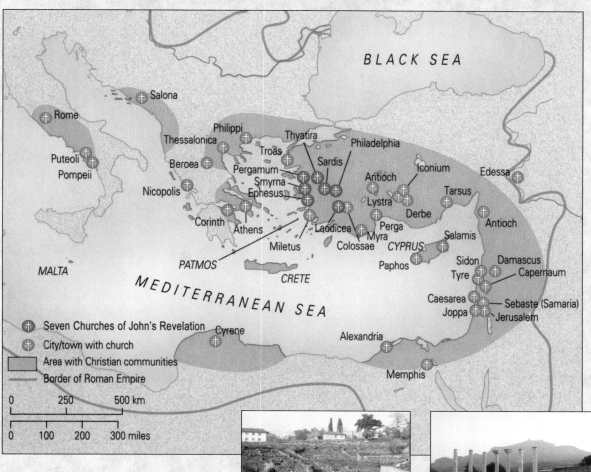

BLACK SEA

Salona
Rome
Philippi
Thessalonica   Thyatira   Philadelphia
Troas
Beroea   Sardis
Puteoli   Pergamum   Iconium   Edessa
Pompeii   Smyrna   Antioch   Tarsus
                Ephesus   Lystra
Nicopolis   Derbe   Antioch
                                    Perga
Corinth   Laodicea   Myra   Salamis
        Athens   Colossae   Myra
                Miletus   CYPRUS   Sidon   Damascus
PATMOS   Paphos   Tyre   Capernaum
MALTA   Caesarea   Sebaste (Samaria)
        MEDITERRANEAN SEA   CRETE   Joppa   Jerusalem

⊕ Seven Churches of John's Revelation   Cyrene
⊕ City/town with church   Alexandria
▨ Area with Christian communities
— Border of Roman Empire   Memphis

0   250   500 km
0   100   200   300 miles

"'Remember then from what you
have fallen, repent and do the works
you did at first. If not, I will come
to you and remove your lampstand
from its place, unless you repent.'"
(Rv 2: 5)

Smyrna

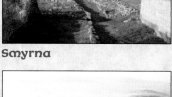

Sardis

Pergamum

Philadelphia

Ephesus

Thyatira

Laodicea

SUPPLEMENTARY READING

Eusebius, *History of the Church*, Book 3

2. His words are as follows: "Woe unto them that are with child, and to them that give suck in those days! But pray ye that your flight be not in the winter, neither on the Sabbath day. For there shall be great tribulation, such as was not since the beginning of the world to this time, no, nor ever shall be."

3. The historian [Josephus], reckoning the whole number of the slain, says that eleven hundred thousand persons perished by famine and sword, and that the rest of the rioters and robbers, being betrayed by each other after the taking of the city, were slain. But the tallest of the youths and those that were distinguished for beauty were preserved for the triumph. Of the rest of the multitude, those that were over seventeen years of age were sent as prisoners to labor in the works of Egypt, while still more were scattered through the provinces to meet their death in the theaters by the sword and by beasts. Those under seventeen years of age were carried away to be sold as slaves, and of these alone the number reached ninety thousand.

4. These things took place in this manner in the second year of the reign of Vespasian, in accordance with the prophecies of our Lord and Savior Jesus Christ, who by divine power saw them beforehand as if they were already present, and wept and mourned according to the statement of the holy evangelists, who give the very words which he uttered, when, as if addressing Jerusalem herself, he said:

5. "If thou hadst known, even thou, in this day, the things which belong unto thy peace! But now they are hid from thine eyes. For the days shall come upon thee, that thine enemies shall cast a rampart about thee, and compass thee round, and keep thee in on every side, and shall lay thee and thy children even with the ground."

6. And then, as if speaking concerning the people, he says, "For there shall be great distress in the land, and wrath upon this people. And they shall fall by the edge of the sword, and shall be led away captive into all nations. And Jerusalem shall be trodden down of the Gentiles, until the times of the Gentiles be fulfilled." And again: "When ye shall see Jerusalem compassed with armies, then know that the desolation thereof is nigh."

7. If any one compares the words of our Savior with the other accounts of the historian [Josephus] concerning the whole war, how can one fail to wonder, and to admit that the foreknowledge and the prophecy of our Savior were truly divine and marvelously strange?

"And they marched up over the broad earth and surrounded the camp of the saints and the beloved city; but fire came down from heaven and consumed them, and the devil who had deceived them was thrown into the lake of fire and brimstone where the beast and the false prophet were, and they will be tormented day and night for ever and ever." (Rv 20: 9-10)

VOCABULARY

APOCALYPSE
The book of Revelation.

ESCHATOLOGY
The study of the end of time.

LITURGY OF THE WORD
The first part of the Mass. Within it the Scriptures are read and interpreted by the deacon or priest. It parallels the liturgy of the Jewish synagogues.

LITURGY
The whole mystical body, Christ the head and his members, worships the Father and continues the effects of his death and resurrection by which he accomplished our salvation.

NEW JERUSALEM
The heavenly city, of which all the faithful are citizens.

REVELATION
The name of the last book of the New Testament, so called because it contains the things that were revealed to St. John.

SCROLL
A long roll used for writing made out of papyrus, leather, or parchment. Most books and letters were written on scrolls in the time of the New Testament.

TITUS
The Roman general whose army captured and destroyed Jerusalem. He later became emperor.

TRIBULATION
A time of trial and distress.

STUDY QUESTIONS

1. When did the early Christians expect the world to end?

2. What did come to an end during their lifetimes?

3. Who was Florus?

4. Who succeeded Vespasian as general against the Israelites?

5. What disaster in 70 A.D. brought the world of the Old Covenant to an end?

6. Where did the Christians flee before the fall of Jerusalem?

7. Why had the Christians fled to Pella before the siege?

8. What two sources can we use to begin to comprehend the heavenly liturgy?

9. How many parts is the book of Revelation divided into, and how do these parts correspond to the Mass?

10. What was John's vision of heaven after he saw the open door?

11. What does the number of 144,000 people represent in Revelation?

12. What happens when the seventh seal of the scroll is broken?

13. In the symbolism of Revelation, who is the Bride of Christ?

14. In the symbolism of Revelation, who is the Ark of the New Covenant in Revelation 12:1-2?

15. Who is the child in Revelation 12?

16. What is the number of the two-horned beast that John sees rise out of the ground?

17. Where will the faithful dwell at the end of time?

18. Why is there no temple in the New Jerusalem?

19. According to the words of Christ, when will the end of the world come?

20. What happened to all the churches listed in Revelation?

PRACTICAL EXERCISES

1. It is has been often said, "hindsight is 20/20." There are many times in our lives when Jesus "knocks on the door" to our hearts, but we fail to open the door. Take a moment to remember the times that you did not open the door. How has this taught you to be better prepared for when Jesus calls you?

2. The Mass has been revealed to be "heaven on earth." How has this affected your attitude as you participate in the liturgy? Do you express proper respect in attitude, attentiveness, and dress? What are ways you can more fully experience this wonderful gift with reverence and gratitude?

3. Jesus told his disciples, "Watch, therefore, for you know neither the day nor the hour" (Mt 25:13). Examine yourself and your life. Are you awaiting the coming of the Lord with vigilance, or taking time for granted? Are you completely satisfied with the way you treat yourself and others? Take time to determine ways you can better prepare yourself for your own death and the end of the world.

FROM THE CATECHISM

1038 The resurrection of all the dead, "of both the just and the unjust" (*Roman Missal*, EP I (Roman Canon) 88), will precede the Last Judgment. This will be "the hour when all who are in the tombs will hear [the Son of man's] voice and come forth, those who have done good, to the resurrection of life, and those who have done evil, to the resurrection of judgment" (Jn 5:28-29). Then Christ will come "in his glory, and all the angels with him....Before him will be gathered all the nations, and he will separate them one from another as a shepherd separates the sheep from the goats, and he will place the sheep at his right hand, but the goats at the left....And they will go away into eternal punishment, but the righteous into eternal life" (Mt 25:31, 32, 46).

1138 "Recapitulated in Christ," these are the ones who take part in the service of the praise of God and the fulfillment of his plan: the heavenly powers, all creation (the four living beings), the servants of the Old and New Covenants (the twenty-four elders), the new People of God (the one hundred and forty-four thousand) (cf. Rv 4-5; 7:1-8; 14:1; Is 6:2-3), especially the martyrs "slain for the word of God," and the all-holy Mother of God (the Woman), the Bride of the Lamb (Rv 6:9-11; Rv 21:9; cf. 12), and finally "a great multitude which no one could number, from every nation, from all tribes, and peoples and tongues" (Rv 7:9).

2788 Since the Lord's Prayer is that of his people in the "endtime," this "our" also expresses the certitude of our hope in God's ultimate promise: in the new Jerusalem he will say to the victor, "I will be his God and he shall be my son" (Rv 21:7).

Endnotes	
1. Mt 24:34.	4. Mt 24:34-35.
2. Mt 24:15-16.	5. Rv 1:9-11.
3. Dn 11:31.	6. Rv 2:5.

How To Read The Bible

We must remember that God, the ultimate author of the whole Bible, knew the plan of salvation from the beginning. The Holy Spirit intended even the oldest parts of the Old Testament to be read in the light of the Incarnation, the coming of Jesus Christ.

Chapter 30

How To Read The Bible

The authors of the sacred texts did not write the same way modern authors write.
To understand what they meant to say, we need to understand the way they saw the world.

The Bible Is Literature

- **The sacred authors used literary techniques to express their meaning.**
- **We must understand those literary techniques to understand the whole meaning of Scripture.**

According to an ancient tradition, one can distinguish between two *senses* of Scripture: the literal and the spiritual, the latter being subdivided into the allegorical, moral and anagogical senses. The profound concordance of the four senses guarantees all its richness to the living reading of Scripture in the Church. (CCC 115)

In Chapter 1, when we first began our walk through the Bible, we learned one essential thing that we must remember: the Bible is *literature*. It uses literary forms and techniques to convey its meaning. We have to understand how those forms and techniques work, or we cannot understand the meaning the inspired authors wanted us to get out of their books.

We also need to remember that the Bible is *ancient* literature. Even the most recent books of the New Testament were written almost two thousand years ago. The authors of the sacred texts did not write the same way modern authors write. To understand what they meant to say, we need to understand the way they saw the world.

When we read any literature, including the Bible, one rule is most important: **Understand the literal sense first.** The *literal sense* is what the sacred writer, inspired by the Holy Spirit, wanted to express. It is usually interpreted to be the immediate and direct meaning of the text.

Literal is different from *literalistic*. Scripture often speaks in a symbolic or metaphorical way. Often the original readers would have understood the symbol or metaphor right away. It may be more difficult for us, because thousands of years have gone by since the books of the Bible were written; but to understand the literal sense of Scripture it is necessary to understand when the writer is speaking symbolically or metaphorically.

For example, the book of Revelation—as we saw—describes heaven in symbolic terms. Are there really golden lampstands and bowls of incense in heaven? Probably not. Until we reach it, heaven is far beyond our comprehension. The sacred author, therefore, describes heaven in terms that would have been familiar to a first-century reader—so we can have some understanding of it. The *literal sense* of Revelation, then, is not just the symbols, but also the *meanings* of the symbols.

We also have to remember that the sacred authors used different literary techniques to make their point, and understanding those literary techniques is part of understanding the literal sense.

When we analyzed the creation story in Genesis, we saw that the author has very carefully built it up to show us that God created the universe as a temple:

SABBATH COVENANT WITH CREATION		
Sun and Moon *rule over*	**Birds and Fish** *rule over*	**Humans and Animals** *rule over*
Day and Night	**Sky and Sea**	**Land and Vegetation**

Because the author conveyed so much meaning by the literary construction of the book, the *literal sense* of Genesis is in that careful *literary analysis*. Without understanding how it works as literature, we don't get the real message intended by the sacred author: that all creation is a temple for the worship of God.

Spiritual Senses

The Church also teaches us to interpret Sacred Scripture in *spiritual* senses. The Holy Spirit often puts more meaning into a passage than the sacred authors knew they were writing.

For example, Jesus Christ quoted the first line of Psalm 22 as he died on the cross. The psalm is attributed to David, who probably described his own feelings in one of his many times of trouble. Yet it describes so well the sufferings of Christ on the cross that no Christian can read it without thinking of the Son of David, the Messiah:

> Yea, dogs are round about me;
> a company of evildoers encircle me;
>   they have pierced my hands and feet—
> I can count all my bones—
>   they stare and gloat over me;
> they divide my garments among them,
>   and for my raiment they cast lots.
> (Ps 22:16-18)

The tradition of the Church tells us that there are three spiritual senses to look for in Scripture.

1. The **allegorical** or **typical** sense shows us how people and events in salvation history point forward to other times. For example, when we read the story of Abraham sacrificing Isaac, we say that Isaac is a "type" of Christ, because the sacrifice of Isaac shows God at work in a way that would reach its ultimate fulfillment in the sacrifice of Christ.

2. The **moral** sense (or "tropological" sense) shows us how we can use the things the heroes of Scripture did as a pattern for our own lives. By seeing the moral content of their actions, we learn to turn toward good and away from evil.

3. The **anagogical** sense shows us how the events we see in Scripture point upward to what we will know in heaven. Through the things that are seen, we come to understand the things we cannot see yet. With those glimpses of the reality of the Kingdom of God, we build up our own hope.

> A medieval couplet summarizes the significance of the four senses:
>   The Letter speaks of deeds;
>   Allegory to faith;
>   The Moral how to act;
>   Anagogy our destiny.[1] (CCC 118)

When we look for the spiritual senses of a passage in Scripture, we must be careful not to forget the literal sense, since "all other senses of Sacred Scripture are based on the literal," as St. Thomas Aquinas pointed out. But the literal sense is not the only sense. We must remember that God, the ultimate author of the whole Bible, knew the plan of salvation from the beginning. The Holy Spirit intended even the oldest parts of the Old Testament to be read in the light of the Incarnation, the coming of Jesus Christ.

Look To The Church For Guidance

Many things in Sacred Scripture are hard to understand. Often different people interpret the same verse of Scripture in exactly opposite ways. How can we know which way is right?

As Catholics, we have the Church to guide us. Jesus Christ left his apostles his authority to teach; the bishops, the apostles of today, still carry on that teaching tradition.

The teaching authority of the Church keeps us from making serious mistakes in the interpretation of the Bible. Because the teaching tradition of the Church goes back to the time when the Bible was written, we know what the books of the Bible were really intended to tell us. Because the Holy Spirit dwells in the Church and guides it, and because Christ himself gave to the apostles his teaching authority, which has been passed down through the Church, the Church's teaching on matters of faith and morals is infallible.

One of the best places to find the teaching of the Church is the *Catechism of the Catholic Church*. All the doctrines of the Church are explained there, with references to the Scripture passages they come from. Whenever you have doubt about what a Scripture passage means, you can often find the answer in the Catechism.

Your priest is also a good person to talk to. Most priests will be delighted to see you sincerely trying to understand the Scriptures, and will give you as much help as they can.

What To Read First

Every book in the Bible is important, but not every chapter of every book is meant to be read through as though it were a novel. Your telephone directory is important, and so is your dictionary; but you don't read them through front to back. Instead, you take the information you need from them when you need it.

Every part of the Bible has to be understood in the context of the rest of the Bible. The New Testament makes no sense without the Old Testament, and the Old Testament is revealed in the New Testament.

> Christians therefore read the Old Testament in the light of Christ crucified and risen. Such typological reading discloses the inexhaustible content of the Old Testament; but it must not make us forget that the Old Testament retains its own intrinsic value as Revelation reaffirmed by our Lord himself (cf. Mk 12:29-31). Besides, the New Testament has to be read in the light of the Old. Early Christian catechesis made constant use of the Old Testament (cf. 1 Cor 5:6-8; 10:1-11). As an old saying put it, the New Testament lies hidden in the Old and the Old Testament is unveiled in the New (cf. St. Augustine, *Quaest. in Hept.* 2, 73: PL 34, 623; cf. DV 16). (CCC 129)

Still, we have to start somewhere. The best place to start is with one of the Gospels. Many Christians like to start with St. Luke. Luke is a great storyteller, and his Gospel was written especially for people who knew little about Jewish customs and traditions.

Genesis and Exodus are rightly placed at the beginning of our Bible, because they prepare the way for everything that follows. Genesis tells how God created the world, how sin entered the world, and how God chose one particular family to be his particular people. Exodus tells how that family became a nation, how God gave that nation the mission of bringing his word to the rest of the world, and how that nation failed in its mission. The rest of salvation history depends on this background.

The best place to start reading the Bible is with one of the Gospels. Many Christians like to start with St. Luke. Luke is a great storyteller.

"Every sincere act of worship or devotion revives the spirit of conversion and repentance within us and contributes to the forgiveness of our sins."

Pray

All these suggestions are useless, though, unless you approach the Bible with the right spirit.

The Bible is the Word of God. As the Word came to us in the flesh in the Eucharist, it comes to us in the words of Scripture. We need to remember that we are approaching the Word of God, and treat it with the reverence it deserves.

A good way to start is by praying for guidance before you read any part of Scripture. But that is only a beginning. You need to be living a life of prayer. Make time for praying at the beginning and the end of every day. Make prayer a part of your life, not an occasional indulgence.

Go to Mass regularly. Soon you will be able to see Scripture come to life in front of you whenever the Mass is celebrated. The more familiar you are with the Mass, the more you will feel at home in Scripture. You will recognize passages in Scripture from hearing them at Mass. The Mass is salvation history alive and present today.

Prayer, the Mass, and Scripture all go together. We need all of them to receive the Word of God in its fullness. If this book has helped you see how God's plan is still working through the Church today, then act on what you know. Go to Mass. Set aside time to pray. And spend more time with the Scriptures.

> Reading Sacred Scripture, praying the Liturgy of the Hours and the Our Father—every sincere act of worship or devotion revives the spirit of conversion and repentance within us and contributes to the forgiveness of our sins. (CCC 1437)

SUPPLEMENTARY READING

Vatican II, *Dei Verbum* 21-22, 25

The Church has always venerated the Scriptures just as she venerates the body of the Lord, since, especially in sacred liturgy, she unceasingly receives and offers to the faithful the bread of life from the table both of God's Word and of Christ's Body. She has always maintained them, and continues to do so, together with sacred tradition, as the supreme rule of faith, since, as inspired by God and committed once and for all to writing, they impart the Word of God Himself without change, and make the voice of the Holy Spirit resound in the words of the prophets and Apostles. Therefore, like the Christian religion itself, all the preaching of the Church must be nourished and regulated by sacred Scripture. For in the sacred books, the Father who is in heaven meets His children with great love and speaks with them; and the force and power in the word of God is so great that it stands as the support and energy of the Church, the strength of faith for her sons, the food of the soul, the pure and everlasting source of spiritual life. Consequently, these words are perfectly applicable to sacred Scripture: "For the word of God is living and active" (Heb 4:12) and "it has power to build you up and give you your heritage among all those who are sanctified" (Acts 20:32; see 1 Thes 2:13).

Easy access to sacred Scripture should be provided for all the Christian faithful. That is why the Church from the very beginning accepted as her own that very ancient Greek translation of the Old Testament which is called the Septuagint; and she has always given a place of honor to other Eastern translations and Latin ones, especially the Latin translation known as the Vulgate. But since the Word of God should be accessible at all times, the Church by her authority and with maternal concern sees to it that suitable and correct translations are made into different languages, especially from the original texts of the sacred books. And should the opportunity arise and the Church authorities approve, if these translations are produced in cooperation with the separated brethren as well, all Christians will be able to use them.

Therefore, all the clergy must hold fast to the sacred Scriptures through diligent sacred reading and careful study, especially the priests of Christ and others, such as deacons and catechists who are legitimately active in the ministry of the Word. This is to be done so that none of them will become "an empty preacher of the Word of God outwardly, who is not a listener to it inwardly" since they must share the abundant wealth of the divine Word with the faithful committed to them, especially in the sacred liturgy.

"...the Church...has always given a place of honor to...the Latin translation known as the Vulgate." (Dei Verbum 22)

VOCABULARY

ALLEGORICAL SENSE

The spiritual interpretation of Scripture that shows how people and events in salvation history point forward to other times. The allegorical sense of Abraham sacrificing Isaac is God's sacrifice of his own son, Jesus.

ANAGOGICAL SENSE

The spiritual interpretation of Scripture that shows how events in Scripture point to what will be in heaven.

CATECHISM OF THE CATHOLIC CHURCH

A book containing a summary of Catholic teaching.

LITERAL SENSE

The meaning of Scripture based on the meaning of words in the literary and historical context.

MORAL SENSE

The spiritual interpretation of Scripture that shows us how the heroes of Scripture portray a pattern for our own lives.

SPIRITUAL SENSE

The interpretation of Scripture that sees not only the words of the text but also the people, things, and events they describe as signs. The spiritual senses flow out of the literal meaning of the words. The three kinds of spiritual sense in Scripture are the allegorical, moral, and anagogical senses.

STUDY QUESTIONS

1. What is the Literal sense?

2. List and define the three spiritual senses of the Bible.

3. What three sources should be read in preparation for reading the Bible?

4. What prayer does the Church recommend to lay people?

PRACTICAL EXERCISES

1. A concordance is a book which lists all the words in the Bible and their location by chapter and page. Do you think the use of the concordance would make reading the Bible easier?

2. What is the best method to guarantee you would set time aside to read the Bible every day? Make a list of "to do's" which will assist you to read the Bible.

3. As preparation for a lifetime of reading Sacred Scripture, see if you can find these well-known passages:

a. The "Our Father" or Lord's Prayer.

b. The parable of the Prodigal Son.

c. "I am the bread of life."

d. Elijah's contest with the prophets of Baal.

e. Abraham's willingness to sacrifice Isaac.

f. The prophecy that Israel's ruler would come from Bethlehem.

FROM THE CATECHISM

112 Be especially attentive "to the content and unity of the whole Scripture." Different as the books which compose it may be, Scripture is a unity by reason of the unity of God's plan, of which Christ Jesus is the center and heart, open since his Passover (cf. Lk 24: 25-27, 44-46).

113 **2.** Read the Scripture within "the living Tradition of the whole Church." According to a saying of the Fathers, Sacred Scripture is written principally in the Church's heart rather than in documents and records, for the Church carries in her Tradition the living memorial of God's Word, and it is the Holy Spirit who gives her the spiritual interpretation of the Scripture ("according to the spiritual meaning which the Spirit grants to the Church" (Origen, Hom. in Lev. 5, 5: PG 12, 454D).

125 The Gospels are the heart of all the Scriptures "because they are our principal source for the life and teaching of the Incarnate Word, our Savior" (DV 18).

133 The Church "forcefully and specifically exhorts all the Christian faithful…to learn the surpassing knowledge of Jesus Christ, by frequent reading of the divine Scriptures. 'Ignorance of the Scriptures is ignorance of Christ'"(DV 25; cf. Phil 3: 8 and St. Jerome, Commentariorum in Isaiam libri xviii prol.: PL 24, 17b).

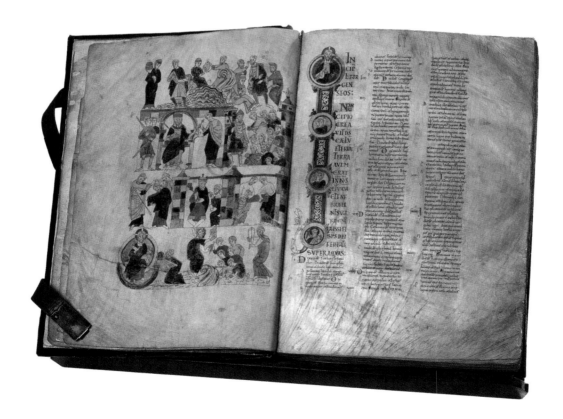

Endnote

1. Lettera gesta docet, quid credas allegoria, moralis
   quid agas, quo tendas anagogia; Augustine of Dacia,
   Rotulus pugillaris, I: ed. A. Walz: Angelicum 6 (1929) 256.

Art and Photo Credits

Art and Photo Credits

Art and Photo Credits

121 (top right) *The Merneptah Stele;* Cairo Museum, Egypt
122 *Joseph Explaining the Dreams of Pharaoh,* Jean Adrien-Guignet, Musée des Beaux-Arts, Rouen
123 *Joseph and His Brothers,* Franz Anton Maulbertsch; Museum of Fine Arts, Budapest
124 *Jacob Blessing the Children of Joseph,* Rembrandt; Staatliche Museen, Kassel

Chapter 7

127 *The Gathering of the Manna,* Guido Reni; Cathedral, Ravenna
129 *The Finding of Moses By Pharaoh's Daughter,* Sir Lawrence Alma-Tadema; Private Collection
130 (top) *Rameses II,* Abu-Simbel, Egypt; Pictorial Library of Bible Lands; Todd Bolen, photographer
130 (bottom) *Temple of Rameses II,* Abu-Simbel, Egypt; Pictorial Library of Bible Lands; Todd Bolen, photographer
131 *Scenes from the Life of Moses* (detail), Sandro Botticelli; The Sistine Chapel, Vatican
132 *Sunrise from Jebel Musa,* Sinai, Egypt; Pictorial Library of Bible Lands; Todd Bolen, photographer
133 *St. Catherine's Monastery,* Sinai, Egypt; Pictorial Library of Bible Lands; Todd Bolen, photographer
135 *The Fifth [Seventh] Plague of Egypt,* William Turner; Indianapolis Museum
136 *The Death of the First Born,* Sir Lawrence Alma-Tadema; Rijksmuseum, Amsterdam
137 *Madonna and Child with the Lamb of God,* Cesare da Sesto; Museo Poldi Pezzoli, Milan
138 *Wilderness of Paran,* Negev; Pictorial Library of Bible Lands; Todd Bolen, photographer
139 *Rameses II And His Chariot,* Abu-Simbel, Egypt; Pictorial Library of Bible Lands; Todd Bolen, photographer
140 Corbis Royalty Free Image
141 *The Miracle of Manna* (detail), Tintoretto; Scuola di San Rocco, Venice
142 *Moses,* José de Ribera; Chiesa della Certosa di San Martino, Naples
145 Folio 70r, *History Bible;* Hofbibliothek, Vienna
146 *Returning the Ark to Israel,* G. Auvergne; Biblia de San Luis de Francia, Catedral Biblioteca, Toledo, Spain; Archivo Oronoz
148 *The Ghent Altarpiece: Adoration of the Lamb* (detail), Jan van Eyck; Cathedral of St Bavo, Ghent

Chapter 8

149 *Moses on Mt. Sinai, Ark of the Covenant and Building the Tabernacle,* Persian Manuscript;
    Island of San Lazaro, Venice; Archivo Oronoz
150 *Adoring the Golden Calf,* Raphael; The Loggias, Vatican
151 Egyptian Statue of Apis; The Senusret Collection, Santa Barbara, California
152 Cow goddess Mehit-Weret from Tutankhamen's tomb; Luxor Museum, Egypt
153 *Moses Destroying the Golden Calf,* Andrea Celesti; Palazzo Ducale, Venice
154 Jebel Musa Steps of Repentance, Sinai, Egypt; Pictorial Library of Bible Lands; Todd Bolen, photographer
155 *The Children of Israel in the Wilderness,* Raphael; The Loggias, Vatican
156 Leviticus Scroll, Shrine of the Book, Israel Museum
157 *Nahal Zin,* Negev; Pictorial Library of Bible Lands; Todd Bolen, photographer
158 *Moses Causes Water to Gush from the Rock,* Raphael; The Loggias, Vatican
160 (left) King George III, AG Archives
160 (right) *Rameses II as Osiris,* Luxor Museum, Egypt; Pictorial Library of Bible Lands; Todd Bolen, photographer
162 *Tabernacle In the Wilderness,* Timna Park, Israel; Pictorial Library of Bible Lands; Todd Bolen, photographer
162 *Arad Iron Age Holy of Holies,* Biblical Negev; Pictorial Library of Bible Lands; Todd Bolen, photographer
163 *Solomon's Temple in Jerusalem,* Pedro Comestor; Miniature, National Library, Madrid, Spain; Archivo Oronoz
164 Biblia Judia de Perpiñan: *Hebrews,* Folio 12v-13; National Library, Paris, France; Archivo Oronoz
166 *Ark of the Covenant and the Dedication of the Tabernacle;* Bible of Milan, Academia de Historia, Madrid, Spain; Archivo Oronoz

Chapter 9

167 *David and Uriah,* Rembrandt; The Hermitage, St. Petersburg
168 *Jordan River South of Sea of Galilee;* Pictorial Library of Bible Lands; Todd Bolen, photographer
169 *View Over Jericho and Jordan Valley;* Pictorial Library of Bible Lands; Todd Bolen, photographer
170 (top) *Crossing the River,* Raphael; The Loggias, Vatican
170 (bottom) *Jericho Neolithic Tower;* Pictorial Library of Bible Lands; Todd Bolen, photographer
172 *Jericho Panorama from Cypros;* Pictorial Library of Bible Lands; Todd Bolen, photographer
173 *Shechem Baal Berith,* Samaria; Pictorial Library of Bible Lands; Todd Bolen, photographer
176 *Gideon's Victory Over the Midianites;* Biblia de San Luis de Francia, Catedral Biblioteca, Toledo, Spain; Archivo Oronoz
177 *Mt. Tabor Aerial from Northwest,* Jezreel Valley; Pictorial Library of Bible Lands; Todd Bolen, photographer
178 *Samuel,* Midwest Theological Forum Archives
179 *Nebi Samwil,* Israel; Pictorial Library of Bible Lands; Todd Bolen, photographer
183 *Michmash Cliffs;* Pictorial Library of Bible Lands; Todd Bolen, photographer
184 *Saul and David* (detail), Erasmus Quellin II; Museum of Fine Arts, Budapest
185 *Saul's Robe Speared By David,* G. Auvergne; Biblia de San Luis de Francia, Catedral Biblioteca, Toledo, Spain; Archivo Oronoz
186 *David Contemplating the Head of Goliath,* Orazio Gentileschi; Galleria Spada, Rome
187 *Saul Attacking David,* Guercino; Galleria Nazionale d'Arte Antica, Rome
188 *Saul and Samuel,* Gothic Miniature, Academia de Historia, Madrid, Spain; Archivo Oronoz

Art and Photo Credits

Art and Photo Credits

Art and Photo Credits

Art and Photo Credits

Art and Photo Credits

Index

Index

Index

Index